National Intelligencer Newspaper Abstracts 1868

Joan M. Dixo

HERITAGE BOOKS
2009

HERITAGE BOOKS
AN IMPRINT OF HERITAGE BOOKS, INC.

Books, CDs, and more—Worldwide

For our listing of thousands of titles see our website
at
www.HeritageBooks.com

Published 2009 by
HERITAGE BOOKS, INC.
Publishing Division
100 Railroad Ave. #104
Westminster, Maryland 21157

Copyright © 2009 Joan M. Dixon

All rights reserved. No part of this book may be reproduced or transmitted in any form or by any means, electronic or mechanical, including photocopying, recording or by any information storage and retrieval system without written permission from the author, except for the inclusion of brief quotations in a review.

International Standard Book Numbers
Paperbound: 978-0-7884-4788-4
Clothbound: 978-0-7884-8106-2

NATIONAL INTELLIGENCER NEWSPAPER
WASHINGTON, D C
1868

TABLE OF CONTENTS

Daily National Intelligencer, Washington, D C, 1868: pg 1

Abraham Lincoln-monument: 120
Alaska: 97
American Medical Association: 137
American sculptors in Italy: 5
Army Officers: 108
Astor, Wm B: 364
Assassination of Prince Michael: 216
Baltimore, Md-flood: 242; 245
Board of Police: see index page 436
Boat Little Western disaster: 197
Bureau of Indian Affairs: 1
Churches in Washington: 360-362

Commencements:	Academy of the Visitation: 212
	Brookeville Academy: 232
	Columbian College: 197
	Georgetown College: 210
	Georgetown College-Medical Dept: 80-81
	Rock Creek College, Ellicott City, Md: 208
	St Vincent's Academy, Washington: 199

Court Martial of Gen M Bache: 61
Court Martial of Capt Napoleon Collins: 61
Dead of 1867: 3

Death of Col Timothy P Andrews: 79
Death of John Jacob Astor-son: 22
Death of Cmder Richmond Aulick: 192
Death of Hon Portus Baxter: 72
Death of Rear Admr Henry H Bell: 57
Death of Mrs Anne E Bronaugh: 42
Death of ex-Pres Buchanan: 157; 166; 169
Death of Christopher Carson [Kit Carson]: 165
Death of Julia Dean Cooper: 77
Death of Louis Wm Dorsey: 18

Death of Chas Loring Elliott, portrait painter: 281
Death of Admr Engle: 51
Death of Philip R Fendall: 54
Death of Gen Peter Force: 26; 30
Death of Thos H Ford: 69; 71
Death of Hon Francis Granger: 291
Death of Robt Ball Hughes, sculptor: 77
Death of Rev B F B Leech: 36
Death of Jas Maize McCrae: 404
Death of Capt Jas McDaniel: 38
Death of Mr Samuel M McKean: 45; 122
Death of Samuel McKenney: 63
Death of Lt McKenzie: 4
Death of an Indian Princess: 269
Death of Lt Cmdr J H Reed: 57
Death of Capt Rohrer: 32
Death of Gioacchino Rossini, composer: 383
Death of Very Rev Benedict J Spalding: 260
Death of Hon Thaddeus Stevens: 264; 274
Death of Benjamin Ogle Tayloe: 96
Death of Ulysses Ward: 104
Death of Mr Jos Williamson: 28
Death of Hon David Wilmot: 90
Dickens, Charles [sister-in-law]: 52
Ferry boat Hamilton & ferry boat Union disaster: 387
Funeral of Brvt Col Wm S Abert: 73
Funeral of Wm M Ellis: 91
Funeral of Mrs Louise Morris Eustis: 56
Funeral of Brvt Maj Michael J Kelly: 62; 65
Funeral of Detective Wm M Kelly: 22
Funeral of Brvt Maj Gen Henry C Maynadier: 415
Funeral of Wm C Rives: 132
Funeral of Maj Geo B Simpson: 62
Funeral of Col John S Williams: 183
Gen Custer accused of murder: 19
Georgetown election: 65
George Washington's will: 299
Greenleaf's Point: 372-373
Grenap, Benj C-monument: 77; 112
Howland case [Robinson, Green, Mardell]: 381-382
Impeach the President: see index page 461
Improvements in Georgetown: 313
Improvements in Washington: 199
Incomes in N Y: 147

Incomes in Washington, D C: 141-146
Indian Wars: 406-407
Industrial Home School officers/cmte: 360
Invalid Pensions: 173; 178-179; 217-219
London era of actresses: 43
Jurors-Washington: 63-64; 136; 172; 348
Liquor licenses: 400; 402
Marriage of Robert T Lincoln: 316; 330
McKinley, Dr Samuel E: 287
Meridian Hill real estate sales: 14
Midshipmen: 140
Military Cadets: 249-250
Municipal Officers-Alexandria & Fredericksburg, Va: 122
Murder of Andrew Rowland: 354
Navy promotions: 424
Oak Hill Cemetery, Gtwn: see index page 475
Officers of the screw frigate Franklin: 274
Orphans Court-Judge Pursell: see index page 476
Pastoral changes-Washington: 283
Propellar Hippocampus disaster: 301
Providence Hospital: 314
Railroad accident-Albany, N Y: 351
Railroad accident-N Y: 121
St Paul's Day: 27
Schools in Washington: 377
Scott, Lt Gen Winfield-monument: 227
Sedwick, Maj Gen John-monument: 347
Ship General Grant disaster: 101
Sir Walter Scott's manuscripts: 266
Steamer City of Boston disaster: 212
Steamer Hibernia disaster: 413
Steamer Magnolia disaster: 92; 93-94
Steamer Morning Star disaster: 193-194
Steamer Sea Bird disaster: 115; 123; 263
Steamer United States & steamer America collide: 408-409
Suicide of Mrs Augustus H Dickens: 426; 428; 429
Vanderbilt, Cornelius: 277
Washington City advertisements: 395-398
Washington City Charter: 32-33
Index: pg 432

> Dedicated to our talented granddaughter:
> Samantha Aubrey Dixon
> Born: Sep 12, 1990
> Columbia, Howard Co, Md

PREFACE
Daily National Intelligencer Newspaper Abstracts
1868
Joan M Dixon

The National Intelligencer & Washington Advertiser is hereafter the Daily National Intelligencer. It was the first newspaper printed in Washington, D C; Samuel H Smith, the originator. The same was transferred to Jos Gales, jr on Aug 31, 1810; on Nov 1, 1812, the paper was under the firm of Jos Gales, sr, & Wm W Seaton. The Library of Congress has microfilm of the paper from the first issue of Oct 31, 1800 thru Jan 8, 1870, the final paper. The Evening Star Newspaper of Jan 10, 1870 reports: The Intelligencer is discontinued: the proprietor, Mr Alex Delmar, says that having lost several thousand dollars, & being in poor health, he has resolved to discontinue its publication.

Included in the abstracts are advertisements; appointments by the President; Hse o/Rep petitions; passed Acts; legal notices; marriages; deaths; mscl notices; social events; military promotions; court cases; deaths by accident; & maritime information-officers-crews. Items or events which might be a clue as to the location, age or relationship of an individual are copied.

No attempt has been made to correct the spelling. Due to the length of some articles, it was necessary to present only the highlights of same. Chancery and Equity records are copied as written.

The index contains all surnames and *tracts of lands/places*. Maritime vessels are found under barge, boat, brig, frig, schn'r, ship, sloop, steamboat, tugboat, yacht or vessel.

ABBREVIATIONS:
AA CO	ANNE ARUNDEL COUNTY
CMDER	COMMANDER
CMDOR	COMMODOR
ELIZ	ELIZABETH
ELIZA	ELIZA
MONTG CO	MONTGOMERY COUNTY
PG CO	PRINCE GEORGE'S CO
WASH, D C	WASHINGTON, DISTRICT OF COLUMBIA

BOOKS IN THE NATIONAL INTELLIGENCER NEWSPAPER SERIES: 1800-1805/1806-1810/1811-1813/1814-1817/1818-1820/1821-1823/1824-1826/1827-1829/1830-1831/1832-1833/1834-1835/1836-1837/1838-1839/1840/1841/1842/1843/1844/1845/1846/1847/1848/1849/1850/1851/1852/1853/1854/1855/1856/1857/1858/1859/1860/1866/1867/1868/1869-Jan 8, 1870. SPECIAL: CIVIL WAR 2 VOLS, 1861-1865

DAILY NATIONAL INTELLIGENCER NEWSPAPER
WASHINGTON, D C
1868

WED JAN 1, 1868
Mr Chas Dickens has an effectual mode of dealing with the numerous applications for his autograph. Applicants receive a printed answer, saying: "To comply with your modest request would not be reasonably possible."

Cooper & Latimer, aucts, sold the south 20 feet of lot 11 in square 901, improved by a 2 story frame house & a large brick bake house, on 7th st, between south G & I sts, to Richd L Cropley, for $1,000.

On Monday S W Grant, employed in the jewelry establishment of Mr Benj De Wolff, Pa ave, under the Metropolitan, was arrested for abstracting from the store of his employer articles of jewelry, valued at $5,000. Some he gave to a lady friend, others he sold.

Bureau of Indian Affairs; the following persons have presided over the ofc, viz:
Elbert Herring, of N Y, appointed ___, 1833.
Carey A Harris, of Tenn, appointed Jul 4, 1836.
T Harley Crawford, of Pa, appointed Jan 31, 1839.
Wm Medill, of Ohio, appointed Oct 28, 1845.
Orlando Brown, of Ky, appointed Jul 1, 1849.
Luke Lea, of Miss, appointed Jul 1,1 850.
Geo W Manypenny, of Ohio, appointed Mar 13, 1853.
Jas W Denver, of Calif, appointed Apr 17, 1857.
Chas E Mix, of D C, appointed Jun 16, 1858.
A B Greenwood, of Ark, appointed Jun 12, 1860.
Wm P Dole, of Ill, appointed Mar 13, 1861.
Dennis N Cooley, of Iowa, appointed Jul 10, 1865.
Lewis V Bogy, of Missouri, appointed Nov 1, 1866.
N G Taylor, of Tenn, appointed Mar 29, 1867.

Orphans Court-Judge Purcell, Dec 31, 1867. 1-First & final account of Saml Norment, adm of Sophia Harvey, dec'd, approved & passed. 2-First account of Matilda Roberts, guardian of Chas R Reynolds, minor child of Chas A Reynolds, & heir of Annie _ Reynolds, dec'd, approved & passed. 3-Will of Francis Lowndes filed & admitted to probate, & Richd P Jackson qualified as executor; bond $1,000. 4-Jerome B Dorman took out letters of administration on the personal estate of Anthony Dorman, dec'd; bond $800. 5-An account of the personal estate of Wm Richards, by his administrators, was received & filed.

Criminal Court-Judge Olin. 1-Carter Jones, petit larceny: guilty. 2-Saml Hanson, petit larceny; guilty: sentenced to 4 months in the county jail. 3-Jonathan Waters, petit larceny; guilty: 3 months in the county jail. 4-Chas Ellis, assault & battery; guilty: 2 months in county jail. 5-Mancey Dunning, indicted for grand larceny, in stealing property to the value of $150, property of Wm J Austin, was found guilty & sentenced to the Albany penitentiary for 15 months.

John Van Riswick vs Edw Lynch et al. Equity 982. Parties to this cause & creditors of the said Edw Lynch, to appear at my ofc on Jan 8 next, 40 La ave, & I shall proceed to state the account of the trustees, the claims of creditors, & distribution of the fund.
–Walter S Cox, auditor

Chicago, Dec 31. Judge A Warrington, one of the ablest lawyers of the State, died at his residence, in this city, today, aged 57 years.

Dissolution of partnership. The limited partnership existing heretofore under the firm of Mohun & Son, is this day, Jan 1, dissolved by mutual consent. –Francis Mohun, Francis B Mohun The undersigned have formed a copartnership to carry on the Lumber business under the name of Francis Mohun & Sons. –Francis Mohun, Francis B Mohun, Philip Mohun [Lumber Dealers, Canal, between 12th & 13th sts.]

Supreme Court of D C, Equity 534. John Bateman et al vs Jane E Bateman et al. Statement of account & distribution of funds Jan 8, 3 P M. –Walter S Cox, auditor

Orphans Court of Wash Co, D C, Dec 31, 1867. In the case of Eliza McDuell, excx of John McDuell, dec'd, the executrix & Court have appointed Jan 28th next, for the final settlement of the personal estate of the said dec'd, of the assets in hand.
-Jas R O'Beirne, Reg/o wills

Dept of the Interior, U S Patent Ofc, Wash, Dec 26, 1867. Ptn of Wm H Seymour, of Brockport, N Y, praying for the extension of a patent granted to him Mar 18, 1854, for an improvement in Harvesters, for seven years from the expiration of said patent, which takes place on Mar 28, 1868. -T C Theaker, Com'r of Patents

Dept of the Interior, U S Patent Ofc, Wash, Dec 26, 1867. Ptn of B G Fitzhugh, of Ellicott City, Md, praying for the extension of a patent granted to him Mar 28, 1854, for an improvement in Harvesters of Grain, for seven years from the expiration of said patent, which takes place on Mar 28, 1868. -T C Theaker, Com'r of Patents

Dept of the Interior, U S Patent Ofc, Wash, Dec 14, 1867. Ptn of Lavinia L Bartlett, admx of the estate of Russell D Bartlett, dec'd, of Bangor, Maine, praying for the extension of a patent granted to him Mar 14, 1854, for an improvement in Machines for making Shovel Handles, for seven years from the expiration of said patent, which takes place on Mar 14, 1868. -T C Theaker, Com'r of Patents

THU JAN 2, 1868
Indian Territory: the flag was raised on old **Fort Cobb**, in Dec 20, by Maj Shanklin, for the first time since it was torn down by the Confederates under Gen Price, in 1862. **Fort Cobb** is now the headquarters of the Ouschita agency.

The dead of 1867: Boston Journal: Ex-Govn'r Andrew, of Mass; ex-Govn'r Hunt, of N Y; Hon Geo Evans, of Maine; ex-Govn'r Jos A Gilmore, Rev David Dudley Field, Rear Admiral Ringgold, Cmdor Paulding, Mr Wright, U S Minister to Berlin; Hon Albert Smith, of Maine; Chief Justice Wayne, of the U S Supreme Court; Gen Thos F Meagher, ex-Govn'r John A King, of N Y; ex-Pres Day, of Yale College; Senator McDougall, Prof Chas King, Elias Howe, the inventor of the sewing machine; ex-Chancellor Walworth, of N Y, Rear Admiral Sloat, Gen Griffin, Admiral Palmer, & Prof Chester Dewey. The literary world mourns the departure of those whose names in this country were esteemed by thousands. N P Willis, died at Idlewild; Byron Forceythe Wilson died here; Thos Bulfinch, the author of The age of Chivalry, etc; Fitz Greene Halleck, the poet, & Catherine Maria Sedgwick. Among the artists we may recall Jacques Burkhardt, the life-long friend of Prof Agassiz; W H Furness the artist; Sallie St Clair, the actress; Paul Julien, W F Brough, Ira Aldridge, Nantier-Didice, & Avonia Jones. Among the writers & journalists: Jas F Otis, of N Y & New Orleans press; Chas F Browne ["Artemus Ward,"] the writer & lecturer, & Geo Wilkins Kendall, of the New Orleans Picayune. The scientific world: Prof A D Bache, Superintendent of the U S Coast Survey; Prof Faraday, of England, the eminent chemist, & Earl Ross, astronomer.

All persons are cautioned against receiving a note drawn by J G Naylor, in favor of Wm Bradley, for $654.25.

Dr Noble Young, an old & well-known practitioner of medicine of Wash City, has been appointed by Warden Heustis as physician to the jail, vice Dr Duhamel, removed.

Yesterday Franklin Lodge No 2, Knights of Pythias, the Grand Lodge & Magenenu Encampment I O O F, attended the funeral of their deceased brother, Mr Manning Hadly, a well known citizen of the Navy Yard section of Wash City.

The N Y Tribune of yesterday says: The family of Judge Richd Busteed received a telegram yesterday from Mobile, informing them that the Judge was on his death-bed, his case having been pronounced hopeless by 3 physicians who were attending him. Mrs Busteed & 2 children, a son & daughter, 13 & 21 years of age, & his brothers Geo & Wm H Busteed, took the earliest train for the South.

Gen Kenton Harper, who founded & for 13 years conducted the Staunton [Va] Spectator, died on Christmas night, aged 66 years. The deceased served gallantly in the Mexican war, & on the secession of Va he espoused the Southern side.

Mrd: on Dec 31, 1867, at the residence of the bride's father, by Rev J C Smith, D D, assisted by Rev P D Gurley, D D, Benj F Winslow, of Pittsford, Vt, to Mary P Middleton, daughter of Mr Robt W Middleton, of Wash City, D C.

Mrd: on Dec 30, 1867, in Balt, Md, by Rev Dr J M Wilson, John F Olmstead, of N Y, to Hannah M Story, youngest daughter of the late Wm Story, of Indiana.

FRI JAN 3, 1868

Pittsburgh Commercial, Dec 31. Mr Chas H Parker, the popular conductor of the Johnstown accommodation train, Pa railroad, met with his death yesterday at the hands of a drunken desperado, Saml Hull, who was a passenger in his charge. Hull refused to give Parker his ticket, & when Parker rang the bell for the train to stop, Hull drew a knife & plunged it into the body of Parker, who expired almost immediately, without uttering a word. The murderer walked off the train. The body of Parker was brought to his residence in Conemaugh, where he leaves a young wife, to whom he was wedded about 6 months ago. Mr Parker was about 28 years of age, a courteous & obliging conductor, & a faithful ofcr of the company. Hull is about 25 years old. He was captured Dec 31.

The friends of Hon John P Stockton will regret to hear of the death of his eldest daughter, Sadie, which occurred yesterday at Trenton, after a brief but painful illness.

News from China & Japan. 1-Cmdor Jas T Watkins died on board the ship **Costa Rica**. 2-Gen Von Valkenburg, the minister to Japan, was married on Nov 25 to Mrs Schayer, of N Y. 3-The body of Lt McKenzie, of the U S ship **Hartford**, who was killed by the savages, has been removed from Tai Wing to Hong Kong, & will be sent home to America. 4-The body of Mrs Hunt, wife of the captain of the bark **Rover**, who was killed by the savages, has been recovered.

Criminal Court-Judge Olin. Anthony Bundy, indicted for an assault & battery, with intent to kill Margaret Foster on Aug 18 last, was found guilty as indicted, with a recommendation to the mercy of the Court.

Mrd: on Jan 2, at the Church of the Epiphany, by Rev Dr Hall, Mr L Howland Coit, of N Y, to Miss Mattie F, daughter of Hon J F Hartley.

Mrd: on Dec 31, 1867, by Rev Mr Lightner, Saml J Matur, of Fairfax Co, to Miss Anna E Carroll, of Wash, D C.

Died: on Jan 2, Hiram Thomas, eldest son of Jerome & Mary E Browne, aged 16 years. His funeral will be Friday at 2 o'clock P M, from the residence of his parents, 334 10th st.

Board of Police meeting yesterday, applications for restaurant licenses were reconsidered & rejected: Jos Freundt, John Thomas, & Jas Cole. New applications rejected: Jas Darity, Robt Lynch, Jos Torrens, Wm Musgrif, & John Mitchell. The application of Ellen Collins & Mary Sullivan, of Gtwn, were rejected. Jas A Dodd was reappointed an additional patrolman for 90 days, to do duty in the Centre Market.

Mr A J Halleck, a brother of Gen Halleck, is supposed to have been lost in the steamer **Raleigh**.

Miss Ida Hillgren is a new Swedish prima donna, who is said to be more talented & more beautiful than Jenny Lind, or Christina Nillson at the best. She is singing at the Royal Theatre in Stockholm.

Hon Col Henry C Lowther, who died on Dec 6, was the father of the British House of Commons, having been member for Westmoreland Co nearly 50 years in succession, or since 1818. He was heir presumptive to the Earldom of Lonsdale; was at the battle of Coronna in 1809, & served under Wellington in Spain in 1812 & 1813.

St Louis, Jan 2. Advices from Silver City, Indian Territory, gives accounts of the campaign of Gen Crook, in Southern Oregon, against the Indians. On Nov 28 a severe fight occurred near South Fork, in which 19 soldiers were killed, one of whom, Lt John Madigan, lived in Jersey City, & another, Carl Bross, in Newark, N J.

Newark, N J, Jan 2. Thos Welch was hung today for the murder of Patrick Tormey on Jul 4 last. Jas Kane & his brother, Patrick Kane, & brother-in-law, named McMovens, were stabbed at Montclair, N J, on New Year's evening by 3 desperadoes, named Taylor, & 2 brothers, Mulhany. All of the latter have been arrested.

Mobile, Ala, Jan 2. Judge Busteed's wounds are now healing, & his recovery is now considered certain. His physicians think he will be confined to his room for some weeks.

SAT JAN 4, 1868
Mr Wm H Eddins, mail agent between this city & Weldon, N C, died yesterday at the Metropolitan Hotel. He was taken sick on Sunday last with a serious affection of the bowels, & although every attention was given him, the disease proved fatal. He was a native of Charlotte, N C, & respected by a large circle of friends & acquaintances.

W Lilly, 540 7th st, has just received a large stock of overshoes. [Ad]

Mrd: on Jan 1, by Rev O Hutton, at the residence of the bride's uncle, Judge Bowie, of Montg Co, Md, Mr H C Bowie to Miss Anna J Holland.

Mrs Gen Price has received $10,000 on her late husband's life policy.

American sculptors in Italy, at least of those resident in Rome & Florence: Mr Story, Mr Rheinhart, Mr Ives, Mr Rogers, Mr Mosier, Mr Haseltine, Mr Horatio Stone, Miss Hosmer, Miss Whitney, Miss Foley, Miss Lewis, Miss Freeman, Miss Stebbins, Mr Ball, Mr Hart, Mr Mead, Mr Jackson, Mr Powers, Mr Colby, & Mr Connelly. Some of those at Rome have commissions of the value of many thousand dollars, & none of them are without engagements which will keep them for some time employed.

Chancery sale of a brick house & lot, by decree of the Supreme Court of D C, in Chancery, in the cause of Lloyd vs McGlue et al, Dec 13, 1867, No 1,100; public auction, on Jan 16 next, of the west part of lot 1 in square 121, on F st, with a comfortable brick dwlg house. –Saml E Douglass, Asbury Lloyd, trustees -John B Wheeler & Co, aucts

The colored man, named Jones, who was convicted of rape upon a white woman of Fred'k, Md, was on Wednesday sentenced to be hung.

U S Marshal's sale: Jan 23, of all Thos McNanny's right, title, claim, & interest in & to lot 17, in square 68, Wash City, with improvements, the property of Thos McNanny, & will be sold in favor of Isaac Herzburg. –David S Gooding, U S Marshal, D C

MON JAN 6, 1868
Mr Geo W Childs, the popular proprietor of the Phil Ledger, presented his editors & reporters with $50 each as a Christmas gift.

Orphans Court-Judge Purcell, Jan 4, 1868. 1-First & final account of John D McPherson, adm of Chas F Robertson, dec'd, & 2nd account of Jos R Keen, guardian to Arthur L & John G Keen, were approved & passed. 2-Eliz Pyles, appointed guardian to orphans of Thos E Pyles, dec'd; bond $3,000. Mary F Essex, guardian to the orphan of John F Essex; bond $5,000. 3-The last will & testament of J A McLaughlin was filed & admitted to probate. 4-The first account of Mary Thacher, admx of Jas Thacher, was filed. 5-The will of Christopher Friess was filed, fully proven, & admitted to probate & record. 6-Exceptions were taken & filed to the first & final account of John D McPherson, adm of C F Robertson, by Danl Wormer, through his counsel, Robt Leech, which were sustained by the Court.

We regret to state that our old & highly esteem fellow citizen, Mr John Johnson, sr, is lying at his home seriously ill. He is a victim of pneumonia; aged 72 years; a good citizen, & Christian gentleman. In early life he was addicted to some extent, to the use of intoxicating liquors. This habit he conquered, & for long years past has been an earnest worker in the temperance cause in this district.

Lt Thos J Simpson, [formerly of the Confederate army,] of Loudoun Co, Va, is now in Wash City. He was of Ashby's cavalry, & was taken prisoner. After his liberation, at the close of the war, he was wounded in the shoulder & hip in a fight with a captain of the Union army, at Columbus, Ohio, growing out of a threat by the latter to kill any man of Ashby's command. Simpson grasped the half-discharged pistol & turned it upon his opposer, killing him. He was some time in prison before his trial, at Little Rock, when he was acquitted.

Mrd: on Jan 2, at St Aloyisus Church, by Rev Fr Lynch, S J, Jas Elverson, of Phil, to Sallie R, daughter of the late Eli Duval, of Annapolis, Md. [Header: Elverson-Duvall.]

Orphans Court of Wash Co, D C, Jan 4, 1868. In the case of Roberta A Pywell & Atwell Cowling, excs of Richd Gudgin, dec'd, the executors & Court have appointed Feb 1st next, for the final settlement of the personal estate of the said dec'd, of the assets in hand. -Jas R O'Beirne, Reg/o wills

Chicago, Jan 5. The jury in the Ticknor divorce case brought in a verdict yesterday, granting the divorce asked for by Mrs Ticknor. A motion for a new trial has been entered.

Orphans Court of Wash Co, D C, Jan 4, 1868. In the case of August Schroeder, adm of Rita Triay, dec'd, the administrator & Court have appointed Jan 28 next, for the final settlement of the personal estate of the said dec'd, of the assets in hand.
-Jas R O'Beirne, Reg/o wills

Dept of the Interior, U S Patent Ofc, Wash, Dec 28, 1867. Ptn of Harriet C B Bigelow, adm of the estate of Chas H Bigelow, dec'd, of Pittsfield, Mass, praying for the extension of a patent granted to said Chas H Bigelow May 20, 1854, for an improvement in mode of manufacturing Turbine Wheels, for seven years from the expiration of said patent, which takes place on May 30, 1868. -T C Theaker, Com'r of Patents

TUE JAN 7, 1868
Wm Mitchell Gillespie, LL D, Prof of Civil Engineering in Union College for 23 years, & author of several standard works in his profession, died in N Y on Jan 1, 1868.

Criminal Court-Judge Olin. 1-Agnes White, petit larceny: sentenced to 20 days in the county jail. 2-Philip Lucas, petit larceny, guilty: sentenced to 2 months in the county jail. 3-John M Smith, alias Slim Jim, larceny; nolle pros. 4-Robt Jones, larceny; guilty. 5-Julius Wallace, assault & battery; guilty of assault only: fined $10; in default of payment to go to the county jail for 2 months. 6-Ann Dorsey, indicted for keeping a bawdy house; nolle pros. 7-Geo McCauley, grand larceny, arraigned & plead guilty. 8-Chas Boyd, larceny; guilty; one month in the county jail. 8-Saml Roberts & Henry Harvey, larceny; verdict guilty. Roberts sentenced to 3 months; Harvey to 1 month in the county jail.

Mr Edw Pagels, for several years past ticket agent at the Balt depot in this city, has resigned to connect himself with mercantile interests of Balt. Mr Geo E Pagels, his brother, who has been employed in that ofc, has been appointed the ticket agent.

Hiram Ulysses Grant was born on Apr 27, 1822, at Point Pleasant, Clermont Co, Ohio. His father was of Scotch descent, & a dealer in leather. Ulysses was the eldest of 6 children. When he entered the military academy at West Point, at age 17, the Congressman who procured his appointment giving his name, by mistake, was Ulysses S Grant. Simpson was the maiden name of his mother, & was also borne by one of his younger brothers. This doubtless occasioned the error. Young Grant applied to the authorities at West Point & the Sec of War to have the blunder corrected, but the request went unnoticed. His comrades at once adopted the initial U S in his behalf, & christened him Uncle Sam-a nickname that he never lost in the army; & when he graduated in 1843, 21st in a class of 39, his commission of brevet 2nd lt & his diploma both styled him Ulysses S Grant; by which name he has since been known.

Orphans Court of Wash Co, D C. In the matter of Jas McSherry, guardian to his minor children, Helen W, Mary C, & Jas C McSherry, heirs of Mrs Helen M McSherry, dec'd, the guardian reported that he sold parts of lot 1 in square 570, as follows: eastern part to Jas L Barbour for $2,238.28; western part to same for $1,641.40; middle part to J W Colby for $3,133.59. –Wm F Purcell, Judge of the Orphans Court of D C.
-Jas R O'Beirne, Reg/o wills

Dept of the Interior, U S Patent Ofc, Wash, Dec 28, 1867. Ptn of Jas Buell, exc of the estate of Jas McGregor, jr, dec'd, of N Y, N Y, praying for the extension of a patent granted to said McGregor on Apr 11, 1854, for an improvement in the construction of Tea & Coffee Pots, for seven years from the expiration of said patent, which takes place on Apr 11, 1868. -T C Theaker, Com'r of Patents

WED JAN 8, 1868
Orphans Court-Judge Purcell. 1-First & final account of Wm King, Geo W Beall, & Jenkin Thomas, excs of Peter Von Essen, filed & passed. 2-John Cameron gave bond in the sum of $8,000 as exc of the late will of Jas McWilliam. Sureties, Geo W Goodall & John McGrann. 3-Harriet A Brown gave bond in the sum of $5,000 as admx of John B Brown. Sureties, Z Richards & John R McClellan. The will of John B Brown was filed & admitted to probate & record. 4-The will of Truman Lynch was admitted to probate. 5-Martha Custis gave bond in the sum of $8,000 as guardian of the minor children of John H Upshur. Sureties, B W Kennon & Robt Dicks.

Criminal Court-Judge Olin. 1-Henry Yost, indicted for receiving stolen goods; guilty. 2-Wm Robinson, petit larceny; guilty, sentenced to the county jail for 30 days. 3-Geo Williams, grand larceny; guilty; sentenced to Albany Penitentiary for 2 years & 3 months. 4-Wm H Shenig, petit larceny; arraigned & pleads guilty. Geo R Schenig, his recognizance, to appear at next term of court to hear judgment. 5-Danl Rice was found guilty of assault & battery only. H D Terry for defence.

Mrd: on Jan 2, at the residence of the bride's mother, by Rev Fr Kane, of St Patrick's Church, Wm Cranch McIntyre, to Fannie, daughter of the late Elexius Simms, all of Wash City.

Augusta, Jan 7. Foster Blodgett, postmaster, has been suspended, & G W Summers has been appointed special agent to take charge of the Augusta post-office. A petition is being circulated among the citizens, which will be presented to Gen Meade, asking for the removal of Blodgett as military mayor of Augusta.

Miss Letitia Christian Tyler, born in the Presidential Mansion at Wash, the beautiful & accomplished grand-daughter of the late Pres John Tyler, & the oldest daughter of Robt Tyler, so distinguished for his zeal & eloquence as the champion of Irish nationality & independence, & a trusted leader of the old Democratic party before the war, is now engaged in type-setting, in the employment of the Advertiser newspaper, Montgomery, Ala. This brave girl shows that her blood descends from a resolute & fearless stock.

Orphans Court of Wash Co, D C, Jan 7, 1868. In the case of Geo Magruder, adm of Peter W Magruder, dec'd, the administrator & Court have appointed Feb 1st next, for the final settlement of the personal estate of the said dec'd, of the assets in hand.
-Jas R O'Beirne, Reg/o wills

Dept of the Interior, U S Patent Ofc, Wash, Jan 2, 1868. Ptn of Morris Mattson, of N Y, N Y, praying for the extension of a patent granted to him Apr 4, 1854, for an improvement in Enema Syringes, for seven years from the expiration of said patent, which takes place on Apr 4, 1868. -T C Theaker, Com'r of Patents

THU JAN 9, 1868
Furnished or unfurnished rooms for rent, with or without board, on D, east of 7th st. Apply on the premises to Mrs Chaffee.

Wm N Rand, late Treasurer of Madison Co, Indiana, is a defaulter to the amount of $22,500.

Mrd: on Jan 8, in Wash City, by Rev Addison, of Trinity Church, Wm D Mack, of Mich, to Ella S, daughter of Douglass Moore, of Wash City.

Died: on Jan 7, Robt H Owen, aged 56 years. His funeral will be from his late residence, 84 First st, between Fred'k & Fayette sts, Gtwn, on Thu at 3 o'clock.

Orphans Court of Wash Co, D C, Jan 7, 1848. In the case of Wm E Roberts, adm of Ann Roberts, dec'd, the administrator & Court have appointed Feb 1st next, for the final settlement of the personal estate of the said dec'd, of the assets in hand.
-Jas R O'Beirne, Reg/o wills

Dept of the Interior, U S Patent Ofc, Wash, Jan 2, 1868. Ptn of Carmi Hart, of Bridgeport, Conn, praying for the extension of a patent granted to him Apr 4, 1854, for an improvement in Machine for Cutting Veneers, for seven years from the expiration of said patent, which takes place on Apr 4, 1868. -T C Theaker, Com'r of Patents

FRI JAN 10, 1868
Criminal Court-Judge Olin. 1-Edw Edwards, convicted of assault & battery. Sentenced to pay six cents fine. 2-Chas Hawes, indicted for assault & resisting Ofcr Kimmell, in Dec last; guilty; recommended to the mercy of the Court. 3-Timothy Gleason, indicted for assault & resisting Ofcr Edmonson; guilty. 4-John Turner, petit larceny; not guilty. 5-Timonty Jackson, alias Jas Jackson. Bench warrant ordered. 6-Danl Rice, convicted of assault & battery, fined $10, & in default of payment to be confined in county jail for 30 days. 7-John Wesley, larceny. Bench warrant issued. 8-John Simpson, grand larceny. Guilty of stealing one pipe of the value of $30, & believe him to be under the age of 16 years. 8-Henry Johnson, alias Stokely, petit larceny: guilty; sentenced to 3 months in the county jail. 9-Frank L Heck, petit larceny: not guilty. 10-Kate Thompson; indicted for keeping a bawdy house: not guilty. 10-Jeremiah Johnson, petit larceny; guilty; sentenced to county jail for 2 months.

The Senate, yesterday, confirmed the following nominations:
J Guy Foreman, postmaster at Erie, Pa.
Thos N Lee, postmaster, Hancock, Mich.
Davis K Noyes, postmaster, Baraboo, Wisc.
Geo W Tabler, postmaster, Martinsburg, West Va.
Oscar Minor, collector of customs for the Dist of Texas, vice Kent, dec'd.
John C Cartwright, U S Atty for the Dist of Oregon.
The Senate rejected the following nominations:
Edmund Cooper, Assist Sec of the Treasury.
Jas Robbins, postmaster, Penn Yan, Pa.
Lemuel D Evans, collector internal revenue 4th Dist, Texas.
Wm J Clark, surveyor of customs for the port of Saybrook, Conn.
Alex'r K Lowry, register of the land ofc, Marysville, Calif.
Wm C Houser, postmaster, Mechanicsburg, Pa.
Danl Burnman, postmaster, Milton, Pa.
Wm D Foutz, assessor internal revenue, 2nd Dist of Indiana.

Chas C Jewett, superintendent of the Boston Public Library, died suddenly yesterday.

Mr Saml Nicholson, inventor of the pavement bearing his name, & other devices, died in Boston on Jan 6, 1868. [Jan 13th newspaper: Mr Saml Nicolson, inventor of the Nicolson pavement, an improved steering apparatus for vessels, & other contrivances, died in Boston, on Monday, after a brief illness, at the age of 76 years. He was a native of Plymouth, Mass.] [Note the two spellings of Nicholson/Nicolson.]

Equity Court-Judge Wylie. 1-Ruppert vs Keenan et al. Order appointing Wm T Keenan guardian ad litem. 2-McPherson, adm, vs Warner et al. Order giving cmplnt leave to file amended bill; application for injunction to be heard Jan 10, 1868. 3-Pepper et al vs Seaton et al. Order for the appearance of dfndnts. 4-Williams et al vs Upshur et al. Order appointing Robt Dick guardian ad litem. 5-Perry Straitner vs Eliz Straitner. Order warning dfndnt to enter appearance. 6-Whitney vs Frisbie. Order taking supplemental bill pro confesso, & certifying the case to the court in general term, to be heard in the first instance.

U S Jail, Wash, Jan 9, 1868. Fifty dollars reward for the apprehension & delivery of the following named prisoners: Ezekiel Chancy, Wm H Elrod, & Jos Glenn.
-Wm H Huesties, Warden U S Jail.

Mrd: at St Patrick's Church, by Rev Fr Kane, Lt Frank H Harrington, U S Marine Corps, to Rosa, daughter of John F Callan. [No date given-current item.]

Died: on Thu, Mrs Nannie W Barclay, wife of Mr John R Barclay, & daughter of Gen Jas A Ekin, Deputy Quartermaster General U S army. Religious service will be held at the family residence, 361 11th st, between L & M, this day at 1½ o'clock.

Died: on Nov 21, 1867, at Oxford, Miss, Mrs Sallie A Owens, wife of Capt A T Owens, formerly Miss Sallie A Davis, of Wash City.

Memphis, Jan 7. A terrible affair occurred at Dyersburg, West Tenn, on Tuesday. Sheriff Parkington attempted to arrest an old man named Duncan on the street. Duncan drew a pistol & fired, shooting off the Sheriff's thumb. Parkington's son, who was standing near, fired a pistol, killed Duncan, whose son, coming up at the same moment, fired, killing young Parkington instantly, whose father, seeing his son slain, drew his pistol & shot young Duncan through the heart. Further trouble is apprehended, owing to the extensive relations of both parties.

Burlington, Vt, Jan 9. The Rt Rev Bishop Hopkins, presiding bishop of the Protestant Episcopal Church of the U S, expired at the Episcopal residence, at Rock Point, this afternoon, aged 76 years. [Jan 15th newspaper: Bishop Hopkins was of English extraction, but was born in Dublin, Jan 30, 1792, so that at the time of his death he was 76 years old. His parents emigrated to this country when he was only 8 years old. He married a daughter of Caspar Otto Muller, a retired merchant of Balt, but previously of Hamburg, Germany.]

SAT JAN 11, 1868
Balt, Jan 9. Miss Jenny Busk met with a brilliant reception at her last concert here tonight. She was repeatedly encored by the large audience. She goes hence to Washington.

The funeral of Mrs Nannie W Barclay, daughter of Gen Jas A Ekin, took place yesterday from the residence of her father. Among the prominent personages present were ex-Sec Stanton, & Generals Rucker, Dane, & Perry. The scene, in which an idolizing husband, parents, & other members of the household gathered to look for the last time upon the form, beautiful in death, of wife, daughter, & sister. The services were conducted by Dr J G Butler, of the English Lutheran Church, of which the deceased was a member, assisted by Dr Tustin; Rev J M Johnston made the concluding prayer. The remains were followed by the family & a large retinue of friends to the depot, & were thence conveyed by special car to Pittsburgh, Pa, for interment in the family burying ground.

<u>The President sent to the Senate yesterday the following nominations:</u>
Chas G Greene, Assist Treasurer at Boston, vice T P Chandler, whose commission will expire on Jan 18, 1868.
Jos E Smith, Collector of Customs for Wiscasset, Maine.
Thos J Kinsella, Collector of Internal Revenue for the First Dist of Illinois.
Geo C Getchell, Assessor of Internal Revenue for Third Dist of Maine.
Wm M Post, Assessor of Internal Revenue for the Twelfth Dist of Pa.
Wm J Britton, Assessor of Internal Revenue for the First Dist of Miss.
Thos M Reynolds, Assessor of Internal Revenue for the Twenty-fourth Dist of N Y.
H Warren Rose, Receiver of Public Moneys at Sacramento, Calif.
Edw B McPherson, Receiver of Public Moneys at Boonville, Missouri.
Chas Mundoe, Register of the Land Ofc at Tallahassee, Florida.

Burlington, Vt, Jan 10. The funeral of Bishop Hopkins will take place in this city on Jan 15. A large attendance of bishops & clergymen of the U S & Canada are expected.

Guisseppi Guidicini died in N Y on Wed. His was the first artist of note that introduced fresco painting into this country.

Died: on Jan 10, Mrs Catharine Caldwell. Her funeral will take place on Sunday next, at 2 o'clock P M, from the residence of her husband, 40 Pa ave.

C V Culver, late senior partner of the firm of Culver, Penn & Co, has been rearrested on the complaint of Dr A G Egbert, of Mercer & Co, charging fraud & embezzlement.

Dept of the Interior, U S Patent Ofc, Wash, Jan 4, 1868. Ptn of B J La Mothe, of N Y, N Y, praying for the extension of a patent granted to him Apr 4, 1854, for an improvement in Railroad Cars, for seven years from the expiration of said patent, which takes place on Apr 4, 1868. -T C Theaker, Com'r of Patents

Dept of the Interior, U S Patent Ofc, Wash, Jan 4, 1868. Ptn of Benj A Lavender, of Halifax, N C, & Kate Lowe, admx of the state of Henry Lowe, dec'd, of Balt, Md, praying for the extension of a patent granted to said Benj A Lavender & Henry Lowe, Apr 4, 1854, for an improvement in Treating Cane Fibre for Paper & other purposes, for seven years from the expiration of said patent, which takes place on Apr 4, 1868. -T C Theaker, Com'r of Patents

MON JAN 13, 1868
The trial of Lt John C Braine, who is charged with piracy in seizing the steamer **Chesapeake**, will take place on Jan 17, 1868.

Orphans Court-Judge Purcell, Jan 11, 1868. 1-The first & final account of John D McPherson, adm of Chas F Robertson, dec'd, was approved & passed. 2-Catharine Johnson gave bond in the sum of $1,600, & was appointed guardian to the orphans of Robt Johnson. Sureties, Isaac Davenport & John W Reed. 3-The last will & testament of J Manning Hadley, late of Wash Co, was filed for probate. 4-A list of the debts of the late Saml Tilston was returned by his executor, Abraham Wyckoff. 5-Mary Dorothea Friess & Christian Widenayer gave bond in the sum of $1,000 as excs of the last will of Christopher Friess. A E L Keese & John Widenayer, sureties. 6-In re. Estate of Patrick Callan, dec'd. Citation against Kate Callan, widow, to appear & show cause why she should not take out letters of administration.

Equity Court-Judge Wylie. 1-J W P Myers vs Jane C Myers et al. Appointing trustee to sell property. 2-Martha C Williams vs Custis P Upshur. Order referring cause to Auditor. 3-Joslin vs Joslin. Order extending time for taking testimony 20 days.

A negro, known as "Old Father Robinson," is living in Detroit, at the age of 114 years. He fought in the Revolutionary war, & again at New Orleans, under Jackson, in 1815.

Criminal Court-Judge Olin 1-Susan Brokenborough; grand larceny of $130; not guilty, on account of her tender age. 2-Nicholas Foreman, assault & battery on an ofcr; guilty, 4 months in jail. Same, petit larceny; nolle pros. 3-John Williams, petit larceny; guilty; jail for 2 months. 4-Wm Marshall, petit larceny; guilty. Lewis Fox, grand larceny; guilty. John Thomas, petit larceny, guilty, jail for 2 months. 5-The Judge recommended the discharge of the following prisoners: Miss Davison, charged with larceny; Geo Shiner, for assault & battery; Thos Gailor, for embezzlement.

Mrd: on Jan 7, at St Aloysius Church, by Rev Fr Kelly, S J, Maurice M Quinlan, of N Y, to Emma F Redmond, of Wash, D C. No cards.

Died: on Jan 10, at the residence of his brother-in-law, Richd B Mohun, Louis William, aged 29 years, only & beloved son of Mrs Anna Hanson Dorsey & the late Lorenzo Dorsey. His funeral will take place on Jan 13 at 10 o'clock, from St Aloysius Church.

Albany, N Y, Jan 12. Judge Wm B Wright, of the Court of Appeals, died suddenly at Congress Hall tonight, of disease of the kidneys. He was on the bench Thursday.

Farm for sale in Chas Co, Md, by power of atty from the parties entitled, the undersigned will offer at public sale, in the village of Piscataway, on Jan 30, that valuable farm of which Geo S Harris, formerly of said county, died seized & possessed, upon Mattawoman Run; consists of 275 acres, more or less; with a dwlg & 2 barns & other out-bldgs thereon. –Jno W Mitchell, Atty for the owners.

Mortgagee's sale on the premises, near Colesville, Montg Co, Md, on Jan 18. By power of atty from Barbara A Close, excx of Christian Close, & under a power contained in a mortgage from Jonathan R Cronice & Emily C Cronice, to Christian Close, dated Jul 21, 1864, will sell at public auction, on the premises, all the property described in said mortgage, being parts of several tracts of land-part of *Good Luck*; *Peach Lot*; & *Beaver Dam*-containing 151 acres, in all, of land, more or less, being the same land conveyed by Dr Benj Berry to said Jonathan R Cronice, by deed dated Mar 11, 1863, & recorded in Liber J G H No 9, folios 248 & 249. This farm is improved by a brick dwlg, in good repair, & all necessary out-houses; situated 12 miles from Wash & 5 miles from Beltsville. Apply to M Bannon, Atty for Barbara Close, excx of Christian Close, 32 St Paul st, Balt, Md.

Orphans Court of Wash Co, D C, Jan 11, 1868. In the case of Lelia M Talburt & Duncan S Walker, adms of Jas W Brown, dec'd, the administrators & Court have appointed Feb 8 next, for the final settlement of the personal estate of the said dec'd, of the assets in hand. -Jas R O'Beirne, Reg/o wills

Dept of the Interior, U S Patent Ofc, Wash, Jan 5, 1868. Ptn of Danl W Shares, of Hamden, Conn, praying for the extension of a patent granted to him Aug 1, 1854, for an improvement in Cultivator, for seven years from the expiration of said patent, which takes place Aug 1, 1868. -T C Theaker, Com'r of Patents

Dept of the Interior, U S Patent Ofc, Wash, Jan 6, 1868. Ptn of L Otto P Meyer, of Newtown, Conn, praying for extension of a patent granted him Apr 4, 1854, for an improvement in Treating Caoutchouc & Vulcanized Gums, for 7 years from the expiration of said patent, which takes place Apr 4, 1868. -T C Theaker, Com'r of Patents

Dept of the Interior, U S Patent Ofc, Wash, Jan 4, 1868. Ptn of Jas McCarty, of Reading, Pa, praying for the extension of a patent granted to him Apr 4, 1854, for an improvement in Heating Skelps for the manufacture of wrought-iron Tubes, for seven years from the expiration of said patent, which takes place Apr 4, 1868. -T C Theaker, Com'r of Patents

TUE JAN 14, 1868
The President yesterday sent to the Senate the name of Hon S S Cox as Minister to Austria.

Real Estate sold. R M Hall sold yesterday, at his Exchange, 7th & D sts, a large portion of the *Meridian Hill* property, comprising several squares & parts of squares, to J T Stevens, for $65,000. Cooper & Latimer, aucts, sold at auction yesterday, a small frame dwlg on 20th st, between E & F sts, to W M Prince, for $650.

Mrs Hubbard, of Port Dallhousie, Canada, has received $7,000 remuneration for the loss of her husband, who was killed at the Angola accident-$4,000 from the railroad company, & $3,000 on an accident insurance policy. A sister of Chas Lobdell, who was slaughtered by the Lake Shore railroad accident at Angola, has become hopelessly insane. She resides at Bridgeport, Conn.

Mr Searle is now completing an elegant summer residence for Hon Montgomery Blair, which is located at *Silver Spring*, a short distance out 7th st. The house is 40 feet wide by 50 feet deep, 3 stories & basement, a handsome French roof, with a large tower surmounting the whole. The structure is of red brick, with trimmings of the American bldg block, light color. It is provided with balconies & piazzas. Messrs Turton & Lowry were the contractors, & they have, under Mr Searle's supervision, erected one of the finest country houses in the District.

Died: on Jan 6, in Wash City, of paralysis of the heart, Miss Mary Foster, of Waterville, Maine, in her 34th year.

Criminal Court-Judge Olin. 1-John Ward; petit larceny; guilty; motion for a new trial. 2-Fanny Duvall, alias Carter; grand larceny; guilty; sentenced to Albany penitentiary for 18 months. 3-Perry Duvall; grand larceny; nolle pros. 4-Henry Lee; grand larceny; not guilty. 5-Moses Clarke; petit larceny; sentenced to county jail for 8 months.

Jefferson Davis & wife left New Orleans on Sat last, for Natchez, Miss.

WED JAN 15, 1868
Criminal Court-Judge Olin. 1-John Fearce, alias Thomas; grand larceny; guilty. Sentenced to Albany penitentiary for 18 months.

The President yesterday sent the following nominations to the Senate:
John D Hopkins, to be Collector of Customs for the Dist of Frenchman's Bay, Maine, vice Wm B Peters, removed.
Bion Bradbury, Collector of Customs at Portland & Falmouth, Maine, vice Israel Washburn, jr, whose commission expires on Jan 19, 1868.
Kellian V Whaley, Collector of Customs at Brazos de Santiago, Texas, vice Richd L Robinson, dec'd.
Wm F Kilgore, to be 3rd lt Revenue Cutter Service, vice Geo Gerrard, dec'd.
Reuben S Torrey, Collector Internal Revenue for the 8th Dist of N Y, vice A M Wood, resigned.
Butler H Bigby, Collector Internal Revenue for the 8th Dist of N Y, vice Thos Smith, to be removed.
Thos B Asten, Assessor of Internal Revenue 8th Dist of N Y, vice Anthony J Bleecker, to be removed.
John G Clark, of Iowa, to be Receiver of Public Moneys at Des Moines, Iowa, vice Thos Seeley, resigned.
Fanny Vandergriff, to be postmistress at the Univ of Va, vice David Vandergrift, resigned. [Note the two spellings of Vandergriff/Vandergrift.]
Jas M Nibbing, postmaster at Finley, Ohio, to fill a vacancy.
RH O'Farrall, postmaster at Chico, Calif, vice Bidwell, dec'd.

Orphans Court-Judge Purcell. 1-Catharine Callan gave bond in the sum of $500 as admx of the personal estate of Patrick Callan. John O'Toole & Michl Carpenter, sureties. 2-The will of John Graham was fully proven & admitted to probate. He names his wife, Mary Graham, excx. 3-Bernard Geier gave bond in the sum of $4,000 as exc of the will of Loring Thomas. Mathias Alleg & Chas Walter, sureties. 4-Wm A Ward gave bond in the sum of $800 as guardian to the infant child of John L Lancaster & heir of Rose M Lancaster. Wm H Ward & Saml T Drury, sureties.

Mrd: on Jan 14, at the Epiphany Church Parsonage, in Wash City, Rev C H Hall, D D, Wm H Andrews, 30th U S infty, to Fannie Eliz, daughter of F A Jones, of Gtwn, D C.

N Y, Jan 13. Jas H Leveridge, record teller of the City Bank, a defaulter. Rumor placed the amount anywhere from forty to four hundred thousand dollars. The detectives are on his track.

Newark, N J, Jan 14. John Dempsey, tried at Morristown for the murder of Kean Carroll, at Boonton, has been convicted of murder in the second degree, & was sentenced to the State prison for 16 years.

Dept of the Interior, U S Patent Ofc, Wash, Jan 10, 1868. Ptn of Jas L Cathcart, of Gtwn, D C, praying for the extension of a patent granted to him Apr 18, 1854, for an improvement in Attaching Propellers to the Driving Shaft for 7 years from the expiration of said patent, which takes place on Apr 18, 1868. -T C Theaker, Com'r of Patents

Orphans Court of Wash Co, D C. Letters testamentary on the personal estate of Maria Miller, late of Wash Co, D C, dec'd. –Ch J Miller, exc

Dept of the Interior, U S Patent Ofc, Wash, Jan 9, 1868. Ptn of Saml J Parker, of Ithaca, N Y, praying for the extension of a patent granted to him Apr 11, 1854, for an improvement in Sewing Machines for seven years from the expiration of said patent, which takes place on Apr 11, 1868. -T C Theaker, Com'r of Patents

Chancery sale of valuable wharf property in Gtwn, on Jan 30; public auction, under a decree of the Supreme Court of D C, passed in a cause in which J W P Myers was cmplnt & Jane C Myers et al were dfndnts, all that valuable wharf property belonging to the estate of the late Chas Myers, fronting 41 feet on the south side of Water st, in Gtwn, & running back that width to the channel of the Potomac river, the said property being between Congress & Jefferson sts. –Jane C Myers, J W P Myers, trustees -Thos Dowling, auct

THU JAN 16, 1868

Mr J Price Kepner, for a number of years in charge of the statistical subdivision of the Surgeon General's Ofc, has received the appointment of Chief Clerk of the Record & Pension Bureau of that ofc, vice Geo S Pringle, who resigned the position to pursue the business of solicitor of claims.

Circuit Court-Judge Wylie. Mary Gorman vs Corp of Wash. Brent & Lovejoy for the plntf; Bradley for the dfndnt. This is a case where the Corp built a bridge across the Tiber in Jackson alley, which caused the water to overflow, & swept away part of the house, & destroyed the furniture of the plntf. She lays her damages at $5,000. Still on trial.

Equity Court-Judge Wylie. 1-In re-Margaret Cronin, [lunatic;] order for rule on P H Donegan. 2-Borland vs Hollidge; decree appointing five com'rs to partition real estate.

Chancery sale of valuable real estate; by decree of the Supreme Court of D C, in Equity No 1,002, wherein Perequine Echols et al are cmplnts & Jos Carter et al dfndnts: sale on Jan 30, on the premises, part of lot 3 in square 243; suitable for a handsome residence. -John J Johnson, trustee -Cooper & Latimer, aucts

Orphans Court of Wash Co, D C. Letters testamentary on the personal estate of Lorenz Thoma, late of Wash Co, D C, dec'd. –Bernard Geier, exc

Dept of the Interior, U S Patent Ofc, Wash, Jan 10, 1868. Ptn of Stephen Bazin & Jas A Bazin, of Canton, Mass, praying for extension of a patent granted to them Apr 25, 1854, for an improvement in Machinery for Laying Rope, for seven years from the expiration of said patent, which takes place on Apr 25, 1868. -T C Theaker, Com'r of Patents

FRI JAN 17, 1868
Equity Court-Judge Wylie. 1-Echols et al vs Carter & Binckley. Appointing J J Johnson trustee to sell, & directing dfndnt to convey to cmplnt a certain lot, & to surrender possession. 2-Edmonston vs Cammack. Order substituting Geo F Appleby trustee, in place of W J Stoze, dec'd.

Criminal Court-Judge Olin. 1-Henry T Johnson arraigned for the murder of Thos S Smoot on Jun 30, 1866, & pleaded not guilty, & asked to be tried by the country.
2-Jos Wm N Zimmer, for the murder of Chas Dumas, Sep 18, 1867, on 17th st, near N Y ave, was arraigned & plead not guilty. Having no friends & no money, the Court assigned Messrs Norris & Fendall to defend him.
3-Wm Eldridge & Cpl John C McClelland were arraigned for the murder of Geo Williams on Sep 12, 1867, in a restaurant kept by Rutherford, at 2nd & Pa ave. The former of these having no counsel, the Court assigned Messrs Mattingly & Carusi to defend him.
4-Geo McCauley was convicted of petit larceny, & was next arraigned on the charge of assault & battery with intent to kill Thos Kinsley on Jan 10. The jury brought in a verdict of guilty of assault with intent to kill. Mr Adams moved for a new trial, & the Court reserved the sentence until after he had heard the reasons for a new trial. The Court said he had a fair & impartial trial. McCauley was sentenced to the Albany penitentiary for 8 years, to commence at the expiration of the 5 years to which he was already sentenced.
5-Henry Plater, grand larceny of goods of the value of $35, the property of John W Digg, from his house, in Gtwn, on West st, on Dec 24, was found guilty of the larceny of a flask only, valued at forty cents; jail 2 months.
6-Jas M Jackson, for the larceny of brass & iron, the property of the U S Gov't, on May 14 last, valued at $15.50. Trial postponed due to the absence of a witness.
7-Ezekiel Chancy, Chas Miller, Jos H Garrett, & Frisby Wyants on trial for assault & battery with intent to kill Benj Whiting on a canal boat on Dec 10 last, excepting the first-named, who was one of the parties who escaped from the jail a few nights since.
8-The grand jury recommended, & the judge discharged, John Hard, now held for assault & battery on David Buell.
9-Rosetta Watkins, petit larceny; nolle pros.
10-Bryan Carroll, robbery; recognizance forfeited.
11-Edw Corydon, surety for $1,000; bench warrant issued.

Cincinnati, Jan 15. The death of E Leghton, an old & well-known pork & beef packer of this city, was announced on Change today. He died suddenly, of apoplexy.

The Senate yesterday confirmed the following nominations:
Wm M Post, to be assessor of internal revenue for the 12th Dist of Pa.
B F Chandler, chief engineer in the navy.
Edw B McPherson, receiver of public moneys at Booneville, Missouri.
Jas M Castello, receiver of public moneys at Fair Play, Colorado.
The Senate rejected Saml P Daniels, receiver of public moneys at Indianapolis.

Died: on Jan 16, of paralysis, Mrs Ann Powers, in her 73rd year. Her funeral will take place on Jan 18 at 2 o'clock P M, from her late residence, 540 12th st west.

Died: on Jan 14, at *Avallon*, his place of residence, in PG Co, Md, Mr Washington Custis Calvert.

Meeting of the Board of Police last evening. Henry E Norris, John J Hill, & Jas Offutt were appointed additional privates for 90 days. The following ofcrs, for neglect of duty & violating the rules of the force, were sentenced as follows: Pvt John S Waugh, fined $5; Pvt Wm H Lusby, to be reprimanded & fined $10; Pvt Henry Nash, for intoxication, dismissed the force; Pvt Wm E Dunn, for insubordination, dismissed; Pvt John Boyle, for neglect of duty, fined $5; Pvt Chas P Hopkins, conduct unbecoming an ofcr, to be reprimanded & fined $10; Pvt Saml T Cronin, for conduct unbecoming an ofcr, violating rules & regulations, to be reprimanded, dismounted, transferred, & fined $30; Pvt Fred'k Peaster, violating general orders, fined $10; Pvt Thos J Burrell, for conduct unbecoming an ofcr, dismissed the force. Alfred Borden & John Zirwes were appointed privates, vice Nash & Dunn dismissed. The following applications for licenses to sell liquor were rejected: R A Golden & Bro, Jas Laws, Chas Hagemann, Patrick Corcoran, John Smith, Wm Taylor, & Edw Abner.

Proposed addition to Gtwn. It is proposed by a number of the leading capitalists of Gtwn to add to the limits of that city the large area of ground now owned by Richd S Cox, north of the new cut road, & west of Fayette st. These gentlemen propose to form a joint stock company, who will open streets through the entire property, consisting of 65 acres, & divide it off into bldg lots for private residences. The corporate limits extend along the north side of this property two-thirds its length from Fayette st. The property offers magnificent sites for residences.

Patents to Washingtonians the past week. 1-For a method of manufacturing illuminating gas, to Lori Stevens. 2-For an improved Hume tug-buckle, to Ludwig Wetzell. 3-For a time alarm, to be operated by an ordinary watch, to Louis Baum, of Wash, D C.

Dept of the Interior, U S Patent Ofc, Wash, Jan 13, 1868. Ptn of Nelson Gavit, of Phil, Pa, praying for the extension of a patent granted to him May 9, 1854, for an improvement in Machinery for Cutting Paper, for seven years from the expiration of said patent, which takes place on May 9, 1868. -T C Theaker, Com'r of Patents

Dept of the Interior, U S Patent Ofc, Wash, Jan 14, 1868. Ptn of Julia M Colburn, admx de bonis non, of Jas H Stimpson, dec'd, who was exc of Jas Stimpson, dec'd, of Balt, Md, praying for the extension of a patent granted to said Jas H Stimpson, as exc aforesaid, Oct 17, 1854, & ante-dated Apr 17, 1854, for an improvement in Vessels for Holding Liquids, for seven years from the expiration of said patent, which takes place on Apr 17, 1868. -T C Theaker, Com'r of Patents

SAT JAN 18, 1868
Obit-died: on Jan 10, at the residence of his brother-in-law, Richd B Mohun, in PG Co, Louis William, aged 29 years, the only & beloved son of Mrs Anna H & the late Lorenzo Dorsey. He was a grandson of the late Judge Owen Dorsey, of Balt; & also of the late Rev Wm McKenney, chaplain U S N, of Gtwn. Mr Dorsey was for some years a clerk in the Gen Post Ofc Dept, & continued in ofc up to the time of his decease, except for one

year's interval, 1864, when he volunteered in the army, & was reinstated in ofc when his time expired. He was a member of the Catholic Church, & was consoled by all the divine sacraments of his faith. His funeral ceremonies took place at St Aloysius Church, where mass for the repose of his soul was celebrated by Rev Wm Cleary, S J, assisted by Rev Chas Stonestreet, S J, & Rev John Kane, of St Patrick's. Mrs Kretchmar's glorious voice, as she sang the "De Profundis;" the anthem, "I know that my Redeemer liveth," & the requiem, "Rest, spirit rest," adding to the touching solemnity of the occasion. His body was deposited at *Mount Olivet Cemetery*, where it rests in hope. Requiescat in pace.

Mr John J Bogue, in Gtwn, real estate agent, has sold the frame dwlg on First st, between Fred'k & Fayette sts, the property of Mrs Henry Johnson, to Mrs Brown, for $1,100.

Gen Custer accused of murder. The Leavenworth Conservative, of last Thursday, states that on Wednesday Gen Geo A Custer & Lt W W Cook were put upon preliminary examination there, for the alleged murder of Chas Johnson, private in company K, 7th U S cavalry. Capt R M West, of company K, testified: Custer was lt colonel of the regt, & Cook a 1st lt in it. Johnson died near *Fort Wallace*, on Jul 19th & 20th last. Up to 2 P M of the 7th he was on duty as private in witness' company. At that time six men were seen leaving the camp. Two mounted parties were ordered by Gen Custer to pursue & bring none of them in alive. A Gov't wagon returned, bringing 3 men who had been shot, one of whom was Johnson. He was very feeble, & seemed to be suffering very much from a wound in the head. The wound which seemed to affect him most was a pistol bullet wound entering the side of the head near the right temple & ranging downward, coming out near the left side of the windpipe. He had another wound in his body, & one in his arm. He was shot in the Territory of Colorado, Jul 7, 1867. Witness applied to Gen Custer for medical attendance for the wounded men, & was told that they were deserters, & a deserter was not entitled to any consideration. Witness urged that the wounded men receive surgical attendance, which was allowed after some further conversations. Witness did not see the shooting, but heard the firing. Lt Cook was in one of the pursuing parties. He told witness he had done some of the shooting, & hoped none of the wounded would die. Johnson was hale & hearty before the shooting. A detail of his company buried him, & witness read the Episcopal burial service at the grave. Clement Willis, one of the deserters, testified that he saw Lt Cook shoot Johnson with a pistol. Miles Moylan, 1st lt & adjutant, also said that an order was given to bring none back alive, & thought Lt Cook was present when it was given. When the message came that 3 were wounded, Gen Custer ordered a wagon sent after them, & a medical ofcr was in attendance before Col West's request. The substance of the Gen's reply to this request was that the men could have necessary medical attendance.

Munson Hill Farm for sale: 175 acres, with good dwlg house, large barns, carriage house, & other outbldgs. This farm is in Fairfax Co, [near Falls Church,] Va. It was in full cultivation last year, & is only sold on account of the recent decease of its late owner, T B Munson. –Robt W Fenwick, 7th & F sts, Wash, D C.

MON JAN 20, 1868
Sales of property in Anne Arundel Co, Md. The Annapolis Gaz announces that the following property has recently been sold in A A Co: for the heirs of Dr Stephen Gambrill, a farm at *Gambrills' gate*, on the Annapolis & Elkridge railroad, containing 230 acres, for $7,270, to Henry Joyce, of A A Co. Also, the country seat of John Cummings, to Maj Frank Larned, U S A, for $7,250. It contains 20 acres, & is fairly improved, situated in A A Co, adjoining Maj Bond, Gen Elzey, M Bannon, & others. Also, a country seat at *Jessup's Cut*, containing 17 acres, with good improvements, to Col John L Smith, of Balt, for $8,500. Also, a farm near Elkridge Landing, containing 140 acres, to B Boyle, at $31 per acre. Also, the farm of the late Richd J Jacobs, near Annapolis Junction, to Mr Wm Anderson, of A A Co, at $46 per acre. Also, an improved tract adjoining the above, to Thos A *Jacob, containing 128 acres, at $32 per acre. Also, a small market farm of 18 acres, to Allen Warfield, of A A Co, for $1,200.
[*Jacob/Jacobs-copied as written.]

At 3 o'clock yesterday there was a large funeral procession from First st to St Aloysius Church, in respect to the memory of Mr John Caldwell, a popular & promising youth, aged about 16 years, & son of Mr Caldwell, an employee in the Congressional Bindery. He was an excellent youth, & much beloved. Fr Wiget performed the funeral services as required by the Roman Catholic Church.

On Sat last a negro woman, employed as a washerwoman, went to the house of Mr Winninger, at Ferry Point, near Norfolk, & in his absence assaulted his wife, Mrs Fanny Winninger, with a hatchet, leaving her for dead, & then robbed the house. This fiend was afterwards arrested & a portion of the stolen money recovered-some $500 in all, although more than $1,000 was stolen, besides a gold watch & valuable papers. Mrs Winninger may possibly recover, but her wounds are very severe.

Detective Wm M Kelly, well known & much beloved member of the detective corps of the Metropolitan Police force, died on Sat last. Since Jan 8 Mr Kelly has been lying very ill at his residence, on 8th st, with a severe attack of typhoid pneumonia. His sufferings were terrible the week before his death. He has been connected with the force since its organization, both as a private & as a detective ofcr. The funeral of Mr Kelly will take place this afternoon. The relatives & friends are to assemble at his late residence, 306 8th st, & accompany the remains to the E st Baptist Church, from whence the funeral cortege will move shortly after 2 P M.
+
Died: on Jan 18, Detective Wm M Kelly, of the Metropolitan Police force, of typhoid pnuemonia, aged 31 years, 4 months & 17 days. His funeral will take place from the E st Baptist Church this afternoon, at 2 o'clock. Friends & relatives of the deceased will attend at his late residence, 306 8th st, between L & M sts, at 1:30, & accompany the remains to the church.

Died: on Jan 17, of dropsy, Mr Nathan C Woodward, aged 53 years. His funeral will take place from his late residence, 354 10th st, between L & M sts, on Jan 20, at 11 o'clock A M. [Maine papers please copy.]

Died: on Jan 17, at the residence of Col H W Wharton, of Balt, Edw Wharton, of Wash, D C, in his 49th year. His funeral will take place at the residence of Col Wharton, 45 McCullough st, on Jan 21, at 8 A M. Interment to be in Phil.

Died: on Jan 17, Alex'r H Cross. His funeral will be from the residence of Mrs Riddall, corner of 21st & H sts, today, Monday, at 12 o'clock M.

Thos Dowling, auct, yesterday sold lot 213, in Beatty & Hawkins' addition to Gtwn, fronting 15 feet on the west side of Fred'k st, between 5th & 6th sts, & having a depth of 96 feet, & improved by a 3 story brick, & a frame store & dwlg house, to Michl Lynch for $1,455.

Circuit Court-Justice Wylie, Jan 18, 1868. 1-The jury in the case of Gormon vs the Corp of Wash, brought in a verdict for plntf-$100 damages.

Equity Court-Judge Wylie. 1-O & M Donn vs Orlando H Donn et al. Decree to sell real estate of Thos C Donn, dec'd. 2-Geo W Uttermehle vs R H Hall et al. Former decree pro confesso, made final, & trustee appointed to recover property. 3-Catherine Bauman vs Frank T Jones et al. Upon hearing bill, answer, & amended bill, the Court enjoined the trustee from selling on the 20th, as advertised, on condition of cmplnt's paying cost of advertisement.

Orphans Court-Judge Purcell. 1-Third account of Geo A Bohrer, exc of Dr Benj S Bohrer, filed. 2-Third account of Sarah Jane Burch, [now Davis,] guardian to the orphans of Jos A Burch, filed. 3-An account of the personal estate of Dr Benj S Bohrer, by Geo A Bohrer, exc, filed. 4-First individual account of Julia A Forrest, guardian to Ellen R Forrest, orphan of John Forrest, dec'd, filed. 5-First individual account of Julia A Forrest, guardian to Chas F Forrest, orphan of John Forrest, filed. 6-First general account of Julia A Forrest, guardian to John W, Chas F, & Ellen R Forrest, filed. 7-Eighth & final account of Wm B Kibbey, exc of John B Kibbey, filed. 8-Sixth general account of Thos Cogan, guardian to the orphans of Owen Murray, filed. 9-R Snowden Andrews gave bond in the sum of $1,400, as administrator of the personal estate of Geo T Andrews. T P Andrews & Eliza H Andrews, sureties. 10-Harriet D Leonard gave bond in the sum of $500, as guardian of the orphan of Fernando F Franklin. E S Pond & Henry Briggeman, sureties.

The heirs of the late John A Washington, of Va, have begun a suit in Chicago for the recovery of $100,000 worth of real estate in that city, which was owned by Washington at the time he was shot in Va, in 1861. A Chicago lawyer made his way through the lines, & finding the Washington heirs, represented that the estate would be confiscated if it remained in their name, & had it deeded to him for safety. He has since refused to restore it-hence the suit.

Springfield, Mass, Jan 19. Gen Humphreys, the famous confidence man, who eloped with Miss Kenyon to Cincinnati last summer, has been sentenced to 10 years in prison. He pleaded guilty to the indictments for obtaining money under false pretences.

Dissolution of copartnership under the name of Gault & Williams, Slate Roofers, this day by mutual consent. Matthew Gault will continue the business, having purchased his partner's interest-10th & La ave. —Matthew Gault, Wm Williams

Several months ago Col Schaaf, of the U S army, shot & killed Col Sheppard, a citizen of Ala, at Mount Vernon Arsenal, near Mobile. The murder was pronounced a most cowardly affair. He has recently been tried by a court-martial, & sentenced to pay a fine of $300, & to be imprisoned at *Fort Pulaski* for 6 months.

Pittsburg, Jan 18. Fireworks exploded this morning in the confectionery of Knable & Schrock, on Smithfield st, occasioned by the friction of a falling box of fireworks. John Schrock, a son of one of the proprietors, was fatally injured. Nancy Campbell & Fred Ramsey were killed by suffocation.

Chicago, Jan 19. A young woman named Eliz Stang was arrested yesterday, for attempting to poison her father, mother, brother, & sister, by putting strychnine in their coffee. They were all in a dangerous condition, but are now recovering. The girl acknowledged having purchased the poison, but asserted it was at the instance of her mother, who she charges put it in the coffee.

Executor's sale at auction of improved real estate & household furniture, by order of the Orphans Court of D C; as exc of the last will & testament of Lorenz Thoma, dec'd, late of Wash, I shall offer at public auction, on Jan 31, part of lot 3 in square 715, improved by 2 frame dwlg houses, 2 stories high; situated on the east side of First st, between I & K sts. -Bernard Geier, exc -John B Wheeler & Co, aucts.

Orphans Court of Wash Co, D C. Letters testamentary, c t a, on the personal estate of Josiah Melvin, late of Wash Co, D C, dec'd. —Maria L Melvin, admx c t z

Supreme Court of D C, Jan, 1868. Equity 988. Geo W Miller et al, cmplnts, vs John W Van Hook et al, dfndnts. Summons were issued in this cause for John Fox, Harriet Fox, F X Ward, & Wm Ward, dfndnts in this cause, & said summons returned "not to be found." Said absent dfndnts to appear on the first rule day occurring 40 days after this day; otherwise the cause will be proceeded with as in case of default. -R J Meigs, clerk

John Jacob Astor, the second son of John Jacob Astor, the millionaire, died in this city yesterday, in his 65th year. In early youth Mr Astor gave much intellectual promise, but, at about age 17, he accidentally fell, striking on his head, & thus his mental faculties were impaired. His father, after vain efforts to effect his restoration, built on 14th st, near the North River, a mansion for his accommodation. It occupies one entire block, & is surrounded by a high fence, to prevent prying & curious eyes from seeing the movements of the occupants. On the death of the father one of the principal items in his will was a provision intrusting the younger John Jacob to the care of a physician in whom he placed implicit confidence, & settling a handsome income upon the 14th st mansion.
–N Y Tribune

A telegraphic despatch from Santa Fe announces the said intelligence that Mr A Baldwin Norton, Superintendent of Indian Affairs for New Mexico, died at Santa Fe, on Jan 10. He was a brother of Senator Norton, of Minnesota.

TUE JAN 21, 1868

The funeral of the late Detective Wm M Kelly took place yesterday from his late residence on 8th st, between L & M sts; remains were conveyed to the E st Baptist Church, there they were deposited in front of the pulpit; coffin was of mahogany, lined with fine merino, & furnished with silver handles, engraved with Masonic emblems, the square & compass & 5 pointed star; the corpse was attired in a plain black suit, & the countenance looked very natural, the disease having apparently wasted Mr Kelly but little. The pall bearers were Messrs Clarvoe & Miner, of the detectives; Britt & Peters, of the police; Skippon & J Cross, of the Masons, & Richards & Keese, of the Schuetzen. After the ceremonies the remains were placed in the hearse, & followed by a long line of carriages. The funeral cortege proceeded to **Glenwood Cemetery**, where the body was consigned to its last resting place.

On Friday 5 negroes came to the store of Mr M A Muldrow, in Darlington Dist, & told Mr Sugs that they were there to purchase goods. The wife of Mr Sugs, in an adjoining room, became suspicious of them and went to the house of Mr Wyndham, & requested him to come to the store, in case there was trouble. He complied, taking a gun with him, & as he opened the door, was fired upon by the negroes. He repaired to Mr Muldrow's house, & they two went to the store & found all quiet. Mr Sugs was lying dead on the floor. Messrs Muldrow & Wyndham went to the house of the latter, where they found Mr Wyndham's father-in-law dangerously shot twice in the head, & his wife in 3 different places on the person by the same party of negroes. –Charleston Courier

Gen J B Magruder, late of the Confederate army, voluntarily presented himself in the clerk's ofc of the U S Circuit Court on Friday, & proposed to take the oath of allegiance to the Gov't of the U S. The oath was administered by Com'r White. -N Y Herald

The new Galt House at Louisville, Ky, will cost $1,200,000, & will be finished by Jul next.

Chicago, Jan 20. The Chicago Times pronounces for the nomination of Geo H Pendleton for the Presidency of the Democratic Nat'l Convention.

Trustee's sale of a small tract of land lying between Rock Creek & Tennallytown, in Wash Co, D C; by deed of trust to the undersigned executed by Wm T Collins, in order to secure the payment of certain promissory notes, as therein set forth, & as is shown by reference to said deed of trust, recorded in Liber R M H, No 3, folios 163 thru 165, in the land records of said county: sale on Feb 21, on the premises, part of a tract called *Azadia/Axadia*, containing 2½ acres. The property is east of the Rockville road, about 1 miles west of *Peirce's Mill*. –A C P Shoemaker, trustee -Jos F Kelley, auct

WED JAN 22, 1868
Orphans Court-Judge Purcell. 1-Rosanna Korts gave bond in the sum of $2,000 as guardian of the orphans of Jefferson B Korts, dec'd. W J Murtagh & Thos E Lloyd, sureties. Rosanna Korts gave bond in the sum of $2,400 as admx of the personal estate of Jeff B Korts. Sureties, Wm J Murtagh & Thos E Lloyd. 2-An account of the personal estate of John Lange, by Zachariah F Borland, administrator, filed.

Court in General Term. 1-M Laura Larner vs Andrew J Larner. This is an appeal from the decree of the Circuit Court appointing Jos H Bradley, jr, guardian to minor children of the parties to the suit, & enjoining & restraining the dfndnt from interfering with cmplnt or her minor children. The Court reserved its decision. 2-Echols et al vs Catharine Barrett. An execution was issued against Thos J Barrett, in his lifetime, & lot 4 in square 836, belonging to Barrett, was sold under said execution. Barrett gave money to John Hazel to buy in the lot at the marshal's sale, & hold it for him. After Barrett died Hazel conveyed the lot to Catharine Barrett, widow of said Thos J Barrett. The heirs of Barrett bring suit to recover from Catharine Barrett, on the ground that she did not give Hazel any consideration for the conveyance. Thompson & Davis. The Court confirmed the decree of court below, on the ground of want of proof of non-payment of consideration. 3-On motion of R S Davis, R McBrainey, of Kansas, was admitted any attoyney of this court.

N Y Tribune. Gen Grant as a Presidential candidate. Some of our friends are quite too fast in asserting the American people are eager to demand & nominate military candidates to the Presidency, merely because of their military record, in preference to civilians. [The Tribune then proceeds at much length to show wherein military aspirants for the Presidency failed.] On the whole, therefore, we are disposed to deny that the American people are very easily brought to elect Presidents from among merely military men, who have given no evidence of statesmanship.

Mr John Henry, of Charlotte, Va, the last survivor, save one, of the children of Patrick Henry, & owner of the old family seat & burial place of the great orator, died at his residence at **Red Hill** on Jan 7, in his 72nd year, of paralysis.

51st Anniversary of the Colonization Society was held last evening at Wesley Chapel. H B Latrobe, pres of the society, presided; Mr Wm C Cappenger, one of the secretaries. Since the last annual meeting, 8 vice presidents of the society have died, viz: Dr Stephen Duncan, of Miss; Hon Washington Hunt, N Y; Rev Joshua Soule, D D, Tenn; Hon Jos A Wright, of Indiana; Freeman Clark, of Maine; Wm H Brown, of Ill; Hon Jas M Wayne, of Ga; & Rev Jeremiah Day, D D, of Conn.

Mrd: on Jan 21, at Wash, D C, by Rev Dr Addison, of Trinity Church, Chas M Robinson, of Hardwick, Mass, to Antonia Hill, daughter of S S Benedict, of N Y C.

Died: on Jan 19, at Boston, in her 72nd year, Mrs Sarah Justice Browne, widow of Wm Browne, of Wash City.

THU JAN 23, 1868
District Supreme Court. U S, use of J D McPherson, adm *de bonis non*, with the will annexed of Timothy Winn, dec'd, vs Blagden & De Selding. This is an action to recover from the sureties on the bond of Rebecca Winn, the former admx *de bonis non*, with will annexed, of Timothy Winn, the sum of $4,941,79, which she collected as said admx, & for which she failed to account. Letters of adm *de bonis non*, with will annexed, after her death were granted to J D McPherson, who brings the suit. [Jan 25th newspaper: The opinion of the Court, to the effect that the Md statute, as interpreted by the tribunals of that State, & according to its evident legislative intendment, debarred the administrator de bonis non from exercising any jurisdiction over the assets of the deceased converted into money, even though not distributed by the former administrator. Therefore it is res adjudicata, & the demurrer is sustained.]

Equity Court-Judge Wylie. 1-Collins vs Collins. Order appointing R R Crawford guardian *ad litem*.

Mrd: on Jan 16, at the residence of the bride's father, by Rev Wm H Laney, Benj C King, of Wash Co, D C, to Fannie L Gibbs, eldest daughter of Jas L Gibbs, of Montg Co, Md.

Mrd: on Jan 14, at Trinity Church, by Rev Mr Addison, Jos S Worthington, of the Pension Ofc, to Sarah E Andrus, of Wash Co, daughter of Geo Naylor, dec'd.

Mrd: on Jan 14, at Trinity Church, by Rev Mr Addison, Eugene M Hammond, of New Market, Fred'k Co, Md, to Minnie O, 2nd daughter of Milton M Welsh, of Wash, D C. No cards. [Balt Sun & Fred'k [Md] Citizen copy.]

On Monday last Dist Atty Carrington gave notice in the Criminal Court that the trial of John H Surratt had been assigned for Feb 24, & that Judge Pierrepoint & Hon A G Riddle had been retained by the prosecution to assist at the trial.

Justice Morsell yesterday committed to jail for court Chas O'Rourke, on the charge of killing his wife, Sarah O'Rourke, at Reynolds' Barracks, on Jan 16. He stoutly denies that he was the cause of her death; & states that she fell off the bed & struck her head, the concussion injuring her brain & causing her death.

FRI JAN 24, 1868
A girl, aged 13, Susan Trout, died in Columbus, Ohio, on Sunday, from lockjaw, caused by over-exertion while skating.

Patents to Washingtonians issued last week. To Saml Carusi, for improved postage stamp. To Edgar C McCeney, for lock-catch & stopper.

Equity Court-Chief Justice Cartter. In Chambers. Owens vs Owens et al. Order giving cmplnt leave to withdraw receipts, on filing certified copies.

Nominations sent to the Senate yesterday:
Dwight Bannister, to be a paymaster in the army.
Leslie Combs, marshal for the dist of Ky, in place of Wm A Merriwether, whose term will expire.
John M Johnson, marshal for Va, in place of John Underwood, whose term has expired.
John B Pennington, atty for the dist of Delaware, in place of John L Pratt, resigned.
Wm H Townsend, of Rhode Island, pension agent at Providence, in place of Wm C Townsend, resigned.
John S Hoolehan, postmaster at Honesdale, Pa.
Geo A Rawlings, postmaster at Old Point Comfort, Va.
H G Lohse, collector of customs for Gtwn, S C.
Henry Miller, assessor internal revenue for the 4th Dist of Ohio, in place of Jas H Hart, dec'd.
Jos B McCarnant, assessor of internal revenue for the 10th Dist of Pa, in place of Jacob Carmony, confirmed, but whose commission has been upheld.
David H Abell, assessor of internal revenue for the 25th Dist of N Y, in place of Lewis Peck, to be removed.
Jas H Cluberla, assessor of internal revenue, for the 5th Dist of Maine, in place of Nathl H Joy, to be removed.
Solomon P McCurdy, Chief Justice of the Supreme Court of Utah, in place of John Titus, whose commission has expired.
Enos D Hoge, associates Justice of the Supreme Court of Utah, in the place of Solomon P McCurdy, appointed Chief Justice.
Ambrose Campbell, of Mich, register of the land ofc at Marquette, Mich, vice Jos W Edwards, to be removed.
Danl Sigler, of Indiana, register of the land ofc at Natchitoches, La.

Gen Peter Force died at his residence, in this city, yesterday, in his 78th year. He had been confined to his room, quite low with a general debility, resulting from disease of the stomach, for some 2 months, & gradually sunk into his last slumber. He was in the full possession of his reason to the last, though he was unable to speak during the day on which he died. A telegrapic communication was announced to him from his only daughter, Mrs Jones, who resides at **Fort Wayne**, Ind, that she was coming to be with him. She had been sick, & not expected to come. Gen Force leaves 5 children, 4 sons & a daughter. Two sons reside in Alabama; one, Dr Wm Q Force, is a resident of Wash City, & the other, Gen M F Force, a resident of Cincinnati, Ohio, & upon the judicial bench of that State-was one of the generals who came into this city at the head of his command in Gen Sherman's army on their march homeward from the sea at the close of the war. Peter Force, an American journalist & historian, born in N J, Nov 26, 1790; removed to N Y when a child, became a printer, & resided in that city till, in Nov, 1815, he removed to Wash, D C; in 1820 he began the publication of the Nat'l Calendar, an annual volume of national statistics, which he continued until 1836; from 1823 to 1830 he published the Nat'l Journal; from 1836 to 1840 he was Mayor of Wash, & afterwards president of the Nat'l Institute for the Promotion of Science.

Died: on Jan 22, at Boston, Mass, Mr Wm L Hodge, of Wash City, in his 79th year.

Died: on Jan 23, in his 73rd year, Jos Williamson, native of Brancaster, England, & for the last 47 years a resident of Wash City. His funeral will be on Jan 26, at 3 P M, from his late residence, 440 M st north, between 13 & 14th sts west.

Hon Wm L Hodge died on Wed; for many years a resident of Wash City. He was, we believe, at one time engaged in commerce in New Orleans, & was conspicuously connected with the press of that city. He was Assist Sec of the Treasury under Gen Taylor's administration. At the time of his decease Mr Hodge must have been well stricken in years.

Jos Platz's Restaurant & Dining Rooms: 355 Pa ave, opposite Metropolitan Hotel, Wash, D C.

Copartnership under the name of Wm Dowling & Co, is this day dissolved by mutual consent. Saml Cropley will settle accounts. –Saml Cropley, Wm Dowling, John M Stake

Orphans Court of Wash Co, D C, Jan 21, 1868. In the case of Wm H & O H Morrison, excs of Wm M Morrison, dec'd, the executors & Court have appointed Feb 18 next, for the final settlement of the personal estate of the said dec'd, of the assets in hand.
-Jas R O'Beirne, Reg/o wills

House for rent, 339 18th st & K sts, with double parlors; gas in all rooms. Inquire at 263 F st, between 13th & 14th sts. –T A McLaughlin

SAT JAN 25, 1868
St Paul's Day, Jan 25. The festival of the Conversion of St Paul was observed in London in the reign of Philip & Mary, 1555, with processions with the children of all the schools in London, with all the clerks, curates, & parsons, & vicars, in capes, with their crosses; also, the chair of St Paul's, & divers bishops, in their habits, & the Bishop of London, with his pontificals & cope, bearing the sacrament under a canopy, with the Mayor & Alderman in scarlet with their cloaks & all their crafts in all their best array. The union of Princess Margaret, of England, eldest daughter of Henry VII, to James IV, of Scotland, on St Paul's Day, 1502, resulted in the union of the two kingdoms which has been so long at enmity with each other. She was at that time but 13¼ years old, & was united to the King of Scotland, as represented by his proxy, Patrick, Earl of Bothwell. She was of tall stature, had lively eyes, smooth arms, beautiful hands, golden hair, & a tongue enriched with various languages. The birth of Burns, who first saw the light on Jan 25, 1759, in a small cottage, near Bridge of Doon, 2 miles from Ayr, has, above all other events, made St Paul's Day hallowed in the heart of all who worship at the shrine of genius & of inspired song. The strains of Burns touch all hearts. He has uttered words with divine inspiration, such as had scarcely been equaled by any other mortal pen. It is an effecting circumstance that Burns, dying in poverty, & unable to remunerate his medical attendant otherwise, gave him his pair of pistols as a memorial of their friendship. Dr Maxwell, who proved a generous friend to the poor bard's widow & children retained the pistols until his death, in 1834, after which they were sacredly, for some years, preserved by his sister. At her death they passed to the Society of

Antiquaries, of Scotland, in whose museum in Edinburgh they are now kept in an elegant coffer, but open to the inspection of the public.

Wm Jones, a Chicago millionaire, died a few days since.

Gen Leslie Combs, of Ky, has been nominated to the Senate as U S Marshal for that State. This "boy hero of the war of 1812," although now full of years & full of honors, has never before sought any ofc except at the hands of the people.

Mr Jos Williamson, a hightly esteemed citizen of the First Ward, died on Thu at his late residence, on M st. He was a native of Brancaster, England, & for the last 47 years a resident of Wash City. He was for many years attached to the military household of the late Gen Winfield Scott, between whom & himself there existed a warm personal regard. He was in his 73rd year. His funeral will take place tomorrow. Three citizens have left within 24 hours: Gen Peter Force, 78; Col Wm L Hodge, 79; & Mr Williamson, 73. [Jan 27th newspaper: the funeral of the late Jos Williamson took place yesterday from his residence on M st, between 3rd & 4th sts. The remains were interred in *Glenwood Cemetery*.]

Court in General Terms. Edw M Linthicum vs Alex'r Ray. John A Wills for appellant; Davidge & Cox for appellee. This case involves the right of the plntf to use the wharf of the dfndnt for shipping coal & other commercial purposes, in connection with a lot owned by the plntf situated on Water st, Gtwn. The controversy turns mainly on the question as to the time when the respective rights of the parties, under whom the plntf & dfndnt severally claim, began. The dfndnt claims that his right originated under both the deed of trust or mortgage from the Lowndeses to Templeman, made in 1800, & under the deed of trust to Smith, in 1807. The plntf contends that the dfndnts rights to the wharf did not arise until 1807, under the deed to Smith, & that in the meantime, in 1804, his [the plntf's] right to the use of said wharf originated in the deed of conveyance made by the Lowndeses to the Johnses, granting the lot & joint right to use the said wharf, now controverted for the first time since its origin by the dfndnt. The dfndnt first alleges that the near of the wharf to the Johnses, granted by the deed of 1804, was a mere easement in gross, not assignable, & consequently never acquired by plntf. Secondly. That if the plntf had any right, he was guilty of *laches* in its assertion. Thirdly. That if the plntf had any right, it was an equitable right, & he should have gone into a court of equity to enforce it; & that he has no standing in a court of law. The cmplnt combatted the dfndnt's propositions. The argument was chiefly confined to the effect & construction of the deeds of trust made by the original parties, & the validity of the sales thereunder by the trustees in said deeds.

Mrd: on Jan 14, in Balt, by Elder W J Perrington, Mr Chas Edmonston, of Wash, to Miss Fannie E, daughter of the late John Berryman, of Balt, Md.

Mrd: on Jan 14, in Balt, by Elder W J Perrington, Mr Jos Hunt & Miss Mary E, daughter of Jas C Conn, of Howard Co, Md.

Died: on Jan 23, Peter Force, in his 78th year. His funeral will take place from the Baptist Church, on 13th st, between G & H sts, on Jan 26, at 2 o'clock P M.

Died: on Jan 24, at her residence in Wash City, after a long & painful illness, in her 76th year, Mrs Harriet Flagg, a native of the State of Maine, but for the last 14 years a resident of Washington, a devoted & beloved mother, & for nearly 60 years a professor of the Christian religion. Blessed are the dead that die in the Lord.

Died: on Jab 24, Maud Hancock, daughter of John & Sue Hancock, aged 23 months. Her funeral will be from the residence of her parents, 239 Pa ave, on Jan 26, at 2 o'clock P M.

Alex'r Stadfeldt, aged 15 years, committed suicide on Monday, by hanging himself with a towel to a peg, at his parent's house, 163 Fourth st, N Y. The family cannot assign any cause for the act.

In Syracuse, N Y, on Nov 20, Jos Nolan received a slight scratch on the back of the hand barely enough to draw blood, from the teeth of a small dog which he drove out of his grocery. The scratch healed & left no scar. A week ago numbness of the fingers & pain through the arm, with a strong distaste for water, induced him to call a physician. His symptoms grew worse & he died after 4 or 5 days of hydrophobia.

Valuable lot on Second st, between D & E sts, at auction. In the matter of the petition of Jas McSherry, guardian of Helen N McSherry, Mary C McSherry, & Jas C McSherry, minor heirs of Thos Carbery, dec'd. In pursuance of a decree of the Orphans Court of Wash Co, D C., the undersigned will offer at public auction, on the premises, Feb 4, part of lot 1 & 6 in square 570, fronting 45 feet, more or less, on said Second st, & running back by that width 167 feet 6 inches to an alley. –Jas McSherry, guardian
-Jos F Kelley, auct

MON JAN 27, 1868
Meeting of the Oldest Inhabitants of the District, was held at 1 P M, of which Gen Force was an honored member; Col J S Williams presided, & J C Brent, acted as secretary. Dr J B Blake stated the meeting was called to take action in regard to the decease of their associate; & on his motion, Messrs Lewis Johnson, Jenkin Thomas, & John F Callan, were appointed a cmte to draft resolutions for the action of the association, in regard to the death of Gen Peter Force, associate & friend. Mr Jas Clephane spoke of the early life of the deceased in Wash City, where, with Mr Davis, he established what was for a long time the only book store in the city. Mr J Carroll Brent spoke of Gen Force as being one of the first members of the Nat'l Monument Society, & the last survivor of those who organized the association, on Sep 26, 1833. He was one of the original members of the Oldest Inhabitants; he spoke of the connection of the deceased with the Society of Nat'l Sciences & his labors. Mr Jenkin Thomas appropriately spoke of his acquaintance with the deceased.

The funeral of Gen Force took place from the 13th st Baptist Church at 2 o'clock yesterday. The pall-bearers were Hon Richd Wallach, Dr John B Blake, J Carroll Brent, Dr Wm Gunton, Thos Blagden, Prof Jos Henry, Geo W Riggs, & J C McGuire. The funeral cortege wended its silent way to *Glenwood Cemetery*, where the remains were deposited in the receiving vault, for future interment.

Accident on the Boston & Providence Railroad on Sunday; rear portion of the train was thrown from the track by a broken rail. Mr E E Shepardson, of Providence, injured; Henry A Guild, of Attleboro, badly cut on the arm; Thos Hawkins & wife, of Providence, he was slightly injured & she was seriously cut-both taken to the Mass Gen Hospital; Mrs Swan, of Providence, slightly injured; Miss Lucy Rice, slightly injured; Patrick Dolen, of Portland, Me, injured in the back & hip; John Mulharn, of Dedham, a brakeman on the train, arm broken & head & foot badly jammed. Mrs Swan was on her way to Boston, in answer to a telegram from her husband, who is lying at the hospital, not expected to live. -Boston Journal, Monday

The funeral of Mrs Rebecca Edmonston, an elderly & highly esteemed lady of the Third Ward took place from Wesley Chapel at 2 o'clock yesterday. The funeral discourse was delivered by the pastor, Rev Dr Ames, & after the services the body was taken to *Glenwood Cemetery* for interment.

Orphans Court-Judge Purcell, Jan 25, 1867. 1-Second account of John S Paxton, guardian to Mary & Catharine Barron, orphans of Josiah Barron, dec'd, approved & passed. 2-The last will & testament of John Graham, heretofore filed & partially proven, admitted to probate & record. 3-In the matter of Geo Poole, dec'd, 3 affidavits were filed by Louisa Poole, stating that she was sister & next of kin to deceased, & the seal of the Justice of the Peace at Dublin, [Thos Henry Barton,] duly certified to by Wm B West, U S Consul at that place. 4-In the matter of the estate of Chas F Robertson, dec'd, ordered, by consent & agreement of all parties, that the funds now in the hands of John D McPherson, adm of the said Chas F Robertson, dec'd, be paid over to David P Moore.

Mrd: on Jan 9, in Portsmouth, Va, at St John's Episcopal Church, by Revs Okeson & Geer, Edw S Duvall, of Wash, D C, to Jeannie D Parker, of the former place.

Died: on Jan 25, Francis Walter Harvey, youngest son of Wm M & Lottie Harvey, aged 18 months. His funeral will be from the residence of his parents, 441 9th st, today, at 2½ o'clock P M.

Phil, Jan 26. Saml W Roop, formerly of the firm of Billings, Roop & Co, a well known & highly respected merchant, died yesterday.

Louisville, Jan 26. John H Harvey, senior editor & proprietor of the Louisville Democrat, died today.

Orphans Court of Wash Co, D C, Jan 23, 1868. In the case of Fred'k Voll, exc of Jacob Snyder, dec'd, the executor & Court have appointed Feb 22 next, for the final settlement of the personal estate of the said dec'd, of the assets in hand. -Jas R O'Beirne, Reg/o wills

Dept of the Interior, U S Patent Ofc, Wash, Jan 22, 1868. Ptn of Henry Clark, of Cedar Keys, Fla, praying for the extension of a patent granted to him Apr 25, 1854, for an improvement in machine for Feeding Sheets of Paper to Printing Presses, for seven years from the expiration of said patent, which takes place on Apr 25, 1868.
-T C Theaker, Com'r of Patents

TUE Jan 28, 1868
Lord Ranelagh, of London, has been summoned to pay 29s & costs for smoking on the Metropolitan railway.

John H Harney, of the Louisville Democrat, has been gathered to his fathers; at about 60 years of age he has left journalism to his successors. He was born & raised in Bourbon Co, Ky, & afterwards was professor of mathematics, & then president of Hanover College, Indiana; in 1848 he went to Louisville, Ky, & established the Democrat. For several months past, Mr Harney has been an invalid, & the paper has been conducted with marked ability by his son, Wm Wallace Harney, & Wm E Hughes. [No death date given-current item.]

Mr Jos Gill, for many years a citizen of the 6th Ward, departed this life on Sunday, & his funeral is this afternoon. He has for a long time been employed in the Navy Yard. He was a prominent member of the Red Men, Odd Fellows & Rechabites.

Died: on Jan 26, at Farley, near Brady Station, Va, Asa D Wood, of dropsy, in his 59th year. [Buffalo & Brooklyn, N Y, papers please copy.

Messrs Wall & Co, on Sat, sold part of lot 4 in square 448, 18 feet front by 135 deep, with a 2 story brick house, fronting on M st, between 6th & 7th sts, to W B Wylie, for $3,515. Also, part of lot 6 in square 516, 17 feet front on I st, between 4th & 5th sts, with a depth of 142 feet, with a 2 story brick house, to C H Carpenter, for $2,505.

The cable announces the death of Chas John Kean, the distinguished tragedian in London, on Thu last, in his 57th year of his age. He was born in Waterford, Ireland, Jan 18, 1811; was the son of the celebrated Edmund Kean, one of the greatest tragedians on the English, or indeed, the world's stage. In 1842 he was married to the accomplished actress, Miss Ellen Tree. Mr Kean left a large fortune. –N Y Herald

The body of Capt Rohrer, who mysteriously disappeared from Pottsville, Pa, 2 months ago, it is ascertained, was thrown into a coal-slope 500 feet deep, & filled with water. The son of one of the partners disclosed the crime, & all the parties implicated have been arrested. The motive of the murder is supposed to have been the securing of a lease of a valuable coal mine. The partners are Smith & Albrighton.

Major Davis, of Mass, formerly of Gen Butler's staff, committed suicide at Honk-Kong, China, Nov 24, 1867, by shooting himself in the head. Cause, pecuniary embarrassment.

London, Jan 27. The trial of Sir Culling Eardley, for bigamy, was concluded today. The testimony given showed that the accused had married Miss Emily Florence Magee, in N Y, in 1859; that in 1867 he married Miss Eliz Allen in St George's Church, Hanover Square, London, & the second marriage took place while the first wife was living. The jury brought in a verdict of guilty. The prisoner was sentenced to imprisonment for 18 months at hard labor.

WED JAN 29, 1868
The Senate confirmed the nomination of Hezekiah G Wells as consul at Manchester, England.

Nominations by the Pres sent to the Senate yesterday: Hon Wm D Bishop, of Conn, to be Com'r of Patents; J Ross Browne, to be Minister to China; Francis Price, of N J, to be Consul General at Havana; & L E Webb, of Wisc, Superintendent of Indian Affairs for New Mexico, vice Norton, dec'd.

Orphans Court-Judge Purcell. 1-Wm Q Force gave bond in the sum of $65,000 as adm of the personal estate of Peter Force, dec'd. Wm Gunton & Geo W Riggs, sureties. 2-Third & final account of Moses Kelly, adm of Jos Ingle, filed. 3-First & final account of M V B Bogan, guardian to John A Johnson, filed. 4-First & final account of Geo S Parker, exc of Clara Nisbet, filed. 5-An account of the personal estate of Geo Pool, by Saml E Arnold, adm, filed. 6-First & final account of Eliza McDuell, excx of John McDuell, filed. 7-Wm Lynch gave bond in the sum of $500 as adm of John Lynch, dec'd. J F Buel & Alfred Green sureties. 8-*In re*. Lorenz Thoma, dec'd. Citation against Bernard Gier, to show cause why he should not amend the inventory returned by him as executor.

Court in General Term. Wm F Purcell vs Gilbert S Miner & wife. The cmplnt, in his original bill in this suit, mentioned Mrs Miner, who holds the legal estate in the property in question as Mary V Miner, when her right name was Virginia A Miner. The cmplnt then filed a new bill against Mrs V A Miner, joining G S Miner, her husband, *pro forma*.

City Charter. We the undersigned, citizens of Washington, property holders & tanpayers, do most respectfully, yet earnestly, protest against the passage by the Board of Aldermen & Common Council of the city of any resolution requesting Congress to renew or extend the charter of the city of Wash. We are in favor of Congress excercising exclusive legislation in all cases whatsoever over the District of Columbia.

Z C Robbins	Wm B Todd	Wm H Ward
L Clephane	H D Cooke	John O Evans
A C Richards	Geo H Plant	Richd Lay
D L Eaton	Moses Kelley	J H Lathrop
B H Stinemetz	S P Brown	Z M P King
Riggs & Co	M H Stevens	Jas Y Davis

Francis H Smith	D K Cartter	McGill & Witherow
Philp & Solomons	Andrew Wylie	W Wall
Wm G Metzerott	A B Olin	John T Mitchell
Nathl Wilson	A G Riddle	John C McKeldon
Michl Green	J C Kennedy	John Markriter
Chas Bradley	A T Kiekhoefer	Fitzhugh Coyle
Henry Bradley	Geo W Riggs	Wm M Shuster & Bro
Jno H Semmes	M W Galt	H Semken
Wm B Riley & Co	Alex R Shepherd	Lockwood
Jos L May & Co	J F Brown	Hufty & Taylor
John Alexander	Thos Blagden	G F Schafer
John G Clarke	Kilbourn & Latta	P J Horwitz
John Lenthall	Geo Savage	H A Chadwick
B F Isherwood	Wm S Huntington	Peter Parker
Jas Sykes	John L Kidwell	W B Kibbey
D W Tomlinson	C C Willard	Owen Thorn & Co
J J Coombs	Wm H Philip	Claggett & Sweeney
Job W Angus	Wm F Mattingly	J F Callen
W D Shepherd	M Wm Beveridge	R M Hall
A N Trunnel	Wm Galt	Benj F Morsell
C McGolgan	Z D Gilman	John Q Willson

Vicksburg, Jan 28. Sgt Gilbert H Bates, of Wisc, who made a bet to carry the stars-and-stripes from Vicksburg to Washington unarmed & without money, started hence at 11 A M. An immense crowd, headed by the Mayor & Common Council & many prominent citizens, accompanied him some distance, & bade him farewell with good wishes.

St Louis, Jan 28. The examination of Isaac M Ruth for an assault with intent to kill Seymour Voultair on Nov 15, terminated today. Ruth was bound over in $1,000 bond to answer the charge before the grand jury. The testimony shows that Ruth fired the first shot; that he had in many ways interfered in the private affairs of Voultair's family, & had been the cause of much of the trouble between Voultair & his wife.

Balt, Jan 28. Dr A G Moore, of this city, was shot by Mrs Edw A Pollard today. Mr Pollard left the Maltby House some weeks since, & Mrs Pollard has been unable to ascertain where he is. Today she called on Dr Moore, an intimate friend of Pollard, & during the interview a difficulty occurred, resulting in the shooting of Moore. The wound is not dangerous. Mrs Pollard refused to give bail, & was committed to jail to await the action of the grand jury.

Nashville, Jan 28. The suit of Margaret Bark, against the Nashville & Louisville railroad for $10,000 damages, was taken up in Circuit Court today. Her husband was accidentally killed on the road in 1866.

Shocking accident at Chattanooga, late on Sat night, when Miss Maria Daily & Miss Kate Harrington, returned from spending the afternoon together, returned to the residence of Miss Daily. Being cold, Miss Daily attended to start a fire in the stove, & when she poured some oil into the stove, the oil exploded. Both ladies were severely burned. They died early on Sunday morning. –Knoxville [Tenn] Press & Herald, Jan 21.

Sale of valuable real estate; by decree of the Supreme Court of D C, on Jan 18, 1868, in the case of Oliver & Marcellus Donn vs Orlando H Donn & others, Equity No 974; sale of the following real estate belonging to the heirs of the late Thos C Donn, deceased; part of lot 6 in square 518, with 3 story brick house, fronting on H st, & two 2 story frame houses, fronting on said alley or Wash st. –John E Norris, trustee -Green & Williams, aucts

Orphans Court of Wash Co, D C. Letters of administration on the personal estate of Peter Force, late of Wash Co, D C, dec'd. –Wm Q Force, adm

Dept of the Interior, U S Patent Ofc, Wash, Jan 24, 1868. Ptn of John Myers & Robt G Eunson, of N Y, N Y, praying for the extension of a patent granted to him May 23, 1854, for an improvement in Machines for Sawing Thin Boards, etc, for seven years from the expiration of said patent, which takes place on May 23, 1868.
–A M Stout, Acting Com'r of Patents

Mr Henry Palmer, one of the business managers of Niblo's Theatre, N Y, is lying very ill of brain fever at the Westminster Hotel.

Mrs Deborah Cass Silliman died recently in Santa Cruz Co, Calif, in her 86th year. She was a sister of Gen Lewis Cass, & widow of Hon Wyllis Silliman, late of Zanesville, who was the publisher of the first newspaper started in Marietta, Nov 30, 1801.

At Leavenworth, Kansas, on Sat last, Judge Adams rendered a decision in the case of the State vs Gen Custar & Lt Cook, charged with the murder of Wm Johnson, a private of Co K, U S Cavalry, in favor of the dfndnts. The point made by the defence, claiming want of jurisdiction, was not sustained. The principal point decided was that Gen Custar marched from Riverdale Station, Colorado Territory, to ***Fort Wallace***, under orders from his superior ofcrs, & did not "flee from justice," as charged in the indictment.

THU JAN 30, 1868

Mr Chas Dickens has engaged rooms at Welcker's on 15th st, & the second & third floors of thie establishment have been assigned for the use of Mr Dickens & his attendants.

Gen J J Dana, of the Quartermaster's Gen's Dept, was yesterday summoned by telegram to Massachusetts, his father, Dr Saml L Dana, having fallen on the ice & broken his hip in 2 places. Dr Dana is well known in the scientific world by his life long devotion to the science of chemistry, & his books on agricultural chemistry.

Victor Hugo derives a large revenue from the sale of his autograph at ten francs each.

Mr Chas Francis Adams has the largest private library in New England, 19,000 volumes.

Brigham Young has pronounced an edict against tea & coffee. The prohibition is universal, so far as the Mormons are concerned.

Orphans Court of Wash Co, D C, Jan 28, 1868. In the case of Jos F Kelley, exc of Mary Farrar, dec'd, the executor & Court have appointed Feb 29 next, for the final settlement of the personal estate of the said dec'd, of the assets in hand. -Jas R O'Beirne, Reg/o wills

John Caldwell, a member of the Chicago police force, stepped into a saloon on Clark st, in that city, & was invited to take a glass of cider, & died 3 hours afterward. He had twice arrested the keeper of the saloon for violations of the law, & suspicions are entertained that revenge prompted the saloon proprietor to poison him.

FRI JAN 31, 1868
Cmdor Vanderbilt is bldg a residence, which will occupy 2 lots, on the easterly corner of Fifth ave & Fortieth st, N Y. It is a brown stone, nearly square on the ground; 3 stories high, with stables in the rear.

Mrd: on Jan 29th, at Grace Church, Balt, Md, by Rev Mr Randolph, Frank S Robertson, of Va, to Ella, 2nd daughter of John P Wheeler, of Wash, D C. No cards.

Died: on Jan 29, of dropsy, Mrs Mary R Mitchell, widow of the late Thos Mitchell, in her 51st year.

St Anna's Hall, a select school for young ladies, is in successful operation.
–Rev O Hutton, A M, Brookeville, Montg Co, Md.

A negro named Lewis Washington has been sentenced, at Indianapolis, to pay a fine of $2,000, & suffer 2 years' imprisonment for marrying a white woman.

SAT FEB 1, 1868
The great novelist of this generation, Mr Chas Dickens, will commence his readings in Carroll Hall, on Monday evening next, with the "Christmas Carol" & "The Trial from Pickwick."

N Y, Jan 30. Last night Mr Benj F Beech, of Brooklyn, went to the residence of Miss Annie Graham, to whom, it appears, he has been for a considerable time attached, & in her presence shot himself through the head with a revolver. His wound is of such a character as to preclude all hope of his recovery. Mr Beech made some observations to Miss Graham, showing that he was actuated by jealousy. All the parties are highly respectable.

Rev B F B Leech, a Methodist minister, well known in Wash City, died yesterday. He was the son of Mr D D T Leech, of the city post ofc, who, for many years past, has resided on I st, between 8th & 9th sts. The deceased is a younger brother of Rev Geo V Leech, now stationed at East Wash Church, & Rev S V Leech, stationed at Annapolis, & commenced his services as a minister of the Gospel by assisting the last brother when he travelled Severn Circuit, about 3 years since. About two years since he was appointed on Elkridge Landing Circuit, the senior minister being Rev M L Hawley. The deceased had been in ill health for some months, his disease being consumption, & 2 months since he was brought home from Elkridge Landing, Md, since which time he has kept his bed & gradually wasted away. In his last moments he was unable to speak, but seemed to recognize his relatives & friends who surrounded his bedside. His funeral will take place from the Foundry Church tomorrow afternoon.
+
Died: on Jan 31, in his 23rd year, Rev B F B Leech, late junior preacher on the Elkridge Landing circuit, Balt Conference. His funeral services will take place at the Foundry Chapel on Sunday at 3 P M.

In Gtwn, Mr Thos Dowling, has sold the valuable wharf property belonging to the estate of the late Chas Myers, fronting 41 feet on the south side of Water st, running back that width to the channel of the Potomac river, between Congress & Jefferson sts, to Francis Wheatley, for $4,000.

Mrd: on Dec 30, at the M st M E Church, by Rev Wm V Tudor, Mr Wm H Rollins, of Balt, to Miss Catherine E Marll, of Wash, D C.

Mrd: on Jan 23rd, at St John's Church, by Rev F D Goodwin, Jas M Boyd, of Univ of Va, to Bettie, eldest daughter of Anthony Lawson, of Wytheville, Va.

Mrd: on Jan 29, by Rev O Pernichief, Dr Saml J Radcliffe, of Wash, to Florence C, daughter of Dr Joshua Riley, of Gtwn.

Vermont papers record the death of Hon Norman Williams, of Woodstock, by paralysis. He was one of the most prominent citizens of the State. [No death date given-current item.]

John G Whittier, the poet, has been seriously ill several weeks at his residence in Amesbury, Mass, but is now improving in health.

Magnificent Rosewood parlor suites, French-plate mirrors, silk damask curtains, French clocks & candelabras, mantle ornaments & figures, walnut bookcase & sideboard, Brussels carpets & rugs, bed linen, & chamber furniture, etc, at auction, on Feb 10, at the residence of the late Sir Fred'k Bruce, 30 L st, between 24th & 25th sts.
-Cooper & Latimer, aucts

The Readings of Mr Charles Dickins, as condensed by himself. Price 25 cents each. For sale at Philp & Solomons, Metropolitan Book Store, 338 Pa ave, between 9th & 10th sts.

Public sale: by deed of mortgage from John G Morsell & Mary E Morsell, his wife, to the undersigned, recorded among the land records of Wash Co, D C, & those of PG Co, Md; sale on Mar 19, of 100 acres, more or less, & of which John Veitch died seized & possessed; adjoins the lands of the heirs of John C Rives; the bldgs are new. The property is 3 miles from Wash. Will be shown by N C Stephen, at Bladensburg, atty. –Fletcher B Veitch, John W Veitch, Margaret Veitch, Isabella Veitch, Mary A Veitch, Eliz Boyle.

Hon Joel Parker, at the head of the law school in Harvard Univ, has tendered his resignation in consequence of advancing years. Prof Parker has been connected with the University for 21 years.

Miss Anna C Jagerisky has completed the undertaking of skating for 30 consecutive house in Detroit.

MON FEB 3, 1868
It is said that Henry J Raymond is to write a history of Gen Grant, assisted by Wm Swinton.

Mr Chas Reade is 54 years old, but, it is said, announces that the best part of his literary life is before him.

A service of silver plate has just been completed in New York, which is to be presented by Geo Peabody to Cyrus W Field, as a recognition of the eminent services of the latter in connection with the Atlantic Cable. There are 12 pieces. On the opposite sides of each dish are medallion likenesses of Messrs Peabody & Field; & appropriate inscriptions. The entire weight is 700 ounces, its cost about $4,000.

Orphans Court-Judge Purcell, Feb 1, 1868. 1-The third & final account of Wm E Roberts, adm of Ann Roberts, dec'd; & first & final account of Robt R Pywell & Atwell Cowling, excs of Richd Gudgin, dec'd; & second & final account of Zephaniah Jones, guardian to Richd L Jones, orphan of Richd J Jones, dec'd, were approved & passed. 2-The last will & testament of Manning Hadley, heretofore filed, fully proven. He names Catharine Hadley, Saml Cross, P W Harbin, & T S Denham, excs. 3-Bernard Geier gave bond in the sum of $600 as adm of the personal estate of Justina Thoma. Emil S Fredrich & Frank Lottar, sureties. 4-First & final account of Geo Magruder, adm of Peter W Magruder, filed. 5-The will of Augustus F Berry was filed & fully admitted to probate. He bequeaths all his estate, real & personal, to his wife, Henrietta Berry, in fee simple, & names her as his excx. 6-*In re*. Estate of Jacob Lowenthal. Citation against John B Hutchinson, exc, to appear & amend inventory. Case postponed until Feb 15, for final hearing, with consent of all parties.

M Madison Morton, author of "Poor Pillicoddy" & a host of other successful farces, is giving public readings in England.

Why did Mr John Jacob Astor, the richest man in N Y C, bequeath in his will to Fitz Greene Halleck, the poet, for many years an intimate friend, & confidential clerk, only the pitiful sum of $200 a year. Explanation: Halleck often used to joke Mr Astor about his accumulating income, & perhaps rather rashy said: "Mr Astor, of what use is all this money to you? I would be content to live on a couple humdreds a year for the rest of my life, if I was only sure of it." The old man remembered that, & with a bitter satire reminded Halleck of it in his will. -N Y Ledger

Mrd: on Jan 23, in St John's Church, Gtwn, D C, by Rev O Perinchief, Dr Danl Weisel, U S A, to Isabel, daughter of Geo Waters, of Gtwn.

Parafine has been successfully used in England for the purpose of preserving fresco wall paintings. Frescoes that were crumbling away became quite solid when saturated with parafine dissolved in mineral turpentine, further experiments in the application of which are being made.

During Price's raid into Missouri in 1864, a skirmish took place on the line of Chariton & Howard Counties, in which one of the Confederates was left on the ground dangerously wounded in the neck. Miss Sarah J Smith, a school teacher, seeing the wounded man, went to him & stanched his wounds, probably saving his life. She remained with him until near nightfall, when he requested her to leave, as his companions would probably come & take him away. He said that he was known by the name of Tucker, but his real name was H C McDonald, & he was from Louisville, Ky. Next morning he was gone. A few days ago, the Glasgow [Missouri] Times says, Miss Smith, [who still resides in the neighborhood,] received a letter from the administrator of H C McDonald, sr, informing her that she was named in the will of the dec'd as the legatee of $50,000, in consideration of her having saved the life of his nephew & only heir, the H C McDonald named in connection with the incident of 1864.

For rent or lease: the late residence of W C Calvert, dec'd, adjoining Forestville, 8 miles from Wash, on the road to Marlboro; 85 acres well enclosed, with a comfortable dwlg & ample outhouses, in good repair. Inquire on the premises, or at 284 G st, Wash. [No name given for contact.]

Col Rose, the ofcr who was tried & acquitted by a court of inquiry at Richmond, Va, some time ago, for alleged misconduct in the supervision of the elections, was attacked at his quarters on Thur, by a soldier of his own regt, who fired his musket at him, making a bullet hole through his coat sleeve. The Colonel immediately clinched with the man, struck him on the head with the gun stock, breaking his skull so that he probably will not recover.

In Sandusky, on Friday, Henry Shade, employed in a saw mill, got his clothing entangled in a shaft-coupling, & before the machinery could be stopped, was killed.

Orphans Court of Wash Co, D C. Letters of administration on the personal estate of Justina Thoma, late of Wash City, D C, dec'd. –Bernard Geier, adm

TUE FEB 4, 1868
Funeral of a prominent Cherokee. Capt Jas McDaniel, late of the 2nd Indian regt, U S volunteers, died on Feb 1st, of pneumonia, after an illness of 3 days. He was a member of the delegation of Cherokees at present in Wash City on business for the Cherokee nation. Rev Dr Gray conducted the funeral ceremonies, which took place at 415 E st. Among the distinguished persons in attendance were Hon N G Taylor, Com'r of Indian Affairs; Chas E Mix, chief clerk Indian Bureau; Gen Thos Ewing, Col Parker, of Gen Grant's staff, & others. The corpse was taken to the *Congressional Cemetery*, preceded by a company of soldiers, & followed by a considerable number of carriages.

Harrisburg, Jan 31, 1868. Railroad accident this morning on the Pa railroad, owing to the breaking of a rail, which left Pittsburg, destined for N Y by way of Allentown, & one car destined for Phil. The only person killed was Mrs Anna Duggen, late of 167 Pa ave, Pittsburg. The husband of this woman & her brother, together with Patrick Hughes & a party, were on their way to Calif. The husband had his hands & face slightly burned. Injured: Mrs Georgia Adams, Phil; J Mausen, Indianapolis; Mrs Mary Crouse, Kansas; W Wiekel, N Y; Herbert Noonson,jr, Phil; W W Powell, N J; L Chase, Mich; Mrs Gen Rodman & daughter, Ill; J Buzzer, Lancaster.

Dickens, it is reported, has sent $1,000 to Mrs Clemm, the mother-in-law of Edgar A Poe, who is an inmate of a charitable institution in Balt, & has been for years in extremely indigent circumstances.

The suicide of Rev Mr Brush, of Delaware, Ohio, was committed on Sunday while his congregation was quietly awaiting his appearance to conduct the opening exercises of the regular quarterly meeting. He was found hanging dead in his barn. Another clergyman, Rev Mr Ryan, at Marysville, in the county adjoining Delaware, also committed suicide the same Sunday, by cutting his throat. Insanity is alleged in both cases, & in the last named it had been for some time apparent. [Feb 11th newspaper: Rev Brush was in the habit of taking morphine, & desired to leave it off; considered the habit degrading; was given to him by a physician for a latent cancer of the tongue; he made an effort on his own to stop, but he was temporarily overpowered & yielded.]

The trial of Gen Geo W Cole on indictment for the murder of L Harris Hiscock will positively take place at Albany about March 1st.

Geo M Dent, a brother-in-law of Gen Grant, is a candidate for Delegate to Congress from Arizona.

Mrd: on Jan 30, by Rev Mr Leich, Thos P Orme, of South River, Md, to Mary A Dobbins, of Wash City.

Trustee's sale of improved property in Uniontown, D C; by deed of trust, executed by Geo W Duvall to secure the payment of certain promissory notes as therein set forth, as shown by reference to said deed, which is recorded in Liber N C T, No 4, folios 239 thru 242, of the land records for Wash Co, D C: sale on Mar 6, of a parcel of ground near the Navy Yard Bridge, on the south side bounded by J M Koenig's lot, on the east by the Potomac river, containing 34,000 square feet of ground more or less, being lots 793 thru 801; & also a piece of ground, 100 feet by 113½ feet, improved by a good dwlg house & barns. –Wm F Mattingly, trustee -Fitch & Fox, aucts

Dept of the Interior, U S Patent Ofc, Wash, Jan 15, 1868. Ptn of E G Allen, of Boston, Mass, praying for the extension of a patent granted to him Oct 27, 1857, for an improvement in Steam Pressure Guages, for seven years from the expiration of said patent, which takes place on Oct 27, 1871. –A M Stout, Acting Com'r of Patents

Dept of the Interior, U S Patent Ofc, Wash, Jan 15, 1868. Ptn of E G Allen, of Boston, Mass, praying for the extension of a patent granted to him Nov 22, 1859, for an improvement in Combination Steam Guages, for seven years from the expiration of said patent, which takes place on Nov 22, 1873. –A M Stout, Acting Com'r of Patents

WED FEB 5, 1868
Wash Corp: Act for the relief of Mary Flynn, excx of the late Simon Flynn, dec'd. That the sum of $65.83 be refunded to Mary Flynn, that amount, the same having been erroneously paid as taxes. Approved, Jan 24, 1868.

Maggie Miller has been paid $1,000 for a new play.

Col Edmund Cooper, Acting Assist Sec of the Treasury, will resign his position in a few days.

Died: on Feb 4, Mrs Harriet H Spalding, widow of the late Wm R Spalding, aged 65 years. Her funeral will be on Thu at 3 o'clock, from the residence of her daughter, on Conn ave, between K & L sts.

Supreme Court of D C, Equity 969. Eliz A Scrivener et al vs Thos S Powell. Statement of the trustee's account & distribution of funds: Feb 14, 3 P M. –Walter S Cox, auditor

Supreme Court of D C, Equity 887, Docket 8. Caroline McAlister vs Chas L McAlister et al. Ratify & confirm reported sale. –R J Meigs, clerk [No particulars.]

THU FEB 6, 1868
The Ripley [Miss] Advertiser of Jan 18th contains an obituary notice of Mrs Lovey Blount, who died a few days ago, at the advanced age of 102 years, 4 months & 25 days.

The President sent to the Senate yesterday the following nominations:
T W Scott, of Tenn, to be Consul at Metamoras.
Alex Willard, to be Consul at Guamas.
O G Rose, to be Consul at Schwerin.
John J Fisk, to be Consul at Leith.
Saml Comfort, to be Postmaster at Lewisburg, Pa.

During the past week the following patents were issued to citizens of Washington:
To John A Frey, for a lamp.
To Emil Cornley, for a sewing machine.
To Edw A Ellsworth, for a method of mixing mortar & cement.
To: Danl E Somes, for an apparatus for making ice for cooling air & liquids.
To Thos J Phillips, for a tool for opening barrels.

A man named Tom Malone was shot & mortally wounded, last Friday, in the Criminal Court in Memphis, during the examination of some witnesses in a murder case. Some say that he shot himself; others, that he was shot by another person.

Mrd: on Feb 4, at the Metropolitan Hotel, by Rev P D Gurley, D D, Mr J D Bigger to Mrs L M Showell, both of Md.

Mrd: on Feb 5, at St Aloysius Church, by Rev Fr Wiget, Mr Geo Chance to Miss Lottie E Ballenger. [Alexandria & Wilmington, Del, papers please copy.]

Dept of the Interior, U S Patent Ofc, Wash, Feb 1, 1868. Ptn of Mahlon Loomis, of Wash, D C, praying for the extension of a patent granted to him May 2, 1854, for an improvement in Plates for Artificial Teeth, for seven years from the expiration of said patent, which takes place on May 2, 1868. -A M Stout, Acting Com'r of Patents

Louisville, Ky, Feb 5. Jos Bloom Gail, assist teller of the U S depository of this city, was arrested yesterday for embezzling Gov't money to the amount of $12,000. He made a written statement acknowledging his guilt, & stating that he had spent the money.

N Y, Feb 5. Wm Walker, John Smith, & Danl Cooper were arrested yesterday for counterfeiting the five-cent coin of the U S. The machinery, metals & dies, & a lot of coin were captured.

FRI FEB 7, 1868
Confirmations. The Senate Monday confirmed the following nominations: 1-Gideon H Hollister, of Conn, to be Minister Resident & Consul at Hayti; to fill a vacancy. 2-Wm R Kinney, of Ky, & Geo A Maguire, of Mo, to be com'rs, to reimburse Indiana for moneys expended in enrolling, equipping, & provisioning militia to aid in the suppression of the rebellion. 3-Wm F Turner to be Chief Justice of the Supreme Court of Arizona, his former Commission having expired.

Senator Guthrie, of Ky, although unable to take his seat, refuses to resign.

John Develin has been found guilty, in N Y, of defrauding the Gov't of $600,000 in whiskey distilling.

Public sale on Feb 8, the Farm of John P Edmonston, 2½ miles from Laurel, PG Co, Md, containing 127 acres, with fair improvements. Apply to M Bannon, 32 St Paul st, Balt.

At 2 o'clock yesterday, Richd P Strong, U S A, of Oregon, & Miss Marion Smith, of Wash City, were united in the bonds of matrimony, by Rev Dr Lewis, at St John Church. The ceremony was witnessed by a large concourse of friends & distinguished personages. The happy pair, with their attendants, left the city for N Y on the 4:30 P M train.

Criminal Court-Judge Fisher. Trial of J W N Zimmer for the murder of Chas Dumas was concluded yesterday. The jury returned with a verdict of manslaughter, & was discharged. The prisoner was remanded to jail.

Died: on Feb 6, in Gtwn, D C, in her 83rd year, Mrs Anne E Bronaugh, widow of the late John W Bronaugh, of Stafford Co, Va. Her funeral will take place from the residence of her son, 55 Second st, on Feb 8 at 1 P M. [Richmond papers please copy.]
[Feb 8th newspaper: Mrs Anna E Bronaugh, was the daughter of Danl & Sarah McCarty, of **Cedar Grove**, & the grand-daughter of Col Danl McCarty, of **Mount Air**, & of Col Geo Mason, of **Gunston Hall**, Fairfax Co, Va. Both her grandfathers were of Revolutionary memory. She was married to John W Bronaugh on Oct 27,1803. Her husband died on Mar 17, 1834, aged 62 years, leaving her with 6 children. Since then she has struggled with adversity. Though born & reared in affluence, she has borne with Christian fortitude & resignation. She was a devoted mother. –An Old Friend]

Edwin Booth, during his late season of 30 weeks, averaged $3,000 a week.

The widow of Gen Miramon has, with her children, taken up her residence at Vienna. She is to receive a pension from the Austrian Gov't.

On Wed morning a solemn high mass of requiem was celebrated at St Joseph's Church, N Y, commemorative of the death of the wife of Gen Danl E Sickles.

Norwich [Conn] Bulletin, Feb 3. Explosion of burning fluid at the house of C N Chapman, in Leffingwelltown, [Bozra] 3 miles from the city. Present were Dr Erastus Leffingwell; his son about 16 years of age; a girl named Mary Murphy, & Mr Chapman's daughter, both about 11 years old; & a young man named Ross, who resides in the neighborhood. The Murphy girl died Sunday; the Chapman girl is very dangerously burnt, & cannot long survive. The boy, although not much burned, is delirious, & is seriously injured internally. It is feared he inhaled the flames.

Orphans Court of Wash Co, D C, Feb 4, 1868. In the case of Jas Fuller, adm of Thos Chessem, dec'd, the administrator & Court have appointed Feb 29th next, for the final settlement of the personal estate of the said dec'd, of the assets in hand.
-Jas R O'Beirne, Reg/o wills

Dept of the Interior, U S Patent Ofc, Wash, Feb 1, 1868. Ptn of Conrad Leibrich, of Phil, Pa, praying for the extension of a patent granted to him May 2, 1854, for an improvement in Trunk Lock Hasps, for seven years from the expiration of said patent, which takes place on May 2, 1868. -A M Stout, Acting Com'r of Patents

SAT FEB 8, 1868

Cooper & Latimer, aucts, sold to Mr John Baker, for $9,000, parts of lots 15 &16 in square 293, & improvements, consisting of a 3 story brick house, on the s w corner of 12th & D sts. John J Bogue, real estate agent, Gtwn, has sold the 2 small brick houses, corner of Green & Dunbarton sts, belonging to Mr Philip May, to Miss Julia Hawkins, for $3,000 cash. Messrs J B Wheeler & Co, aucts, sold 2 frame houses on First st east, between I & K sts, one to Chas Lockbeiller at $850, & the other to Patrick McCormick at $955. The prices were considered fair in that location.

It is now postively stated & believed that Mrs Lincoln is laboring under an aberration of mind. Her conduct has been very strange. She recently sold all the furniture in her house, & has two old men as guards, believing she will be murdered. Her mania is for selling things, & a dread lest she come to want. All her friends think she is harmless, & her removal to a lunatic asylum would increase her derangement. –Hartford Post, [Rad]

The London Era gives a list of actresses who have become members of the Peerage & Barronetage of England: Anastasia Robinson, a vocalist of some eminence, in the early part of the last century, married the Earl of Peterborough. Lavinia Fenton, afterwards Duchess of Bolton in 1729 retired from the stage, & died in 1760, aged 52. Eliz Farren became Countess of Derby. Miss Harriet Mellon, afterwards Duchess of St Alban's, made her first appearance at Drury Lane Theater as Lydia Languish, in Sheridan's comedy of "The Rivals," Jan 31, 1795. Miss Louisa Brunto, Countess of Craven. She made her first appearance at Covent Garden Theatre. Died Sep 3, 1860, aged 78. Miss Mary Bolton, afterwards Lady Thurlow, made her first appearance as Polly in "The Beggars' Opera," Oct 8, 1806. Married Edward, Lord Thurlow, in 1813. Miss Marie Foote, Countess of Harrington, made her first appearance at Covent Garden Theatre. Miss Katharine Stephens, Dowager Countess of Essex, made her first appearance at Covent Garden Theatre as Mandane, in Dr Arne's opera of "Artaxerxes," in Sep, 1813. Married in 1838 the fifth Earl of Essex, who died in 1839. Miss O'Neill, born in 1791, made her first appearance at Covent Garden Theatre as Juliet on Oct 6, 1814. Retired from the stage & married Wm Wrixon Beecher, Dec 18, 1819. On the death of his uncle, Mr Beecher succeeded to a very ancient baronetcy, & his wife became Lady Wrixon Beecher. Miss Nisbett [maiden name Louisa Mordaunt] first appeared at Drury Lane. Married Sir Wm Boothby, Bart, Oct 15, 1844, who died Apr 21, 1846. Lady Boothby died at St Leonard's, near Hastings, Jan 16, 1858.

Hon Anson Herrick, formerly member of Congress from N Y C, & for many years proprietor & publisher of the Sunday Atlas, & naval storekeeper, died on Wednesday.

In a quarrel in Louisville, M V Yates was stabbed R Bull. Yates died 2 or 3 days ago.

The steamer **George Leary**, of the Bay Line, collided with the schnr **Peter A Keyser**, off Old Point, yesterday, & cut her in two. The schnr went down immediately, in the darkness, three of her crew were drowned. The captain & crew were picked up by Leary & brought to this city. The men lost were: Patrick Dougall, John McGill, & a negro man, Wm Hill. –Norfolk Day Book, Feb 5.

Equity Court-Judge Olin. Langtry vs Estill. Decree appointing J D McPherson & Geo F Appleby trustees to sell.

Criminal Court-Judge Fisher.
Perrie Prandel was found guilty of an assault & battery on a child named Edith Smart.
Wm Johnson, assault & battery, guilty.
Wm Johnson, petit larceny, nolle pros.
John St John, indicted for beating his wife on Jan 31st last, not guilty.
Wm H Gantt, petit larceny, not guilty.
Chas Wheeler, petit larceny, bench warrant issued.
Wm Jones, larceny, not guilty.
Foster Bailey, larceny, guilty.

Mscl news: 1-Minister Thornton has a wife & 3 children. 2-The mill to which Henry Clay carried his grist still remains. 3-Mrs "Stonewall" Jackson has received $15,000 from the sale of the life of her husband. 4-Ina Hillgen, a Swedish maiden, is said to excel Jenny Lind as a vocalist. 5-W E Hughes, of the Louisville Democrat, has recently sold his magnificent farm of about 500 acres, in Jefferson Co, 8 miles from Louisville, with all the stock, to T Ten Broeck, the distinguished turfman. 6-Wm Brandon, in St Louis, has recovered a verdict of $1,250 damages against D J Jocelyn, a dentist, who broke his jaw bone, & otherwise damaged him in the process of extracting some teeth. The dentist asked for a new trial. 7-In Westport, Mo, Belle Barnard, daughter of Rev Jeab Bernard, was dangerously wounded on Jan 28, by a pistol which had been left in a bed she was engaged in making, discharged by accidentally falling to the floor. The ball passed entirely through her body, above the right lung.

Mr Chas Dickens yesterday visited the *Executive Mansion*, & was presented to the President, with whom he had a short interview. He spent some time in examining the various rooms & the conservatory.

John Gest, one of the New Ulm [Minnesota] murderers, has been found guilty, & sentenced to be hanged on Apr 3 next. Several others are to be tried for the same offence.

Sale of valuable real estate, by decree of the Supreme Court of D C, in Equity No 1,169, Echols et al vs Carter et al; sale on Feb 20, on the premises, lot 1, with improvements, in square 213, located at N & 13th sts. It will be divided: the west 25 feet of the lot, running back 100 feet. The next adjoining 50 feet front, with the same depth, improved by a handsome double cottage, 2 stories & an attic, with outbldgs. Lastly, the east 25 feet front of said lot, by the same depth of 100 feet. Title perfect. —John J Johnson, trustee

At a Circuit Court continued & held for Fluvanna Co, at the Court house thereof, on Sep 12, 1867: Hervey Oliver, plntf against the children of Robt Oliver, dec'd, whose names, ages, & number are unknown; Anne E Fariswe, John M Harlowe, Mary Ann Harlowe, John L Harlowe, infant son of Lewis Harlowe, dec'd; John M Hawlowe, the children of Mary Howard, dec'd, whose names, ages, & number are unknown; Stephen Furgerson, Brockman & Ann Eliz his wife; Wm N Oliver, Geo H Oliver, Benj Bebb, & his 4 infant children, viz: Ann Eliz, Demetrius, John F, & Jas Bebb; & John Sclater, sheriff of Fluvanna Co, & as such administrator of Robt Oliver, dec'd, of Mary Howard, dec'd, & Lewis Harlowe, dec'd, dfndnts. In obedience to a decree rendered in the foregoing cause on Sep 12, 1867, the parties interested are to appear at the next term of the Court, to be held in Apr, 1868, & show cause, if any they can, why the report of Hervey Oliver, com'r & receiver, filed in this cause should not be confirmed.
—Hervey Oliver, Com & Receiver

Dept of the Interior, U S Patent Ofc, Wash, Feb 3, 1868. Ptn of Philander Shaw, of Boston, Mass, praying for the extension of a patent granted him May 2, 1854, & reissued Jul 17, 1860, for an improvement in Air Engines for seven years from the expiration of said patent, which takes place on May 2, 1868. -A M Stout, Acting Com'r of Patents

MON FEB 10, 1868
Mr Saml M McKean, disbursing clerk in the Sec's Ofc, Treasury Dept, died at his residence, on 17th st, Sat, in his 79th year, after an illness of 2 weeks. He entered the Treasury Dept in 1817 as clerk, & was appointed disbursing agent in 1830, which position he held until the reorganization of the Dept in 1853, when he was made disbursing clerk, & held this position at the time of his death. His total service in the Dept was 51 years. For some months past he had been complaining, but attended to the duties of his ofc until about 2 weeks since. Mr McKean was the son of Chief Justice McKean, of Pa, & a grandson of one of the signers of the Declaration of Independence. His funeral will take place tomorrow at 4 o'clock P M, from St John's Episcopal Church.
+
Died: on Feb 8, S M McKean, in his 79th year of his age. His funeral will be from St John's Church on Tuesday afternoon, at 4 o'clock punctually.]

Court in General Term. *In re.* Geo L Sherwood was fined $31 by Justice Buckey for violating a Gtwn Corp ordinance, & upon his refusal to pay said fine, was committed to jail. He was brought out under a writ of habeas corpus, & by agreement of the counsel the case was referred to the court in banc.

The testimony in the case of Wm L Rynerson, did, on Dec 15, 1867, at the Exchange Hotel, in the city of Santa Fe, state the cause of the death of John P Slough, by a pistol shot fired from Rynerson's hand. Rynderson boarded at the Exchange & Slough sometimes took meals there. Judge Slough had called Rynerson a lying son of a ___, & Rynerson wanted him to take back what he had said. Slough said he did not propose to take anything back.

Col R M Johnson has been appointed postmaster at **Fort Dodge**, Kansas.

Fourteen Camels, raised in Texas, to be shipped to N Y, & placed in the Central Park in that city. Some years ago a lot of camels were imported by the War Dept for use in transportation of supplies across the desert regions of New Mexico; & the lot referred to came from that stock, having been raised in **Camp Vere**, Texas.

Orphans Court-Judge Purcell, Feb 8, 1868. 1-John H Bird was granted letters testamentary upon the personal estate of Wm Bird; bonds $4,000. Sureties: R H Graham & J Yates. 2-Catharine Cross & P W Harbin gave bond in the sum of $4,000 as execs of Manning Hadley. Wm Morgan & E J Klopfer sureties. Last will of Manning Hadley admitted to probate. 3-The last will of Jas Gill was fully proven. He names Dr S A H McKim sole executor. 4-First account of Osceola C Green, guardian to Hilda Leach, filed. 5-First general account of Lawrence Scott, guardian to Isaac W & John R Scott, filed. 6-The last will of Eliz A Cross filed.

On Thur Past Master Noble D Larner, of Lafayette Lodge No 19 was presented with a magnificent Past Master's Jewel of solid gold. Mr Larner then presented to the lodge a very valuable Masonic relic of the Revolution; a beautifully worked Masonic apron, with all the jewels of the order worked upon it in the most elegant manner, & very tastefully designed & executed. This was the apron owned by Jacob Gideon, sr, who came to this country from Germany, & was Gen Washington's favorite bugler. This he wore in the well remembered Continental Lodge, & afterwards in the lodge at Phil, before the Gov't was removed to Wash. He died at the age of 85, Mar 3, 1841, & presented this apron to Mr Crowley, & he presented it to Grand Sec Larner. It will be placed in a fine frame & hung up on the Masonic Hall.

Two Americans, named Cooke & Pillow, enroute for Tuxhuan, were murdered by Mexicans near Victoria. They were emigrants from Waco, Texas.

Mrd: on Jan 2, by Rev Mr McKim, in Annadale, Fairfax Co, Va, Maj H P Burroughs, son of the late P W Burroughs, of N Y, to Miss Alice M Summers, daughter of the late Warren Summers, of Fairfax Co, Va.

Died: on Feb 7, at Wash, D C, Mrs Rebecca L De Leon, widow of the late Dr M H De Lyon, of Columbia, S C, in her 72nd year. [Balt, Richmond, & Charleston papers please copy.]

Died: on Feb 8, Josephine C, wife of Thos Thompson, aged 29 years. Her funeral will be on Feb 10, at 3 o'clock P M, from 367 Pa ave.

Died: on Feb 7, at New London, Conn, Milton Passmore, infant son of Cmder R B Lowry, U S navy.

Died: on Feb 9, Sophia M, daughter of the late Wm G Ridgely, of Gtwn. Her funeral will take place on Tuesday, Feb 11, at 2 o'clock P M, from the residence of her mother, 16 1st st.

Crawshay, the wealthiest iron manufacturer of England, who died some months ago, left an estate valued at L7,000,000.

Pliny Jewell & wife of Hartford, Conn, father & mother of the Republican candidate for Govn'r in Conn, have started on a hundred mile sleigh ride to N H, disdaining railroads & such modern devices.

Judge Busteed has recovered from his wounds, & is again holding court in Mobile.

Designing to change business, I offer at private sale my entire stock of Boots, Shoes, & Store Fixtures. The store is located at 278 Pa ave. Apply to the proprietor, on the premises, T W Howard, 278 Pa ave, near Kirkwood House.

The **Rose Hill Estate**, the property of the late Maynadier Mason, 4½ miles from Alexandria, containing 360 acres, with a fine Mansion House, barns, stables, granary, servants' house, etc, for sale or rent. If not sold privately, it will be offered at public auction on Mar 2, 1868. Possession immediately. Inquire of L B Taylor, Atty-at-Law, Alexandria, Va, or the undersigned at Haymarket, Prince Wm Co, Va. –R F Mason, exc

Orphans Court of Wash Co, D C. Letters of administration on the personal estate of Maning Hadley, late of Wash Co, D C, dec'd. –Catharine Hadley, Sam Cross, Philip W Harbin, excs

Dept of the Interior, U S Patent Ofc, Wash, Jan 24, 1868. Ptn of Fred'k G Schaum, adm of the estate of Fred'k Schaum, dec'd, of Balt, Md, praying for the extension of a patent granted to said Fred'k Schaum, Apr 25, 1854, for an improvement in Glass Furnaces, for seven years from the expiration of said patent, which takes place on Apr 25, 1868.
-A M Stout, Acting Com'r of Patents

Capt Redington Stetson has obtained a lease for 7 years of the Astor House, in N Y.

Gen Forrest has filed a peition of bankruptcy in Memphis.

Gen Albert Pike lectured on " Masonry" in New Orleans, on Wed night.

Maj Rogers, of the Boston Journal, has purchased for $280,000 the old <u>Joy's Bldg estate</u>, whereon to erect a new publication ofc.

Jas Reed, a member of the N Y Assembly, dropped dead on Sat, while standing at the bar of Grosts & Duff's restaurant, in N Y.

TUE FEB 11, 1868
The President yesterday nominated Chas K Tuckerman, of N Y, to be Minister Resident at Greece.

John Gray, of Brookfield township, Noble Co, Ohio, who is supposed to be the last surviving soldier of the Revolution, was 101 years of age on Feb 6.

Miss Greenough, aged 17 years, was burned to death on Sunday, at Burlington, Vt, her clothes taking fire from the explosion of a kerosene lamp.

A young lady named C Mills, living at 1,119 Ellsworth st, Phil, was fatally burned on Sunday by the explosion of a kerosene lamp.

Hahyaktakee, the principal member of the Japanese troupe, now performing in N Y, died on Sat night.

In Lafayette, Indiana, on Tuesday, Mrs Smith, widow of Mr H W Smith, was burned to death. She had gone to sleep while reading, & the candle set fire to the bed clothes.

Yesterday the Gtwn Fire Com'rs awarded the contract for bldg a new hose-carriage for the Fire Dept to John J Cooke. The price fixed is $498.

Dr J Gilliams, one of the founders of our Academy of Natural Sciences, died on Feb 4. He was near 85 years of age; born in Phil; was intimate associate & friend of Chas Lucien Bonaparte, the ornithologist. –Phil North American

Chas Dickens was 56 years old on Friday.

Charlotte Cushman has sent home from Italy three beautiful works of art as a present to the Boston Music Hall.

A few days ago Mrs Cooke, of Madison Co, Ala, put arsenic in her dough, mistaking it for soda, & the consequence was the death of the whole family-herself, her husband, & 3 children.

Madame de Morny, the widow of Duke de Morny, has become a member of the Catholic Church, & is about to enter in a matrimonial alliance with the richest grandee of Spain, The Duke de Seato.

The President has recognized Chas Walcott Brooks as Consul of Japan at San Francisco; & Geo C Reid as Vice Consul at Denmark for the State of Va, to reside at Norfolk.

Trustee's sale at auction of handsome residence, with fashionable & elegant parlor, chamber, dining-rm, & library furniture, & 600 volumes select books; by deed of trust to me from Jos B Stewart, dated Jan 30, 1867, recorded in R M H No 29, folios 217 etc, of the land records for Wash Co, D C; at public auction, for cash, on the premises, 319 K st, between 12th & 13th sts, on Feb 17, at 10 A M.-Albert G Hall, trustee
-J B Wheeler & Co, aucts

Dept of the Interior, U S Patent Ofc, Wash, Feb 4, 1868. Ptn of Wm Baker, of Utica, N Y, praying for extension of a patent granted him May 16, 1854, & reissued on Sep 22, 1863, for an improvement in Clap Board Joints for seven years from the expiration of said patent, which takes place on May 16, 1868. -A M Stout, Acting Com'r of Patents

WED FEB 12, 1868
The President yesterday sent to the Senate the nomination of Chas Robinson, of Vt, as Consul to Quebec. In executive session yesterday the nominations of Gen Leslie Combs, as Marshal of Ky, & W D Bishop as Com'r of Patents, were rejected.

Renewal of the Attempt to Impeach the President. Wash, Feb 9, 1868. The publication of the correspondence between the President & Gen Grant in relation to the surrender of the War Dept to Stanton has at last furnished sufficient grounds in the estimation of the Radicals to induce the inauguration of new inquisition, looking to the impeachment of the President.

Friends of Hon Cassius M Clay, in Ky, have learned that he has offered his resignation as Minister to Russia, & will return home by May 1st.

Mr W E Finch, a mail agent on the Opelousas railroad, has been arrested in New Orleans for robbing the mails. When arrested 35 letters were found in his possession, one of which contained $331.

Mrd: on Feb 11, at the Church of the Ascension, by Rev Dr Pinkney, John C Whitnell to Maggie S, daughter of the late J S Miller. No cards.

Died: on Feb 9, in Wash City, Dr Sherburne F Dodge. His funeral services at 74 Missouri ave, today, Wed, at 11 A M.

Died: on Feb 10, after a long & painful illness, Mrs Christiana E Duval, consort of the late Maj M Duval, of Balt Co, Md. Her funeral will take place on Feb 13, at 10:30 A M, from the residence of her brother-in-law, Bladen Forrest, 78 First st, Gtwn.

Susan Dinin has another husband.

H F Handy, considered last year one of the very richest men of Cincinnati, has petitioned for bankruptcy.

Madame Juarez has been fined for not having lights upon her carriage while traversing the streets of the Mexican capital at night.

A daughter of John Alson, aged 3 years, while walking on Jefferson st, Memphis, on Friday, was seized by a negro woman & carried off. So far the police have been unable to gain any clue to her whereabouts.

Supreme Court of D C, Equity No 983. Sonnenschmidt et al vs Fugitt et al. Report of trustee's account & distribution of fund; Feb 17, 3 P M. –Walter S Cox, auditor

Supreme Court of D C, Equity No 895. Wm H Wood et al, cmplnts, vs Geo W Wood et al, dfndnts. It is ordered that the report made by the Aduitor, & the manner of distribution of the proceeds of the sale of the real estate of Mary Wood, dec'd, be ratified & confirmed. –Olin, Justice -R J Meigs, clerk

Boston, Feb 11. The elegant mansion of Edw N Perkins, Jamaica Plains, with a portion of the furniture & costly paintings, was destroyed by fire last night. The loss is estimated at $70,000, partially insured.

N Y, Feb 11. This morning a German, Albert Garagnon, called at the house of Henry Strauss, 141 13th st, & asked to see a girl named Sophia Walt. After conversing with her for a short time, he drew a revolver & fired at her twice, neither shot taking effect. He then drew a razor & cut his own throat, expiring almost instantly. The unfortunate man was actuated by jealously.

Dept of the Interior, U S Patent Ofc, Wash, Feb 6, 1868. Ptn of Albert Fink, of Louisville, Ky, praying for the extension of a patent granted to him May 9, 1854, for an improvement in Bridges, for seven years from the expiration of said patent, which takes place on May 9, 1868. -A M Stout, Acting Com'r of Patents

Fortress Monroe, Feb 11. The revenue cutter **Noesha** was burned up on Chesapeake Bay on Friday, off Wycomico River. Two of the crew, John Grennel, cockswain, & Wm Stroud, master at-arms, were drowned.

THU FEB 13, 1868
The Senate yesterday confirmed Gen Noah L Jeffries as Register of the Treasury.

Royal B Milliken, editor & publisher of the Vt Record & Farmer, was found dead in his bed at Brandon, on Friday morning.

Gen & Mrs Dix, in Paris, are giving receptions on Sat evenings.

Victor Hugo amuses his leisure by water-color drawing & counting up his income.

Norfolk, Va, Feb 12. The revenue cutter **Northerner** has arrived here with the officers & men of the burned steamer **Neusho**.

Orphans Court-Judge Purcell, Feb 11, 1868. 1-Second account general, & second account of the personal estate of Jas B Leach, dec'd, by Louisa K Leach, [now Norton,] admx. First general & first final account of Augustus Schroder, adm of Rita Tuay, dec'd, & guardian to orphan children of R R & R Tuay; first & individual account of the same, guardian to orphan of the same, were approved & passed. 2-Last will & testament of Jas E Bliss, consitituting & appointing his wife sole executrix & guardian to the minor children, was filed & partially proven. Sylvia L Bliss, widow, took out letters testamentary; bond $6,000; H I King & Chas H Bliss, sureties.

Equity Court-Judge Olin. 1-Swain vs Swain et al; order appointing Geo W Langley guardian *ad litem*. 2-Adams vs Adams et al; decree appointing Wm M Matthews trustee to sell.

FRI FEB 14, 1868
The objections made to the ratification of the sales of the real estate of the late John Contee, which were elaborately argued in the Circuit Court of PG Co, Md, have been overruled by the Court of Appeals. The sales made by the trustees have thus been confirmed. This real estate was bought by R B B Chew & Danl Clark, trustees, by Mr J R Wilson, now residing in Phil, & was purchased from him by Jonathan T Walker, of Wash City. This decision by the Court of Appeals gives him a clear title to the property, which is one of the finest estates in PG Co, Md.

Mrd: on Feb 11, at St Paul's Church, PG Co, Md, by Rev Dr Marbury, John M Roberts to Alice C Connick, both of PG Co, Md. No cards.

Admiral Engle died at Phil on Wed, in his 69th year. At the commencement of the war he brought home from China the steamer **Hartford**. [Feb 17th newspaper: He was a native of Delaware Co Pa; entered the naval service in 1814; during the Mexican war he commanded the ship **Princeton**, & distinguished himself for his activity & skill in the blockading squadron; large portion of his service had been on land, connected with the various naval boards; at the outbreak of the rebellion Admiral Engle was sent out ot China to assume command of the steamer **Hartford**, & brought that famous ship home; was put in command of the Phil navy yard; his last service was as govn'r of the Phil Naval asylum, a post which he held until superseded by Admiral Paulding. Admiral Engle married a sister of Bishop McIlvaine, & his widow & 3 children survive him.]

Harrisburg, Feb 13. Govn'r Geary has granted a full pardon to Wm Muser, editor of the Sunday Mercury, convicted of libel on Wm B Mann, Dist Atty of Phil.

The President has sent to the Senate the following nominations:
Lt Gen Wm T Sherman, to be general by brevet in the army of the U S, for distinguished courage, skill, & ability displayed during the war of the rebellion.
Chas M Tuttle, assessor of internal revenue for the 24th Dist of N Y; Moses S Foot, collector of the 1st Dist of Ala; Hazard Stevens, collector of Wash Territory; Horace G Storms, assessor of internal revenue for the 1st Dist of Ohio; Geo Otis Allen & W B Jones, assist surgeons in the navy; Henry Gillem, deputy postmaster, Hazleton, Pa; Chas P Wannall, justice of the peace, Dist of Columbia.

Board of Police. The resignation of Pvt Saml T Crown was received & accepted. Pvt John D Nutting, charged with gross neglect of duty, was dismissed the force. Pvt Fenton D Paxson, charged with violating the rules & regulations of the force, was fined $25 & ordered to be reprimanded. Pvt John C Mansfield, charged with neglect of duty, was dismissed the force. Pvt Chas N Proctor, charged with conduct unbecoming an ofcr, was ordered to be reprimanded. Pvt Alfred Borden, for neglect of duty, was fined $10. Pvt C L Green, same offence, fined $10. The following were appointed additional privates for 90 days: E G Townsend, for duty at Kendall Green Barracks. Henry C Jones, at Metropolitan Hall. Wm H Snyder, between 10th & 12th st, & E & B sts. John L Daily, at the depot of the Wash & Gtwn Railroad Co. The following named men were appointed additional privates on the regular force: Chas G Langly, Jas B Boyle, Z Offutt, & F M Doyle. The application of Thos Manning for restaurant license was rejected, as was also the applications of Wm Musgrif, Jas Cole, Casper Herbert, Alois Mueller, Geo Nachman, & John Carrigan, of Wash, & Anthony Rodier, of Gtwn.

Cable announces the death of Sir David Brewster; he was born at Jedburgh, Scotland, on Dec 11, 1781, & was, therefore, at the time of his death in his 87th year. During 1810 he was married to one of the daughters of Mr J Macpherson, the translator. Mrs Brewster died in 1850, & he was married a second time, in 1857, to a Miss Purnell. No ancient or modern discoverer has done more to make the study of natural science attractive than Brwester. –N Y Tribune [No death date given-current item.]

A Western paper says that Dickens has a sister-in-law residing in Chicago, the widow of Augustus Dickens, who was a clerk in the Illinois Central Land Ofc for some 10 or 12 years, & died 2 or 3 years ago. Augustus was the favorite brother of Chas in the time of his early literary triumphs, & it was from him that he derived his *nom de plume* of Boz. Mrs Dickens, it it added, is keeping a boarding house, & is barely able to support herself & children. [May 5th newspaper: A despatch from Chicago says it may not be improper to state that the story, sent by a London correspondent to the Boston advertiser, to the effect that the widow of Augustus N Dickens, is living in England, a sufferer from ill-health, & tenderly cared for by Chas Dickens, is untrue in all its parts. Mrs Dickens is now, as she has been for several years, living at 568 North Clark st, Chicago, on an exceedingly small patrimony. She has never received a dollar, not even a word of comfort from Mr Chas Dickens since his brother's death.]

Appointments in the Treasury Dept. Maj Bushrod Birch, formerly 4th class clerk in the ofc of disbursing clerk, Sec's ofc, Treas Dept, has been appointed disbursing clerk, vice Saml M McKean, dec'd. Mr H C Niles has been transferred from a 4th class clerk in the temporary roll appointment bureau, to a permanent position of like grade, vice Birch, promoted.

Worcester, Mass, Feb 13. Byron Wilson, aged 17 years, was killed by the cars at Junction Station this morning. He was riding on the cars to school, when he fell at the railroad crossing, & both of his legs were crushed.

SAT FEB 15. 1868
Mr Wm W Corcoran returned to Wash City on Thursday, bringing with him for sepulture the remains of his only beloved daughter, Mrs Louise Morris Eustis, who died after a fatal illness in Europe. The funeral will take place from Mr Corcoran's residence on next Monday at 3 o'clock P M. The friends of the family are invited to attend.

Gen John A Green has been nominated as a Democratic candidate for Mayor of Syracuse, N Y.

The President has pardoned E Farran, who held the position of admiral in the rebel navy during the rebellion. The pardon was granted on the recommendation of Govn'r English, Senator Dixon, of Conn, & other prominent citizens.

Mobile, Feb 14. Died: Hiram T Henry, the oldest printer of Mobile, this morning, aged 62 years.

John W P Myers vs Jane C Myers, Geo Murray, et al. No 1,015 Equity, Docket 8. The trustees reported they sold the wharf property belonging to the late Chas Myers, fronting 41 feet on the south side of Water st, to Francis Wheatley, for the sum of $4,000, & he has complied with the terms of sale. –A B Olin -R J Meigs, clerk.

Dept of the Interior, U S Patent Ofc, Wash, Feb 11, 1868. Ptn of Wm H Mitchell, of N Y, N Y, praying for the extension of a patent granted to him May 16, 1854, for an improvement in Machinery for Composing Type, for seven years from the expiration of said patent, which takes place on May 16, 1868. -A M Stout, Acting Com'r of Patents

Dept of the Interior, U S Patent Ofc, Wash, Feb 10, 1868. Ptn of Edw Brown, of Waterbury, Conn, praying for the extension of a patent granted to him May 16, 1854, for an improvement in Machines for Making Hinges, for seven years from the expiration of said patent, which takes place on May 16, 1868. -A M Stout, Acting Com'r of Patents

MON FEB 17, 1868
Criminal Court-Sat. Henry Johnson found not guilty for the murder of Thos Smoot. The crowd assembled applauded at the verdict. Johnson left the court-room with his friends.

Phil, Feb 16. Wm M Swain, the founder of the Public Lodger newspaper, of this city, died this morning, aged 59 years, after a long illness. He was the founder of the Balt Sun; a native of Onondaigua Co, N Y; for 8 years was president of the Magnetic Telegraph Co; & for many years director in the American Telegraph Co. He possessed great intellectual ability & force of character. [Feb 21st newspaper: Phil, Feb 20. The remains of the late Wm M Swain, were interred in *Woodland Cemetery* this morning. The deceased, it is believed, has left no will, & his large estate will be divided between his widow & 2 sons.]

The *Astor House* hotel rents for $55,000 a year.

Mr Philip R Fendall expired at his residence in Wash City, at the advanced age of 73 years. Some months since this gentleman was prostrated by disease. He was born in Alexandria, Va; graduated at Princeton College in 1815 with distinction, taking the first honor of the class; came to the bar in Alexandria, then a part of D C; removed to Wash City; filled important positions. Mr Fendall married Miss Young, of Alexandria, a sister-in-law of ex-Senator A G Brown, of Mississippi. This lady has been some years deceased. Mr Fendall leaves a family of 9 children, 6 sons & 3 daughters. For the last 2 months Mr Fendall has been wholly confined to his house. He had a hearty breakfast & about 1 o'clock he was suddenly seized with convulsions, & died in a few minutes. [Feb 18th newspaper: The funeral of the late Philip R Fendall will take place from his residence, 4½ st & La ave, on Thu at 12 o'clock M. The remains will be taken to *Glenwood Cemetery*, & temporarily placed in the receiving vault, for removal to Alexandria for interment, in accordance with his wish.] [Feb 21st newspaper: The spacious mansion was crowded with ladies & gentlemen, & among the many eminent persons present was Judge Dunlop & Morsell, of the old Circuit Court, the latter now being in his 94th year; Judges Cartter, Olin, Fisher, & Wylie, of the present court; & Messrs John Marbury, the oldest member of the bar; W W Corcoran, Dr Wm Gunton, J M Carlisle, Dr Peter Parker, Thos Blagden; John A Smith, late clerk of the Circuit Court; Rev Dr Samson, of Columbia College; Rev D Sunderland, Capt Junius Boyle, & many others. The coffin was of black walnut, covered with fine black broadcloth; lined with fine white merino; the mountings of the casket were of silver of neat design. Upon the lid was a massive silver plate, inscriped: "Philip Richard Fendall. Born at Alexandria, Va. Died at Washington, D C, February 16, 1868." Rt Rev Bishop Johns, of Rhode Island, accompanied by Rev D Pinckney, of the Church of the Ascension, & Rev B Peyton Brown, of the Foundry Church, took their places near the coffin in seats prepared for them. The burial service of the Episcopal Church was read by Bishop Jones & Dr Pinckney. Bishop Johns said that over 50 years ago, they stood side by side in the class-room. At the conclusion, the coffin lid was screwed down by Mr Harvey, the undertaker, & was borne to the hearse by the pall-bearers: Dr John B Blake, Judge Dunlop, Judge Wylie, J Carroll Brent, Walter Lennox, Dr J F May, W S Mitchell, J B H Smith, & J C McGuire. The remains were followed by a long line of carriages, & the funeral procession wended its mournful way to *Glenwood Cemetery*, where the remains were place in the receiving vault for future interment.]

Gen J B Steedman has resigned the collectorship of internal revenue in New Orleans, to take effect May 15.

Equity Court-Justice Olin. 1-Young et al vs Goodrick et al. Decree appointing A Lloyd trustee to sell.

Orphans Court: owing to the illness of Judge Purcell on Sat, there was not session of the Orphans Court.

Appointment of Catholic Bishops: Phil, Feb 16. Yesterday the appointments of the following bishops for the diocese of Phil were received from Cardinal Barnabe, at Rome: The Pope has designated the following: Rev Wm O'Harra, of St Patrick's Church, to be Bishop of Scranton; Rev L F Shanahan, of Medea, Pa, to be Bishop of Harrisburg; & Rev Dr Brecker, of Richmond, Va, to be Bishop of Wilmington, Delaware.

Hon S S Marshall, present Representative in Congress from the 11th Dist of Ill, announces himself as a candidate for re-election.

On Friday the wife of Col G T Gibbings was killed at Galveston, Texas, by jumping from a carriage whilst the horses were running away.

Mr Geo Ticknor Curtis does not desire the place of Minister to Great Britain. He suggests his friend, Hon Robt C Winthrop, as the right man for the place.

The Albany Argus states that Hugh J Hastings, of that city, has purchased the interest of Thurlow Weed in the N Y Commercial Advertiser. He has had long experience in newspaper management.

In Howard Co, Mo, on Sat, a son of Mr Harry Dickerson, 9 years old, attempted to release a hog which had got fastened in a gate, when a number of other hogs attacked the boy, & he was so mangled & bruised that he died the next day.

TUE FEB 18, 1868
Fire last night in the carpenter shop of Mr J Geo Naylor, La ave, oppostie 5th st; shop was filled with doors, inside blinds, & other finely-worked lumber, which were totally destroyed, & was a large amount of paints & oils, the property of Mr T A Brown, whose painting establishment was in the bldg. The law ofc of Mr Asbury Lloyd, adjoining, was damaged by water, but his valuable papers were saved. The loss of Mr Naylor, who owned the bldg destroyed, will be about $7,000, of which there is but $400 in insurance. [Feb 20th newspaper: A large force of workmen were busy yesterday rebldg the carpentering establishment of Mr J Geo Naylor; he is a well known builder of our city.]

Fortress Monroe, Feb 17. The propeller **Lynhaven**, of Norfolk, blew up yesterday. Loss about $5,000. No insurance. No lives lost.

The execution of Ottawa G Baker took place on Feb 14 at Omaha, for the murder of Woolsey D Higgins, in Nov last. The criminal was 26, 5 feet 10 inches high, light complextion, prominent Roman nose, born in Richmond, Va, & was employed by Wm R King & Co, wholesale grocers, 2 years ago, as porter. While thus employed, on Nov 22, 1866, he murdered Higgins, the book-keeper, then sleeping in the same bed, robbed the safe, & set the bldg on fire, which resulted in the destruction of an entire block. The execution was witnessed by six to eight thousand persons. Baker wrote a confession several weeks ago, but begged the confessor not to publish it till after his death. He killed Higgins by striking him with 2 blows across the forehead with an axe.

Gen Grant has rebought the farm, near St Louis, which he used to cultivate.

The funeral of Mrs Louise Morris Eustis, the only child of our esteemed fellow-citizen, W W Corcoran, took place yesterday from her father's residence. At 3 o'clock the spacious halls & parlors of the mansion were thronged with the friends of the deceased, gathered to pay the last sad tribute of respect to the memory of one who in life enjoyed the most estimable regard of all who had the pleasure of coming within the circle of her acquaintance. Orphan children from the different asylums in Wash City were there. Mrs Eustis loved to visit these institutions, dispensing gifts. The remains, enclosed in a metallic coffin, were place on a pedestal in the centre of the north parlor. On the lid, surrounding the massive silver plate was inscribed: "Louise Morris Eustis, born March 20th, 1838. Died December 4th, 1867." The services were conducted by Rev Dr Pinckney, rector of the Espicopal Church of the Ascension. The coffin was then removed to the hearse by the pall-bearers: Messrs J B H Smith, Col Jas G Berret, Jas M Carlisle, Geo W Riggs, Dr Jas B Blake, Gen Park, Dr Thos Miller, Col R D Cutts, Wm A Gordon, Maj Lee, & Mr Harrison. The remains were taken to *Oak Hill Cemetery*, Gtwn, & placed in the mausoleum. The funeral cortege was one of the largest ever seen in Washington.

The President yesterday sent the following nominations to the Senate:
Danl Garrison, assessor of internal revenue for the 1st Dist of N Y.
Chas H Hall, assessor of internal revenue for the 32nd Dist of N Y.
Thos Sim, marshal for the dist of S C.
R H Smith, U S atty for West Va.
Wm C Burt, postmaster at Murfreesboro', Tenn.
Jas W McDonough, postmaster at Galveston, Texas.
Jos H Moore, postmaster at El Paso, Ill.
Geo T Martin, postmaster at Santa Fe, Mexico.
Wm M Baine, postmaster at Jackson, Ind.

WED FEB 19, 1868
Orphans Court of Wash Co, D C, Feb 18, 1868. In the case of Edw Keefe & Thos McGrath, excs of Thos Johnson, dec'd, the executors & Court have appointed Mar 14 next, for the final settlement of the personal estate of the said dec'd, of the assets in hand.
-Jas R O'Beirne, Reg/o wills

By telegram from San Francisco the death is announced of Rear Admiral Henry H Bell, commanding the U S Asiatic squadron. He, together with a boat's crew of the men of the flagship **Hartford**, drowned by crossing the bar at the mouth of the Osaka, Japan, on Jan 11 last. Admiral Bell was born in the State of N C, from which State he was appointed to the navy on Aug 4, 1823. After becoming a midshipman he was promoted, by slow degrees, until he had attained the rank of commander, which he held at the time of the breaking out of the war. He had been in the service 43 years, 23 of which he spent at sea.
+
Lt Cmder J H Reed, was drowned at the same time with Admiral Bell. He was a native of Mich, & entered the service on Sep 28, 1859. During the rebellion he was at the passage of ***Fort Jackson & Fort St Philip***, & the Chalmatte batteries, & ran the batteries at Vicksburg twice. He was in the engagement with the rebel ram **Arkansas**, the siege of Port Hudson; ran the batteries at Grand Gulf twice, & was on the iron-clad during their operations off Charleston & Stone river. Both ofcrs were much esteemed by all who knew them. [Mar 11th newspaper: Admiral Bell was accompanied by his Flag-Lt Reed & 13 men; 3 of the sailors were saved. On Mon Cmdor J R Goldsborough, now senior in command of the Asiatic squadron, issued a notice that the funeral of those lost would take place on 14th. Tues was very calm, the bay still. Some 50 marines, under command of Capt Forney, landed at 10 A M, & took their position on the beach; at 11 A M the first gun was fired from the ship **Hartford**, & the procession, under the command of Lt-Cmder Higgenson, moved slowly towards the shore. The entire population arrived on the beach & took their places in the procession. The band of the ship **Ocean** had been loaned for the occasion. Gen Paul Frank, the American Consul, was in attendance, with the Vice Govn'r of Hiogo, & many Japanese ofcrs. Upon the landing of the bodies the line took up its march for the cemetery; the bodies were all lowered at one time into the graves, & a volley fired by the marines. Then the procession returned to the beach & dispersed.]

Died: on Feb 18, Grace, the infant of C & E S Ingle, aged 18 months.

Orphans Court of Wash Co, D C, Feb 18, 1868. In the case of Edw C Dyer, dec'd, adm of Mary E Dyer [by his executors, S E Boarman & Thos J Fisher,] the administrator & Court have appointed Mar 14 next, for the final settlement of the personal estate of the said dec'd, of the assets in hand. -Jas R O'Beirne, Reg/o wills

Orphans Court of Wash Co, D C. In the case of Sylvester B Boarman & Thos J Fisher, excs of Edw C Dyer, dec'd, the executors & Court have appointed Mar 11th next, for the final settlement of the personal estate of the said dec'd, of the assets in hand.
-Jas R O'Beirne, Reg/o wills

Dept of the Interior, U S Patent Ofc, Wash, Feb 13, 1868. Ptn of Elias Ingraham, of Bristol, Conn, praying for the extension of a patent granted to him Dec 3, 1861, for an improvement in Design for a Clock Case, for seven years from the expiration of said patent, which takes place on Dec 3, 1868. -A M Stout, Acting Com'r of Patents

Orphans Court of Wash Co, D C. Letters of administration on the personal estate of Wm Binning, late of the U S army, dec'd. –S M Owen, adm

An Eastern man named Tucker purchased some land where the village of Hudson, Mich, is now located, in 1837, & subsequently sold it, giving deeds without his wife's signature. Mr Tucker died in 1842, & his wife now claims her right of dower [one third] in all this land, which is now covered with valuable bldgs. The matter has been placed in the hands of attys, & creates considerable excitement among property owners there.

THU FEB 20, 1868
Miss Anne Proctor, who was captured by the Cheyenne Indians 20 years ago, is now stopping near Emporia, Kansas. She escaped only a short time since. She thinks some of her family live in South Kansas, but does not know where.

Jacob Barker's pictures were sold in New Orleans last week for $2,695.

The late Wm M Swain, founder of the Phil Ledger, left over three millions of dollars to his two sons.

The U S Supreme Court, to which an appeal had been made, has sustained the will of Mrs Abigail Loring, of Boston, who devoted $171,000 to various charitable institutions.

Mrs Weaver, the insane woman who recently murdered her 5 children, & who was in jail at Pembroke, Ontario, committed suicide on Monday by hanging herself to the door of her cell.

Govn'r Geary has signed the bill repealing the charter & confiscating the property of the Gettysburg Asylum Lottery.

Criminal Court-Chief Justice Carter: cases disposed of yesterday: 1-Wm Smith & John Green, larceny, not guilty. 2-Perry Jones, Jas A Snowden, Louis Snowden, Stephen Taylor, indicted for larceny: found gulty. 3-Jas Garrity, assault & battery, fined $25. 4-A *nolle pros* was entered in the case of Louisa Deitz & John Matthews.

Equity Court-Justice Olin. In the claim of Edw L Walker vs John K O'Neil, of interference with patent, both claiming to be the inventors of a patent horse hay fork, the Com'r of Patents, Hon T C Theaker, decided in favor of Walker, & hence the appeal.

Phil, Feb 19. About midnight at 23rd & Market sts, Patrick McLaughlin was stabbed to the heart in a scuffle by Michl Carey, who boarded at the house of the former. The former was employed at the skating park, & coming home late found himself locked out, when he attempted to break open the door, & after being assaulted by his wife a scuffle ensued, which resulted in his death. Carey has been arrested.

Buffalo, N Y, Feb 19. Three men, Geo Morrison, Thos Thompson, & Wm Alexander, were capsized in an open boat yesterday, in the Niagara river, & drowned.

Orphans Court-Judge Purcell, Feb 18, 1867. 1-The will of Eliz A Cross, heretofore filed for probate, was exhibited & partially proven. 2-In re. estate of Jacob Lowenthal, dec'd. On motion of A G Riddle, for widow, Thos H Ford & S S Hinckle were cited to appear & give testimony. Hinckle returned non est. 3-The inventory of the personal estate of Mary Ann Fearson, dec'd, was returned by Mary Julia Barrett, collector. 4-Third account of Susannah Carrico, adms of Jas Carrico, dec'd. 5-Fourth & final accounts of Wm H & O H Morrison, excs of Wm H Morrison, dec'd, relating to Louisa Culver, dec'd, were approved & passed. 6-The will of S M Kean was filed & fully proven. He gives all his property to his wife, M T McKean, & names her sole excx. 7-Saml W Owen gave bond in the sum of $800 as adm of Wm Benning, dec'd; Col A A Hosmer & Wm L Dove, sureties.

Ada Isaac Menken's volume of poems, just published in Paris, is dedicated to "my friend Charles Dickens."

Mr Berryer, the father of the French bar, has entered his 79th year.

On Sat, near this village, Mr Timothy Ryan was killed by the accidental discharge of his gun, in drawing it through or over a fence he had hurriedly crossed while in pursuit of game. The load entered his head, & he died instantly. A little son was with him, & a faithful dog guarded his body, refusing to permit strangers to approach his master until some members of the family came to pacify him. Mr Ryan was an industrious & honest man, & has left a widow & 5 small children. –Marlboro Gaz

Mrd: on Jan 8, at the British Embassy in Paris, & afterwards at the Madeleine, Temple Kirkpatrick, Sec in the British Legation at Berlin, to Sylvia Livingston, widow of Wm S Drayton, of the U S navy, & daughter of the late Mortimer Livingston, of N Y.

Mrd: on Feb 11, by Rev M V Tudor, Mr John H Hennage, of Va, to *Indiana P Drish, daughter of the late Grafton Powell. [Feb 21st newspaper: John H Hennage, of Va, was married to India P Drish, daughter of the late Grafton Powell. *The change was Indiana to India.]

Orphans Court of Wash Co, D C, Feb 18, 1868. In the case of John H Semmes, adm of Louisa Collins, dec'd, the administrator & Court have appointed Mar 17 next, for the final settlement of the personal estate of the said dec'd, of the assets in hand.
-Jas R O'Beirne, Reg/o wills

Dept of the Interior, U S Patent Ofc, Wash, Feb 14, 1868. Ptn of Ward Eaton, of N Y, N Y, praying for the extension of a patent granted to him May 16, 1854, for an improvement in Machine for Cutting Glaziers' Points, for seven years from the expiration of said patent, which takes place on May 16, 1868. -A M Stout, Acting Com'r of Patents

Chas Reade says one novel in two years is as much as he can attend to.

FRI FEB 21, 1868
The President's order assigning Lt Gen W T Sherman to the command of the new dept of Atlantic, with headquarters in Wash, D C, has been revoked by the President.

Gen McClellan has gone to Florence from Vienna with his wife, whose health requires the change.

Fire last night in the stable belonging to Patrick Deely, F & 3rd sts south. The loss is about $100. The only horse in the stable was rescued with some difficulty.

Capt Travis, the famous pistol shooter, is giving lessons in pistol practice to the ladies of Youngstown, Ohio.

Madame Antoine Cruzat, of one of the leading families of the old Creole population in New Orleans, died a few days ago, at the age of 92.

Cyrus W Field sailed for Europe on Wed to complete arrangements for the consolidation of the Atlantic Telegraph Co with the Anglo-American Co.

Mary Ann Duffin, 60 Mulberry st, N Y, died on Wed of injuries received by an oil lamp explosion. On Friday an agent of "non-explosive oil" was trying to convince her of the merits of his articles when it exploded.

Gen McFerran, Depot Quartermaster, on G st, between 17th & 18th sts, in Wash City, has received information that the bodies of Maj Simpson, Pay Dept, & Maj Michl J Kelly, 4th U S cavalry, U S army, who died in Texas of yellow fever, would arrive at Balt & Ohio depot in Wash City this morning. Gen McFerran has made suitable arrangements for the reception of the bodies.

Criminal Court-Chief Justice Carter. 1-Jas Hill, indicted for the larceny of $2 from Jesse Coats, on Nov 2 last: not guilty. 2-Henry Wheeler, indicted for the larceny of one shawl, of $7 value, the property of Dernelman & Blout, on Jan 12 last; jury unable to agree, the Dist Atty entered a *nolle pros*. 3-Julius Finnicum, recognizance forfeited. Bench warrant issued. 4-Thos Lucas, indicted for receiving stolen goods, knowing them to have been stolen: not guilty. 4-The trial of Jas A Becket, for murder, will be taken up today.

Circuit Court-Judge Wylie. The case of Jas C Hyland et al vs Savage. This is an action for meane, accruing for the possession of a lot on H st, between 8th & 9th sts, from 1838 to 1866. It appears that the lot was vacant, & sold for taxes in 1838, & purchased by parties through whom Mr Savage claims title. But the law applying to tax sales had not been strictly carried out in the sale, & this lot was some time ago recovered by action in ejectment from Mr Savage, & the suit is now brought to recover the rents & profits received during its occupancy by Savage. Damages laid at $20,000.

Died: on Feb 19, in Balt, Jas Maddox, [formerly of **Ford's Theatre**, Wash] in the 30th year of his age.

Died: on Feb 20, after a few weeks illness, Lavinia A, eldest daughter of Jas Clephane. Her funeral will take place from the residence of her brother, on G st, between 12th & 13th sts, on Feb 22, at 12 o'clock M. [Star & Express copy.]

Obit-died: Saml M McKeean, on Feb 8, in Wash City, having nearly completed four-score years; born in Pa; was the grandson of Govn't Thos McKean, one of the signers of the Declaration of Independence. Mr McKean became a member of St John's Episcopal Church some year or two ago, under the ministrations of the pastor, Rev Mr Lewis. –C

Freehold, N J, Feb 10. Col Wm D Davis, late president of the Freehold & Janesburg railroad, & a prominent citizen of Monmoth Co, died here last night.

Spring Mill property for sale; by decree of the Circuit Court of Loudoun Co, Va, pronounced Oct 19, 1866: sale on Apr 25, the *Big Spring Mill* property, containing 43 acres of land, with brick dwlg house, a large warehouse, the remains of the burnt mill, among which are a large Iron Mill Shaft. The Mill Site: the purchaser can by 150 acres of land adjoining it if he should desire to do so. Apply at Leesburg, Va, to John Janney, A H Rogers, Matthew Harrison, Com'r of sale. –John L Rinker, auct

Madame Petipa, the favorite dancer of St Petersburg, has drawn the great Russian lottery prize of 75,000 roubles.

The late Prof Faraday kept a record of his experiments. The last one was numbered 16,541.

At a court-martial held in N Y Jan 3, Capt Napoleon Collins, of the navy, was tried for allowing the U S steamer **Sacramento** to run upon a shoal at the mouth of Kathapaloun river, on the coast of Coromondel, where she was wrecked. Capt Collins sentence was yesterday approved by the Sec of the Navy, in a general order: to be suspended for the term of 3 years from rank & duty, during which period of time he shall receive only the pay of ofcrs of the grade of capt on the retired list; his suspension from rank only to affect his promotion to a high grade; & to be publicly reprimanded by the Sec of the Navy. Capt Collins is the same ofcr who commanded the ship **Washusett** when she entered Bahia Bay, Brazil, & captured the rebel pirate Florida, & for this act he was then promoted to the rank of lt cmder. Gen M Bache, executive ofcr of the **Sacramento**, was also court-martialed for the same offence, & sentenced to be suspended for one year, & to be publicly reprimanded by the Sec of the Navy.

SAT FEB 22, 1868
Mark Twain, the well-known humorist, will lecture this evening at Forrest Hall, in Gtwn.

Phil, Feb 21. Jos R Ingersoll, a well-known lawyer, died here yesterday, aged 82 years.

Yesterday afternoon, about 5 o'clock, as Mr Geo W Wood, of Richmond, Indiana, with his nephew, was on his way to the Balt depot, he fell at 3rd & Pa ave & expired immediately. Ofcr Offutt had the body removed to the 7th precinct station house, & Dr Geo M Dove was called in, & gave his opinion that the deceased died from disease of the heart or affection of the brain. Hon Geo W Julian & Hon M C Kerr, Reps from Indiana, were informed of the death of Mr Wood, & placed the body in charge of Undertaker Harvey, who will forward it to his family. Mr Wood was about 40 years of age, & for some time was editor of a paper at Richmond, Ind; of late years he had devoted his attention to the invention of a chromotype press, & had recently received patents for improvements on the same. He leaves a wife & 4 children.

Funeral of military ofcrs: the bodies of Maj Geo B Simpson, late paymaster U S army, & Maj Kelly, late of the 4th U S cavalry, who died last summer in New Orleans from yellow fever, were consigned to Gen Van Vliet, U S quartermaster at Balt, who forwarded them to Wash City. They were taken care of by Messrs Harvey & Co, undertakers, & that of Maj Kelley was conveyed to their warerooms for future interment. The funeral of Maj Simpson took place at once; funeral procession was formed, with Cos B D C & F, 44th U S infty, with the regimental band, recently organized, led by Wagner, under command of Brvt Lt Col Shea, the companies being commanded by Lt Porter, Capt Tyler, Lt Crosby, & Brvt Capt Marcott; carriages containing the pall bearers: Brvt Lt Col Taylor, Maj Truesdale, Maj Dyer, Maj Vroman, Lt Col Robinson, Brvt Lt Col Potter, Brvt Lt Col Wright, & Brvt Lt Col Walcott; carriages containing the family connections & friends of the deceased; among others, Maj Gen B W Brice & Brig Gen A B Eaton. The remains were taken to **Mount Olivet Cemetery**, where they were interred with military honors, after the services of the Catholic Church had been performed.
+
Died: The remains of Brvt Maj Michl J Kelley, capt 4th U S cavalry, who died of typhoid fever in Texas on Aug 13 last, having arrived in this city, his funeral will take place from the residence of his brother, Mr Richd Kelly, 29 Ind ave, on Feb 24 at 10 o'clock.
+
[Feb 24th newspaper: the funeral of the late Maj Kerr, whose body arrived here on Friday with that of Maj Simpson, will take place today, moving from his late residence, 29 Indiana ave, at 10 o'clock this morning, to St Aloysius Church, where requiem mass will be celebrated by Rev Fr Kelly, brother of the dec'd, at 11 o'clock, after which the remains will be interred at **Mount Olivet Cemetery**.]

Five negroes have been imprisoned in Fairfax Co jail, charged with the murder of Mrs Patsy Mills, on Leesburg pike, near Wash. She was nearly 75 years of age. Robbery was the instigation to the murder.

Mrd: on Feb 19, by Rev Dr Pinckney, of Ascension Church, Leonard L Nicholson, of Wash City, to Susie C Brawner, daughter of Jas L Brawner, of Chas Co, Md. [Port Tobacco Times copy.]

Mrd: on Feb 20, at the residence of the bride's father, in Balt, Md, by Rev Dr Grammer, Thos B Valentine, of San Francisco, Calif, to Marie A, daughter of Jas Dull. No cards.

Died: on Feb 21, in Gtwn, D C, Saml McKenney, in his 77th year of his age. His funeral will be from his late residence, 124 Dunbarton st, tomorrow, Sunday, at 3½ P M. [Mar 2nd newspaper: Obit-died at his residence, in Gtwn, D C, Feb 21, Saml McKenney, in the 78th year of his age. In early life he was married to Miss Mary Ann Foxall, daughter of the late Henry Foxall. Mr McKenney was an earnest Christian, & although a member of the Methodist Episcopal Church from his youth, his spirit was truly Catholic, & in sympathy with evangelical Christianity in all its denominational forms. As a father his affection was intense; as a friend his attachment sincere.]

Dept of the Interior, U S Patent Ofc, Wash, Feb 17, 1868. Ptn of Frederic Howes, of Boston, Mass, praying for the extension of a patent granted to him Jun 20, 1854, for an improvement in Extra Yard to Topsails, for seven years from the expiration of said patent, which takes place on Jun 20, 1868. -A M Stout, Acting Com'r of Patents

The boiler of the tug-boat **James A Wright**, exploded at N Y on Mon; the capt, Silas A Dakin, & pilot, Benedict Fisher, with one of the crew, were thrown into the air, landing on the deck of the bark **Gangenolf**, which the tug was towing at the time of the disaster. Both are very seriously injured.

MON FEB 24, 1868
Meeting of the Oldest Inhabitants Association of the District was held on Sat; Col Williams, 1st vice pres of the society, presided, with Mr Nicholas Callan as sec. Mr John F Callan, as chairman of the cmte of arrangements reported that the cmte had requested Mr J Carrol Brent to read certain letters written by Gen Washington during the Revolution, on the birthday of the Father of his Country. Mr Lewis Johnson presented a copy of the Ulster Co Gaz, which was published in 1800. Mr John F Callan, on behalf of Mr W W Cox, presented a parchment signed by Thos Jefferson, dated 1802, it being the original appointment of Robt Brent, as the first Mayor of Washington.

Criminal Court-Chief Justice Cartter. Names of the jurors drawn at the Mar term:

C J Brewer	D V Burr	Jas L Owens
David McClelland	W H Tenney	Jas W Johnson
Richd Kelly	John R Pierce	F S Cissell
W B Hurdle	Richd J Cook	Saml Craton
Geo Green	H C Litchfield	John D West
C H Wiltberger	Thos E Smithson	Geo W Parker
Oliver Craig	Benj F Van Horn	J D Dement
Jas Dement	Ira Richards	
Petit Jury:		
Richd Emmons	W C Magee	John W Simms
Robt W Waters	C E Upperman	Edw C Adams
J A Hamilton	John R Arrison	A E P Hilton

W N Young	Henry McIntosh	W H Gunnell
Wm Houndschild	J Norment	J W Angus
W H Hanner	Jos Tuturville	Jacob J Fink
John W Law	John E Carter	Saml H Donaldson
August Acker	John Alexander	W M Keefe
W J Dyer	Alex'r Patterson	

Senator Sprague is going to build a very large cotton factory in Wilmington, Del.

Stewart, Vanderbilt, & Astor, within a few weeks, invested about $10,000,000 in up-town N Y real estate.

Elder Hiram B Clawson has just married the 4th daughter of Brigham Young. He had had previously married the prophet's eldest daughter. Besides being a high dignitary of the church, he is lessee & manager of the Salt Lake Theatre.

Miss Sarah Schofield died in Port Huron, Mich, on Feb 15, at the age of 103 years. She bore her hundred years with more apparent ease than women usually do at 60, & managed her business up to the time of her death.

TUE FEB 25, 1868
Mrd: on Feb 23, by Rev Fr Boyle, Mr Edw Cullinan to Mrs Eliz Gibson, widow of the late Joshua Gibson, all of Wash City.

Danl Clarke, Atty-at-Law, 417 N Y ave, Wash, D C.

Bowie & Williams, Attys-at-Law, Rockville, Md. –Richd J Bowie, Richd M Williams

Bosts & Poston, Attys-at-Law, Plant's Bldg, 15th & N Y ave, Wash, D C.
-Chas T Botts, Chas D Poston

Wm W Boyce, [formerly of S C,] Atty-at-Law, 281 G st, Wash.

Columbia Dispensary for Women & Children, N & 14th sts; in connection with **Columbia Hospital**, opened for the treatment of outdoor patients, who are supplied with medicine, medical & surgical treatment free. -Prof F Howard, Prof J H Thompson, Dr Ashford.

Providence Hospital, under the charge of the <u>Sisters of Chariety</u>, 2nd & D sts south, Capitol Hill. Medical Staff attending, physicians: D R Hagner, M D; John C Riley, M D; Wm Marbury, M D. Surgeons: J F Thompson, M D; C M Ford, M D; N S Lincoln, M D. Advisory & Consulting: Grafton Tyler, M D; W P Johnson, M D; F Howard, M D; Thos Miller, Johnson Eliot, C H Liberman. –Sister Loretta O'Reilly, Superior

Henry R Searle, Architect: ofc, 471 E st, oppostie Gen Post Ofc.

WED FEB 27, 1868

The impeachment of the Pres of the U S. The Republicans have impeached the President of high crimes & misdeameanors. It was understood last night that the Impeachment Cmte of seven were afraid to trust their case upon the single ground of the removal of Stanton, & had determined to rake among the dry bones of the two previously repudiated attempts at impeachment for charges against the President.

Gtwn election was held on Monday, & resulted in: Aldermen: Geo Hill, jr, T A Newman, Levi Davis, Jenkin Thomas, John W Branaugh. Common Council: Dr Chas H Cragen, Benj Darby, C S Ramsburg, Edw Shoemaker, Chas S English, John H Newman, Wm R Collins, L L Clements, Chas F Peck, J B Weller, C T Edmonston. These gentlemen were elected on what was known as the Corporation ticket, & are pledged as in favor of a Corporation market.

Orphans Court-Judge Purcell. 1-Harriet E Marsh gave bond in the sum of $2,000 as guardian of the orphans of Alfred J Webb. A F Cunningham, A K Walsh, & O W Marsh, sureties. 2-Lucinda Hess gave bond in the sum of $500 as admx of J J Hess. Valentine Hess & G W Scroggins sureties. 3-Benley Daughton gave bond in the sum of $3,000 as guardian to the orphans of Saml Warner. Wm I Shepherd & Harris Daughton, sureties. 4-First & final account of Thos E Baden, adm of Eleanor Baden; first account of Christian Lederer, guardian to Emma & Lilly Lederer; first account of Edw Simms, adm of Jos Reynolds; & the first & final accounnt of G W Sampson, adm of Robt Newman, were filed.

Criminal Court-Chief Justice Carter. Jas Beckett, convicted of manslaughter in causing the death of Thornton, was sentenced to 8 years in the Albany penitentiary.

Died: on Feb 24, Gustavus W Shipley, 3rd son of the late Benj Shipley, of Md. His funeral is this afternoon from the residence of his brother-in-law, E F Simpson; 398 E st.

Died: on Feb 24, Edw C Eddie, aged 38, Register of Deeds for the Dist of Col; a native of N Y, but a resident of this District for the last 15 years. His funeral will be from his late residence, on H st, between 12th & 13th sts, on Feb 27, at 11 A M.

Obit-Maj M J Kelly. The remains of Brvt Maj M J Kelly, capt 4th U S cavalry, were on Monday removed to **Mount Olivet Cemetery**, to repose beside the ashes of a good & amiable mother. His distinguished gallantry won for him the admiration of his companions in arms. Painful as was the parting of brother from brother, it was softened by the hope of soon meeting again. Maj Kelly died on Aug 13 last, of typoid fever, in the wilds of Texas. Requiescat in pace.

A young man, Wm Roche, an operator for the Franklin Telegraph Co, N Y, has been arrested & put under $500 bonds for divulging the contents of a private message sent by that line from Washington.

Rosa Verner Jeffrey, Vice Regent of Ky for the **Mount Vernon Ladies' Association**, has issued an appeal to the peope of that State for a few hundred dollars to keep *Mount Vernon* & the association from ruin. She says Miss Cunningham, the Regent, is at *Mount Vernon*, broken in health, ruined in fortune, & in want of the common comforts of life.

Trustee's sale, by deed of trust from John Fox & wife & John W Vanhook & wife, dated Apr 26, 1859, recorded in the land records for Wash Co, D C, in Liber J A S No 173, folios 269 thru 273, conveying certain property to the undersigned trustee, to secure the payment of Wm Ward of certain debts therein mentioned; public auction on Mar 28 next: parcel of land called *Uniontown* by said parties of the first part, & known as *John W Vanhook's Hill*, containing 8 acres, 3 rods, & 1 perch, more or less, being part of the ground which, by deed recorded among the land records of Wash Co, D C, in Liber J A S, No 78, folio 114, was granted & conveyed to Enoch Tucker & wife to the said John Fox & John W Vanhook, jointly with John Dobler, the interest of the said John Dobler being conveyed to the said John Fox & the said John W Vanhook by deed dated Mar 13,1857, with bldg improvements, rights, privileges, & appurtenances thereunto belonging. -Frank X Ward, trustee

Supreme Court of D C; equity 495, Docket 7. Barrand et al vs Ransone et al. Report of the sales made by Will Y Fendall, trustee, of lots 20 thru 25, of square 169; confirm & ratify same. –A B Olin, Justice -R J Meigs, clerk

Dept of the Interior, U S Patent Ofc, Wash, Feb 20, 1868. Ptn of Geo T Bigelow, adm of the estate of Saml Nicolson, dec'd, of Boston, Mass, praying for the extension of a patent granted to him Aug 8, 1854, for an improvement in Wooden Pavements, for seven years from the expiration of said patent, which takes place on Aug 8, 1868.
-A M Stout, Acting Com'r of Patents

THU FEB 27, 1868
Mrs Mary A Peaslee, an inmate of the insane asylum, at Augusta, Maine, was shockingly murdered on Monday by Mrs Catherine Hurley, another inmate, during a fit of frenzy.

Died: on Feb 25, in Wash City, Mrs Cecilia Wynne Stevens, widow & relict of John Stevens, in her 69th year.

Died: on Feb 25, Michl Doyle, a native of Queen's county, Ireland. His funeral is this afternoon at 3 o'clock, from 199 G st.

Died: on Feb 26, Samuel Owen, youngest son of Benj & Virginia Prosise, aged 3 months & 26 days. His funeral will take place at the residence, 348 D st, between 9th & 10th sts. [Leesburgh Mirror & Balt Sun will please copy.]

Phil, Feb 26. Maj Gen Geo A McCall died yesterday at West Chester, & will be interred at Christ Church, Phil, Sat. He served in the Mexican war, & organized & commanded the Pa reserves during the Peninsula campaign, & was captured before Richmond.

Chancery sale on Mar 17, of the **Lichau House**, situated on part of lot 13 in square 490, with bldgs & improvements thereon. Chancery sale of personal property at the Lichau House, [La ave, near 6th st west,] by decree of the Supreme Court of D C; in Equity No 904, wherein Chas G Hall is cmplnt & Henry Lichau et al are dfndnts; sale on Oct 30th of excellent furniture & kitchen ware. -Eugene Carusi, A Thos Bradley, Wm John Miller, Thos E Lloyd, Asbury Lloyd, trustees -Cooper & Latimer, aucts

Phil, Feb 26. Levi Morris, of the firm of Morris, Tasker, & Morris, iron workers, of this city, was accidentally killed this morning by being run over on the Pa railroad below Rosemount. He fell from the train while in motion, & his headless remains were discovered by the engineer of the next train.

FRI FEB 28, 1868
Cooper & Latimer, aucts, sold the east half of lot 2 in square 161, improved by a two story brick bldg, to Mr Chas Hartman, for $1,900; also, the west half of lot 2, improved with a 2 story bldg, to Helena Hartman, for $1,450. This property is on the north side of L st, between Conn & 18th st west.

Yesterday as a lad, Charley Donaldson, was skating on the Tiber Creek, between C & D sts, his little sister, who was with him, ventured upon a portion of ice which was weak & broke from her weight. Her cries for help brought her brother to assist her, & he also fell into the water. He was carried by the current under the ice, where he smothered before assistance could be rendered. The little girl was rescued, & the body of Charley was soon found. The corpse was carried to the residence of the boy's parents, on Indiana ave, between 2nd & 3rd sts.

Hazel's Hotel & Livery Stables, 168 Beall st, Gtwn, D C. -Wm C Hazel [Ad]

It is understood that Gen Lorenzo Thomas, Sec of War ad interim, was examined by the Impeachment Cmte yesterday, without eliciting any point upon which the impeachers can hang a charge of any kind against the President.

Reading, Pa, Feb 27. Wm Leavan, a member of the night police of this city, while assisting another ofcr to carry to jail 3 Irishmen who were drunk, was kicked in the abdomen, the effect of which he died in the Mayor's ofc a short time later. Leaven was 60 years of age, & leaves a large family.

Mrd: on Feb 26, at the residence of the bride's mother, by Rev Mr Gray, Cornelia Kavanaugh, of Wash, D C, to Capt J J Hinds, of Decatur, Ala. [Alabama papers please copy.]

Board of Metropolitan Police: meeting yesterday. Henry M Lowry, an additional private at the Nat'l Safe Deposit Co's ofc, & Jas W Kitchen, in Gtwn, were recommissioned as additional privates. Chas G Eckloff was reappointed as additional private, to do duty at Coombs' Hall, on Pa ave; & Geo W Nokes was appointed a private on the force, vice Jas H Gordon, placed on the retired list. In the case of Pvt Peter W Farley, charged with neglect of duty, complaint dismissed; Saml W Koontz, charged with violating rules & regulations, & Lawrence Rossiter, same charge, both fine $5; Privates Chas P Hopkins & Thos Price, charged with violating the rules & regulations, were both ordered to be reprimanded.

Died: on Feb 27, Louisa Nowlan, widow of the late Thos Nowlan. Her funeral will be from the residence of her daughter, 42 Water st, between Jefferson & Congress sts, Gtwn, D C, this afternoon, at 3 o'clock.

Died: on Feb 26, in Balt, after a protracted illness, Thos F Semmes, aged 75 years. His funeral will take place from the residence of Mrs John B Semmes, 392 G st, on Feb 28, at 11 o'clock A M.

Sir Fred'k Bruce left personal property to the amount of $350,000.

Gen Robt E Lee, who has steadily refused to write a book on the late war, has just completed the manuscript of his long meditated memoirs of his father, commonly called "Light-Horse Harry."

On Sat last Isaac Dutton was cut entirely in two by a circular saw, about 3 miles from Morgantown, Indiana.

Supreme Court of D C; Equity 349. Danl R Dyer vs Mary Ann Perkins, Mary Greenwell, Robt Greenwell, Geo W Perkins, et al. The above cause is referred to me in inquire into the material allegations of the bill & the necessity for a sale of the property mentioned in the proceedings. Meet at my ofc on Mar 2 at 3 o'clock. –Walter S Cox, auditor

Dept of the Interior, U S Patent Ofc, Wash, Feb 26. 1868. Ptn of Thos A Steadman, adm of the estate of Thos S Steadman, dec'd, of Lyons, Mich, praying for the extension of a patent granted to said Thos S Steadman, May 23, 1854, & reissued in 3 divisions-Jun 29, 1860, Jun 5, 1866, & Jun 20, 1865, for an improvement in Clover & Grass Seed Harvesters, for seven years from the expiration of said patent, which takes place on May 23, 1868. -A M Stout, Acting Com'r of Patents

Cincinnati, Feb 27. Patrick Ross, who some 8 years ago murdered a lady of rank in Ireland for her property, & for whom the British Gov't offered L750, was arrested in this city several days ago. Today he attempted suicide by cutting his throat, & is in a critical condition.

SAT FEB 29, 1868
The President sent to the Senate the following nominations: John H Broadhead, of Pa, com'r under the act of Mar, 1867, to reimburse the State of Indiana for money expended for the U S in enrolling, equipping, & provisioning militia to aid in the suppression of the rebellion; Jos H Rowland, marshal for the Western Dist of Ark; Chas Van Winkle, marshal for the Dist of Va, vice John Underwood, whose commission has expired; Thos Hood, atty for the Dist of Wisconsin.

The nomination of Gen Wisewell to be Com'r of Internal Revenue, was yesterday rejected by the Senate.

Hammack's Hotel, 200 & 202 Pa ave, between 14th & 15th sts. On the European plan. Meals served at all hours. The bar is stocked with the best liquors & wines.
-Thos Green, proprietor

Yesterday morning about 10 o'clock, Mr Lewis Thomas fell dead at his residence, on G st south, from the effects of an appoplectic stroke. Mr Thomas was in the 58th year of his age, & had been a resident of the 7th Ward for over 40 years. He had been engaged in the wood & coal business, & was esteemed by all who knew him. [Mar 2nd newspaper: Lewis Thomas died on Feb 29, in his 60th year of his age. His funeral is Mar 2 at 2 o'clock, from his late residence, G & 10th sts, on the Island.]

Died: on Feb 27, in Gtwn, after a brief illness, Mrs Mary D Abbott, wife of Geo D Abbott, & daughter of the late John N Moulder, of Wash City. Her funeral will take place from her late residence, on Bridge st, Gtwn, at 3 o'clock this afternoon, the 29th.

Died: on Feb 28, after a long & painful illness, Chas C Weeden, in his 30th year, eldest son of Henry A & Anna M Weeden. His funeral will take place on Sat at 2 o'clock P M, from the residence of his parents, 221 Pa ave, between 14th & 15th sts.

Cmte of Impeachment expected to present to the House today articles of impeachment. A despatch to the N Y Commercial Advertiser, says: It is given out that there will be six articles of impeachment as follows:
First: Declaring that the President had violated the Consitution in making a removal while the Senate was in session.
Second: That he had made this removal contrary to the tenure-of-ofc act.
Third: That he had appointed Gen Thomas as Sec of War while there was another legal Secretary.
Fourth: That he had conspired with Lorenzo Thomas to obtain possession the War Dept by military force.
Fifth: That he had conspired with or endeavored to get ofcrs of the army to disobey the laws of his country & enter into a conspiracy to get the legal Sec of War out of ofc.
The sixth article has not been completed.
The cmte do not take up any act of the President prior to the removal of Mr Stanton.

Died: on Friday, Magdaline, daughter of Wm H & Adelaide Sweeney, aged 1 year.

N Y, Feb 28. The Board of Presbyters appointed to try Rev Stephen H Tyng, jr, for a violation of a canon of the Protestant Episcopal Church, found Mr Tyng guilty, & have sentenced him to receive a public admonition from the Bishop, in accordance with the provisions of the diocesan canon.

MON MAR 2, 1868

Hon Thos H Ford, of Ohio, died on Sat, at his residence on Capitol Hill, of purpura, a disease that is very painful & generally fatal. He was born in Rockingham Co, Va, on Aug 23, 1814, & was in his 54th year. When quite young his family removed to the State of Ohio, & he became a resident of the town of Mansfield, Richland Co, Ohio. In 1853 he was elected Lt Govn'r of the State. In 1863 he came to Wash City & commenced the practice of his profession. In June last he connected himself with Metropolitan Division Sons of Temperance, & soon became a power in the temperance community, having done much by his example & his eloquent speeches to spread the temperance reform in this District. Govn'r Ford leaves a wife, daughter, & 3 sons, besides a large circle of friends, to mourn his loss. His funeral will take place today from Wesley Chapel, F & 5th sts. [Mar 20th newspaper: The remains of Hon Thos H Ford arrived in Mansfield on Sat, & were removed on Sunday to the Methodist Episcopal Church, where a funeral was preached by Rev J A Mudge, & eulogy pronounced by Hon Barnabas Burns, who had been intimately acquainted with him for more than 40 years.]

Robt Watson Williams, a young man of fortune, who died in N Y last week, bequeathed to a young colored man employed in the ofc of the N Y Times, the sum of $50,000.

Died: on May 1, Wm H Watson. His funeral will take place from his late residence, G & 19th sts on Tues, at 11 A M.

Died: on Feb 27, at Balt, after a brief Illness, Mrs Catharine B Senseney, in her 71st year, widow of the late Jacob Senseney, of Winchester, Va.

Chancery sale of valuable real estate on Lafayette Square: by decree of the Supreme Court of D C, in a cause wherein John S Gittings & others were cmplnts, & Wm B B Cross & others dfndnts; in Equity, No 1,093: public auction on Mar 24, of part of square 186, in Wash City, fronting on H st north 54 feet 9 inches, running back that width 131 feet 1 inch, to a 20 foot alley; with a 3 story double-front brick house, built in the best style; & a brick stable. This property adjoins the residence of W W Corcoran & fronts directly upon Lafayette Square & the President's House. –J Carter Marbury, trustee -W L Wall & Co, aucts

Orphans Court of Wash Co, D C. Letters of administration on the personal estate of Philip B Fendall, late of Wash Co, D C, dec'd. –W Y Fendall, Reginald Fendall, adms

Orphans Court of Wash Co, D C, Feb 29, 1868. In the case of Carlotte L Munck, admx of Christian H Munck, dec'd, the administratrix & Court have appointed Mar 28th next, for the final settlement of the personal estate of the said dec'd, of the assets in hand.
-Jas R O'Beirne, Reg/o wills

TUE MAR 3, 1868
Died: on Mar 1, Henry Baldwin, in his 65th year. His funeral will be on Mar 3 from the Church of the Epiphany. [No time given.]

Died: on Mar 1, Wm H Watson. His funeral will take place from his late residence, G & 19th sts, this morning at 11 A M.

Died: on Mar 2, Chas A Melcher, eldest son of Andrew D & Mary J Melcher, in his 34th year.

Died: on Mar 1, in Wash City, after a brief illness, Clara Story, aged 2 years, 7 months & 10 days, only child of Eliza L & Albert S Greene, U S navy.

The funeral of ex-Govn'r Thos H Ford took place yesterday, from his late residence, A st & Dela ave. The corpse was encased in a walnut coffin, covered with black cloth. The services were conducted by Rev Mr Ames, pastor of Wesley Chapel; pall-bearers were: Hons John Sherman & T C Theaker, C H Snow, C Wendell, J H Bradley, Judge Cartter, Gen Eckly, & J J Coombs. The cortege escorted the remains to the *Congressional Cemetery*, where they were placed in the receiving vault until arrangements can be made to take them to Ohio.

Col Danl E Sickles, of the 5th infty, has been ordered to report, without delay, to Maj Gen Hancock, & to take command of the 20th U S infty.

WED MAR 4, 1868
Edwin Booth became so much excited in playing "Macbeth" at Chicago, that he severely cut Nagle [Macduff] in the combat scene.

Chas Dickens entertained about 30 literary gentlemen of Boston & suburban cities at supper, at the Parker House, on Sat evening. The affair was a peculiarly elegant one, the room & table being decorated in the most expensive & lavish manner with flowers.

Private sale of a good & substantial Family Carriage, & also a Nice Buggy, with pole, in good order, together with a pair of sound, safe, & well-broken Horses. Apply to John Purdy, 5 4½ st, between C & La ave.

Chancery Sale: by deed of trust from John Douglas to Jas McClery, dated Oct 18, 1843, in the cause of the Nat'l Metropolitan Bank vs Henry Douglas et al; Equity No 875; auction on Apr 6, on the premises, at 15th & G sts, part of lot 5 in square 223, with valuable improvements. –Walter S Cox, trustee -Cooper & Latimer, aucts

Died: on Mar 3, in Wash City, in her 75th year, Miss Casandra Luvigne Cannon, of Alexandria, Va. Her funeral will be from the house of Mrs M M Bangs, 357 D st, near 9th, at 10½ o'clock, on Mar 5. Burial in Alexandria. [Alexandria papers please copy.]

Dept of the Interior, U S Patent Ofc, Wash, Feb 27, 1868. Ptn of John Brown, of N Y, N Y, praying for the extension of a patent granted to him May 30, 1854, for an improvement in Hot Water Apparatus, for seven years from the expiration of said patent, which takes place on May 30, 1868. -A M Stout, Acting Com'r of Patents

THU MAR 5, 1868
The loss by fire of Barnum's Museum is estimated at $400,000. The giraffe, valued at $20,000, will die from its burns. The museum was insured for $150,000. Two tigers were burned, valued at $25,000. The giantess loses $3,000. Twenty-two animals were saved, & twenty-eight burned. Mr Barnum announces his intention of selling off the Broadway property, & bldg a far more spacious museum farther up town. N Y Times says: Mr Barnum, rising at the Fifth-ave Hotel about 8 o'clock Tues, concluded to look at the morning papers, & there first learned of the event of the night. Coming to the scene about 10 o'clock, he gave directions for the relief & care of his human monstrosities, cowering almost naked in the rear part of Taylor's restaurant. He spoke confidently of the future.

Hon Portus Baxter, late a Rep in Congress from Vt, died in Wash City, this morning, of pneumonia. He was a member of the 37th, 38th, & 39th Congress, declining a re-election to the 40th Congress. His death was sudden & unexpected. His funeral service will take place on Sunday, from his late temporary residence, corner of G & 18th sts. [Mar 6th newspaper: The funeral of the late Hon Portus Baxter will take place on next Sunday afternoon, at 3 P M, from the corner of G & 18th sts. His remains will be temporarily deposited at **Oak Hill Cemetery**, Gtwn, until such time as it will be proper to convey them to their final resting place, in his own beloved Green Mountain State. A meeting of his friends will be held this evening at 8 o'clock, at 453 9th st, near the Herndon House, to make arrangements for attending his funeral. It is hoped that every Vermonter will be present.]

The 46th annual commencement of the National Medical College took place on Tues at the 13th st Baptist Church. The degree of M D was conferred upon the following graduates: M Bruckheimer, Baden, Germany; J P Richardson, N Y; Jas L Luddarth, Va; C C H Fenwick, Md; H F Krumme, Nebraska; E M Schaeffer, D C; Benedict Thompson, Md; & Wm L Rider, of Va. Rev Dr Samson presented the diplomas; music by the 12th infty band; valedictory was delivered by Wm L Rider, M D, of the graduating class.

Dept of the Interior, U S Patent Ofc, Wash, Feb 28, 1868. Ptn of Thos T Jarret, of Horsham, Pa, praying for the extension of a patent granted to him May 30, 1854, for an improvement in Hay Elevators, for seven years from the expiration of said patent, which takes place on May 30, 1868. -A M Stout, Acting Com'r of Patents

Justices of the Peace for this District. Messrs E J Klopfer, E L Corbin, & W G Brock were on Tues confirmed by the Senate as justices of the peace in & for the Dist of Col. The commisions of the following justices expired yesterday: J W Barnaclo; Jas Cull, police magistrate; Saml Douglas; Henry Lyles; Chas Walter, police magistrate; J Rutherford Worster; C P Wannall; C P Webster. Justices B W Ferguson's & G L Giberson's commission will expire on Mar 9. The nomination of Saml T Crown, formerly a police ofcr, has been sent to the Senate for confirmation.

Boston, Mass, Mar 4. Geo L Crumnut has been convicted for firing the high school house at Brighton, & sentenced to the State prison for life.

Supreme Court of D C, in Equity No 1,203; docket 8. P Fleury Herard, cmplnt, vs Harvey Lindsley, David Saunders, Saml Chase Barney, et al, dfndnts. On the motion of the cmplnt, by John D McMcPherson, his solicitor, it is ordered that the dfndnts, David Saunders & Saml Chas Barney, appear on or before the first rule day occurring 40 days after this day; otherwise the cause will be proceeded with as in case of default.
-A B Olin, justice -R J Meigs, clerk

FRI MAR 6, 1868
Danl Lord, an eminent lawyer, died in N Y yesterday.

Isaac Montose was found lying in a hovel on the outsirts of Wash City, literally dying by inches from exposure to the weather. He was taken to the station, but although everything was done for his accommodation, he died yesterday. He was but lately from Palmyra, Wayne Co, N Y, where it is said his friends reside. The ofcrs promptly telegraphed thither, & are now awaiting an answer.

Died: on Mar 4, at his residence, **Beall's Manor**, Montg Co, Md, Isaiah F Beall, in his 45th year of his age. His funeral is today, Friday, at 2 o'clock P M.

Supreme Court of D C, Mar 4, 1868. Equity 974, Docket 8. Oliver & Marcellus Donn vs Orlando H Donn et el. The trustee, John E Norris, reported sale made by him in the above entitled cause; to be confirmed & ratified. –A B Olin, Justice -R J Meigs, clerk [No other details.]

For sale or rent, a new house, containing 10 rooms, on the east bank of the Potomac; attached to it about 14 acres of land. Price, $10,000. Address J Fenwick Young, **Giesboro**, near Wash City, D C.

SAT MAR 7, 1868
The President yesterday nominated to the Senate Jas R Roche to be Register of Deeds for Wash Co, to fill a vacancy.

Boston, Mar 6. The third trial of Frank McArena, for the murder of Mary Greary, resulted in a disagreement of the jury, after 18 hours' deliberation.

The remains of Brvt Col Wm S Abert, Major 7th Regt U S cavalry, who died of yellow fever, at Galveston, in August last, were quietly buried in the ***Rock Creek Church Cemetery***, on Wed, by the side of his wife, who died of the same disease a few days before him, & near the body of his father, the late Col J J Abert. An escort of U S cavalry accompanied the remains to their final resting place. Members of his family, with his two little children, were present, & Rev Mr Buck, pastor of the church, read the committal portion of the burial service.

Died: on Mar 6, Frank Tenney, youngest son of W H & Eliza Tenney, aged 14 years. His funeral will be from the residence of his parents, 163 West st, Gtwn, on Mar 8, at 3 o'clock P M.

Boston, Mar 6. Ball Hughes, the sculptor, is dead. [No other information.]

Supreme Court of D C, Mar 6, 1868. Equity 1,179, Docket 8. N M Miller vs New Mexico Mining Co. A summons has been issued in this cause, & returned *non est* as to A Rencher. Said Rencher is to appear on or before the first rule day, occurring 40 days after this day; otherwise the cause will be proceeded with as in case of default.
-A B Olin, Justice -R J Meigs, clerk

Dept of the Interior, U S Patent Ofc, Wash, Feb 29, 1868. Ptn of Levi Dederick, of Albany, N Y, praying for the extension of a patent granted to him Jun 6, 1854, for an improvement in Hay Presses, for seven years from the expiration of said patent, which takes place on Jun 6, 1868. -A M Stout, Acting Com'r of Patents

N Y, Mar 6. Julia Dean Hayne, the actress, died suddenly this morning at the residence of her father-in-law. She was in the 37th year of her age.

MON MAR 9, 1868
The Phil Press says that "Grant & impeachment is now the battle cry." Has Gen Grant joined in it? Has he expressed any opinions on the subject of impeachment? If he has, we must have mislaid the paper containing it." -N Y Times, [Rad]

The improvements at the Arsenal grounds are being carried on; the walls of the penitentiary have been taken down, & the workmen are engaged in removing the yard wall. The offices are left standing; the west elevation, on Potomac, will be entirely renovated, surmounted with a modern French roof. A portico will surround it, with gardens, walks, & carriage drives, for the headquarters of Gen Ramsay. The cost will be about $25,000. The east wing will be handsomely fitted up as a residence of Maj Fred'k Whyte, the storekeeper & paymaaster of the Arsenal.

Mrd: on Mar 3, at the residence of Dr H Magruder, in Gtwn, D C, by Rev A M Randolph, of Balt, Mr S Arriss Buckner, of Loudoun Co, to Miss Helen P Fitzhugh, of Falmouth, Va. [Fredericksburg papers please copy.]

Circuit Court-Judge Wylie. In the case of McPherson vs Barrett & wife, the jury found affirmatively on the first two issues, viz: That Mary Ann Fearson, at the time of executing her will, was of sound & disposing mind & memory; & negatively on the two last issues, viz: That undue influence was exerted over the said Mary Ann Fearson to procure the execution of said will, & that she was not in a condition, property to make disposition of her estate. The will is therefore declared valid, & the probate stands.

Orphans Court-Mar 7, 1868. 1-The will of the late Edw Wharton, bequeathing his estate to his wife & daughter, was filed & proved, & Mrs Wharton also filed a request that her brother, Edw Shippen, of Pa, be appointed exec. Letters of administration *c t a* were issued to Mr Shippen; bond $20,000. 2-A record of the proceedings in the Circuit Court in the case of Barrett et al vs McPherson et al, involving the will of the late M A Fearson, was filed, showing that the will was sustained, & letters testamentary were issued to Mrs Barrett; bond $5,000. 3-Letters of administration on the estate of Marcus Long were issued to Jas W Plant; bond $300. 4-A copy of the proceedings of Oriental Lodge of Odd Fellows, instructing the Noble Grand of the Lodge, Jacob Miller, to apply for letters of administration on the estate of Jas B Morand, a member of the Lodge, was received. Also, a ptn of Morris Murphy, at whose house deceased died, making the same request. Also, one from clerks in the Pension Ofc asking that letters be issued to Chas M Tompkins. 5-A ptn was presented to the court by Mr Jas Ray, representing that during the lifetime of his wife, Bridget Ray, she placed a note paid to him in bank to her own credit, & asks the Court to take some action to enable him to receive this money. The judge decided that the wife, having been a married woman, & having no separate estate, the husband is entitled to the amount. 6-The last will of Mary Ann Fearson was filed in open court. 7-The first general account of Geo Brown, guardian of the orphans of Wm Brown, deceased, was filed & approved. 8-The third & final account of Susana Carrico, guardian to the heir of Jas Carrico, dec'd, was approved & filed. 9-*In re*. Estate of Thos Tucker. Attachment issued against Chas S English for contempt of court in not appearing according to citation. Partly excused by Court on paying costs of attachment. 10-The examination of witnesses in the Lowenthal will case was taken up, & the remainder of the session occupied in hearing the evidence.

Criminal Court-Chief Justice Cartter. 1-Geo Smith alias Geo Butt; larceny, guilty: sentenced to 60 days in jail. 2-Ellen Nolan: keeping a bawdy house: guilty. 3-Mary McCavrin, larceny of goods, the property of Cornelius Wendell: guilty: 18 months in the penitentiary. 4-John Nelson, larceny; plead guilty: sentenced to 1 week in jail. 5-Geo Keating; 2 indictments for larceny; nolle pros entered by Dist Atty in one; plead guilty to the other: sentencd to one week in jail. 6-Sandy Parker; larceny; not guilty.

Orphans Court of Wash Co, D C, Mar 7, 1868. In the case of Mariah C Emrich, admx of Peter Emrich, dec'd, the administratrix & Court have appointed Apr 4 next, for the final settlement of the personal estate of the said dec'd, of the assets in hand.
-Jas R O'Beirne, Reg/o wills

Louisville, Mar 8. Horrible murder here yesterday. Wm Kriel, a butcher, seized his wife by the throat, thew her violently on the floor, & drawing a six-barreled revolver, fired. The ball entered just below the ear, causing instant death. Kriel then place the pistol to his head & fired, but the ball glanced, inflicting a trifle wound. At this moment a sister of Mrs Kriel entered the apartment, whereupon Kriel again fired the pistol at his head & ran, but was captured after a short chase. Mrs Kriel, having received inhuman treatment from her husband, had gone to live temporarily with her mother. Kriel met her there yesterday, & becoming enraged at her conduct killed her.

Trustee's sale of property on Capitol Hill, known as Casparis' Hotel; by deed of trust executed on Aug 22, 1866, by Jas Casparis, recorded in Liber R M H, No 21, folio 201, of the land records of Wash Co, D C: public auction, on the premises, on Apr 2 next; the described lots of ground in square 688, to wit; the whole of lot 15, the western half of lot 16, & the whole of lot 6. The former two lots are improved by a large Hotel Bldg, on A st south, & fronting the Capitol grounds. Title perfect. –Fred P Stanton, trustee
-Cooper & Latimer, aucts

Orphans Court of Wash Co, D C, Mar 7, 1868. In the case of Louisa Libbey, adm of Jos Libbey, dec'd, the administratrix & Court have appointed Apr 4 next, for the final settlement of the personal estate of the said dec'd, of the assets in hand.
-Jas R O'Beirne, Reg/o wills

Orphans Court of Wash Co, D C, Mar 7, 1868. In the case of Chas A James, exc of Matilda S Holmead, dec'd, the executor & Court have appointeed Apr 4 next, for the final settlement of the personal estate of the said dec'd, of the assets in hand.
-Jas R O'Beirne, Reg/o wills

Dept of the Interior, U S Patent Ofc, Wash, Mar 2, 1868. Ptn of Edw Harrison, of New Haven, Conn, praying for the extension of a patent granted to him Jun 6, 1854, & reissued Nov 16, 1858, for an improvement in Grinding Mills, for seven years from the expiration of said patent, which takes place on Jun 6, 1868. -A M Stout, Acting Com'r of Patents

Dept of the Interior, U S Patent Ofc, Wash, Mar 2, 1868. Ptn of Caleb Swan, exc of the estate of Danl Hayward, dec'd, of Easton, Mass, praying for the extension of a patent granted to said Danl Hayward Aug 29, 1854, for an improvement in the Manufacture of India Rubber, for seven years from the expiration of said patent, which takes place on Aug 29, 1868. -A M Stout, Acting Com'r of Patents

Dept of the Interior, U S Patent Ofc, Wash, Mar 3, 1868. Ptn of Jacob Senneff, of Phil, Pa, praying for the extension of a patent granted to him Aug 22, 1854, for an improvement in Machines for Casting Metallic Eyes or Mails of Heddles for Looms, for seven years from the expiration of said patent, which takes place on Aug 22, 1868.
-A M Stout, Acting Com'r of Patents

Orphans Court of Wash Co, D C. Letters testamentary on the personal estate of Mary Ann Fearson, late of Wash Co, D C, dec'd. –M Julia Barrett, excx

Dept of the Interior, U S Patent Ofc, Wash, Mar 3, 1868. Ptn of Jacob Senneff, of Phil, Pa, praying for the extension of a patent granted to him Jul 18, 1854, for an improvement in Weavers' Heddles, for seven years from the expiration of said patent, which takes place on Jul 18, 1868. -A M Stout, Acting Com'r of Patents

TUE MAR 10, 1868
Queen Victoria is an indefatigable knitter.

Died: on Mar 9, of consumption, Eliz H Craven, only surviving daughter of the late Isaac Craven. Her funeral will be from the residence of her mother, 416 __ st, on Wed, at 3 P M.

Julia Dean Cooper, well known actress, died yesterday, at her residence in this city, in her 37th year; she was born in the town of Pleasant Valley, Duchess Co, in this State, Jul 30, 1830, where she lived until she was 12. Her father, Jas Dean, was an actor, & her mother was the well-known Western actress, Mrs Drake, who, at the time of her marriage with Mr Dean, was the widow of Fosdick. In 1842 Mr Dean took Julia to Cincinnati, where he had settled permanently, having abandoned his professional career. Miss Dean attended school at the Mount Auburn seminary. She made her debut in Cincinnati at Shier's theatre, Jul 21, 1845; in 1856 she married Dr Hayne, of Charleston, S C, a son of Senator Hayne, who was so effectively beaten in the celebrated debate with Danl Webster. On the death of Dr Hayne she reappeared on the stage, & performed for the most part in Calif. About 2 years ago she married Mr Jas G Cooper, of this city. Her death was not unexpected. She leaves her husband & 6 children to mourn her loss. -N Y Herald, 8th [Mar 11th newspaper: It is stated that Julia Dean died in childbirth. She left very little property, her first husband having squandered the fortune she possessed when married.]

Robt Ball Hughes, the sculptor, died at his residence in Dorchester on Thu; had been ill several months of a most painful disease. He was born in London, Jan 19, 1806, & came to this counrty in 1820; resided for a time in N Y; removed to Boston. The statue of Bowditch in Mt Auburn; Uncle Toby, & the Widow Wadman in the Athenaeum; & Oliver Twist, now in the possession of the Duke of Devonshire, at Chatsworth, are among some of his fine works. The Dead Christ in the Catholic Church at south Boston, which was burnt a few years since; Fisher Boy, & other works, have also been much admired. Mr Hughes leaves a family who inherit some of his talents. -Boston Post

Wanted: a Farm hand & wife. Good references required. Apply at Delwig & Bailey's, 8th & E st, near the Navy Yard. –L Bailey

U S Marshal's Ofc: sale of the west half of lot 51, in square 183, in Wash, D C, with improvements thereon, seized & levied upon as the property of Nathl B Myers, & will be sold to satisfy execution No 4,350, in favor of Michl Gore. –D S Gooding, Marshal, D C

Supreme Court of D C, No 974. Oliver & Marcellus Donn vs Orlando H Donn & others. All parties interested in trustee's account, appear on Mar 14, 10 A M. —Walter S Cox, auditor

Dept of the Interior, U S Patent Ofc, Wash, Mar 4, 1868. Ptn of Chas F Martine, of Boston, Mass, praying for the extension of a patent granted to him Jun 6, 1854, & reissued Dec 25, 1855, & again reissued Aug 27, 1867, for an improvement in Sofa Bedsteads, for seven years from the expiration of said patent, which takes place on Jun 6, 1868. -A M Stout, Acting Com'r of Patents

WED MAR 11, 1868
On Apr 6 the monument created to Benj C Grenup, in *Glenwood Cemetery*, will be dedicated. Mr Grenup was killed some years ago by being run over by the suction of the Columbia company, as he, with others, were on the way to a fire. The dedicatory services will be in charge of the Columbia Association, which has held its organization intact ever since the disbandment of the old volunteer dept.

Manchester, N H, Mar 10. The dwlg of Dennis McCarthy was burned last night, & Miss Hannah Sullivan, aged 20 years, perished in the flames.

Chancery sale of real estate, by decree of the Supreme Court of D C, passed Dec 6, 1867, in Chancery No 1,092, of which Eliza A Weber is cmplnt & Mary A Weber et al, are dfndnts: public auction, on the premises, on Apr 2, of lot 17 in square 162, on 18th st, with brick house & bakery thereon. —M Thompson, trustee -Green & Williams, aucts

Orphans Court of Wash Co, D C. Letters of administration on the personal estate of Heman L Chapin, late of Wash City, D C, dec'd. —Catharine V Chapin, admx

THU MAR 12, 1868
The Senate yesterday confirmed the nomination of J Ross Browne to be Envoy Extraordinary & Minister Plenipotentiary to China; & Chas K Tuckerman to be Minister Resident at Greece.

Mark Twain sailed for Calif yesterday.

Died: on Mar 10, Robt R Alymer, in his 47th year. His funeral is on Mar 13 at 9:30 A M, from his late residence, 399 13th st. [Petersburg papers please copy.]

Died: on Mar 9, of pneumonia, Mrs Julia A Hilton, wife of Mr Jos H Hilton, in her 64th year. Her exertions for the well-being of her sorrowing husband, children, & grandchildren, & other near relatives were constant & untiring. She is now at rest.

For sale: new furniture of residence at 471 L st. Apply to Wm Coppinger, 469 L st.

For sale: the farm lately owned & occupied by Benj Bohrer, dec'd, is offered for private sale by the heirs. This farm is 2½ miles from Laytonsville, Montg Co, Md, contains 192½ acres, & adjoins the lands of Col Lyde Griffith, Wm G Darby's heirs, & others. Improvements consist of a good 2 story dwlg house, with back bldg, new stabling & all necessary out-bldgs, in good order. Apply to Wm A Darby, residing near the premises, or to John S Bohrer, Bloomfield, Loudoun Co, Va.

Trustee's sale of valuable property on N st, between 4th & 5th sts; by decree of the Supreme Court of D C, in the case of Utermehle vs Minor et al, No 1,106 Equity, docket 8, substitutes Fred'k Schmidt as trustee in place of Chas H Utermehle, made Aug 30, 1864, recorded in the land records of Wash Co, D C, Liber N C T No 52, folios 471 thru 173; sale on Mar 23 next, of lot 25 in square 513, with all improvements.
-Fred'k Schmidt, trustee -Green & Williams, aucts

On Sat, near Anderson, Indiana, the murderer Geo Stotler, went to the house of an old man, Mr Eisnagle, & requested the loan of a horse, & he was refused. Stotler became enraged, & Mr Eisnagle's sons, 16 & 19, undertook to eject him from the house, when a scuffle ensued, during which Stotler stabbed & killed both boys. Stotler was arrested yesterday, & is now in jail, at Anderson. Stotler is said to be a desperate character.

Died in this city, on Mar 11, Col Timothy P Andrews, of the U S army, aged 74 years. When quite a youth, unbeknown to his father, he repaired to the Patuxent river, where Cmdor Barney's flotilla was flagship, & tendered his services to the Cmdor in any situation in which he could be useful. The Cmdor employed him as an aid. He was appointed a paymaster in the army in 1822, til 1847; resigned to take command of the regt of voltigeurs, raised for the Mexican war; distinguished in the battle of El Molino, was brevetted a brig general for gallant & meritorious conduct in the battle of Chapultepec; on the close of the war he was reinstated as paymaster, & in 1851 was promoted to the position of Deputy Paymaster Gen. He succeeded the late Paymaster Gen Larned. His funeral will take place from his late residence, 447 14th & G sts, on Friday next, at 12 o'clock M.

FRI MAR 13, 1868
Henry Stanbery resigns the ofc of Atty General of the U S, to take effect Mar 12, 1868. During the Cabinet meeting the Pres appointed Mr Browning, Sec of the Interior, to be Acting Atty General.

A young lady, Adrienne Anderson, died in Chicago on Monday, from the effects of chloroform, while suffering the amputation of an arm.

Wm Henry Augustus Bissell, D D, Rector of Trinity Church, Geneva, N Y, was elected Bishop of Vt by the Episcopal Convention in Burlington, on Wed.

Green & Williams, aucts, sold a 2 story frame house & lot on 4th st west, between L st & N Y ave, to Mr Andrew J Riley, for $1,500.

The Senate yesterday confirmed the following nominations:
Lewis Wolfley, assessor of internal revenue for 1st Dist of La, vice Jas Ready, removed.
Henry Montague, postmaster at Whitewater, Wisc.
Robt M Lindsey, postmaster at Boise City, Idaho.
Chas Van Winkle, marshal for the dist of Va.
Thos Hood, atty for Wisc.
Geo T Martin, postmaster at Santa Fe, New Mexico.
T W Scott, of Tenn, consul at Matamoras.
Wm C Burt, postmaster at Murfreesboro, Tenn.
Saml K Allen, of N Y, & Saml Mercer, of Pa, to be 2nd lts in the Marine Corps.
Lt Col M R Kintzing to be colonel, Maj Thos G Field to be lt col, Capt David M Cohen to be major, 1st Lt Henry A Bartlett to be captain, & 2nd Lt Albert B Young to be 1st lt in the Marine Corps.

Died: on Mar 12, of typhoid fever, Sarah Ellen, beloved wife of Robt W Goggin, aged 36 years. Her funeral will take place from the residence of her husband, 635 M st, this evening, at 3 o'clock.

Died: on Mar 12, in Wash City, Mrs Sarah Shields, aged 68 years. Her funeral will take place Sat at 3 o'clock P M, from the residence of her son-in-law, Geo McCauley, 437 5th st, between D & E sts.

Died: on Mar 12, Annie Phoebe, wife of W Chace, & daughter of the late Capt Carothers, of Pittsburg, Pa, in her 28th year. Her funeral will take place from 504 11th st this afternoon, at 3 P M.

Died: on Mar 11, at Lowell, Mass, Saml Luther Dana, M D, LL D, aged 72 years.

Died: on Mar 10, at Lancaster, Ohio, of heart disease, Mary Duncan, aged 26 years, wife of John A Hunter, & daughter of the late Hon Danl Duncan, of Ohio.

Nineteenth Commencement exercises of the Medical Dept of the Gtwn College took place on Wed at Wall's Opera House; Prof Noble Young, M D, president of the faculty; & Rev B A Maguire, were introduced. Prof Johnson Eliot, M D, dean of the faculty, announced the names of the graduating class, as follows:

J Lee Adams, D C
J F R Appleby, D C
Andrew Rothwell Brown, D C
C V N Callan, D C
Jespyr Edwin Cheney, Ill
Abner H Cull, D C
Ira J Culver, Pa
John G Davis, Ky
Julian W Dean, D C
J Henry Demeritt, N H
Wm S Dixon, D C
Robt H Edwards, Ohio
Stuat Eldridge, Wisc
Geo A Fitch, West Va
J Lee Adams, D C
Danl S Foster, Pa
Geo N French, N H
Wm G Green, N Y
Joel C Green, Kansas
Jas J F Houston, Pa

Dallas Johnson, D C	Chas E Prentiss, D C
Benj C Jones, Pa	Wm D Putnam, Ohio
S B LeCompte, N Y	Henry W Sawtelle, Maine
Jas B Littlewood, Ill	Geo A Skinner, Ind
John O Marble, Maine	Solomon S Stearns, Maine
John Edwin Mason, N H	John J Stephens, N Y
Jas C McConnell, Ohio	Geo H Stone, N Y
Hugh Henry McIntyre, Vt	John Thatcher, N Y
Chas P Nalley, D C	John Walter, D C
Lewis E Newton, D C	Saml R Ward, Vt
Alex'r Osburn, Va	Chas Warren, Ill
Henry C Pierson, N J	Geo M Wellman, Mass
John Waterman Porter, Ill	Walter H Wells, Md

Reception cmte did much to the enjoyment of the occasion; their names are: Messrs Jas M Duncan, Wm Ward, Wm H Ross, Albert D Kingsbury, Ralph Bell, H C Porter, T S Beale, W W Miller, J T Winter, A W Abbott, M C Wallace, & J T Diggs.

Board of Police-meeting last evening. Application of Danl J Byrne for a license to sell liquor was rejected. Henry J Fox & Jonathan M Clarkson were appointed privates on the force. Chas Fink was appointed an additional private for 90 days to do duty at Campbell's Barracks. Pvt John Ogden, for intoxication, was dismissed the force. Pvt D W Jarboe, for violation of orders, was fined $2. Pvts W L Lloyd & Wm T Kelly, for neglect of duty, were fined $5. Pvt Benj Ross, charged with conduct unbecoming an ofcr, was fined $10, & ordered to be reprimanded. The resignation of Surgeon John B Keasbey was received, & Dr Patrick Croghan was appointed surgeon of the force, to fill the vacancy. Pvt Chas Wesley Thompson was appointed to a position on the detective force to fill the vacancy by the death of the late Detective Wm M Kelly.

Phil, Mar 12. During the progress of a fire here this morning, a wall fell, killing Edw Hanks, & seriously wounding Geo Harman, both members of Spring Garden Co. Other firemen were injured.

N Y, Mar 12. Rev Wm Wall's Female Institute at Englewood, N Y, was burned today. Loss, $20,000.

Phil, Mar 12. Geo W Childs, proprietor of the Phil Lidger, has purchased a lot at the corner of 5th & Chestnut sts, 28 x 110 feet, for $72,000. This is the highest price ever paid in this city for a lot of similar size.

Gen Hooker & wife are in Rome.

Lord Broughan has lost the use of his limbs & tongue.

Mr S B Hayman, an American Express messenger on the Hamilton & Dayton train, due at Concord on Wed, was knocked senseless, by some persons unknown, who entered the car with false keys after the train left Lockland, & took the package containing $20,000. He was very seriously injured. The money belonged to parties in Indiana & Illinois.

SAT MAR 14, 1868
The name of the town of <u>South Danvers</u>, Mass, is to be changed to Peabody.

Mrs Kate Warn, a celebrated female detective, & head of the female dept of Mr Pinkerton's agency for 13 years, has died lately. Many stories of her skill are told by the Chicago papers.

Probably suicide. Yesterday Mr John W Wells, residing at 384 5th st, attempted suicide by shooting himself in the head. Dr Eliot pronouced the wound fatal. Mr Wells was still alive last evening. He was for years a clerk in the Interior Dept; his health became much impaired about a year ago; he received the appointment of Indian agent for Montana Territory, & only several weeks since returned from that Territory, greatly improved in health. He was to have left for Montana on Apr 1. He is in his 50th year of his age, & leaves a wife, 2 sons, & 3 daughters. No cause can be assigned for the attempt at self destruction. Mr Wells was highly esteemed. [Mar 16th newspaper: Mr John W Wells died from the effects of the wound on Sat noon at his residence. The funeral will take place this afternoon at 2 o'clock. <u>Same paper</u>-Died: on Mar 14, suddenly, John W Wells, in his 50th year. His funeral is this day, at 2 P M.] [Mar 17th newspaper: The funeral of Mr J W Wells took place yesterday; services conducted by Rev Dr J C Smith, of the Fourth Presbyterian Church, assisted by Rev Mr Johnson, of the Assembly's Church. Pall bearers: Dr Gooden, John Ball, Wm Lord, Col Tekner, of the Treas Dept, Geo Stoddard, formerly of the Indian Bureau, & Wm Redstrake.]

The funeral of the late Col Andrews, ex-Paymaster Gen, U S A, was attended yesterday by a large number of army ofcrs & many of our respectable citizens. The funeral cortege left the late residence of the dec'd at 12 M for ***Rock Creek Church Cemetery***, where his remains were interred by those of his wife, who died 2 years before him. Among the pall-bearers were Mr Corcoran, Dr Blake, Dr King, of the army; paymaster Gen Brice & Dr Fred May.

Orphans Court of Wash Co, D C. Letters of administration w a, on the personal estate of Edw Wharten, late of Wash Co, D C, dec'd. –Edw Shippen, adm w a

MON MAR 16, 1868
Mr John J Bogue sold the 2 story frame house on north side of First st, between Fayette & Fred'k sts, Gtwn, to Miss Gibbons, of Wash, for $1,150 cash. Also, the 2 story frame house, No 18, on the north side of Prospect st, belonging to Robt Hunter, to Mrs Joyce, of Wash, for $2,000 cash.

Gen Geo W Lew, general Treasurer of Rhode Island, is a defaulter to the amount of $4,000. He has resigned, & Saml A Parker has been placed in charge temporarily.

The funeral of the late Rev W J Eliot, post chaplain at *Fort Washington*, took place on Sat, from the residence of Mrs Upperman, 488½ 12th st, near F st. Rev Mr Butler, of the Lutheran Church, officiated. The remains were interred in the *Congressional Cemetery*. The dec'd was in his 43rd year; was a native of Tenn; was attached to a Minnesota regt during the war; & leaves many friends & acquaintances in Wash City, among the warmest was Pres Johnson & his family. He was a widower & leaves 3 children.

Orphans Court-Judge Purcell, Mar 14, 1868. 1-The last will & testament of the late Timothy P Andrews, late Paymaster Gen of the U S army was filed for probate. To his son, Albert S Andrews, was bequeathed $10,000, when he arrived at age; to his granddaughter, Emily J Marshall, a tract of land in La, containing some fourteen or sixteen hundred acres; to his daughter Caroline & son Albert, to be equally divided between them, all his silver ware, assets of property beyond or more than sufficient for payments of debts, said surplus to be shared among his children & grandchildren. He appointed Saml Early his sole executor. He further bequeathed to his daughter, Caroline, the sum of $3,000, in addition to any gifts, conveyances, or trusts. 2-The last will & testament of Mary Helen Fenwick was filed & fully proven. The testator names her 2 daughters, Mary Ann & Juliana Fenwick, executrices. 3-N H Miller gave bond in the sum of $600 as adm of J A Montrose; Jas Maguire & Geo Capron, sureties. 4-Second & final account of Robt W Fenwick, guardian, filed & passed. 5-John C Dyer in account with E C Dyer, adm of M E Dyer, by S B Boarman, & F J Fisher, excs, filed & passed. An account of the personal estate of the same party was filed & passed. 6-Chas P Culver gave bond in the sum of $5,000 as guardian of the orphans of L E Culver, dec'd; Alex'r H Stephens & F B Culver, sureties. 7-John Hitz gave bond in the sum of $400 as adm of Jacob Markwalder; W G Metzerott & W F Mattingly, sureties. 8-Henry Baldwin gave bond in the sum of $800 as adm of Henry Baldwin, sr; A H Young & Wm Manadier, sureties. 9-Harriet C Bradford gave bond in the sum of $1,000 as guardian to the orphan child of Brazilla Betts, dec'd; C A Bradford, W S Johnson, & W G Parks, sureties. 10-The will of Sarah L Henry filed & partially proven. The testator appoints her son, Richd Henry, her executor.

Equity Court-Justice Olin. 1-Bayley against Bayley: order appointing N Carusi guardian. 2-McDonald against Pratton: order of final ratification of trustee's sale & reference to another. 3-Foot et al against Phillips: order ratifying sale & for distribution. 4-Davidson against Wash & Gtwn railroad Co: argument closed & case submitted.

Chancery sale of very valuable improved real estate at the corner of N Y ave & 10th st west; by decree of the Supreme Court of D C, Equity No 1,050, wherein Yates & Selby are cmplnts, & Geo Seltz et al, are dfndnts: public auction on Apr 6 next, all the estate, right, title, & interest of Geo Seitz of & into part of lot 1 in square 343, in Wash City. -Saml L Phillips, trustee -W L Wall & Co, aucts

Died: on Mar 15, Mrs Frances A Farwell, wife of ex-Govn'r L J Farwell, of Wisc, & daughter of Gen A N Corss/Corse, aged 37 years. Her funeral will take place at 486 E st, between 5th & 6th sts, on Tuesday at 11 o'clock A M.

Dept of the Interior, U S Patent Ofc, Wash, Mar 6, 1868. Ptn of Finley Latta, adm of the estate of A B Latta, dec'd, of Cincinnati, Ohio, praying for the extension of a patent granted to him Jun 6, 1854, for an improvement in Steam Generators, for seven years from the expiration of said patent, which takes place on Jun 6, 1868.
-A M Stout, Acting Com'r of Patents

Orphans Court of Wash Co, D C. Letters of administration on the personal estate of Jacob Markwalder, late of Wash City, D C, dec'd. –John Hitz, adm

Orphans Court of Wash Co, D C. Letters of administration on the personal estate of Henry Baldwin, sr, late of Wash Co, D C, dec'd. –Henry Baldwin, jr, adm, 456½ 9th st

Orphans Court of Wash Co, D C, Mar 14, 1868. In the case of Marian E C King, admx of Henry King, dec'd, the administratrix & Court have appointed Apr 11 next, for the final settlement of the personal estate of the said dec'd, of the assets in hand.
-Jas R O'Beirne, Reg/o wills

Gen Grant's income is said to be $30,000 per annum.

Ex-Govn'r Henry S Foote was received into the communion of the Methodist Church, in Nashville, on Sunday last.

The new St James Hotel, in Boston, is 6 stories high, extending 190 feet on Newton st, & 215 feet on James st. The hotel is leased to Jas P M Stetson, late of Astor House, N Y.

TUE MAR 17, 1868
The Impeachment Cmte yesterday, for the second time, subjected to a 3 hours' examination Col Wm G Moore, private secretary of the President. It appears to be the design of the impeachers to "pump" thoroughly all those whom they suspect may be called as witnesses for the defence in the impeachment trial, with a view to prepare themselves for what these witnesses may have to say, so as to expedite the progress of the trial, & hasten the attainment of the goal, upon reaching which they have staked all their hopes.

The ***East Capitol barracks***, covering the square between 2nd & 3rd sts east, & East Capitol st & A st south, have been demolished & the lumber removed. These barracks were erected during the early part of the war for the accommodation of the troops poured into the city at that time, & who were frequently obliged to remain here for several days before arrangements could be made for sending them to the front.

Rev Wm Hamilton on Sabbath preached his farewell address of the ministry to the congregation of the McKendree Chapel. He reviewed the 50 long years he has spent in the ministry.

Died: on Mar 16, Wm M Ellis, in his 62nd year. His funeral will take place from the First Presbyterian Church on Thu, Mar 19, at 2½ o'clock. [Phil Ledger please copy.]

+

Death of well known citizens. Mr W M Ellis & Mr Wm Slade. Mr Ellis was born in Phil, & came to Wash City with his parents when an infant, & has resided here all his life, except about 4 years. For many years he was in the Navy Yard here, in full charge of the machine dept. He was one of the best scientific mechanics in the country; served years ago in the City Councils for several terms; a prominent member of the Masonic fraternity, & was elevated to grand master of the Dist. For 40 years he was a devoted member of the 4½ st Presbyterian Church, from which he will be buried Thu, 2:30 P M.

+

Mr Wm Slade, steward at the Executive Mansion, died at his residence, on Mass ave, yesterday, after an illness of some weeks. The dec'd was a colored man, & for many years was the porter of the old Indian Queen Hotel, [now the Metropolitan,] when it was in charge of the late Jesse Brown. He was appointed to a position in the Treasury Dept,& has held positions, confidential & responsible, including that he filled at his death. He was one of the founders of the Colored Presbyterian Church, on 15th st, & was prominent in every effort to advance the interests of his race. Pres Lincoln appointed him a messenger at the White House, & Pres Johnson promoted him to the post of steward. He was about 50 years of age, & leaves a wife & several children.

Dept of the Interior, U S Patent Ofc, Wash, Mar 9, 1868. Ptn of Thos Allender, exc of the estate of John Allender, dec'd, of West Hampton, Mass, praying for the extension of a patent granted to said John Allender Jun 20, 1854, for an improvement in Metalic Grommets, for seven years from the expiration of said patent, which takes place on Jun 20, 1868. -A M Stout, Acting Com'r of Patents

Dept of the Interior, U S Patent Ofc, Wash, Mar 9, 1868. Ptn of Chas Parker, of Meriden, Conn, praying for the extension of a patent granted to him Jun 20, 1854, for an improvement in Cast-Iron Vices, for seven years from the expiration of said patent, which takes place on Jun 20, 1868. -A M Stout, Acting Com'r of Patents

Hon Robt C Winthrop is in Rome.

Lord Lytton has entirely recovered his hearing which has been very bad, under the treatment of a surgeon in Paris.

Mr & Mrs Howard Paul are enjoying extraordinary popularity in Scotland. They acted & sung one night to an audience of more than 3,000 persons.

The estate of Elias Howe, jr, of Bridgeport, the great sewing machine inventor, is represented insolvent. He was reported to be worth over $1,000,000.

Marshal's sale on Mar 26, all David R Smith's right, title, claim, & interest in & to the improvements on the 17 feet front by 30 feet deep of lot 25 in square 490, on 4½ st, having a lease to run about 2 years & 6 months, in Wash City, seized & levied upon as the property of David R Smith, garnishee of John W Walker, & will be sold to satisfy Execution No 4,253, in favor of Jas B Simpson. –D S Gooding, U S Marshal D C

Marshal's sale on Mar 21, of one sorrel horse, seized & levied upon as the goods & chattels of Washington Hurdle & will be sold to satisfy Execution No 4,1059, in favor of Nathl B Mosely vs Henry M Hurdle & W R Hurdle. –D S Gooding, U S Marshal D C

I will sell **Rock Hall**, the farm on which I reside, containing 740 acres of strong limestone land with 1/5th in timber; situated 5 miles s w of Charlestown; the Bull Skin Run stream passes through the middle of the farm. I will also sell my **Millville Flour Mills**, with 91 acres of land; lie 4 miles n e of Charlestown. The dwlg house is large, with 9 rooms. Address the undersigned at **Summit Point**, Jefferson Co, West Va. –Thos H Willis

Dept of the Interior, U S Patent Ofc, Wash, Mar 11, 1868. Ptn of Fred'k H Bartholomew, of N Y, N Y, praying for the extension of a patent granted to him Jun 20, 1854, & reissued Nov 13, 1860, numbered 1,071 & 1,072, for an improvement in Method Governing the Action of Valve Cocks, for seven years from the expiration of said patent, which takes place on Jun 20, 1868. -A M Stout, Acting Com'r of Patents

WED MAR 18, 1868
Orphans Court. 1-Last will of Wm L Hodge was filed & partially proven & admitted to probate as to personalty. The testator names Sarah B Hodge & J Ledyard Hodge, excs. 2-Geo J Seufferle gave bond in the sum of $300 as guardian to the orphan Thos C Davis. B L Jackson & John H Semmes sureties. 3-First individual account of Julia Ann Forest, guardian to John W & Ellen R Forrest; the first account of Julia Ann Forrest, admx of John Forrest; & the third account of John Marbury, exc of Ellen Carter were filed & passed. 4-Anna E McCleary gave bond in the sum of $10,000 as admx of personal estate of Morven J McCleary, dec'd. John Keyworth & Lewis J Davis sureties. 5-Ellen Eddie gave bond in the sum of $10,000 as admx of the personal estate of E C Eddie, dec'd.

Criminal Court-Chief Justice Cartter. Rachel Webster, indicted for the larceny of clothing, valued at $10, property of Eliza Boyd: guilty. Sentence: fined $5; not paid; ordered into commitment. 2-Timonty J Hurley, indicted for removing spirits from distillery to a place other than a bonded warehouse, on Dec 20 last: verdict guilty; capias to hear judgment. There were 5 other indictments against the same party for a violation of section 31of act of Jul 13, 1866, on all of which he was guilty. 3-Catherine Nickens, petit larceny: not guilty. 4-Isaac Mills, indicted for the larceny of $40 from Lewis C Kengla, on Mar 7 last, in the Northern Liberty Market. Verdict guilty; sentenced to Albany penitentiary for 18 months. 5-Geo Hays, assault & battery. Verdict guilty;

recognizance forfeited. 6-Jefferson Simms, indicted for an assault & battery on John Chrisman; verdict not guilty. 7-John Chrisman, indicted for an assault & battery on Jefferson Simms; verdict guilty as indicted, with a recommendation to the mercy of the Court.

The President yesterday sent to the Senate the following nominations, vz::
L M Newton, collector of customs, Genesee, N Y.
Henry H Green, assessor of internal revenue, Territory of New Mexico.
John Hancock, collector of internal revenue, First Dist of La.
Julius Newberg, collector of internal revenue, Territory of Idaho.
W W Willis, collector of internal revenue, Second Dist of Miss.
Mahlon Wilkinson, Indian agent, Upper Missouri.
Franklin Hanen, jr, assist treasurer at Boston, Mass.

Yesterday Mr Jas L Barbour was the purchaser *Lichau House*, for the sum of $9.000. It is located on Louisiana ave, near 6th st, & the sum it was sold for is considered very reasonable.

Mrd: on Mar 3, at the residence of the bride's uncle, Richd Lott, of ___dgeton, N J, by Rev P D Gurley, D D, of Wash, D C, Isaac Hackett, of the latter city, to Abigail R Clawson, of Woodstown, N J. No cards.

Monday night a valuable sword, worth $10,000 to $15,000, on exhibition at the museum in the Patent Ofc, was stolen from the case containing most of the relics of Gen Washington. The stolen sword was presented by the Viceroy of Egypt to Cmder Biddle, of the U S navy, many years since, & was studded with diamonds. The scabbard, of gold, was stolen several years ago, along with a gold snuff box & other jewels, a portion of which were recovered. –Star [Mar 23 newspaper: The sword was found in Manhattanville, N Y, on Sat; the thief was a young man known as Mr Lewis, & by others at Capt W N Murphy. About 3 weeks ago he received an appointment in the Patent Ofc, & has been employed as one of the door-keepers of the museum room. He is about 5 feet 7 inches in height, hav several scars, from gunshot wounds, upon his face. He will be brought to Wash City at once.]

Clerks promoted in the Treasury Dept, since Mar 1. Register's Bureau: Ros A Fish, I H Beatty, J T W Durand, F A Carr, Wm Guilford, J Fox, & G W Bradford, all to 4th class clerks. Sec's Ofc: C A Wilson & J C R Clarke, to 2nd class. 3-First Auditor's Ofc: C A Taylor to their class, & W P Marsh to 2nd class.

Trustee's sale of 3 story brick dwlg with side lot adjoining, on I st, near 19th st; by decree passed by the Supreme Court of D C, in Chancery No 514, wherein Anna L Derrick is cmplnt & Anna P Derrick et al are dfndnts; public auction, on Apr 13, 1868, on the premises, lot 9 in square 106, in Wash City. –Ann P Derrick, trustee -Fitch & Fox, aucts

Orphans Court of Wash Co, D C. Letters of administration on the personal estate of Edw Crittenden Eddie, late of Wash City, D C, dec'd. –Ellen Eddie, admx

Changes in the Fire Dept: C McDermott appointed extra-man, vice Wm S Scott, resigned; Wm S Scott, appointed supernumerary, vice C McDermott, permoted; Wm Brooks, appointed supernumerary, vice C C Langley, resigned. Jas Hess was appointed supernumerary, vice John Entwisle, dropped.

Spring Fashions. –Sarah A Chevalier, M D, 1123 Broadway, N Y. [Ad]

Edwin Booth is said to earn $90,000 a year.

Capt Travis, the famous shot, has opened a pistol gallery at Youngstown, Ohio.

Madame Lind Goldschmidt has been passing the winter at Cannes, France. The climate of England does not agree with her.

THU MAR 19, 1868

The fact that the Senate generously concluded to grant President Johnson a whole week, & one working day over, to prepare for his defence in the most important trial which has ever taken place in America, is rather distasteful to some gentlemen of the advanced Radical persuasion. –Cincinnati Commercial, [Rep]

The President sent to the Senate yesterday the following nominations: J B Hubble, collector of internal revenue for Montana Territory; A Huggon, U S Atty for the dist of Idaho; Saml E Douglass, justice of the peace for the Dist of Columbia.

The funeral of the late Wm Slade took place at his late residence, on Mass ave, yesterday; among those in attendance was Pres Johnson, Mayor Wallach, Marshall Brown, Dr J F May, Dr Palmer, Dr John B Blake, Mrs Patterson, & Mrs Stover, the daughters of the Pres. The religious services were conducted by Rev Byron Sunderland, assisted by Rev J C Smith, D D, Dr Tustin, Rev Mr White; & also Rev Danl Muse & Le Grimes, [colored.] The pall-bearers were Messrs C Denhane & W G Finney, [white,] W Lewis, E Cruse, & J Thos Jefferson, [colored.] The remains were moved to the *Harmonial Cemetery*, adjoining *Glenwood*. [The post mortem examination revealed that his heart had swelled to 3 times its natural size, weighing 38 ounces, & it had burst into 3 parts.]

Chicago, Mar 17. During the storm last evening a frame dwlg, Miller & Dayton sts, occupied by Adam Walter, was blown down. Walter was seriously injured, & his wife was instantly killed.

T M Harvey, the oyster man, is making a complete "shell road" of 11th st, from the avenue to C st. This street improvement is a good one, &, barring the effluvia which arises from the shells, [& which will soon pass off,] meets the approbation of all those of our citizens who have noticed it.

Literary Life and Works of Jas K Paulding. Compiled by his son, Wm I Paulding. N Y. Chas Scribner & Co. 1867-8. Jas K Paulding was born at Great Nine Partners, Dutchess Co, N Y, Aug 22, 1778, in the midst of the Revolutionary war. His father, a prominent Whig, was compelled to flee from Tarryton, their home, by reason of the Tories; & while his family was in this exile this son was born. His father lost his property in the war, & died in poverty in 1825, at the age of 90, his mother dying in 1830, at 89. Paulding died in Hyde Park, on the Hudson, Apr 6, 1860, at nearly 81 years. His life-long bosom friend, Washington Irving, preceding him by about one year to the tomb, & at nearly 77 years of age. Paulding & Washington Irving, & his eldest brother, Wm, whose wife was Paulding's sister, in 1807 entered into partnership in a serial publication intended to satirize the ways of the hour in N Y-to simply instruct the young, amuse the old, reform the town, & castigate the age. For most of his life Paulding lived in N Y C, & for several years prior to 1837 he was Navy Agent at that port. He was appointed sec of the Board of Navy Com'rs Apr 28, 1815, & held that place about 8 years. On Jun 25, 1838, he was commissioned Sec of the Navy, & took up his residence in Washington, retiring on Mar 4, 1841. He later retired to a country seat at *Hyde Park*, on the Hudson, where he died in 1860.

Patents to Washingtonians during the past week:
To Benj Chambers, jr, for an improved letter balance.
To John Wagner, for mode of attaching horse shoes.
To Jos P Milburn, for a tumbler washer.
Two patents to Adolph Ott, assignor to Antoino Pelletier, the first for a process of extracting precious metals from ores, the second for an appartus for extracting precious metals.

Equity Court-Judge Olin. 1-Maguire vs Miller et al; decree appointing A Lloyd trustee to sell. 2-*In re*. Worthington's estate; order of reference to auditor. 3-Merrill vs Kent, order of publication.

Criminal Court-Chief Justice Cartter. 1-Trial of Wm Eldridge, indicted for the murder of Geo Williams, Sept last, in Rutherford's restaurant, 2nd st, was commenced with the following jurors being sworn: Henry McIntosh, Leonard Gordan, John W Morsell, August Ockert, Bladen Forrest, Robt A Waters, Jas Tultavull, C C Anderson, Jacob J Fink, Peter Hepburn, Thos M Adams, Chas H Anderson. Eldridge went into the saloon with McClelland, & met the dec'd, Geo Williams, who belonged to the same regt, when McClelland & Williams got to sparring, McClelland was knocked down, & Williams, it is alleged, struck the accused, when the latter drew a knife, & stabbed him, causing his death. The trial is in progress. The Dist Atty entered a *nolle pros* as to McClelland, the evidence in now way implicating him in the murder.

Died: on Mar 18, Mary Adeline, daughter of the late Surgeon Whelan, U S Navy. Her funeral will take place from St Aloysius Church on Mar 20, at 10½ o'clock A M.

Died: in Wash City, after a short illness, Mrs Mary A Stephenson, wife of Jos Stephenson, in her 58th year. Her funeral will take place from Ryland Chapel, 10th & D sts, at 2 o'clock on Mar 19. [No death date given-current item.]

Died: on Mar 16, Mrs John G Schott. Her funeral will take place from her late residence, 362 B st, Capitol Hill, on Friday afternoon, at 2 o'clock.

Died: on Mar 16, Wm M Ellis, in his 62nd year. His funeral will take place from the First Presbyterian Church, 4½ st, on Mar 19. [Phil Ledger please copy.]

Buffalo, N Y, Mar 18. Chas H Spencer, late of the Albion, N Y, committed suicide this evening by shooting himself through the head.

A Mons Didier Balthazer D'Ourches has bequeathed the French Academy of Medicine $5,000 as a prize to the scientific man who invents the method of discovering the certain signs of death.

Supreme Court of D C, Equity 1,207-Docket 8. John H Merrill, cmplnt, vs John Kent, dfndnts. On motion of cmplnt, by McPherson & Appleby, his solicitors, it is ordered that the dfndnt cause his appearance on or before the first rule day occurring 40 days after this day, otherwise the cause will be proceeded with as in case of default. –A B Olin, justice

Columbia, S C, Mar 18. Sgt Bates, with his flag unfurled, arrived here this evening. Hundred awaited his arrival on the banks of the Congaree river. He was welcomed by Major Melton on behalf of the citizens, & escorted to Wickerson's Hotel.

FRI MAR 20, 1868
Hon David Wilmot, one of the Justices of the Court of Claims, died at his home in Towanda, Pa, of paralysis, on Monday last. He was born at Bethany, Wayne Co, Pa, Jan 20, 1814; educated at Bethany Academy & at Aurora, N Y; subsequently studied law & was admitted to the bar in 1834; in 1844 elected member of Congress from the Bradford dist, Pa, & severed several consecutive terms. His greatest celebrity was derived from his introduction, in 1848, of the proviso excluding slavery from the territory acquired from Mexico, ever since known as the Wilmot proviso. In 1860, after Cameron, he accepted the position of Sec of War under Lincoln; elected to the U S Senate to fill the unexpired 2 years of Mr Cameron's term in that body. In 1863 he was appointed by Mr Lincoln one of the Justices of the Court of Claims, which position he held at the time of his death.

The President has directed that the Territory of Alaska, heretofore under Gen Halleck, in the Dept of the Pacific, be made a separate military dept, to be known as the Dept of Alaska, & Brvt Maj Gen Jeff C Davis has been assigned to the command of the same.

Mr Thos Woodward, Coroner of Wash Co, is again prostrated by a severe illness, & is lying very low. Mr Woodward being of an advanced age, & greatly enfeebled by past bad health, it is thought he will not survive this attack.

The funeral of the late Wm M Ellis took place yesterday from the 4½ st Presbyterian Church. The pall-bearers were: Messrs Robt Clark, Jas Nokes, Josiah Essex, C W Bennett, Campbell, & Robt Carter. The service was conducted by Rev Byron Sunderland & Rev John Chester. The choir of Dawson Lodge of Masons, consisting of Messrs J B Dawson, Ball, Stewart, Sheriff, S V Noyes, Jos Hodgson, Griffin, & others, chanted the beautiful "Remember thy Creator in the days of thy youth." The procession having been formed, the funeral cortege wended its solemn way to the *Congressional Cemetery*.

The Marlborough Gaz says: "We learn that the Court of Appeals has at last finally decided the Craufurd case in favor of the heirs represented by the late Dr Blackburn. The personal property will now be distributed at once." We understand that Mrs Kearney, of this city, widow of the late Dr Kearney, of the navy, is one of the heirs of this estate, which is one of the largest in PG Co.

The mansion belonging to the estate of the late Gen Winfield Scott, at Elizabeth, N J, was sold at auction, on Wed, for $11,900.

Thos Dowling, auct, on Wed, disposed of the following property at auction, in Gtwn, formerly belonging to Mrs E M Mosher: lot 30 on High st, to W Selden, for $1,320; lot 29 on High st, to John Wagner, for $1,280; north half of lot 28, High st, to W Selden, for $620; south half of lot 28, High st, to J McDaniels, for $600; lot 27 on High st, to J W Haney, for $800; lot 26 on High st, to W H Hilleary, for $920; south part of lot 207, High st, to D O Donovan, for $1,236; middle part of same lot to J H McDaniels, for $1,064; north part of same lot to Mr M McCormick, for $115; lot 24 on High st, to Catharine Stoub, for $2,360; south part of lot 220, on Market st, to J H McDaniels, for $900; part of lot 11 on High st, improved by a brick bldg, to R E Talbot, for $2,500. The sales were well attended, & the bidding brisk.

Mr Saml Gardner, the electrician, has submitted a proposition before the Cmte on Accounts of the House of Reps to light the hall of the House by electricity, as the dome is now lighted. Mr Gardner estimates the first cost for fixtures, etc, at $7,800, & that the cost per year of lightning by this system would not exceed $100. It is being considered by the cmte.

Equity Court-Judge Olin. 1-Keating vs Keating: order of reference to C Ingle, special auditor, to report on partition. 2-Alman vs Huntly: order of reference to examiner, J J Johnson, to report on transfer of mail contract. 3-Allen vs Allen: order of publication against absent dfndnt. 4-Cragin vs Osborne: order appointing John S McKenney, guardian *ad litem*.

Albany, N Y, Mar 19. On Tuesday Henry Verschel, a soldier, who belonged to N Y, but was stopping temporarily at the Soldiers' Home in this city, was beaten by rowdies on Madison ave, & died today. No arrests have been made.

Springfield, Mass, Mar 19. Lucius H Tenney, the defaulting teller of the First Nat'l Bank of Greenfield, was sentenced today to 5 years imprisonment in the State prison.

Kansas City, Mo, Mar 18. Andrew McGuire, a noted guerrilla connected with the late bank robbery at Richmond, Mo, was taken from jail at his place last night, hung by a party of 6 persons in disguise, calling themselves a vigilance cmte.

N Y, Mar 18. The action for libel, brought against Moses S Beach, of the Sun, by Mary Boker Dean, was commenced in the Brooklyn city court yesterday. The dfndnt acknowleged he published the alleged libellous article, but claims that it was not done maliciously.

Cincinnati, Mar 19. Explosion of the steamer **Magnolia**, on Mar 18. Killed, missing, & lost: Capt Prathers, Jas Stevens, 2nd engineer; Perry Miller, 2nd mate; Wm Evans, bartender; Mary Capin, chambermaid; John Rees, Ohio; Wm Evans, boatman; Miss French, Mason Co, Ky, supposed to be drowned. R Bradley, Ripley, Ohio, lost. Injured: Henry Clark, Adams Express Co, badly. Mr Gardner, one of the owners of the boat, badly hurt. Mr Burton, bartender, badly bruised. There were fully 140 people on the **Magnolia**, 80 of whom are lost. A full list cannot be obtained, as the papers & books were destroyed.

Nashville, Mar 19. 1-Dr L D Nagle, late of Indiana, was arrested today for kidnapping a negro boy & sending him off as a servant to some member of the Legislature. 2-Shooting affair between Henry C Barr, policemen, formerly a member of Stokes' cavalry, & Col J W Lawless, formerly of the 5th Ky cavalry, now a clerk at the workhouse. Several shots were exchanged. Lawless is mortally wounded.

For sale or rent: farm of 110 acres, in Montg Co, Md, near Sandy Spring, with fine improvements; double house, containing 17 rooms; water at the door. P Palmer, on the place, of Edw L Palmer, 28 Bowly's Wharf, Balt. -Jno D McPherson, 430 D st, Wash City.

The Ohio Senate has passed resolutions ejecting Thos C Jones, Senator from the 8th Dist, on the ground that he was elected by negro votes. The seat was awarded to Henry M Onderdock, his Democratic competitor, who was immediately sworn in.

SAT MAR 21, 1868
A telegram from Crown Point, N Y, states that on Wed, Capt Raine, the lighthouse keeper, assisted by his son, in attempting to draw his 2 daughters across Lake Champlain to Chimney Point, in a sleigh, broke through the ice, & all were precipitated into the water. The son first gained the firm ice, & saved his father, but the ladies fell under the sleigh, & their dead bodies were recovered 2 hours later. They were 18 & 30 years of age. The eldest leaves a husband & 2 children.

The President yesterday sent the following nominations to the Senate:
Homer G Plants, U S Atty for the Southern Dist of Fla.
John S Watts, Chief Justice of the Supreme Court of the Territory of New Mexico.
Peter A Callan, assist surgeon in the navy.
J O P Burnside, 2nd Auditor of the Treasury, vice B French, to be removed.
John R Drabell, Assessor of Internal Revenue 2nd Dist of West Va.
Edw H Smith, Collector of Internal Revenue 1st Dist of S C.
Walter E Carlin, Assessor of Internal Revenue 10th Dist of Ill.
Monroe A Blanchard, Pension Agent at Portland, Maine. [This nomination was subsequently confirmed.]
Wm M Daily, of La, Receiver of Public Moneys at New Orleans.
Capt August L Case, to be cmdor.
Cmder A B Caldwell, to be capt.
Cmder Henry K Davenport to be capt.
Lt Cmders Stanton & B B Taylor, to be cmders.

Cincinnati Gaz, Thu. Explosion of the steamer **Magnolia**. Thy Maysville packet, the steamer **Magnolia**, was built in Cincinnati, & received her finishing touches in Oct, 1859; her original owners were G Molen, J H Procter, David Gibson, O F Shaw, & A & V Shinkle. She was 200 feet in length, 33 feet beam, & 6 feet depth of hold, & would carry 518.82 tons. Her boilers were inspected by Capt Fisher, the U S inspector, on Dec 11 last, & were found to be in excellent condition, a certificate of the same having been given. Capt J B Purcell happened to be out in the river with a skiff, & was one of the first at the rescue. The names of the injured left at Calif are as follows:
Miss Ellen Eckelman, M D Ridenour, Col Chas Marshall, Mason Co, Ky, slightly.
Mrs Wiles & daughter, Ripley, Ohio, slightly burned.
Rufus Martin & lady, of Ky, slightly bruised.
Mr A N Fulton, of Ohio, slightly.
W D D Kerr, of Higginsport, Ohio, slightly bruised.
Geo W Kerr, of Bridgetown, Ind, no doubt, fatally injured.
Jerome Stevens, 2nd engineer, slightly.
Fred'k Cox, editor of the Flemingsbury [Ky] Democrat, badly bruised, scalded, lower jaw being broken.
C D Armstrong, of the same place, slightly injured.
G H Hustin, Berlin, Ky, lower body badly scalded.
T F Jones, Smith's Landing, Ky, arm broken.
Andy Connor, pilot, slight bruises.
Alex Elliott, 2nd clerk, bruised.
O F Shaw, 1st clerk of the boat, laid over during the trip, was not on board.
L E Rolman, Indiana, slightly scalded & bruised.
Wm D Ross, Ky, slight injuries, as did also Thos F Jones, of this city. Known to be lost were Capt J H Prather, the cmder of the steamer. He was asleep in his stateroom & he was probably killed instantly, his body blown into the water.
Wm Evans, assist barkeeper, waiting on a customer at the time, the two were never seen afterwards.

John Rose, farmer, residing near Felicity, Ohio, known to be lost.

Mrs Lapan, residence in this city, was lost. Mr Stevens, 2nd engineer, it is supposed was instantly carried into eternity.

Miss Retta French & her sister, two young ladies, during the past few days had been visiting friends & relations in the city, on their way to their home in Mason Co, were lost.

Benj Bradford, of Ripley, Ohio, a young man just returning from school, it is supposed was blown over board & drowned.

Perry Miller, 2nd mate, & the 1st mate [not named] are supposed to have been lost. Brought to this city: Mr Levi & Mrs Baker, of Ripley, Ohio, slightly scalded; Geo Prather, clerk & brother to the Capt; John Jackson, [colored] steward of the boat, badly scalded; Jerome Stevens, 1st engineer, badly burned & scalded; Henry Clark, messenger of the Adams Express Co; one leg broken & one arm dislocated. Clark is lying in a dangerous condition. J B Gilliman, of Ripley, Ohio, had 2 ribs broken, & was slightly scalded; J R Hawes, of Minerva, Ky, had 2 ribs broken, & was badly bruised. Geo Wilder of Higginsport, was badly scalded. At the Metropolitan Hotel were several who were on board at the time of the catastrophe: Capt John Law, of Aberdeen, Ohio, slightly injured; Wm Burton, barkeeper of the **Magnolia**, slightly bruised & burned; Thos Curran, of Dover, Ky, badly scalded; Geo L Gillis, Covington, Ky, uninjured; Mrs Fits, of Higginsport, Brown Co, Ohio, safe. At the Spencer House we found Mr A C Hull, a manufacturer at Pittsburg. Mr Hull had hardly recovered from some slight bruises he received on the Indianapolis & Cincinnati railroad, when the train he was on was thrown from the track at Whitewater bridge on Tuesday by the storm. He escaped with slight injury. He is an elderly gentleman, & fortunately his trunk was waiting for him when he arrived at the Spencer House. We learn from eye witnesses that the dead bodies of Mr D H Murphy & Benj Broadland, both of Ripley, had been sent up the river on the ship **Mary Ament**. Three of the injured, viz: Stephen Shorter & Green Johnson, both colored; Chas Lewis, white, were conveyed to the Commercial Hospital. Shorter died at 7 o'clock. His remains were taken to the home of his parents, 144 East 5th st. He was about 25 years of age. Green Johnson, a colored man, aged 23, was scalded all over the body; the physicians did not think he would live through the night. Chas Lewis, white, was terribly scalded & had a hole in the back of his head. His recovery is extremely doubtful. A German, Myers Ocha, on his way to Maysville, for the collection of some outstanding debts, died a short time after being taken to his residence on Race st, near 5th. His occupation was that of a drover. He leaves & wife & 5 children to mourn. We have since learned that Mr Jos Beatty, a merchant doing business in Second st, was among the lost. L McCowan, from New Richmond, is also in Calif, in a dangerous condition; badly scalded.

The swift steamer **Arrow** has been purchased by Mr Jas Sykes, of Willard's Hotel, & she is to be under the command of Capt Thos Stackpole, well known as the "steamboat man." On Monday next regular trips will commence to **Mount Vernon**, leaving this city daily at 10 o'clock, [Sundays excepted,] stopping at Alexandria, **Fort Foot**, & **Fort Washington**.

Rev B Speke has just received a bequest of $3,000 a year.

Criminal Court-Chief Justice Cartter. 1-Saml Jackson; assault & battery: not guilty. 2-Henry Dougherty; larceny; recognizance forfeited; bench warrant issued. 3-Alex Clendening; assault & battery with intent to kill; recognizance forfeited; bench warrant issued. 4-John T Crismond, who was convicted of an assault & battery some days ago, fined $50 & costs. 5-Henry Wair & John Bracker, indicted for cheating, found guilty. Bracker sent to jail for 2 weeks, & Wair for 1 day. 6-Jas M Smith, indicted for breaking into the house of Dement & Howell on Mar 7 last, & stealing articles valued at $3.40; guilty; sentenced to the penitentiary for 5 years. 7-John Wagner & Conrad Sauer, indicted for burglary & for stealing property to the value of $228 from Louis Kettler on Feb 16 last, pleaded guilty; sentenced to the Albany penitentiary for 3 years each. 8-Thos H Newton; assault & battery; recognizance forfeited; bench warrant issued. 9-Chas F Daily; larceny; guilty; sentenced for 30 days. 10-Augustus Buss; false pretences; pleads guilty; sentenced to Albany penitentiary for 1 year, the execution of the sentence to be postponed until Mar 26.

Equity Court-Judge Olin. The case of Hessler vs Dixon occupied the attention of the Court yesterday.

Chas A Dana & Gen J H Wilson, the captor of Jeff Davis, are to write a life of Gen Grant.

The Internal Revenue Dept decides that the proceeds of Mr Dickens' reading are not liable to the two percent tax which some assessors have levied upon them.

The equestrian, Carlotta de Berg, while riding in a N Y circus on Tuesday, fell from her horse & broke her arm & leg, & so seriously injured herself internally that she is not expected to recover.

Paris has a new lady violinist, Mme Norman Neruda, who is said to be equal to Paganini. She was born in Prague, educated at Vienna, & married a Swede. She is 28 years of age, & appeared in a concert when only seven.

MON MAR 23, 1868
Messrs J B Wheeler & Co, aucts, sold lot 11, in Reservation C, on Md ave, near 4½ st, to Mr John E Kendall, for $1,343.76.

John Ward was hanged at Windsor, Vt, on Friday, for the murder of Mrs Griswold, at Willotson, near Burlington, in Aug, 1866.

Cork, Mar 21. Capt Mackay was been sentenced to imprisonment at hard labor for a term of 12 years.

Baseball. A meeting of the Nat'l Club was held on Friday last, when Mr Geo Fox, the champion player of America was presented with a very handsome & costly silver ball. The presentation was made by Mr M A Tappan in behalf of the club.

From South America; N Y, Mar 23. Arcbishop Herron died on Feb 6.

Orphans Court-Judge Purcell, Mar 21, 1868. 1-The will of Wm L Hoge was fully proven & admitted to probate. 2-The will of Newman Shelton was fully proven & admitted to probate. 3-The will of the late Wm Slade, bequeathing his estate to his widow, & naming her & his brother-in-law, W P Parke, excs was filed. 4-Letters of administration on the estate of the late Edw Maynard, of Knoxville, Tenn, were issued to Horace Maynard; bond $2,500. 5-Letters of administration, with the will annexed, on the estate of the late Newman Shelton to Judson T Cull; bond $800. 6-Annin G Chevallie was appointed guardian to the orphan of Henry Chevallie, late of Richmond; bond $3,500. 7-The first accounts of S B Bowman, guardian to orphans of E C Dyer, dec'd; & 2nd account of Martha J Troxel, [now Sran,] guardian to orphans of Jos P Troxel; & first & final account of Wm Guipe, exc of Margaret Mackel, were offered & passed.

Louisville, Mar 22. John Arnold, sec of the Hope Ins Co, has been arrested on a warrant sworn out by D G Bly, president of the company, charging Arnold with embezzling $7,000 of the company's funds. Arnold gave bail in $8,000.

Obit-died: on Feb 26, at Rome, Italy, Benj Ogle Tayloe, the eldest surviving son of the late Col John Tayloe, of *Mount Airy*, Va, & Wash City; born at Annapolis, May 21, 1796, in the house of his maternal grandfather, Govn'r Ogle, of Md; received his preliminary academical education at Phillips' Exeter Academy, & was graduated at Harvard Univ in 1815; in 1817 he visited Europe as an attache of the American Ambassador to the Court of St James, Hon Richd Rush. He enjoyed the advantages of the society of the higher circles of the British metropolis. From there he went to Paris; toured Germany & Italy. In 1824 he married Miss Julia Dickinson, of Troy, N Y, daughter of Hon John D Dickinson, of N Y C, & for many years the Representative of the Rensselaer Dist in the U S Congress. After a brief stary at *Mount Airy*, his ancestral estate, on the banks of the Rappahannock, he removed to this city, & to the house which thenceforward became his permanent abode. Renowned as the *Octagon*, the residence of his father, had been in the preceding generation, the house of Mr Tayloe, on La Fayette square. In 1846 Mr Tayloe had the misfortune to lose his wife, the mother of his children, all at that time of tender age After the lapse of several years Mr Tayloe married Miss Phoebe Warren, of Troy, N Y, a lady of extraordinary loveliness of character, with the rarest of Christian virtues. On the breaking out of the late unhappy war Mr Tayloe was the possessor of a large amount of land & personal property in the Southern States. Through the result of that war his losses were enormous. Many of his nearest relatives were reduced from affluence to comparative poverty. In May, 1866, Mr Tayloe, accompanied by his wife & son, sailed for Europe, & spent some months at Leamington Spa, in England, for the benefit of his health, went on the Continent, where he remained until his death. He long suffered from a tendency to paralysis. In Nov last, while in Paris, he received a severe blow in the death of a beloved daughter, Mrs Perry, of Cumberland. Mr Tayloe was descended through a long & honorable lineage from many of the most distinguished families in Va & Md, from the Carter, the Lees, the Wormleys, the Ogles, & the Bladen. –W M W

Died: on Mar 20, after a long illness, of consumption, J W Steel, in his 32nd year.

Criminal Court-Judge Olin. 1-Edw M Magee, petit larceny; recognizance forfeited; bench warrant issued. 2-Jos Smith, petit larceny; verdict guilty; sentenced to 60 days in jail; a *nolle pros* was entered in another case against Smith. 3-Wm Bell, petit larceny; verdict guilty; sentenced to jail for 30 days. 4-J Harris & A J Fitzpatrick, indicted for the larceny of two overcoats, one having in the pocket a draft for $50; verdict guilty; sentenced to Albany Penitentiary for 3 years. 5-Jas Colemen, assault & battery on Laura Thomas, alias Cissel, on Mar 14 last; verdict guilty; sentenced to jail for 3 weeks. 6-Leo Jackson, assault & battery; verdict guilty; sentenced to two weeks in jail.

Panama: N Y, Mar 22. Gen Plant, Pres of the State of Panama, died on Mar 4th, it is supposed of poison. Don Juan Dias acted as President ad interim.

TUE MAR 24, 1868
Died: on Mar 23, Geo E Falconer, in his 27th year. His funeral will be from the residence of his father, Ralph Falconer, 280 7th st, between L & M sts, on Mar 25 at 2 o'clock.

Balt, Mar 23. Jefferson Davis arrived here on the steamer **Cuba** from Havana.

Orphans Court of Wash Co, D C, Mar 21, 1868. In the case of John B Blake, exc of Johnson Hellen, dec'd, the executor & Court have appointed Apr 18 next, for the final settlement of the personal estate of the said dec'd, of the assets in hand.
-Jas R O'Beirne, Reg/o wills

Supreme Court of D C; No 778. Henry McLeod et al vs Eugene McLeod et al. Statement of the trustee's account, on Mar 28. –Walter S Cox, Auditor

The Answer of the President of the U S, Andrew Johnson, to the impeachment articles, exhibited against him by the House of Reps of the U S covered a large portion of this newspaper.

WED MAR 25, 1868
The President's message in regard to ***Alaska***. The Gov't Printing Ofc has just issued the message of the Pres of the U S in answer to a resolution of the House, together with all the correspondence in relation to Russian America. Minister Clay, at St Petersburg, writing to Mr Seward, says: I congratulate you upon this brilliant achievement, which adds to the vast territory of our Union whose ports, whose mines, whose waters, whose furs, whose fisheries are of untold value, & whose fields will produce many grains, even wheat, & become hereafter in time the seat of a hearty white population. I regard it as worth at least five millions of dollars, & hereafter the wonder will be that we ever got it at all. The document includes the reports of the Sec of War & the Sec of the Treasury, together with numerous official statements showing the character of the country in all particulars.

Gen Hancock has received information that his son, who is at school at New Haven, Conn, is in ill health, & has leave of absence for 4 days to visit him. He will leave here tomorrow morning, stopping at Balt until the afternoon train North, to attend to private business there.

Quite a large audience of ladies & gentlemen were in attendance at Trinity Church yesterday to witness the nuptials of Capt Edw Stanford, son of Mr W H Stanford, of Wash City, & Miss Mary McNabb, of *Giesboro*. The ceremony was performed by Rev Dr Addison, rector of Trinity, at the close of which the happy couple proceded to the cars for a honeymoon trip North.

St Louis, Mar 24. Cora James, alias Samantha Procter, notorious here & in Chicago for bringing suits against all sorts of persons on trivial grounds, was arrested here today on a charge of being a common scold, & in default of bail committed to jail. She came here to attend to a suit against the Democrat, which was thrown out of court for want of security for costs.

Jackson, Miss, Mar 24. Wm M Estelle, a prominent lawyer of Miss, was assassinated last night. The supposed assassin has been arrested. [No name given.]

Died: on Mar 23, Geo E Falconer, aged 27 years. His funeral will be from the residence of his father, Ralph Falconer, 280 7th st, between L & M sts, on Mar 25, at 2 P M.

Died: on Mar 15, at his residence, *Willow Grove*, Montg Co, Md, Roger Brooke, in his 59th year of his age.

Jas Finnigan, who arrived in Buffalo on the Grand Trunk railroad on Friday, stabbed 3 passengers just before the train reached the depot. He was arrested. Chas Short & J R Ludwig, of Buffalo, are stabbed slightly, & W J McCarthy, of Port Clabourne, Canada, severely in the shoulder & back. Finnigan was supposed to be insane.

Hunter's Mill for sale; by decree of the Circuit Court of Fairfax Co, Va, rendered in the suit of E O Powell, etc, vs Hunter, etc, at Jun term, 1867; the undersigned Com'r will sell on Apr 20, 1868, his property which lies immediately on the A L & H railroad; contains 138½ acres of land; the entire tract will be sold subject to the right of dower of Mrs Mary A Hunter, to that portion which has been allotted her, & includes the dwlg-house. Her right can be bought on reasonable terms. –Thos Moore, Com'r of sale

Supreme Court of D C; No 1,141 Equity, docket No 5. In the matter of the estate of the late Wm Worthington. The accounts of Saml Stott, the trustee, have been referred to me for settlement, with directions to approve of a new trustee in the place of the said Saml Stott. Parties interested to appear at my ofc, 36 La ave, Mar 31, 12 o'clock M.
-C Ingle, Special Auditor

Excellent household & kitchen furniture at auction on Mar 30, at 340 N Y ave, between 9th & 10th sts, including Grover & Baker's Sewing Machine, & one Rosewood Case Piano, 6¾ octave, made by Oliver Dixon & Co. -Cooper & Latimer, aucts

Orphans Court of Wash Co, D C. Letters testamentary on the personal estate of Wm Slade, late of Wash Co, D C, dec'd. –Josephine L Slade, Wm P Parker

Orphans Court of Wash Co, D C, Mar 24, 1868. In the case of Michl F Moran, exc of John McGarvey, dec'd, the executor & Court have appointed Apr 21 next, for the final settlement of the personal estate of the said dec'd, of the assets in hand.
-Jas R O'Beirne, Reg/o wills

THU MAR 26, 1860
The Senate yesterday confirmed, among other nominations, John G Bond, to be capt in the revenue service, & R M Sherman to be marshal for the District of Rhode Island.

Pres nominated Cmdor Jos Lanman to be rear admiral in the navy, vice Palmer, dec'd.

Cincinnati, Mar 25. C Adoe, Prussian Consul, & an old resident, died last night.

Mr Saml Strong, whose case has been in the Court of Bankruptcy for some time, & who was arrested under a requisition from the Govn'r of Va, & who was discharged from arrest by Judge Fisher under a writ of habeas corpus, has been adjudged a bankrupt, & obtained a final discharge. The following requisition was filed yesterday in the Clerk's ofc of the county; Headquarters First Military Dist, State of Va, Richmond, Va, Mar 12, 1868. To Hon Chief Justice of the Supreme Court, Court of the Dist of Columbia. "Whereas it appears by the annexed document, which is hereby certified as authentic, that Samuel Strong stands charged with the crime of obtaining signatures to writings under false pretences, with intent to defraud, committed in the city of Richmond, in this state & military district, & it having been represented to me that he had fled from justice, & taken refuge in the Dist of Col. Now, therefore, I, Major General J M Schofield, commanding the First Military Dist, State of Va, do hereby require, in pursuance of the provisions of the Constitution & laws of the U S in such cases made & provided, that the said Strong be apprehended & delivered to Wm H Southall, who is hereby authorized to receive & convey him to the First Military Dist, State of Va, that he, may be dealt with according to law. J M Schofield, Maj Gen. Commanding First Military Dist, State of Va. The Chief Justice ordered a warrant for the arrest of Strong to be issued, & the case will probably be heard today. [Mar 30th newspaper: Mr Saml Strong arrived in this city from Albany & surrendered himself to the Marshal, in response to the warrant issued by Judge Cartter on Thursday, under a requisition from Gen Schofield, commanding the First Military Dist.]

Mrd: on Mar 25, at St Aloysius Church, by Fr C H Stonestreet, Jos S Jones to Emily F Wiley, daughter of the late T P Brown, all of this city.

Circuit Court-Judge Wylie. Uttermehle vs Uttermehle et al Brent, Merrick, & Norris. Davidge, Caruis, & Cook. This is an action of replevin. The dfndnts represent the estate of Chas H Uttermehle, dec'd. When he died a certain number of U S bonds & Corp stock, amounting in the aggregate to $30,000, was found deposited in the box of said dec'd in the Nat'l Metropolitan Bank by his administrator. The father of the dec'd, the plntf, claims that the dec'd was acting as his agent, & that the bonds in question were placed in the hands of the dec'd for safe-keeping by the plntf. The plntf demanded from the executors the delivery of these bonds, but they refused to make such delivery, & therefore, the plntf replevied. The case is before this court to settle the question of title as to the said bonds. [May 27th newspaper: The case was settled by compromise. The property replevied is to be equally divided among the parties, & the costs of suit are to be borne equally by each.]

Criminal Court-Chief Justice Cartter. 1-A *nolle pros* was entered by the Dist Atty Carrington in each of the following cases: 1-Hysum Dodson, indicted for an assault & battery on Roberta Douglass, on Jan 8 last. 2-O'Hare Allen, indicted for larceny of $20, the property of Chas Willis, on Dec 17 last. 3-Mary C Brooks, indicted for receiving stolen goods, knowing them to have been stolen, to the amount of $122, the property of Thos Mears, on Feb 14 last. 4-Wm King, indicted for stealing two horses of the value of $300, the property of Geo P Fisher, on Feb 15; & for stealing 2 horses of the value of $400 each, the property of S A H Marks, on Feb 10; & for stealing two horses of the value of $350 each, the property of Chas E Mix, on Jan 21 last.

Orphans Court-Judge Purcell, Mar 24, 1868. 1-The second account of Edw Sunnis, adm of the estate of Jos Reynolds, dec'd, was approved & filed. 2-Horace Maynard took out letters of administration of the late Edw Maynard; bond $5,500. 3-The will of the late Nancy Schott, bequeathing, after directing that tombstones shall be erected over the graves of her husband, son, & self, $2,000 to her grand-daughter, Lilly A Moss, & the residue of her estate to her daughter, Anns V Moss, who she appoints as executor, was filed & fully proven. 4-Letters testamentary were issued to A V Moss, who gave bond in $8,000. 5-A renunciation of the right to the appointment of guardian to the minor children of Lewis Thomas was received from Margaret Thomas, & in her stead, Geo C Henning qualified; bond $3,000. 6-Mary Ann Ellis was granted letters testamentary upon the personal estate of the late Wm M Ellis; bonds $10,000. Sureties, S T Ellis, T A Richards, & Geo B Smith. 7-The last will of Mr Slade was admitted to probate. 8-Ann E McClery gave bonds, & was appointed guardian to the orphans of the late M J McClery. 9-The will of Sarah L Henry was admitted to probate.

Trustee's sale of valuable bldg lot on I st north, between 4th & 5th sts west, at auction; by decree of the Supreme Court of D C, in Chancery, cause No 960, wherein Wm Trueman is cmplnt, & Fred'k Iddins et al are dfndnts; public auction on Apr 17, on the premises, the west half of lot 9 in square 516. Also, the east half of the west half of lot 8 in same square. –John N Oliver, trustee -J B Wheeler & Co, aucts

Dept of the Interior, U S Patent Ofc, Wash, Mar 16, 1868. Ptn of Jas Brayley, adm, & Mary Pitts, admx, of the estate of John A Pitts, dec'd, of Buffalo, N Y, praying for the extension of a patent granted to said John A Pitts Jul 4, 1854, for an improvement in Horse Power, for seven years from the expiration of said patent, which takes place on Jul 4, 1868. -A M Stout, Acting Com'r of Patents

FRI MAY 27, 1868
Board of Metropolitan Police Com'rs was held last night. 1-Jas Lynch was appointed a police magistrate, vice Jas Cull, whose commission had expired. 2-The applications of Benj Conley & August Horsch for license to sell liquors were reconsidered & rejected. 3-The application of Mrs Doratha Gerhardt & Geo Fauth were rejected. 4-Sgt B F Barker, for conduct unbecoming an ofcr, was dismissed the force. 5-Pvt Laurence Rossiter, for conduct unbecoming an ofcr, was fined $5. 6-Chas E Smith & Wm W Mills were appointed privates on the force.

Wreck of the ship **General Grant**-the survivors lived on the Auckland Isles for 18 months. It was night when the ship drifted into a giant cave, 400 feet deep, crushing its sides. When daylight came the boats were lowered; there were, including 24 of a crew, 83 passengers in all, among whom were 6 ladies & about 20 children. Of these there escaped from the sinking ship 4 male passengers, 10 seamen, one female, the stewardess, 15 in all. The capt of the ship was last seen in the Miezzen-topmast crosstrees; within a few moments of disappearing he waived his handkerchief as au adieu to those who were in the boats. They reached Port Rose; camped there; & the fire they lit that night was not allowed to go out for 18 months. They were badly off for clothing, food, & water. They were attacked with dysentery. On Jul 11th they came upon Capt Musgrave's hut; their joy was turned to disappointment as everything had been carried away. In Sept, after being on the islands for over 4 months, they were all attacked with a sickness that made their bellies swell, & then their limbs; somewhat resembled scurvy. They learned afterwards that it was a disease known to old whalers as the "cobbler." On Oct 6 a ship was seen. They were on an island at the time which they called *Rabbit Island*. They lit fires and gave chase to the boat, without success. The ship passed & was not seen again. On Sep 3 old David McClellan died. He had worked with them & suffered with them. On Nov 19, 1867, the man on the look out saw a sail. The signal fires were lighted without delay, but the smoke did not appear to attract notice. On the 21st the brig **Amherst** was sighted. The boat was launched, as observed from the brig, & the sufferers were taken on board, & treated by Capt Gillroy & his ofcrs & men with kindness & consideratioon. They were taken on to Southland, New Zealand, where they were hospitably received & provided for.

Archduke Henry, of Austria, who violated what was thought to be princely propriety by marrying Mile Hoffman, the actress, has lost his command & a large part of his revenue in consequence, & the bishop who granted the dispensation had been severely reprimanded.

A Dr Maynard has left by will one-tenth of his net estate to the poor of Balt, for the purpose of procuring fuel, food, raiment, & other necessaries that might be required.

U S Marshal's sale on Apr 4, at the Livery Stabel of Tray, on Congress st, Gtwn, D C, one bay horse, & one buggy & harness, seized & levied upon as the goods & chattels of Jos M Parish, & will be sold to satisfy execution No 4,521, in favor of C D Spaids. –D S Gooding, U S Marshal, D C.

Orphans Court of Wash Co, D C. Letters of administration, d b n, on the personal estate of Lavinia Boyle late of Wash Co, dec'd. –John F Ennis, adm, d b n

SAT MAR 28, 1868
Abraham Pushee, of Lebanon, the well-known musician & teacher of dancing, died in Lebanon, on Thursday, aged 77 years. About the first of the month while directing a dancing party at Norwich, Vt, he had a stroke of paralysis. He recovered to a great extent, in the course of a few days, but on Thursday he had another attack, which he survived but a few hours. He was a distinguished member of the Masonic fraternity, holding at the time of his death the position of High Priest of the Royal Arch Chapter. He was buried on Sunday with high Masonic honors. –N H Patriot

Mrd: Mar 14, at the residence of the groom's parents, in St Paul, Minn, by Rev J Matlocks, Jas Edw Froiseth to Miss Sarah Gilbert, both of St Paul.

Died: on Mar 26, at Gtwn, D C, Josiah, infant son of Hon Saml J & Fanny W Randall.

Providence Journal. On Wed morning the residence of Mr Albert Hubbard, cashier of the Scituate Nat'l Bank, in North Scituate, was entered by 4 men, who proceeded to his bedroom, held a lantern & a pistol to his face, ordered him to get up & give them the keys of the bank & of the bank vault. He was then gagged, handcuffed, bound, rope put around his neck, & was tied his wife & son. Two remained at the house & the other two went to the bank. The keys alone would not open the vault. They returned to the house, & holding a pistol to the head of the cashier, marched him over to the bank, compelling him to open the vault, when they despoiled it of its entire contents, which included $10,000 in bonds, about $800 in specie, & various bills of $5,500. Only a special deposit of $1,000 was left. The robbers made their escape. Since writing the above: the robbers were disguised, except one who had a German accent, stoutly built, average height, with a mustache. The pursuers, 4 in number, included Dr Chas H Fisher, president of the bank. One of the parties concerned in this robbery is suspectd to have been Jack Hartley, a notorious & skilled putter-up of heavy jobs of this character. [Mar 30th newspaper: On examination, it was found that the total loss will not exceed $30,000.]

Among recent deaths in Europe are those of Lord Byron, cousin & successor to the poet; Mrs Geo Combe, daughter of the great Mrs Siddons, & widow of the author of the "Constitution of Man;" & Madame Sophie Schroeder, who 70 years ago was a famous actress on the German stage.

Miss Hosmer's statue of Thos H Benton is soon to be put up in Lafayette Park, in St Louis. The structure upon which the statue is to stand is to be massive, & the extreme height of the statue from the ground will be about 20 feet.

MON MAR 30, 1868
Another proposed street railroad in Wash. On Friday the bill was introduced in the House of Reps, & will probably pass through Congress. The bill creates Augustus B Stoughton, John Little, John L Kidwell, Geo H Plant, LeRoy Tuttle, G W Hopkins, R M Hall, & their associates & assigns, a body corporate under the name of the Connecticut Ave & Park Railway Co, with authority to construct a single or double track, commencing at the intersection of 17th st & Pa ave, & running northward on the west side of 17th st to H st, thence along 17th st to Conn ave, along Conn ave to the intersection of Boundary st, thence along the country road from the said intersection, thence on any road opened, or which hereafter be opened west of the 14th st road, to, within, or through the proposed public park to the county line of Wash Co. Additional roads will be considered.

Orphans Court-Judge Purcell, Mar 28, 1868. 1-Several applications were made for administration on the estate of Jas B Morand, who recently died at Dorsey's Hotel, but the Court decided that letters of administration should be granted by consent of all parties, & they were accordingly granted to De W J C Duhamel, who gave bond in the sum of $2,500. Jas Bryan & Geo Howard sureties. 2-The will of the late Robt B Aylmer was filed, fully proved, & admitted to probate. He bequeaths his estate to his wife, Margaret, whom he also appoints excx, & letters testamentary were issued to her; bond $10,000. 3-An exemplified copy of the last will of Mary Ann Brown, of Cranstown, R I, was filed & admitted to probate & record. The testatrix bequeaths to her daughter Lorena, all her real estate in Wash City. She names Edw M Thurston, of Providence, R I, exc. 4-Ellen Biddie gave bond in the sum of $8,000 as guardian to the orphans of E C Eddie, deceased. John B Bryan & R C Bryan sureties.

A new indictment found against Jefferson Davis. Richmond, Va, Mar 28. The U S grand jury has found a new indictment against Jefferson Davis. It covers 50 pages, & details all his offences since the opening of the rebellion.

For sale: I will sell 40 acres of land near Falls Church, on reasonable terms. For particulars address Thos Moore, Atty-at-Law, Fairfax Co, Va. –Wm H Sewall

Orphans Court of Wash Co, D C. Letters testamentary on the personal estate of Robt R Aylmer, late of Wash Co, D C, dec'd. –Margaret Aylmer, excx

Dept of the Interior, U S Patent Ofc, Wash, Mar 12, 1868. Ptn of Horace Smith & D B Wesson, of Springfield, Mass, praying for the extension of a patent granted to them Feb 14, 1854, & reissued on Oct 10, 1854, this application having been authorized by act of Congress, for an improvement in Fire-arms, for seven years from the expiration of said patent, which takes place on Feb 14, 1868. -A M Stout, Acting Com'r of Patents

Wash Corp-Mar 23, 1868. 1-Cmte of Claims: bill for the relief of Lewis Block; of Alfred Chinn; of Wm Buckley; of Francis Buhler; each were passed. 2-Cmte on Wharves: bill granting permission to G W Linville to erect a wharf.

Hon Jas Harlan, accompanied by Mrs & Miss Harlan, has left Wash City to visit his father in Indiana. The elder Mr Harlan is seriously ill, & is far advanced in years.

The dwlg of Hon Chas Dudley, at Agency, Wapello Co, Iowa, was destroyed by fire Friday night, & 3 of his sons perished in the flames.

Cornelius Vanderbilt is supposed to be worth $75,000,000. A large proportion of his means are invested in railroad stocks & securities.

In the Ticknor divorce case, in Chicago, a decree has been entered giving the lady the custody of the children & $3,000 alimony.

Judge Ebenezer Starnes accidentally shot & killed himself, while hunting near Augusta, Ga, a few days ago. He served for a number of years as Atty Gen & afterwards as one of the judges of the Supreme Court of the State.

Miss Olive Logan was arrested in Columbus, Ohio, on Wed, on a warrant issued by Mayor Bull, for not having procured a city license to lecture there. Miss Logan pleaded her own case, &, after paying the license, left the city.

TUE MAR 31, 1868
St Louis, Mar 30. 1-In the Supreme Court today, the case of Gen Grant vs Jos White, for unlawfully retaining possession of a farm near this city, belonging to Mrs Grant, was decided in favor of plaintiff. 2-The Court also decided the case of Edw S Rouse, State & county collector, vs the Washington Univ, for State & county taxes, in favor of Rouse. The Court held, that under the new law, the University must pay taxes, notwithstanding its charter provides for perpetual exemption.

Mar 30, 1868. Senate. Impeachment trial; opening argument was by B F Butler for the House managers. [This is to provide you with the date the proceedings commenced; coverag in the newspaper is very extensive.]

Hoop-skirts are now restricted to street wear in Paris.

Carl Formes has begun his career as an actor at Wurtzburg.

Bishop Stevens, of Pa, has been made permanently lame by his late accident.

The Appletons have offered Dickens $25,000 for his next novel.

King Ludwig, of Bavaria, left a fortune of eight & a half million dollars.

Another of our old & most valued citizens has gone from us. Ulysses Ward, sr, died yesterday at the residence of his son-in-law, Saml Norment. Born of English parentage near Rockville, Md, Mr Ward has been for more than 50 years a resident of the Dist of Col, & by his industry, engergy, enterprise, & example, had contributed largely to the promotion of the prosperity of Wash City. Commencing life as a mechanic, he became one of our principal builders, & by a life of industry & untarnished integrity, amassed a large fortune. He was an active & devoted member, & for 40 years a local minister of the Methodist Episcopal Protestant Church. His ardent advocacy of the temperance cause earned for him years ago the title of the "Hero of Temperance." During 1846 & 47 he edited the Columbia Fountain. At the time of his death he was president of the Mutual Fire Ins Co. He died ripe in years, having attained his 76th year.

+

Died: on Mar 30, in great peace, Rev Ulysses Ward, aged 76 years. His funeral will be from the residence of his son-in-law, Saml Norment, 50 Missouri ave, on Wed afternoon, at 2½ o'clock without further notice. [Apr 3rd newspaper: The funeral of the late Ulysses Ward: the pall bearers were Rev Dr W Hamilton, Rev W C Lipscomb, Messrs Jas A Kennedy, M G Emory, J C McKelden, J Van Riswick, P W Browning, & C H Lane. Other ministers present were Revs B P Brown, Gillette, DeHaas, J G Butler, & Parker. The services were conducted by Rev Dr Drinkhouse, of the Methodist Protestant Church, 9th st. The remains were conveyed to *Glenwood Cemetery*, where they were interred.]

Seventy-two cardinals compose the *Sacred College* at present-6 bishops, 50 priests, & 16 deacons. Twenty-three hats are vacant. During the reign of the present Pope, 84 cardinals have died. The oldest cardinal in the archbishop of Toledo, who is 86; the oldest in the ecclesiastical office has worn the hat 36 years.

In Syracuse, N Y, a little daughter of C C Downing died of hydrophobia on Friday. She was bitten 5 weeks before by a pet Newfoundland, but exhibited no symptoms of the fatal poison which took possession of her system, until 2 days before her death.

Sydney Hydeley, 18 years old, shot his cousin, Carrie May Billings, at Wynantsville, near Troy, N Y, on Friday. He was handling his gun carelessly, when it was discharged, accidentally, of course, the ball entering her forehead, & she fell dead.

Buffalo, Mar 30. Abraham Mills, the canal boat capt who murdered Pat Malone, in this city, in Aug, 1867, was brought here from Grand Rapids, Mich, & lodged in jail this afternoon. Mills claims he stabbed Malone in self-defence, & fled from fear of popular vengeance.

Died: on Mar 19, in Brooklyn, N Y, Chas F Thomas, jr, aged 26 years & 11 months.

St Mary's Retreat, a select school for young ladies, near Bryantown, Chas Co, Md. Miss W Martin, formerly Principal of St Mary's Institute, Chas Co, & Mrs A Hughes, of Balt, have perfected arrangements to accommodate a limited number of boarders. Address Miss Martin, as shown above, or Mrs Agatha Hughes, Balt Post Ofc.

Public sale of valuable house & lot in the village of Piscataway, in PG Co, Md; by decree of the Circuit Court for PG Co, Md, sitting in Equity: public sale, in Piscataway, on Apr 24, all that lot or tract of land, with bldgs thereon, owned by Dr Geo F Harris, late of said village. –C C Magruder, jr, trustee Upper Marlborough, Md.

Dept of the Interior, U S Patent Ofc, Wash, Mar 20, 1868. Ptn of Warren Shaw & Parley G Green, of Wales, Mass, praying for the extension of a patent granted to them Jun 20, 1864, for an improvement in Tentering Cloth, for seven years from the expiration of said patent, which takes place on Jun 20, 1868.

WED APR 1, 1868
Wash Corp. 1-Ptn of Benj Evans, asking to place a paling in front of his property, 5 feet from the bldgs line: referred to the Cmte on Police. 2-Ptn of R A Golden & brother, asking a paved footway: referred to Improvements Cmte. 3-Ptn of Albert Bouldin & others: referred to the Improvements Cmte. 4-Ptn of Maria Maguire, for a remission of a fine: referred to the Claims Cmte. 5-Ptn of Wm Walter, asking the privilege of carrying on the business of coach & carriage factory on s e corner of 14th & D sts: referred to the Police Cmte. 6-Resolution directing that the property belonging to the estate of the late John P Pepper be not advertised for taxes until the fact of its being in arrears shall have been ascertained: adopted. 7-Police Cmte: bill granting permission to S C & E Wroe to erect an iron railing in front of their property, on 22nd st: passed. Also, a bill granting the same privilege to Danl Hunter; to Thos H Syphax; & to August Schemborn. 8-Claims Cmte: bills for the relief of Sarah A Johnson & Thos Lucas, were severally rejected. 9-Bill for the relief of Christopher Hololan, remitting a fine of $20 imposed on him for alleged violation of law, in selling liquor without license: passed. 10-Cmte on Wharves: bill grainting permission to G W Linville to build a wharf. 11-Ptn of Conrad Fauntz & John Gibson, asking permission to erect a wharf on the Potomac river, between 13th & 13½ sts: presented.

Mlle Nilsson, the famous Swedish singer, will soon visit this country.

Died: on Mar 31, Miss Anne Mangan, in her 20th year. Her funeral will be today at 3 o'clock P M, from the residence of her aunt, corner of 4th st west & G st north.

Died: on Mar 31, of consumption, Mr Isaac Reed, aged 63. His funeral will take place from his late residence, 497 First st, near Md ave, on Apr 2, at 3 o'clock P M.

New Orleans, Mar 31. Brvt Brig Gen L D Watkins, colonel of the 20th infty, died suddenly of congestion of the brain on Sunday. He was a son-in-law of Gen Rousseau.

Selma, Ala, Mar 31. Judge Pope, of the 12th circuit of Alabama, was arrested yesterday at Jacksonville by the military authorities, & confined, for failure or refusal to execute the jury orders. Judge Pope was an original, & has been all the time a true Union man.

Orphans Court of Wash Co, D C. Letters of administration on the personal estate of Morven J McClery, late of Wash City, D C, dec'd. –Anna E McClery, admx

Dept of the Interior, U S Patent Ofc, Wash, Mar 21, 1868. Ptn of John Taggart, of Boston, Mass, praying for the extension of a patent granted to him Jul 4, 1854, for an improvement in Machine for Excavating Earth, for seven years from the expiration of said patent, which takes place on Jul 4, 1868. -A M Stout, Acting Com'r of Patents

Dept of the Interior, U S Patent Ofc, Wash, Mar 24, 1868. Ptn of Edw Lindner, of N Y, N Y, praying for the extension of a patent granted to him Jun 27, 1854, & reissued in two divisions Dec 23, 1856, for improvement in Magazine, Repeating, & Needle Gun, for seven years from the expiration of said patent, which takes place on Jun 27, 1868. -A M Stout, Acting Com'r of Patents

THU APR 2, 1868
Staff Ofcrs appointed: orders issued by Gen Hancock: Headquarters Military Division of the Atlantic, Wash, D C, Mar 31, 1868. 1-Brvt Lt Col W G Mitchell, capt 37th infty, aide de camp, is hereby announced as Acting Assist Adj Gen, at headquarters Military Division of the Atlantic. 2-Brvt Maj Gen S S Carroll, lt colonel 21st U S infty, is hereby announced as Acting Assist Inspector Gen of the Military Division of the Atlantic. –W G Mitchell, Brvt Lt Col U S Army, Acting Assist Adj Gen

Died: on Feb 4, 1868, at his residence, 14 High st, Holywood, county Down, Ireland, Charles O'Callaghan, youngest son of the late Jas M Fordyce, of Belfast, aged 24 years.

Died: on Wed, Enoch Edmonston, aged 19 years & 5 months, son of the late Elijah Edmonston. His funeral will be from his mother's residence, 536 Mass ave, near 4th st, on Friday afternoon, at two o'clock.

St Michael's, Talbot Co, Md, a delightful dwlg house & grounds at private sale; on the Chesapeake; the house is nearly new, newly painted, & in complete repair; has 8 rooms, kitchen, outbldgs, carriage-houses, stables; complete with one acre of ground. The property has an extensive water front on St Michael's river. Also, a number of town lots. –John Chew Gibson, M D, St Michael's, Talbot Co, Md

Dept of the Interior, U S Patent Ofc, Wash, Mar 22, 1868. Ptn of Geo Hand Smith, of Rochester, N Y, praying for the extension of a patent granted to him Jul 18, 1854, & reissued Aug 14, 1866, for an improvement in Process of Making Steel Direct from the Ore, for seven years from the expiration of said patent, which takes place on Jul 18, 1868. -A M Stout, Acting Com'r of Patents

FRI APR 3, 1868
The Senate yesterday rejected the nomination of John Hancock, the brother of Maj Gen Hancock, as collector of internal revenue for the first district of Louisiana.

For sale: 3 story brick house, 48 3rd st, between Market & Fred'k sts, Gtwn. Will give 5 years' time if desired. Inquire for key at 52 2nd st. –R W Downman, Real Estate Broker, 511 7th st.

The following is a correct list of the ofcrs of the army on duty in the dept of Wash, as also the troops under their command: Commandant, Brvt Maj Gen W H Emory.
The following are the staff ofcrs of Gen Emory:
Brvt Col J H Taylor, A A G
Brvt Brig Gen Jos Roberts, A A I G, & discharging ofcr
Brvt Maj Gen Eugene A Carr, acting judge advocate
Brvt Brig Gen J C McFerran, chief quartermaster
Brvt Col Geo Bell, chief commissary of subsistance
Brvt Col L A Edwards, Medical director
Brvt Maj M H Stacey, Brvt Lt Colonel C B Atchinson, & Brvt Capt R H Montgomery, aides-de-camp.
The following is the list of the troops & where stationed:
At **Sedgwick Barracks**, Brvt Capt R H Montgomery in command; field, staff, band, & detachment 5th U S cavalry.
At **Russell Barracks**, Brvt Maj W J L Nicodemus in command; companies A, D, E, G, H, & I, 12th infty.
At **Reynolds Barracks**, Brvt Maj H Gardner in command; 44th regt U S infty.
At **Lincoln Barracks**, Brvt Brig Gen Geo P Buell in command; companies A, B, C, G, H, & I, 29th U S infty.
At **Fort McHenry**, Md, Brvt Brig Gen H Brooks in command; companies C, D, E, & H, 4th artl.
At **Fort Washington**, Md, Brvt Col John Mendenhall in command; companies A & M, 4th artl.
At **Fort Foote**, Md, Brvt Col Richd Lodor in command, company I, 4th artl.
The garrison of Washington is under Lt Col Geo W Wallace, 12th U S infty.

The subscriber offers at private sale his Plantation, on which he now resides, containing 565 acres, more or less, in the 7th Election District of PG Co, Md; with a large frame dwlg house, recently built with all requisite out-bldgs, including tobacco houses. If not disposed of at private sale before Sat, May 2 next, it will be offered at public sale, at the store house, on the place. –Stephen Belt

Admx's sale of horses, mules, carriage, oak & pine ofc furniture; by order of the Orphans Court of Co, D C., at auction, all the personal effects of the late Lewis Thomas, dec'd, at the wood yard, corner of Md ave & 8th st west. One half of the schnr **Flounder**, her sails, tackle, & apparel, in good order & condition. –Margaret Thomas, admx
-J B Wheeler & Co, aucts

SAT APR 4, 1868
Mr Benj F Wade, the expectant President of the U S, in place of Andrew Johnson, is one of the champions of the women's rights party.

The President on Tuesday accepted the following resignations: Lt Col Fred Townsend, 9th U S infty, [brevet brig gen U S army.] Capt Jas R Brownlow, 8th cavalry. Capt John P Macy, 10th U S infty. 1st Lts Louis H Fine, David J Scott, & Egbert Olcott. 2nd Lts Wm A Clark, Porter Hooden, Earl J Rogers, John A Arthur, & Geo Darrow.

Gen Emory, cmder of the Dept of Wash, has issued the following order: Headquarters Dept of Wash, D C, Mar 31, 1868. The following assignments to duty at these headquarters are announced to take effect Apr 1, 1868: Brvt Maj Gen E A Carr, major 5th U S cavalry, as Acting Assist Inspector Gen & Discharge Ofcr. Brvt Lt Col A J McNett, capt 44th U S infty, as Acting Judge Advocate of the Dept. They will be respected accordingly. By command of Brvt Maj Gen M H Emory. –J H Taylor, Assist Adj Gen

Chas Dickens will leave N Y in the Cunard steamer **Russia**, for England, on Apr 23.

Cooper & Latimer, aucts, sold part of lot 16 in square 41, improved by a 2 story frame house, on 23rd st west, between H & I sts, to Jos McGilton, for $1,445.

Mrd: on Apr 2, at the Foundry M E Church, by Rev Mr Brown, Brvt Maj R C Parker, capt 12th U S infty, to Miss Ellen Morgan, of Wash City.

Mrd: on Mar 26, at *Oland Farm*, Stafford Co, Va, the residence of the bride's mother, by Rev Chas B Young, Geo W Sensner, U S N, of Balt, Md, to Isabella B Frazier, of Va. No cards.

Harrisburg, Pa, Apr 3. Thos Hanlon, one of the Hanlon brothers, gymnasts, was arrested here this morning for drunkenness, but was found to be insane, & was discharged. Shortly afterwards he was again arrested for attempting to murder 3 boys accompanying him, & was placed in the county prison. He attempted to commit suicide by butting his head violently & repeatedly against an iron pipe. Six men were required to secure secure him. [Apr 6th newspaper: Hanlon, the acrobat, died of his injuries this morning. His brother takes his body to N Y tonight.]

Capitol Hill Presbyterian Church: recent meeting, election of trustees: G A Bohrer, pres; D McNair, sec; J R Arrison, treasurer; Messrs Parsons, Zimmerman, Nicholson, & Lainhart. The congregation have voted an increase of the pastor's salary of $300 per annum.

Trustee's sale of a lot on north side of south C st, between 2nd & 3rd sts, at auction, by deed of trust executed by Jas Buckley, in order to secure the payment of a certain promissory note: sale on Apr 14, on the premises, part of lot 2 in square 577, said lot fronting 36 feet on south C st, running back that width 120 feet. –Dennis Blaney –Jos F Kelley, aucts

Patents issued the week ending Mar 24th, 1868, to Washingtonians: To Jearum Atkins, for a caliper; to Jas W Byrnes, for composition pavement for streets; to Chas Rowland, for a car seat.

MON APR 6, 1868
Providence, R I, Apr 5. Jas E Engly, who plead guilty to a conspriacy to rob the Union Express Co of $300,000, was yesterday sentenced to 8 months' imprisonment.

Miss Mary A Levers, of Jackson township, Wood Co, Ohio, is 12 years old, & weights 225 pounds. She is still growning.

Died: on Apr 4, Wm A Franklin, aged 35 years. His funeral will take place from his late residence, corner of 1st st east & B st north, this evening at half past 3 o'clock.

At St Vincent's Orphan Asylum, 10th & G sts, on Sat, Isabella Boyd, while cleaning a third-story window, the shutter, against which she was leaning, flew open, & the child fell to the pavement, a distance of nearly 30 feet. It was found that no bones had been broken, but whether internally injured the physician could not determine. Yesterday she was better, & will undoubtedly recover.

The Cincinnati authorities have forbidden Harry Gurr, the wonderful swimmer, to make the leap of 50 feet from the suspension bridge into the Ohio, which he had advertised to perform.

Trustee's sale of a valuable square on Boundary st between 11th & 12th sts; by decree of the Supreme Court of D C, in Chancery No 1,155, wherein Martha C Williams is cmplnt, & Custis P Upshur et al, are dfndnts: public auction on Apr 22, in front of the premises, square 302, in Wash City, containing 96, 912 square feet of ground.
–W L Dunlop, trustee -Cooper & Latimer, aucts

Orphans Court of Wash Co, D C. Letters of administration on the personal estate of Mary Sullivan, late of Wash Co, D C, dec'd. –H Duval, admx

TUE APR 7, 1868
Rev Dr M L Olds, rector of Christ Church, East Washington, has been recommended to seek the medicinal benefits of the waters of St Albans, Vt, on account of a serious complaint with which he is afflicted.

Yesterday the Associated Bricklayers of Wash City, headed by Prosperi's Band, attended the funeral of Mr Wm Kinsley, who died quite suddenly on Sat last. Mr Kinsley was well known in this city as a gentleman of intelligence, & a thorough master of his profession.

Died: on Apr 6, of congestion of the brain, Richard Suton, son of Richard S & Eliz Smith, aged 3 years, 9 months & 22 days. His funeral will be from the residence of his father, 429 E st, on Wed, at 11 o'clock. [Boston & Phil papers please copy.]

Died: on Apr 5, David Lyles, in his 30th year, formerly of Westbury, Wilts, England. His funeral will be from the residence of S S Watts, 661 Md ave, between 13½ st & 14th st, at 3 o'clock, this evening. May he rest in peace.

On Sunday, at the Arkendale fishery, owned by Messrs Beasley & Thomas, about 3 miles this side of Aquia Creek, the details of a terrible disaster were received from Mr Wm H Thomas, who was at the fishery at the time. On Sunday 13 colored men, all hailing from Washington, employed at the Arkendale fishery, were drowned while returning from the seine-boat to the shore. The boat being overloaded, the wind high, with considerable sea, the boat swamped in water 7 feet deep. [The foreman had been instructed to bring only 4 or 5 at a time; the order was not heeded.] The men who lost their lives were good men. They were Geo Thompson, alias Mulligan, Jeff Butler, Jos Bulger, John Fitzhugh, Robt Hollon, Wm Ware, Jas Thompson, John Mason, Cornelius Clayton, Jas Thomas, Jas Bell, Lewis Magruder, & Jas Starks. Nearly all these men have families in this city, & resided in the 7th Ward. Measures will be taken to provide for the destitute wives & children of these unfortunate men.

For sale: lot of ground on Wash st, Gtwn, D C, 120 feet with a dept of 90 feet on Dunbarton st. This is one of the most desirable bldg lots in Gtwn, & is capable of division into 4 good bldg lots. Apply to Wm D Cassin, Atty for owner.

Orphans Court-Judge Purcell, Apr 4, 1868. 1-The will of the late Edw Walsh, bequeathing his property to his wife, was filed & partially proven. 2-Letters testamentary were granted to E M Thurston on the estate of Mary Ann Brown, late of Rhode Island; bond $1,000. 3-First distribution of the personal estate of Jos Libbey, by Louisa Libbey, admx, filed. Second account of Louisa Libbey, admx of Jos Libbey, dec'd, filed & passed. 4-Distribution of the personal estate of Matilda S Holmead, by Chas A James, exc, filed. First & final account of Chas A James, exc of Matilda S Holmead, filed & passed. 5-Second account of R T Morsell, adm of Ann E Beall, filed & passed. 6-Hannah Duval gave bond in the sum of $3,000 as admx of Mary Sullivan, dec'd. Jas Ragan & Owen Libby sureties. 7-B B Gallaher gave bond in the sum of $350 as adm of Jos Gibbings. J S Gallaher & F A Gallaher, sureties. 8-Fred Spindler gave bond in the sum of $500, as adm of Catharine Goldschmidt. August & Andrew Gross, sureties.

For sale: choice suburban property; 4th st, north of & adjoining Columbian College grounds, & opposite the Stone estate. Lt Gen Sherman & Senator Sherman each have acre lots, with a view to make handsome improvements. Horse railroad cars will run by, as the track is to be laid during the summer. Plat, price, terms, etc, at our office.
–Kilbourn & Latta

Died: on Sunday, John Bainbridge Henry, son of the late John B & Nancy Douglas Henry, of Jefferson Co, Va.

Denver city papers announce that Rynderson, a member of the New Mexico Legislature, who killed Chief Justice Slough in that Territory last fall, has been acquitted.

Literary entertainment. Mrs Cornelia D Mitchell will give Recitations & Readings at Odd Fellow' Hall, on Thu next, at 8 o'clock. Voice & instrumental music by Mrs Lizzie Pope & Miss Jennie Pugh. Tickets to be had at Ballantyne's & Shepherd's Book Stores.

WED APR 8, 1868
Montreal, C E, Apr 7. This morning news was received from Ottawa, relative to Hon Thos D'Arcy McGee, who was shot dead on the steps of his residence. He had just left the House, with other members, & about to unlock the door of his residence, when he was shot from behind & instantly killed. The assassin was so close that the hair of McGee's head was burned by the flash from the pistol which killed him. Rewards for the arrest of the assassin. [His brother, Jas E McGee, is a resident of N Y C; he left for Montreal last evening.] [Apr 9th newspaper: Ottawa, Canada, Apr 8. Two men, named Whelan & Doyle, were arrested last night on suspicion of having been concerned in the murder of D'Arcy McGee. The suspicions against them are very strong. The body of McGee was this morning conveyed to the Roman Catholic Cathedral, where the funeral services were performed, after which the remains were sent by a special train to Montreal, attended by the members of the Cabinet & other distinguished men as pall-bearers. The cause of the assassination is generally attributed to Fenianism, which Mr McGee had done so much to expose in Canada. The family of Mr McGee will be amply provided for by the Gov't.] [Apr 24th newspaper: Iran Baptist La Croix, who says he saw the shot fired which killed D'Acy McGee, has been subjected to a searching cross examination as to the facts, & his testimony remains unshaken. He has seen Whalen in jail & identifies him. La Croix is an ignorant Frenchman, but he tells a straightforward & connected story.]

On May 6, 1856, Benj C Grenup, a member of the Columbia Engine Co, was killed while proceeding to a fire. His death was caused by being run over by the "suction," while passing down Capitol Hill. He was a young man universally beloved by his associates, & in his memory they have erected over his grave in **Glenwood Cemetery**, a very beautifully designed monument, which will be dedicated on the anniversary day of the sad accident. The monument has on one side a striking representation of the accident, & was designed by an Italian artist, Galfardi, who commenced the work, but, returning to Italy, it was completed by Mr Chas Rosseau, of Wash City. The work cost the company $3,000.

Count De Waldeck, an artist in Paris, is 102 years old, & is still painting.

London, Apr 7. The assassination of Flores, Pres of Uruguay, is confirmed. He was murdered in Montevideo shortly after his return from the allied camp on the Rio Parano.

Special sale of elegant estate: ***Strawberry Hill***, adjoining the U S Naval Academy, at Annapolis, on the Severn River, 240 acres, at public auction, on Apr 23 next. The improvements are very extensive, & would now cost over $25,000.
—F W Bennett & Co, aucts

U S Marshal's sale, Apr 28, all the dfndnt's right, title, claim, & interest in & to the southern part of lot 10 in square 583, fronting 29 feet 9 inches on 3rd st, running back said width 92 feet, with improvements thereon, in Wash City, seized & levied upon as the property of John Howett, & will be sold to satisfy execution No 4,255, in favor of S L Morrison & John L Shaw, use of D L Morrison. —David S Gooding, U S Marshal D C

Dept of the Interior, U S Patent Ofc, Wash, Apr 1, 1868. Ptn of Jonathan Ball, of Elmira, N Y, praying for the extension of a patent granted to him Jul 11, 1854, for an improvement in Mode of Connecting Water-pipes, for seven years from the expiration of said patent, which takes place on Jul 11, 1868. -A M Stout, Acting Com'r of Patents

Orphans Court of Wash Co, D C, Mar 14, 1868. In the case of Marian E C King, admx of Henry King, dec'd, the administratrix & Court have appointed Apr 11 next, for the final settlement of the personal estate of the said dec'd, of the assets in hand.
-Jas R O'Beirne, Reg/o wills

Office of ***Glenwood Cemetery***, Wash, D C, Mar 30, 1868. On & after Sep 29 this office will be removed to the entrance of the Cemetery at the head of North Capitol st.
-G Clendenin, Superintendent

THU APR 9, 1868
Drowned, on Apr 5, at Arkandale Landing, Va, Chas B Butler. His funeral will take place this evening at 3 P M.

Equity Court-Judge Olin. 1-Curtis et al vs Smoot: appointed Jedediah H Lathrop trustee to sell. 2-Kobb vs Kobb: divorce a vinculo matrimonii. 3-Bogan vs Varnell et al: appointing W F Mattingly trustee to release. 4-Swain vs Swain: appointing R T Morsell trustee to sell.

Indianapolis, Ind, Apr 8. 1-A man named Timothy Murphy was accidentally killed on the Bellefontaine railroad yesterday. 2-Two young men, named Leach & Lindsay, fought a duel at Keekomo yesterday. After exchanging two shots their friends interfered, & the affair was settled. Neither party was injured.

Cardinal Bonaparte's new title is Saint Puderitius.

The death of Phineas H Young, son of Brigham Young, is announced by Salt Lake city papers. He was an excellent painter, it is reported, & aged only 20 years.

Trustee's sale of valuable real estate; by decree of the Circuit Court for PG Co, Md, in Equity, in the case of Thos A L Mitchell vs Henry W Darnall & wife; public sale on Apr 30 next, on the premises, near the residence of Mr Richd N Darnall about 2 miles from the village of Bladensburg, parcel of land No 4, 58½ acres, which was allotted to the said Henry W Darnall by com'rs appointed by said court to divide the real estate of Francis L Darnall, dec'd. –N C Stephen, trustee

Executor's sale of Corp stock, Chesapeake & Ohio Canal money, gold watches & diamonds at public auction, on Apr 13; belonging to the estate of the late Andrew Small. Terms cash. –John A Ruff, exc -Green & Williams, aucts, 526 7th st.

Dept of the Interior, U S Patent Ofc, Wash, Apr 2, 1868. Ptn of Geo A Leighton, of Lawrence, Mass, praying for the extension of a patent granted to him Jul 11, 1854, for an improvement in Sewing Machines, for seven years from the expiration of said patent, which takes place on Jul 11, 1868. -A M Stout, Acting Com'r of Patents

Chancery sale of valuable real estate at 14th & K sts, opposite Franklin Square, known as The ***Rugby House***; by decree of the Supreme Court of D C, in which Curtis & others were cmplnts, & Smoot dfndnt, Equity No 1,190; public auction on May 11 next, on the premises, part of square 248, being lots 21 & 22, known as The ***Rugby House*** property, fronting 51 feet 8 inches on K st, running back of that width 147 feet to a 30 foot alley; improved by a 4 story double brick house. –J H Lathrop, trustee
-Cooper & Latimer, aucts

FRI APR 10, 1868
Boston, Apr 8. Mr Chas Dickens gave his final reading in Boston this evening, in Tremont Temple, before one of the largest & most cultivated audiences that ever greeted him in this country. He read "Dr Marigold" & "Sairey Gamp," with a spirit & life, showing that he felt the magnetic charm of the friendly faces around him. He was again & again greeted with applause.

Economical Bldg Assoc: election of ofcrs: Geo H Plant, pres; N W Burchell, vice pres; H A Willard, J W Barker, John P Hilton, W S Thompson, H C Gill, & D Wesley Middleton, directors; N Callan, treasurer; C Storrs, atty, & Fred Koontz, sec.

The residence of Mr O'Hare, at Linden Grove, [known also as ***Shepherd place***,] about 4 miles from Wash City, was totally destroyed by fire on Wed. The fire caught from the chimney; loss is estimated at about $5,000. Messrs Taylor & Bell, connected with the Treasury Dept, who had just gone out to spend the season, lost most of their wardrobe & books.

St Louis, Apr 9. On Mar 23 Mr Worrell & party escaped to Indian Spring ranche, & the entire party started for Cottonwood ranche, & were attacked by 60 Indians, & after a long fight ensued, Hooper, David Dumpter, & another man, [name unknown,] were killed.

Equity Court-Judge Olin. 1-Morrison vs Harris et al: order appointing guardian ad litem for Wm Jenkins.

Chicago, Apr 9. The side-wheel steamer **Sea Bird**, belonging to the Goodrich line, which left Milwaukie last night, was burned off Waukegan this morning. Vessel & cargo a total loss. It is supposed that all on board were lost. The vessel was valued at $70,000; no insurance. [Apr 11th newspaper: About 100 persons on board, including 8 or 10 ladies & 7 or 8 children. From the statement of one of the persons rescued it appears that all on board became demoralized, even the ofcrs, & no effort was made to lower the small boats. The only survivors, as far as known, are C A Chamberlain & Edwin Hannebury, passengers from the ship **Sheboygan**. Chamberlain states that he was looking over the side of the steamer, & saw a porter come out of the ladies' cabin with a scuttle of coal & ashes, & going to the bulwarks, near where a quantity of miscellaneous freight was stored, he threw the contents overboard. In about a quarter of an hour he heard an alarm of fire & saw flames issuing from this pile of freight. Capt Yates, of the schnr **Cordelia**, states that when off Waukegan he saw a burning steamer, was distant from her 4 or 5 miles; bore down to her & recused 2 passengers in the water. The following are the names of those on board, as far as ascertained: G B Davidson, Robt Scott, Geo Nieman, Thos Carpenter, Peter Sullivan, G A Goss, L Lincoln, Edwin Neighbor, H Comstock, Rome, N Y; Geo W Emery, & S C Watkins, clerk. Ofcrs: Capt, John Louis; first mate, Richd Hocklin; 1st engineer, Thos Honchen; clerk, Jas Hodges; steward, John Morrison. Crew: M Morrisey, M Malone, John Glennon, Jason & Jas Rourke, & J Burns, cook & assistant; H Simpson & J Brennan, cabin boys. The following embarked at Sheboygan: H A Gaylord & wife, W G Mallory, Mrs E E Sharpe, John O'Brien, T Stein, D C Daggett, Edwin Hunneburg, L Packard, Dr L Bock, Edw Proomskall, Henry Uilrich Glenubuth, A C Chamberlain & Mrs S C Sprague, both of Sheboygan Falls; O Perry, of Detroit; M Gallagher, of Xenia, Ohio; Mr Roeper/R_eper & wife, & J M Leonard, of Chicago; F Lester, wife & children, & 2 travelling agents, names unknown.]

Selma, Ala, Apr 9. This evening John P Howard, a one armed ex-Confederate soldier, was shot from his horse & instantly killed, about 4 miles from this city, on the Burnsville road. The assassin has not been apprehended. This is the 5th white man murdered since the war, in the immediate vicinity.

Mrd:Apr 8, by Rev Benj F Ball, Geo F Reeves, of N Y, to Emily W Wells, of Wash, D C.

Columbus, Ga, Sunday. Our community was painfully startled on Tuesday by the announcement that the notorious G W Ashburn had been killed on the previous night. Almost a year ago, upon the advent of the present military garrison, this mischievous emissary of the Radical faction made his appearance in our city, with the openly-avowed determination to commence an active crusade against the white people of the State of Ga.

The funeral of Gen Orlow Smith, in Edford, Henry Co, Ill, on Mar 22, was attended by over 1,200 persons in 200 vehicles, the procession being over 2 miles long. He was colonel of the 65th Ohio infty, & received wounds at Chickamauga & Franklin.

Notice to Jas Campbell & Wm Campbell, or if they be dead, then to their descendants: you are required to attend at my ofc, in Staunton, Va, on or before Jun 1, 1868, prepared then & there to assert & establish your claims to distribution in the estate of Nancy Carroll, dec'd, late of said town of Staunton, who some time since departed this life, intestate & without issue. By order of the Circuit Court of Augusta Co, Va.
-J N Hendren, Com'r of said court

By deed of trust executed to me, as trustee, by Martha Washington on Jul 25, 1867, recorded on Dec 27, 1867, in Liber E C E No 25, ofc of Register of Deeds & Land Records of D C, to secure payment of certain indebtedness in said deed described, I will sell in front of the Auction-room of J T Coldwell & Co, Pa ave & 4½ st, at public outcry, for cash, on Apr 20, all the right, title, interest, or estate of said Martha Washington in & to all these pieces or lots of ground in said city, known as lots 14 & 15, in John Van Riswick's subdivision of square 471, being the same lots of ground which were conveyed to J C Shelan by J Van Riswick & wife by deed dated Dec 1, 1864, subject to a reservation-contained in deed of said Shelan to Wm Washington & Martha Washington, to date Nov 28, 1806, & recorded in the Ofc of the Register of Deeds & Land Records in said District; of a framed house & lot of ground therewith, fronting 20 feet, & running back 24 feet, at L st & an alley, between 6th & 7th sts. –M J Saffold, trustee
-J T Coldwell & Co, aucts

Dept of the Interior, U S Patent Ofc, Wash, Apr 4, 1868. Ptn of Henry Outcalt, of Wilmington, Ohio, praying for the extension of a patent granted him Jul 11, 1854, for an improvement in Mode of Contructing Metallic Roofing, for 7 years from the expiration of said patent, which takes place on Jul 11, 1868. -A M Stout, Acting Com'r of Patents

SAT APR 11, 1868
For sale: ten burial sites in ***Congressional Burying Ground***, very eligibly situated adjoining the grounds of B F Middleton, & fronting the principal ave. Price, $5 gold per size, or $50 gold. Apply at Wall & Co's, aucts.

Died: on Apr 10, Good Friday, Eleanor, wife of Peter Conlan, aged 67 years. Her funeral will take place from her late residence, corner of 3rd & G sts, on Apr 13, at 9:30 o'clock A M, to proceed to St Aloysius Church, when a solemn mass will be offered up for the repose of her soul. [Herald, Star, Express]

Died: on Apr 9, Julia R, beloved wife of Dr J C R Clark, in her 28th year. Her funeral will be on Apr 12 at 3 o'clock P M, from her late residence, 292 Delaware ave.

Died: on Apr 9, Mrs Ann A Kervand, widow of the late Lazar Kervand. Her funeral will take place from St Alban's Church, on Apr 11, at 2:30 P M.

Chancery sale of improved property at the Navy Yard; by decree of the Supreme Court of D C, passed on Apr 8, 1868, in Chancery, Mary V Swain vs Mary A Swain et al; public auction on Apr 23, of the original lot 18 in square 977, in Wash City, with a good two story frame house; fronts 45 feet 4 inches on M st south, between 10th & 11th sts, & extends back to a 30 foot public alley. –R T Morsell, trustee -Cooper & Latimer, aucts

Handsome elegant furniture & accessories at public auction on Apr 23, at houses 391 & 393 G st, between 3rd & 4½ sts, lately occupied by J E Bliss, dec'd.
-Green & Williams, aucts

Supreme Court of D C, in Equity No 1,117. Jas L Barbour et al vs Catharine Morgan et al. The creditors & others interested are to appear on Apr 15: report of the amount of indebtedness of Bernard Morgan, dec'd, the names of the creditors, & the sufficiency or insufficiency of the personal estate of the dec'd. –Walter S Cox, auditor

MON APR 13, 1868
Orphans Court of Wash Co, D C, Apr 11, 1868. In the case of Ursula Corcoran, admx of John L Corcoran, dec'd, the administratrix & Court have appointed Mar 9 next, for the final settlement of the personal estate of the said dec'd, of the assets in hand.
-Jas R O'Beirne, Reg/o wills

Dept of the Interior, U S Patent Ofc, Wash, Apr 8, 1868. Ptn of Collins B Brown, of Upper ____, Ill, praying for the extension of a patent granted to him Jul 11, 1854, for an improvement in Harvester Rakes, for seven years from the expiration of said patent, which takes place on Jul 11, 1868. -A M Stout, Acting Com'r of Patents

Mrd: on Apr 8, in Portland, Maine, by Rev John T G Nichols, of Saco, assisted by Rev B H Bailey, of Portland, Everett F Throop, of Cincinnati, Ohio, to Mary J C Abbot, eldest daughter of Geo J Abbott, U S Consul at Sheffield, England.

Died: on Apr 11, Jennie D, daughter of the late Thos Brown. Her funeral will take place at 3 o'clock this evening, from the residence of her mother near Rock Creek Church.

TUE APR 14, 1868
Hon Jas Guthrie was stricken with paralysis at Louisville, Ky, on Thursday last, & serious fears of the result are entertained by his family & friends.

Dept of the Interior, U S Patent Ofc, Wash, Apr 8, 1868. Ptn of Albert S Southworth, of Boston, Mass, praying for the extension of a patent granted to him Apr 10, 1855, & reissued Sep 25, 1860, for an improvement in Plate Holder for Cameras for seven years from the expiration of said patent, which takes place on Apr 10, 1869.
-A M Stout, Acting Com'r of Patents

Died: on Apr 11, at Langley, Va, Angelique Lesiardi, wife of Henry Johnson, in her 64th year.

Chancery sale of valuable improved real estate near 14th st west fronting almost directly on Pa ave; by decree of the Supreme Court of D C, in Chancery No 1,048; Stoneman et al vs Hardesty et al; public auction on May 6 next, on the premises, the real estate which was of the late Cornelius McLean, dec'd, being parts of lots 7 & 8 in square 254, in Wash City, which has been divided into two parts, improved by a brick bldg. The second lot is improved by a brick bldg now occupied by P Venneren as a hotel & restaurant.
-Geo H Williams, trustee -Cooper & Latimer, aucts

WED APR 15, 1868
The following confirmations were made by the Senate yesterday:
Robt A Marmion, of West Va, to be assist surgeon in the navy.
2nd Assist Engineers H D McEven & David Jones, to be 1st engineers.
3rd Assist Engineers R D Taylor & C F Nagle, to be 2nd assist engineers.
Cmdor John Lanman, to be rear admiral on active list from Dec 8, 1867.
Maj Chas G McCawley, to be lt colonel in Marine Corpsl
Wm S Weiles, of N J, to be assist surgeon in the navy.
Portias P Bielby, of N Y, to be assist surgeon in the navy.
Porter A Cullom, to be assist surgeon in the navy.
Alex'r Spaulding, to be Collector of Internal Revenue for the 8th Dist of N Y.
Killian V Whaley, to be Collector of Customs for the Dist of Brazos de Santiago, Texas.

Annual election of vestrymen for Trinity [P E] Church, 3rd & C sts: chosen-Wm M Morrison, Theodore E Ebaugh, H I Alvord, & Thos L Moore, who, with Maj J C Cash, John H Semmes, John P Franklin, & A Baldwin, members of the old board, constitute the vestry for the ensuing year. The wardens of the church are Messrs D W Middleton & Wm B Todd. At the Church of Ascension, [Rev Dr Pinckney,] the following were elected for the ensuing year: J B Dodson, H S Davis, N W Burchell, Judge Chas Mason, Henry Reynolds, W M Shuster, C B Baker, & J T Stewart. Mr John Duncanson was re-elected register.

Lotts, the young comedienne, is engaged to be married, it is said. Her full name is Charlotte Crabtree.

Mr Dickens is said to have sent home $80,000 in gold, as part of his profits.

C M Norton, colored, is a candidate for Congress from the 1st district of Va.

Dr Gurley, pastor of the N Y ave church, sails for Calif next week on account of his health. The pulpit will be filled during his absence by Rev Mr Reed, of Ohio. Rev R W Lowrie, of the Church of the Incarnation, returned to the city on Sat last, after a brief sojourn in Fla, whither he went for the benefit of his health.

Richmond, Apr 14. Gen Schofield today appointed Wm M Berkeley Mayor of Alexandria, & a full set of city ofcrs & Councilmen for that city. He also appointed a new City Council for Fredericksburg.

Orphans Court-Judge Purcell. 1-First & final account of Marcellus Morrice, adm of Thaddeus Morrice, filed & passed. 2-Distribution account of the personal estate of Henry King, by Marian King, admx. 3-The will of Saml Harrington Raybold was filed. The testator gives all his estate to his wife, Ann E Raybold, with the exception of $6,000 to his aunt, Harriet R Palmer. He appoints Hon Geo P Fisher exc. 4-The will of Jane S Burrass was filed for probate. The testatrix bequeaths all her estate to Isabella S Turpin, & names her sole excx. 5-The will of Ann E Kervand was filed for probate. The testatrix names her son Jas L Kervand as exc. 6-*In re*. Estate of Jacob Lowenthal, dec'd. The exception heretofore filed to the returns made by the executor of said deed, & to certain claims filed against said estate. This cause being heard, it was ordered that the return of the executor, under oath, is admitted as evidence, & the Register of Wills is hereby ordered to state the account of said executor, & to make a pro rata distribution to creditors, it being shown that the estate at present is insufficient to pay all debts. The Court is further of opinion that the sums of money given to the wife of said deceased in the lifetime of the testator is not chargeable against the executor in this procedure. It was further ordered that the exceptions filed to the claims of the Nat'l Bank of the Metropolis are overruled; also, the exceptions filed on Apr 11, by executor of said dec'd, through his attys, Chipman & Co, to the claims of Natalie Myerson, A G Ridder, Dr Hansmann, & T H Ford. 7-*In re*. Estate of Sarah Edelin, dec'd, & the ptn of Mary J Harris, T J Edelin, & E C Carrington, collector, for letters of administration of said estate, heretofore filed, & to which a demurrer was filed on Apr 11, by C H Winder, as next friend of Mary L Black. In this cause it is ordered that the demurrer be sustained, & that no administration be granted until the appeal prayed & awarded by the Supreme Court of D C be decided.

Notice. Being unable to carry on my business in consequence of continued ill-health, I shall offer my entire Stock of Goods at auction on May 4 next. Fine Family Groceries, Liquors, Wines, etc. –Richd J Ryon, 481 9th st.

Chancery sale of valuable property in Wash City; by decree of the late Circuit Court of D C, & of the Supreme Court of D C, in a cause between John R Woods & others against Richd G Briscoe, heirs & others, in Equity, No 1,117; sale on May 8, on the premises, of part of lot 9 in square 382, fronting on 9th st, between the canal & La ave, with a 3 story brick bldg. South third of lot 11 in square 408, fronting on 8th st, between D & Market Space, with a 3 story brick bldg. –Wm R Woodward, trustee -Green & Williams, aucts

Gettysburg, Pa, Apr 14. Rev H L Baugher, D D, Pres of Pa College, died this evening. He has been connected with the college since its erection, & has been president 18 years.

Moses Febrey, contemplating a change of business, will offer at public sale, on Apr 25, his Farm, in Alexandria Co, Va, containing 88 acres, more or less, 5 miles from Washington. Improvements consist of a 2 story frame dwlg house of 6 rooms, with outhouses. –Fitch & Fox, aucts

The Academy of Sciences of Paris has elected Sir Roderick Murchison as Foreign Associate, in place of the late Mr Faraday.

Orphans Court of Wash Co, D C, Feb 18, 1868. In the case of Bridget Cullinane & Patrick Cullinane, adms of Michl Cullinane, dec'd, the administrators & Court have appointed May 12th next, for the final settlement of the personal estate of the said dec'd, of the assets in hand. -Jas R O'Beirne, Reg/o wills

Dept of the Interior, U S Patent Ofc, Wash, Apr 9, 1868. Ptn of Hymen L Lipman, of Phil, Pa, praying for the extension of a patent granted to him Jul 11, 1854, for an improvment in Eyelet Machines, for seven years from the expiration of said patent, which takes place on Jul 11, 1868. -A M Stout, Acting Com'r of Patents

Mr Wm Wheatley, the actor & theatrical manager, has sold out his interest in Niblo's Theatre, N Y, to Jarret & Palmer, his partners, for $100,000. He intends to retire from business altogether. The arrangement to date from Sept next.

THU APR 16, 1868

Washington: Abraham Lincoln Monument was dedicated yesterday; the monument is 38 feet in height, to the top of the statue; it rests on a solid foundation of blue rock, 6 feet in depth; the base is an octagon, 6 feet in height, & about 7 feet from side to side. It represents Lincoln standing with his left hand resting on the emblem of Union, the Roman Facii, his head erect, with a slight inclination forward, & right hand partially open, as in the attitude he was wont to take in addressing an audience. The design was first made in clay by Mr Flannery last summer, & was subsequently cast in plaster. Mr Lot Flannery, the designer of the monument & the scupltor of the statue, is a young man of 27 years; since his boyhood he has resided in Wash City, which he claims as his home. Mr Flannery has achieved a number of successes of art, among which is the admired monument over the victims of the arsenal explosion, at the *Congressional Cemetery*. The site selected for the monument, is exactly in the centre of 4½ st, & directly in front of the central portico of the City Hall.

Chancery sale of valuable real estate; by decree of the Supreme Court of D C, passed on Oct 7, 1867, in Equity No 920, in which Margaret A Eckels & Lewis G Eckels are cmplnts, & Catharine Barret et al are dfndnts, we will sell, at public auction, on May 11 next, lot 16 in square 836, on 6th st, between D & E sts, with a frame dwlg house. And by decree of the same Court passed on Apr 14, 1868, in Equity No 1,105, between the same parties, we will sell at public auction, May 11, lots 3 & 5 in square 836; said lot 3 fronting on D st, with a good frame house; & said lot 5 fronting on 5th st, with a frame bldg. -M Thompson, R S Davis, trustees -Green & Williams, aucts

Dept of the Interior, U S Patent Ofc, Wash, Apr 10, 1868. Ptn of Rebecca R Gillett, admx of the estate of Thos W Gillett, dec'd, of Chicago, Ill, praying for the extension of a patent granted to John Matthews, as assignee of the said Thos W Gillett, Jul 11, 1854, for an improvement in Apparatus for Corking Bottles, praying for the extension of a patent granted to him, which takes place on Jul 11, 1868. -A M Stout, Acting Com'r of Patents

N Y, Apr 15. Terrible disaster this morning 16 miles west of Port Jervis, on the Erie railroad; cars were thrown off the track by the breaking of a rail, down an embankment 20 feet. List of the casualties: <u>Killed</u>: Ephraim Hoyt & wife, of Vanango Forks, N Y; Mary E Cobb, of Hornellsville, N Y; Enos Blossom, Susquehanna Depot; a child of Mrs Tisdell, of Ithica, N Y; H B Corwin, supposed to be of Urbana, Ohio; J S Dunham, of Binghampton, N Y; C K Loomis, of Buffalo; Eli Knapp, of Jamestown, N Y; Thos Burrington, of N Y C; an unknown man, woman, & boy. <u>Wounded</u>: Henry Hention, of Danville, N Y, legs broken; S B Foreman, of Elmira, N Y; C W Harris, of Cochran, Ind; Lewis Barker, of Bates, N Y, in the head; S W Horton, of Salem, Wisc, in side & head; S P Snow, of Bleaksburg, Iowa, head & breast; Tobias Aldrige, head; G W Baker, Ithica, N Y, shoulder; G G Lapham, of Syracuse, N Y, back & head; Mrs C R Beardsley, Hudson City; G Hartman, Hudson City, N J; C V Tiffany, Danville, N Y, badly injured; A L Oliver, N Y C, leg broken; A L Smith, of Hornellsville, N Y, badly injured; Mrs C C Reynolds, of Hornellsville, N Y, badly injured; Rogers Corning, of N Y; W Hodge Corning, of N Y; W P Decker, of Waverly, N Y; A Palmer, of Ripley, N Y, internally injured; L J Fitzgerald, N Y C; A T Kingsley, of Portland, N Y; M Goodman, of Buffalo; S Sweet, of Middletown, N J; J Heenan, of Louisville, Ky, badly injured; M R Reay, of Middletown, N Y; J Henderson, of Rome, Ohio, badly injured; J B Alsier, of Rome, Ohio, badly injured; J B Alsier, a boy, of Cincinnati, Ohio; E R Newton, of Corry, Pa, badly injured; N W Galsey, of Addison, N Y; A T Gilbert & wife, of Mercer, Pa, badly injured; Mary Stewart, of Mercer, Pa, badly injured; J S Ramsey, of St John's City, mashing in the back & head; A Cleaver, of N Y C; 3 children of S P Snow, all seriously injured; C R Moncrieff, of N Y C, badly injured; D Lyons, of Binghamton, N Y, internally injured; D Lyons, of Binghamton, N Y, internally injured; J B Florid, of Chenang, N Y, badly burned; A S Bigelow, a boy, of Ithica, N Y; Mr Gunther, of N Y, badly injured; Geo Furnace, of the Metropolitan Hotel of N Y C, badly wounded; Misses Maggie & Emma Hoyt were both badly hurt, & their father & mother killed; D B Steens, of Cayuga, N Y; Mrs H Bailey, of Longville, Ohio; I T A Jewett, of N Y C; J Decker, of Elmira, N Y; C C Donahue, Buffalo, N Y; Austin Woodruff, Randolph, N Y; J Dubois, a boy; an unknown woman, who has a baggage check numbered 506; C W Douglass, division superintendent, badly hurt; Fairman Spencer, a partner in the Elmira Advertiser; Henry Hanlin, of Danville, N Y, leg broken; & G M Harris, of Indiana.

Mrd: on Apr 14, at Ryland Chapel, [M E Church,] by Rev J N Coombs, Mr Hugh S McLeod to Miss Alice E Adams, both of Wash City. [San Francisco Bulletin please copy.]

Died: on Wed, after a short illness, Mrs Mary Anatasia Eckloff, wife of Christian A Eckloff, in her 22nd year. Her funeral will be on Apr 17 in the morning, from the residence of her mother, 492 Mass ave, to proceed thence to St Aloysius Church, where the funeral service will take place.

Sale of fine first-class residence on Gtwn Heights, on the n w corner of High & 8th sts, adjoining the grounds of Col Kurtz, & opposite the residence of T C Cox. Apply to Chas M Matthews, 51 Congress st, Gtwn, D C.

FRI APR 17, 1868
Appointment of Municipal ofcrs for Alexandria & Fredericksburg. The following appointments were made by Gen Schofield on Tuesday. Alexandria: Mayor, Wm N Berkeley, vice Latham; Auditor, T A Stoutenburgh, vice Hurdle; Corp Atty, S Fergusson Beach, vice Smoot; Gauger of Casks, etc, Isaac Lovejoy, vice McClish, resigned; Inspectors of Lumber, E S Boynton, vice McNight, & W E Howard, vice Vincent; Collector, J C O'Neill, vice Fossett; Assessor, P G Henderson, vice Campbell; Surveyor, Robt Bell, vice Ficklin; Chief Engineer of Fire Dept, Ed Hughes, vice Kell; Superintendent of Gas, Geo C Hughes, vice McKnight; Aldermen, L D Harman, Jas L Dyson, John C Clark, Robt Bell, sr; Common Council, Lewis McKenzie, Anthony Moran, Lewis Stern, David Turner, W D Massey, Jas M Stewart, E White, Wm Arnold; Inspector of Flour, L D Anthony. Fredericksburg: Common Councilmen: G W Eve, vice Thos F Knox; L C Frost, vice Jas H Bradley; L C Beardsley, vice Jas McGuire; D E Ellis, vice E M Braxton; C E Hunter, vice Jas W Ford; Wm C Morrison, vice Geo W Wroten; Wm Jefferies, vice Jos W Sener; P Couse, vice John J Young.

N Y, Apr 16. Wm C Forbes, a well-known theatrical manager, formerly of Charleston & other Southern cities, died on Tuesday last at his residence in Brooklyn.

For rent: in Gtwn, large 3 story brick dwlg, with extensive back bldg, 58 High st, containing 19 rooms; for rent about June 1. Apply on the premises. –Eliza M Mosher

Dept of the Interior, U S Patent Ofc, Wash, Apr 11, 1868. Ptn of Lavinia L Bartlett, admx of the estate of Russell D Bartlett, dec'd, of Bangor, Maine, praying for the extension of a patent granted to said Russell D Bartlett Jul 11, 1854, for an improvement in Machine for Making the Heads of Shovel Handles, for seven years from the expiration of said patent, which takes place on Jul 11, 1868. -A M Stout, Acting Com'r of Patents

SAT APR 18, 1868
Saml M McKean, who departed this life at his residence in Wash City on Feb 8, 1868, was 78 years of age. He was a native of Pa, his ancestors having been among the earliest colonists of that State, & associated most conspicuously in its public history. His Grandfather, Thos McKean, was one of the signers of the Declaration of American Independence, & Govn'r of the State, & his father, Jos B McKean, having been one of the judges of the Supreme Court of the State. Mr McKean was in public service till the close of his life.

Mrd: on Apr 16, in St John's Church, Gtwn, by Rev O Perinchief, Lt E N Chester, 4th artl, U S army, of Buffalo, N Y, to Bessie, daughter of A H Dodge, of Gtwn.

Died: on Apr 16, Mrs Margaret Deeble, wife of Edw Deeble, in her 82nd year. Her funeral will be from the residence of her husband, 428 G st, between 9th & 10th sts, this morning, at 11 o'clock.

Died: on Apr 16, Chas Demonet, [confectioner,] aged 57 years. His funeral will be from his late residence, 173 Pa ave, between 17th & 18th sts, on Sunday, Apr 19, at 1:30 P M.

Hon Jas Guthrie, who was stricken with paralysis at Louisville, on Thursday, was pronounced decidedly better by his physicians on Saturday.

Jas H Leonard, whose alleged escape from the wreck of the steamer **Sea Bird** constituted a thrilling chapter in that tragedy, is believed to be an impostor. He is not recognized by any known survivors, & his stories are very contradictory. His attempt to start a contribution in his own behalf has strengthened suspicions. It is thought he purposely threw himself into the lake, & appeared with ice upon his garments in order to aid his deceptions.

Supreme Court of D C, Apr 17, 1868; Equity No 1,260. Mary C Rupley, cmplnt, vs Chas J Rupley, dfndnt. It is ordered that the dfndnt appear on or before the first rule day, occurring 40 days after this day; otherwise the cause will be proceeded with as in case of default. –R J Meigs

Trustee's sale of to beautifully located bldg sites, each containing between 5 & 6 acres; on the road leading to the **Soldiers' Home** & Rock Creek Church; by decree of the Supreme Court of D C, in Chancery No 1,044, substituting me as trustee, I shall sell, at public auction, on the premises, two lots of ground in Wash Co, D C, the same being part of **Turkey Thicket**. It is near the lands of Messrs E J Middleton, Henry Queen, & Conway Robinson. –W Y Fendall, trustee -J T Coldwell & Co, aucts

U S Marshal's sale on May 7 next, all Wm Bowen's right, title, claim, & interest in & to that part of lot 1 in square 529, at 3rd & G st, with improvements; seized & levied upon as the property of Wm Bowen & will be sold to satisfy execution No 3,968, in favor of Fred'k G Bletz. –D S Gooding, U S Marshal, D C

Dept of the Interior, U S Patent Ofc, Wash, Apr 11, 1868. Ptn of R H Garrigues, adm of the estate of L A Dole, dec'd, of Salem, Ohio, praying for the extension of a patent granted to him said L A Dole Jul 25, 1854, for an improvement in Arrangement for Lathe Chuck, for seven years from the expiration of said patent, which takes place on Jul 25, 1868. -A M Stout, Acting Com'r of Patents

Dept of the Interior, U S Patent Ofc, Wash, Apr 11, 1868. Ptn of Wm S Chapman, of Wilmington, Dela, praying for the extension of a patent granted to him Aug 8, 1854, for an improvement in Preventing Rattling in Carriages, for seven years from the expiration of said patent, which takes place on Aug 8, 1868. -A M Stout, Acting Com'r of Patents

MON APR 20, 1868
On Apr 16, during a heavy thunder shower, Rev John B McKinnon, a young Presbyterian minister, & Mr Lauchlin McLaurin, of Laurinburg, Richmond Co, N C, were instantly killed by lightning.

Maj L Engle, express messenger of the Merchant's Union, on Fri night, was pushed against a hot stove in his car, on the N Y Central Railroad, by a falling box, & was unable to extricate himself. His cries were not heard until the train was stopped, 10 some minutes later, & when taken out he was found severely burned. It is doubtful if he recovers.

Capt Andrew K Long, brevet lt colonel in the Commissary Dept, [who has for some time past been one of the President's private secretaries,] was yesterday ordered to duty at **Fort Harkens**, Kansas.

The marriage of Miss Kate Dix, daughter of Gen Dix, to Mr Walsh, a well known merchant in the Japan trade, took place at Paris on Friday.

Died: on Apr 2, at **Needwood**, Fred'k Co, Md, the residence of her father, the late Saml L Gouverneur, Eliz Kortwright, wife of Grafton D Spurrier, in the 43rd year of her age.

Handsome furniture & accessories at public auction, on Apr 27, at the residence of Mrs Harriet M Sullivan, 472 7th st west, between E & F sts. –Fitch & Fox, aucts

Property in Gtwn for sale at auction on Apr 22; on the north side of West st in Gtwn, D C, long known as the ***Chesley property***; with a one brick & one frame bldg.
–John Marbury, Fendall Marbury, trustees -Thos Dowling, auct

Orphans Court of Wash Co, D C, Apr 18, 1868. In the case of Edgar Patterson, adm of Robt S Patterson, dec'd, the administrator & Court have appointed May 12 next, for the final settlement of the personal estate of the said dec'd, of the assets in hand.
-Jas R O'Beirne, Reg/o wills

Circuit Court for PG Co; in Equity, Apr Term, 1868. Henry C Kirkwood & others vs Mary J Kirkwood & others. On Apr 17, 1868 private sale was made by M J Kirkwood & Wm R Woodward, trustees; the land was sold for $8,300. [No other details.] -D Ford, D R Magruder, Assoc Judges -Henry Brooke, Clerk of the C C Court for PG Co, Md.

TUE APR 21, 1868
The statuette of Gen E D Baker, which now adorns the spacious aisle of Messrs Galt Brother's jewelry store, is one of the most admirable gems of art that has ever been seen in Wash City, & has just been received from the Eternal City, where is was executed by a well known Washingtonian, Dr Stone, who is also the sculptor of several of the finest pieces of statuary that adorn the Capitol. It is pronounced as an eloquent resemblance of the illustrious Senator. In several weeks it will be taken to San Francisco, to the residence of Col R J Stevens, for whom it was executed.

Springfield, Mass, Apr 20. Three fires occurred in this city this morning, within 2 hours of each other. Henry E Cobleigh has been arrested as the incendiary. Horace Kimball, a negro, was burned to death in a barn.

Wm Graham, an Irishman, aged about 40 years, residing in Temperance alley, was found dead in his bed yesterday. A young man, J P Coffee, was arrested on suspicion of having been engaged in a quarrel with the deceased, but an examination of witnesses showed that Graham died from the effects of habitual drunkenness, & Coffee was released.

Order issued by Gen C H Howard, directing that the frame bldg known as ***Wisewell Barracks***, corner of O & 7th sts, shall be torn down, & the material used in constructing dwlgs for colored people on square 1054, between 14th & 15th sts east, & C & D sts north.

Maj E G Townsend has been relieved from duty as Superintendent of ***Kendall Green Barracks***, & will proceed to Va, where he has received an appointment as agent of the Freedmen's Bureau for that State.

Mrd: on Apr 20, in Wash City, by Rev W W Williams, of Gtwn, D C, Maj Gen E A Hitchcock, late of the U S A, to Miss Martha R Nichols, of Nashville, Tenn.

Died: on Apr 20, John Berdine King, infant son of P H & M E King, aged 6 months.

U S Marshal's public sale, for cash, May 18, all Chauncey H Snow's right, title, claim, & interest in & to lot 11 in square 247, in Wash City, with singular improvements thereon, seized & levied upon as the property of said Chauncey M Snow, & will be sold to satisfy execution No 3,69_, in favor of the Ocean Nat'l Bank of N Y against Cornelius Wendell, Chauncery H Snow, John F Coyle, & Wm F Spalding. –D S Gooding, Marshal, D C

U S Marshall's public sale, for cash, on Apr 25, in front of Henry Middleton's Livery Stable, on 6th st west, near the canal in Wash City, D C, two cows seized & levied upon as the goods & chattels of Wm Norris, & will be sold to satisfy execution No 4,354 & 4,355, in favor of Seligman P_fferling. D S Gooding, U S Marshal, D C

Beautiful residence in Va for sale; wishing to remove to Leesburg, the county seat, I will sell my farm, ***Captiol Hill***; contains 20 acres; the dwlg house is of brick, large & well built containing 12 rooms. A farm adjoining may be purchased with it on reasonable terms. Address Arthur L Rogers, Atty-at-Law, Middleburg, Va.

The Senate yesterday confirmed Hedgeman Slack to be U S Marshal for West Va, & rejected Minard H Faily to be surveyor general for Calif.

Mr John J Bogue, real estate agent, yesterday sold to Mr A H Herr the two story brick house on the corner of Cherry & Potomac sts, for $3,000 cash.

WED APR 22, 1868
Cmdor Vanderbilt, now in his 76th year, is one of the handsomest men in N Y. He has a skin & complexion almost as fair as a woman's. He dresses very neatly, always wears a white cravat & a ministerial cut out, & would be taken by 99 in 100 for a preacher.

Patents to Washingtonians during the week of Apr 14. Swing cradle, to Patrick P Carroll; induction-cell apparatus & circuit breaker, to Chas Grafton Page; water elevator, to Wm H Castle; cement for coating wood, to Antonio Pelletier; paper file, to Eldridge J Smith & Benj H Cheever; apparatus for manufacturing illuminating gas, to Levi Stevens; & paper file, to Edmund W Woodruff & Geo C Green.

Orphans Court-Judge Purcell, Apr 21, 1868. 1-Margaret A Falconer gave bond in the sum of $2,400 as admx of Geo E Falconer, dec'd. Ralph J Falconer & Thos Evans, securities. 2-The will of Edwin W Moore, of Texas, was filed, fully proven, & admitted to probate & record. The testator names Emma M Cox sole excx. 3-The will of Ann E Kervand was fully admitted to probate & record. 4-The will of Chas Demonett was filed, fully proven, & admitted to probate. The testator devises all his property, real & personal, to his wife, Ida Demonett, & names her sole excx. 5-Ellen Sarsfield gave bond in the sum of $400 as admx of Lawrence Sarsfield, dec'd. Thos Sarsfield & Bartley Sarsfield, sureties. 6-Second general & individual accounts of August Schroeder, guardian to Jas E & Rita Triay, filed & passed. 7-Emma M Moore gave bond in the sum of $1,000 as excx of Edwin W Moore. C H Smith & Mary Saunders sureties.

Mrd: on Apr 21, in St Patrick's Church, by Rev J J Keane, Chas Cons Callan to Ida A, daughter of Henry S Benson.

Died: on Apr 21, Wm Seaman Beare. His funeral will be at the Church of the Incarnation, N & 12th sts, this afternoon, at 4 o'clock.

Dept of the Interior, U S Patent Ofc, Wash, Apr 13, 1868. Ptn of Elliot Savage, of Meriden, Conn, praying for the extension of a patent granted to him Nov 21, 1854, & reissued in two divisions Sep 27, 1859, for an improvement in Machine for Threading Screw Blanks, for seven years from the expiration of said patent, which takes place on Nov 21, 1868. -A M Stout, Acting Com'r of Patents

Orphans Court of Wash Co, D C, Apr 21, 1868. In the case of John A Ruff, exc of Andrew Small, dec'd, the executor & Court have appointed May 19 next, for the final settlement of the personal estate of the said dec'd, of the assets in hand.
-Jas R O'Beirne, Reg/o wills

Orphans Court of Wash Co, D C, Apr 21, 1868. In the case of Mary E Stinemetz & Benj H Stinemetz, excs of Saml Stinemetz, dec'd, the executors & Court have appointed May 19 next, for the final settlement of the personal estate of the said dec'd, of the assets in hand. -Jas R O'Beirne, Reg/o wills

Orphans Court of Wash Co, D C, Apr 21, 1868. In the case of Thos Miller, exc of John D Hammack, dec'd, the executor & Court have appointed May 19 next, for the final settlement of the personal estate of the said dec'd, of the assets in hand.
-Jas R O'Beirne, Reg/o wills

THU APR 23, 1868
Gen T C Hindman was brought before the U S Circuit Court in Little Rock, Ark, on Apr 13, on an indictment for treason. The case was continued until the next term of the court, & Gen Hindman was held to bail in the sum of $5,000, which he gave at once.

Robt Toombs is about to leave for Europe to attend to an important lawsuit in which he is interested.

Hon Chauncey Jerome, of New Haven, whose clocks have made his name known world wide, died on Monday, after a brief illness, in the 76th year of his age.

Bishop Hawks, who died in St Louis on Sunday, had been the Episcopal Bishop of Missouri for 22 years. He was born in Raleigh, N C.

Hon Jas F Wilson, of Iowa, chariman of the House Judiciary Cmte, has written a letter declining a renomination to Congress.

Yesterday, the First Presbyterian Church, on 4½ st, presented a brilliant array of the beauty & fashion of the metropolis, prominent among whom were the Pres of the U S & his accomplished daughter, Mrs Patterson. The occasion was the marriage of Thos M Shepherd to Miss Bettie E Page, daughter of the late Y P Page, of Wash City. The ceremony was performed by Rev Byron Sunderland, D D, pastor of the church, assisted by Rev Jno C Smith, D D. The happy pair received the congratulations of their numerous friends, & took the afternoon train to N Y & Boston.

Mrd: on Apr 13, Easter Monday, in Savannah, by Rt Rev John W Beckwith, D D, Jos Packard, jr, of Va, to Laura Dillon, eldest daughter of Wm Bennett, of Burke Co, Ga.

Cincinnati, Ohio, Apr 22. Jacob Morris, for many years editor of the Western Star, Warren Co, died at Lebanon, Ohio, yesterday, aged 70 years.

N Y, Apr 22. 1-Chas Dickens sailed on the steamer **Russia** today for Europe. There was a large crowd of people on the wharf, & considerable enthusiasm was manifested.
2-Anthony Trollope, the celebrated English novelist, arrived today on the steamer **Scotia**.

Chancery sale of valuable improved property on N Y ave between 14th & 15th sts; by decree of Supreme Court, in Equity, No 1,262, wherein Anna E McClery & Ida McClery are cmplnts, & Kate _ & Eva McClery are dfndnts; auction on May 14 next, on the premises; lot 3 in square 222, with handsome double 2 story brick house, the late residence of Morven J McClery, dec'd. –Ann E McClery, trustee
-W L Wall & Co, aucts

Orphans Court of Wash Co, D C. Letters of administration on the personal estate of John H Snyder, late of Wash Co, D C, dec'd. –Susanna J Snyder, admx

FRI APR 24, 1868
Hon Alex'r W Buel, a prominent citizen of Detroit, died on Sat last, aged 56 years. He was a native of Castlebar, Rutland Co, & graduated at the Vt Univ in 1831. He has held many ofcs of public trust in city & county, was a member of the State Legislature 4 terms, & in Congress from 1849 to 1854.

In Gtwn, Mr Thos Dowling sold the lot on the n e corner of West & Valley sts, 106 feet front by 110 feet deep, known as the *Chesley property*, together with improvements, consisting of one brick & one frame dwlg, to Jos L Simms, for $4,400.

Yesterday, in the Criminal Court, the ptn of Hugh Hughes for the discharge of his son, Thos J Hughes, a minor, from the service of the U S army, was argued before Chief Justice Cartter, but the Court held the matter under advisement.

Died: on Apr 22, in Wash City, E W Farley, in his 44th year. His funeral will be from McKendre Church, on Mass ave, between 9th & 10th sts, tomorrow, Apr 24, at 3 o'clock.

Died: on Apr 23, Israel M Jackson, sr, in his 77th year. His funeral will take place from his late residence in PG Co, Md, on Sat, at 10 A M.

Madrid, Apr 23. Narvaez, the Prime Minister, died early this morning.

SAT APR 25, 1868
Green & Williams, aucts, sold the south half of lot 17 in square 163, fronting on 18th st west, with brick house & bakery thereon, to Fred'k Harman, for $1,625. Messrs W L Wall & Co, aucts, sold part of lot 8 in square 569, fronting 15 feet on E st, between 1st & 2nd sts, running back 100 feet to an alley, with improvements, to Mr John Hendrickson, for $1,400.

Police promotions & appointments; meeting held Thu. Messrs John T Howe & J B Stoops were appointed privates on the force. John S Hill & C W Okey were appointed additional privates for 90 days. Michl O'Callaghan was promoted to a sergeantcy, as was Pvt Saml B Clements. Mr Clements has for some time past been on duty as clerk in charge of the records of the detective force. We are pleased to make the announcment that the Board has recognized his claims to promotion, & elevated him to a sergeantcy.

Chicago, Apr 23. Telegram from *Fort McPherson* says that a party of Indians made a dash upon a company of men cutting wood yesterday, killing Jas Brown, Gus Hall, Geo Kline, & Jos Vert. E Hoffman was scalped & badly wounded by an arrow. A boy, named Tanney, aged 14, was dangerously wounded.

Died: on Apr 22, in Phil, of consumption, Wm David Dowling, of Wash City, D C, in his 29th year.

Died: on Apr 20, in N Y, Eva Monteith, infant daughter of Leonard & Minnie Huyck, aged 5 months & 4 days.

G W Bey, a poor Illinois boy, drew the prize of a house & lot, valued at $15,000, in a St Louis lottery on Monday.

Trustee's sale of valuable real estate, by decree of the Supreme Court of D C, in the case of John M Keating & others vs Sarah A Keating & others, Equity No 1,209, the undersigned, appointed trustees by said decree to make sale of the interest of the widow & heirs of all the real estate of the late Geo W Keating dec'd, will offer at public auction, on the premises, on May 19, the following: all that tract of land lying in Wash City, adjoining the lands of the late Jos Gales & others & lying along Lincoln ave, containing 29 acres & 30 perches, except a part retained as a family grave-yard by Jas Moore, supposed to be about half acre, & a right of way to & from the same; & also the part that has been taken in widening Lincoln ave supposed to be about 1 acre. The improvements consist of a large & substantial 3 story dwlg house with 2 spacious porticoes, extending around the entire bldg; also a very large brick bldg used formerly as a slaughter house. On May 2, on the premises, will be sold 3 lots & the improvements in Wash City, described as: part of original lot 1 in square 329, near 11th st, having thereon a 3 story brick house. –John E Norris, Walter S Cox, Wm Emmert, trustees -Green & Williams, aucts

Valuable residence on 6th st west near the City Hall for sale, on May 4 next, on the premises, built by Mr David Saunders, & lately occupied by Mr Geo E Kennedy; lot fronts 36 feet 4 inches on 6th st; being part of lot 22 in square 457, containing about 2,400 square feet of ground. Title indisputable, & immediate possession given.
-Fitch & Foy, aucts

MON APR 27, 1868

Orphans's Court-Judge Purcell, Apr 25, 1868. 1-Anne E Robinson gave bond in the sum of $5,000 as guardian of the orphans of Jas H Robinson, dec'd. David Hepburn & Thos K Gray, sureties. Anne Robinson gave bond in the sum of $400 as admx of Jas H Robinson, dec'd. David Hepburn & T K Gray sureties. 2-John Thompson gave bond in the sum of $100 as guardian to the orphan of John & Mary E Ray, dec'd. E P Ross & Jas Guinity sureties. Same, as guardian to orphan of John Conner; bond $400; same sureties. 3-The will of Ann Crouse was filed & fully proven. The testatrix names M V Buckey exc. 4-First & final account of Maria C Emrich, admx of Peter Emrich, filed & passed. 5-Distrubutive account of the personal estate of Peter Emrich, by M C Emrich, admx, filed & passed.

Died: on Apr 25, Chas M Fay, in his 23rd year. His funeral will be from the residence of his father, Julius A Fay, at 19th & G sts, on Apr 28, at 11 o'clock A M.

Died: on Sunday, Chas Edwin Green, aged 28 years. His funeral will be from the residence of his mother-in-law, Mrs Lambright, 387 9th st, near I, Tuesday at 4 o'clock.

Richmond, Va, Apr 26. A despatch from Charlottesville announces the death of Wm C Rives, a native of Nelson Co, Va, former U S Minister to France, & Senator from Va, aged 75 years. [Death date not given-current item.]

Louisville, Apr 26. Jos Bloomgart, who embezzled $120,000 from the Gov't here some time ago, returned yesterday from N Y, under arrest, & was brought before U S Com'r Ballard. Bloomgart waived examination, &, in default of $150,000 bail, was committed to jail. 2-Mrs Prentice, wife of Geo D Prentice, of the Louisville Journal, died today. 3-The ceremony of <u>decorating the graves</u> of confederate dead occurred at *Cave Hill Cemetery* yesterday. Several hundred persons were present.

U S Marshal's sale on May 2 next, of goods & chattels, seized & levied upon, & will be sold to satisfy execution No 4,353, in favor of Geo W Berry & Co. –D S Gooding, U S Marshal, D C, per Green & Williams, aucts [Owner of goods & chattells not given.]

Chancery sale of highly valuable property, 544 Pa ave, by decree of the Supreme Court of D C, passed in a cause wherein John W Ciaflin et al are cmplnts, & Benj F Dyer et al are dfndnts, Equity 527, sale on May 18 next, on the premises, part of lot 3 in square 575, in Wash City. –A Thos Bradley, trustee -Cooper & Latimer, aucts

TUE APR 28, 1868
For **Mount Vernon**: the steamer **Arrow**, Thos Stackpole, cmder, will leave foot of 7th st daily at 10 A M, [Sundays excepted,] touching at Alexandria, **Fort Foote & Fort Washington**, returning about 4 P M. Fare for the trip, including admission to the mansion & grounds, $1.50. –Jas Sykes, Gen Superintendent, Ofc, Willard's Hotel.

Orphans Court of Wash Co, D C, Apr 25, 1868. In the case of Alex'r H Loughborough, exc of Hamilton Loughborough, dec'd, the executor & Court have appointed May 19th next, for the final settlement of the personal estate of the said dec'd, of the assets in hand. -Jas R O'Beirne, Reg/o wills

Dept of the Interior, U S Patent Ofc, Wash, Apr 20, 1868. Ptn of Horace Woodman, of Biddeford, Maine, praying for the extension of a patent granted to him Dec 8, 1857, & reissued Dec 8, 1857, for an improvement in Cleaning Top Cards of Carding Machines, for seven years from the expiration of said patent, which takes place on Aug 1, 1868. -A M Stout, Acting Com'r of Patents

Dept of the Interior, U S Patent Ofc, Wash, Apr 20, 1868. Ptn of Polly Hunt, of Jersey City, N J, admx, & Geo W Hunt, of Newburgh, N Y, praying for the extension of a patent granted to said Walter Hunt Jul 25, 1854, & reissued in 4 divisions: Nov 29, 1864; Feb 7, 1865; Apr 4, 1865; & Jul 10, 1866, for an improvement in Shirt Collars, for seven years from the expiration of said patent, which takes place on Jul 2, 1866.

WED APR 29, 1868
Miss Lizzie L, daughter of Hon John P Hale, was married on Apr 7, at the U S Legation at Madrid, to Edw V Kinsley, of West Point.

Richmond, Va, Apr 28. 1-Gen Schofield today appointed Joh E Stokes mayor of Portsmouth, & a list of councilmen for that city. 2-John Millward, one of the proprietors of the Spotswood Hotel, on Tuesday week intimated to some friends that they would not see him again, & has since been missing, until this afternoon, when he was found in the canal, with a bullet in his head. 3-Robt Boone, a son of Bishop Boone, was accidentally shot & killed at Halifax Court House, on Saturday, by a companion.

Mrd: on Apr 28, at Laurel, Md, by Rev Dr Young, Mr Jos L Seymour, of Phil, to Miss Mollie J Pilson, of Laurel. No cards.

Died: yesterday, Effie Hamline, youngest daughter of Wm H & Lizzie S Pope, aged 1 year, 10 months & 18 days. Her funeral will be from her parents' residence, 230 6th st, between M & N sts, on Apr 30, at 11 A M. [Express]

Orphans Court of Wash Co, D C. Letters testamentary on the personal estate of Ann E Kervand, late of Wash City, D C, dec'd. –Jas L Kervand, exc

Orphans Court of Wash Co, D C. Letters testamentary on the personal estate of Chas Demonet, late of Wash Co, D C, dec'd. –Ida M Demonet, excx

Dept of the Interior, U S Patent Ofc, Wash, Apr 21, 1868. Ptn of Chas A Wakefield, of Pittsfield, Mass, praying for the extension of a patent granted to him Jul 25, 1854, for an improvement in Seed Planters, for seven years from the expiration of said patent, which takes place on Jul 25, 1868. -A M Stout, Acting Com'r of Patents

Dept of the Interior, U S Patent Ofc, Wash, Apr 21, 1868. Ptn of Griffith Lichtenuhaler, of Limestonville, Pa, praying for the extension of a patent granted to him Jul 25, 1854, for an improvement in Cultivators, for seven years from the expiration of said patent, which takes place on Jul 25, 1868. -A M Stout, Acting Com'r of Patents

THU APR 30, 1868
A special train will leave Alexandria, Va, this morning for Leesburg, to convey such persons as desire to witness the solemn services of consecrating Rev Francis M Whittle, of Ky, as Assist Bishop of Va, which service will take place this afternoon. Bishop Johns is to officiate upon the occasion.

Mr Peter Berry, the lessee of a portion of the wharf at the foot of 6th st, has been appointed the agent for the steamer **Express**, of the Wash & Balt Transportation Co's line. The agency was formerly in charge of Messrs Bryan & Bro, avenue grocers.

Gardner has, with his usual success, produced 2 very fine life-size photographs of the late Detective Wm M Kelly, of the Metropolitan force. One of these pictures has been presented to the widow of Mr Kelly, & the other framed & placed in the Detective Ofc at Police Headquarters.

St Louis, Apr 28. Wm Glasgow, a member of the firm of Glasgow Brothers, a heavy grocer in this city, has just won half of the capital prize in the Madrid lottery, amounting to $75,000 in gold. Mr Glasgow has been spending the winter in Havana, where he purchased the ticket.

Castalia, Albemarle Co, Va, Apr 28, 1868. Yesterday evening the funeral of Hon Wm C Rives took place at *Castle Hill*, in the presence of a large number of his friends & neighbors, including very many of the colored people. Rev E Boyden, rector of the parish, assisted by Rev W C Butler, of Charlottesville, performed the services in the house & at the grave. The last resting place of the deceased statesman & patriot is a plateau of ground with southern exposure, not far from the lawn leading up to the mansion house. An affectionate daughter placed a cross of white flowers on the grave of her beloved father. The death of Mr Rives is the first, with the exception of an infant daughter, 40 years ago, that has occurred in his family since his marriage, a period of 50 years. He was a Virginian, pure & simple. Before he died, Mr Rives had been enabled to complete the 3rd volume of his life of Jas Madison, bringing it down to the termination of the administration of Gen Washington, leaving the 4th volume to be completed by some other hand. -Monticello

Died: on Apr 28, Mrs Jane Bates Copeland, of McConnellsville, Pa, widow of the late Thos K Copeland, of Pittsburg, Pa, in her 82nd year. Her funeral will be from the residence of her daughter, Mrs Smallwood, 581 8th st, [Navy Yard] Apr 30 at 2 P M.

Died: on Apr 28, at Washington, in her 75th year, Sarah, wife of Wm Hogan. Her funeral services will be at St John's Church at 4:30 P M, on Thursday. Her remains will be taken to N Y for interment.

Dept of the Interior, U S Patent Ofc, Wash, Apr 24, 1868. Ptn of Edw W Brown, formerly of Fall River, Mass, praying for extension of a patent granted him Jul 25, 1854, & reissued Mar 14, 1868, for an improvement in Looms, for 7 years from the expiration of said patent, which takes place on Jul 25, 1868. -A M Stout, Acting Com'r of Patents

Cincinnati, Ohio, Apr 29. 1-T F Langstaff has been arrested & brought to this city from Bay City, Mich, on the charge of embezzling $17,000 from Cameron, Story & Malone lumber dealers. The alleged embezzlement took place in 1857. 2-C W Adams, of Cleveland, Ohio, committed suicide at the St Nicholas Hotel this afternoon.

San Francisco, Apr 29. The schnr **Growler**, the property of the new fur company, was wrecked on the Northern coast; 12 lives were lost. The vessel was destined for Sitka, with a valuable cargo on board. Seven bodies have been recovered. [No names given.]

Trustee's sale at auction of valuable lots in the 7th Ward; by deed of trust from John Crowley & wife & Thos Coleman & wife to be subscriber, dated Nov 12, 1866, recorded in Liber R M H, No 25, folios 234; public auction on May 21, in front of the premises, the south half of lot 36 & all of lot 37 in square 498, in Wash City, fronting 37 feet & 6 inches on 4½ st west, & a depth of 125 feet to a 20 foot alley. –W B Todd, jr, trustee –J B Wheeler & Co, aucts

Household & kitchen furniture at auction on May 2, by order of the Orphans Court of Wash Co, D C, by the undersigned excx of the last will & testament of Benedict Swain, dec'd, late of Wash Co. Mrs M Antonette, excx -Cooper & Latimer, aucts

Excellent household & kitchen furniture at auction on May 6, at the residence of the late Dr S C Smoot, 128 Pa ave north, between 19th & 20th sts. –Fitch & Fox, aucts

FRI MAY 1, 1868
The Chicago Journal says: "Gen Grant has already promised some appointments: his brother-in-law, Judge Dent, is to be Minister to Mexico." If we believed a word of this- but we don't- it would show that this is a fine time for office hunters. What with Johnson's appointments, Wade's appointments, & Grant's appointments, every one ought to be able to get a good fat place. –N Y Times

Hypolite Roux, a member of Sincerity Lodge, I O O F, of N Y, died on Wed at the residence of his brother, Victor Roux, proprietor of the Everett House, where he was on a visit. He fell a victim to consumption at the early age of 24. His remains are taken in charge by the Metropolis Lodge, No 16, who will attend his funeral in a body this afternoon at 2 o'clock.
+
Died: on Apr 29, of consumption, Hypolite Roux, aged 24 years, son of Victor & Margaret Roux, of France. His funeral will take place from the residence of his brother, Victor Roux, at the Everett House, F st, between 14th & 15th sts, today, at 2 P M.

Six American sculptors have taken up their residence in Florence: Powers, Ball, Hart, Mead, Connolly, & Jackson. Powers, in fact, has become a part of Florence to every American traveller. He first came to Florence in 1838. He is best known at home by his statue of Henry Clay, which has been erected both in Ky & New Orleans.

Mrd: on Apr 29, at Orange Court House, Va, by Rev Dr Handy, of the Presbyterian Church, at the residence of the bride's mother, Maj E A Belger, U S A, to Willis Louise, youngest daughter of Mrs M L Payne, of Va. No cards.

Richmond, Apr 30. Gen Schofield has appointed Allen McDowel mayor of Lynchburg, Va, & a list of officers for that city.

Chicago, Apr 30. Geo F Carpenter, express agent of the Merchants' Union Express Co at Davenport, Iowa, was robbed & murdered in this city last night by an unknown assassin.

SAT MAY 2, 1868
A Balt despatch says that young Jerome Bonaparte, of the French army, has sailed for America to visit his parents & grandmother. The latter is now in her 86th year, & resides in that city.

The trial of Edwin Kelly, for the murder of Thos J Sharpley, was concluded in N Y on Thursday. A verdict of not guilty was rendered, & the accused was allowed to depart.

Mrs A E Hammond was put under the influence of chloroform, in order to have some teeth extracted, in Ontario, Knox Co, Ill, on Thursday last, & before this operation could be completed she died.

Winchell, the broker, who is missing from Springfield, Mass, leaves large liabilities unprovided for-the amount being variously estimated at $20,000 & upwards. His wife, a niece of ex-Vice President Hamlin, loses about $5,000 of her separate property.

Gen Canby, commanding in South Carolina, recently sent a party of soliders to arrest Riddick Carney, who, in 1866, while under arrest for murder, killed Lt Kenyon & escaped. Carney & his friends resisted the soliders, killing two & wounding Maj Lyman. He was then killed, as was also his son, & his son-in-law was badly wounded.

Mrd: on Apr 28, at Trinity Church, by Rev Thos Addison, Capt Edw Field, U S army, to Minna, daughter of Dr Noble Young, of Wash City.

Died: on Apr 30, at the Academy of the Visitation, Fred'k, Md, Miss Mary C Daly, daughter of Jas Daly, aged 17 years. Requiescat in Paca. Her funeral will be from the residence of her father, Vt ave & L st, today, May 2, at 4 o'clock P M.

The congregation of Grace Church parish have chosen the following gentlemen as wardens & vestrymen for the ensuing year: Senior warden, Joshua J Cookey; jr warden, E H May; vestrymen, Arthur Yeatman, S B Taylor, Cornelius Jacobs. Chas Hadaway, J L Kidwell, C Neale, Geo Taylor, & C F Hurlburt. C F Hurlburt was appointed register, & Cornelius Jacobs treasurer. At an election for delegate to the diocese convention, to be held at Balt, May 27, C F Hurlburt was chosen, with Jos Gordon as alternate.

Vicksburg Times of Apr 22. Recent murder of a family at Omega Landing, on the Mississippi river; four negroes were determined to kill a man named Keenan, for the purpose of obtaining money they supposed he had just received for a lot of wood. On Apr 11th Keenan was shot by one of the negroes. Finding nothing in his pockets, they went to his house & killed his wife & son with an axe, & tied a daughter, a little girl, to a bed, & set it on fire. The murderers were pursued, & two of them were captured. While the ofcrs were conveying them to prison, a mob of negroes seized them, & at once made a fire & roasted the criminals to death.

Public sale, by decree of the Circuit Court of PG Co, in Equity, on May 21, at Collington P O, near the premises, all the real estate of which the late Elisha Duvall died seized & possessed, containing about 120 acres. This property adjoins the lands of Mrs Ann D Worthington, Joshua P Clarke, & others, 2 miles from **Collington**. Improvements are a small but new dwlg house & necessary outbldgs. –C C Magruder, jr, trustee

Valuable property in Gtwn at public sale, by deed of trust, dated Jul 1, 1867, from Lawrence M Closs/Close to the subscriber, recorded in Liber E O M No 16, folio 123, of the land records for the Dist of Col; public sale on Jun 8, of part of lot 41, fronting 35 feet on Market Space. –R P Jackson, trustee -Thos Dowling, auct

MON MAY 4, 1868
Geo Willner, Paperhanger & Upholsterer, 464 9th st, between D & E sts, Wash, D C.

Orphans Court-Judge Purcell, May 2, 1868. 1-Susan G Walker gave bond in the sum of $1,000 as guardian to the orphans of Wm Walker; Richd Walker & Jas Barker, sureties. 2-Anne Cathcart gave bond in the sum of $2,000 as guardian to the orphan of T J Cathcart; T P Barclay & J J Peabody sureties. 3-J W Somers gave bond in the sum of $6,000 as guardian to the orphan of J W Elliott; C H Law & Cyrus Birge sureties. 4-Mary Cassel gave bond in the sum of $400 as admx of Patrick Deely; Thos Cassel, Matthew Byrne, & R R Pyewell sureties. 5-The will of Edw W Farley was filed & fairly proven. 6-The will of Louise Warren was filed.

Newark, N J, May 2. The U S ofcrs arrested 3 notorious counterfeiters, whose headquarters are at Newton, N J: Gustavus Zeouth, Geo A Julian, & Henry Schaffer. Two other men, Jas E Lawrence & John Stucher, both of N Y State, were arrested here last night for passing counterfeit money.

E L Davenport, the tragedian, sailed for Calif on Friday.

Supreme Court of D C, Apr 30, 1868; in Equity No 1,252, Docket 8. Henry S Davis vs Danl A Veitch et al. The suit is instituted for the purpose of procuring a confirmation of the sale of lot 14 in square 762 in Wash City, the property of the late Wm Veitch, dec'd, made by the cmplnt; & subpoena having been issued against the dfndnts on Apr 6, 1868, & returned by the Marshal of D C on Apr 10, 1868, "not to be found," as to Danl A Veitch, John A Veitch & Mary V Humphries, on motion of John E Norris, solicitor for the cmplnt. Absent dfndnts are to appear on or before the first rule day occurring 40 days after this day; otherwise the cause will be proceeded in as in case of default.
-A B Olin, Justice -R J Meigs, clerk

TUE MAY 5, 1868
Eminent teacher, Wm H Seavey, died suddenly last week in Boston. He was a native of Maine, a graduate of Bowdoin College, in the class of 1844, & leaves a wife, a Boston lady, & one child to mourn their irreparable loss.

Yesterday Messrs Fitch & Fox sold at auction the 4 story brick house fronting on 6th st west, between D & E, owned by Geo E Kennedy, for $15,925, to D S Stewart. The sale was largely attended by our substantial citizens.

Jurors drawn for the May term of the Circuit Court:

Jos F Brown	Richd H Williams	Danl Harbaugh
Wm Reed	W F Seymour	J C Parker
Zachariah Williams	S Hermen	P J Collison
Jacob Aigler	G W Goodall	Henry Boswell
Martin M Potts	S H Bacon	J P Richardson
D M Beall	John Wilson	Geo T Raub
G C Nichols	Geo T Langley	G L Sheriff
W R Clarke	John M Washington	Simon Mead
Louis Dietrich	Jas Caldwell	

Buffalo Courier, May 2. Last Tuesday the fine propeller **Governor Cushman**, H W Thompson, master, arrived here from Milwaukie. Directly in front of the Sturges elevator, opposite the foot of Wash st, she began the process of winding. The capt was standing on the wheel-house, & within were the two wheelsmen, Thos Farrell & Thos J Franey. The engineer, H S Gilbert, & the assist engineer, Jos Gray, were at their posts, as were most of the deck hands. Several of the ofcrs & crew were quietly sleeping. A tremendous explosion from the engine room stunned the ears of all on board. Killed: Peter McDermail, fireman; Barney Lester, Frank Smith, Lewis Anderson, & Herman Fromming, deck hands. Killed & Missing: H S Gilbert, 1st engineer; John Dworak, Wm Ebert, H G Stewart, Geo Lewis, & Jeremiah Mare, deck hands. Wounded: Capt H W Thompson; Patrick Brashahan, fireman; & Jos Gray.

Chancery sale of valuable bldg lots at 1st & Mass ave & 2nd st, between E & F sts north; by decree of the Supreme Court of D C, dated Nov 14, 1867, wherein Caroline McAlister is cmplnt, & Chas E McAlister et al, are dfndnts; Equity No 887; public auction on May 27 next, of lots 26 & 27 in square 568, in Wash City. –A Thos Bradley, trustee -Green & Williams, aucts

Dept of the Interior, U S Patent Ofc, Wash, Apr 29, 1868. Ptn of Benj Bray, of Salem, Mass, praying for the extension of a patent granted to him Sep 5, 1854, for an improvement in Spring Rollers for Window Curtains, for seven years from the expiration of said patent, which takes place on Sep 5, 1868. -A M Stout, Acting Com'r of Patents

WED MAY 6, 1868
Messrs J B Wheeler & Co sold lot 16 in S P Brown's subdivision, of part of *Pleasant Plain mill*, on 14th st, 100 feet front by 270 feet deep, to Dr F Howard, for $1,215. Messrs Fitch & Fox, aucts, sold at auction yesterday the 2 story brick house & lot on F st north, between 6th & 7th sts, the residence of the late Wm Dalton, for $10,300, to Wm J Sibley.

Gen Schofield has removed Jos Mayo, Mayor of Richmond, & appointed Geo Cahoon in his place.

Orphans Court-Judge Purcell, May 5, 1868. 1-Martha E Bellis gave bond in the sum of $500 as guardian to Chas H Wilson. John Bellis, H O Hood, & F A Conrad, sureties. 2-Alex'r Hay gave bond in the sum of $10,000 as administrator of Marie Armadie. Chas Mellier, Augustus B Stoughton, & W S Teel, sureties. 3-The will of Geo F Hartshorn was filed for probate. The testator names his wife, Sarah G Hartshorn, excx. 4-The will of Rachel Clements was filed for probate.

Died: on May 5, in his 57th year, Prof Chas Grafton Page, M D, Examiner in the Patent Ofc. His funeral will be from his late residence, 253 F st, at 12 o'clock M, on May 7.

Died: on May 4, Charles Albert, infant son of L F & Mary C Clark, aged 8 months. His funeral will take place on May 6 at 10 o'clock A M.

19th Annual meeting of the American Medical Association was held yesterday at Carroll Hall, on G st, Wash; called to order by the president, Dr S D Gross, of Phil; prayer offered by Rev Dr Pinckney, of Wash City. Permanent sec, Dr W B Atkinson, of Phil, was at his post. On the platform were Vice Presidents Prof Post, of N Y; Dr Atlee, of Pa; Prof H R Storer, of Boston; & Dr C C Cox, of Md. Dr Grafton Tyler, of Gtwn, delivered the address. Cmtes called: Opthalmology, Dr Jos S Hildreth, Ill; Cultivation of the Cinchona Tree, Dr J M Toner, of D C; Surgical Diseases of Women, Dr Theophilus Parvin, Indiana; on Rank of Medical Men in the Navy, Dr N S Davis, Ill; on Insanity, Dr C A Lee, N Y; on American Medical Necrology, Dr C C Cox, Md; on Leakage of Gas Pipes, Dr J C Draper, N Y; on Plan of Organization, Dr C C Cox, Md; on provision for the Insane, Dr C A Lee, N Y; on Climatology & Epidemics of Maine, Dr J C Weston; of New Hampshire, Dr P A Stockpole; of Vt, Dr Henry Janes; of Mass, Dr Alfred C Garratt; of R I, Dr C W Parsons; of Conn, Dr E K Hunt; of N Y, Dr W F Thomas; of N J, Dr Ezra M Hunt; of Pa, Dr D F Condie; of Md, Dr O S Mahon; of Ga, Dr Juriah Harriss; Missouri, Dr Geo Engelman; Ala, Dr R Miller; Texas, Dr T J Heard; Ill, Dr R C Hamil; Ind, Dr J F Hibberd; D C, Dr T Antisell; Iowa, Dr J W H Baker; Mich, Dr Abm Sager; Ohio, J W Russell; Calif, Dr F W Hatch; Tenn, Dr Jos Jones; West Va, Dr E A Hildreth; Minn, Dr Saml Willey; on Clinical Thermometry in Diptheria, Dr Jos G Richardson, N Y; on the Treatment of Diseases by Atomized Substanced, Dr A G Field, Iowa; on the Ligation of Arteries, Dr Benj Howard, N Y; on the Treatment of Club-foot without Tenotomy, Dr L A Savre, N Y; on the Radical Cure of Hernia, Dr G C Blackman, Ohio; on Operations for Harelip, Dr Hammer, Mo; on Errors of Diagnosis in Abdominal Tumors, Dr G C E Weber, Ohio; on Medical Education, Dr A B Palmer, Mich; on Medical Literature, Dr Geo Mendenhall, Ohio; on Prize Essays, Dr Chas Woodward, Ohio. Resolved: The resignation of Dr Julius Homberger, of N Y, be accepted, & that all further consideration of him, or of his peculiar methods of procuring practice, be indefinitely postponed. Drs N P Tallifero & Buckner preferred charges against Dr A G Field, of Iowa. Matter laid over for investigation. A reception at the residence of Hon Schuyler Colfax took place from 9 until 10.

Mrd: on May 5, at the Church of the Ascension, by Rev Dr Pinckney, Mr Geo A McIlhenney, of Wash City, to T Virginia Smith, of Alexandria, Va.

On Sunday night Patrick Laughlin & his wife, living at Great Bend, Pa, went away from home, leaving their 6 children in charge of a girl aged 16 years. During the evening the shanty took fire, & the girl awakening seized two of the children & carried them safely out. Returning for the others, she became suffocated with the smoke.

Dr Gabor Naphegyi, who was arrested some days ago for an alleged forgery, by which he obtained $50,000 from Columbus Powell, of Broad st, N Y, was honorably discharged on Monday, the prosecution not being prepared to proceed in the matter. He made an informal statement, showing that the money was obtained in his capacity of Santa Anna's secretary, for that old veteran's use in carrying out revolutionary schemes against Mexico.

For rent: the dwlg over the wine store of Messrs Thos Russell & Co, north side of Pa ave, between 12th & 13th sts. –S B Boarman, trustee of R C Dyer, at the Bank of Washington.

Trustee's sale of a valuable Farm in Culpeper Co, within a few miles of Brandy Station & Culpeper C H, Va; by deed of trust executed by John Taylor & wife to the undersigned, as trustee, dated Feb 11, 1861; public auction, on the premises, on Jun 3, of a certain tract of land, in Culpeper Co, Va, containing 700 acres, the same that was bought by John Taylor, of Jeremiah Morton, & the larger part of the very valuable farm known as **Stillmore**, formerly owned by John Taylor, & at present occupied by Messrs John F Lewis, M Blackburn, Jas W Crawford, & Francis M Young. The improvements consist of a commodious dwlg, with other bldgs, all in good condition. The debt secured by the deed is $8,000, with interest thereon from Feb 11, 1861 to the day of sale, & the deed requires the sale to be for cash sufficient to pay the same. –Jas Pleasants, trustee

Orphans Court of Wash Co, D C, May 5, 1868. In the case of Jos E Nourse & Wm Nourse, excs of Mary R Nourse, dec'd, the executors & Court have appointed Jun 2 next, for the final settlement of the personal estate of the said dec'd, of the assets in hand. -Jas R O'Beirne, Reg/o wills

Cincinnati, May 5. A despatch to the Commercial from Delaware, Mo, says on Sunday 3 boys, sons of Henry Forge, were out in a field, when a difficulty arose between them, & the older one smashed the heads of his younger brothers with an axe, killing one outright, & leaving the other nearly dead. At the approach of their father the oldest boy ran to a barn & hung himself dead.

Phil, May 5. Cmdor Ridgely, U S N, died today at the St Lawrence Hotel. He was born in Ky, but his residence was in Balt, though on duty in this city at the time of his death.

Orphans Court of Wash Co, D C, May 5, 1868. In the case of Jos E Nourse & Wm Nourse, excs of Michl Nourse, dec'd, the executors & Court have appointed Jun 2 next, for the final settlement of the personal estate of the said dec'd, of the assets in hand.
-Jas R O'Beirne, Reg/o wills

THU MAY 7, 1868
An insane woman, Ann Cooney, was run over & killed by a train on the Bellefontaine road on Thursday, about 8 miles from Indianapolis. It appears that Mrs Cooney had a son who was one of the Fenian army that invaded Canada, & was captured & sentenced to 21 years' confinement. The fate of her son unsettled her reason, & she has ever since been wandering about in a demented condition.

On Tuesday, at the Church of the Ascension, on H st, between 9th & 10th sts, was filled with a brilliant audience to witness the nuptial services of Mr Geo A McIllhenny, the gentlemanly engineer of the Wash Gas Light Co, & Miss Jennie Smith, one of the fair belles of our sister city of Alexandria. The attendants were Messrs Jas D Clary & Jas F Russell, two of the courteous clerks in the Gas Co's ofc, & Misses Alice Armstrong, of Alexandria, & Ella Adams, of Wash. The bride & bridesmaids were attired in white silk dresses, with flowing trails, while the groom & his attendants wore the customary black, with white vests. Rev Dr Pinckney performed the solemn ceremony which made the twain one. The happy couple proceeded to the depot & took the 4:30 P M train for a bridal tour of the principal cities of the North.

Messrs Kilbourn & Latta, of Wash City, sold a lot of ground, 51 feet by 150 feet deep, on F st, between 13th & 14th sts, for the sum of $25,000, W P Dole, late Com'r of the Indian Bureau, the purchaser.

Died: on May 6, in Wash City, Edward, infant son of Hon Edward & Annie C McPherson.

Died: on May 5, in Wash City, Harvey Cruttenden, in his 80th year. His funeral will be from his late residence, 5 K st, between 8th & 9th sts, Thursday, at 3 P M.
[May 8th newspaper: Mr Cruttenden resided in the Northern portion of the city, beloved & respected by all who knew him. By industry & perserverance he amassed a considerable fortune, & owned a large amount of real estate in the locality in which he has had his residence for a long period.]

Utica [N Y] Herald, Apr 28. Horrible & sickening tragedy on Sat last, at Pond Hill, about 4 miles east of Camden village. A little girl, 8 years of age, daughter of Levi Sanders, was brutally outraged, near her father's residence, & then her throat was cut & her head mashed in with a stone. Her parents found her dead body. Wm Henry Carswell, age 26 years, who lived nearby, was arrested & charged with the murder of the little girl. He was found at the residence of his brother-in-law. The murdered girl was second cousin to Carswell. When his father asked him if he murdered the little girl, he told his father that he did not. There are other suspects, one of them is a negro.

Appointments of Midshipmen at large for the year 1868, just ordered by the President:

N T James, Calif	Jacob Medary, Ohio
Rogers H Galt, Va	Danl F Baker, Maine
John C Fremont, jr, son of an ofcr	Thos F Dixon, Pa
Robt H Fletcher, son of an ofcr	Chas E Fox, son of an ofcr
Lewis Pitcher, son of an ofcr	Wm Pohlmeyer, Md

The Pres also ordered that Geo D McCarty be transferred from cadet engineer.

Haverhill, Mass, May 6. Saml Mills was hung today for the murder of an old man named Mexwell, at Franconia, N H. He hung for 30 minutes & life was declared extinct.

Redwood for sale; the undersigned offers this desirable farm for sale; situated about 1 mile from Culpeper C H, Va; contains 400 acres of good land; the dwlg contains 9 rooms, in fine condition; outbldgs are numerous. Price, $45 per acre, on reasonable terms. Address Shackelford, Spilman, & Garden, Law Agents, Warrenton, Va.

FRI MAY 8, 1868
The Oldest Inhabitants' Association meeting on Tuesday; Capts Chauncey Bestor & S Masi, & Messrs John F Callan, Jenkin Thomas, & Wm Prentiss were appointed a cmte to make arrangements for the approaching Jul 4th anniversary. Additions to the museum of the association were presented by: Mr J Carroll Brent, on behalf of Mr Thos Blagden, presented a list of names of the original subscribers to the stock of the Commercial Co of the City of Wash, formed in 1808. Mr Brent also presented, in behalf of Mr Howard Keyworth, a complimentary invitation from J Roberts, Mayor of Alexandria, dated Oct 11, 1824, to Judge Thurston, to dine with Gen Lafayette at Clagett's Hotel, at that place. Mr F R Dorsett presented the spawls which he had taken from the cavity of the corner-stone of the Nat'l Wash Monument before it was laid. Mr J F Callan presented a history of the Baptist institutions in Wash City, the first of which was organized in 1862.

Patents to Washingtonians during the past week: to Chas De Hass, for a mode of roofing bldgs. To John T Parson, for roadway pavement, who claims a baked or burned clay paving block as a new article of manufacture. To Danl E Somes, for an apparatus for consuming smoke & gas & increasing draught in boiler furnaces. To Josiah Humphrey, for a sadiron holder.

Mrd: on May 5, at Middleburgh, N Y, the residence of the bride's father, by Rev J S Lott, B D Hyam, of Wash City, to Mary Boardman, youngest daughter of Dr S B Wells.

Dept of the Interior, U S Patent Ofc, Wash, May 2, 1868. Ptn of Bradford S & Chas M Pierce, of New Bedford, Mass, praying for the extension of a patent granted to him Aug 1, 1854, for an improvement in Moulds for Cement or Earthern Tubes, for seven years from the expiration of said patent, which takes place on Aug 1, 1868.
-A M Stout, Acting Com'r of Patents

Mr Jas N Ball is hard at work preparing the corner stone of the new Masonic temple, which is to be laid with appropriate ceremonies on May 20.

The income tax of Dist of Col: Incomes about $10,000:

Marshall Brown, $22,021
Thos Blagden, $10,125
W W Corcoran, $36,423
Sarah H Coltman, $23,329
Henry D Cooks, $82,421
D W Middleton, $10,005
J C McGuire, $13,530
Margaret Freeman, $24,200
M W Galt, $10,773
Wm Gunton, $10,579
Wm Helmick, $14,487
A H Herr, $15,370
W P Johnson, $13,315
Moses Kelly, $12,115
A T Keickhoefer, $10,128
Edw W Linthicum, $12,600
Phineas Lawrence, $18,028
Benj Lawrence, $18,020
Edw H Linthicum, $12,606
W G Metzerott, $13,183
Saml Norment, $10,259
Saml V Niles, $15,617
Andrew H Potts, $14,890
Geo H Plant, $17,992
Chas F Peck, $16,252
Alex Provest, $22,848
Geo W Riggs, $47,045
Geo W Riggs, trustee, $18,551
Alex'r Ray, $27,491
A S Solomons, $11,234
A R Shepherd, $24,876
W H Tayloe, $33,214
Geo W Utermehle, $15,589
Jos C Willard, $27,340
Henry A Willard, $13,756
C C Willard, $12,285

Incomes below $10,000 & above $5,000:
Jas Adams, $5,479
J H Aulick, $9,740
Columbus Alexander, $6,151
John Alexander, $7,403
Mrs M J Blair, $5,746
J W Boteler, $6,568
B Bayliss, $6,650
Jos Bryan, $5,608
Jas L Barbour, $5,149
Mrs Frances Blanchard, $9,511
Geo T Brown, $8,340
G W Cochran, $5,523
H A Chadwick, $6,251
E C Carrington, $5,830
Jas M Carlisle, $8,400
T J Durant, $8,564
Jas W Denver, $7,201
Geo A Delafield, $5,388
Cornelia A Dikeman, $5,636
Jas Dunlap, $5,602
W D Davidge, $5,573
John O Evans, $5,298
John R Elvans, $9,468
M G Emery, $9,129
Michl Green, $6,672
A Green, $5,156
Mrs S A Greeves, $6,751
W Galt, $5,871
W M Galt, $9,998
Jos Holt, $6,745
E D Hartley, $5,719
F Howard, $6,253
G J Johnson, $6,929
Lewis Johnson, $5,067
Wm B Kibbey, $7,125
J E Kendall, $6,786
Wm King, $6,031
J C Kennedy, $7,085
Amos Kendall, $8,673
F A Lutz, $8,966
J H Lathrop, $9,686
John T Lenman, $8,939
W H Lowry, $5,057
Geo Lowry, $5,499

F B Mohun, $5,615
W S Mitchell, $9,209
Francis Mohun, $7,463
John R Murray, $6,059
J McPherson, exr, $8,000
W F Mattingly, $5,066
J C McKelden, $6,849
A L Merriman, $5,520
R T Merrick, $7,117
Francis Mohun, $7,463
John T Mitchell, $5,256
John Markriter, $5,337
Dr J F May, $5,558
John Marbury, $8,299
J G Naylor, $5,777
Wm Orme, $6,967
F Philp, $8,466
John Purdy, $7,929
Mrs Ann Pickrell, $5,004
A Provest, exc & trustee, $5,099
Henson A Resley, $5,534
W S Reese, $5,163
L Savage, $7,033
John Saul, $6,922
A M Smith, $6,961
A B Stoughton, $7,687
Danl Smith, $6,438
John H Semmes, $6,562
Geo F Schaffer, $8,792
Riley A Shinn, $8,701
P Thyson, $6,664
W B Todd, $5,834
Theodore Wheeler, $6,148
W R Woodward, $5,887
Wm Wilson, $9,117
Mrs Martha Ann Winter, $5,220
John G Worthington, $7,602
Jas S Welsh, $5,328
Francis Wheatley, $5,004
W Wall, $6,686
Mark Young, $6,240

Incomes between $2,000 & $5,000:

N Acker, $4,502
T H Alexander, $2,291
Sidney Andrew, $2,639
John Angerman, $2,000
Geo C Ames, $2,029
Geo W Adams, $3,820
C M Alexander, $4,260
J D Bond, $2,000
Chas Bradley, $2,508
W H Burt, $2,716
J F Bridget, $2,589
John A Bundy, $2,361
Catharine C Boyle, $2,383
Thos F Barnes, $2,488
A T Britton, $2,540
Benj Beall, $4,577
Mrs Eliza Barry, $2,248
Mrs Susan M Burche, $2,960
M W Beveridge, $5,370
M V B Bogan, $3,131
J B Blake, $3,047
D W Brown, $2,942
Geo E Baker, $2,557
Henry Baldwin, $2,339
Henry Beard, $2,006
W O Berry, $2,490
N W Burchell, $2,875
John W Bulkley, $2,118
Peter F Bacon, $2,461
P W Browning, $3,020
S Bacon, $2,242
W E Brown, $4,523
W D Baldwin, $2,608
C B Baker, $4,067
Jos A Blondon, $2,000
P T Berry, $3,550
J H Bradley, sr, $3,761
H S Benson, $4,852
Jos Borrows, $4,416
W H Brett, $2,000
W B Boggs, $2,921
Fred Bates, $4,805
Geo A Bailey, $4,084
W H Baldwin, $2,000
Edw Baldwin, $2,000
Wm Bates, $4,805

W W Burdette, $2,475
Jas W Barker, $3,277
C A Beavans, $2,600
D J Bishop, $4,006
W C Bestor, $2,432
W F Bascom, $3,010
A P Brown, $2,594
Jos F Brown, $4,000
S P Brown, $4,000
A Cluss, $2,189
Jos C Clayton, $3,508
W E Clark, $2,160
W H Campbell, $3,023
Chirs Cammack, $2,000
R A Crawford, $3,116
Mrs C Cruit, $2,011
Henry M Copp, $2,275
S D Castleman, $2,484
Same as guardian, $3,465
Dr Geo C Clymer, $2,519
Mrs U Corcoran, $2,013
W S Cox, $4,056
Richd D Cruit, $2,000
D E W Carter, $4,757
Benj Charleton, $2,243
W McL Cripps, $2,912
John E Cox, $2,600
C B Church, $4,186
N Carusi, $2,159
C F Cunningam, $2,374
R B Clark, $3,015
T E Clark, $3,008
J H Clark, $2,511
Jerome Callahan, $2,600
Edw Dunn, $2,624
W W Danenhower, $2,171
Dr Donaldson, $2,121
Henry F Davis, $2,222
H S Davis, $2,353
W A Dunlap, $3,892
John Dickson, $4,322
Henry Dickson, $2,376
W H Dougal, $2,463
T J Davis, $2,094
Benj Darby, $2,502

Peter M Debant, $2,343
Jas Y Davis, $3,910
B D DeWolff, $2,835
John Davidson, $2,126
W P Dole, $2,650
W H Dempsey, $3,519
Ed Droop, $3,723
Gen Demick, $3,132
W H Dougall, $2,463
Jas B Dodson, $3,000
L J Davis, $4,114
Mrs Georgeana Davis, $2,193
Wm Egan, $3,241
Rudolph Eichern, $4,798
D S Evans, $2,958
Dr J Eliot, $2,460
J F Ellis, $2,466
Chas Edmonston, $4,754
Thos Evans, $2,279
Gen Thos Ewing, jr, $4,700
*M G Emery, $9,129
Anton Eberly, $2,481
Jos Fugitt, $2,702
W A Fenwick, $4,083
J W Fitzhugh, $2,009
R W Fenwick, $4,972
Saml Fowler, $3,675
Chas Ford, $3,500
J E Fitch, $2,529
Thos Francis, $2,957
Georgiana L Force, $2,599
C M Ford, $2,343
Bladen Forrest, $2,503
Adam Gaddis, $2,797
Lemuel Gaddis, $2,625
Geo F Gulick, $3,123
Mrs S Green, $3,040
E M Gray, $4,087
John Grinder, $4,153
T J Galt, $2,713
H J Gray, $2,70
H M Gunnell, $2,290
W H Godey, $4,822
Walter Godey, $4,838
G W Goodall, $2,476

Wm Guinard, $4,102
L A Gobright, $2,000
Bernard Hays, $3,750
F J Heiberger, $3,380
T M Hanson, $2,939
Geo C Henning, $2,345
C Hertzberg, $3,465
W H Harrover, $2,297
Geo W Humphrey, $2,004
John Hitz, $2,074
W W Hough, $2,810
Gen D Hunter, $4,229
Prof J Henry, $3,723
Anthony Hyde, $3,165
G Hill, jr, $2,500
W E Howard, $2,251
A Heitmilier, $2,602
Dr Hagner, $3,200
J A Hamilton, $2,509
J C Hall, $3,255
J C Harkness, $4,832
T L Hume, $4,086
Wm Heine, $2,065
Henry Ingle, $2,433
Susan Ireland, $4,253
Chas Just, $2,244
C B Jewell, $2,002
W C Johnson, $3,246
B L Jackson, $3,684
H Kilburn, $2,340
Saml Kerr, $2,675
Jos F Kelly, $2,152
Mrs M A Kerr, $2,041
Maria G Knight, $2,300
John L Kidwell, $2,122
W Scot Ketchum, $2,347
J M Latta, $2,562
C H Lieberman, $2,727
Dr H Lindsley, $4,068
Dr H Lindsley, as guardian, $4,104
De Witt C Lawrence, $4,039
Robt Leech, $2,348
Robt Leslie, $4,938
S P Lee, $3,825
Mrs Louisa Libbey, $2,469

M B Lattimore, $2,003
Jos Libbey, $4,147
John E Libbey, $3,792
Alfred H Lee, $2,433
W Linkins, $2,002
Mrs A Lindsley, $2,868
J C Lewis, $2,048
J W Maury, $2,703
Wm McLean, $2,187
S A H Marks, $3,649
W H Morrison, $3,260
D W Mahon, $3,821
J M Mason, $4,910
John McCullom, $4,625
Horatio Moran, $2,000
J A Milburn, $2,014
G O McIllheny, $2,360
Mary Moore, $2,803
B F Moxley, $2,496
Benj Miller, $4,055
Dr Lewis Mackall, $2,878
Dr H Magruder, $4,173
W D C Murdock, $3,568
E M Mosher, $3,523
John Marbury, jr, $3,013
John Moore, $2,717
J H McDaniel, $2,000
D C McDowell, $2,040
Geo Mattingly, $2,862
Dr T Miller, $4,447
N C McKnew, $4,345
R J Meigs, sr, $2,853
Francis Mattingly, $2,334
L D Mears, $2,953
Thos McGill, $4,605
Geo E Noyes, $4,167
Thos A Newman, $2,256
Mrs Sarah Otterback, $3,340
John L Owens, $2,000
Edw Owen, $4,439
L J O'Toole, $3,290
G W Phillips, $3,252
H Polkinhorn, $2,900
A Pollak, $2,266
Jos L Pearson, $4,571

A H Pickrell, $2,486
Esau Pickerell, $2,555
Ebenezer Peck, $2,329
A E Perry, $4,029
Mrs C Pierson, $2,129
Jas Pilling, $3,079
Edgar Patterson, exc, $4,072
W F Quicksall, $2,270
J Riley, $2,584
John H Ruff, $2,545
C Ruppert, $3,105
G A W Randall, $3,113
B W Reed, $3,317
C F E Richardson, $2,270
T A Richards, $4,048
A Richards, $3,835
A K Randall, $4,901
David F Robinson, $2,015
Dr Joshua Riley, $4,416
Jefferson Rives, $4,828
Franklin Rives, $4,430
Bushrod Robinson, $2,021
Z C Robbins, $4,927
W Ruggles, $3,398
Jos Saxton, $2,474
Geo B Smith, $2,208
John A Smith, $2,358
P J Steer, $2,174
F H Smith, $2,176
H Sempkin, $3,392
Ed Simms, $2,658
Jas H Shreeve, $2,546
Mrs Harriet M Sullivan, $3,148
B H Stinemetz, $4,743
Jas J Shedd, $2,633
H Clay Stewart, $2,849
Eliz J Stone, $4,984
H C Swain, $3,276
John A Stephenson, $2,713
L Sutgreaves, $2,863
M H Stevens, $4,903
Jas G Smith, $3,378
W B Sibley, $2,935
Mrs Angelica Simpson, $2,262
S H Stevens, $4,150

Jos T Stevens, $4,150
A T Shriver, $2,033
Admiral Jos Smith, $3,367
Herbert Schutter, $3,505
C A Schneider, $2,470
Geo Seufferle, $2,120
Chas H Shelly, $2,233
Mrs Emma D E N Southworth, $4,200
John H Smoot, $3,483
Wm M Shuster, $4,604
Mary F Stone, guardian, $3,239
John H Stewart, $4,083
John J Sullivan, $2,384
R K Stone, $2,064
Saml Stott, $2,207
Christian Schneider, $2,188
Lewis Schneider, $2,431
Wm Stickney, $2,555
John W Simms, $3,148
W S Shepherd, $2,165
Enoch Totten, $3,145
Franck Taylor, $3,179
Michl Talty, $3,499
Zachariah Tobriner, $2,300
Henry Thorn, $2,025
Columbus W Thorn, $3,366
Jas Towles, $2,482
Wm S Thompson, $2,473
Elias Traverse, $3,275
C C Tucker, $4,554
Washington Tilley, $2,927
Jas S Topham, $2,386
S Ogle Tayloe, by agent, $4,872
John Van Riswick, $2,320
Wm Wurdeman, $3,107
John Wise, $2,137
Washington B Williams, $3,779
H M Waterson, $3,317
Wm H West, $2,358
John F Webb, $3,829
H N Wadsworth, $3,080
Mrs Ellen F Woodhull, $3,685
John Welcker, $4,413
Capt H A Wise, $2,662
Wm B Webb, $2,991

Jesse B Wilson, $4,283
Jas Wallace, $3,805
Henry Weaver, $2,137
Wm A Ward, $2,027
Chas Wheatley, $3,259
G E Wheatley, $3,259

Geo Waters, $4,594
Patrick White, $4,346
Jas M Witherow, $4,485
Richd Wallach, $4,037
Chas B Young, $2,000
Henrietta E Young, $2,611

Trustee's sale of a valuable house & lot in the village of Bladensburg; by decree of the Circuit Court for PG Co, Md, in Equity, passed in the case of Wm B Todd vs John A Soper & wife, & Robt Coltman; public sale on May 28 next, on the premises, now in the occupancy of the said John A Soper, a large & comfortable bldg, with about 1 acre of land attached to it; would be a most desirable residence to a gentleman doing business in Wash City. –N C Stephen, trustee

Dept of the Interior, U S Patent Ofc, Wash, May 2, 1868. Ptn of Bradford S & Chas M Pierce, of New Bedford, Mass, praying for the extension of a patent granted to him Aug 1, 1854, for an improvement in Moulds for Cement or Earthern Tubes, for seven years from the expiration of said patent, which takes place on Aug 1, 1868.
-A M Stout, Acting Com'r of Patents

SAT MAY 9, 1868
Meeting of the police commissioners on Thursday: The resignations of Pvt Augustus H Voss, of the sanitary force, & Pvt Fenton D Paxson, were received, & accepted. The application of Augustus Hosch for liquor license was reconsidered, & again rejected. Hamlet Dixon was reappointed an additional private for 90 days, to do Jury at Wisewell Barracks. John D Kidwell was reappointed an additional private for 90 days, to do duty on Pa ave, between 12th & 14th sts. F L Payne was reappointed an additional private for 90 days, to do duty on the square bounded by 9th & 11th sts, & Pa ave & C st. Thos L Salkeld was appointed a private on the force.

Chicago Tribune, thus speaks: The unwelcome intelligence comes from Washington that Johnson may not be convicted & removed. It is asserted that Mr Fessenden has publicly announced that he is preparing an argument showing why the Acting President should be acquitted upon the first 3 articles-he regarding the others as of no account. It only requires 7 Republicans voting with the copperheads to defeat impeachment.

Mrd: on Apr 21, at Portland, Maine, by Rev W H Fenn, Chas B Bailey, of Wash City, to Miss L *_ Chase, daughter of S C Chase, of Portland. [*This could possible be an "A".]

Died: on May 8, at Wash, D C, Mrs Eliz Selden Eaton, wife of Brvt Maj Gen Amos B Eaton, Commissary General of Subsistence. Her funeral will be at the house of Prof Danl E Eaton, at New Haven, Conn, on May 10.

Excellent household & kitchen furniture at auction on May 15, at the late residence of Edw McPherson, 298 H st, between 17th & 18th sts. -Cooper & Latimer, aucts

Cincinnati, May 8. Pat Matthews, a negro, while attempting to carry coal from the residence of C G McPhersons, was shot by a trap gun & mortally wounded.

Large incomes: some of the returns made in the 8th Dist of N Y: Aaron Arnold, $152,752; Loring Andrews, $110,805; Robt Bonner, proprietor of the N Y Ledger, $238,411; August Belmont, $94,687; Stewart Brown, $200,889; David Dorrs, $127,595; Amos R Eno, $196,490; Robt Goelet, $117,986; Peter Goelet, $210,547; Benj Hutton, $159,656; Thos Roosevelt, $101,569; Moses Taylor, $293,780; John D Wolfe, $111,241; Jas Gordon Bennett, $167,000.

MON MAY 11, 1868

Tomorrow the Senate, acting as the court of impeachment, will proceed to pronounce a verdict upon the articles charging Pres Johnson with "high crimes & misdemeanors."

Letters received by the Prussian Legation show that the report that the Baron Holstein has recently been killed in a duel near Brussels is untrue.

Wm Garrett, of Greenville, S C, had a desperate fight with a stallion a few days ago. The animal tore several pieces of flesh from Garrett's side & arm, knocked him down, & kicked & otherwise injured him so that he died in a few hours.

Green & Williams, aucts, sold part of lot 9 in square 382, fronting on 9th st, between the canal & La ave, with a 3 story brick house thereon, to John Rock, for $4,150. They also sold the south third of lot 11 in square 408, on 8th st, between D & Market Space, with a 3 story brick house, to P G Leizer, for $5,350. The same auctioneers sold lot 40 in square 83, on north I st, between 1st & North Capitol sts, with a 3 story brick front house, to Eliz Culinan, for $5,200 cash; part of lot 3 in square 421, with a frame dwlg, fronting on M st north, between 7th & 8th st, to S Groding, for $3,000. Also, part of lot 3, with a good 8 room house, fronting on I st north, between 4th & 5th sts west, to H L Turner, for $2,800.

The cornerstone of the school house to be erected by St Matthew's parish, on K st, between 14th & 15th sts, was laid yesterday; Dr White, paster of St Matthew's Church, conducted the ceremonies; address was delivered by Rev B A Maguire, president of Gtwn College. The bldg, 64 feet x 30 feet, will be of brick 3 stories in height, & will cost about $15,000.

The First Congregational Society of Wash was organized under a charter passed by Congress over one year ago. The organization was affected some time previous under the auspices of Rev Dr Boynton, the pastor. The church is being erected under the direction of Mr Henry R Searle, the well known architect of Wash City. The brick & stone-work will be under the direction of Mr Thos Harvey; carpenter work under Mr J W Rumsey. The cost of the church edifice & ground will be about $100,000. The bldg cmte are Gen O O Howard, J W Rumsey, R H Stevens, D L Eaton, C S Mattoon, & L Watson. The trustees, who by the charter have legal control of the church property, are D M Kelsey, Gen O O Howard, Dr H Barber, A T Langley, & W F Bascom.

Rev J A Walter, the esteemed pastor of St Patrick's Church, is homeward bound, having left Rome on Apr 15. He will spend a short time in Ireland, & expects to leave Cork on May 31st, & arrived in N Y about Jun 12th. His health has improved.

Orphans Court-Judge Purcell, May 9, 1868. 1-Geo P Fisher filed his renunciation of the executorship of Saml H Raybold, Isaac Keeler & J E Dexer renounced their right to administer on W J Keeler's estate in favor of Geo C Chipman. 2-The second & final account of the excs of John T Sullivan, dec'd, was approved & passed. 3-The will of the late C G Page, bequeathing his estate to his wife, Priscilla W Page, whom he names as executor, was fully proven & admitted to probate, letters on the estate being issued to Mrs Page; bond $1,500. 4-R B Mohun gave bond in the sum of $4,000 as administrator of L W Dorsey, Francis Mohun, & F B Mohun, sureties.

The death of Lord Brougham, the veteran English statesman, is announced in our cable despatches. Henry Lord Brougham was born in Edinburgh, in Sep, 1778; was a companion of Jeffrey, Murray, Scott, & Wilson, & one of the founders of the Edinburgh Review. As a lawyer he has managed more important cases than all the rest of the bar. [May 12th newspaper: Lord Brougham's demise took place at his beautiful villa, Louise Eleonore, near Cannes, France, overlooking the Mediterranean sea. He was born on Sep 19, 1779-he does not seem to be certain of his own age. He was descended from an ancient & highly respectable Westmoreland family, & was through his mother the grand nephew of the well known historian, Wm Robertson. No death date given-current item.]

Stephen Conroy shot Albert Townsend at Hoboken on Friday for seducing Mrs Conroy, & then tried to beat out the brains of his wife with the butt of the pistol.

Chas Ross, a sailor, 19 years old, was carried on Sat from the ship **Ansel** to the Pa hospital, in an almost dying condition, the effect of long confinement & deprivation of food & drink. He had stowed himself away before the vessel left Liverpool, & was without nourishment for 14 days. His feet were frost bitten, making it necessary to amputate both legs. It is not supposed he will live.

The well known **Crutchett Cottage**, n e corner of North Capitol st & C st north, at auction. On May 19, we will sell lot 3 in square 683, with the **Crutchett Cottage** thereon. Also, lots 2, & 4 thru 8, immediately adjoining the above. We will sell lot 9 & 10, & part of lot 8, in square 685; lot 1 in square 722; & parts of lots 3, 5, & 6 in square 630. -Cooper & Latimer, aucts

Boston, Mass, May 9. The accounts of Jas D Martin, cashier of the Nat'l Hide & Leather Bank of this city, have been found to have been made up on false figures for some time past. The defalcation will not exceed $50,000. Mr Martin was placed under temporary arrest; released & put in charge of a deputy sheriff.

Premptory sale of the entire balance of the very superior stock of fine liquors, wines, brandies, champagne, sirup, coal, & sperm oil, platform scales, at auction: at the store of R J Ryon. —W L Wall & Co, aucts

Dept of the Interior, U S Patent Ofc, Wash, May 5, 1868. Ptn of Alex'r Hay, adm of the estate of M C A Mellier, dec'd, of Phil, Pa, praying for the extension of a patent granted to said Mellier, May 26, 1857, [said patent was also granted in France Aug 7, 1854, & in England Oct 26, 1855,] for an improvement in making Paper Pulp, praying for the extension of a patent granted to him Aug 7, 1868. -A M Stout, Acting Com'r of Patents

Boston Traveller: murders at Hampton Falls, N H, on Thursday night. Mr Brown, a wealthy farmer, & his wife, Mrs Brown, both about 75 years old, were attacked by a hired man named Pike, with an axe. Pike had been discharged by Mr Brown about a week ago. Their son lived close by, & Mr Brown was able to give him details of the murderous assault & robbery. Mrs Brown died May 9; Mr Brown still survives, with little hopes of recovery. The evidence against Pike is conclusive. [May 14th newspaper: Boston, Mass, May 13. Pike, who was arrested on the charge of murderously assaulting Thos Brown & wife at Hampton, Mass, has confessed the murder & robbery.] [Oct 31st newspaper: Plymouth, N H, Oct 30. Josiah L Pike, convicted of the murder of Mr & Mrs Thos Brown, of Hampton Falls, was sentenced to be hung the second Tuesday of Nov.]

Edw Pason Weston, the pioneer & best known of American pedestrians, is in town, preparing to walk from Bangor, Maine, to St Paul, Minn, & return to Buffalo, N Y, making in all 5,000 miles, to be completed in 100 consecutive days. —N Y Tribune

TUE MAY 12, 1868
The town of **_South Danvers_**, Mass, has decided, by 133 majority, to change its name to "Peabody," it having been the birthplace of that charitable millionaire.

Gen Schofield on Sat appointed Wm B Payne Mayor of Danville.

Selma, May 11. Ryland Randolph, who has been tried before a military commission here for an offence against the civil rights bill, was released from confinement this evening.

Boston, May 9. Some time ago Miss Belinda M Nelma, of this city, sued Danl D Kelly, a wealthy & extensive shipbuilder of this city, & formerly a member of the city gov't, for $20,000 damages for breach of promise of marriage. Yesterday a verdict for the plntf was returned, & the damages were fixed at $3,000.

Mrd: on May 10, by Rev Fr Jamieson, Michl Keliher to Mary Sullivan, both of Gtwn, D C.

Died: on May 10, Wilkerson G Williams, in his 62nd year. His funeral will be this evening at 3 o'clock, instead of 10 in the morning, as mentioned in the evening papers.

Judge Caton, of Illinois, has accumulated an estate of $1,500,000 since 1852, in the telegraph business. His franchise in Illinois, Iowa, & Minnesota has been leased to the Western Union Co at a rental of $90,000 a year for 50 years.

Savannah, May 11. The mate of the schnr **Walton**, which arrived at Portland, Me, reports the loss overboard of Capt J J McCall, off Cape Hatteras, on May 1st; also, the loss of two of the crew, who went out in a boat in search of the captain.

Richmond, May 11. Gen Schofield has appointed G W Gunn the Mayor of Winchester.

Supreme Court of D C, May 11, 1868; Equity No 1,155. Martha E Williams vs Custis P Upshur et al. Wm L Dunlop, trustee, reported he sold square 302, to John W Starr, of the firm of Starr & Metcalf, for $8,358.66, & Starr has complied with the terms of sale.
-A B Olin, Justice -R J Meigs, clerk

Orphans Court of Wash Co, D C. Letters of administration c t a, on the personal estate of Chas Grafton Page, late of Wash Co, D C, dec'd. –P W Page, admx c t a.

Orphans Court of Wash Co, D C, May 9, 1868. In the case of Susan L Hall, admx of Edw Hall, dec'd, the administratrix & Court have appointed Jun 2 next, for the final settlement of the personal estate of the said dec'd, of the assets in hand.
-Jas R O'Beirne, Reg/o wills

WED MAY 13, 1868
Mr Wm Chambers, the Edinburgh publisher, is busy on his autobiography, which will appear some time during the present year.

Col A G Hazard, powder manufacturer of Enfield, Conn, died in N Y on Thursday.

Yesterday Mrs E Schultz was on her way to the Centre Market in a wagon accompanied by her daughter-in-law, when near the corner of 6th st & La ave, one of the traces broke & the horse took fright. Mrs Schultz jumped from the wagon & fell against the curbstone, breaking her arm & cutting her forehead badly. She was carried to the ofc of Justice Barnaclo, when Dr Toner was called & gave her medical aid. She was then conveyed to her residence on H st.

Mrd: on May 12, at the M st Methodist Church, by Rev Wm V Tudor, Chas B Bayly to Miss Mary V Howard. No cards. [Star & Express.]

Mrd: on Feb 28, by Rev John C Smith, minister of the Fourth Presbyterian Church, at his residence, Washington, Woolman Gibson, of Fayette, Missouri, to Miss Addie Richardson, of West River, Md.

For sale: Pianos, just received by steamer **Knight**. –W G Metzerott & Co, Sole Agents of Steinway Pianos, & Mason & Hamlin's Cabinet Organs.

U S Marshal's sale on Jun 2 next, of all the right, title, claim, & interest in an undivided half of that part of square 349, in Wash City, with the bldgs thereon; also, at the foundry on same lot, I will sell half interest in steam engine, boiler, blow pipe, & cupola; seized & levied upon as the property of Absalom A Crockston & Geo H Moore, & will be sold to satisfy execution No 4,235, in favor of Jas T Close use of S F Brown.
–D S Gooding, U S Marshal, D C

Dept of the Interior, U S Patent Ofc, Wash, May 8, 1868. Ptn of Albert G Safford, of Boston, Mass, praying for the extension of a patent granted to him Aug 8, 1854, for an improvement in Applying Springs to Window Sashes, for seven years from the expiration of said patent, which takes place on Aug 8, 1868. -A M Stout, Acting Com'r of Patents

Dept of the Interior, U S Patent Ofc, Wash, May 8, 1868. Ptn of Sarah W Reed, admx of the estate of Chesney Reed, dec'd, & Jane E Mould, admx of the estate of Brooks K Mould, dec'd, of Chicago, Ill, praying for the extension of a patent granted to Chesney Reed & Brooks K Mould, on Aug 8, 1854, for an improvement in Ventilating Railroad Cars, for seven years from the expiration of said patent, which takes place on Aug 8, 1868. -A M Stout, Acting Com'r of Patents

Dept of the Interior, U S Patent Ofc, Wash, May 9, 1868. Ptn of Jacob Senneff, of Phil, Pa, praying for the extension of a patent granted to him Jan 13, 1852, & an additional improvement granted Jul 20, 1852, for an improvement in Metallic Heddies, for 7 years from the expiration of said patent, which takes place on Jul 13, 1866; this application having been authorized by act of Congress. -A M Stout, Acting Com'r of Patents

The celebrated <u>Trotting Stallion</u>, Washington, will stand the present season for a limited number of Mares, from Apr 1, 1868, to Aug 1, 1868, at the Willard Hotel Stables, corner of D & 14th sts, at $30 per season, payable at the time of service.
–G F King, Willard's Hotel Stables, Wash, D C.

THU MAY 14, 1868
Supreme Court of D C, May 13, 1868; Equity No 1,271. Moncure Robinson vs Sidney A Bradley et al. This suit is instituted for the purpose of procuring the conveyance of the fee simple of the tract of land in Wash Co, D C, known as the ***Agg Farm***, & the ***Vineyard***, the property of the late Buckner Thruston, dec'd, to the cmplnt, the holder of the leasehold, by the dfndnts, the heirs-at-law of said Thruston; & subpoenas having been issued against the dfndnts on May 1, 1868, & returned by the Marshal of D C, on May 1, 1868, "Not to be found," as to Chas M Thruston, Helen K Tidball, Edw M Tidball, Jeanette B Logan, S R Logan, Alfred B Thruston, Sidney Thruston, Gates P Thruston, Eliza Houk, Geo W Houk, & Dickenson P Thruston, on motion of W L Dunlop, solicitor for the cmplnt, it is ordered that the dfndnts last named appear on or before the first rule day occurring 40 days after this day, otherwise the cause will be proceeded with as in case of default. –A B Olin, Justice -R J Meigs, clerk

Established in 1844: Andrew J Joyce & Co, Carriage Manufacturers, 477 & 479 14th st.

In the Criminal Court yesterday, before Chief Justice Cartter, the argument upon the motion to admit John H Surratt to bail was resumed. Mr Merrick read: the prisoner is poor; he has no means whatever; his brother has none; his sister is under the disadvantages of great physical debility, supporting herself by her own exertions, in Wash City. Bail overruled-capital case.

Wm T Lee, a clerk in the Gen Post Ofc, has been arrested & held in $5,000 bail, on the charge of robbing the mail. Detectives McDevitt & Thompson made the arrest.

The following is the list of the Board of Visitors selected to attend the annual examination of the U S Naval Academy, at Annapolis, which commences on May 20: Rear Admiral Chas H Bell, U S navy, president; Cmdor T P Green, U S N; Capt J E M Mullany, U S N; Surgeon Phillip Lansdale, U S N; paymaster S F Dunn, U S N; Chief Engineer Wm H Shack, U S N; Prof Chas Davies, LL D, U S Military Aacdemy, West Point; Hon John Scott, Lt Govn'r of Iowa; Lucien A Hagans, Wheeling, West Va.

FRI MAY 15, 1868
Roses, climbing plants, shrubs, dahlias, etc at auction, on May 15, at the corner of Pa ave & 11th st, Star Bldg. A Jardin, Florist -Cooper & Latimer, aucts

Impeachment. Read by Senator Fessenden in the secret session of the Senate on Mondy last. Mr Edw M Stanton was appointed by Pres Lincoln during his first term, which expired May 4, 1865. By the terms of his commission he was to hold "during the pleasure of the Pres for the time being." Pres Lincoln took the oath of ofc, & commenced his second term on the same May 4, & expired Apr 14th of the succeeding Apr. Mr Johnson took the oath of ofc as Pres on the day succeeding the death of Pres Lincoln. Mr Stanton was not reappointed Sec of War by either, but continued to hold under his original commission, not having been removed. How, under these circumstances, did the act of Mar 2, 1867, affect him?

N Y, May 14. A motion was made in the U S Court today to liberate on bail Confederate Naval Ofcr J C Braine. Decision reserved.

Valuable improved real estate at auction; by decree of Supreme Court of D C, passed in Equity No 1,222, wherein Margaret Bayley et al are cmplnts, & Mary E Bayley et al are dfndnts: sale May 25 next, lots 6, 7, & part of lot 2 in square 257, fronting 91 feet 8 inches on north D st, between 13½ & 14th sts west; with a brick stable, frame carriage-house & outbldgs thereon. –Eugene Carusi, trust -Cooper & Latimer, aucts
+
The same, in Equity No 1,095, will sell at public auction, on May 26, on the premises, lots 3, 4, 5, & 9, in square 941, at East Capitol & 9th sts. The above real estate is situated in a rapidly improving location, where property is eagerly sought after.
–Eugene Carusi, trustee -Cooper & Latimer, aucts

Died: on May 14, suddenly, Dr Wm O Lumsdon, aged 63 years. His funeral will be from his late residence, Gay st, Gtwn, May 16, Sat afternoon, at 4 o'clock.

SAT MAY 16, 1868
Edw W Belt, of PG Co, Md, writer & speaker, departed this life, at his residence in this village, last night, after a brief illness. His private life, like his public, was unblemished. –Marlboro' Prince Georgian of yesterday.

City News: We regret to announce the death of our aged fellow citizen, Col W B Randolph, which occurred at his late residence, 284 G st, yesterday. At the time of his death he was in the 81st year of his age; for many years connected with the Treasury Dept, having received an appointment in 1808; was over 20 years chief clerk; an ofcr in the war of 1812; for many years the inspector general of the militia of this district; & was an Old Line Whig. His funeral will take place tomorrow at 3 o'clock, from the Church of the Epiphany. His remains will be interred in **Oak Hill Cemetery**.
+
Died: on May 15, Col Wm Beverly Randolph. His funeral will take place from the Church of the Epiphany, G st, tomorrow, Sunday, at 3 P M, to which the friends of the family are invited without further notice.

Died: on May 9, at the residence of his mother, near Bladensburg, Md, Perrie W Eversfield, in his 36th year.

Mrd: on May 14, by Rev Mr Perrinchief, John R Livermore, of Houghton, Mich, to Eliz, daughter of Thos Antisell, M D, of Wash City.

I will open my Summer Boarding-house on Jun 1; acommodations for 100 boarders; situated 5 miles from Washington & Alexandria, near the Loudoun & Hampshire railroad. –Dervis Bailey, of Va -Wash, D C

For sale or exchange for city property, the Farm called **Summerfield**, in Northumberland Co, Va, of about 219 acres; with a large 2 story brick house in good repair, new barn, corn-houses, ice-house, etc. Apply to Dr D R Hagner, 209 H st.

Promotions in the Treasury since May 1. Sec's Ofc: G W Taylor, Benj Austin, J S Langworthy, & Julius Frank, from 1st to 2nd class; C C Walden, G G Lyons, J W Hubbard, from 2nd to 3rd class. Internal Revenue: W C McGowan, T J Gardner, L A Conner, J A McKnight, P H Rheinhard, & E D Tracey, from 1st to 2nd class; J W Huntington, J A Joyce, & A H Sawyer, from 2nd to 3rd class; Walcott Lay, from 3rd to 4th class. First Auditor's Ofc: Geo T Cottrell, from 1st to 2nd class. Treasurer's Ofc: P H Eaton & W T Parker, from 2nd to 3rd class. Register's Ofc: F Y Commager & Alex'r Burns from 1st to 2nd class; W A Whidney, from 2nd to 3rd class. Fifth Auditor's Ofc: C H Cutler, from 1st to 2nd class.

N Y, May 15. Chas Jefferds, who murdered John Walton & John W Matthews, Jun 30, 1860, was killed by some unknown person yesterday in State Prison at Sing Sing, where he was imprisoned for life. He is supposed to have had some money in his possession. An inquest will be held today.

MON MAY 18, 1868
President Johnson received on Sat & yesterday a large number of despatches from all parts of the country, congratulating him on his acquittal.

Orphans Court-Judge Purcell, May 16, 1868. 1-Mary Farrell gave bond in the sum of $500 as guardian to Bridget O'Halloran, minor. Terence O'Brien & Jas J Farrell, sureties. 2-E C Carrington gave bond in the sum of $15,000 as administrator of Sarah Edelin. Nath Wilson & John H Johnson, sureties. 3-Mary A Edmonston gave bond in the sum of $500 as guardian to the orphans of Elijah Edmondston. Jas Bowen & W E Brown, sureties. 4-Ninth account of John Little, guardian to Julia Little, filed & passed. 5-Distribution account of the personal estate of John L Corcoran, by Ursula Corcoran, admx, filed & passed. First & final account of Ursula Corcoran, admx of John L Corcoran, filed & passed. 6-The will of Primus Leman was filed for probate. He names Susan Leman executrix. 7-The will of Johanna Ahern was filed & fully proven. The testatrix names Patrick Sullivan executor. 8-The will of Harvey Cuittenden was filed & fully proven. He named John H Goddard & Mary, his wife, executors. 9-Anne Turner gave bond in the sum of $300 as guardian to the orphans of Albert Turner. H E Phelps & Elbert Turner, sureties. 10-Eliz A Scrivener gave bond in the sum of $500 as guardian to W H Scrivener, a minor. John C Schafer & F A Jones, sureties. 11-Wm H Wheeler gave bond in the sum of $300 as guardian to Eliza Ann Taylor, a minor. Isaac Lander & John West, sureties. 12-Margaret S Morse gave bond in the sum of $300 as administratrix of P C Wenderstraut. C S Wallach & R L Wallach, sureties.

Died: on May 17, Ellen, wife of Wm Young, aged 81 years. Her funeral will be from her late residence, B st, between 12th & 13th sts, Island, this afternoon, at 3 o'clock.

Chancery sale of very valuable improved real estate at N Y ave & 10th st west; by decree of the Supreme Court of D C, in Equity No 1,050, wherein Yates & Se_by are cmplnts & Geo Seitz et al are dfndnts; public auction on May 28 next, of all the estate, right, title, & interest of Geo Seitz of & into part of lot 1 in square 343, in Wash City, D C, with its bldgs & appurtenances. –Saml L Phillips, trustee -W L Wall & Co, aucts

Dept of the Interior, U S Patent Ofc, Wash, May 13, 1868. Ptn of Joshua Gibbs, of Canton, Ohio, praying for the extension of a patent granted to him Aug 15, 1854, for an improvement in Ploughs, for seven years from the expiration of said patent, which takes place on Aug 15, 1868. -A M Stout, Acting Com'r of Patents

TUE MAY 19, 1868
One hundred guns were fired in Springfield, Mass, on Sat night, & 100 at Westfield last night, in honor of the acquittal of Pres Johnson.

Boy lost. A little son of Mr John C Hatter, corner 20th & P sts, First Ward, has been missing since Monday morning, & any information for his recovery will be kindly received in the Loan Branch Treasury, or at the above named home of Mr Hatter.

Died: on May 17, Henry M Lowry, U S N. His funeral will take place from the residence of C Calvert, 342 19th st, at 11 o'clock A M today.

Died: yesterday, Jennie, youngest child of J P & J Crutchett, aged 3 years & 9 months. Her funeral will take place from the residence of her parents, 6th & D sts, this day at 2 o'clock P M.

WED MAY 20, 1868

On Friday afternoon last, a youth named Judson Gilman Tabler, aged 14 years, while engaged in fishing from the Long Bridge, fell into the river & was drowned. He was the son of Mr Jacob Tabler, who is well known & esteemed in this community. Who can imagine the feeling of his two brothers, the one a cripple, who saw him vainly struggle with the angry element & sink to rise no more, while they were unable to extend a saving hand. No trace has been found of the body as yet.

Worcester, May 19. Patrick Brenner was run over by a locomotive at Munich today, & killed.

Orphans Court-Judge Purcell, May 19, 1868. 1-Filed & passed: first & final account of M F Moran, exc of John McGarvey. 2-First distribution account of the personal estate of Andrew Small by J A Ruff, exc. First account of J A Ruff, exc of Andrew Small. 3-First distribution & first account of the personal estate of Hamilton Loughborough by A H Loughborough, exc. 4-First & final account of J B Hutchinson, exc of Jacob Lowenthal. 5-Ed P Walsh gave bond in the sum of $5,000 as guardian to Michl & Thos Duley, minors. 6-Pat Sullivan gave bond in the sum of $500 as guardian to the orphans of John & Johanna Ahera. 7-The last will of Primus Leman was filed for probate. He names his wife Susan executrix. 8-The will of Timothy Downey was filed & partially proven. He names Patrick Downey, exc. 9-First account of Ursula Corcoran, guardian to Emma & Alice Corcoran, minors, filed & passed.

Dissolution of co-partnership in the Livery & Sales Stable Business, this day, by mutual consent. Jas Keleher will settle the firm. –Jas Keleher, Robt R Pywell

The cost of the impeachment trial of President Johnson is estimated at $400,000. -Albany Argus

The income of Senator Chandler, of Mich, last year, is returned at $43,000.

Mrs Jessie Benton Fremont has been selected to unveil the bronze statue of her father, in St Louis, on May 27.

Geo T M Davis, brother-in-law of Geo Francis Train, who was murdered near Cheyenne, in the mountains, on May 4, had but lately established business in that region, & was a contractor for ties on the railroad. He was at his store at the time of the murder, & was about starting to take the train for Omaha, when a half breed named Brown, lately employed by the company, called on Davis for pay for some work done. He was referred to the cashier, which did not satisfy him. Some words followed, & Brown instantly shot him, & he fell dead. His remains were taken to N Y C for interment.

Extensive sale of valuable real estate within one mile of Wash City, being the residence of the late Washington Berry, called *Metropolis View*; by decree of the Supreme Court of D C, in Equity, wherein Middleton et al are cmplnts & Berry et al are dfndnts; public auction on Jul 11 of *Metropolis View*, located at the terminus of Lincoln ave, opposite *Glenwood Cemetery*, containing 342½ acres, more or less, being the homestead of the late Washington Berry. Property divided into lots, each containing from 5 to 31 acres. Lot 20 is improved by a comfortable frame dwlg & stable. Lot 33 is improved by a good 2 story frame dwlg & necessary out-bldgs. Lot 31 is improved by a large & commodious first class brick dwlg in good condition, the residence of the late Washington Berry, with numerous out-bldgs. Mr Magruder, who resides upon the premises, will show the house.
–John A Middleton, Thos W Berry, trustees -W D Davidge, atty
-Cooper & Latimer, aucts

U S Marshal's sale of a tract of land called *Woodley*, in Wash Co, D C; beginning at a stake of the original tract as conveyed by Lorenzo Thomas to Rachel A E Bowen, together with improvements. Also, I will sell the whole of square 720; lot 8 in square 683; lots 9 & 10 in square 635, in Wash City, with improvements. Seized & levied upon as the property of Robt J Walker & will be sold to satisfy executions Nos 410 & 411, trials Jan term 1868, in favor of the Bank of the Metropolis, & _evington Smith, excx of Richd Smith, vs Robt J Walker. –David S Gooding, U S Marshal, D C

Supreme Court of D C, Equity; Herbert P Curtis et al vs Anne E Smoot. Ratify sale reported by J H Lathrop, trustee; amount of sale to be $34,000. –R J Meigs, clerk

Dept of the Interior, U S Patent Ofc, Wash, May 14, 1868. Ptn of Wm D Andrews, of N Y, N Y, praying for the extension of a patent granted to him Aug 22, 1854, for an improvement in Centrifugal Pumps, for seven years from the expiration of said patent, which takes place on Aug 22, 1868. -A M Stout, Acting Com'r of Patents

Dept of the Interior, U S Patent Ofc, Wash, May 14, 1868. Ptn of Horatio N Gambrell, of Balt, Md, & Thos D Bond, of Wash, D C, administrator of the estate of Singleton F Burgee, dec'd, praying for the extension of a patent granted to said Singleton F Burgee, Feb 27, 1855, antedated Aug 22, 1854, & reissued Nov 17, 1857, for an improvement in Carding Machine, for seven years from the expiration of said patent, which takes place on Aug 22, 1868. -A M Stout, Acting Com'r of Patents

THU MAY 21, 1868

Nothing is more discreditable in the vindictive war which has been waged against the President than the part which Gen Grant has played, both as a willing tool of the Radical faction, & as the champion of his own immediate interest. Ever since the exposure of his duplicity in the Stanton matter he has sought any mode of revenge by which he might inflict injury, in retaliation for the loss of public regard resulting from that development. Hence he has been one of the most active & urgent impeachers, disregarding the propriety of his position & his duty as a subordinate to the consitutional Cmder-in-chief of the army & navy.

Yesterday was a day long to be remembered by the Masonic fraternity of Wash, it being selected by the Grand Lodge of the District for laying the corner-stone of the Masonic Temple now in course of construction at the corner of 9th & F sts. Grand Chief Marshal: Mr McGowan. Assist Grand Chief Marshals: Myers, Wheeler, Hable, Lashhorn, J P Crowley, & Saunders.

Died: on May 14, in Jersey City, N J, in her 38th year, Mrs Catharine R King, wife of T G King, & daughter of the late John McNerhany, of Wash City.

Illness of Ex-Pres Buchanan. The Lancaster Intelligencer states that the condition of Mr Buchanan's health is very critical. He is confined to his bed, & allowed to see no one.

Trenton, N J, May 29. In the U S Dist Court, the death of Benijah Deacon, U S marshal for N J, on Tues, at Mout Holly, was announced, & the court adjourned. He was appointed during Lincoln's first term.

Missing, my son, Locaste Rodier, left home at 8 o'clock morning to attend school, since which time he has not been seen. He is between 11 & 12 years of age, very intelligent, & quick at answering when spoken to; has quite a scar over his right eye; had on, when he left home, brown cassimere pants, black cloth jacket, white shirt, & slouch hat. Any information will be thankfully received by his distressed parents. A liberal reward will be paid for any tidings concerning him. – P Louis Rodier, 22nd st, near N Y ave.

Augusta White Sulphur & Alum Springs, [formerly known as Stribling's,] 3 miles from Staunton, Augusta Co, Va, will be open for visitors Jun 1. –J A Hefelfinger, proprietor

Auction sale of the magnificent estate, in Columbia Co, N Y, 5 miles from the city of Hudson, known as **Stramore Hall**, or **Livingston Manor**; the mansion is in form a Greek Cross, 125x108 feet, with hall 70x20 feet, & cross hall 68x8 feet, built of brick rough cast; with gas, water-closets, bathrooms, billard room, & laundry room. The stable is 70x80, with stalls for 10 horses, besides box stalls, & contains apartments for servants & room for carriages. -Adrian H Muller, aucts, 7 Pine st, N Y.

FRI MAY 22, 1868
Green & Williams, aucts, sold part of lots 1 & 14 in square 488, at E & 5th sts, improved by a 3 story dwlg, to G W Utermehle, for $8,410. W L Wall & Co, aucts, sold yesterday, a brick house & lot on 12th st, between E & F sts, fronting 23 feet on 12th st, running back 75 feet, with improvements, to Geo W Harvey, for $6,190.

Equity Court-Judge Olin. Varnell vs Rainey et al. Order appointing N Callan guardian ad litem to infant.

The old burying ground formerly attached to St Peter's Catholic Church, which is located on H st, near the boundary line, is being obliterated. For some days past Frank Sands, undertaker, has been removing the remains from the old ground to *Mount Olivet Cemetery*. Those persons who can identify the graves of deceased relatives & friends can have them reinterred in such cemeteries as they may name.

Drowned: on May 15, Judson Gilman, son of Jacob & Eugene B Tabler, aged 14 years & 2 days. His funeral will take place from the residence of his parents, C st, between 12th & 13th sts, this morning, May 22, at 10 o'clock. [May 23rd newspaper: The body of J Gilman Tabler, was found Thursday by 3 young men, Henry Reagan, Robt Carroll, & Lewis Maugle. It was carried to the residence of his sorrow stricken parents.]

Elegant first class private residence on Gay st, & brick warehouse on Prospect st, at public auction on May 28, in front of the premises, part of lot 62 fronting 28 feet 6 inches, more or less, on the north side of Gay st, between Wash & Congress sts, adjoining the residence of the late Wm Redin. The improvements consist of a large first class brick dwlg house, No 78, containing 12 rooms, bathroom, china closets, two cellars, gas & gas fixtures throughout the house, range, hot & cold water, washtubs, & all modern improvements. Possession given immediately. Also, part of lots 89 & 90, fronting 30 feet on the north side of Prospect st near High st, by a depth of 100 feet, improved by a substantial Brick Warehouse. Title perfect. -Thos Dowling, auct

Dept of Interior, U S Patent Ofc, Wash, May 15, 1868. Ptn of Solomon S Gray, of Boston, Mass, praying for extension of a patent granted him Aug 22, 1854, for an improvement in Machine for Planing Lumber "out of Wind" for 7 years from expiration of said patent, which takes place Aug 22, 1868. -A M Stout, Acting Com'r of Patents

Dept of the Interior, U S Patent Ofc, Wash, May 15, 1868. Ptn of Sarah W Flanders, of Newburyport, Mass, admx of the estate of Jos F Flanders, dec'd, & Jeremiah A Marden, of Boston, Mass, praying for the extension of a patent granted to them Aug 29, 1854, for an improvement in Leather Splitting Machines, for 7 years from the expiration of said patent, which takes place on Aug 20, 1868. -A M Stout, Acting Com'r of Patents

SAT MAY 23, 1868
Col Hazard leaves an estate of $2,000,000.

War Dept, Adj Gen's Ofc, Wash, Nov 14, 1864. Army Gen Order No 282. Ordered by the President-That the resignation of Geo B McClellan as major general in the U S army, dated Nov 8, & received by the Adj Gen on the 10th instant, be accepted as of Nov 8. By order of the Pres of the U S. E D Townsend, Assist Adj Gen.

Fort Benton, Apr 26. Helena [Montana] Gaz. 1-About 4 miles above **Camp Cook**, one of the proprietors, Nath Crabtree, was out looking for his cattle & was attacked by a party of red devils, & being without arms to defend himself, was pierced with 7 arrows; his men found him in a dying condition. He formerly lived in Jackson Co, Mo.
2-*Fort Ellis*, Montana, Apr 25. Leroy Wyette, age 21 years, was ruthlessly murdered by hostile Indians in order to secure his horse. Capt La Mott ordered out Lt Chance with a detachment to aid a citizen in his search for the body of his companion, who was also killed by the Indians. They returned without succeeding in finding it.

Mrd: on May 21, at the residence of R W Fenwick, by Rev H P Deckert, assisted by Rev S F Bittinger, Rev A A E Taylor, of Gtwn, to Miss Lucy E, daughter of the late T B Munson, of *Munson's Hill*, Va. No cards.

Metropolitan Police Board Thursday. Henry M Lowry was recommissioned as additional private to do duty at the Nat'l State Deposit Co, for 90 days. Wm Flammers was appointed an additional private, to do duty at Schuetzen Park, for 90 days. Francis F McCathran was appointed a private on the force, vice F D Paxton, of Gtwn, resigned. Francis M Skinner was appointed a private on the force, vice A H Voss, resigned.

Fauquier White Sulphur Springs, Va, wil be opened for visitors on Jun 10th. The hotel will be in charge of Mr Thompson Tyler. –Cornelius Boyle, M D

Boston, May 22. Hern Regney sentenced to imprisonment for life for killing Thos A Cleary on Jul 4th last.

Dept of the Interior, U S Patent Ofc, Wash, May 15, 1868. Ptn of Jos H Tuck, of Brooklyn, N Y, praying for the extension of a patent granted to him Jun 16, 1855, & also granted in England Aug 25, 1854, for an improvement in Packing for Stuffing Boxes, etc, for seven years from the expiration of said patent, which takes place on Aug 25, 1868. -A M Stout, Acting Com'r of Patents

Who killed impeachment. Impeachment was privately slain by the conviction of one-third of the Senate that the offences of the President were political differences instead of usurpations.

MON MAY 25, 1868
Died: on May 23, Hattie P, aged 4 years, youngest daughter of Jerome & M E Brown. Her funeral will take place on May 25 at 2 o'clock P M, at the residence of her parents, 334 10th st.

Died: May 18, in Brookline, Mass, Delia, only daughter of Hon Ginery Twichell, aged 20 years.

Advertisement for several weeks in the newspapers of the U S: Two millions pounds sterling for the heirs of Wm Harrison, of London, who emigrated to America about 1796. Address Rd Stafford, No 4 Lincoln's Inn, London. Countless number of Harrisons asserted their relationship, but applicants failed to verify their claim. Among others bearing this respectable name is a Mr David R Harrison, a married man, about 70 years of age, the father of a large family of children. He resides at Harlem, & for many years has been employed as an engraver by the American bank Note Co, 142 Broadway, in this city. This individual to whom the fortunate legatee is indebed for the bestowal of this immense wealth was an uncle, a brother to David's father. He began life a poor boy, but when young he engaged in the East India trade, & amassed a golden treasure; a sum equal to $14,000,000 in greenbacks. Among other relatives of David is Mr Lafayette F Harrison, the well known proprietor of Irving Hall, who is a full cousin.
-N Y Times, 21st

Hon W H Barnum, member of Congress from Conn, is still very ill at his home. His reported recovery was erroneous.

Elegant household & kitchen furniture at auction on May 29, at the residence of Dr Verdi, 151 West st, between Congress & High sts, Gtwn. -Thos Dowling, auct

N Y, May 24. The body of Capt A Depeyster, late Govn'r of the Sailors' Snug Harbor, at Staten Island, who has been missing since Jan 23 last, was found on Sat at Port Johnson, Hudson Co, N J.

Rev John C Lyon died suddenly at Catonsville, Balt Co, on May 21, aged 67 years. He was a minister in the Methodist Episcopal Church for over 40 years, & the founder of the German Methodist Church in America. He was a fine linguist, scholar, & author.

Orphans Court-Judge Purcell, May 23, 1868. 1-First & final distribution account of M E & B H Steinmetz, excs of Saml Steinmetz, dec'd, filed & passed. 2-First acount of Jos Hubley Ashton, adm of Adam Count Garowski, filed & passed. 3-First & final account of H J McLaughlin, guardian to Mary Ann Keating, filed & passed. 4-Second general & second individual accounts of S E Douglass, guardian to J F & H C Douglass, filed & passed. 5-Susan Leman gave bond in the sum of $300 as administratrix of Thos Leman; John Dewdney & Terrence Drury, sureties. 6-The will of Primus Leman was admitted to probate & record.

TUE MAY 26, 1868
Died. Thomas-on May 25, Lewis Foulk, aged 5 years. His remains will be sent to Cincinnati for interment. [May 27th newspaper correction: Died: on May 25, Lewis Foulke Thomas, aged 53 years. His remains will be sent to Cincinnati for interment.]

Obit-died: suddenly, in her 82nd year, at the residence of her son, John K Clement, Sunbury, Pa, Mrs Hannah Kay, relict of Evan Clement, of N J. [No death date given- current item.]

Guardian's sale of real estate, by decree of Orphans Court of D C., in the case, ex parte, of Mary F Emerson, guardian of Mary Homer Emerson, orphan child of Chas Emerson, dec'd; public auction on Jun 8 next, of lot 10 in square 338, fronting 20 feet on north O st, having a depth of 80 feet, being the corner of 11th & O sts.
-Mrs Mary F Emerson, guardian -Green & Williams, aucts

Dept of the Interior, U S Patent Ofc, Wash, May 19, 1868. Ptn of Abner Whiteley, of Springfield, Ohio, praying for the extension of a patent granted to him Jan 8, 1856, for an improvement in Track Clearers to Grass Harvesters, for seven years from the expiration of said patent, which takes place on Aug 22, 1868. -A M Stout, Acting Com'r of Patents

Dept of the Interior, U S Patent Ofc, Wash, May 21, 1868. Ptn of Danl Halladay, of Batavia, Ill, formerly of Ellington, Conn, praying for the extension of a patent granted to him Aug 29, 1854, for an improvement in Governor for Windmills, for seven years from the expiration of said patent, which takes place on Aug 23, 1868. -A M Stout, Acting Com'r of Patents

Alex'r Dumas makes from $150 to $200 a year in selling his own autograph.

Robt Browning's new poem will have the distinction of being the longest poem in the English language.

Brigham Young is having 7 state carriages made for him in N Y.

Mrs Priest, of Licking Co, Ohio, died on Sat last, at the advanced age of more than 100 years. She was born in Culpeper Co, Va, & in removing to the Muskingum Valley, about 20 years ago, walked the entire distance of about 400 miles, carrying an infant child.

Anne Leech, the widow of the famous English artist John Leech, died recently, leaving two delicate orphan children totally unprovided for. She had been living upon the pension awarded to her by Lord Palmerston, but this, of course, stops with her death.

WED MAY 27, 1868
New Haven, May 26. The decree in the Judd divorce case dismisses the petition of Mrs Judd, & grants the cross petition of Dr Judd, & gives him the custody of the children.

Died: on Sunday last, at Flushing, N Y, Mrs Margaret Drake, wife of Willard Drake, formerly of Wash City. Her funeral will take place from the residence of her son-in-law, Geo S Gideon, 374 8th st, corner of K, today at 12 o'clock.

The parties in the famous breach of promise case, just decided at Providence, R I, by a verdict of $1,500 for the plntf instead of the $100,000 asked, were Mrs Delia M Albro, a widow of 40, & Thos J Hill, 60 years old, & a widower, after being twice married.

Extensive stock of hardware, cutlery, tools, etc, at auction, on May 29 & 30, at J E Shields' Store, 331 Pa ave, between 6th & 7th sts. -Green & Williams, aucts

Chancery sale of real estate; by decree of the Supreme Court of D C, passed on Oct 7, 1867, in Equity No 920, in which Margaret A Eckels & her husband, Lewis G Eckels, are cmplnts, & Catharine Barret et al are dfndnts, we will sell, at public auction, on Jun 17, lot 4 in square 837, fronting on I st north, between 5th & 6th sts, Wash City, D C.
-M Thompson, R S Davis, trustees -Green & Williams, aucts

Orphans Court of Wash Co, D C. Letters of administration on the personal estate of Cloreviere Bohrer, late of the State of Va, dec'd. –Geo A Bohrer, adm

Orphans Court of Wash Co, D C, May 26, 1868. In the case of Mary E Russell, admx of Alfred Russell, dec'd, the administratrix & Court have appointed Jun 23 next, for the final settlement of the personal estate of the said dec'd, of the assets in hand.
-Jas R O'Beirne, Reg/o wills

Orphans Court of Wash Co, D C, May 26, 1868. In the case of Laurence A Gobright, exc of Prudence S Aiken, dec'd, the executor & Court have appointed Jun 23 next, for the final settlement of the personal estate of the said dec'd, of the assets in hand.
-Jas R O'Beirne, Reg/o wills

Dept of the Interior, U S Patent Ofc, Wash, May 21, 1868. Ptn of Phillippines Brackenridge, of Natrona, Pa, admx of the estate of Edw Stieren, dec'd, praying for the extension of a patent granted to said Edw Stieren Dec 12, 1854, for an improvement in Treating the Mother-water of Salines, for seven years from the expiration of said patent, which takes place on Dec 12, 1868. -A M Stout, Acting Com'r of Patents

THU MAY 28, 1868
Oak Hill Cemetery. The annual meeting of Lot-Holders owning 300 square feet or more, will be held in the Chapel at the Cemetery on Monday, the 1st of June, at 5 o'clock P M, for the election of a Board of Managers for the ensuing year. –J W Deeble, Sec

Mr Christopher Heise, a member of the Equal Division Sons of Temperance, died on Tuesday, at his residence in the bldg at Mass & N Y & 7th st. He has resided for many years in this community; for some time past he has been incapacitated by disease. His widow is entirely without means, & the membership decided to make all arrangements for, & defray all the expenses attendant upon his funeral. He will be buried this afternoon at 4 o'clock, from his residence. The dec'd was a brother of Mr Jos L Heise, formerly of Wash City, now of Phil, who has been telegraphed of the fact of his brother's demise.

Trustee's sale of valuable bldg lots on I st north, between 4th & 5th sts west, at auction; by decree of the Supreme Court of D C, Chancery No 960, wherein Wm Trueman is cmplnt, & Fred'k Iddins et al are dfndnts; public auction on Jun 18, of the east half of the west half of lot 8 in square 516. –John N Oliver, trustee -J B Wheeler & Co, aucts

Trustee's sale of valuable improved property & brewery on Pa ave & 9th st; by decree of the Supreme Court of D C, wherein Wm G Staetter is cmplnt, & Catharine Baumann, excx of the last will & testament of Paul Baumann, dec'd, & others are dfndnts, the same being Equity cause No 1,069; public auction on Jun 18, the whole of lots 1, 2, 18, 19, & 20, in square 924, with brewery bldgs & vaults, & the other improvements thereon. –W F Mattingly, Fred Schmidt, trustee -Green & Williams, aucts

FRI MAY 29, 1868
Baron Rothschild is said to have made $2,000,000 by his recent transactions on the Bourse.

M Andre L'Heritier, editor of the Courrier des Etats Unis, died in N Y on Wed, after a protracted illness. He was only 28 years of age.

Last Lt M F Maury will soon come back to take his professorship in the Va Military Institute.

Died: on May 28, Thos Byrne, aged 45 years, after a long & painful illness. His funeral will take place from his late residence, corner of 14th st & Ohio ave, this afternoon at 3 o'clock P M.

Died: on May 27, one of the oldest & most respected citizens, after a long & most painful illness, Wm Clarke. His funeral will be this afternoon at 4 o'clock, from St Peter's Church, Capitol Hill.

Mr Henry F Dickens, son of the well known Charles, has made his appearance as a public reader in Kent. No opinion is expressed as to the merits of the performance.

SAT MAY 30, 1868
Nominations by the Pres sent to the Senate yesterday:
Henry Stanbery to be Atty Gen of the U S, to fill a vacancy caused by resignation.
Thaddeus P Mott, of N Y, to be Minister Resident of the U S to Costa Rica, vice Albert Gallatin Lawrence, recalled.
H G Worthington, of Nevada, to be Minister Resident of the U S to the Argentine Republic.
Rear Admiral John A Dahlgren, to be Chief of the Bureau of Ordnance, vice Capt Henry A Wise, resigned.
Cmdor Thos Turner, to be rear admiral in the navy, on the active list, from May 27, 1868.
Capt Alex'r M Pennock, to be a cmdor in the navy, on the active list, from May 6, 1868.
Capt John L Worden, to be cmdor in the navy, on the active list, from May 27, 1868.

Confirmations & Rejections:
Confirmations: A Huggan, to be U S Atty for Utah; Homer G Plantz, U S Atty for the Southern Dist of Fla; W W Thatcher, Assessor of Internal Revenue, 8th Dist of Tenn; A K Osborne, Collector of Internal Revenue, 5th Dist of Wisc; Franklin Haven, jr, Assist Treasurer, Boston, Mass.
The following were rejected: Thos Sim, to be U S Marshal, S C; Joel B McCamant, Assessor of Internal Revenue, 10th Dist of Pa; Jas B Hubble, Collector of Internal Revenue, Montana; Solomon P McCurcy, Justice of the Supreme Court of Utah; 1st Lt Frank Barr, revenue service, to be captain in same.

Worcester, Mass, May 29. The venerable ex-Govn'r Levi Lincoln died at his residence in this city this morning, in his 86th year.

An inquest was held yesterday by Justice Harper, on the body of a German woman, Mary Arnold, who died very suddenly on Wed last, at the residence of her son-in-law, Chas Hohonan, 290 N Y ave. Verdict: she came to her death from a stroke of paralysis, with which she was attacked on May 27, & died the same day. She was without means.

Mrd: on May 28, at the 4½ st Presbyterian Church, by Rev Dr Sunderland, assisted by Rev Geo H Smyth, of the Sixth st Church, Mr Wm H Fletcher, of Winchester, Va, to Mary E Ward, daughter of the late Jos D Ward, of Wash City. No cards.

Died: on May 27, of consumption, Susan Amelia Heinecke, daughter of Saml & Joanna R Heinecke, formerly of Wash City, aged 19 years. Her funeral will take place from the residence of her uncle, Jas W Barker, 423 H st, on May 31 at 3 o'clock P M.

Obit-died: on May 14, at his residence in Upper Marlboro, Md, Hon Edw W Belt, in his 35th year. Mr Belt graduated with the highest honors of his class at the College of St James, Md, in 1852; studied law & in 1854 was admitted to practice. He was known for his moral excellence as brother, husband, & parent, who, in the sacred sanctuary of their darkened homes, bear in silence & tears, the bitterness of their inconsolable grief.

Plymouth, May 27. Cornelius Holmes, brother of Alex'r Holmes, formerly president of the Old Colony railroad, was found murdered this morning, in a by road near the back entrance of the cemetery, in the adjoining town of Kingston, his brains being beaten out. Mr Holmes was quite a wealthy man, his property has been mostly held in trust. It is known that he received quite a large sum of money yesterday, which was found upon him. No positive clue has yet been obtained of the murderer.
+
[May 30th newspaper: Plymouth, Mass, May 29. Saml M Andrews, at whose house, in Kingston Co, Holmes stopped the evening before he was murdered, has been arrested on suspicion of being the murderer. The arrest causes much surprise, Andrews being highly respected among townspeople, a deacon in the Baptist Church, & an intimate friend of the murdered man.]

U S Treasury Dept, May 27, 1868. Lewis Foulke Thomas, who died on May 25, was a grandson of the renowned journalist & bibliophilist, Isaiah Thomas, whose name has so long been a household word in New England, & he had, therefore, a just claim to honorable lineage & hereditary talent. Born in the West, to which his father had removed in early life, his youth was spent in that free & vigorous land.

MON JUN 1, 1868
Orphans Court-Judge Purcell, May 30, 1868. 1-The will of the late W B Randolph was filed & partially proven. He leaves his estate to his widow, & nominates her as executrix. 2-Letters of administration were issued to Eliz C Westerfield, on the estate of David Westerfield; bond $600; Isabella Higgins, on the estate of Wm Higgins, bond $60,000; Sarah B Hodge & J Ledyard Hodge, qualified as executors of W L Hodge; bond $10,000; Isaballa Higgins was appointed guardian of the orphans of the late Wm Higgins; bond $60,000.

A letter from *Fort Lyon*, Colorado, announces the death of Christopher Carson, better known throughout the U S as Kit Carson. He died on May 23, from the effects of the rupture of an artery in his neck. The deceased was born in Madison Co, Ky, on Dec 24, 1809, & was consequently in his 59th year. When quite a child his parents emigrated to Missouri, where he was reared. At age 15 years he was apprenticed to a saddler, but disliking the trade, & being of a wild, roving disposition, he left his master two years after, & started on a hunting expedition. For 8 years he pursued the arduous & dangerous career of a trapper, when he was appointed hunter to **Bent's Fort**, in which capacity he continued for 8 years longer. Returning to Missouri at the end of this time, for the pupose of seeing his family, he met Gen Fremont, & promptly accepted an offer to join his exploring expedition. His reputation as a mountain trapper & guide had, by this time, become extended, his name being connected with many daring feats. In 1847, he was a lt in the U S army, & attached to the rifle corps, & during the rebellion he was promoted from rank to rank until he reached that of brevet brigadier general. As an Indian fighter, he was, perhaps, unequaled. A splendid shot, he is said never to have failed to kill a redskin that he fired at, & the number that fell beneath his aim must have been numerous. During the rebellion he served principally in New Mexico, where he distinguished himself by his untiring prosection of hostilities with his savage foes, then at war with the Government. [Jun 8th newspaper: *Fort Lyon*, Colorado Terrotory. Christopher Carson-Kit Carson: For many weeks past his condition prompted Dr H R Tilton, surgeon at the post, to bring him to the post for treatment, &, notwithstanding the greatest care, his death took place suddenly at 4:15 P M May 23, 1868. The saddest picture in his long, eventful career, was to witness a devoted, loving wife crossing the mountains to welcome him home from the States, & dying suddenly just at their fond meeting. This was more than even the lion hearted Carson could bear. Side by side they now sleep their last sleep beneath the green turf of those distant Plains. His children mourn the loss of a true patriot, gallant soldier, & a devoted father.]

New Merchants' Line of Steamboats, E C Knight, John Gibson, will run during the Winter between N Y, Alexandria, Washington, & Gtwn. Apply at the ofc of the company, corner of N Y ave & 17th st, below the Navy Dept. –J W Thompson, Pres

Supreme Court of D C, May 28, 1868; Equity No 901. Chas G Ball vs Henry Lichau et al. The trustees reported they sold part of lot 13 in square 490 to Jas L Barbour, for the sum of $9,000. –A B Olin, Justice -R J Meigs, Clerk

To John W Hibbs, Jas E Hibbs, Geo E Moore, & Chas Haslup. In a certain chancery suit depending in the Circuit Court of Louisa Co, in which Jas M Teice & Robt S Ellis are plntfs, & you & others are dfndnts, by a decree in said court, rendered on Sep 24, 1867, it was ordered, that if the debts due to the plntfs respectively by you for the purchase of the lot known as the ***Old Parsonage Lot***, lying near the Court-house of said county, should not be paid within 6 months from the date of the said decree, that the undersigned, as com'r, should sell the said lot for that purpose, sufficient to pay the costs of said suit, which is required to be in cash. –Henry W Maury, Com'r; Louisa Co, Va, May 14, 1868.

TUE JUN 2, 1868
The telegraph of yesterday brought the intelligence of the death of ex-Pres Jas Buchanan, who died at his residence, ***Wheatland***, in Lancaster, Pa, on June 1st. He was 78 years of age; the 15th Pres of the U S; born in Franklin Co, Pa, Apr 22, 1791; educated at Dickinson College, graduating in 1809, & having studied law with Jas Hopkins, of Lancaster, he came to the bar in 1812. [One account says he was ill for 4 weeks.]

Boston, Jun 1. 1-A young man, Nehemiah Ball, was arrested in Mansfield, Ohio, on a requisition from the Govn'r of Mass, charged with robbing Rufus Marion, of Concord, Mass, of $20,000. He was brought here today. He is said to be a graduate of Harvard College. 2-Minister Anson Burlingame, Chinese Minister, spent Sunday with his father-in-law, Mr Livermore, at Cambidge.

Died: on May 31, K H Lambell, of heart disease, in his 53rd year; a native of Wash, & the only son of the late Wm & Sophia Lambell, of Wash City. His funeral will take place at his late residence, 750 N J ave, on Tuesday afternoon, at 3:30 o'clock.

$10 reward for lost white terrier slut, with a light brindle patch over the right eye. To be returned to Henry Howard, 280 I st between 16th & 17th sts.

Orphans Court of Wash Co, D C. Letters of administration on the personal estate of David Westerfield, late of Wash Co, D C, dec'd. –Eliz E Westerfield, admx

WED JUN 3, 1868
The Queen of Spain sold a necklace to Madame Mussard for L35,000. The ex-Queen of Naples has followed her example, & sold a pearl & diamond necklace, which had been in the Neapolitan royal family for several generations, to a celebrity of the world of Anonymous of Paris, for L15,000.

Miss Charlotte Cushman is expected to return to the U S next month.

The body of Mr Wm Doolittle, who committed suicide on Friday last, by jumping from the steamer **Keypont** into the Potomac, was recovered on Sunday last by the crew of that vessel, as they were on their return trip. It was taken on board & brought to Wash City, when it was placed in ice until Monday morning, & then sent, by way of the Balt & Ohio railroad, to his friends in Balt.

Orphans Court-Judge Purcell, Jun 2, 1868. 1-Letters testamentary were granted to Sarah L Randolph upon the estate of Wm Randolph; bond $7,000. 2-Geo Mattingly qualified as guardian to the orphan children of Danl Rowland. 3-The will of Wm B Randolph was received & admitted to probate 4-The third & final account of Thompson Ragan, guardian to Henry Ragan, was approved & passed. 5-Mary H Rowland relinquished her right as guardian to the minor children of Danl Rowland.

Mrd: on Jun 2, at the Fourth Presbyterian Church, by Rev John C Smith, Mr Frank Smith to Miss Maggie C Bentley, both of Wash City. No cards.

Died: on May 28, in New Orleans, La, at the residence of Col Geo G Garner, Col Wm L Wynn, of Assumption Parish, La, aged 69 years & 2 months.

Lancaster, Pa, Jun 2. Mr Buchanan's funeral will be on Jun 4 at 3 P M.

Delicious strawberries, fresh gathered, grown at my nursery, can be had daily at my store, 446 7th st, opposite the U S Patent Ofc. –John Saul

Maj Gen Hooker was expected to arrive in N Y from Europe yesterday. It is reported that while his own health is not improved, that of his wife is broken down.

Mr Crabtree, the father of the actress, Lotta, left St Louis Sat night, after having plundered his daughter's trunk of $25,000 in Gov't bonds, $10,000 in greenbacks, & all her jewelry. He proposes to go to England, & take his ease. [Jun 10th newspaper: N Y, Jun 9. Crabtree, the father of Lotta, the actress, has been indicted by the grand jury of this county, on complaint of his daughter, for taking away her property, the proceeds of her professional services. He stands committed to trial without bail.]

Bakery for sale together with the property: ground 95 feet by 130 feet, with a 2 story brick dwlg containing 5 rooms, including store shelving, show cases, & counters, roomy bake house 16 feet x 20 feet, with oven capacity to bake 500 loaves at one heat & all tools necessary to go right to work; one horse & wagon, stables & outhouses. Title indisputable. Apply to Wm Guinand's Coal Ofc, 1st & B sts, Capitol Hill.

Orphans Court of Wash Co, D C. Letters testamentary on the personal estate of Wm B Randolph, late of Wash Co, D C, dec'd. –Sarah L Randolph, excx

Orphans Court sale by catalogue of the marble statuary, library, valuable old oil paintings, engravings, wines, table & bed linens, etc, the property of the late Chas Carroll Mactavish, at auction; by order of the Orphans Court for Balt City, at store 161 West Balt st, on Jun 11 at 10 o'clock. Terms cash. Marcella Mactavish, excx of Chas Carroll Mactavish, dec'd. –Thos P Yearley, Atty -Saml H Gover, Auct, 84 Balt st.

Supreme Court of D C, Equity 1,176. Perry Elliott, Catharine Elliott, Jas Frizzell, & others, vs Mercy Ann Frizzell, Viemma Serene Frizzell, Isaiah H Frizzell, Wm M Frizzell. It will be for the advantage of the infant dfndnts & other parties to sell the real estate of John C Frizzell, dec'd, described in the will. Parties interested to appear at my ofc on Jun 6 at 12 o'clock. –Walter S Cox, auditor

Dept of the Interior, U S Patent Ofc, Wash, May 26, 1868. Ptn of Clark Alvord, of Courtland, Wisc, praying for the extension of a patent granted to him Nov 21, 1854, for an improvement in Hand Brick Moulds for seven years from the expiration of said patent, which takes place on Nov 21, 1868. -A M Stout, Acting Com'r of Patents

THU JUN 4, 1868
Murder yesterday on Pa ave, between 4½ & 6th sts: Mr John Henry Faulkner, son of Mr W H Faulkner, residing on Mass ave, between 6th & 7th sts, was killed by an unknown negro man, whose identity is not known. The altercation was over angry words that passed between the two of them.

An English paper records the death of Lt Pollard, the gallant midshipman who avenged Nelson's death at the battle of Trafalgar. Sixty years after the battle he had arisen to the rank of lt, & then, when attention was called to his case, a grateful government elevated him to the grade of commander, but with no increase of pay.

Shooting affair last night resulted in the instant death of Thos *Kelleher, a bookbinder, by a pistol shot fired by a companion, Lep Turpin, who in company with Henry Dubant, had been with the deceased during the evening; all were intoxicated. The announcement of the facts threw a pall over the spirits of many of our citizens, to whom all of the participants are well known. [Jun 5th newspaper: Thos H *Kellaher was about 42 years of age, & had been a resident of Wash since 1853, contantly engaged at his trade of bookbinder, & leaves a wife & 3 children. Turpin is about 29 years of age, a harness maker by trade, well known in the city, especially in the neighborhod in which the homicide took place; for several months he has not been at work. A singular coincidence that the deceased & Faulkner, who was killed the night before, were bosom friends, & were frequently together.] [Jul 25th newspaper: Levin Turpin, one of the principals in the terrible Kelleher homicide, was sentened to 8 years' hard labor in the penitentiary.]
*Two spellings of Kelleher/Kellaher

Mrd: on Jun 2, in St Ann's Church, Annapolis, by Rt Rev Bishop Whittingham, H E Offley, of Gtwn, D C, to Mary, eldest daughter of Rev Dr Nelson, of Annapolis. No cards.

Died: on Jun 3, by a wound inflicted by the hand of an assassin, John H Faulkner, aged 32 years. His funeral will be from the residence of his father, Wm H Faulkner, 439 Mass ave, on Jun 5 at 3 o'clock P M.

FRI JUN 5, 1868
Funeral of the ex-Pres Buchanan; the family carriage of Mr Buchanan conveyed his immediate mourners, including Mrs Johnson, formerly Harriet Lane. Rev Edw Buchanan, brother of the deceased, was present with his entire family. The mansion of *Wheatland* was thrown open to the public; the body was placed in the hall, while the family occupied the room in which Mr Buchanan died. The ex-Pres was dressed in a satin shroud, white necktie & high collar, as in life. The place of burial stands on the opposite side of the city from *Wheatland*. He directed the following inscription to be cut in his tombstone: "Here rest the remains of James Buchanan, fifteenth President of the United States, born in Franklin County, Pennsylvania, April 23, 1791. Died at his residence, at *Wheatland*, Lancaster County, Pennsylvania," & adding the day of my death, which is now so near. Mr Buchanan's last words were, "Oh, Lord Almighty, as Thou wilt."

Mrd: on Jun 4, at the residence of Mrs Lindsay, by Rev Dr Hall, Geo Peabody, late of Ohio, to Emma, youngest daughter of the late Dr Louis Lindsay, of Winchester, Va. No cards. [June 6th newspaper: Mrd: on Jun 4, at the residence of Mrs Lindsay, by Rev Dr Hall, Geo Peabody Este, of Ohio, to Emma, youngest daughter of the late Dr Louis Lindsay, of Winchester, Va. No cards.]

Mrd: on Jun 2, at the Foundry Church, by Rev MrTudor, Mr Jas H Reed, late of Westmoreland Co, Va, to Miss Emma J Clokey, of Wash City.

Died: on Jun 3, Catherine O'Brien, of Limerick, Ireland, of dropsy, in her 81st year. [Limerick & Vienna, Austria papers please copy.]

Supreme Court of D C, Jun 4, 1858; Equity 109, Docket 7. Hagner et al vs Randall et al. Alex'r B Hagner, trustee, reported he has sold lot 13 in square 141, to John Wilson, for $8,000. –A B Olin, Justice -R J Meigs, clerk

Supreme Court of D C, Jun 4, 1868; in Chancery; No 1,296 Equity, Doc 9. Lorinda A Etheridge vs Jas Etheridge. A subpoena has been issued in the above cause, & returned *non est*; on the motion of the plntf by R S Davis, her solicitor, ordered that the dfndnt cause his appearance to be entered herein or or before the first rule day occurring 40 days after this day, otherwise the cause will be proceeded with as in case of default.
-A B Olin, Justice -R J Meigs, clerk

SAT JUN 6, 1868
The President sent to the Senate yesterday the following nominations: F T McMahon, Minister Resident at Paraguay; W H Parker, Sec Idaho Territory; J Mason, Justice of the Peace, Dist of Columbia.

The Senate yesterday confirmed the following nominations: H G Worthington, of Nevada, to be Minister Resident at the Argentine Republic, vice Asboth, dec'd. Alfred Allen, of Ky, Consul at Foo Chow, China. Thos B Asten, Assessor of Internal Revenue for the 8th Dist of N Y, vice Bleecker, to be removed. Cmdor Thos Turner, rear admiral on the active list, & Capt John L Worden, commodore.

We are glad to report that Master Geo Handly, who was dangerously wounded, & reported dead yesterday, is now considered out of danger by Dr P Crogan, who has been in constant attendance since he was wounded.

Died: on Jun 5, at her residence, **Brentwood**, near Wash, Mrs Catharine Pearson, widow of the late Hon Jos Pearson, aged 77 years. Her funeral will take place from **Brentwood** on Jun 8 at 1 P M. Friends & acquaintances are invited to attend, & will find carriages in waiting in front of St John's Church at 12 o'clock.

Died: on Jun 6, at the residence of her grandson, Wm W Grant, after a long & painful illness, Mrs Catharine Wagoner, in her 97th year. Her funeral will be on Sunday afternoon next, at 3 o'clock, at the German Lutheran Church, Gtwn, D C. [Balt, Hagerstown, Md, & LaCrosse, Wisc, papers please copy.]

An infant daughter of Mr Jas J Rogers, 4th st, Brooklyn, died on Friday night in consequence of being bitten the previous day by a pet black & tan pup. It is supposed that the infant died rather from the effects of fright than the bite, which did not appear to be of a serious nature.

A young girl, only 14 years old, named Christadora Deuer, poisoned herself in Waukesha, Wisc, last week, because of her father's intemperance & neglect. She left a note: I have taken poison-you know why.

Walter Harper, our esteemed fellow citizen died on May 14, suddenly, at the Hotel Corona d'Italia, Florence, Italy. His travelling companion [Mr Hutchings, the artist] was out for a short time, & on his return found him dead in his room. He died of disease of the heart. His funeral was attended by the few Americans then in Florence. The services were performed by Rev Dr Van Nest, of the American Church. He was buried in the Protestant cemetery. He was for more than 50 years a resident of this city.

Miss Josephine Davis, of Poland, Maine, on a visit to friends in Auburn, Maine, died suddenly on Sat, while walking from one room to another. She was a dwarf, being but about 3 feet in height, & weighing 54 pounds. She was about 35 years of age. She was about the size of an ordinary child of 2 years.

MON JUN 8, 1868
Louisville, Jun 7. Alex'r C Bullett, for 30 years associated with the press of this country, died here yesterday.

Green & Williams, aucts, have sold lots 50 thru 57, 59 & 60, fronting on Webster ave, being part of a tract of land owned by Geo W Caton, dec'd, to Saml Hoover, at five cents per foot. Also, 2 valuable lots at the n e corner of 9th & G sts north; one lot adjoining Smith's church, 25 feet front by 100 feet deep, to J M Duncanson, at \$1.62½ per foot; the next adjoining lot 25 feet by 100 feet deep, to W A Cunningham, at \$1,82½. Cooper & Latimer, aucts, sold part of lots 1 & 17 in square 686, on First st east, near the corner of B st north, to Thos Ewing, at .50 per square foot. Messrs Galligan & Townshend, aucts, sold lot 8 in square 518, 22 feet front by 94 feet deep, improved by a frame house, fronting on H st, between 4th & 5th sts, to E Williams, for \$3,450. Messrs Hall & Ross [late R M Hall's Real Estate Exchange] have sold the farm, containing 105 acres, on the new Bladensburg road, opposite the *Metropolis View* property, about $3/4^{th}$ a mile from Boundary st, to Chas Stewart, late of N Y, for \$22,000.

Meeting last Friday of the Nat'l Union Bldg Association; the following elected ofcrs: Pres-Saml Bacon; Vice-Pres-N D Larner; Treasurer-R T Morsell; Sec-W T Johnson; Atty-R T Morsell. Directors: Messrs Jos Fry, W M Barry, J H Halley, R T Morsel, Saml Stalley, Wm Lord, H M Dallenger, W H Bailey, & H O Hood.

The beautiful park of the Washington Scheutzen Association will be opened today with appropriate ceremonies; six months ago the association purchased of Mrs Lindsley her farm of 12 acres located on 7th st road, for the sum of \$36,000-\$3,000 per acre. The Washington <u>Scheutzen Verein</u> is an organization numbering about 286 members, among whom are many of our best known German & American citizens. Some of our wealthiest citizens are members of the association. The president is Mr B Henze, one of our German fellow citizens. The hotel on the grounds is neatly fitted up with an immense dancing pavilion; shooting galleries, bowling alleys, & ample stabling. Superintendent is Mr Christian Worsch. Mr Lafayette Jacobs & his brother will perform & walk the tight rope. The brothers Jacobs, under the name of the Denville brothers, have achieved quite a reputation in other cities for their proficiency in their line of entertainment. A splendid band of the 12th U S infty, under the leadership of Prof Dansch, has been engaged. Prof Schroeder, with his fine string band, will furnish the music for the dancing community.

Justice O E P Hazard was before the Supreme Court of the District in General Term in Sat, to answer to the rule laid upon him to show cause why he should not be removed from ofc for appropriating money collected by him for the Gov't. Mr Thos Feinour, clerk of the Police Board, being sworn, testified that Justice Hazard has never made any returns to Headquarters whatever of fines, etc, by him collected as a magistrate during the past year. Chief Justice Cartter: this is a case without apology. The dfndnt has, for one whole year, appropriated to himself the money of the Gov't, & has continually & protractedly acted in utter disregard of his duty as an ofcr, & incontempt of the law, & thus designedly. He is therefore removed from office. Judge Olin said he fully concurred in the opinion expressed, & that the respondent should be indicted for a misdemeanor. He hoped the grand jury would act on this case, & show to the public that their rights would be protected.

Alanson H Reed charged by Mr Fred Depro, special agent of the Post Ofc Dept with having used the U S post ofc at Wash, D C, in connection with other persons unknown to the U S Gov't at the present time, for the purpose of defrauding postmasters & others in different towns of various sums of money under false & fraudulent pretence. Mr Reed pleaded not guilty to the charge.

Jurors drawn for the June Term of the Criminal Court. Grand Jurors: [C-City; c-county; G-Gtwn.]

Jas S Stettinius-C
Geo W Cheseline-C
H N Easby-C
Geo E Dement-C
Robt J McFarland-C
Peter Bopp-C
Christian F Schmidt-C
Geo S Hepburn-C
J Nicholson-G
Pierce Shoemaker-c
Wm Davis-c

R E Miller-C
Geo D Young-C
Jas T Cross-C
Lewis Schwing-C
Reuben D Dietrick-C
A R Shepherd-C
John H Howard-C
Frank Linkins-C
A P Snyder-C
Chas Ossinger-C

Petit Jury:
T A Newman-G
J F Wollard-C
Wm Jones-C
Jas Vanderwerken-G
John W Ray-c
Jos Gerhardt-C
John T Hill-C
Chas Milburn-c
J F Young-c
Richd M Hall-C
Jas F Young-C
Henry Queen-c
John S Cragin-C

Chas H Hall-C
M L Noerr-C
Geo Sonnenschmidt-C
D T Johnson, C
Saml Williams-C
Wm J McDermott-C
David Ullman-C
Saml Wallach-C
Jos R Cassin-C
Jas Goddard-G
John W Wetherell, C
Reuben A Bacon, C
Wm Vernon-G

Orphans Court-Judge Purcell, Jun 6, 1868. 1-Margaret Bond gave bond in the sum of $2,000 as admx of Thos Byrne, dec'd. Matthew Byrne & A J Joyce, sureties. 2-A T T Donn gave bond in the sum of $1,000 as guardian of Oscar Martin. O H Donn & M A Donn, sureties. J J Waters gave bond in the sum of $1,000 as administrator of R H Owens. Richd J Jackson & G H Bohrer, sureties. 3-Thos Jenkins gave bond in the sum of $500 as guardian to orphans of R L Jenkins. A J Joyce & J T Boisseau, sureties. 4-The following accounts were filed & passed: Account of the personal estate of A J West, by Margaret West, admx. Sixth account of Andrew Jackson, guardian to his infant children. Account of the personal estate of B S Bohrer, by G A Bohrer, exc. Final account of the excs of Mich & Mary R House, dec'd. 5-The will of Wm O Lumsden was partially proven. 6-The will of the late Thos Byrne, beqeathing his property to his wife &

children, & if they die without issue, to St Vincent's, St Joseph's Orphan, & St Ann's Infant Asylums, was filed & partiall proven, & letters testamentary issued to Margaret Byrne, excx; bond $2,000.

Mrd: on Jun 4, at Duddington, Wash City, by Rev Fr Boyle, Ira Nichols Burrett, of Pa, to Eliz A, daughter of the late Maj A A Nicholson, U S M.

Died: on Jun 6, Orville T Gilman, of Salem, Wash Co, N Y.

House of Reps-Jun 6: 1- Cmte on Invalid Pensions, made a large number of reports. Bills passed, granting pensions to the following persons:
Margaret Davis, widow of Wm H Davis, late acting surgeon, 18th Missouri volunteers.
Eliz Cassidy, widow of Lt Michl Cassidy, 69th Pa infty.
Louisa M Willeston, widow of Sgt Saml P Willeston, 4th Mass battery
Esther Graves, late a nurse in the army, [allowing $8 a month from Jan, 1865.]
Mary Atkinson, mother of a late quartermaster U S navy
Fred'k Denin, father of Wm F Denin, 9th Maine volunteers
Jos B Roden, late 16th N Y volunteer.
Eliza Matthews, mother of Jos W Matthews, late 109th Pa volunteers.
Wm F Nelson
Lucinda J Letcher
Julia A Barton, widow of W M Barton, 7th Ky volunters.
Julia Carroll, widow of Edw Carroll, 29th Mass volunteers
Cornelia Peaslee
Mary Cover
Melinda Ferguson, widow of Jas Ferguson, 1st Ky cavalry
David Duhigg, father of the late Lt Duhigg, 1st Vt artl.
Mary Merchant
Mary A Felardo, widow of Onesimus Felardo, 125th N Y volunteers
Geo Truax, 1st Va volunteers
Phoebe McBride, mother of Thos McBride, late 87th Ill volunteers.
Harriet E Shears, widow of John T Shears, late 57th Ill volunteers
Wm H Blair, late 12th Miane volunteers.
Christopher M Cornesser, Independent Iowa House Guard
Sarah Webb, widow of Wm R Webb, 1st Tenn volunteers.
Bridget W McGrorty, widow of Lt McGrorty, 5th Minnesota volunteers.

On Sat last our townsman, Chas Knap, with his estimable wife, started upon a European tour, attended by the heartfelt good wishes of a host of truly devoted friends. Mrs Knap is an invalid, & the trip is hoped to be beneficial to her health.

Balt, Jun 7. 1-Milton B Rogers was arrested today, & confessed having obtained $2,105 within 2 months past on forged checks in the name of Brooks & Rogers, wholesale shoe dealers, from the Western Nat'l Bank of this city. 2-The North German ship **Hermit**, from Bremen, brings 283 German emigrants, all in good health.

Orphans Court of Wash Co, D C, Jun 6, 1868. In the case of Adaline Lusby, admx of Jas Lusby, dec'd, the administratrix & Court have appointed Jun 30th next, for the final settlement of the personal estate of the said dec'd, of the assets in hand.
-Jas R O'Beirne, Reg/o wills

The Senate on Sat confirmed the following nominations:
Wm L Howard, of Ala, to be receiver of public moneys at Mobile.
John H Brodhead, com'r to adjust the claims of Indiana for expenses incurred in the late war.
Nathan Goff, to be U S Atty, for West Va.
Capt Pennock, to be cmdor in the navy.
Cmder N B Harrison, to be capt in the navy.
Lt Cmder Wm P McCann, to be cmder in the navy.
Alfred T Lacy, to be collector of internal revenue for the First Dist of Louisiana, vice Steadman, resigned.
W W Randall, of Wisc, to be consul at Taleshusno.
John W Haverstack, to be 1st lt in the marine corps.
Mahlon Wilkinson, of Dakota, to be Indian agent for Upper Missouri.
Oliver Mungen, to be consul at Turk's Island.
Brig Gen Jas H Carlton, to be major general by brevet, for meritorious services during the late war.
The Senate rejected the following nominations:
Geo B McClellan to be Minister to England.
Colby Knapp, to be collector of internal revenue for the 8th Dist of Illinois.
Julius T Newburg, to be collector of internal revenue for Idaho.
Josiah Durham, to be assessor of internal revenue for the 3rd Dist of Mass.
Chas S Hull, to be collector of customs for the Dist of Stonington, Conn.
Walter E Carlin, to be assessor of internal revenue for the 10th Dist of Illinois.

TUE JUN 9, 1868
We're constantly Manufacturing & have on hand the Largest Stock & Greatest Variety of Sole Leather & Dress Trunks, with McMurray's Patent Stays. Buy at the Practical Manufactory, 500 7th st, East Side. –Jas S Topham & Co

Mrd: on Jun 2, at Chambersburg, Pa, by Rev Dr Mowry, T B Wigfall, of Va, to Mary Aston Chambers, daughter of the late Jos Chambers, of that place. No cards. [Richmond papers please copy.]

Died: on Jun 8, Mrs Ann Allen, in the 6_th year of her age. Her funeral will be from the M E Church on 4th st east at 4 o'clock this evening, Jun 9.

Died: on Jun 8, in Wash City, Cmder Richmond Aulick, U S navy, aged 40 years. His funeral will be on Jun 10th, from his late residence on 19th st between I & K sts.

Died: on Jun 8, D B Wylie, a native of Scotland, & member of the Richings' Opera Troupe. His funeral will take place today at 2 P M, from St Aloysius Church.

Capt Jerome Napoleon Patterson Bonaparte is at the N Y hotel. He came by the last steamer, & is going to Balt.

H Pugh, Merchant Tailor, has removed from 474 14th st to his new store 2_6 Pa ave, between 14th & 15th sts.

Valuable mortgaged real estate in PG Co, Md, for sale: by power of atty from Saml Meakin dated May 30, 1868, filed in the Clerk's ofc of the Circuit Court of PG Co; public sale at the Court-house in Upper Marlboro, PG Co, on Jul 8, all that piece or parcel of land in said county known as *Prospect Hill*, the same being composed of several tracts or parts of tracts of land called *Donald's Grove, Holliday's Choice, Bowie's Purchase, Riley's Neglect*;] *Jones' Loss/Less*; contained in all about 560 acres. Being the tract of land first described in a mortgage from Geo W Duvall of Geo & wife to said Saml Meakin, dated May 21, 18_4, recorded in the land records of said county. –Peter W Crain, Atty for Saml Meakin.

Supreme Court of D C, Equity 1,048; Docket 8. Stoneman et al vs Hardesty et al. G H Williams, trustee, reported he sold the real estate in the above mentioned cause. -A B Olin, Justice -R J Meigs, clerk [No details given.]

Orphans Court of Wash Co, D C, Jun 6, 1868. In the case of Robt H Ives, exc of Chas Morris, dec'd, the executor & Court have appointed Jun 30th next, for the final settlement of the personal estate of the said dec'd, of the assets in hand. -Jas R O'Beirne, Reg/o wills

Dept of the Interior, U S Patent Ofc, Wash, Jun 1, 1868. Ptn of Wm H Akins & Jos C Burritt, of Ithaca, NY, praying for the extension of a patent granted to them on Sep 19, 1854, for an improvement in Calendar Clocks, for seven years from the expiration of said patent, which takes place on Sep 19, 1868. -A M Stout, Acting Com'r of Patents

WED JUN 10, 1868
Jas Malady & wife were murdered at Seaforth, Canada, on Sunday. Their son has been arrested for the crime.

The schnr **Evening Star** capsized off Goderich, Canada, on Sunday, & the captain & one of the crew were drowned.

Ofc of Internal Revenue, Treasury Dept, Wash, D C, Jun 8, 1868. Sir: In pursuance of a purpose known to my friends for several months past, I hereby tender to you the resignation of my office, to take effect on the qualification of my successor; who shall be nominated by yourself & confirmed by the Senate. –E A Rollins, Com'r [To Andrew Johnson, Pres of the U S.]

J C Southall has sold the Charlottesville Chronicle, & retired from the editorial profession.

Mrd: on May 14, by Rev R T Howlett, Mr John H Gardner, of Wash, to Miss Ellen C Fraunces, of Phil. [Phil papers please copy.]

Mrd: on Jun 4, at *Oland Farm*, Stafford Co, Va, the residence of the bride's mother, by Rev Chas B Young, Henry C O'Bannon, of Falmouth, Va, to Lizzie Frazier, of Va.

For sale or let, a beautiful country residence on Elk Ridge, Howard Co, Md, one mile from the Relay House, Balt & Ohio railroad; contains 63 acres; frame dwlg, well built, with parlor, dining room & library on the first floor; 8 rooms on the 2nd floor; a summer kitchen adjoins the dwlg; with a barn, stable, spring-house, servants-house-4 rooms, chicken-house, ice-house, coal sheds, & cistern. -Edwin A Lewis, [Care of O Morton Stewart] 52 S Gay st, Balt, Md.

Yesterday a lady named Miss E Byron attempted to drown herself in the canal at the foot of 12th st; several men who were standing near the bridge, at once proceeded to rescue her. It was with difficulty they succeeded. She was taken to the Central Guard House, where Dr P Croghan attended her. She once before made a similar attempt & was prevented. The reason assigned was family difficulties.

Cavendish, Vt, Monday evening last. Mr Albina Knights, wife of Horatio Knights, & Miss Ellen M Cary, both operatives in Jas Felton's woollen mill, proposed to cross the mill pond in a boat, the water being high, & the current strong, from so large a flow over the dam. They both were drowned while their friends on the shore stood powerless.

THU JUN 11, 1868
Real estate sales: Danl Rawlins purchased part of lot 29 in square 904, on 8th st west, with a brick house thereon, for $1,825. J E Merrell/Herrell purchased part of lot 4 in square 876, on south E st, with a frame dwlg house, for $1,450. Moses Kelley bought lot 12 in square 183, fronting 27 feet on 17th st, between L & M sts, at 27 cents per square foot. Albert Gleason was the purchaser of a strip of land, land allotted for a private road from Piney Branch road to the land allotted to the Widow's Dower, said road being near Columbian College, for 8 cents per foot. Thos Dowling, auct, Gtwn, sold the brick house, with a large back bldg, 54 Bridge st, the residence of the late Jas Fullalove; lot is 24 feet front by 120 feet deep, to John Thecker, for $4,010. A lot, improved by a 4 room house, at the s e corner of 25th & I sts, was sold to Thos Riley, for $465.

The funeral of Cmder Richmond Aulick took place yesterday, from his late residence, 258 north I st, & was attended by Pres Johnson, Secretaries Welles, Schofield, McCulloch, Postmaster General Randall, Gen Grant, & ofcrs of the army & navy.

Mr Blakely, inventor of the gun bearing his name, & his wife, are among the victims to yellow fever in Lima, Peru. In the middle of last month the daily mortality was between two & three hundred, & nearly three thousand were in the hospitals.

Phil, Jun 10. John S Warner, sr, a veteran of the war of 1812, & a well known silversmith of this city, died yesterday, aged 71 years.

Montpelier, Vt, Jun 10. Maj Chas W Upham, paymaster in the U S navy, was found dead in his bed here this forenoon, aged 50 years.

Troy, N Y, Jun 10. Patrick Callahan, who had been on trial here for the murder of Patrick Dunn, 2 years ago, was convicted of murder this afternoon.

Worcester, Mass, Jun 10. Asa Hapgood, the veteran conductor & proprietor of the N Y & Boston sleeping cars, died at his residence in this city today.

Mrs John Wood is not to return to this country, as reported, at present. She expects to manage a theatre in London next winter.

Robt Heller, whose real name is W H Palmer, is in the English bankruptcy court, with liabilities amounting to L2,665, principally in this country. The final meeting is to be held on Jun 19.

The library of M Brunet, the book collector, has been sold in Paris by auction, & realized 305,825 francs. Two volumes of Rabelais brought 3,750 francs, & a copy of Machievel's work on Peace & War was sold for $5,000 francs.

Trustee's sale of valuable property near the Balt & Wash Railroad; by deed of trust from Saml C Crauford & wife, recorded in Liber F S No 5, of the land records of PG Co, Md; public sale on Jul 3 next, the property now in the possession of said Crauford, & whereon he resides, containing about 106 acres; improved by a commodious frame dwlg, erected within a few years past, in good repair, & all necessary out-houses. –N C Stephen, trustee

Dept of the Interior, U S Patent Ofc, Wash, Jun 5, 1868. Ptn of Elias Ingraham, of Bristol, Conn, praying for the extension of a patent granted to him Sep 3, 1861, for an improvement in Design for Clock Case Front, for seven years from the expiration of said patent, which takes place on Sep 3, 1868. -A M Stout, Acting Com'r of Patents

Gen Saml F Cary, M C, from Cincinnati, delivers the Fourth of July oration before the Young Men's Association of Albany.

FRI JUN 12, 1868
Messrs Wall & Co have sold part of lot 2 in square 396, improved by a 2 story frame house, on Q st north, between 8th & 9th sts west, to John Paxton, for $1,470.

Nominations by the Pres transmitted to the Senate yesterday: C K Hall, collector of customs, Dist of Texas; J C Forsyth, collector of internal revenue, 15th Dist of N Y; E C Darlington, collector of customs, Dist of Yorktown, Va; C J Barbour, appraiser of merchandise, Port of Portland, Me; H M Lee, assessor of internal revenue, 3rd Dist of Mass; Henry Naylor, member of the Levy Court, in place of Owen Thorn, whose name is withdrawn.

Died: on Jun 11, Mrs Julia A Davis, wife of S R Davis, of the Adjutant General's Office, aged 28 years. Her funeral is today, at 4 P M, at his residence, 137 8th st, between P & Q.

The Barnum's Museum property in N Y was sold at auction on Wed for $432,000.

Bloomington, Ill, Jun 11. A C Haldredge, formerly of Monroe Co, N Y, & for 4 or 5 years past clerk in the Ashley House, in this city, jumped from a 4th story window of the Ashley House this forenoon, alighting on his head, & killing himself instantly. Delirium tremens was supposed to be the cause.

Dissolution of partnership between McNeir & Nicholson, Real Estate Brokers, by mutual consent, in consequence of the withdrawal of Mr L L Nicholson. The business will be continued as usual by Mr Wm McNeir. –Wm McNeir, L L Nicholson

N Y, Jun 11. Don Antonio Jose de Irisor_i, Minister Plenipotentiary of Guatemala & San Salvador, died at his residence, 80 State st, Brooklyn, yesterday.

SAT JUN 13, 1868
House of Reps: 1-Cmte on Invalid Pensions: bill passed, granting pensions to the following named persons:
Michl Hennessy, Platte Co, Missouri
Kate Higgins, of Louisville, Ky
Sarah J Rogers, widow of Hugh S Rogers, 50th Ohio
Catherine Ginnsler, mother of John Ginnsler, 149th Pa volunteers
Margaret Fillson, widow of a soldier of the 79th Indiana volunteers
Jane E Rogers, widow of Capt Jas B Rogers, 64th U S colored troops
Patrick Collins, 20th Indiana
Barbara Weisse, widow of Michl Weisse, 9th Michigan
Martha Anne Wallace, widow of Brig Gen W L Wallace
Joanna L Shaw, widow of John E Shaw, 14th Maine
Anna H Pratt, mother of Capt Wheelock, 55th Mass
Bartlet & Carrie Edwards, children of David W Edwards
Jas A Guthrie, 16th Ill volunteers, in the Mexican war
Hannah K Cook, widow of Lt Cook, 119th Pa
John Morley, 7th N H
Ruth Barton, widow of Albert G Barton, hospital steward, U S army
Frederika Brielmayer, widow of Wm Brielmayer, 2nd Ohio heavy artl
Johannah Connolly, mother of Eugene Connolly, 20th Mass

Minor children of Michl Travers, 74th Ohio
Widow & minor children of Jas Cox, 1st Ohio heavy artl
Mother of Andrew J Gittings, 1st Md cavalry
Owen Griffin, foster father of Jas Griffin, 22nd Wisc, & of John Griffin, 17th Wisc
Margaret, mother of John B Lewis, 12th Conn, enrolled under the name of Clarence L Ingersoll
Mary, widow of Wm Brown, 37th Iowa
Ether Fisk, widow of John D Fisk, 2nd N Y veteran cavalry
Wm O Dodd, Missouri Home Guard
Widow & minor children of Solomon Goss, 65th Ohio
Sherman H Cowes, 19th Conn
Widow of Jas Corcoran, 5th N Y infty, [Senate bill]
Caroline E Thomas, [Senate bill]
Michl Kelly, 1st Vt battery
Caroline & Margaret Swartwort, sisters of the late Cmdor Swartwort, [at rate of $30 per month]
Geo Bennett, 6th Mich, [Senate bill]
Ellen, widow of Jas Curry, 39th Illinois
Matthew C Griswold, 1st lt, 20th N Y cavalry
Widow & minor children of Hiram Hitchcock, hospital steward, 18th Wisc
Orlina Walters, widow of Lt Elisha Walters, 7th provisional regt enrolled Missouri militia
Eliz, widow of Wm Richardson, 5th Ky cavalry
Margaret C, widow of Jesse K Long, 28th Ky
Jas Rooney, 7th Missouri cavalry
Chas Hamstead, West Va State Guards, afterwards 7th West Va volunteers
Children of Garrett W Freer, special agent in the provost marshal's ofc, 13th Dist of N Y, [same pension as the minor children of a 2nd lt]
Widow & minor children of John D Doty, late contract surgeon
Widow of Brvt Lt Col Webster, 4th U S artl

Gilbert S Giberson was yesterday confirmed by the Senate to be justice of the peace for the District of Columbia.

The President yesterday sent to the Senate the following nominations:
Hon Reverdy Johnson, Senator from Md, to be Minister to England.
L Newton Richinson, Superintendent of Indian Affairs, Southern superintendency.
Alex'r M Mahew, Dist Atty for Territory of Montana.
D F Dennison, of Phil, Associate Justice Supreme Court of Wash Territory.
L M Robinson, Superintendent of Indian Affairs.
Jos McConnell, of Ill, Com'r under the act to reimburse the State of Indiana for moneys expended to equip militia during the war.

Mr J Ross Browne, our new Minister to China, sailed for Calif yesterday, en route to the scene of his duties. –N Y Tribune

Gen Prim says Queen Isabella, of Spain, has 15 illegitimate children.

Wash Spaulding, negro barber, in Louisville, leaves an estate of $165,000.

Ex-Govn'r Buckingham, of Conn, recently elected U S Senator, lies dangerously ill in Illinois.

Mrd: on Jun 11, at St John's Church, by Rev Mr Lewis, Geo W Bonnell, of Newark, N J, to Miss Mollie V Degges, of Wash City. [Newark papers please copy.]

Dept of the Interior, U S Patent Ofc, Wash, Jun 8, 1868. Ptn of Gardner Chilson, of Boston, Mass, praying for the extension of a patent granted to him Sep 26, 1854 & reissued Sep 27, 1764, for an improvement in Furnaces or Heat Generator & Radiator, for seven years from the expiration of said patent, which takes place on Sep 26, 1868. -A M Stout, Acting Com'r of Patents

MON JUN 15, 1868
The President on Sat sent to the Senate the following nominations:
Michl Coyle Drenham, of Pa, to be assistant surgeon in the navy.
Wm Brours, to be surveyor of customs for Hannibal, Mo.
Geo J Anthony, to be collector of internal revenue for the Dist of Kansas.

Died: on Jun 14, Mr R J Ryon, in his 51st year. His funeral will be from his late residence, 399 E st, between 9th & 10th sts, on Tues, at 3 o'clock P M. [Star]

Died: on Jun 13, Mary, daughter of Mary & the late Chas Draine, in her 18th year. Her funeral will be on Tues at 10 o'clock A M, from the residence of her mother, 390 10th st, between N Y ave & 10th sts.

Died: on Jun 14, after a long & painful illness, Col John S Williams, in his 84th year. His funeral will take place on Jun 16 at 1 o'clock P M, from the Church of the Ascension. [Balt & Hagerstown papers please copy.]

TUES JUN 16, 1868
New Jewelry Store of Wm M Galt & Bro; bldg has a front of 31 feet 8 inches on Pa ave, running back 85 feet, & 70 feet in height, a deep cellar under the whole bldg. The site is the property of Messrs Fred'k Pilling, Jos Shillington, & M W Galt & Bro.

Mrd: on Jun 11, at the residence of the bride's father, at Tarrytown, N Y, Lt Alex'r Macombs Miller, U S A, to Anna Grant, daughter of Wm S Wilson.

Died: on Jun 14, Mr R J Ryon, in his 51st year. His funeral will be this afternoon at 3 o'clock, from his late residence, 399 E st, between 9th & 10th sts.

Died: on Jun 3, in Brooklyn, N Y, Mr Gold S Silliman, in his 91st year.

Died: on Jun 14, of consumption, Georgie L Force, eldest daughter of Wm Q Force. Her funeral will be from the residence of her father, 478 10th st, this afternoon, at 5 o'clock.

Criminal Court-June Term. Grand Jurors: Hiram T Litchfield, A T Clark, John A Borland, Thos R Veasey, David P Glasco, John Chisein, Wm Richards, W A Boss, of Wash; Jas Gosler & W S Dixon, Gtwn. Petit Jurors: Alfred Hall, John T Cassell, Abraham Depue, Chas Hackman, Arnold Holstein, Geo A Hall, Christopher Cammack, Benj J Wood, J D Morrison, J R McCatran, Robt Patterson, Saml Cross, of Wash; J J Bogue & Jas Ridgway, Gtwn.

The will of the late ex-Pres Buchnan filed in the Register's ofc, at Lancaster, Pa. The following are the bequests: $2,000 to the poor of Lancaster City, in addition to $4,000 previously donated; $1,000 to the Presbyterian Church, Lancaster, of which dec'd was a member; $5,600 to Esther Parker, housekeeper of the deceased-being in addition to $2,000 heretofore given her; $2,000 to Martha J Lane, widow of Jas B Lane, deceased; Peter Hilliery, Mary Smithgall, & Lizzie Stoner, servants, $100 each. The books, plate, & furniture to Mrs Harriet L Johnson, Rev E Y Buchanan, & J Buchanan Henry, to be divided equally among them, allowing Esther Parker $200 out of the amount. The balance of the estate, real & personel, is directed to be divided among his heirs as follows: one-fourth to Mrs Harriet L Johnson, one-fourth to Rev E Y Buchanan, neither of whom is to be charged with considerable advancements which have been made to them, & the balance to J Buchanan Henry, son of his sister, Harriet B Lane, & to the three sons of his nephew, Jas B Lane, dec'd; Mary E Durham, daughter of his sister, Mary Yates, deceased; to Maria B Weaver, Jessie Magaw, [formerly Jessie Weaver,] Jas B Weaver, & John B Weaver. The testator states that whilst feeling full confidence both in the integrity & business capacity of Edw E Johnson, the husband of my niece, Harriet Lane Johnson, I yet deem it prudent to secure to her a maintenance against the unforseen contingences of future years. For this purpose I appoint my hereafter named executors, Hiram B Swarr & Edw Y Buchanan, or the survivors of them trustees or trustee, & direct them to retain in their hands, & invest & manage to the best advantage, free & discharged from the debts & control of her said husband, two-thirds of the amount bequeathed her as my residuary legatee. The testator appoints Rev Edw Y Buchanan, his brother, & Hiram B Swarr, to be the executors of his last will & testament. The **Wheatland** property is given to Harriet Lane Johnson, niece of the testator, for which she pays $12,000 out of her residuary share of the estate. The will is dated at **Wheatland**, Jan 27, 1866, & a codicil of Aug 9, 1867, provides that Wm B Reed is to have $1,000 to pay the expenses & secure the publication of a biographical work of deceased, & to Mrs Mary L Reed, wife of Wm B Reed, the deceased gives $5,000, a legacy for her separate use & benefit, as a compensation for the work of Mr Wm B Reed has undertaken to perform. All the deceased private papers, correspondence, etc, are directed to be given to Mr Reed for this purpose. The estate estimated at $300,000.

Detroit, Mich, Jun 15. During a severe storm at Gravehaven yesterday, the house of Alex'r Van Zanwick was struck by lightning, & Mr Van Zanwick & a boy named Balgaria were killed.

Balt, Jun 15. Wm R Hunt, of the firm of Hunt & Co, died here yesterday. He was one of the most prominent & successful dry goods merchants in this city.

N Y, Jun 15. An examination of the case of Isaac H Davis, Collector of the 4th Dist, charged with perjury by one Davis, resulted today in the honorable discharge of the accused, & Davis has been arrested & held in $1,000 bail on the charge of perjury.

Sale of valuable estate: by deed of trust from Govn'r Wm Grason; public sale, on the premises, on Jun 25 next; 2 most desirable farms, containing in the whole 530 acres of land. These Farms are situated in Queen Anne's Co, on the bold waters of Wye river. **The Home Farm**, for many years the residence of Govn'r Grason, contains 380 acres of land; double frame dwlg, having 8 rooms; a kitchen, smoke-house, barn, granary, stable, & ice-house. The **Brick House Farm**, adjoining the **Home Farm**, contains 180 acres, improved by an ordinary brick dwlg, having 3 rooms; a granary, corn-house, & stable, all in good order. –P G Hopper, Lloyd Tilghman, trustees

Supreme Court of D C, Equity 1,072-Docket 8. Emily Wiley vs Marshall Brown, Geo Prentice, & Nannie Haw. Ordered that the dfndnt Nannie Haw, cause her appearance to be entered herein on or before the first rule day occurring 40 days after this day; otherwise the cause will be proceeded with as in case of default. –A B Olin, Justice -R J Meigs, clerk

WED JUN 17, 1868
Brvt Major Gen Thos E Wood, colonel 2nd U S cavalry, has been placed upon the retired list of the army, a board of examination having found him physically incompetent to discharge the duties of his office, on account of wounds received in battle. Gen Wood is retired with the full rank of major general his disability resulting from long & faithful service.

Yesterday, in the eastern section of Wash City, Quartermaster Sgt Wm A Wilker, of the Marine Corps, committed suicide by shooting himself through the head. This happened upon the porch of the bldg occupied as the officer's barracks at the marine garrison. Two of the watchmen at the Navy Yard, Messrs Overby & Batham, in going to their homes, found the body of Wilker lying on the porch, with the pistol, a heavy 6 barrel revolver, lying near his right hand, with but one load discharged. The deceased had been a sgt in the marines for 30 years. He resided on E st, between 6th & 7th sts, & leaves a wife & two children, bright twin boys, 12 years of age. He was about 54 years of age, a native of Pa, & a member of the Syracusan Lodge, No 10, Knights of Pythias; Naval Lodge, No 4 of Masons, & of the Schutzen Verein, & was greatly esteemed.

The funeral of Col John S Williams took place yesterday from the Church of the Ascension, on H st. He was one of the oldest inhabitants. He was a member of the Episcopal Church; the son of Gen Otho H Williams, of Wash Co, Md, a revolutioanry officer of distinction. The deceased early in life entered the army under the command of Gen Jas Wilkinson; subsequently resigned his commission, & took up his residence in Gtwn prior to the war of 1812; through which he took an active part in the cause of his country; was upwards of 30 years a Gov't clerk. He died at his residence on Jun 14, at the ripe age of 83 years, in full assurance of Christian faith.

Newark, N J, Jun 16. Isabella Decamp, aged 17 years, died this morning from the effects of arsenic taken because of parental interference in a love affair.

Mrd: on May 28, at **Red House**, Buckingham Co, Va, the residence of Jas B Ficklen, by Rev Wm S Thompson, Dr E Jacquelin Harrison, of Cumberland, to Miss Susan M Ficklen.

Died: on Jun 15, Ann Hilbush, in her 75th year, consort of the late Jacob Hilbush. Her funeral will be on Wed at 3 o'clock, from her late residence, 241 H st, between 17th & 18th sts west.

Died: on Jun 15, of consumption, Sarah M Baukhages, wife of Fred'k E Baukhages, & daughter of Rev P Sweet, in her 30th year. Her funeral will be on Wed evening at 4 o'clock, from the Presbyterian Chapel, West st, Gtwn.

Died: on Jun 16, at the residence of his son, Z W Cromwell, Mr Richd Cromwell, of Montg Co, Md, in his 66th year. [Rockville [Md] papers copy.]

Jackson, Miss, Jun 16. Gen Humphries has been removed, & Maj Gen Adelbert Ames appointed Provisional Govn'r. Atty Gen Hoover has been relieved by Capt Jasper Myers. Both of the appointees are officers of the Federal army.

Phil, Jun 16. 1-Timothy Heenan, murdered here last week, came to his death at the hands of Gerald Eaton. 2-No clue to the murderer of Newton Stewart.

According to the Saturday Review, the only 3 women endowed with a true poetical faculty who have lived in England during the present century are Mrs E B Browning, Christina Roseti, & Emily Bronte.

Trustee's sale of valuable property fronting on M st south, between 3rd & 4½ sts; by deed of trust from Henry Muth & wife to me, recorded in Liber E C E No 22, folio 166, of the records of Wash City, D C; public sale on the premises, Jul 6 next; the east part of lot 6 in square 544, in Wash City, fronting 25 feet 5 inches on M st south; improved by a commodious frame dwlg, erected within a few years past, & a large stable in the rear, with side & back alley. –J M Busher, trustee -John B Wheeler & Co, aucts

Frank Lawlor, the actor, sailed for Europe on Saturday.

Supreme Court of D C, in Equity No 741. Julia V Ragan, cmplnt, vs Thompson Ragan et al, dfndnts. On motion of the cmplnt, by M Thompson, her solicitor, it is ordered by the Court that the sale made & reported by the said Julia V Ragan, guardian, be ratified & confirmed. -A B Olin, Justice -R J Meigs, clerk

Orphans Court of Wash Co, D C, Jun 16, 1868. In the case of Adolphus Linde_kohl, exc of Eliz Morison, dec'd, the executor & Court have appointed Jul 14 next, for the final settlement of the personal estate of the said dec'd, of the assets in hand.
-Jas R O'Beirne, Reg/o wills

THU JUN 18, 1868
Orphans Court-Judge Purcell, Jun 16, 1868. 1-Ellen McFadden gave bond in the sum of $1,500 as guardian to the orphans of Wm McFadden. J P Kersey & Geo Wright sureties. 2-Wm Hogan gave bond in the sum of $30,000 as administrator of Sarah Hogan. E P Gaines & W V J Mercer sureties. 3-The will of Lewis Browner was filed for probate. He names Jane Browner excx. 4-The will of Wm O Lumsden was admitted to probate & record. 5-The will of Wm Clark was filed for probate. The testator makes bequests to St Patrick's Church, St Vincent's Orphan Asylum, & then divides the balance of his estate between his grand-daughters, share & share alike. He names Henry A Clark executor. 6-The will of Owen Munsen was filed for probate. He appoints his wife Caroline excx. 7-The following accounts were filed & passed: Second account of Eliza McDuell, excx of John McDuell. Second & final account of John H Johnson, guardian to minor son of S C Espey. Distribution & first account of personal estate of H C Spalding by Jas Fullerton, adm. Distribution account of the personal estate of John Vierbuchen by Sophie Pohlers, admx. Second Account of Mary Baron, guardian to the orphans of Simon & Ann Branson. First & Final account of E C Carrington, collector of the personal estate of Sarah Edelen.

Equity Court-Judge Olin. 1-Fowler vs Whelan et al; decree appointing C A Buckey trustee to sell. 2-Maguire et al vs Mille et al; order ratifying trustee's sale *nisi*. 3-Swain vs Swain; final ratification of trustee's sales; confirming report of auditor & for distribution. 4-Finch et al vs Way et al; order of reference to auditor to report on propriety of sale.

Buffalo, Jun 17. A deaf & dumb man, Andrew Klief, was killed on the Central railroad last night. His head was completely severed from his body, & the trunk was mangled.

Model Shoe Store: the establishment of Geo B Wilson, 502 7th st, under Odd Fellows' Hall. The finest variety that can be found in Washington, is now on hand.

Plymouth, Jun 17. Deacon Andrews has confessed to his counsel that he killed Cornelius Holmes, claiming to have done it in self-defence. A confession in writing will be submitted to the grand jury, with a view to justify an indictment for manslaughter.

Phil, Jun 17. The Press Club of Phil today elected A M V McKean, editor of the Public Ledger, President, for the ensuing year.

The funeral of Quartermaster Sgt Wilker, of the Marine Corps, took place yesterday from his late residence, on G st, between 6th & 7th sts east, & was accompanited by the Syracosian Lodge, Knights of Pythias, No 10, Heald's band, & Wash Naval Lodge of Masons, with the Marine drum corps. The remains were interred in the ***Congressional Cemetery***.

Died: on Jun 17, Miss Catharine W Polk, a native of Somerset Co, Md, but for many years a resident of Wash, D C. Her funeral will take place at 485 12th st, between F & G at 5 o'clock this evening.

Concord, N H, Jun 17. Mr Webster, engineer on the Vt Central railroad was killed yesterday, by his head striking against a bridge. He is a brother of Webster, who was recently killed by a collision on the same railroad.

Hon Wm Hancock died at his residence in Dudley, Mass, on Jun 14, aged 76 years. Col Hancock was a lineal descendant of John Hancock of Revolutionary memory. He was State Senator for several years, & was largely interested & occupied with town affairs during his active life.

Hon Jas Guthrie has resigned the presidency of the Louisville & Nashville railroad, a position which he has held for a number of years. The charter requires that the president of the company shall sign all its bonds, & this, from the state of his health, Mr Guthrie is unable to do.

Trustee's sale of valuable improved lot on 4th st near Fred'k, in Gtwn; by decree of the Supreme Court of D C, in Chancery No 1,293, Docket 9, wherein John Fowler et al are cmplnts & Franklin & Chas Whelan are dfndnts; public auction on Jul 2 of part of lot 175, in Beatty & Hawkins' addition to Gtwn. –Chas A Buckey, trustee -Thos Dowling, auct

Dept of the Interior, U S Patent Ofc, Wash, Jun 9, 1868. Ptn of Norman C Harris, of Poultney, Vt, praying for the extension of a patent granted to him Apr 24, 1855, for an improvement in Manufacture of Slate Pencils, for seven years from the expiration of said patent, which takes place on Apr 24, 1869. -A M Stout, Acting Com'r of Patents

Dept of the Interior, U S Patent Ofc, Wash, Jun 11, 1868. Ptn of John Mabie, of English Neighborhood, N J, praying for the extension of a patent granted to him Oct 3, 1854, for an improvement in Pen & Pencil Case, for seven years from the expiration of said patent, which takes place on Oct 3, 1868. -A M Stout, Acting Com'r of Patents

FRI JUN 19, 1868

Mr Richd B Nixon, of this city, has been appointed financial clerk in the ofc of the Sec of the Senate, in the place of Sayles J Bowen. Mr Nixon has been an attache of the City Post Ofc under Mr Bowen for some time.

Capt Chas Mather, of Portsmouth, N H, committed suicide on Tues evening by tying a stone weighing 40 pounds to his ankles, confining his hands behind with handcuffs, & then jumping into the water. He was about 40 years of age, & has manifested symptoms of insanity at times. He has been an active seaman, & had commanded an English steamer.

Hon Wm D Sohier, a distinguished member of the Suffolk bar, died on Thurs last, at the advanced age of 80 years. He was of Huguenot descent, & universally respected for his integrity & learning. His wit was proverbial, & by his death one of the most brilliant & admirable of the old school lawyers & gentlemen of Boston passes from the stage.

Francis Todd, about 21years of age, was bitten in the hand by a small dog, in New Haven, 2 or 3 weeks ago, & died on Monday last of hydrophobia. The wound in his hand was very slight, & no ill effects were apprehended until Sunday, when it first grew painful. [Jun 20th newspaper: Francis Todd leaves a wife, having been married a few months ago to a young lady in Darby. He was son of Mr A Todd, of New Haven, Conn.]

The court of impeachment at Albany on Friday acquitted Robt C Dorn, canal com'r of N Y, of the charges preferred against him. He was charged with complicity in a combination made by contractors, & with letting a repair contract to the highest instead of the lowest bidder. The vote stood 8 for conviction & 19 for acquittal.

Meeting of the Board of Police: the applications of C J Menden, Edw McCarthy, & Jas A Powers, for restaurant licenses were rejected. The official bond of Justice E L Corbin was received & approved. Thos Young was appointed an additonal private for 90 days, to do duty at the Centre Market. L S Pond was appointed a private in the force, vice A D Hilton, resigned.

Equity Court-Judge Olin. 1-Adams vs Carroll et al; decree of sale. 2-R C Hewett vs Wash City Orphan Asylum et al; decree appointing trustee to execute release. 3-Nicholas E Young vs Julia A Young; divorce a *vinculo matrimonii*. 4-Devaughn et al vs Devaughn et al; order appointed Geo W Mitchell guardian *ad litem*. 5-May et al vs May et al; decree appointing Wm Y Fendall trustee to sell.

Died: on Jun 18, Ralph Sterrett, infant son of John T & Louisa Sterrett Fenwick, aged 18 months. His funeral will be this afternoon, at 5 o'clock, from the residence of his parents, 171 south F st, between 4½ & 6th sts.

Richmond, Jun 18. A G Barbee, a celebrated Va sculptor, died in Rappahannock Co on Jun 16 of cancer.

Chateau Lafitte, whence come the famous wines, is to be sold by auction, the upset price being 70,312 francs a hectare, equal to $7,000 an acre. At this rate the estate would bring something more than five million francs.

Orphans Court of Wash Co, D C. Letters of administration on the personal estate of Sarah Hogan, late of Wash City, D C, dec'd. –Wm Hogan, adm

Chancery sale of real estate; by decree from the Supreme Court of D C, in Equity 920, in which Margaret A Eckels & her husband Lewis G Eckels are cmplnts, & Catherine Barnett et al are dfndnts; public auction on Jul 9, of all of lot 4 in square 837, with 2 two story frames houses, with back bldgs, having 6 rooms each-will be sold separately; property fronts on north D, st the corner of 6th st east & Md ave. –M Thompson, R S Davis, trustees -Green & Williams, aucts

Prof Seeley, the author of "Ecce Fomo," has started a new magazine, "The London Student."

SAT JUN 20, 1868
Explosion of fire engine on Jun 17th, N Y; street almost instantly filled with steam; just at the time a number of people were coming out of the Bowery Theatre. Injured: Patrick W Hand, engineer of steamer, badly scalded; John Conway, fireman; Edw Roach, fireman, scalded & arm broken; John Clarrisson, shock & badly scalded; Collis Lightbody; Lyon Vetter; John McGuire, badly scaled & thigh broken, resided at 75 Mott st; Frank Clarke, slightly hurt; Jas Sullivan; Louis Storms, bad scald; Jas Macken, scalded; Thos Keating; Theodore Bates, compound fracture of both bones of left leg-lived at 596 Grand st; Stephen Wooldridge; Fred'k Roscol, arm broke-185 Clinton st; Jas Broderick, scalded & leg broken; Frank Evers, thigh broken-lives at 15 Bowery; Thos Cronin, scalded-lives at 17 Doyer st; Thos Foley, scalded; Robt Scholer; Jas Laden, aged 13 years; Thos O'Donnell, aged 17 years. Five persons were killed but their names were not ascertained.

Died, at his residence, 164 F st, on Jun 18, 1st Lt Jas D Graham, 2nd U S cavalry, & aide de camp to Maj Gen Hancock, cmder of the Military Division of the Atlantic. Lt Graham was appointed a cadet at large in 1860, & graduated with honor at West Point, in Jun, 1865. He was appointed 2nd lt in the 13th U S infty, & was subsequently transferred to the 2nd U S cavalry, & promoted during the war to a 1st lt for gallant conduct. Lt Graham was in his 25th year, & had been afflicted but a short time with homorrhage of the bowels. The day for the funeral has not been designated, the father of the deceased being a resident of New Orleans, & is expected to reach here Monday. Gen Hancock will issue in the meantime an order detailing the funeral escort. [Jun 24th newspaper: The funeral of the late Lt Jas D Graham, took place yesterday from St Matthew's Church; Rev Fr De Wolf-celebrant & Fr O'Neale-deacon. Acting pallbearers: Col Wilson, Col W G Mitchell, Lts Miller, Rathbone, Plummer, & Totten. Eight sgts carried the coffin to the hearse. The remains were put in a special car & conveyed to Balt for interment.]

Miss S J Bradford purchased part of lot 7 in square 821, fronting on 4th st east, near D st south, at 26 cents per foot.

A new marble statue of Mr Lincoln, executed by Mrs Ames, of Boston, has been placed in the Rotunda, near the door leading to the Senate. It is pronounced by good judges to be an excellent likeness of Mr Lincoln, & an admirable work of art. Mrs Ames & her sister, Mrs Lippincott ["Grace Greenwood,"] are among the notables now in Washington.

Hiram Miller, who has been on trial at Woodstock, Vt, for the murder of Mr & Mrs Joshua Gowing, in Jul last, was convicted on Friday, & sentenced to be hung on the last Friday in June, 1869.

Mobile Register of Friday last: N E Thomas, editor of the Choctaw Herald, was murdered in a most cowardy manner by Joshua Morse, the Atty Gen elect of the scalawag oligarchy which the so-called Congress at Washington has just voted to recognize as the lawful government of what was the State of Alabama. He was assisted by one Wm Gilmore, a less eminent member of the gang of renegade white men, but well enough known. Mr Thomas has not been backward in expressing his opinion of these creatures. Gilmore brought on an altercation; Thomas fired a pistol at him; Morse, who kept in the background, first a double barreled gun at Thomas, lodging 38 buckshot in his body, causing death in an half an hour. Both assassins fled. We also learn that Mr Pierce, oversee of the plantation of Mrs McCormick, formerly Mrs Lewis, was found dead on the road, having been shot & his head shockingly beaten with a club. No trace of his murderers has been found, but public opinion connects the deed with a difficulty he has recently had with a man named Davis.

Rev Mr Lambert Young, of Frankfurt, a young German Catholic priest, was interceded with by a prominent lawyer of that city, Mr Scott, to repair to the jail for the purpose of preventing violence to the negro who was accused of outraging, & then brutally murdering a young girl, some months ago. Mr Young repaired to the jail just in time to prevent violence upon the jailor by the mob; he then retired. The mob returned & burst open the jail; the prisoner was taken off an executed. –Louisville Democrat [Jun 22nd newspaper: Fr Lambert Young who was confined to jail for not testifying, was released on bond on Monday last. Fr Young was dangerously attacked with erysipelas about 3 years ago, & his confinement in jail caused the disease to break out again. The bond was fixed at $1,000 for 10 days, or such time as he may have fully recovered.]

Chancery Sale of Valuable Improved Real Estate near 14th st, & fronting almost directly on Pa ave & west of the Nat'l Theatre; by decree of the Supreme Court of D C, in Chancery No 1,048, Stoneman et al vs Hardesty et al; public auction on Jul 13, of the estate of the late Cornelius McLean, dec'd, being parts of lots in square 254, in Wash, on E st; with improvements now occupied by P Vermeren as a hotel & restaurant. This property is in the square immediately east of Willard's Hotel. –Geo H William, trustee -Cooper & Latimer, aucts

Phil, Jun 19. Gustavus Riddle, recently from N Y, threw himself from the 5th story of a house on Water st, & died on the way to the hospital. He is said to have a brother in Balt.

MON JUN 22, 1868
The following nominations were sent to the Senate on Saturday by the President:
Capt W W Moore, to be postmaster of this city, vice Sayles J Bowen, whose commission has expired.
Richd W Mellen, to be collector of customs, Dist of Teche, Sate of Louisiana.
Geo Hubbard, collector of customs, Dist of Stonington, Conn.
John L Treanor, assessor internal revenue, 5th Dist of Ky.
Thos B Price, collector internal revenue, 3rd Dist of Md, vice W Prescott Smith, who has accepted another position.
Thos S Pettit, assessor internal revenue, 2nd Dist of Ky.
John C French, of Kansas, agent for Indiana in New Mexico.
Henry C Myers, of Louisiana, receiver for public moneys for dist of lands subject to sale at Natchitoches, La.
Andrew J Moulder, of Calif, to be surveyor general of that State.

Real Estate Sales. Saml Norment purchased part of lot 9 in square 382, on 9th st, between the canal & La ave, with a 3 story brick house thereon, for $3,125. Norment also purchased part of lot 11 in square 408, fronting on 8th st, between D & Market Space, with a 3 story brick house, for $4,950. Jos Pheffer purchased a 3 story brick house & lot on 4th st, between I & K sts, for $1,900.

The 4½ st Presbyterian Church [Rev Byron Sunderland, D D] the oldest church of this denomination in Wash City, was the scene last evening of the ordination of 5 new officers: G P Patch, to be elder, C B Jewell, E Champlin, Jas M McNair, & Lester E Ross, to be deacons.

The renovation of Christ Church [P E] in Gtwn, commenced in May, 1867, has just been completed; the old church was erected half a century ago; the style is Byzantine & the bldg is 2 stories in height. Contractor & builder, John W Webster, Wash; brick work, Andrew Barbour, Gtwn; lumber by Evans & Pickrell, Gtwn; painting by R McLean, Wash; glass work, by Wm Vaughn, Wash; tin work by Geo W Berry, Wash; slating by J H Montgomery, Wash; pews by H W Hamilton & Co, Wash; carpets by W S Mitchell & Co, Wash; stone work by M G Emory, Wash; iron work by Gray & Noyes, Wash, hardware by M J Adler, Gtwn; architects & superintendents, Hutton & Murdoch, Balt, Md.

Johns Hopkins, the wealthiest man in Balt, now approaching octagenarian life, has made his will, bequeathing a million & a half, with a magnificent suburban estate, for a great university; as well as another million for a hospital in the city.

Mrd: at Omaha, PG Co, Md, by Rev Dr Hodges, Dr Benj L Bird to Nannie Ogle, daughter of John Hodges. [No wedding date given-current item.]

Alfred Lee, an old & respected colored citizen of Gtwn, died at his residence on Sat in his 63rd year. He was for several years subject of apoplectic attacks, & was seized with congestion of the lungs Sat morning, & died in less than half an house. By his prudence & industry he amassed quite a fortune; his estate probably largely exceeds $100,000. He was born & raised in Gtwn, & worked in early life in a brick-yard, but for 30 years past has been engaged in the feed business. His funeral will take place Tuesday next. [Jun 24th newspaper: Alfred Lee, who died on Jun 20, 1868, was buried on Jun 23 in the *Harmonial Cemetery*. His late residence was 43 Bridge st, Gtwn. Rev Dr Maden, of Alexandria, officiated.]

Died: on Jun 20, at Gtwn, D C, I Tisdale Wheeler, son of Mrs H A & the late Gen Thos T Wheeler, aged 20 years. His funeral will take place from the residence of his mother, 13 3rd st, this afternoon, at 5 o'clock.

Died: on Jun 20, Jennie Lillian, infant daughter of Geo H & Henrietta F Denman, aged 11 months & 20 days. Her funeral will take place on Jun 22, at 2 o'clock, from the residence of her parents, 381 N Y ave, between 12th & 13th sts. [N Y papers please copy.]

Died: on Jun 20, after a brief but severe illness, Emily, youngest daughter of D D T & Phoebe T Leech. Her funeral will be from the residence of her parents, 470 I st, on Jun 22 at 4 P M.

Died: on Sunday, Catherine Rosalia, infant child of John & Mary Ann Doran, aged 3 months & 12 days. Her funeral will take place from the residence of her parents, 274 9th st, between M & N sts, this afternoon at 4 o'clock.

Near Van Buren, Hancock Co, Ohio, the other day, two sons of Thos G Carr, took their father's gun, with the intention of going hunting. Mr Carr had left the ramrod in the barrel, & when the boys endeavored to draw it out, the gun was discharged, driving the ramrod through the body of one of the boys, killing him almost instantly.

Troy, N Y, Jun 19. Col Henry A Mercer, of Chicago, & formerly of this city, who was a passenger from N Y on the steamer **Connecticut** last night, took an overdose of chloroform to quiet a neuralgic affection, & was found insensible in his berth this morning. He died at 11 o'clock.

Chancery sale of valuable lots at auction; by decree of the Supreme Court of D C, passed in a cause wherein Riggs & Co are cmplnts, & the widow & heirs of the late Thos Smith are dfndnts, [having been substituted as trustee instead of the late Wm Reding;] public auction on Jul 15 next, of lots 37, 38, 40 thru 46, in square 182, fronting on R I ave, between 16th & 17th sts. –Wm R Woodward, trustee -Cooper & Latimer, aucts

Orphans Court of Wash Co, D C. Letters of administration on the personal estate of Wm Clarke, late of Wash Co, D C, dec'd. –Henry A Clarke, exc

Administrator's sale at auction of household & kitchen furniture, carriage, horses, wagons & carts, & 2 milch cows, at the late residence of K H Lambell, dec'd, 750 N J ave, near south L st, the Personal Effects of the said dec'd. –Richd Wallach, adm of K H Lambell, dec'd. –J B Wheeler & Co, aucts

Orphans Court of Wash Co, D C, Jun 20, 1868. In the case of Martin Burke, adm of John Burke, dec'd, the administrator & Court have appointed Jul 18 next, for the final settlement of the personal estate of the said dec'd, of the assets in hand.
-Jas R O'Beirne, Reg/o wills

A few persons can be accommodated with board, on very reasonable terms at Waverley Seminary, a mile & a quarter from College Station, on Balt & Ohio railroad. References required. Apply to Miss M Keech, Branchville, PG Co, Md.

Nashville Banner, Jun 18. From Detective Barmore, who returned from Russelville, Ky, yesterday, we learn of a shocking tragedy that occurred there yesterday. At the close of the war Capt McCarty, of the Confederate army, returned home, & having no money with which to purchase citizens' clothing continued to wear his uniform. This seems to have been distasteful to Maj N C Lawrence, then of the Federal army, & an ofcr of the Freedman's Bureau, at Russelville. The latter, with 2 or 3 soldiers, forcibly took possession of his gray coat & commanded him to keep his d__d mouth shut. McCarty reported the action of Lawrence to the post commandant, who rebuked Lawrence for having gone outside of his duty, & ordered him to return the coat. From this sprang ill feelings which resulted last Tuesday in the death of Lawrence, & in McCarty receiving a mortal wound at the hand of his enemy. Lawrence fired at McCarty, inflicting a mortal wound, McCarty rushed at Lawrence, succeeded in getting the revolver from him, & shot & killed him with his own revolver. McCarty was soon arrested, but being in critical condition, was taken to a house nearby.

Mrs Rhoda Berg, a widow 76 years of age, died in Chelsea, Mass, a few days since, from the effects of a slight scratch upon her hand by a tame rabbit. A most painful death ensued 10 days after the occurrence.

Orphans Court-Judge Purcell, Jun 20, 1868. 1-Wm Helmick gave bond in the sum of $400 as administrator of Jas A Downey, dec'd. A J Downey & F Schmidt sureties. 2-The will of Benj Miner was filed for probate. He names his wife executrix. 3-The will of Wm Clarke was admitted to probate, & record, & letters testamentary issued thereon. Henry Clarke gave bond in the sum of $1,500 as executor of Wm Clarke, dec'd. J T Given & A J Harvey sureties. 4-The following accounts were filed & passed: First individual & 4th general accounts of J B Monroe, guardian to David M, Charlotte L, & Mary C Monroe. Sixth account of John Shanahan, guardian to Catharine, Timothy, & John Scanlon. 5-The Miller will case is set for a hearing next Saturday.

Criminal Court-Judge Wylie. Mary Butler, indicted for the larceny of one $100 note, U S Currency, from O B Beckwith, on Apr 30 last, was sentenced to the Albany penitentiary.

In Chambers-Justice Wylie. 1-Heiskell vs Heiskell et al; order appointing commission to obtain answer of absent infant dfndnts. 2-Hicks vs Pepper et al; order appointing Henrietta P Pepper guardian to infant dfndnt.

TUE JUN 23, 1868

Obit-died: on Jun 8, Cmder Richmond Aulick, U S navy, at his residence, in Wash City, & on Jun 10th his remains were consigned to the tomb with the military honors due to his rank in the naval service. For a long time an invalid; for some years prevented from mingling freely in society as his genial nature would have prompted. He was the eldest son of Cmdor John H Aulick; entered the navy, at age 15, Oct 19, 1840. Among the first who graduated at the Naval Academy at Annapolis, where he was distinguished by bearing away the first honors of his date. He served on the schnr **Nautilus**-1846; the brig **Washington**-Feb, 1847. In Nov, 1847, reported to Lt W F Lynch for special duty & accompanied him in the exploration of the river Jordan & the Dead Sea. In Dec, 1849, he was ordered to the sloop **Marion**, at the East India station, as acting master, & promoted to acting lt, Aug 21, 1850. Jun 15, 1852, he was ordered to the Naval Observatory; joined the Mediterranean squadron as acting master of the ship **Saranac**, & promoted to be master, Apr 28, 1854. Ordered again to the Naval Observatory, & in Jun, 1859, ordered to join the Pacific squadron, on board the ship **Wyoming**; but, before sailing, he was detached, sick, Aug 3, 1859. In Dec, 1858, he was on board the steamer **Ariel** as a passenger, with his wife, returning from Europe, with many passengers & a valuable cargo. The ship encountered a terrific storm, the captain was killed & the mates disabled. Lt Aulick, at the insistance of the passengers, took command & brought the ship safely to N Y. Soon after his return from Europe, in 1858, he received an injury which caused the loss of his left leg. He was attached to the Bureau of Ordnance in Oct 1864; appointed assist chief of that bureau in Jun, 1863, serving until Congress abolished the office, after the close of the late war. He was promoted to lt cmder Jul 16, 1862, & to the rank of cmder Mar 3, 1865. He was an ardent lover of the Union, & never faltered in his devotion to its flag & in the future of his country. –B M B

Cleveland, Ohio, Jun 21. The steamer **Morning Star**, hence for Detroit, collided with the bark **Cortland**, 30 miles from her, last night, & both sunk. The officers were all saved except Mr Jas Morton, the clerk of the **Morning Star**, who was seen to go down with Mrs Hackett, the wife of Capt Hackett, a passenger. Saved: Capt Lawton, Geo C Tripp, Thos Anderson, M Frederick, Wm Smith, Jas Henson, Andrew Brough, David Slater, John Thompson, J Kenyon, 2nd Mate J D Smith-all of the bark **Cortland**. Capt Viger, J Havlick, 2nd Engineer John Russell, Thos Flannagan, L Bang, John Smith, John Stevens, John Saxton, P Kelley, J Burns, P Barrett, John Conant, F Crindall, J Distin, A Curry, H Gayson, P Fallon, 2nd Mate D McLaughlin, 1st Mate D McLaughlin, Wheelsman H Brady, & B Dempsey-all of the **Morning Star**. Names of the passengers: Mrs Ellen Chittenden, of Chicago; Mrs Capt Burke, of Cleveland; Capt Hackett, of Detroit; H N Gurley, of Marietta; Mr Downey, of Detroit; J Poulliet, of Detroit; P Pomeroy, of Bay City; Capt Blanchard V Horgesky, of Rochester, N Y; S A Thorp, of N Y; W H Smith, of N Y; J Donovan, of Chicago; C J Newman, of Wash, D C; W B Watson & Capt Harbottle, of Hamilton, Ontario. Several of the crew of the steamer whose names are not known were saved. The following are known to be missing: Mrs Hackett, of Detroit; Jas Moreton, clerk of the steamer **Morning Star**; Maj Wm Hutchinson, of Detroit; the Miss Carrie Patchen, & Miss Minnie Patchen, of Troy, N Y; Albert Iddings, of Cleveland; Mrs Wamlet, of Cleveland; Mrs Parker & child, of Marietta, Ohio; Capt Ballantine & wife, of Detroit. One of the boats of the **Morning Star** is still out, & may contain other survivors. [Jun 24th newspaper: additional names of those: John Kayne, mate; G C Tritt, Jos Hanson, Aug Seward, J L Smith, & W S Conklin-all brought in by the steamer **R N Rice**. Additional missing persons to above list: Mrs L B Wamelink, Cleveland; Capt Ballentyne & wife, Detroit; Mrs John H Garrett & daughter, 5 years old; Chas Schroeder, Cleveland; Mrs Searle & child, Collingwood, Canada; a son of Mrs Liston, of this city, aged 10 years; Mrs Addis, chambermaid of the **Star**; Moses Lontain, cabin boy; Geo ___, fireman; & a deck hand. Note: Some names are duplicates-different spelling. Edw McDonald, a lumber merchant of Chicago, was on the **Star** at the time, & jumped overboard, he was in the water about 2 hours; had a life preserver. John H Garrett, of Detroit, [brother of Henry N Johnson, of this city & formerly a resident here,] was on board with his wife & little daughter. When the water rose to their feet they stepped overboard, he saw nothing of his wife & child again. Mrs Garrett was formerly Miss Sallie A House, of Lockport, N Y; the little girl, Mabel, was 5 years old. Mr Albert Iddings, who is among the lost, was the youngest son of Mrs Iddings, widow of the late Hiram Iddings, of the late firm of Edwards, Iddings & Co, grocers on Water st. The dec'd was about 20 years of age. Mrs Wamelink, who is among the lost, was the widow of the late L S Wamelink, formerly a grocer of this city. She resided on Lorain st. The Misses Patchen had been visiting the house of Mr Edwards, in Cleveland, the eldest, Caroline, aged about 23, had been a bridesmaid at the recent wedding of Mr Cole & Miss Tiffany. They were sisters, the youngest, Minnie, just from boarding school, & not quite 19 years of age, daughters of T W Patchen, a prominent banker of Troy, N Y, & former resident of Buffalo. This has been a shock to their invalid mother & devoted father. Mr Perry A Tietsort, of Detroit, was probably the first man that went overboard. He was picked up after 2 hours in the water by the schnr **Ada Medora**, of Detroit, Capt McIntyre. Mrs Searle, of Collingwood, Canada, who had been on a visit to Mrs Liston, of this city, was probably drowned, with a child of her own, & also a little boy 10 years old, the son of Mrs Liston, who was accompanying his aunt to her home. Maj Wm Hutchinson, special agent of the Treasury Dept at Detroit, became exhausted in the water, & died on reaching the steamer **Rice**. The **Morning Star** was built at Trenton, in 1862, by Alvin Turner, & was worth about $150,000. There was no insurance on her. She was thorougly overhauled last winter, at an expense of $8,000 to $10,000, making her as good as new.]

Dept of the Interior, U S Patent Ofc, Wash, Jun 15, 1868. Ptn of Wm Thornley, of Phil, Pa, praying for the extension of a patent granted to him Sep 19, 1854, for an improvement in Safety Washer for Securing Wheels to Axles, for seven years from the expiration of said patent, which takes place on Sep 19, 1868. -A M Stout, Acting Com'r of Patents

$10 reward for estrayed or stolen red Buffalo Cow, if returned to Owen, 9th st, just beyond the boundary line.

Supreme Court of D C, Equity No 341-Docket 7. Matilda Grammer vs Wm B Todd & Henry Probasco. Trustees, Wm B Todd & Henry Probasco, reported they sold, on Jun 1, 1868, lots D, H, M, & N, in square 164, for $3,557.75, to Jno W Thompson, who has since complied with the terms of the sale. –A B Olin, Justice -R J Meigs, clerk

WED JUN 24, 1868
The Senate yesterday confirmed Edw C Johnson, of Md, [son of Hon Reverdy Johnson,] to be Assist Sec of the American Legation at London.

The Pres transmitted to the Senate yesterday the following nominations: Edwin O Perrin, of N Y, to be Chief Justice of the Supreme Court of the Territory of Utah; Cmder John C Febiger, to be capt in the navy from May 6, 1868, vice Capt A M Pennock, promoted; & Cmder Pierre Crossty, to be a capt in the navy from May 27, 1868, vice Capt John L Worden, promoted; 2nd Assist Engineer John J Bissett, to be a 1st assist engineer in the navy, to fill a vacancy in that grade. The following were also nominated to be 3rd lts in the revenue service of the U S: Jos M Simms, vice Calvin L Hooper, promoted to 2nd lt; Robt M Clark, vice John Davison, promoted to 2nd lt; John Owen, vice Jas McVey, 3rd lt, dec'd.

Examination day last Monday in the female intermediate school of the First District, which for 3 years has been under the instruction of Miss Helen E Williams. Sixteen girls were transferred to the most excellent female grammar school, under the charge of Miss Annie E Evans: Effie McFarlane, Clara Lesh, Annie Dutton, Fannie Sypherd, Jeannie King, Lizzie McGuffin, Mary Rohrer, Annie Clarke, May Blackeston, Mary Clark, Ella Backenbaugh, Lizzie Clark, Annie Turton, Nettie Combs, Clara Fitzgerald, Isabel Thompson. Premium scholars: Effie McFarlane, Clara Lesh, Annie Dutton, Annie Hazard. Exemplary Conduct & Punctuality: Nettie Combs, Mary Rohrer, Ella Beckenbaugh, Maggie Epler, Nellie Hutchinson, Mattie Greason. Attention to Study & Improvement: Clara Fitzgerald, Fannie Sypherd, Annie Turton. Penmanship: Lizzie Clark. Neatness: Carrie Davis. Vocal Music: Nettie Lenman. Miss Annie I Hazard, age 15 years, won the scholarship in the Business College for the ensuing year, by reason of her superior penmanship.

St Matthew's Church was thronged yesterday with a brilliant assemblage of ladies & gentlemen, to witness the marriage of Miss F, daughter of Columbus Alexander, & Mr Jas F Russell. The ceremony was performed by Rev Dr White, pastor of the church, assisted by Rev Fr De Wolf. Groomsmen: Dr W O Alexander, brother of the bride, Mr Jas D Clary, & Mr W B Orme; bridesmaids: Miss Lulie Libbey, & Miss Mattie Micks, of Gtwn, & Miss Nannie Thomas, of Fairfax. The reception was at the residence of the bride's father. The bridal party left for the North last evening.

Oak Hill Cemetery. At the annual meeting of lot holders owning 300 square feet or more, last Monday, the board of managers elected John Marbury, again as president. We have only to add that Mr Corcoran's princely munificence, consisting of the original grounds, chapel, superintendent's residence, stone wall along the Rock Creek front, & iron fencing around the enclosure, which altogether cost, 20 years ago, about $62,000, has realized his expectations, & proved to be for the purpose a much needed endowment. We are sure the inhabitants of his native city unite in wishing long life, health, & happiness to W W Corcoran. At this very meeting a request from Mr Corcoran for the election of one named friend, to be appointed to the present board, which has, with one exception, become entirely new, by deaths & resignations, since Mr Corcoran's appointing & transfer, was refused by the proxy vote of several lot owners. We are at a loss to understand how anyone would be willing to place themselves before the public in so unenviable a position, & we can only regard such an ungrateful spirit as unworthy the dignity of the man who seeks for the repose of his own loved departed the peace & serenity of a place made beautiful & endowed by his public benefactor for the consolation of us all mutually in the present, & our future resting place. "Till morning break and pierce the shade."

N Y, Jun 23. Rev J M Raphael, an eminent Jewish divine, died today at his residence in this city, aged 60 years.

Mrd: on Jun 23, by Rev Theodore Appel, of Lancaster, Pa, J Bingham Woodward, of Bordentown, N J, to Anna E Appel, of Wash City.

Died: on Jun 23, at Wash, D C, Wm Hogan, son of Wm V I & Sophia H Mercer, aged 3 months & 10 days.

Died: on Jun 22, Ellen Vincent, infant daughter of Wm M & Ellen J Brown, aged 8 months & 2 days. Her funeral will take place at the residence of her parents, 293 8th st, this morning at 9 o'clock A M.

Trustee's sale of real estate; by deed of trust dated Sep 12, 1867, executed by Chas H Holmead, Richd T Martin & Mary E Martin his wife, to me, recorded in Liber E C E, No 16, folios 168 etc, of the land records of Wash Co, D C; public auction on Jul 6, of part of lot 5 of a larger tract known as lot 4, of the ***Widow's Mite***, in said part of lot, being the whole of side lot 5 except a strip of 80-100 of an acre taken off from the west side thereof, the same containing 4 3/10th acres, more or less. –John E Norris, trustee -Green & Williams, aucts [Advertised again in Sep 4th newspaper, to be sold Sep 16.]

Dept of Interior, U S Patent Ofc, Wash, Jun 15, 1868. Ptn of Harry H Evarts, of Chicago, Ill, praying for the extension of a patent granted to him Oct 31, 1854, for an improvement in Shingle Machines for seven years from the expiration of said patent, which takes place on Oct 31, 1868. -A M Stout, Acting Com'r of Patents

Nashville, Jun 23. B H Payne, who was tried in the Criminal Court of Nashvile for the murder of M S Allen, the seducer of his wife, was acquitted today.

Dept of Interior, U S Patent Ofc, Wash, Jun 18, 1862. Ptn of Abner Whitely, formerly of Springfield, Ohio, now of Platte Co, Mo, praying for extension of a patent granted to him Sep 19, 1854, for an improvement in Grain & Grass Harvesters, for 7 years from the expiration of said patent, which takes place on Sep 19, 1868.
-A M Stout, Acting Com'r of Patents

Orphans Court-Judge Purcell, Jun 23, 1868. 1-The will of Georgiana L Force was filed for probate. The testatrix bequeaths $500 to the Wash City Orphans asylum, & the rest of her estate, real & personal, to her father, W Q Force, & names him executor. 2-The will of Patrick Toban was filed for probate. He names his wife executrix. 3-First & final account of L A Gobright, exc of Prudence S Aiken, filed & passed. 4-Letters testamentary, on the will of Benj Miner, were issued to Margaret A Miner. 5-First & final account of Bridget Grau, admx of Wm A Grau, filed & passed. 6-The will of Wm Grey was filed for probate. He names his wife executrix.

Criminal Court-Judge Wylie, Jun 23, 1868. 1-Harris Carroll convicted of petit larceny, & found to be under 16 years of age. 2-Henry Willis guilty of an assault & resisting an ofcr. In 2nd charge, for an assault & battery, a *nolle pros* was entered. 3-Braxton Reynolds plead guilty to petit larceny; sentenced to 30 days in jail. 4-Chas Williams guilty of petit larceny; sentenced to 1 year in jail. 5-John M Shrode guilty of petit parceny. 6-John Thomas convicted of petit larceny. 7-Thos Johnson, alias Dorsey, convicted for petit larceny. 8-Thos Buckley guilty of an assault & resisting an officer.

THU JUN 25, 1868
Hon Saml Hooper has offered his house in Wash City for sale.

Criminal Court-Judge Wylie, Jun 24, 1868. 1-Robt Johnson convicted of petit larceny. 2-John Thomas convicted of petit larceny. 3-Emanuel Dodson & Philip Lancaster, indicted for garroting & robbing Wm Davis; not guilty. 4-John Wilson & Edw Williams, petit larceny. Williams plead guilty. Wilson convicted, & Williams sentenced to 30 days in jail. 5-Anne E Coliwell, keeping a bawdy house; guilty. 6-Lewis Simms, petit larceny; guilty; sentenced to 12 months in jail. 7-Rachel Brown, petit larceny; guilty; recognizance forfeited. *Capias* to hear judgment. 8-Wm Washington & Thos Henry; recognizance forfeited. Bench warrant issued.

Equity Court-Judge Olin. 1-Tisdel & wife vs Drury et al. Order appointing M Thompson & A T Bradley, trustees to sell. 2-Fridley vs Thomas et al. Order appointing W P Lasselle guardian *ad litem*. 3-Mulligan vs Mulligan. Order appointing Jas Henning guardian *ad item*. 4-*In re* estate of Catharine Noonon. Decree confirming com'r report & directing sale.

Forty-fifth annual commencement of Columbian College today at the First Baptist Church, 13th st, between G & H; Rev Drs Samson, Sunderland, & Brown; Profs Schute, Wilson, Fristoe, Clarke, & D G Gillette, & Hon Amos Kendall, present on the stand. Latin Salutatory, by L B Allen, Va; orations by E O Leech, D C; F R Boston, Md; G Y Coffin, D C; S W Handy, Md; F C Bowen, D C; Jas Pollard, Va; W Veirs Bouie, jr, Md; J E Martin, Md; J T Beckley, Md; D D Johnson, West Va; Valedictory Address, Jos H France, jr, D C. Medals for the Davis Prize awarded to: F R Boston; G Y Coffin; L B Allen, J T Beckley, W Veirs Bouie, jr; F C Bowen, S W Handy, Jas Pollard, of the Graduating Class. First prize in Mathematics: L B Allen. Natural Science: J T Beckley; 2nd, W Veirs Bouie; 3rd, Z T Sowers, Va. First prize in Latin: G Y Coffin; 2nd L S Pleasants, D C. Prize in Anglo Saxon: J T Beckley. In Metaphysics: J T Beckley. Bachelors of Art conferred on: L B Allen, J T Beckley, W Veirs Bouie, jr, M Clarke, D C; L J Crendiropulo, Greece; Jos H France, jr, D C; C E Samson, D C. Masters of Art conferred on: Rev J W Custis, A B, N J; D D Johnson, A B, West Va; & Rev J O Kirk, A B, Va. The exercises closed with the benediction.

Boston, Jun 24. The U S storeship **Supply**, Edw Conroy commanding, from China, arrived yesterday, bringing the remains of the late Rear Admiral H H Bell & Lt Cmder J H Reed, who were drowned by the upsetting of a boat on the bar at Hioga, Japan. She also brings the body of Lt Cmder A S Mackenzie, who was killed in the attack on Formosa.

Highly valuable real estate on E st between 6th &7th sts, now occupied by Wm Rutherford, as a marble yard, at auction, on Jul 6, on the premises. This property fronts 69 feet, more or less, on E st, by a depth of 150 feet 1½ inches to a 30 foot alley; improved by a long brick bldg on the rear of the lot. -Cooper & Latimer, aucts

Chicago Times of Monday. The experimental trip of the boat **Little Western** was attended by disastrous consequences, the boat being upset in the trough of the sea, & the capt, Thos Garret, & Henry Chisholm-a newspaper reporter of this city, being drowned. Her design was conceived by Capt Garret, who, for over 18 years, was a sailor on the ocean, for a part of the time commanding a packet between N Y & Liverpool. After a trip in the morning, the capt & those on board were convinced of her ability to ride safely in any sea. Another trip was made in the afternoon with Prof Legendre, one of the owners, being desirous of sailing opposite his residence, ***Cottage Grove***. Six persons embarked: Capt Garret, Prof Legendre, Geo Atkins, [foreman of the Times,] Henry Chisholm, [a newspaper reporter,] R Chester & a boy. The waves were rolling & she was capsized. The coldness of the lake & the violence of the waves benumbed Capt Garret, & his strength failed him rapidly. The accident was observed by a number of persons at ***Cottage Grove***, & steps were immediately taken to rescue them. Capt Garret's life was extinct before assistance was afforded, & his body was taken on board a tug. Mr Chisholm was the only one in the cabin, & the cabin being filled, became unmanageable & rolled over on her side. The others were rescued, Garret & Chisholm being the only ones who were lost.

Obit-died: on Jun 5, 1868, Mrs Catharine Pearson, of Brentwood, D C; daughter of the late Dr Chas Worthington, of Gtwn, D C, who was born Jul 6, 1791. She was married in Jan, 1821, to Hon Jos Pearson, an ex-member of Congress from N C. Her eldest sister was the wife of Hon Wm Gaston, also a representative from S C. Mr Pearson died in Oct, 1834, in Salisbury, N C, while there upon a business errand, leaving his widow with a large family of young children. But one survives her now the wife of Carlisle P Patterson. The rest were taken, one after another, in the freshness of youth, just at the age when a fond & careful mother looks to see the reward of her prayers. One brother also survives her, Mr John G Worthington, of Gtwn, D C. Five years ago she was smitten with paralysis & remained the remainder of her life a helpless cripple, & could hardly endure to be raised from a reclining attitude long enough to have the pillows stirred & changed. Her pastor visited her to give her Holy Communion. When her mind wandered through infirmity, it wandered to her Lord. In the last few months she was seriously enfeebled & social calls were unintelligible to her. Ye who loved her follow her.

Suicide. Chas Welch, about 25, a tinner by trade, & a resident of Balt, committed suicide yesterday by drowning in the Tiber Creek. He was temporarily visiting Washington. He had been addicted to intemperate habits, & was under a temporary aberration of mind when he committed the act. The body was taken to the home of his mother, who resides on 13th st.

Mrd: on Jun 23, at St Matthew's Church, by Rev Dr White, assisted by Rev Fr DeWolf, Miss Fannie, daughter of Columbus Alexander, of Wash, to Mr Jas F Russell, of Toronto, Canada.

FRI JUN 26, 1868
Wedding at the Nat'l Hotel, on the occasion of the nuptials of Senator John B Henderson, of Missouri, to Miss Mary Foote, of Wash City, daughter of Judge Foote, of the Patent Ofc, whose family has been for months residents at the Nat'l. Messrs Benson & Dawson, proprietors, lent their best efforts to make it enjoyable while such ladies as Mrs Ann S Stephens, the authoress, took active part in giving eclat to the event. The newly married couple left last evening for Phil, en route for Cape May. [Same newspaper: Miss Mary Foote, daughter of Hon Elisha Foote, of N Y. Senator Jas F Fowler, of Tenn, & Mr F Arnold, of N Y, groomsmen, Miss Catherine Beach, of Beach, of Saratoga Springs, N Y, & Miss Augusta Foote, sister of the bride, as bridesmaids. Distinguished guests: Pres Johnson & Mrs Senator Patterson, Gen Grant, Sec Seward, Judge Chase, Sec Browning & lady, Senators Hendricks, Sherman, Davis, Hons N P Banks, Jas Brooks, Richd Wallach, Jos Wilson, Com'r of Land Ofc, & lady; Chas E Mix, acting Com'r Indian Bureau; Hon Montgomery Blair, Jonah D Hoover, the Missouri delegation in a body, army & navy officers, & prominent citizens.]

An ordnance Sergeant, named Franseker, stationed at *Fort Ripley*, Minnesota, was burned to death on Wed last, together with his 4 children. In consequence, Mrs Franseker has become insane.

Distribution of premiums at St Vincent's Academy, corner of 10th & G sts, took place yesterday. Gold medals were awarded to the graduates Misses M Crolly, M Cleary, & Rosa Marle. Premiums were awarded to: Bettie Peyton, Isabelle Peyton, J Peyton, Misses Boone, Helen Sheckells, M Zimmerman, M Byrne, Carroll, Linkins, Hollingshead, Sullivan, Mary Seibel, Julia Boone, Wilton, L Boone, Thomas, Newmeyer, Simmons, Allabach, & L Thomas.

Justice Harper held an inquest over the body of Michl Padden, who died very suddenly on Tues at the Union House, 13½ & E sts. He died from a disease of the heart. The dec'd came to this city about 3 weeks since from Boston, where he leaves one child, his wife being dead, & was here to collect a Gov't claim of $800 having served during the late war in the 5th U S cavalry.

Yesterday Mayor Bowen appointed Mr Jos S Martin, of the 6th Ward, Intendant of the Asylum, vice Mr S E C Douglass. Mr Douglass was removed because he had recognized releases for prisoners signed by T E Lloyd, Mayor, etc.

Improvements in Washington. Extensive & beautiful additions, improvements, & alterations of Heney D Cooke's mansion, Gtwn, D C, now the most extensive & beautiful residence in the District. A beautiful church on High st, Gtwn, D C, erected by Henry D Cooke, for the Society of Grace Church, a Beautiful edifice. The magnificent store, 32 feet, iron front, 4 stories high, designed for M W Galt & Bro. Baldwin Bros, builders. Beautiful first class dwlg for Wm Shields, 13th st west, between I & K sts, with brown stone trimmings. N G Starkweather, architect; Messrs Downing & Bro, contractors. Superb cottage residence, 2 stories high, with modern improvements, for Miss Susan Walker, near 7th st Park. Commodious dwlg & drug store, 3 stories high, for J P Hilton; built of brick, with brown stone trimmings, 14th st near M st. Beautiful & commodious dwlg for H A Willard, on K st, oposite Franklin Square; Messrs Wilson & Lewis, builders. First class residence, 15th & I sts, for S P Brown; Mr Robt Hart, builder; Mr Nicholas Acker, stonework; Mr J Collins, brickwork. Country residence, in the Italian architecture, 3 stories high, for Henry D Cooke, Gtwn, D C; Thos M Plowman, contractor. On Stoddard st, Gtwn Heights, there are 8 first-class cottage villas being built, containing each, on the principal floors, 2 parlors, library, & dining-room, butler's closet, servants' stairs, & hall; lots are each 43½ feet front by 135 feet deep. Col A A Hosmer has commenced the construction of a most beautiful city residence on L between 13th & 14th sts; the mansion is in the Italian style of architecture, & has a beautiful tower in front. The 2 story Gothic cottages on T st, corner 17th st, for Henry A Willard, are being built in the eastern style of cottage architecture.

Equity Court-Judge Olin. 1-Susan B Allen vs Thos B Allen; decree of divorce a *vinculo matrimonii*, & divesting property from dfndnt, & vesting it in cmplnt. 2-*In re* estate of Benj Newton; order directing trustees to sell the interest of Francis Newton.

Mrd: on Jun 2, in Greensboro, Ala, by Rev Dr Wadsworth, Mr David J Castleman, formerly of Wash City, to Miss Belle/Belie Sledge, daughter of the late Dr Alex'r Sledge.

Criminal Court-Judge Wylie. 1-Henry Willis, not guilty of assault & resisting an ofcr. 2-Saml Jackson guilty of petit larceny; sentence-30 days in jail. 3-Ann E Colwell, convicted of keeping a bawdy house; fined $200. 4-Henry Prather, alias Geo Henry Prather, convicted of petit larceny; sentenced to 6 months in jail. 5-Geo Washington Barnes was convicted of petit larceny; sentenced to 12 months in jail. 6-Adam alias Pink Jackson, convicted at Mar term of assault & battery; sentenced to pay $27.25 costs.

Died: on Jun 25, after a lingering illness, Margaret Keller, beloved wife of Henry J Keller, in her 29th year. Her funeral will be from the residence of her husband, 328 4th st, above G, on Jun 27 at 4 o'clock P M. [Phil papers please copy.]

San Francisco Alta Calif, May 23. The mortal remains of Hon Jas A McDougall were deposited yesterday in the family vault at *Lone Mountain Cemetery*, within a few hundred yards of where lie entombed the bodies of his Senatorial predecessors, Broderick & Baker. The pall bearers on the part of the citizens were Hons Lawrence Sawyer, O C Pratt, S H Dwinelle, E W McKinstry, Thompson Campbell, Saml Purdy, J W McCorkie, Gregory Yale, John J Williams, S H Brady, John Nugent, & Gen Wm T Wallace.

Valuable private residence at corner of West & Washington sts, at public auction, on Jul 9 next; property now occupied by Gen Peloaza. Improvements are a large brick dwlg house, containing 13 rooms & cellar, with gas & water. -Thos Dowling, auct

Trustee's sale of tract of land in Wash Co; by decree of the Supreme Court of D C, in Chancery, in the cause of Dyer vs Perkins et al; Equity No 349, Docket 7; public auction on Jul 14, of *The Ridge*, containing 27 acres, 2 roods & 4 perches, more or less. This land lies about one mile from *Good Hope Tavern*, adjoining the lands of Thos Jenkins. –Wm F Mattingly, Asbury Lloyd, trustees -Wm L Wall & Co, aucts

Chancery sale of valuable real estate; Willard P Tisdel & wife complnt, vs Mary Drury et al, dfndnts; Equity No 599. By decree in this cause, public auction, on the premises, on Jul 15: the west half of lot 9 in square 268, on D st, between 13th & 13½ sts, Island. Lot 18 in square 465, on 6th st, between D & E sts, Island. Part of lot 7 in square 494. Part of lot 6 in square 494, fronting on 6th st, between D & E sts, Island. -M Thompson, A Thos Bradley, trustees -Green & Williams, aucts

Dept of the Interior, U S Patent Ofc, Wash, Jun 22, 1868. Ptn of Stephen J Gold, of Cornwall, Conn, praying for the extension of a patent granted to him Oct 3, 1854, for an improvement in Warming Houses by Steam, for seven years from the expiration of said patent, which takes place on Oct 3, 1868. -A M Stout, Acting Com'r of Patents

SAT JUN 27, 1868
Columbian College conferred the honorary degree of LL D on Jas C Welling, now president of St John's College, Annapolis; for many years editor-in-chief of this paper.

On Tues the Senate confirmed a number of military nominations, among them the following of interest in this District: E G Fast, D C, to be 2nd lt in the 2nd regt of U S artl; Robt H Patterson, D C, to be 2nd lt in the 1st regt U S artl; Geo B McDermot, D C, to be 2nd lt in 23rd regt U S infty; Chas R Hinton, D C, to be 2nd lt in 25th infty; Lewis Washington & W Coyle Bayliss, D C, to be 2nd lts in the 4th cavalry; Chas H Pettit, D C, to be 2nd lt in 2nd cavalry; Donald McIntosh, clerk in the Quartermaster's Dept, to be 2nd lt in 7th cavalry; R S Fletcher, D C, to be 2nd lt in 5th infty.

Telegram announces the death, on Jun 23, of Brigham Young's right hand man, Heber C Kimball, &, next to the prophet, the chief man among the Mormons. The rank he held was first prophet, & he has been identified with this polygamous people ever since Jos Smith started them on their nomadic & multifarious career. Little is known about his life until 1837, when he became a convert at Kirkland, Ill, & was soon sent, with Orson Hyde, since assassinated, as missionaries to England for the new faith. On his return, a year afterward, he joined his fortunes with the Mormon in Ray Co, Mo. He had 67 sealed to him, & today, as at Chevy Chase, will come "as many widows their husband to bewail."

In the Senate yesterday the bill for the removal of the ***Centre Market House*** was passed. The Com'r of Public Bldgs is to remove within 12 months all the bldgs, sheds, & tenements now located on the Gov't reservation on Pa ave, between 7th & 9th sts, occupied as a city market. The reservation to be preserved in the same manner as other reservations now under his charge. The corporate authorizes the city of Wash to enter upon & occupy as a permanent site for a market-house, a portion of public reservation, along 12th st west to west side of 10th st; cost not exceeding the sum of $2,000, at a rate of interest not exceeding 6%.

Died: on Jun 25, of consumption, Willie C Harte, aged 19 years & 4 months, son of the late Edw & Rosana Harte. His funeral will take place from the residence of his uncle, Rev Alfred Holmead, No 4_6 12th st near F, this afternoon at 3 o'clock.

Chas D Fuller, who was committed to the Conn State prison last fall for 5 years, charged with the theft of $20,000 in bonds from the Hartford Bank, of which he was cashier, presented the Legislature of Conn, on their alleges that he sold the bonds from time to time, at the convenience of B T Abbott, of whom no trace has been found since Nov 10th. Fuller reasserts his entire innocence, & asks for his release as an act of justice.

The counsel engaged to defend the prisoners from Columbus, Ga, now held under arrest by the military authorites at Atlanta for supposed complicity in the Ashburn murder, are A H Stephens, Crawford & Ingram, Moses & Garrard, Smith & Alexander, Mr Waddell, of Columbus; Wm Dougherty, of Atlanta, & H W Hilliard, of Augusta.

St Louis, Jun 26. Judge Wm S Allen, who has been editorially connected with the St Louis Republican for some 12 years, died at his residence, in Franklin Co, on Tuesday last. Judge Allen was born in Mass in 1805; he occupied several prominent positions.

Trustee's sale of valuable farm in Montg Co, Md, 8 miles from Wash City, about ½ mile west of the 7th st road; by deed of trust to the undersigned; recorded in Liber E B P No 3 folios No 131; public auction on Jul 9, at the public house of Thos Moulton, at **Brightwood** on the 7th st road, in the Dist of Col, a large Farm known as **Joseph Park**; containing 134 acres; with a new 2 story frame house containing 4 rooms with never failing springs of running water convenient. –Jos F Kelley, trustee/auct

Harrisburg, Pa, Jun 26. Nicholas Zolinger, a well-known citizen, was run over this afternoon by the passenger train from Phil, & had both legs taken off. The accident occurred with a square of his house. He died in an hour after the accident. He was attempting to cross the track at the time.

U S Marshal's sale on Jul 16, all dfndnt's right, title, claim, & interest in & to lot 6, in Chas Wiltburger's subdivision of square 442, in Wash City, with improvements thereon, seized & levied upon as the property of Fred'k Gaiser, & will be sold to satisfy exectuion 2,079, in favor of John F Behrins. –David S Gooding, U S Marshal, D C

U S Marshal's sale on Jul 16, of all the dfdnt's right, title, claim, & interest to the west part of lot 1 in square 380, being the house & lot on Pa ave, between 9th & 10th sts, now occupied by John R Elvan, as a hardware store, together with all the improvements thereon seized & levied upon as the property of Walter Lenox, & will be sold to satisfy execution 268, in favor of Penniman, Stove, & Knight. –Ward H Lamon, late U S Marshal, D C

New Orleans, Jun 26. An affray occurred in a restaurant last night, in which Major Frank Manney, of Nashville, was stabbed by an unknown man, who made his escape. Manney died instantly. Col Luckett, of Texas, was arrested today as an accessory to the murder of Maj Manney. The assassin is still at large.

Detroit, Jun 26. Rev Dr Duffield died this afternon, aged 74 years. His funeral will take place on Sunday.

Supreme Court of D C, Jun 26, 1868; Equity No 1,183. Ezra L Stevens & Wm W Kirby, cmplnts vs Andrew J Amos et al, dfndnts. It is ordered that the dfndnts Andrew J Amos, Fergus M Blair, Wm Bell, & Jas H Edes, cause their appearance to be entered herein on or before the first rule day occurring 40 days after this day; otherwise the cause will be proceeded with as in case of default. –A B Olin, Justice -R J Meigs, clerk

Supreme Court of D C, Jun 26, 1868; Equity No 1,315-Docket 9. Lucy Reese, cmplnt vs John P Reese, dfndnt. On motion of the cmplnt by J J Coombs, her solicitor it is ordered that the dfndnt cause his appearance to be entered herein on or before the first rule day occurring 40 days after this day; otherwise the case will be proceeded with as in case of default. –A B Olin, Justice -R J Meigs, clerk

Elmwood Home School, near Laurel, M, on the Washington Branch Railroad. Mrs David H Burr will reopen her French & English School for Young Ladies on Sep 28. Mrs Burr, Laurel, PG Co, Md.

MON JUN 29, 1868
Patrick Hughes, aged about 40, employed at Willard's Hotel as a baker, fell from the 5th story of the bldg, on Friday night, & was instantly killed. He was a man of temperate habits. The dec'd had been in the country about 20 years; was a native of Ireland; had two brothers here & one in N Y. His brother John Hughes resides on 1st st, & took charge of the body.

The Senate, on Sat, confirmed the nomination of Martin T McMahon, of N Y, as Minister to Paraguay. The nomination of Gen John E Mulford, as collector for the 3rd Dist of Va, was rejected.

Dr J N Hollywood pleaded guilty of passing counterfeit national currency, in Detroit, on Thursday, & was sentenced to the State prison for 5 years.

Osmond Patten, of Westmoreland, Oneida Co, N Y, was stung over the left eye a few days since, by a honey bee. The sting was taken out, but in about 15 minutes he became dizzy & faint, &, although sensible at times, grew rapidly worse & died in 3 hours.

Miss Laura M *Schaffer, daughter of Christian *Schaffer, residing in Alexandria, on Fairfax st, died yesterday from the effects of burns received the previous evening. She was running down stairs on Sat with a lighted coal oil lamp, & fell, the lamp breaking into fragments, & the flames igniting her clothing. He mother was also severely burned about the left arm in endeavoring to help her daughter. Miss Schaffer was about 23 years of age, engaged to be married to Mr Chas *Tennison, of Alexandria, who was so affected by her death that he attempted to commit suicide yesterday. He shot himself in the head. He was removed to his father's residence, Cameron & Fairfax sts, where Dr Lewis examined the wound; but no hopes are entertained of his recovery. [Jul 1st newspaper: Mr Tenneson, who shot himself on Sunday, died on Monday, after lingering 36 hours. The funeral of Miss Laura *Schafer, his affianced, took place on Monday, from St Paul's Church; the body was interred in the ***Alexandria Cemetery***. Same newspaper-another article: Mr Wm Phillips, who married Miss Schafer's sister, was at the scene of the accident at the time; her grandmother, Mrs Ballenger, a lady of some 80 years, was with her. Mr Phillips threw his coat on her to subdue the flames. Mr Chas *Tennesson, [son of Mr Saml Tennesson,] had been her constant companion for years. *Schaffer/Schafer; Tennison; Tenneson/Tennesson: various spellings.]

Criminal Court-Judge Wylie. 1-John Thoms; petit larceny; guilty; sentenced to jail for 6 months. 2-John R Stewart, John Jefferson, Taylor Triplett, & Edw Brown, indicted for the larceny of a hog, the property of Antoine Rupert, on May 12 last; not guilty. 3-Chas Grant; petit larceny; *nolle pros*. 4-Chas White; petit larceny; guilty; sentenced to jail for 10 days.

Orphans Court-Judge Purcell, Jun 27, 1868. 1-The will of Catherine Pearson was filed for probate. The testatrix appoints C P Patterson, Wm H Philip, & W S Cox, excs. 2-Margaret R Grey gave bond in the sum of $5,000 as admx of Wm Grey. John Prince, & John H Leiffert, sureties. 3-A F Kimmell gave bond in the sum of $5,000 as guardian to the orphan of K H Lambell. John Van Riswick & R Coyle, sureties. 4-The will of Alfred Lee was filed for probate. The testator names John T Lee & John H Johnson, excs. 5-The second account of Saml W Owen, guardian to Kate D Owen, filed & passed. 6-Wm Thomas gave bond in the sum of $2,000, as adm of Benj F Thomas, dec'd. H P Prather & T W Tansell, sureties. 7-A decree was passed finally ratifying & confirming the sale of real estate by Lucinda Hess, guardian to the minors of Jacob Hess, dec'd.

Died: on Jun 28, in her 68th year, Mrs Malinda Smith. Her funeral will be tomorrow at 4 o'clock, from the residence of her son-in-law, Dr Jos Walsh, 493 G st.

Died: Jun 27, at Laurel, Md, John N, son of Henry & Augusta Lovejoy, aged 7 months.

Died: on Jun 27, after an illness of 6 weeks, Charlie Nimrod, infant son of John E & Ethie A O'Brien, aged 7 months & 7 days. His funeral will be from the residence of his parents, 493 L st, between 9th & 10th sts, this afternoon at 3 o'clock P M. [Balt Sun please copy.]

Montreal, Jun 27. Jefferson Davis, while coming down stairs with one of his children in his arms, in the hotel at Lenoxville, fell, & somewhat injured his back. He was unable to attend the convocation of the Bishop's College.

Chas Tucker, [alias Mason,] who served in the army, & for many months at the Custom House, was detected in stealing a quantity of butter. He was discharged, which took effect on Nov 10, 1866. Tucker was tried & convicted at Niagara recently for the murder of his wife, in Buffalo, in Sept, by poisoning her, for a Life Insurance policy of $5,000.

Balt, Jun 28. Miss Caroline F Sturgeon, a highly respected & estimable young lady, aged 22, residing at 414 West Lombard st, was so badly burned this morning from the contact of her clothes with a stove that she died at 4 P M.

Memphis, Jun 28. Geo Kingwalt, attempting to rescue a friend who had been arrested, was mortally shot by Sgt Brown, of the police. Brown was arrested.

Great sale of real estate at auction, by Hall & Ross, [Recently R M Hall,] Real Estate Brokers, corner 7th & D sts: sale on Jul 9, of 105 acres of land, said property is between the places of ***Clark Mills*** & Col Wright Rives; 3 miles from Wash City limits.

Supreme Court of D C, In Chancery No 500. John A Middleton et al vs Eliza T Berry et al. Ratify sales reported by John A Middleton & Thos W Berry, trustees for the sale of the real estate of Washington Berry, dec'd. The report states the amount of sales to be $100,208.59. –A B Olin, Justice -R J Meigs, clerk

Executors of Wm Slade, dec'd, offer for sale a very superior gray Carriage Horse, fine driver in single or double harness, & perfectly kind & gentle. Also, set of Single Harness, & one Family Carriage. –J B Wheeler & Co, aucts, 61 La ave.

TUE JUN 30, 1868
Grant's acceptance of presents from everybody, a dangerous position for a President to be in. Grant is known to be a very self-absorbed, selfish, & grasping man. He takes everything that is presented to him, no matter by whom, or what the supposed consideration. Rich men of the nat'l bank & bondholder stripe have presented him with houses, bond & stocks; sporting men have presented him with horses; gambler presented him with billiard table; dog fanciers with pups; theatre mangagers with dead head tickets; harness makers with saddles & harness; carriage makers with carriages; Russell Jones & Washburne presented him with $5,000 of stock in the Chicago Horse Railway Co. Even poor card-writers presented him with all the visiting cards he uses, for which they get in return letters of thanks in very indifferent English. In fine, "all is fish that come to Grant's net." Let this be thought of when taxpayers are asked to "vote for Grant."

Yesterday, at an early hour, while a number of soldiers were at the house of Geo Callahan, 6th & B sts, Capitol Hill, Mr Callahan was shot by Parick Boyd, the ball passing through Callahan's hand & into his thigh. The shooting was accidental, & Boyd was fined $10 for carrying a concealed weapon, & $5 for disorderly conduct, & in default of payment he was committed to the workhouse.

Died: on Jun 29, Estell Ann, only daughter of Jas & Ella Taylor, aged 4 months & 19 days. [Canada papers please copy.]

Thirty acres of valuable garden land near Uniontown, D C, for sale on Jul 20, on the premises, divided in 3 parts, of 10 acres each. Thos land, the property of C A Krause, is known for its richness & healthy locality. –Chas Kloman, Real Estate Broker, 488 7th st. –Galligan & Townshend, aucts

Chancery sale-valuable real estate on *Lafayette Square*; by decree of the Supreme Court of D C, wherein John S Gittings & others are cmplnts, & Wm B B Cross & others are dfndnts, the same being Equity 1,693; public auction on Jul 23, of part of square 186, improved by a 3 story double front brick house; adjoins the residence of W W Corcoran, & fronts directly upon Lafayette Square & the President's House.
–J Carter Marbury, trustee -W L Wall & Co, aucts

Supreme Court of D C, Equity 1,209. John M Keating et al vs Sarah A Keating et al. Parties in this cause to appear on Jul 6 next, at my ofc, 36 La ave. I shall state the account of the said trustees, & distribute the fund in their hands.
–C Ingle, Special Auditor

WED JUL 1, 1868

Louisville, Jun 30. J C Roy Taylor committed suicide at the St Chas Hotel, Nashville, this morning, by taking opium. Pecuniary troubles are supposed to have been the cause of the suicide.

A visit, a year ago, to the Female Grammar School of the First School Dist of Wash City, under charge of Miss Annie E Evans, left a deep impression on us. It is the kind of school that train girls into the discipline, knowledge, & ideas which make the substratum of truly cultivated, refined, & useful women. It's roll has 60 scholars from age 12 to 16. Mary Wilson, 13, is perhaps the best reader of her age; Hattie Gove, 13, was scarcely less remarkable; Pauline Prince, 13, made a marvelous trio in this important study. Miss Annie E Trumbull, 16, daughter of Thos Trumbull, a Gov't clerk, won the gold medal for the reading of a composition. Premium list: Medal-Annie E Trumbull. Written examinations: Kate Snyder, Mary McGill, & Fannie Calvert. Attention to Study & Improvement: Kate Rawlings, May Wilson, & Jennie Clampit. Exemplary Deportment: Amanda France, Jennie Murphy, Sarah Oliphant, Lottie Swallow, Fannie Sothoron, Janie Turton, Maggie Ballantyne. Neatness: Maude Sharretts. Music, Mary Reiss. Present every day during the year: Kate Rawlings, Annie Trumbull, Ella McMahon, Jennie Hallaran, Fannie Sothoron, & Nora Jones.

The Cleveland Leader says, Mrs Sarah Victor, who has been on trial there for several days past, for poisoning her brother, Wm Paquet, was on Tues found guilty of murder in the first degree. Parquet had been a soldier, & had insured his life, in favor of Mrs Victor, for $2,300. Early in 1867 he came to Cleveland, from Euclid, Ohio, where he had been working, & stopped with his sister. Soon after he was taken sick, & died Feb 4, 1867. Suspicion having been excited as to the cause of his death, the remains were exhumed about a year after his burial, & arsenic was found in the stomach. The father of the murderer & her victim was an ignorant Frenchman, named Parquet, usually called "Old Pocket." The evidence on her guilt was conclusive. The verdict of guilty was returned-she muttered & spoke loudly, called to her sister, & was taken by 2 deputy sheriffs, conducted to her cell, apparently unconscious of her motions. [Jul 6th newspaper: Mrs Victor was sentenced at Cleveland, Ohio, on Friday, to be hanged Aug 28 next.]

Criminal Court-Judge Wylie. 1-The Grand Jury returned a true bill of indictment against Levin Turpin, charging him with the murder of Thos H Kelleher, on Jun 3. Witnesses on the indictment: Dr P Croghan, C Wesley Thompson, J H Dubant, Asbury Lloyd, & Jas A McDevitt. The indictment was read & the prisoner answered "not guilty." Trail set for Jul 8th. 2-Geo Livingstone, guilty of the larceny of $12, the property of Christina Peifner, on May 19 last; sentenced to 6 months in jail. 3-John Schrode, convicted of the larceny of 2 calves; sentenced to 2 months in jail.

Died: on Jun 29, Indiana H, daughter of John B & Sarah J Lord, aged 9 months.

Died: on Jun 30, Bernadine Mary Anastasia, infant daughter of Christian F & the late Mary Anastasia Eckloff.

Orphans Court-Judge Purcell, Jun 30, 1868. 1-The will of Catherine Pearson was filed for probate. The testator names C P Patterson, W H Philip, & W S Cox execs. 2-First account of Geo W McClelland, exc of Jas H Smith. 3-First & final account of Adaline Lusby, guardian to the orphan of Jas Lusby. 4-John H Johnson qualifies as exc of the estate of the late Alfred Lee; bond $125,000.

St Paul, Jun 30. The celebrated <u>Chippewa Chief</u> Hole-in-the-Day was assassinated by being shot, near his own residence, at Crow Wing, on Sat, by 3 Indians of the Pillager band. Cause attributed to pent up jealousy & old grudge. [Jul 3rd newspaper: Hole-in-the-Day was murdered by 3 Beech Lake Indians, while riding in his buggy near his residence. He leaves 6 Indian wives, & one who is white.]

Cleveland Herald, Jun 29. John Cool, a resident of Warrensville, made an attack upon 2 step sons, Edw & Henry Quayle, aged 20 & 18, with a butcher knife, Sat, & Henry died in 4 hours, & Edw cannot live long. They were heirs to the farm where Cool lived, & chose to select a neighbor as their guardian [Mr Thorpe] in preference to their step father, which so excited him that he determined to kill them, their guardian, mother, a few others & then himself. He was arrested before the job was completed, & is now in the county jail waiting a preliminary examination. He had been drinking during the day. His wife was formerly the wife of ____ Quayle, a brother of Robt Quayle, the blacksmith, near Central Market. She is, perhaps a little older than her husband, who is from 42 to 45 years of age, & has never given birth to any children since second marriage. Her children, numbering 4, were the fruit of her first marriage. The two eldest, Edw & Henry were the victims of the assault by their step father. The other children, a boy aged 9, Silas, & a girl, age & name not known, make up the remainder of the family. Silas was the only witness to the stabbing. The boys did not live at home, but were employed as farm hands by the neighbors. He met them on their way home, in front of Thos Cooper's house, where he attacked them in the middle of the road. [Jul 8th newspaper: Cleveland, Jul 7. John Cool, who killed his two step-sons, named Guoyle, at Warrensville, on Jun 27, cut his throat last night in his cell, with a razor borrowed from a fellow prisoner. His trial commenced yesterday.] Note: Quayle/Guoyle. Copied as written.

Trustee's sale of valuable real estate in St Mary's Co, Md; by decree of the Circuit Court of said county, wherein Walter Mitchell was cmplnt & John H Sothoron dfndnt; public auction, on Aug 4 next, at Leonardtown, the estate known as The Plains, supposed to contain 800 acres, more or less; the farm is located on the Patuxent river.
-F Stone, Port Tobacco, Chas Co, Md; Peter W Crain, Balt, Md, trustees

Excellent household & kitchen furniture at auction on: Jul 3, at the residence of Mrs De LaRoche, 143 Wash st. -Thos Dowling, auct

Sale of personal estate; by order of the Orphans Court, passed on Jun 24, 1868, the undersigned, as administrator of Eliz Sibley, late of PG Co, Md, dec'd, will offer at public sale, at the late residence of the dec'd, in Bladensburg district, the following: 3 mules, 3 milch cows, 1 carriage & harness, 1 wagon & harness, 1 carryall & harness, on stack of hay, corn, fodder, horse rake, lot of potatoes; household & kitchen furniture.
–Wm J Sibley, adm of Eliz Sibley

THU JUL 2, 1868
Commencement at Rock Creek College, at Ellicott City, Md, on Monday; college is under the charge of the Brothers of the Christian Schools, an order in the Catholic Church, devoted especially to the education of boys. Present were Rev Dr Coskery, Vicar Gen of Balt; Rev Fr McCarthy, of Wash; Bishop Given, of S C; Rev Frs Foley & McColgan, of Balt; Rev Fr Griffing, of St Chas College, Md, & Judge Merrick, formerly of the Dist of Columbia courts. Bachelor of Science conferred on Wm G Heuisler, Md. Master of Accounts conferred on Francis J McDermott, Md; Chas F Fusting, Md; Jos T Daiger, Md; J Jerome McManus, D C; Jos C O'Neill, Md; John W Lynch, Va. A certificate for proficiency in English Literature was given to Jos T Daiger, Md. There are about 154 students at the college, of whom 20 are from D C. Medals went to Jerome McManus; J Howard Bushnell; W H Collins; P G Young; Jos E Dyer; Chas A Stewart; John L Eliot; W C Clabaugh; Hugh Caperton; R B Mosher; & John Fegan.

John A Enos, about 22 years of age, walked, a few days since, from the monument in Peabody, Mass, to the Eastern railroad depot, in Boston, & return, declared to be a distance of 28 miles, in 5 hours & 38 minutes, an average of a mile in 11 3/4th mins.

Distribution of premiums at St Aloysius parachial Schools for girls took place on Monday; children numbered about 100; Rev Fr Wiget distributed the premiums.
In the evening the distribution of medals & premiums of the Male Parochial School, containing 316 pupils, took place. Music by Beckar's Band; Mr F A Rover was in charge of the exhibition, & Misses Agnes Cleary & M E Eckloff, in charge of the singing classes. In the male schools the gold medal was awarded to Master Wm Hartnett, & a silver one, each, to John Lincoln & Wm Rabbitt. Distribution of premiums in St Dominick's schools, male & female, took place Monday. The distribution of premiums at St Stanislaus Academy for young ladies, took place on Monday afternoon.

Mrd: on Jun 30, in Wash City, by Rev G W Samson, D D, Prof Andrew Tenbrook, of the Univ of Mich, to Mrs Emma Smoot, widow of the late Dr Saml C Smoot, of Wash.

Mrd: on Jun 30, by Rev Fr Boyle, Dr Edw S Kimball to Miss Lizzie M Pearson. No cards.

Died: on Jul 1, Walter Jordan, only son of Wm W & Imogene Graham, aged 9 months. His funeral will be on Jul 2 at 5 P M, from 326 19th st, between I & K sts.

Cincinnati Enquirer, Jun 24. The third attempt at suicide, made yeterday, which was successful, does away with all the secrecy, & we are pained to announce that Dr Chas P Thornton has fallen victim to the suicidal mania. For several months he has been laboring under a fit of melancholy, brought on by an unpleasant termination of a strong attachment he had formed for a certain young woman. For the past few months he had been drinking to excess. On Monday Dr Thornton made a short visit to his father, who resides at Cleves, & appeared quite rational. He retired at an early hour, got up & stabbed himself in the neck, & then in the vicinity of the heart. The noise of his falling on the floor aroused the other members of the family, but it was too late. The deceased was between 35 & 40 years of age. When the war broke out he was appointed surgeon of the 5th Ohio cavalry; after the war he bought out the well known drug stand on the corner of 6th & Elm, where he remained only a short time, as he preferred the labors of his profession.

Dept of the Interior, U S Patent Ofc, Wash, Jun 26, 1868. Ptn of John J Weeks, of Oyster Bay, N Y, praying for the extension of a patent granted to him Sep 26, 1854, which patent was surrendered & application for reissue made in 4 divisions for an improvement in Harvesters & Grain & Grass for seven years from the expiration of said patent, which takes place on Sep 26, 1868. -A M Stout, Acting Com'r of Patents

FRI JUL 3, 1868
Cooper & Latimer, aucts, sold to Dr D R Hagner, for $3,425, lot 15 in square 141, improved by a 2 story pressed brick house, embracing 5 rooms; on the south side of H st north, between 18th & 19th sts west. Mr Wm McMeir, real estate broker, sold lots 13, 14, & 15, in square 245, N & 13th sts, to Col L Sitgreaves, for $10,275.

Mrd: on Jun 30, in Wash, D C, at the residence of Mr P H Hooe, by Rev B A Maguire, Pres of Gtwn College, Mr Caleb C Magruder, jr, of Md, to Miss Bettie R Nalle, of Va.
+
Mrd: also, at the same time & place, by Rev Geo H Horton, of Alexandria, Va, Mr John W Belt, of Md, to Miss Mary D Nalle, of Va. No cards.

Mrd on Jun 25, at Spring Grove, Westmoreland Co, Va, by Rev Mr Wharton, Col John M Fessenden, of Boston, to Mrs S A Richards, daughter of the late Dr Robt Murphy, of the former place.

A collection of nine <u>Cremona violins,</u> made by the late Mr Chas Plowden, has been purchased by a London gentleman for L2,000.

<u>Rittenhouse Academy,</u> Prof Wight, principal, has been on Indiana ave, near 3rd st, for the past 20 years. Exercises were held on Tuesday last. The speeches of Frank T Browning, Stephen Tabor, & John Wight, were well delivered. Oration "Washington" by Master Geo R Milburn; "Lafayette" by Master John H Olcott. Milburn intends to enter Yale; Olcott intends to enter Brown Univ.

Yesterday Christopher Bohlayer, a well known character of the 6th Ward was brought before Justice Lynch, to answer to the charge of assault & battery with intent to kill Ofcr Geo Luskey. Bohlayer had fired at Luskey with a Spencer rifle, the ball entering the left breast & passing over to the right side. Bohlayer was taken to the precinct, in company with his wife; he was committed to jail. He tried to commit suicide by swallowing a large dose of arsenic, but an emetic was admininstered, which saved his life.

Board of Police. Ninety-day privates appointed: C G Eckloff, duty at Harvey's oyster saloon; John L Daily, duty for the Wash & Gtwn Railroad Co; Chas Frick, duty at Campbell Barracks; Francis Quinn, duty at the Ebbitt House. Wm Martin filed his official bond as a justice of the peace. Privates Richd A Frere & Joshua B Stoops were fined $50 each & reprimanded for gross neglect of duty. The applications of the following for liquor licenses were rejected: Danl P Mealey, J B W Seigert, Herman Koppel, & Matthew D Attley.

Dept of the Interior, U S Patent Ofc, Wash, Jun 27, 1868. Ptn of Joel F Keeler, of Pittsburgh, Pa, praying for the extension of a patent granted to him Sep 26, 1854, for an improvement in Platform Scales, for seven years from the expiration of said patent, which takes place on Sep 26, 1868. -A M Stout, Acting Com'r of Patents

SAT JUL 4, 1868
Annual Commencement of <u>Gtwn College</u> on Wed: [the college was used for a long period as a military hospital during the war.] Academic exercises: orations by Jas V Coleman, D Clinton Lyles, Henry A Seyfert, W A Hammond, Sands W Forman, Steph R Mallory, Chas S Abell, & W Tazewell Fox. Valedictory: F J Kieckhoefer, of Wash City. E H White, of Md, of the graduating class, & R Mallory, from Fla, spoke well. The degree of LL D was conferred upon Hon Geo Brent & Hon Robt Ford, both eminent jurists of Md, & both graduates of the College some quarter of a century ago. The degree of A M was conferred upon Jesoyr Edwin Cheney, M D, Ill, & Richd L Carne, Va; Thos M Herran, New Granada; Danl A Casserly, N Y; Frank A Rudd, Va; F P Blair Sands, D C; W Tazewell Fox, Va. The following are the names of the graduating class: Chas S Abell, Md; Needham C Collier, Ga; Wm A Hammond, Va; Francis J Kieckhoefer, D C; D Clinton Lyles, Md; Luis De Puebla, Mexico; Edw H White, Md. The summary of attendance at the college the past year is as follows: Senior dept, 50, jr, 63, preparatory, 139; medical graduates, 47, under medical graduates, 61; total, 360. Medal Scholars belonging to this District: Robt Taylor, John T Hedrick, Wm H Larman, & Frank H Jones. Premium Scholars: Robt Taylor, Nathan Webster, Ferdinand Risque, Chas F Pochon, Chas A Trunnell, Jos S Aylmer, & Vincent A Hubbard. Acceserunt Scholars: Michl T Tuohy, Chas A Ball, Jas Hunter, Jas Collins, Jas H A O'Neill, Franklin Steele, Louis D Mohne, Jas Mackall, Jas Reily, Chas A Heron, Chas R Alexander, Frank H Jones, Jos S Aylmer, Vincent A Hubbard, Edw Godey, Frank T Smart, Jas Dyer, Nathan Webster; Robt V Simms, Louis Thian, Jos M Semmes, John T Hedrick, Ferdinand Risque, Francis J Kieckhoefer, & Chas H Sawyer.

The remains of Rear Admiral Bell were interred at Newburgh, N Y, on Thursday.

Equity Court-Judge Olin. 1-Fridley et al vs Thomas et al; order appointing R H Laskey trustee to sell. 2-B F Wiget vs C E Ryan et al; decree appointing E Carusi trustee to sell.

Potter Palmer, the Chicago millionaire, is about building a grand hotel in Chicago for Mr Geo S Leland.

Died: on Jul 3, Mrs B M Smoot, aged 71. Her funeral will take place on Sunday afternoon at 3 o'clock, from her late residence, 331 Pa ave.

N Y, Jul 3. This afternoon a man named John M Mulhern, who was at work on 79th st, about 2,500 feet from the shooting ground at Schuetzenfeat, directly in line of the targets, was killed by a stray ball. It is not known by whom the shot was fired. This put a stop to the shooting on the grounds today.

Kinderhook, Jul 3. Maj Lawrence Van Buren, brother of Pres Van Buren, & for many years postmaster at Kinderhook, died suddenly yesterday at his residence in this village, in his 85th year.

Phil, Jul 3. Lafayette C Baker, the Gov't detective, died this morning. He leaves a fortune of $200,000.

Valuable bldg lot on south E st, between 7th & 8th sts, Island, at auction; in the Supreme Court of D C, wherein Susan B Allen, cmplnt, vs Thos D Allen, dfndnt, Equity 221; public auction on Jul 9 part of lot 8 in square 464, 25 feet by 100 feet deep.
-S R Allen, -Green & Williams, aucts

MON JUL 6, 1868
Mrd: on Jun 30, in Trinity Church, Wash City, by Rev Jas B Avireth, Mr Chas N Coles, of Winchester, Va, to Miss Fannie Perry, of Montg Co, Md. [Missouri papers please copy.]

Died: on Jul 4, in her 73rd year, Frances, eldest daughter of the late Michl Hogan, formerly consul of the U S at Valparaiso. Her remains will be taken to N Y for interment.

Died: Jul 4, Fred'k B Williams, in his 35th year, leaving a wife & 3 children. His funeral will take place at his mother's residence, 576 8th st, between I & K sts, this afternoon at 4 P M.

Died: on Jul 5, Mrs Cornelia M Boyden, widow of the late Fred'k Boyden, aged 53 years. Her funeral will be at 284 G st this morning at 10 o'clock. Her remains will be taken to Boston for interment. [Boston & N Y papers please copy.]

Died: on Jul 5, Minnie Irene, infant daughter of C M & Annie M Taylor, aged 3 months. Her funeral will take place this afternoon, at 6 o'clock, from the residence of her parents, 330 N J ave. [Balt Sun & Petersburg, Va, papers please copy.]

Died: on Jul 5, Ida Taylor, only daughter of Chas M & Mary S A Taylor, aged 8 weeks. Her funeral is this afternoon at 3 o'clock.

Academy of the Visitation, 10th & G sts, last Friday, has their annual distribution of premiums. Rewards of conduct in the senior circle were bestowed upon: Anna Smith, Fannie Wilson, Fannie Flint, Helen Goolinski, Julia Parsons, Mary Saul, Mollie Williams, Grace Scott, Anna Lauck, Clara Callan, Susie Torney, Clara Drew, Kate Harkness, Victoria LeCompte, Dedie Handy, Anna Bartholow, Bertns Chilton, Rosalie Sprigani, Julia Greer, Annie Waters, Florie Cook. Jr Circle: Lucy Herbert, Fannie Saul, Lizzie Walsh, Susie Watson, Amlia Bastianelli, Maggie Cox, Etta Brent, Mamie Ryan, Elvie Fletcher. Primary Class: Jannie Shacklin, Lizzie Rush, Mamie Clarke, Blanche Elwood, Annie Adamson, Ada Williams, & Elia Farrae. Attention to study & amiable conduct during their short stay in the academy: Josephine Woolard, Rose Hoffer, Ida Phelan, Zaidee Jones, of the senior class; Ella Easby, Delia Jocknick, Mamie Chapman, & Mamie Cromwell, of the jrs. Music: Cecelia Elliot, on the harp; vocal by Mary Polzinhorn; piano, Misses Julia Parsons & Fannie Stoops. Display of varied work by Mary E Jones, Julia De Frees, Mary E Jones, & Fannie Wilson. Water colors by Anna Elliott; ornamental writing: H Goolinski.

On Tuesday, during a heavy thunderstorm, Rev A G Shafer, pastor of the West Deer Township United Presbyterian Church, 10 miles from Pittsburg, was instantly killed by lightning while standing at the corner of his residence. He was 50 years of age, & had been pastor of the church for 30 years.

On Thursday, 3 little girls, Mary Sullivan, Margaret Doherty, & Ann Carroll, while bathing in Poplar Pond, in Douglas st, Brooklyn, got beyond their depth & were drowned. Mrs Doherty, the mother of one of the children, & Jas McGee, who attempted to rescue the children, went beyond their depth & were also drowned.

Boston Journal of Friday. The steamer **City of Boston**, of the Norwich line, from N Y for New London, was run into at midship by steamer **State of N Y**, last night. Dense fog at the time hung over the waters. Mr Caleb P Hoogs, of the Adams Express Co, was in his stateroom at the time of the accident, & ran to ring the bell; he had to climb within reach of it, & strike it with an iron rod. Injured, as far as ascertained: Wm B Hazeltine, agent of Sandford's line of steamers, Boston, severe contusion & internally injured- seriously; J W Edgely, Brookline, scalded internally, not serious; Mrs N B Walker, Jersey City, severe cut in foot; & Henry B Tracy, Norwich, Conn, right hand scalded.

Herr Moscheles, now 75, has just composed a symphonic sonata for 2 pianos & 8 hands, which has been produced with good success at Leipsic.

TUE JUL 7, 1868
House of Reps: 1-Cmte of Claims-bills passed for the relief of: Anthony Bucher; Mark Howard, collector of internal revenue for the 1st Dist of Conn; Capt Thos W Miller, of the Army of the Potomac; N A Shuttleworth, of Harrison Co, West Va; heirs of Jas S Porter, of Hancock Co, West Va; Saml Tibbetts; Geo Kaiser; Jas Hooper; Henry B St Marie, allowing him $10,000 for services & information in the arrest of John H Surratt.

On Jun 26, Rufus Ludwig was executed at Salisbury, N C, for the murder of his wife. He spoke to the people for a very long time; he desperately tried to jump off of the platform, but was held down by the officers, most of them old Confederate soldiers; he fought having the noose put over his head; he finally choken to death from the tight rope.

On Sunday 3 young men, Messrs J F Gladmon, John Donnelly, & T L Cropley, discovered Mr Jas Gray lying helpless from intoxication at Mr Cropley's door, on Bridge st. They took him to his home at Mrs Cleveland's, across the st, at 168 Bridge st, Gtwn, D C. A scuffle ensued, in which the deceased received fatal injuries. T L Cropley was held under bail for a hearing. Donnelly & Gladmon were discharged.

The Association of Oldest Inhabitants, at their meeting on Jul 4, elected as members messrs Mathew Glascoe, John Belt, Francis A Fenwick, Danl Hauptman, John Downing, John McDermott, M Hanson, & John E Neale. Ofcrs were elected for the ensuing year: Pres, Dr John B Blake; Sec, J Carroll Brent. The death of Col John S Williams was then formally announced, & proper expressions of respect to his memory were adopted.

A young man, Dewitt Clinton Van Syckle, a resident of East Liberty, Delaware Co, Ohio, has been arrested in Columbus on the charge of poisoning his father's family & burning his house. The poisoning was done in April, the culprit putting arsenic in some molasses. Fortunately, but a small quantity was partaken of, & no fatal results ensued. Some weeks afterward the homestead was set on fire & burned to the ground. The young man is thought to be insane, & will be taken to a lunatic asylum.

WED JUL 8, 1868
The President sent the following nominations to the Senate yesterday: Lt Cmder Henry Erben, to be cmder in the navy on the active list, vice J C Febiger, promoted; & Lt Cmder Edw P McCrea, cmder on the active list, vice Peirce Crosby, promoted; Edw Willett, to be receiver of public moneys at Sacramento, Calif; Tubman Ayres, to be register of the land ofc, Bois City Idaho, vice R H Brown, resigned; Chas W Burr, to be assessor of internal revenue of the 4th Dist of Va; Louis D Viser, to be assessor of internal revenue for the 3rd Dist of Mississippi.

Ludwig, the North Carolina murderer, in his confession, says his mother & sister made him kill his wife. He shot her, & while his mother held her arms his sister cut her throat. Amiable ladies.

Equity Court-Judge Olin. 1-Pfluger vs Wallach; order for release of certain property from deed of trust. 2-Ridgeway vs Curtis; decree appointing John J Johnson trustee to sell. 3-May et al vs Oilrich et al; decree appointing John F May trustee to sell. 4-Gorman vs Edelin; order substituting Edw Gorman trustee in place of Horace Edelin. 5-In re. Voluntary bankruptcy of Catharine Bauman; order refusing its junction to restrain trustees in equity from selling.

Orphans Court-Judge Purcell, Jul 7, 1868. 1-Annie J Ryon gave bond in the sum of $20,000 as executrix of the will of Richd J Ryon; J H Yeatman, B H Stinemetz & Jerome Brown sureties. Also, a bond in the sum of $6,000 as guardian of her minor children; same sureties. 2-The following accounts were filed & passed: First account of Mary E Russell, adm of Alfred Russell. First account of Wm Queen, guardian to Chas Posey. Distribution account of personal estate of Jas Lusby, by Adeline Lusby, admx. 3-Wm Van Master gave bond in the sum of $300 as administrator in the cases of Saml Cunningham, Michl Cooper, Jos Riley, Edw Bartlett, Stacy Grant, Lyman Reynolds, John J Bellinger, John Castel, Hannah Sohn, Wilde Emerson, D C Connor, & Elijah Hail- all land warrants.

Died: on Jul 6, Mrs Ellen P, beloved wife of J T Kelly. Her funeral will be from her late residence, 20th & H sts, this afternoon, Jul 8, at half past three o'clock.

Died: on Jul 7, suddenly, Martin King, in his 64th year. His funeral will take place from St Peter's Church, on Jul 9 at 9 o'clock A M.

The partnership existing under the firm of Pratt & Turner is this day dissolved by mutual consent. The business of the late firm will be conducted by A S Pratt, 408 7th st, U S Revenue Bldg. E S Turner may be seen at the ofc of Jay Cooke & Co, Wash, D C.

N Y, Jul 7. Peter Cagger & John T Devlin, while riding in Central Park last evening, were thrown from their carriage. Cagger was instantly killed. Devlin's injuries are very serious. His condition is precarious. Mr Cagger was an eminent politician of the State, long identified with the Albany Regency. [Jul 9th newspaper: They drove to the St Vincent Hotel, kept by one of the sons of Mr Chas A Stetson, who is father-in-law of Mr Develin. The hour was late & they were anxious to get home. They were trotting at speed down the west drive when suddenly, the front wheel of the wagon broke, & the vehicle overturned. Mr Develin was conveyed to his residence in 138th st, near the Hudson river. Mr Cagger's friends hastened to St Luke's Hospital, & it was arranged that the body should be conveyed to Albany by the evening boat. A despatch from N Y announced the death of Mr Develin. –Ed Int.]

Cleveland, Jul 7. John Cool, who killed his two step-sons, named Guoyle, at Warrensville, on Jun 27, cut his throat last night in his cell, with a razor borrowed from a fellow prisoner. His trial commenced yesterday.

THU JUL 9, 1868
Died: on Jul 8, Sarah M, beloved wife of David Pool. Her funeral will take place from her late residence 499 Mass ave on Jul 10, at 4 o'clock P M.

Died: at the residence of Dr Maxwell, 128 F st, Robert M, infant son of Lt Cmder T H Eastman, U S N, & Anna H Eastman, aged 6 months. His funeral will be on Friday at 5 o'clock P M. [No death date given.]

Martin King, an old & esteemed citizen of Wash, residing in the Fifth Ward, was prostrated with a violent attack of cholera morbus within a few hours after dinner on Jul 4, but, under medical treatment, was gradually improving until 3 o'clock Tuesday afternoon, when he was suddenly taken with spasms, & died in about 15 minutes. He was born in Montg Co, Md, in 1804, & came to this city when quite a child. He was a printer by trade, & served for a long time with the late Col Force. Thirty-six years ago he entered the ofc of adjutant of marines as clerk, which position he has filled ever since. He was a member of the Association of Oldest Inhabitants, & was universally respected for his sterling worth & upright character. His funeral will take place from St Peter's Church this morning at 9 o'clock.

The Desert News of Jun 25 comes to us in mourning for the death of "one of the saints" –Heber C Kimball. The funeral obsequies were held on the 24th at Salt Lake City; over 8,000 attended; the coffin was borne by 12 bearers, accompanied by the 12 Apostles.

Rockbridge Alum Springs, Va, for sale; by decree in Chancery of the Circuit Court of Augusta Co; property must be sold for partition; public auction on Sep 1, 1868, on the premises. In 1848 it sold for $12,000; & in 1851 for $100,000; to the present owners for $105,000. The estate consists of about 1,100 acres in Rockbridge Co, 25 miles from the Natural Bridge. Descriptive pamphlet with map will be sent on application to the proprietors, at the Springs. –John B Baldwin, Henry B Michie, John Echols, David Fultz, Com'rs. Address Staunton, Va. –Peck & Cushing, aucts

Orphans Court of Wash Co, D C, Jun 30, 1868. In the case of Michele Bright & Eliz Ann Rhodes, excs of Jas Rhodes, dec'd, the executors & Court have appointed Jun 18 next, for the final settlement of the personal estate of the said dec'd, of the assets in hand. -Jas R O'Beirne, Reg/o wills

Orphans Court of Wash Co, D C. Letters testamentary on the personal estate of Richd J Ryon, late of Wash Co, D C, dec'd. –Anna J Ryon, excx

Dept of Interior, U S Patent Ofc, Wash, Jun 20, 1868. Ptn of Ann Winter, of Roundout, N Y, admx, & Wm Winter, of same, adm of the estate of Archibald Winter, dec'd, praying for the extension of a patent granted to said Archibald Winter, Sep 19, 1854, for improvement in Machine for Sawing Firewood, etc, for 7 years from the expiration of said patent, which takes place on Sep 19, 1868. -A M Stout, Acting Com'r of Patents

Dept of the Interior, U S Patent Ofc, Wash, Jun 30, 1868. Ptn of Jules Debauvais, of N Y, N Y, executor of the estate of Victor Beaumont, dec'd, praying for the extension of a patent granted to said Victor Beaumont Oct 3, 1854, for an improvement in Steam Gauge for seven years from the expiration of said patent, which takes place on Oct 3, 1868. -A M Stout, Acting Com'r of Patents

FRI JUL 10, 1868
Horatio Seymour is the people's candidate for the Presidency at the next election. He is a native of Utica, N Y; his father was one of the earlier inhabitants of that city, & a native of Middlebury, Vt; one of the most distinguished citizens of Central N Y, & at the time of his death, which occurred about 35 years ago, held the ofc of Canal Com'r. In 1850 Horatio Seymour was elected Govn'r of N Y by a small majority over Govn'r Washington Hunt. Re-elected in 1852, & in 1862. Govn'r Seymour is about 56 years of age. His wife, a daughter of the late John R Bleecker, of Albany, is universally admired for her intelligence, & loveliness of character. They have no children. Of Mr Seymour's 3 sisters, one married Ledyard Sinclair, of Casenovia; another Mr Shonnard, of Westchester; & another Hon Roscoe Conkling, U S Senator from N Y.

The will of the late Col A G Hazard, offered at the Probate Court in Enfield, Conn, on Sat, appoints Govn'r Bullock, Mrs Hazard, & his daughter, Fanny, executors; gives $75,000 to the library hall to be erected in Hazardville; $5,000 to Hazardville Episcopal Church; $2,500 to the Hazardville Methodist Church; & $2,500 to the South Congregational Society in Enfield. The estate is estimated as valued at nearly a million dollars.

Hon Marcus P Norton, of Troy, has been awarded the sum of $250,000 for the past use of the Norton Post Ofc stamp. The Court of Claims certified their decision to Congress, & asked that a bill might pass covering this amount in favor of Mr Norton. The bill was promptly passed by Congress, & the President's 10 days for signing the same expired on Tuesday. [Jul 11th newspaper: We are informed that there is no truth in this statement, copied from the N Y Times.]

Died: on Jul 9, John A Smith. His funeral will take place from his late residence, 390 C st, this evening at 5:30 o'clock P M.
+
Obit-died: on Jul 9, John A Smith, aged about 76 years. The deceased was a native of Md, but for more than half a century a resident of this District; he witnessed the small beginnings & gradual growth of the metropolis; was for many years connected with the late Circuit Court as deputy or principal clerk; was always devoted to farming & horticulture. He could refuse nothing to his friends. For a year past he has been in declining health, & of late became so feeble that he felt his days to be numbered. Shortly before his death he received Holy Communion. He passed away suddenly from the midst of an affectionate family.

London Times: Assassination of Prince Michael. The impression produced by the savage outrage at Belgrade has thrown into the background every other subject. It is felt in Hungary almost like a family tragedy, for Prince Michael was well known; had spent his youth in exile in Vienna; & in Hungary, he had a fine domain of Jvanka, he had married a Hungarian lady, Countess Julie Hunyday, who, spent several months in England a few years ago; he had kept up those relations. As on almost every afternoon at this season, on Wed, the Prince, in company with his cousin, Anka Konstantinovich, & her young daughter Catharine, about 16, walked about the park. They encountered 3 other persons, well known to them as members of the Radovanovich family, the father & 2 sons. The father was a bankrupt lawyer, from Sabaez, & had been condemned to 20 years' imprisonment, which had been reduced to 7. In spite of this the family thought they had some kind of grievance againt the Prince, as well as his cousin, with whom the father had been in litigation, which was decided against him. The Radovanoviches passed, making the customary salute; & almost as soon as they passed they drew their revolvers & fired at the Prince & the 2 ladies from behind. The Prince, struck by several bullets, fell mortally wounded, as well as the young girl; the mother was shot dead on the spot. Seeing the Prince still breathing, the 3 assassins drew their long stagans & fell savagely upon the porstrate Prince, cutting him about the head & face so as to disfigure him almost completely. Two of the aides de camp, one a son of the late Prime Minister, Garachanin, ran to the spotwhere they were received by shots, one of which broke Garachanin's arm so badly that it afterwards had to be amputated. Still they were able, with others, to arrest the father & one of the sons. The other escaped, but has since been captured.

Erie, Pa, Jul 9. Erie express train, on the Pittsburg & Erie railroad, left Erie last evening, broke through the bridge near Union Mills. The engine, tender, & baggage car got over safely. Two passenger cars went through, making a complete wreck. Mrs J W Fust, of Flat Rock, Seneca Co, was killed. It is thought that the bridge was tampered with, for the purpose of plunder.

Died: on Jul 8, Judge Geo B Way, late of Ohio, in his 57th year. His funeral will be from his late residence, 395 9th st, between H & I sts, this afternoon at 4:30 P M.

Died: on Jul 9, Eva, infant daughter of Wm P & Lizzie Moran, aged 8 months & 15 days. Her funeral will take place from the residence of her parents, 339 21st st. [No date or time given for the funeral.]

Died: on Jul 9, William Young, infant son of Alex'r R & Mary G Shepherd, aged 4 weeks. His funeral will be on Jul 10, at 8 o'clock A M, from 358 10th st.

Dept of Interior, U S Patent Ofc, Wash, May 28, 1868. Ptn of Rebecca A Marcher, of N Y, N Y, excx of Robt J Marcher, dec'd, praying for the extension of a patent granted to said Robt J Marcher, May 22, 1855, for an improvement in Tool for Grooving Mouldings for seven years from the expiration of said patent, which takes place on May 22, 1869. -A M Stout, Acting Com'r of Patents

House of Reps: 1-Cmte on Invalid Pension-granted pensions to the following:
Eliz Lane, mother of John Lane, 12th Mass volunteers.
Rosalinda, widow of Barney McCabe, 40th N Y cavalry.
H L Hall, 97th N Y volunteers.
Eliz G, widow of Rev Saml Hibben, 4th Ill cavalry
Kate, widow of John Higgins, 28th Ky.
Eliza, mother of Col Donnelly, 28th N Y volunteers [$30 per month.]
Mich Reilly, 35th Mass volunteers.
Jane, widow of Peter McNaughton, contract surgeon.
Anne, widow of John Williams, 3rd Wisc cavalry.
Chauncey D Rose, father of Alvin G Rose, 2nd Ohio cavalry.
Hugo Eicholds, 15th N Y heavy artl.
Zadock T Newman, 7th enrolled Missouri militia.
Sarah E, widow of Jas Ball, fireman on the steamer **Vidette**, connected with the Burnside expedition.
Capt Danl Sheets, 17th Ohio volunteers.
Esther C C, widow of Chas F VanGuilder, 1st Vt heavy artl.
Miss Anne E Hamilton, aunt & adopted mother of Jas E & Chas B McKillip, 61st & 62nd Pa.
Stephen T Carver, 49th N Y.
Prescott G Howland, 12th N H.
Martin Burke, 15th N Y heavy artl.
Children of Wm M Wooten, Davies Co Home Guards, Ky militia. [Senate bill, with amendment.]
John Sheets, 12th West Va, [Senate bill, with amendment.]
Widow & child of John P Fetty, 14th West Va, [Senate bill, with amendment.]
Martha, widow of T Stout, Davies Co Home Guards, Ky militia, [Senate bill.]
Obadiah T Plum, 22nd Iowa, [Senate bill, with an amendment.]
Louisa, widow of E P Fitch, capt & assist quartermaster U S volunteers, [Senate bill.]
Annie, widow of Bernard Kelley, 13th N Y heavy artl, [Senate bill.]
Edward, child of Edward Hamel, 8th Kansas volunteers, [Senate bill.]
Wm B Edwards, [increasing pension from $8 to $15 per month, from June, 1866.]
Jonathan H Perry, father of Anthony H Perry, 3rd N J infty.
Wm J Kotty, 21st Missouri volunteers.
Widow & children of Patrick Raffery, 33rd Mass, [Senate bill.]
Anna M, mother of Geo W Howard, 11th N J, [Senate.
Francis T, widow of Maj Gen Israel B Richardson, [increasing pension to $50 per month, from Sep, 1862.]
Barbara, widow of John P Stout, Tenn.
Nancy, widow of Alex'r Cook, Johnson Co, Tenn.
John Lamarsh, 3rd Vt infty.
Catherine, widow of Chas B Skinner, 2nd Pa infty.
Mary J, widow of Jas Truman, 12th West Va infty.
Helen L, widow of John Wolf, 111th N Y infty.
Wm Smith, 10th U S infty.

Eliz, mother of Jas C Lamar, killed while fighting with a Union organization in Ky.
Jos A Fry, 17th Ohio infty.
Thos Stewart, [Senate bill.]
John W Harris, pilot in the service of the U S, [Senate bill.]
Harriet W Pond, widow of ___ Stinson, [Senate bill.]
Lucinda R, widow of Dr Blueford Johnson, of Ill, contract surgeon, [Senate bill.]
Widow & children of Henry Brown, 10th Tenn cavalry, [Senate bill with amendment.]
Minor children of Robt T Weed, 2nd Indiana battery, [Senate bill with amendment.]
Widow & children of Conrad Switzer, 61st N Y, [Senate bill, with amendment.]
Geo T Brien, naval pensioner, [Senate bill, with amendment.]
Patrick Collins, Columbus, Ohio, of the U S railroad construction corps.
John Gridley, 9th Mich.
Catherine, mother of John D Gensler, 119th Pa.
Asa F Holcombe, 29th N Y cavalry.
Emily B, widow of Brig Gen Danl B Bidwell, [increasing pension to $50 per month from Oct, 1864.]
Henrietta, widow of Capt Danl G Nobles, 4th Tenn infty, [Senate bill.]
Catherine, widow of Henry L Eckhard, 5th Missouri, [Senate bill.]
Carrie E, widow of Jas F Burdett, acting assist surgeon, [Senate bill.]
Eliz, widow of H W Steepleton, 6th Indiana legion, [Senate bill.]
Children of Lafayette Cameron, Dist of Col, [Senate bill with amendment.]
Children of Jos Berry, 4th Iowa.
Nine Senate bills, granting back pensions to the widow of John W Jamison, Catherine Wands, Henry Reems, Sylvester Nugent, Eliz Barker, Mary Gerther, Charlotte Posey, & Rebecca Senior.
Alice A, widow of Maj Hiram Dryer, 13th U S infty, [$25 per month.]
Seth Lea, Knox Co, Tenn, [allowing pension as 2nd lt.]
Polly W, widow of W W Cotton, 7th Tenn infty, [granting her pension of capt.]
Children of Wm R Silvey, 2nd Tenn infty.
Jane, mother of Jas C Rook, 3rd Maine infty.
Sarah K Johnson, of Salisbury, N C, [$30 a month.]
Bill for the relief of Gen Ward B Burnett, of N Y, laid on the table.

Ex-Govn'r Grason died on Thursday, at his residence in Queen Anne's Co, Md, at the venerable age of 82 years. He was the first Govn'r elected in Md by the people under the remodelled constitution of the State, & well remembered by the older inhabitants of Md. Prior to that period, 1836-38, Mr Grason served creditably in both branches of the Genr'l Assembly, being identified with the old Democratic party. He served as Govn'r for 3 years & then retired to his estate in Queen Anne's Co. Judge Grason, the present judge of the Circuit Court of Balt Co, is a son of the deceased. –Marlboro Gaz

Richmond, Jul 9. Jeter Phillips, tried for the murder of his wife, was convicted this morning of murder in the first degree. [Nov 5th newspaper: Richmond, Va, Nov 4. Govn'r Wells has respited Phillips, who was to have been hanged next Friday, for 60 days.]

Died: on Jul 9, Francis M, infant son of Mr & Mrs John M Binckley.

Mr John A Smith, a well known citizen of the District, died very suddenly yesterday. He had been in bad health for several months; he was about 76 years of age; a native of Taneytown, Western, Md; came here when about 22; he filled the position of deputy clerk of the Circuit Court of this District for many years, under Col Brent. He was possessed of considerable property& for years resided & worked the farm on which Howard Univ is in course of erection, he having disposed of it to the Univ a year or two since, & was the owner of a fine farm over the Eastern Branch. He leaves a widow & 6 children, 2 sons & 4 daughters. His funeral will take place at 5:30 this afternoon, from his late residence on C st, near 3rd.

Dept of the Interior, U S Patent Ofc, Wash, Jul 1, 1868. Ptn of Gardner S Blodgett & Paul T Sweet, of Burlington, Vt, praying for the extension of a patent granted to him Dec 5, 1854, for an improvement in Oven for Baking, for seven years from the expiration of said patent, which takes place on Dec 5, 1868. -A M Stout, Acting Com'r of Patents

SAT JUL 11, 1868
Thos Dowling, auct, sold the valuable residence, & large lot attached, on the n e corner of West & Washington sts, to Mrs Mary Williams, for $9,125. John J Bogue, real estate agent, sold at private sale the large frame dwlg, 42 Market st, between 1st & Prospect sts, to S Gans, for $2,700 cash; also, lot on east side of High st, on the canal, to F L Moore, for $2,000. Mr Moore will erect on this lot a large warehouse for storage. Also, lot on north side of 2nd st, between Fayette & Lingan sts, to John L Cook, for $800. On this lot Mr Cook proposes to erect a dwlg.

N Y World. Peter Cagger, who lost his life on Monday, was a native of Albany, of Irish parentage, & about 56 years of age; he had been a resident of Albany all his life, where he studied law. Mr Cagger was a peculiar looking man, standing about 5 feet 5, & possessing a smooth florid face, with thin, yellow hair, sparingly covering a large & well developed head; a gentleman of excellent manner & courtly address. He was a leading member of one of the Catholic Churches at Albany, & leaves a wife & family to mourn his loss.

Criminal Court-Judge Wylie. 1-Sarah Jones; petit larceny; pleads guilty; sentenced to jail for 3 months. 2-Jos Black; petit larceny; verdict guilty; sentenced to jail for 6 months. 3-John D Preston, indicted for stealing a horse valued at $100, the property of the U S, on May 15 last; guilty; sentenced to the Albany Penitentiary for 3 years. 4-Thos Talbert, John Patsey & J W Johnson, indicted for riot & effray; guilty; sentenced to jail for 30 days. 5-Jas C Smith indicted for stealing one horse, saddle, & bridle, of the value of $100, the property of John Doyle, on Jun 27 last; pleads guilty; sentenced to penitentiary for 2 years. 6-John Williams, burglary; not guilty. 7-Jas Jones; larceny; guilty; sentenced to jail for 6 months. 8-Jos Smith; larceny; guilty.

Edwin Forrest is reckoned the richest actor in the country, & his fortune is put at $840,000.

Equity Court-Judge Olin. 1-Rupert vs Greir et al; decree appointing Geo Killian trustee.

Mrd: on Jul 2, at the Trinity [M E] Church, in Wash City, Thos L Davis, of Ky, to Miss Sallie C, daughter of Col P M & Susan Henry, of Va. No cards. [Richmond, Lynchburg, & Danville, Va, papers please copy.]

Died: on Friday, Willie, youngest child of Bushrod & L V Robinson, aged 5 months & 15 days. His funeral will take place on Sat at 11 o'clock A M, from 250 10th st. [Star.]

Died: at his residence, 87 Pa ave, between 21st & 22nd sts, Jas Chapman, in his 40th year. His funeral will take place on Jul 12, at St Stephen's Church, at 8 o'clock. Requiescat in pace. [No death date given.]

N Y, Jul 10. Gabriel P Dissosway, contributor for many years past to the religious press, died suddenly yesterday, aged 70 years.

Wanted: a white girl, as Chamermaid or Nurse. Apply to Wm L Downey, H st, between Delaware ave & 2nd st east.

MON JUL 13, 1868
The Senate acted upon the following nominations by the Pres: confirmed-Edw W Willett, receiver of public money at Sacramento, Calif; John C Cox, justice of the peace in Wash, D C; John S Walls, chief justice of New Mexico; E Mayhead, U S Dist Atty for Montana. Rejected-J O P Burnside, 2nd auditor of the Treasury, vice E B French.

The death of Lt Col Wm Dulany occurred at Beltsville, Md, on Jul 4. He was a native of Alexandria, & for more than 40 years an ofcr of the Marine Corps.

On Sat, while a number of men were bathing in the Potomac river, off Easby's ship yard, one of them, Andrew Balmain, was observed to be unable to swim, & seemed in imminent danger of being drowned. He was promptly rescued by some of his companions, & prevailed upon to go on shore & clothe himself. After having donned his apparel, he became quite excited, insisting that he could swim, & threw himself into the river, & was drowned before assisstance could be rendered him. His body was recovered by his horror-stricken companions, & conveyed to the residence of his father, Mr A Balmain, residing on H st, between 18th & 19th sts. Young Balmain was aged about 27 years. The news of his decease will be heard with deep sorrow by his many friends.

Mrd: on Jul 1, at the residence of Chas J Ost, by Rev Wm Pinckney, D D, Edw Thos Boag, of Charleston, S C, to Mary Amelia, oldest daughter of the late Edw Dewees, of Eliz City Co, Va.

Died: on Jul 11, Capt Francis Key Murray, U S N, in his 48th year. His funeral will take place from his late residence, Rockburn, Howard Co, Md, on Jul 14, at 6:30 P M.

Died: on Jul 12, Geo M Harry, in his 39th year. His funeral will take place from the residence of his father-in-law, Jas Shackleford, 217 Pa ave, on Tuesday at 5 P M. [Jul 14th newspaper correction: Geo W Harry]

Died: on Jul 12, George C, son of Henry C & Mary V Bamberger, aged 3 years & 8 months. His funeral will take place from the residence of his parents, 300 Va ave, between 9th & 10th sts, Island, this morning, at 9 o'clock.

A negro man, Harvey Lewis, fell from a window in a house in Prather's alley, between 4th & 5th sts, yesterday. He was so seriously injured that he died yesterday evening.

Dennis O'Hare, charged with the murder of Patrick Hughes, by throwing him out of a window at Willard's, some two weeks since, was dismissed on Sat by Justice Smith, there being no evidence against him.

Annie Rooney, white, & Wm Thomas, colored, charged with robbing John Usher of $14,000 in gold & bonds, have been held to bail in $2,000 each for their appearance at court.

Constantinople, Jul 11. Ishmael Pacha, Viceroy of Egypt, has married a daughter of Abdul Medjid.

Orphans Court of Wash Co, D C. Letters testamentary on personal estate of Benj Ogle Tayloe, late of Wash Co, D C, dec'd. –P W Tayloe, E T Taylor, Geo B Warren, jr, excs

Orphans Court of Wash Co, D C. Letters of administration on the personal estate of Walter Harper, late of Wash Co, D C, dec'd. –John T Mitchell, Richd Petitt, adms

Phil, Jul 12. At the Roman Catholic Cathedral of St Peter & St Paul, this day, Rev Wm O Hooda, D D, was consecrated bishop of the new diocese of Scranton, & Rev J F Shanahan, D D, was consecrated bishop of the new diocese of Wilkesbarre. The Rt Rev Bishop Ward was the consecrator, the attending bishop being L McGill, of Richmond. The services lasted 5 hours.

Nashville, Jul 11. The Nashville Banner received a despatch from Knoxville, stating that Col A M Ashby, late of the rebel army, was shot & instantly killed, yesterday, by E C Camp.

Phil, Jul 12. The nickel works of Jos W Wharton, in Camden, N J, were totally destroyed by fire this evening.

Cincinnati, Jul 11. J B Woodruff, news editor of the Cincinnati Times, was sunstruck yesterday, & died almost immediately.

The Democratic nominee for Vice Pres, Frank P Blair, jr, is the son of Francis P Blair, sr, the veteran statesman & journalist, was born in Lexington, Ky, Feb 19, 1821; educated at Princeton College; admitted to the bar in his native town; removed to St Louis, & commenced practice in 1843. During the war with Mexico he served as a lt of volunteers.

Orphans Court-Judge Purcell, Jul 11, 1868. 1-John W Nairn gave bond in the sum of $500 as the guardian of the heirs of E R Nairn. J W Nairn & W T Griffith, sureties. 2-Jacob Scherer gave bond in the sum of $4,000 as exc of Henry Scherer. Frank Miller & C H Gockeler, sureties. 3-Richd Pettit & T Mitchell gave bond in the sum of $200,000 as adms of Walter Harper. Richd Pettit, G W Riggs, & G H Plant, sureties. 4-Junius J Boyle gave bond in the sum of $4,000 as adm of John Boyle. John F Boyle & C A Stubbs, sureties. 5-Phebe W Tayloe, Edw Thornton Tayloe, & G B Warner, jr, gave bond in the sum of $150,000 as excx of B Ogle Tayloe. Geo B Warren, jr, & W H Tayloe, sureties. 6-The will of Henry Sherer was fully proven & admitted to probate & record. He names Jacob Sherer sole exc & legatee. 7-The will of B Ogle Tayloe was filed, partially proven, & admitted to probate as to the personalty. 8-The first & final account of Sam T Crown, guardian to Susan E Crown, was filed & passed.

Equity Court-Judge Olin. 1-In re. Voluntary bankruptcy of Catharine Bauman; order denying injunction as prayed. 2-Bayly et al vs Bayly et al. Order on Thos McLaughly to comply with terms of sale. 3-Wangman vs Wangman. Order allowing bill filed without deposit, & for alimony.

TUE JUL 14, 1868
Hon Wm Pinkney Whyte, of Balt, has been appointed U S Senator for the unexpired term of Hon Reverdy Johnson.

<u>The President yesterday sent to the Senate the following nominations:</u>
Chas E Ramus, of Kansas, to be Consul at Honolulu
L P Williston, to be Associate Justice of the Supreme Court of Montana Territory
Silas H Axtell, to be Assessor of Internal Revenue for the 3rd Dist of Calif
H L Warren, to be Chief Justice of the Supreme Court of Montana
Adam Rise, to be Assessor of Internal Revenue for the 10th Dist of Pa
Edwin S McCook, to be Collector of Internal Revenue for the 8th Dist of Ill
Selden Conner, to be Assessor of Internal Revenue for the 3rd Dist of Maine
B F Brundage, to be Register of the Land Ofc at Vidalia, Calif
Jas H Wilber, of Oregon, to be Agent for Yakama Indians
Lafayette Head, to be agent for New Mexican Indians
+
The Senate yesterday, confirmed Edw S McCook, collector of internal revenue for the 8th Dist of Ill; & Selden Conner assessor for the 3rd Dist of Maine.

Sir Morton Peto has come out of the bankruptcy court penniless.

The ceiling of the dome of the Senate library in Luxenbourg palace lately fell & destroyed the beautiful painting by Eugene Delacroix which covered it.

A cable despatch announces the death of Saml Lover, the well-known Irish novelist, artist, song writer, & lecturer, at the age of 71. Mr Lover was born in Dublin, in 1797. He wrote the attractive & widley known songs of "Rory O'More," "The Angel's Whisper," "Molly Bawn," & the "Four Leaved Shamrock." In 1856 the British Gov't awarded him a pension of 100 pounds a year, since which time he has lived in retirement.

Yesterday, in the Criminal Court, Judge Wylie, the trial of Levin Turpin, better known as Lep Turpin, indicted for the murder of Thos H Kellaher, on Jun 3 last, was commenced; Messrs John E Norris & R T Merrick for the accused. The jury as selected stands: Saml Wallach, W D Bell, John T Cassell, Jos R Cassin, Jas Goddard, Chas H Anderson, G A Hall, Zachariah Forrest, Thos N Adams, Richd W Wallace, Francis C Iardella, C O Wall, A F Offutt. Dr Patrick Coghan, Jas A McDevitt, John J Peabody, Mr John H Dubant were sworn. Asbury Lloyd, Geo Klerlein, W Thompson, Lt Noonan, Jos Hamlin, G F Hotchkiss, & Horatio Nater were sworn. Court adjourned. [Jul 15th newspaper: W H Gorbutt testified; resided at 8th & E sts; has known the accused for 18 months. W H Hopkins, Capt H R Howlett, Edw Davis, T H Browning, Arthur Shepherd, W H Miller, & Maurice Dubois testified to the good character of the accused, to his having been a mail carrier with the army, employed on the street cars. The jury, after an absence of 15 minutes, came into court, & the foreman announced the verdict of guilty of manslaughter, but not guilty of murder. The prisoner was remanded to jail.]

Died: on Jul 11, Andrew Balmain, aged 24 years. His funeral will take place this afternoon, at 4 o'clock, from the residence of his father, 294 H st, between 18th & 18th sts. [In announcing that Mr Balmain committed suicide, it appears his death was entirely accidental, the coroner's jury having returned a verdict that the deceased came to his death from exhaustion.]

Died: on Jul 13, after a brief illness, Mrs Rebecca Goodrich, aged 91 years. Her funeral is this morning at 9 o'clock, from the residence of her son, Josiah Goodrich, 435 5th st, between D & E sts.

Died: on Jul 13, Maria Sellman, infant child of Wm H H & Katie Ridgely Barclay, aged 6 months. Her funeral will be this afternoon at 6 o'clock, from the residence of her parents, 390 19th st, between F & G sts.

Died: on Jul 13, in Wash City, Mary P Ingle, youngest daughter of the late Jos Ingle. Notice of the funeral tomorrow. [Jul 15th newspaper: died on Jul 13, Mary P Ingle, aged 19 years, daughter of the late Jos Ingle. Her funeral will take place from the residence of her aunt, Mrs E Lindsley, 452 I st, between 9th & 10th sts, this afternoon at 5 o'clock.]

Equity Court-Judge Olin. 1-Annie Cathcart vs Arthur Cathcart. Order of reference to auditor to report on partition. 2-Woods et al vs Briscoe's heirs et al. Order ratifying trustee's sale. 3-Rogerson vs Rogerson. Order for appearance of dfndnt. 4-Patterson *et rex* vs Jay et al. Order appointing of W H Phillip guardian *ad litem*. 4-Paterson *et rex* vs Jay et al. Order or reference to special auditor, C Ingle, to report on propriety of confirming trustee's sale.

Phil, Jul 13. Geo Krouse, aged 16, fired a revolver at Nathl Westcall, aged 14, today, inflicting a serious wound in the breast. Krouse had a few days before stabbed Westcall in the leg, & the last outrage seems prompted by a deliberate attempt at murder.

Sale of very valuable farm about 4 miles from Wash City, on the old Bladensburg road, containing about 110 acres; public auction on Jul 27, of the farm of the late W H Dundas, dec'd, known as "*The Cottage*," improved by a dwlg house, containing 12 rooms, & numerous outbldgs. –W Y Fendall, atty -Green & Williams, aucts

Supreme Court of D C, Equity No 1,227, Docket 5. John R Woods et al vs R G Briscoe's heirs et al. Ratify sales made by Wm R Woodward, trustee, on Jun 10 last, of part of lot 9 in square 382, & part of lot 11 in square 408, to Saml Norment. –A B Olin, Justice -R J Meigs, clerk

Richmond, Jul 13. 1-Gen Stoneman has appointed Jas S Tipton, judge of the 15th Circuit, vice Fulton, resigned. 2-Jas H McGhee, an old citizen of Hanover Co, was killed yesterday.

Dept of the Interior, U S Patent Ofc, Wash, Jul 7, 1868. Ptn of Isaac R Trimble, of Long Green, Md, praying for the extension of a patent granted to him Apr 10, 1855, & ante dated Oct 10, 1854, for an improvement in Wooden Splice-piece for Railways, for 7 years from the expiration of said patent, which takes place on Oct 10, 1868. -A M Stout, Acting Com'r of Patents

WED JUL 15, 1868
Orphans Court-Judge Purcell. 1-Verando E King gave bond in the sum of $12,000 as admintrator of Martin King. John T Hoover & Dennis Callahan sureties. 2-The following accounts were filed & passed: First & final account of J B Monroe, adm of Geo Monroe. Second account of M A Sipes, guardian of Sarah Sipes. First & final account of P G Meem, adm of John Meem. First & final account of Adolphus Lindenkohle, exc of Eliz Morrison. 3-*In re*. Will of Eleanor Miller, dec'd, & the caveat filed against the probate of said will. The hearing in this cause was commenced upon the testimony taken before the Register of Wills, but was not concluded when the court adjourned. Several days will be required to conclude the arguments of counsel. Robt Leech, solicitor for the propounders of the will; M Thompson, for the caveators.

Mrs Kechley's husband died at Memphis last week.

Thos *Meggins, formerly a soldier in one of the Pa regts, & lately a laborer in the Patent Ofc, died very suddenly yesterday morning, in the model room of that bldg. Shortly after he reached the ofc he was observed to be quite sick. The best of attention was immediately given him, but without avail, as he died about an hour afterwards. The city authorities have taken charge of the body. [Jul 16th newspaper: Mr Thos *Magins, who was employed as a laborer in the model room at the Patent Ofc & died suddenly on Tuesday, was buried in the *Congressional Burying Ground*. The attaches of the dept attended the funeral, who also bore all the expenses of the interment.] *Note the two spellings: Meggins/Magins.

Litchfield, Ky, Jun 27. Pleasant W Shields, a boy, was convicted of the murder of his cousin & playmate, Henry Hocker, near Cromwell, Ohio Co, Ky. Yesterday was fixed for the day of execution. The prisoner was taken from the jail by the Sheriff & placed in a car, & then, with Rev Mr Armstrong, Baptist minister, surrounded by a strong guard, went to the place of execution. The prisoner spoke for about 40 minutes, making a full confession of his guilt. The rope was adjusted around his neck, & at precisely 2 o'clock the door fell. He died without a struggle. His body was delivered to his father, & was carried to Ohio Co, to be buried in the same burying ground, alongside his victim. -Louisville Courier

N Y World, Jul 14th. Last evening as 7 young ladies went in bathing in the East river, at the foot of 56th st, one of them, Mary Powers, age 16, slipped off into deep water & was drowned. Frank Beck, aged 14, whose parents reside in avenue A, near 57th st, plunged in to rescue one of the ladies, De Camp, who in turn seized hold of her two sisters, & all 3 were pulled under the water. He succeeded in bringing them up alive, one at a time. He continued to dive for the body of Miss Powers, but was unsuccessful.

The steamer **Stephen Low**, which returned from Dudley's Grove with a large picnic party on board, was nearing the dock at 152nd st, when a girl fell overboard. Police Ofcr Colett jumped into the water to rescue her, but was himself drowned. A panic occurred among the passengers, & all of them rushed to one side of the boat, the guards gave way, & a large number were precipitated into the water. Nine hats were picked up on the water. The body of Ofcr Colett, & that of the girl, whose name is unknown, are still missing. -N Y World

Died: on Jul 14, in his 34th year, Saml Murray. His funeral service will be held at his late residence, 435 10th st, near G st, on Thursday morning at 9 o'clock.

Phil, Jul 14. John P McDevitt, for several years connected with newspapers of this city, died this morning of inflamation of the bowels. He was said to be one of the best phonographic reporters in the country.

St Clement's Hall, Ellicott's Mills, Md, near Balt. Rev J Avery Shepherd, A M, Head Master. The third annual session will open during the first week in Sept.

Brady & Co's Photograph Gallery for sale at auction; by decree passed by the Supreme Court of D C, wherein Matthew B Brady is cmplnt, & Jas F Gibson et al are dfndnts; public auction on Jul 23, on the premises, all the stock in trade, good will, materials, instruments, furniture & fixtures, of the Gallery, on Pa ave, between 6th & 7th sts, over the banking house of Rittenhouse, Fowler & Co. The above Gallery is handsomely furnished & in complete order. Terms of sale: cash. –Wm F Mattingly, Receiver
-Green & Williams, aucts

Dept of Interior, U S Patent Ofc, Wash, Jul 10, 1868. Ptn of Eben N Horsford, of Cambridge, Mass, praying for extension of a patent granted to him Oct 10, 1854, for an improvement in Compounds for Neutralizing Chlorine, for 7 years from the expiration of said patent, which takes place on Oct 10, 1868. -A M Stout, Acting Com'r of Patents

THU JUL 16, 1868
Died: on Jul 14, Mary L McConnell, wife of Geo E McConnell, & daughter of the late Henry C Greenfield, in her 25th year. Her funeral will take place from the residence of her mother, Mrs Greenfield, 11th st east, between Pa ave & G st, this afternoon at 4 o'clock.

Died: on Jul 14, Mary E Murtagh, aged 68 years. Her funeral will take place from the residence of her son, Wm J Murtagh, 497 Md ave, this afternoon, at 2 o'clock.

Died: on Jul 13, Mary P Ingle, aged 19 years, daughter of the late Jos Ingle.

The monument soon to be erected at ***West Point*** over the grave of Lt Gen Winfield Scott, consists of a granite base, 7 feet long, 3 feet wide, & 1 foot 2 inches thick. Upon this rests a single block of Italian marble 6 feet long, 2 feet wide, & 2½ feet high. There is not an ornament about it; not even a moulding to break the severe simplicity & solidity of the massive stone. The following is the inscription:
WINFIELD SCOTT
Born, Dinwiddie County, Va, June 27, 1786.
Died, West Point, N Y, May 27, 1866.
History records his Eminent Services as a Warrior, Pacifi
-cator, and
General-in-Chief of the Armies of the United States.
Medals and an Equestrian Statue, ordered by Congress in
The Capitol
Of his Country, are his Public Monuments.
This stone is a mark of the love and veneration of his
Daughters.
Requiescat in Pace.

Orphans Court of Wash Co, D C. Letters of administration on the personal estate of Martin King, late of Wash Co, D C, dec'd. –Venerando E King, adm

The decease of Capt Mitchell, late proprietor of *Piney Point*, will not interfere with the arrangment for carrying on that favorite resort for this season. Mr Knight Woodley, who is at the head of the establishment, is an old hand at the catering business & will conduct everything to the satisfaction of visitors.

Frank Leslie, the well-known magazine publisher, on Tuesday commenced a suit for a divorce from his wife.

Michl D Lawlor, a clerk in the Interior Dept, & said to be one of the finest penmen in Wash City, died very suddenly at his boarding house, [Mrs Waters, D st, between 6th & 7th sts,] last night. An hour before he was seen on the street, apparently in good spirits. Drs Iardella & Toner were present at the time of his decease, & pronounced his malady congestion of the brain, superinduced by the excessiveness of intoxicating liquors.

FRI JUL 17, 1868
Live black bass are being shipped from St Albans to N H, for purposes of propagation in the waters of that State.

Mrs Armstrong, a lady living at 1st & Indiana ave, was taken with cholera morbus on Monday & died on Tuesday. Her death was supposed to have been caused by the loathsome effluvia from the *Tiber Creek*. She was taken to the Washington Asylum, & is now at the point of death.

The Marshal of the District has arrested Thos L Cropley, Jacob Gladmon, & John Donnelly, of Gtwn, who were, on Wed, indicted by the grand jury for the murder of Jas Gray, on Jul 5, in Gtwn. They were committed to jail.

Equity Court-Judge Fisher. 1-Arthur vs Arthur. Order for dfndnt to pay alimony.

Died: at the residence of Dr Maxwell, 428 F st, in her 86th year, Mrs Anna K, relict of Dr Saml Harris, of Camden, N J. Her remains will be taken to Camden for interment. [Camden, N J papers, & Phil Inquirer, please copy.] [No death date given.]

Died: on jul 15, of congestion of the brain, M D Lalor, aged 36 years, a native of Dublin, Ireland, late clerk in the Dept of the Interior. His funeral will take place today at 5 o'clock P M, from the residence of Mr Waters, on D st, between 6th & 7th sts.

Schenectady, N Y, Jul 16. Cmdor Ganzevoort, of the U S navy, died suddenly, of congestion of the brain, in this city last night, in his 56th year. His funeral will take place on Friday, & the remains will be interred in *Greenwood Cemetery*.

Gen Grant, with his family, is now sojourning on his farm near St Louis, where he will remain several weeks, prior to his departure further West. He is not expected to return to Washington before the middle of Sept.

The President has transmitted to the Senate the following nominations: T J Bowers, to be Chief Justice of the Supreme Court of Idaho, vice J B McBride, resigned; Wm M Stafford to be Associate Justice of the Supreme Court of Montana, vice L E Munson, removed; H Knowles, to be Associate Justice of the Supreme Court of Montana vice L P Williston, whose term has expired, & whose name, submitted to the Senate for reappointment on Jul 13, is withdrawn; A Whittlesey, agent for the Chippewas of Lake Superior, vice D E Webb, appointed superintendent of New Mexico; S Day, to be Surveyor General of Calif, vice L Upson, whose term has expired; W M McCauley, to be Agent for the Flat Heads & other confederated tribes of Indians in Montana Territory, vice John W Wells, dec'd.

Cleveland, Ohio, Jul 16. Govn'r Hays has granted a reprieve to Mrs Victor condemned to be hung on Aug 29, until Nov 29, & ordered her to be removed from the Northern Ohio Lunatic Asylum, Newberg.

Trustee's sale of land in St Mary's Co, Md; by decree of the Circuit Court of St Mary's Co; public sale, at the Court-house door, in Leonardtown, on Aug 4, the farm called *Foster's Neck*, within 2 miles of Plowden's wharf, with nearly 3 miles of shore line, containing 250 acres, more or less. Possession given Jan 1st next. Refer to J R W Mankin, 673 7th st, [Island] Wash. –John F Dent, trustee, Milestown, St Mary's Co, Md.

Trustee's sale of valuable improved real estate on 7th st west, between R & S sts north; & on H st north, between 11th & 12th sts east, in Wash City; by deed of trust from John E Behrins & wife, dated Sep 18, 1867; public auction on Aug 4 next, lot 24 in square 42, with a substantial brick dwlg house; located on 7th st. Also, by virtue of the same deed; sale on Aug 5, of lot 7 in square 982, with a dwlg house, on H st. –R H Laskey, Philip May, trustees -Green & Williams, aucts

Dept of the Interior, U S Patent Ofc, Wash, Jul 3, 1868. Ptn of Abigail L Webster, of Binghamton, N Y, admx of the estate of Benj B Webster, dec'd, praying for the extension of a patent granted to said Benj B Webster Oct 3, 1854, for an improvement in Mosquito Curtains, for seven years from the expiration of said patent, which takes place on Oct 3, 1868. -A M Stout, Acting Com'r of Patents

SAT JUL 18, 1868
Mr A F Kimmell, proprietor of the Kimmell House on C st, between 4½ & 6th sts, died at his residence yesterday, aged 55 years. He had been a resident of Wash for nearly 40 years, & was for a long time engaged in the livery stable business, & subsequently erected the hotel bearing his name, & conducted this business up to the time of his death. He was attacked with paralysis on Sat last, the disease changing to congestion of the brain, which caused his death. He leaves a wife & 4 children.

Herman Kalb, boarding at the Steuben House, on Pa ave, near 2nd st, attempted yesterday to terminate his existence by hanging himself. His efforts were frustrated by Ofcrs Scott, McColgan, & Peaster. Domestic troubles are assigned as the cause of the attempt.

The Senate yesterday made the following rejections & confirmations.
Rejections: Francis Price, of N J, to be consul general of the U S at Havana
Adam Reese, to be assessor of internal revenue for the 10th Dist of Ky
R H Cochrane, to be assessor of internal revenue for the 6th Dist of Ky
Saml Babcock, collector of internal revenue for the 2nd Dist of Conn
Robt H Kerr, U S Marshal for Western Dist of Pa
Thos B Price, collector of internal revenue for the 3rd Dist of Md
Confirmations: Mark B Scull, assessor of internal revenue for the 8th Dist of Pa
Felix M D Nemegezele, of N J, to be consul of the U S at Tabasco
Reuben S Torrey, collector of internal revenue for the 2nd Dist of N Y
Anthony F Campbell, deputy postmaster at Brooklyn, N Y
Thos E Webb, to be naval constructor
Henry Eber & E P McCrea, cmders in the navy
Andrew S Hunter deputy postmaster at Chicopee, Mass
C A B Prescott, deputy postmaster at Holyoke, Mass
Eliphalet Wright, deputy postmaster at Berkshire, Mass
Cornelius A Field, deputy postmaster at Hanover, N H
E R Sprigman, of Pa, consul at Tumbez, Peru

Boston, Jul 16. The neighborhood of Kingston, where Deacon Andrews murdered & robbed old Cornelius Holmes some weeks since, finds there might be another alleged murder that Andrews was responsible for. Some few years ago a mill operative who boarded in Andrews' house disappeared suddenly, & nothing since was ever heard of him. All of his effects were left behind. Andrews took possession of the effects & appropriated them to his use. A few days since a human skeleton was found in the immediate neighborhood, corresponding in size to that of the missing mill operative.

John Leech's widow is dead. Her pension is continued to her children.

Before a West Point cadet can get leave of absence he must take a pledge that he will keep sober the 3 days immediately succeeding his departure & 3 days immediately preceding his return.

Died: on Jul 16, suddenly, Mrs Ann Ward, in her 78th year. Her funeral will be on Sunday next, at 5 o'clock P M, from the residence of her son, Jos Anderson, corner of 24th & H sts.

Died: on Jul 17, of congestion of the brain, Abm Ferdinand Kimmell, aged 55 years. His funeral will take place on Monday next, at 5:30 P M, from Trinity Church.

N Y, Jul 17. Police Ofcr Wm Irving was stabbed last night by an unknown man, while endeavoring to settle a dispute between the latter & a woman. The assassin escaped. The ofcr is not expected to live.

Sandusky, Ohio, Jul 17. P O Ws The War Dept has ordered the immediate removal of the bodies of 200 Confederate ofcrs who died & were buried at *Johnson's Island*, while prisoners of war, to the *Catholic Cemetery*. Their removal will commence on Monday next, under the direction of a Gov't agent. [Jul 22nd newspaper: Sandusky, Ohio, Jul 21. The Sec of War has ordered an indefinite postponement of the removal of the Confederate dead from *Johnson's Island*. Great fears are felt for the health of the city in case the bodies are disinterred during the hot weather.]

Northampton, Mass, Jul 17. Rev Dr Wm Allen, formerly president Bowdoin College, died Thursday, aged 84.

Holyoke, Mass, Jul 17. John Kelly was found drowned in the canal at this place today. He is supposed to have been robbed & murdered.

Dept of Interior, U S Patent Ofc, Wash, Jul 13, 1868. Ptn of John Ross, of Brooklyn, N Y, adm of the estate of Chas Ross, dec'd, praying for the extension of a patent granted to said Chas Ross Oct 17, 1854, for an improvement in Grinding Surface in Mills, for seven years from the expiration of said patent, which takes place on Oct 17, 1868. –A M Stout, Acting Com'r of Patents

Executor's sale of valuable real estate; by authority vested in me as executor by the last will & testament of the late Ann S Milburn, late of St Mary's Co, dec'd; public sale, at the Court House door, in Leonardtown, on Aug 11 next: a Farm containing 265 acres, more or less, at the headwaters of the St George's river. The bldgs consist of a fine new dwlg house, containing 4 rooms on the 1st floor, & 4 good bedrooms on the 2nd; & excellent outbldgs. –Jas C Bean, exc

MON JUL 20, 1868
We regret to announce the sudden death, yesterday, in Wash City, of Mr Leutze, the celebrated artist. His daughter has been with him in this city, while Mrs Leutze is now abroad upon an errand in connection with a high position in the work of art which has been recently proffered to her husband in Europe. Mr Leutze was born in Wurtemberg.
+
Died: on Jul 18, suddenly, E Leutze, aged 52 years. [Jul 22nd newspaper: Emanuel Leutze died of congestion of the brain; born on May 24, 1816, in G___d, Wurtemberg; while an infant, his parents emigrated to this country & settled in Phil, where he was reared & educated; he returned to Germany in 1841; he married a German lady in Dusseldorf; in 1859 he returned to the U S, & took up residence at Washington. Madame Leutze, with the remaining members of the family, being absent in Europe, it is understood that his remains will be deposited in one of the vaults of the *Congressional Cemetery*, there to await burial. –N Y Herald]

Mrd: on Sep 5, 1866, at Hartford, Conn, by Rev Geo B Spalding, Frank W Jones, Pension Ofc, Wash, D C, to Annie C Leonard, daughter of Jason S Leonard, of N Y C.

Nashville, Jul 13. 1-John Rhea was killed by lightning at Gallatin, today. 2-Wm Gustman, a negro, was taken from jail at Franklin yesterday, & shot by a mob. His offense was rape on a white girl & 2 negro girls. 3-A gentleman who saw Hon John Bell, [formerly U S Senator,] a few days ago, reports that he is partially paralyzed, but appears in fair health.

TUE JUL 21, 1868
Examination of Brookeville Academy took place on Jun 30th, before A B Davis, president of the Board of Trustees, & Dr W B Magruder & E J Hall, trustees. Medals for good conduct were awarded to Chas Murray & Wm Action. Prizes were awarded for rank in school: 1st, Chas Rhodes, Fred'k Co; 2nd, Fisher Gore, Carroll Co; 3rd, F Ernst, Wash City; 4th, L Magruder, New Mexico.

The President yesterday sent the following nominations to the Senate:
Hon John I Dawson, of Pa, to be Minister to Russia.
Henry L Watts, of Pa, to be Minister to Austria.
Gen John A McClernand, of Ill, to be Minister to Mexico.
Gen W S Rosecrans, of Ohio, to be Minister to Spain.
Hon Edmund Cooper, of Tenn, to be Com'r of Internal Revenue.
C C Cox, of Md, to be Com'r of Penions.
Elisha Foote, of N Y, to be Com'r of Patents.
W P Wells, of Mich, to be Assist Sec of the Treasury.

Mrd: on Jul 15, in Jackson, Miss, Jas Foster Moore to Julia Catharine, eldest daughter of Col Wm H Terrett, formerly of Wash City-all of Hinds Co, Miss.

Died: on Jul 20, John W, son of Marcellus & Cynthia R Driver, aged 7 years, 3 months & 1 day. His funeral will take place from the residence of his parents, between 3rd & 4th sts, near D, Capitol Hill, at 3 o'clock. [Raleigh, N C papers please copy.]

Died: on Jul 20, after a brief illness, Jos P Sullivan, in his 30th year. His funeral will be from 510 Mass ave, on Wed next, at 2 o'clock P M. [Star & Express copy, & send bill to this ofc.]

Died: on Jul 20, in Gtwn, D C, Florence Templeman, youngest child of Fred W & Frances M Jones, aged 1 year, 7 months & 20 days. Her funeral will take place today, at 5:30 P M, from the residence of her parents, 72 1st st.

Supreme Court of D C; Equity No 1,252-Docket 8. Henry S Davis vs Silas Veitch, Eldridge R Veitch, Mary Humphries & Danl A Veitch et al. Ordered that the decree *pro confesso* against the aforesaid dfndnts be made final, & that the sale by Henry S Davis, the cmplnt, of the property named in the bill, be ratified. –Geo P Fisher, Justice
-R J Meigs, clerk

Our citizens learned yesterday of the death of Mrs Olivia Hooker, wife of Maj Gen Jos E Hooker. She was the sister of Hon Wm S Groesbeck, & a most brilliant woman. Mrs Hooker has been for some time in ill health, & her death was not unexpected.
-Cincinnati Gaz, Jul 18

For sale, the best farm in the Dist of Columbia; Pomona, on 7th st, 108 acres, with several fine bldg sites. Situated between the beautiful estates of Hon F P Blair & Alex'r R Shepherd. The improvements are first class. –John B Clagett

For sale: farm called **Mountain View**, containing 97 acres; in Dranesville, Fairfax Co, Va; with a large dwlg, barn, stabling, carriage, smoke, & ice-houses. Title indisputable. Possession given immediately. –Albert J Wheat, Dranesville, Fairfax Co, Va.

Supreme Court of D C, Equity 1,293-Docket 9. John Fowler et al vs Franklin & Chas Whelan. Chas A Buckey, trustee, reported he sold part of lot 175, in Beatty & Hawkins' addition to Gtwn, D C, to Thos L Hume, for $1,675, & that Hume has complied with the terms of sale. –Geo P Fisher, Jus S C D C -R J Meigs, clerk

Northampton, Mass, Jul 20. Capt G G Wright, an extensive lumber dealer of this town, has absconded, having failed for $30,000, & forged notes on two of his brothers-in-law.

WED JUL 22, 1868
The President sent the following nominations to the Senate yesterday: Jos W Meeks, of N Y, to be consul at Nantes; Darius Atwater, of Conn, consul to Seychelles.

By his fall from a stairway in Montreal the other day, Mr Jefferson Davis was much injured, three of his ribs being broken. He was doing well, however, at last accounts.

Finishing touches are being put on the new splendid grocery store of B W Reed, 393 F st, between 12th & 13th sts. Mr Reed will be returning again to the business in which he was formerly well known in Wash City.

Criminal Court-Justice Wylie. 1-Robt Lane guilty of assault & battery with intent to kill Chas Washington, on Jun 27 last: sentenced to Albany Penitentiary for 2 years. 2-David R Smith, assault & resisting ofcr, *nolle pros*. 3-Robt Lane, guilty of petit larceny. 4-Richd Brown, Wm Limaker, & Geo Butt, indicted for the robbery of money from Martin Gauginagel on May 10 last. Brown found guilty, the others acquitted. 5-Richd Barrell, larceny; recognizance forfeited; bench warrant issued. 6-Michl Flannigan & John Murphy, larceny; recognizance forfeited; bench warrant issued. 7-John Shea, assault & battery; recognizance forfeited; bench warrant issued.

Died: Jul 10, 1868, at the Convent of the Sacred Heart, Havana, Cuba, Madame Florence Poe, a Religious of the Sacred Heart, daughter of the late Geo & Emma M Poe, of Gtwn, D C.

Died: on Jul 21, at Providence Hospital, Dr DeWitt Clinton Wilson, formerly of N J.

Died: on Jul 20, Annie M, only daughter of Wm G & Jane C Steinmetz, aged 8 months & 15 days. Her funeral services will be at **Glenwood Cemetery**, Jul 22, at 5 o'clock P M.

Died: on Jul 20, after a brief illness, Jos P Sullivan, in his 30th year. His funeral will be on Wed next at 2 o'clock P M, from 510 Mass ave. [Star & Express copy, & send bill to this ofc.]

Cincinnati, Jul 21. Philip Clifton, Chas Rosebery, & Val Elliott, arrested for the attempted robbery of the Adams' express car, at Brownstown, Ind, on Jul 10, left here last night under strong guard to be place in the Brownstown jail. When the train reached near Seymour, it was stopped by a mob from that place & vicinity. The mob overpowered the guard & hung the prisoners. [Jul 23rd newspaper: The 3 robbers who were lynched made a full disclosure of their connection with many robberies & murders in that vicinity. Their headquarters was at the Reno House, near Rockford. John Reno is now in the Missouri Penitentiary, & 2 other members of the family are under arrest for robbing the Adams Express Co; & Frank Reno, the most skilful & adroit assassin of the whole family, is at Windsor Canada West. A large reward will be paid by the ofcrs of Adams Express on the delivery of his body at Seymour, Jackson Co, Indiana.] [Jul 30th newspaper: Cincinnati Gaz of Monday. The final scene in the tragedy at Seymour has been enacted; Ellets, Roseberry, & Clifton were hung on Monday last; the 3 were taken on Monday from this city, conveyed to Seymour, arriving about 10 o'clock P M; all was silent at the depot when the train halted; no hint of the tragedy soon to be enacted; the train then sped toward Brownstown & was signaled by a red light, the train stopped. At once it was surrounded by a body of some 200 men, & a detachment went to the express car, where the 3 outlaws were sitting; only 2 pairs of handcuffs, Roseberry being bound with one pair, & Ellets & Clifton fastened together with the other. They were hurried away, & in only a few moments their bodies were dangling, in the black darkness of the night, from limbs in the midst of the forest. The work was not complete. Three of the party engaged in the outrage were yet at large. A description of Moore, Sparks & Jerrell had been sent out in all directions by the detective who was working up the case. Friday these 3 men were found in Mattoon, Ill; all were arrested by the sheriff of the place. They were placed on a train bound for Indianapolis; on reaching that city they were transferred to the Seymour train, to be taken to Brownstown to await their trial. But an engineer sent in advance an ominous despatch: "Shall run over no red lights." The prisoners were taken to Brownstown in a wagon; yesterday the wagon was stopped in the dreary forest, by men disguised with handkerchiefs bound about the brow; the three were taken from the custody of the ofcrs in charge, & were bidden to prepare for death. Again the morning light revealed ghastly corpses hanging from the limbs, the faces of horrid blackness, the eyes starting from their sockets, & their bodies swaying to & fro in the breeze. The Reno family, at the head of these outrages, is now in a fair way to be broken up. Simeon & Wm are new in the jail at New Albany, on the charge of being connected with the Marshfield robbery. Frank, the oldest, the ringleader, has been arrested at Windsor, & will be transferred to Indiana.]

Orphans Court-Judge Purcell. 1-The will of Patrick Toban was filed & fully proven. He names his wife, Catharine Toban, sole excx. 2-The will of Robt Leckie was filed for probate. 3-Walter S Cox & Thos C Cox gave bond in the sum of $150,000 as excs of John A Smith. W H Phillip & Richd S Cox, sureties. 4-J B Gibbs gave bond in the sum of $1,500 as guardian to the heirs of Eliz B Gibbs. Edgar Patterson & R P Dodge, sureties.

Moses Y Beach, former proprietor of the N Y Sun, died at his residence in Wallingford, Conn, aged 68 years. During the Mexican war he was sent to Mexico by Pres Polk as an agent to arrange a treaty of peace. Mr Beach retired from active business some 10 years ago, & went to live in his native town of Wallingford. He has been for years subject to paralysis but the attack by which he was carried off was quite sudden & unexpected. [No death date given-current item.]

Hon Wm Bigler, of Pa, is seriously ill at his residence in Clearfield.

Phil, Jul 21. Henry Dale, a convict, who escaped from the N J State prison during the fire, was captured in this city & taken back to Trenton.

Adm's sale, auction, Jul 21, by order of the Orphans Court of D C, household & kitchen furniture at house 298 south B st, between N J ave & 1st st, the personal effects of the late Martin King. —Verando E King, adm of M King, dec'd -John B Wheeler & Co, aucts

THU JUL 23, 1868
The President yesterday sent the following nominations to the Senate:
Wm Pidgeon, of Ind, to be Sec of the Territory of Idaho.
Reuben O Harmon, of Ohio, to be Consul at the Island of Trinidad.
Levi Howland Cost, to be Consul at Valencia.
Mathew Meigs, of Pa, to be Consul at P____. [Not Paris-too light to read.]
Alvin Hawkins, of Tenn, to be Consul at Havana.
Jacob B Blair, of West Va, to be Minister Resident of the U S at Costa Rica.
Robt Newell, of Idaho, to U S Indian Agent for the Territory of Idaho.
Chas Peters, to be Naval Ofce for the Dist of N Y.
Wm E Wells to be Collector of Internal Revenue, 4th Dist of Va.
Wm Selden, to be Collector of Internal Revenue, 2nd Dist of Va.
Jas Marr, to be Collector of Internal Revenue for the Dist of Montana.

Capt Alex V Fraser died on Jul 22, in Brooklyn, N Y; for many years he was Chief of the Revenue Marine Bureau of the Treasury Dept; commanded the revenue cutter **Lawrence**, built in this city in 1849, under his auspices, during the Secretaryship of Hon Robt J Walker, & was the first Gov't vessel sent to the port of San Francisco, Calif, for the protection of our commerce. Capt Fraser was an ardent & devoted friend, a kind husband & father, & an honest man, the noblest work of God. –T

Criminal Court-Judge Wylie 1-John V Kehl, jr, not guilty of an assault & battery on Agnes Willett, on Jun 11 last. 2-Thos Bowie, not guilty for assaulting & resisting Ofcr Eckloff in the discharge of his duty, on May 26 last. He was found guilty of assault & battery on Robt Miller, on May 30 last, & sentenced to jail for 60 days, & made to pay the costs of prosecution. 3-Charlotte Wilson, assault & battery, *nolle pros.* 4-Ed McCarthy, assault & battery, *nolle pros.* 5-Seth Landsford & Henry Brown; guilty as to Landsford-grand larceny. 6-Chas Langley & Alfred Borden, assault & battery; bench warrant issued. 7-Danl Hannon, assault & battery; bench warrant issued. 8-The Court orders the remission of the sentence of John W Johnson, sentenced to 30 days for riot on Jul 10th.

Equity Court-Judge Fisher. 1-Easby vs Easby; order authorizing the sale of lots 5 & 6 in square 1, at private sale. 2-Howard vs Howard et al; order on Julia McCandless to employ new counsel before next rule day. 3-In re. Involuntary bankruptcy of Chas Howard; order allowing assignee to sell stock of goods at private sale.

Thos Dowling, auct, sold part of lot 72, fronting 82 feet on Water st & 100 feet on Cherry st, with improvements thereon, to Owen Kelly, for $2,700.

Chas Rousseau, [graduate of the Royal Academy of Fine Arts, Brussels] the well known sculptor & marble worker, of Wash City, has just finished a beautiful monument of Italian marble, to be erected in the ***Congressional Cemetery***, to the memory of the late John P Pepper. It stands about 18 feet in height, & the shaft, which rises from the die block, appears covered with a cloth gracefully on the sides, cut in an artistic manner.

Orphans Court of Wash Co, D C. Letters testamentary on the personal estate of John A Smith, late of Wash Co, D C, dec'd. –Walter S Cox, Thos C Cox, excs

Orphans Court of Wash Co, D C. Letters of administration, d b n, on the personal estate of John Boyer, late of Wash City, D C, dec'd. –Junius Boyle, U S N, adm, d b n

Savannah, Ga, Jul 22. Difficulty last night in a drinking saloon, between Mr Robt Hopkins, the tax receiver, & Isaac Russell, deputy sheriff, resulting in the shooting of Hopkins, killing him instantly. Russell claims the shooting was done in self defence.

FRI JUL 24, 1868
Senator Norton, of Minnesota, was married yesterday, in Balt, Md, to Miss Laura Cortlan, daughter of Mr Jas Cortlan, jr, of that city, by Rev Mr Harris, chaplain, U S A, at the residence of the bride's father. The couple left for the North after the reception.

Equity Court-Judge Fisher. 1-Scala vs Scala; order for alimony *pendente lite*.
2-*In re.* Lunacy of Saml A Lee; order to issue commission of inquiry.
3-Bake vs Fant et al; order for Marshal to bring into court infant dfndnt.

The dedicatory ceremony of St Ann's Church of Tenallytown will take place on Sunday. The Gtwn College choir will be in attendance. Rev Dr Clark, of Balt, will preach.

Criminal Court-Justice Wylie. 1-Barney Clinkett; assault & battery; guilty; sentenced to jail for 10 days. 2-John Ferguson; false pretences; not guilty. 3-Gabriel Green; assault & battery; guilty; sentenced to jail for 10 days. 4-Saml Anderson & Henry Johnson, indicted for grand larceny; guilty; sentenced to the penitentiary for 1 year. 5-Mary Strimel; assault & battery; not guilty. 6-Chas Ford, alias Philip Lancaster; larceny; recognizance forfeited; beach warrant ordered.

Mrd: on Jul 21, at the residence of the bride's mother, Harrisburg, Pa, by Rev Dr Keeling, Gilbert B Towles, of Wash City, to Carrie, youngest daughter of the late Jas Gillard, of the former place. No cards. [St Louis papers please copy.]

Died: on Jul 23rd, Cornelia Pr_yn Munson, wife of the late Owen Munson. Her funeral will take place at 412 9th st, on Sat at 5 o'clock P M.

Died: on Jul 22, at Lower Giesboro', Washinton Co, D C, of cholera infantum, Clementina Loretta, aged 10 months, infant daughter of J Fenwick & Nora C Young. Her funeral will take place at St Dominick's Church, Island, on Jul 24 at 8 o'clock A M.

Died: on Jul 7, in Carlisle, Ill, Dr Wm L Fraser, son of A R Fraser, of Alexandria Co, Va.

Phil Telegraph of Wed. The Camden & Atlantic Railroad Co, for the first time, met with a serious accident yesterday, about 1½ miles below Haddonfield; heavy rains washed away under the rails. John Hutchinson, the engineer, was frightly scalded; Wm Hill, fireman, badly scalded; Mr Fernley, hardware merchant on Market st, bruised; Mr Lansingbock, residing at Broad & Cumberland sts, injured. Geo Ferris, Wm C Yates, the forward brakesman, & Jos Bartlett, baggage master, all escaped injury. The engineer, Hutchinson, died. He resided at Atlantic City, & leaves a widow & 2 children.

The President yesterday sent to the Senate the following nominations:
Gen Noah L Jeffries, of Md, to be Com'r of Internal Revenue.
J Irving Burns, to be collector of Idaho Territory.
John A Clark, to be surveyor-general of Utah.

Geo V Foreman, who died in Woodsfield, West Va, on Jun 30, confessed on his death bed that he murdered Miss Isaphine Allen, of Salem township, Monroe Co, in that State, in 1858. Foreman was tried for the murder in 1859, & acquitted. He confessed that he first struck her with a stone which fractured her skull, & had he no intention of killing her. He threw the stone when in a passion. He then carried her to his house, & after ascertaining that her recovery was impossible, took an axe & killed her.

Confirmations & rejection, by the Senate yesterday. Confirmations:
Robt Newell, Indian agent, Idaho.
John Avers, Indian agent, New Mexico.
Albert G Boone, Indian agent, Colorado.
Jas H Wilber, Indian agent, Wash Territory.
Edw T Wood, collector of internal revenue, 3rd Dist, N Y.
Chas Sitgreaves, postmaster, Phillipsburg, N J.
Emmeline A Finch, postmistress, Red Bank, N J.
Mary J Martin, postmistress, Burlington, N J.
John M Keese, postmaster, Rhinbeck, N Y.
Wm B Hed_epeth, postmaster, Union City,Ind.
Elisha P Liscomb, postmaster, Lebanon, N H.
Corydon B Streeter, postmaster, Youngstown, Ohio.
Danl J Bailey, postmaster, Pitthole City, Pa.
Franklin Burrows, postmaster, Millville, N J.
Culver A Barcalow, postmaster, Somerville, N J.
Dorence Atwater, U S Consul at Sychelles.
David M Mills, assessor internal revenue, Dakota.
Wm R Lee, assessor 3rd Dist, Mass.
Henry Shreve, postmaster, Alliance, Ohio.
David B Green, postmaster, Yps_anti, Mich.
Lewis D Viser, assessor 3rd Dist, Miss.
Rejected:
Wm P Wells, Assist Sec of the Treasury.
Moses E Flannagan, assessor of internal revenue 32nd Dist of N Y.
Jos W Weeks, of N Y for Consul at Nantes.
Avery D Bencock, Indian agent for Oregon.
Chas R Reims, of Kansas, Consul at Honolulu.

Jefferson Davis is on his way to Richmond, to consult his old family physician in regard to the injuries he sustained by his last fall.

The skeleton recently discovered in Kingston, Mass, half a mile from the scene of Cornelius Holmes' murder, is supposed to have belonged to a tailor named Jones, who disappeared 64 years ago.

Atlantic City, Jul 23. This afernoon Miss Mary Lawler, daughter of Michl Lawler, of Centre House of this city, & Miss Annie Lavens, daughter of John Lavens, liquor merchant, Grant st, Phil, ventured too far in the surf & both ladies were carried away. Their bodies have yet to be recovered.

Belari, Harford Co, Md, Jul 22. Isaac Moore, colored, attacked a highly respectable young lady, near this town, this morning, with foul intentions. He was arrested & placed in jail. When brought out before the magistrate a mob overpowered the ofcrs, carried off the prisoner, & hung him.

Suicide. Buffalo, N Y, Jul 23. John Wackeman, a Buffalo hardware merchant, cut his throat at Clinton, Canada, yesterday. Domestic trouble is supposed to be the cause.

Portland, Me, Jul 23. The new mill of the Oriental Powder Co, at Gorham, Maine, blew up yesterday, killing Ben Hawks.

SAT JUL 25, 1868
The President nominated yesterday to the Senate J Lyle Dickey, of Ill, & J Hubley Ashley of Pa, to be assist atty general.

The President has accepted the resignation of Brvt Maj Gen Robt K Scott, to take effect from & after July 6.

Died: on Jul 23, Rev Richd Allen, aged 61 years. His funeral will be from the Second Baptist Church, Va ave & 4th st east, on Sunday next, at 4 o'clock P M.

Died: yesterday, John Lawrence Hayes, infant son of John & Anna M Hayes, aged 7 weeks & 1 day. The body will be taken to Phil for interment.

Died: on Jul 24, Mrs Sarah Caton, aged 69 years. Her funeral will take place on Jul 26, at 3 o'clock P M, from her late residence, 361 5th st.

Husband shoots his wife for a burglar; last night in this city. The parties are Mr & Mrs John McAvoy, who reside on Second, between Brunswick & Bladen sts. The night previous the house adjoining their residence had been robbed. Hearing noises in the night he thought his wife was in bed, when he fired at an object, when his wife called out to him, that she had been shot. Her condition is critical; the husband is in despair. -Wilmington Journal, Jul 19.

Upon his own application, Brvt Maj Gen Silas Casey, colonel 4th infty, having served 40 consecutive years, has been, by direction of the President, retired from active service, & his name entered upon the retired list of ofcrs of the grade to which he now belongs.

Balt, Jul 24. The flood subsided today as suddenly as it arose. The water was carried off within the banks of Jones' Falls. A telegram this evening from Ellicott City, formerly *Ellicott's Mills*, reports that the granite mills were carried away & 60 lives lost. Dr Owens' entire family, except himself, were drowned.

Phil, Jul 24. Saml Nicolson, a dry goods merchant on Market st, has been missing since last night. He left the city to visit the falls of Schuylkill, & his boat was found drifting in the river this morning with his hat, coat, & vest. He had with him a gold watch & considerable money, & foul play is apprehended. The river has been dragged, without success.

N Y, Jul 24. Policeman John Linedick was killed by John Real last night, in revenge for previous arrests for intoxication. Real is in custody.

MON JUL 27, 1868
On Sat the following nominations were sent to the Senate:
Chas C Wilson, of Ill, to be Chief Justice of the Territory of Utah.
J J Johnson, to be Collector of Internal Revenue for the 3rd Dist of La.
Luther B Wilson, to be 2nd Auditor of the Treasury, vice E B French, to be removed.
Dorsey B Thomas, to be Collector of Customs at New Orleans.
Lloyd D Waddell, to be Assessor of Internal revenue for the 3rd Dist of Ga.
H L Brown, to be Marshal of the Western Dist of Pa.
A S Paddock, of Nebraska, to be Govn'r of the new Territory of Wyoming; & H G Worthington to be Minister to Uruguay.
The President yesterday sent the following nominations to the Senate:
Wm S Roscrans, Minister to Russia.
Alex'r Cummings, of Pa, Com'r of Internal Revenue.
Simeon M Johnson, Assist Sec of the Treasury.
Chas M Alexander, Postmaster at Wash, D C.
Geo S Stubblefield, Dist Atty for the Middle Dist of Tenn.
Jacob H Meech, Assessor 13th Dist of N Y.
D H Stanton, Assessor 17th Dist of N Y.
John W Smith, Collector 1st Dist of Ark.
Stephen Coburn, Postmaster at Skowkegan, Maine.
Henry C Allen, Postmaster at Indianola, Texas.
H L Stephens, Postmaster at Honesdale, Pa.
Harvey Adams, Postmaster at Lancaster, N H.
A P Turner, Postmaster at Idaho City, Idaho.
M W Wilcox, Postmaster at Mattooh, Ill.
Isaac W Webster, Postmaster at Kenacha, Wis.
Fletcher P Cuppy, Register of Deeds, Dist of Col.
Zaphaniah Spalding, Consul to Honolulu.
W H Wimer, Collector of Customs at New Orleans.
Confirmations:
C C Cox, of Md, to be Com'r of Pensions.
Eisha Foote, of N Y, to be Com'r of Patents.
Saml Milligan, of Tenn, to be Assoc Justice of the Court of Claims.
Henry M Watts, of Pa, to be Minister to Austria.
Wm B Storm, of N Y, Consul at Leeds.
Silas H Axtell, Assessor Internal Revenue, 3rd Dist, Calif.
O H Burnham, Assessor, & Theodore Lidball, Collector of Internal Revenue for the 2nd Dist of Calif.
Robt A Crawford, to be Collector of Customs, Brazos de Santiago, Texas.
Jas Marr, to be Collector of Internal Revenue for the Territory of Montana.
Erastus D Webster, to be Assessor of Internal Revenue, 32nd Dist of N Y.
Henry P Hay, of Tenn, to be sec of Legation at Florence.

Jacob B Blair, of West Va, to be Minister to Costa Rica.
E P Harmon, of Ohio, to be Consul at Trinidad.
J Hubley Ashton, to be Assist Atty Gen of the U S.
Holland Smith, to be Deputy Postmaster at San Francisco.
Rejections: the Senate rejected the following nominations:
Noah C Jefferies, to be Com'r of Internal Revenue.
Nelson Poe, to be Collector of Internal Revenue for the 3rd Dist of Md.
Clark H Gheen, to be Collector of Internal Revenue for the 3rd Dist of Missouri.
John A McClernand, as Minister to Austria.
E O Perrin, as Chief Justice of Utah.

Robinson Crusoe's island now has a population of 19.

On Sat Ofcr Smith found Capt Columbus J Queen lying on the ground; who after being partially restored to consciousness, said that on Friday he was set upon by 3 persons, one white man & 2 negroes, robbed and one of them cut his throat. He was conveyed to the residence of his father-in-law, Mr Thos Noyes, 572 H st, between 4th & 5th sts, where he now lies in a very critical condition. Dr Johnson Eliot expresses his opinion that he will recover.

The body of John Peterkin, one of the 2 men who were drowned by going over Niagara Falls on Jul 12, was found below Suspension Bridge on Thursday, & was recovered Friday. Seneca Devine, the comrade of Peterkin, has not yet been found.

Died: on Jul 25, at her late residence in Wash City, 395 G st, between 6th & 7th sts, of dyspepsia & general debility, Mrs Julia A, wife of Capt Jos A Garretson, in her 59th year. Her funeral services will be held at the house at 5 o'clock P M, from whence the remains will be conveyed to York, Pa, for interment.

Criminal Court-Justice Wylie. 1-Wm Fowler, assault & battery; plead guilty; sentenced to jail until Sep 10th next. 2-Richd Burrell; petit larceny; guilty. 3-Ellen Garrison, petit larceny; guilty; sentenced to jail for 30 days. 4-Henry Richardson; assault & battery; guilty; sent to jail for 6 months. 5-Sonny Gibbs, alias Wm Dougans, indicted for an assault & battery, with intent to kill, with a razor, Emma Williams, on Jul 10 last; was found guilty & sentenced to the penitentiary for 5 years. 6-Richd Mason, alias Cookley, petit larceny; guilty.

Equity Court-Judge Olin. 1-Barbour vs Morgan et al; decree appointing C M Matthews & J F Ennis trustees to sell. 2-*In re*. Jos Clark, a lunatic; order directing issue of writ *de lunatico inquirendo*. 3-Blake vs Fant et al; order appointing Clifton Helen guardian ad litem to Jos Helen.

A land suit lately instituted in Harrison Co, Texas, by the heirs of Gen Albert Sidney Johnson, for 30 leagues of valuable land in that county, has resulted in a verdict in their favor.

Balt flood: Jul 25. The losses by the flood yesterday will be several millions of dollars. Damages to Balt City; bridges swept away at Chas, Monument, Centre, Hillen, Fayette, Bath, & Swann sts, & the wrecking of the Gay, Balt, & Pratt st bridges, is very heavy. Patapsco: Mr Wm Partridge, a mechanic, 60 years old, with his wife & grand-daughter, are lost. Among others, whom the waters have carried away with their houses, are Mr Wm Patterson, wife & son; Mrs Farrer & her 2 grandchildren, Fannie & Emma Duvall; Wm Reese, a wheelwright, wife, son, & daughter. Dr Owings has only 2 children left.

Miss Kate Keathley, the Missouri giantess, who weighed 812 pounds, died a few days since, near St Louis.

Frank Reno, implicated in the express robbery in Indiana, has been arrested at Windsor, Canada, & will be deliverd up to the Indiana authorities.

Hon Edw Frost, a member of one of the oldest families in Charleston, & formerly one of the Circuit Judges of S C, died in Charleston on Tuesday, in his 68th year. He graduated at Yale College in 1820.

Supreme Court of D C, in the matter of the last will & testament of E W Farley, dec'd. On the motion of Isaac L Johnson, it is ordered that the heirs-at-law of said dec'd, appear in this court on or before Aug 18 next, & show cause why the said last will & testament should not be admitted to probate. –Wm F Purcell, Judge of Orphans Court
-Jas R O'Beirne, Reg/o wills

Orphans Court of Wash Co, D C. Letters of administration on the personal estate of Margaret Whitney, late of Wash City, D C, dec'd. –Sallie M Whitney, admx

Orphans Court of Wash Co, D C. Letters of administration on the personal estate of Chas Carroll, late of Balt, Md, dec'd. –C A James, adm

Orphans Court of Wash Co, D C, Jul 25, 1868. In the case of Martha Riordan, excx of Jas Riordan, dec'd, the executrix & Court have appointed Aug 25 next, for the final settlement of the personal estate of the said dec'd, of the assets in hand.
-Jas R O'Beirne, Reg/o wills

TUE JUL 28, 1868
The Senate confirmed the nomination of Lt Col Saml D Sturgis, 6th cavalry, U S army, as brevet brigadier general, for gallantry in the battle of Antietam, & brevet major general, for distinguished service in the battle of Fredericksburg, Va.

The Senate yesterday confirmed the nomination of Col C M Alexander to be postmaster of Wash City, vice Sayles J Bowen, whose term had expired. Col Alexander has long been a resident of this city. We have every reason to believe he will make an excellent postmaster.

The Senate yesterday confirmed the following nominations:
Chas M Alexander, postmaster, Wash
Gen Wm S Rosecrans, Minister to Mexico
Fletcher P Cuppy, Register for D C, vice Edw C Eddy, dec'd.
Enos D Hodge, Assoc Justice-Utah.
Robt White, Justice of Peace, D C
Chas N Felton, Assist Treasurer at branch mint, San Francisco, Calif, vice D W Cheesman, removed.
T Lyle Dickey, Assist Atty Gen of U S
Chas P Heywood, Collector of Int Rev, Missouri
Lewis Wolfley, Assessor of Int Rev, Louisiana
Jas T Shelley, of Tenn, Indian Agent-New Mexico.
Alex'r L Buffington, Receiver-Montg, Ala.
Chas C Wilson, of Ill, Chief Justice of Supreme Court-Utah.
Zephaniah S Spalding, of Ohio, Consul at Honolulu
Saml T Crown, Justice of Peace, D C
The following were confirmed on Sat:
Alvin Hawkins, Consul at Valencia.
Matthew Meigs, of Pa, Consul at Pir ous [Print very light.]
J M Clark, of Ill, Surveyor Gen-Utah.
Wm Selden, Collector of Int Rev for Va.
S Ferguson Beach, U S Atty for Va.
Oscar Buckalew, Receiver-Arizona
Lewis S Hill, Receiver-Utah.
Nicholas Qintinna, Agent of Indians-New Mexico.
Rejections made by the Senate yesterday:
Simeon M Johnson, Assist Sec of Treasury
Rejected on Sat:
Wm B Storm, of N Y, Consul at Leeds.
Chas Peters, Naval Ofcr-N Y.
W P Gould, Additional Paymaster in U S army.
W R Wyatt, Receiver at Montg, Ala.
Nominations:
Geo H Parker, of Iowa, to be Miniser to Ecuador.

Orville Grant, a brother of the General, lives in Chicago, & has just given $100 to a Seymour & Blair club.

Richmond, Jul 27. Reuben J Herndon, who has been confined in jail at Orange Courthouse, charged with the seduction & murder of Miss Mary Lumsden, escaped last night. He left a confession of the seduction, but a denial of the murder. A reward of $500 has been offered for his capture.

B F Morsell & Co have on Jul 1st, taken into copartnership, Mr Wm H Beall, so long known in connection with my business as clerk; 69 La ave near 7th st.

Criminal Court-Justice Wylie. 1-John Hackenyas & Mary Hackenyas, indicted for assault & battery; not guilty. 2-Danl Hannan guilty of assault & battery on Martin Ganin; fined $20 & costs. 3-John Shea, indicted for an assault & battery; fined $50 & costs. 4-Martha Taylor, convicted of grand larceny; sentenced to 1 year in the Albany penitentiary. 5-Richd L Richardson, alias Bob Rets, convicted of larceny of a pair of sleeve buttons, & being the second offence, sentenced to the Albany penitentiary for 3 years. In a second case a *nolle prosequi* was entered. 6-Harriet Hill, alias Mary Jones, indicted for the larceny of a watch chain & pencil case, was convicted & sentenced to the Albany penitentiary for 2 years. 7-Frank Whittington, indicted for petit larceny, found guilty, to be under 14 years of age, & recommended to mercy. 8-John Dwyer, indicted for an assault & battery on Bernard Drew, was convicted & sentenced to pay the cost of prosecution. 9-Jos Smith, convicted of petit larceny, second offence, sentenced to the Albany penitentiary for 1 year.

Mrd: on Jul 23, in Balt, at the residence of the bride's father, 133 St Paul st, by Rev Matthias Harris, Hon D S D Norton, U S Senator, of Minnesota, to Laura, daughter of Mr Jas Cortlan, jr, of Balt, Md.

Died: on Jul 26, Wm H Custis, aged 63 years. His funeral will be from his late residence, 398 D st, at 3 P M, on Jul 28.

Died: on Jul 26, Mrs Ann S Newton, widow of the late Augustine Newton, in her 79th year. Her funeral will be on Jul 28 at 1 o'clock, from the residence of her son-in-law, W D Wallach, 8 Duddington place, Capitol Hill, First st, between B & C sts.

Died: on Jul 27, Frank Louis Green, infant son of Miranda C & the late C Edwin Green. His funeral is today at 4 o'clock P M, from the residence of his grandparent, Mrs Lambright, 387 9th st.

Police Matters: Wm Henry, colored boy aged about 11 years, arrested on charge of stealing 5 valuable gold watches from the pawnbroker shop of Mr Henry Prince, on Pa ave. He was in a cell at Police Headquarters & attempted to escape by making a hole in the floor of the cell.

Supreme Court of D C, in Equity 1,190. Jas Wormely vs Andrew Wormley & others. The above cause is referred to me to report whether it is proper or expedient to sell the real estate mentioned in the proceedings; meeting on Jul 21 at 11 o'clock A M, at my office. –Walter S Cox, auditor

Augusta, Ga, Jul 27. Difficulty this evening between the police & a few citizens; the latter were talking loudly at a street corner, & the police ordered them to desist, when shooting commenced. Alex Phillips, who attempted to prevent the difficulty, was shot in the breast, seriously, but not dangerously. Cornelius Reed was mortally wounded. Wm Dillon, chief of police, was shot in the abdomen. Chas Evans, lt of police, slightly wounded.

Balt flood. Balt Gazette of Monday; waters have entirely subsided; immense destruction by the flood on Friday. The Garrett Cotton Mill, owned by Mr Deford, of this city, valued at $150,000 was a complete wreck & Matthew McCauley, a watchman, was drowned on the premises. As far as can be ascertained, the names of those drowned are given as follows: Mrs Dr T B Owings, 6 children & 3 servants; Wm Patterson, wife, & 5 children; Wm Partridge, wife & niece; Mrs Farren & 2 nieces; Miss Duvall & Mary E Duvall, her niece; Martha McCauley; John Reese & daughter; John Murphy, wife, & child; Mr Gabbrel, wife & child; John Steel; Wm H Fountain, wife & daughter; Mr Snyder. [Jul 29th newspaper: the body of Jas Summers, about 18 years of age, was washed from Lombard st bridge; his body was removed to the residence of his father, 70 Granby st. John Kavanaugh, age 18, employed at the Sisters of Mercy's Institute, at Mount Washington, was drowned; body recovered on Sunday. Mr Wm Partridge's body was found; the body of Mrs Duvall was identified; the bodies of Mr Geo Biden & Mr Peter Hawk were found; also the bodies of Mrs Dr Owings & her infant son; Mrs Ann Stansbury, & a little daughter of Mrs Patterson, of Elliott City. Mrs Dr Owings was recognized by the wedding ring on her finger. Messrs J H Leisher, G T Gambrill, & John W McCormick took charge of the bodies, Coroner Carr having deemed it unnecessary to hold further inquests. In addition to the above the following bodies of persons drowned at Ellicott City have been found & identified: Mrs Gabriel & child; Mr Wm Fountain & wife; Mrs Wm Partridge; Wm, servant of Dr Owings, Kettie Owings, Tommy Owings; Mr Smith Murphy; Mary Lizzie Duvall; Mathias Macauley, child of Murphy; John Reese, Mrs Patterson; Bettie Patterson; Amelia Patterson; Fannie Duvall; Mrs Duvall; Maggie Patterson.] [Jul 30th newspaper: Cmte appointed to collect & receive subscriptions & contributions: Messrs A E Perry, Wm Galt, Geo W Cochran, & Jas Y Davis.]

WED JUL 29, 1868

Orphans Court-Judge Purcell, Jul 28, 1868. 1-The will of the late Ann Crown was filed for probate, bequeathing her estate to her children, & nominating her daughter, Sarah Eliz Crown & John J Johnson, excs. 2-The will of the late Anna K Harris was filed, fully proven, & admitted to probate. She bequeaths her estate to her sisters & nieces, & nominates Dr C D Maxwell, U S navy, executor, to whom letters testamentary were issued. Bond $12,000. 3-Robt Harding gave bond in the sum of $2,000 as guardian of the orphan of John Williams. 4-J E G Tomley gave bond in the sum of $500 as administrator of John Williamson. 5-Letters of administration on the estate of the late Jos P Sullivan were issued to Anna Sullivan; bonds $4,000. 6-The argument as to the validity of the will of the late Eleanor Miller, filed last fall, against which a caveat was filed by Sarah B & Geo Hutton, represented by Col Thompson, was commenced by Judge Robt Leech, who represents the propounders. The testimony in this case, taken last fall, comprises about 50 printed pages, & the argument will likely occupy some days.

Equity Court-Judge Olin. L C Baker vs Corp of Wash, city award for the assassination conspirators. Order making J E Stedpole, excutor of Baker, cmplnt.

Criminal Court-Justice Wylie. 1-Chas C Langley & Alfred Borden; assault & battery, guilty; fined each $50, to be confined till paid. 2-Wm Woody, Edw Woody, & Jas Shearer; indicted for an assault & battery with intent to kill, on John W Frizele, on Apr 19 last. Case on trial.

Died: on Jul 28, Mrs Margaret Golden, widow of the late John A Golden, for the last 50 years a resident of Wash City. Her funeral will be on Jul 30 at 10 o'clock, from St Peter's Church.

Died: on Jul 27, Edw G Guest, of Wash City, aged 44 years. His funeral will be from the residence of Mrs Riddel, 372 H st, this morning, at 9 o'clock A M. [Cumberland, Md, papers please copy.]

Died: on Jul 25, in Gtwn, Mrs Margaret Whann, relict of the late Capt David Whann, in her 90th year.

Residence on Gtwn Heights for sale, now owned & occupied by Mrs Matthews; a first class brick house, quite new, containing 13 rooms, exclusive of bath-room, pantries, etc. Also, a frame cariage-house & stable. Grounds include about 2/3rds an acre, beautifully laid out with lawn & shrubbery; & an orchard & garden. Price, $25,000.
–Fitch & Fox, Real Estate Brokers & Aucts, 470 7th st, opposite the Post Ofc.

By decree of the Supreme Court of D C, in Equity 1,320, wherein Catharine L DeVaughan & others are cmplnts, & Thos H & Eliz M DeVaughan are dfndnts; sale on Aug 6 next, of lot D, in Simson Meade's subdivision of square 408, improved by 2 brick bldgs. Also, the fourth part of lot 5 in square 405, improved by a frame dwlg house. On Aug 7: the east 30 feet of lot 2 in square 487, improved by a brick bldg. On the same day, lot 11 in square 517. –John N Oliver, trustee -Cooper & Latimer, aucts

Orphans Court of Wash Co, D C. Letters testamentary on the personal estate of Anna K Harris, late of Wash City, D C, dec'd. –Chas D Maxwell, adm

Orphans Court of Wash Co, D C. Letters of administration on the personal estate of Jos P Sullivan, late of Wash City, D C, dec'd. –Annie L Sullivan, admx

Orphans Court of Wash Co, D C. Letters of administration on the personal estate of Geo R Thomas, late of Wash City, D C, dec'd. –Benj C King, adm

Orphans Court of Wash Co, D C. Letters of administration on the personal estate of John Williams, late of Wash City, D C, dec'd. –John C G Toombs, adm

Portland, Jul 28. The case of N F Deering, the surviving trustee, against the heirs of the Cmdor Preble estate, was decided yesterday in the Supreme Court in favor of the respondents, releasing them from the trust of nearly $1,000,000.

Jewish Democratic Club in Nashville-Resolution condemnatory of Grant, the Proscriptionist. From the Nashville Banner of Sat. Mr E Levy called to the chair; Mr L Lerman appointed temporary secretary. Whereas U S Grant did, on Dec 17, 1862, while in command of the dept of the Tenn, issue his infamous order No 11, banishing all Israelites, regardless of age or sex, from his lines, thereby casting a reproach upon us as a religious body; & whereas the whole tendency of said order was to stigmatize us as disloyal citizens, unworthy of the protection of our armies, in which we were largely represented as Israelites; & Whereas no such order was every issued in this country against any other denomination, thereby showing plainly his hatred & narrow mindedness toward our people; & Whereas said U S Grant is now before the American people, asking their suffrage for the highest ofc in the gift of the Republic, we think him dangerous to our religious liberty, as by the elevation to that position he would possess even more power to do us harm, & may proscribe other churches who may differ with his mode of worship; thereford, Resolved, That we will not support U S Grant, the man who, when in brief authority, sought to degrade us, & thereby heaping insults on a people who have always been law-abiding & an honor to their adopted country, etc.
Philip Flashman, Chairman, D Bloch, N Nosh, J Godhelp, M Rosenheim, cmte

THU JUL 30, 1868
Miss Emily E Hunt & Mr Otis Crosby received, last evening, the beautiful prizes offered by Mr Wm Ballantyne & W F Brett & Sons to the students of the Consolidated Business College, for greatest improvement during a course of 15 lessons. The gentleman received a rare edition of Shakspeare, in 13 volumes, & the young lady a beautiful ivory fan.

Criminal Court-Justice Wylie. 1-Wm Summers; grand larceny; nolle pros. 2-Frank Washington; assault & battery; nolle pros. 3-Mary Ridner; larceny; nolle pros. 4-Allen Kinney; larceny; guilty; sentenced to 90 days in jail. 5-Chas Ford, alias Phil Lancaster, indicted for larceny, [second offence,] guilty, sent to the penitentiary for 1 year.

Died: on Jul 26, in Gtwn, John Jacob, aged 9 months & 14 days; & on Jul 29, Mary Ellinor, aged 9 months & 17 days, infant children of David & Emma L Auld. Their funeral will take place from the residence of their grandfather, J J Frey, 119 Washington st, Jul 30, at 5 o'clock P M. [Balt Sun please copy. Sun please copy.]

Died; on Jul 29, Edw Lacy, formerly of Ky, but for the past 35 years a resident of Wash City. His funeral will take place on Jul 31, at 12 o'clock M, from the residence of W H Harrover, 406 D st, between 6th & 7th sts.
+
Mr Edw Lacy, an old & much esteemed citizen, died yesterday at the house of Mr Harrover, of whose family he has long been a member. He was near 80 years of age, formerly a successful merchant in Wash City; & retired from active business many years since; a truly noble man; his contributions for religious & charitable purposes were numerous & liberal.

The Wheeling Intelligencer learns that Mr John Robinson, an old & highly respected citizen of Monongahela Co, was stung to death by bees one day last week. Mr Robinson resided 2 miles east of Morgantown.

Easton, Pa, Jul 29. 30th annual commencement of Lafayette College was held today: the degree of LL D was conferred on Jas C Hepburn, missionary in Japan. The degrees of P H D were conferred upon R W Raymond, editor of the Journal of Mining. Valedictory by A B Howell, of N J; address by Hon Galusha A Grow, ex-Speaker of the House of Reps. Govn'r Pollock presided at the alumni dinner.

Double murder committed on a flatboat at Mound City, Ill, on Jul 20, by Refus Adamson, a citizen of New Albany, Indiana, & formerly a soldier in the 66th Indiana regt. The victims were David Southwick & Asa Hodges, both residents of New Albany. Adamson stabbed Southwick while he was asleep, knocked Hodges in the head, & threw him overboard. All the parties, together with Southwick's wife, were living or working on the flatboat. Adamson made his escape in a skiff, threatening to kill Mrs Southwick if she gave the alarm

Augusta, Ga, Jul 29. The remains of Cornelius Redd, killed by the police ofcrs, were interred this afternoon, followed by a large procession of citizens & firemen. It is understood the grand jury found a verdict of murder against the police ofcrs.

Dept of the Interior, U S Patent Ofc, Wash, Jul 23, 1868. Ptn of Barton H Jenks, of Bridesburg, Pa, praying for the extension of a patent granted to him Oct 24, 1854, for an improvement in Looms, for seven years from the expiration of said patent, which takes place on Oct 24, 1868. –Elisha Foote, Com'r of Patents

Pittsburg, Pa, Jul 29. Explosion last night at the Auburn oil works of Lafferty & Waring, resulted in the death of Jas Gonigle, & probably fatally injuring Robt Lafferty, one of the proprietors.

Dept of the Interior, U S Patent Ofc, Wash, Jul 23, 1868. Ptn of John C Schooley, of Cincinnati, Ohio, praying for the extension of a patent granted to him Mar 14, 1855, for an improvement in process of Caring Meat, for seven years from the expiration of said patent, which takes place on Mar 14, 1869. -Elisha Foote, Com'r of Patents

Dept of the Interior, U S Patent Ofc, Wash, Jul 24, 1868. Ptn of Stephen E Booth, of Orange, Conn, administrator of the estate of Sheldon S Hartshorn, dec'd, praying for the extension of a patent granted to said Sheldon S Hartshorn, Nov 7, 1854, & reissued May 26, 1868, for an improvement in Buckles, for seven years from the expiration of said patent, which takes place on Nov 7, 1868. -Elisha Foote, Com'r of Patents

Despatch from Quebec says: The President of the defunct Southern Confederacy, Jeff Davis, together with his family, left this city on Sat in the steamship **Australian**, for Europe.

Appointment of Military Cadets in the army; with the rank indicated below, to date from Jun 15, 1868. Corps of Engineers:
Albert H Payson, 2nd lt, vice Mallery
John G D Knight, 2nd lt, vice Shears, promoted
Richl L Hoxie, 2nd lt, vice Turtle, promoted
Edgar W Bass, brvt 2nd lt
Jas B Mackall, brvt 2nd lt
Richd H Savage, brvt 2nd lt
Wm S Marshall, brvt 2nd lt
Jos H Willard, brvt 2nd lt
Ordnance Dept: Henry Metcalf, 2nd lt, vice Poland, promoted
1st Regt of Cavalry: Wm T Ditch, 2nd lt, vice Rousseau, resigned
Chas F Roe, 2nd lt, vice Stanton, promoted
Co F-Delaney A Kane, 2nd lt, vice Grant, promoted
Co E, 2nd Regt of Cavalry; Christopher T Hall, 2nd lt, vice Neff, promoted
Co D-Wm P Clark, 2nd lt, vice Steel, resigned
Co G-Saml M Swagert, 2nd lt, vice Arthur, resigned
Co L-Joshua L Fowler, 2nd lt, vice Taylor, promoted
Co E-Jas E Batchelder, 2nd lt, vice Macadams, promoted.
3rd Regt Cavalry-Geo W Pyle, 2nd lt, vice Bragg, promoted
Co I, 4th Regt of Cavalry-Jas H Jones, 2nd lt, vice Bayley, promoted
F L Shoemaker, 2nd lt, vice [blank,] promoted to be adjutant of the 5th regt of cavalry
W J Valkmer, 2nd lt, vice Porter, dec'd
Co M-W C Forbush, 2nd lt, vice Cummings, promoted
Co F, 6th Regt of Cavalry-F W Russell, 2nd lt, vice Walker, promoted
Co G-Sumner H Bodfish, 2nd lt, vice the adjutant of the 7th regt of cavalry
Thos J Marsh, 2nd lt, vice Godfrey, promoted
8th Regt of Cavalry, Co G-Harrison S Weeks, 2nd lt, vice Rothermel, dec'd
Co D-Wm H Coombs, 2nd lt, vice Haden, resigned
1st Regt of Artl, Co E-Robt Fletcher, 2nd lt to fill an original vacancy
Jas C Morrison, jr, 2nd lt, to fill an original vacancy
Geo W Desher, 2nd lt, to fill an original vacancy
2nd Regt of Artl-Clarence O Howard, 2nd lt, to fill an original vacancy
Eugene O Fechet, 2nd lt, to fill an original vacancy
3rd Regt of Artl-Frank Heath, 2nd lt, to fill an original vacancy
Paul Dahlgren, 2nd lt, to fill an original vacancy
Chas A Whipple, 2nd lt, to fill an original vacancy
4th Regt of Artl-David D Johnson, 2nd lt, vice Grier, transferred to the 4th artl
Chas R Barret, 2nd lt, vice W P Ham, transferred to the 4th artl
David S Dennison, 2nd lt, vice Hills, transferred to 3rd artl
Alex'r Morton, 2nd lt, vice Wm Pike, transferred to 3rd artl
1st Regt of Infty-John D C Hoskins, 2nd lt, vice Smith, promoted to co A. 3rd Regt of Infty-Chancellor Martin, 2nd lt, vice Wallace, promoted to co F.
5th Regt of Infty-Jas W Pope, 2nd lt, vice Pierce, declined
6th Regt of Infty-Richd E Thompson, 2nd lt, vice Shibant, promoted to co K.

Thos M Willey, 2nd lt, vice Walbridge, resigned
Co B, 10th Regt of Infty-Geo M Harris, 2nd lt, vice Hapwood, wholly retired
Co G, 19th Regt of Infty-Wm P Hall, 2nd lt, vice Thompson, resigned
Co L, 20th Regt of Infty-John B Rodman, 2nd lt, vice Robinett, promoted. Co F, 21st Regt of Infty-Loyal Farragut, 2nd lt, vice Riley, promoted
Co B, 25th Regt of Infty-Patrick T Broderick, 2nd lt, vice O'Brien, promoted
Co B, 26th Regt of Infty-John Pope,jr, 2nd lt, vice Dickinson, appointed 1st lt
Co E, 43rd Regt of Infty-Patrick Fitzpatrick, vice Garretty, promoted to co I.
The general regulations allow 3 months' leave of absence to the graduates of the Military Academy on entering the service. –By command of Gen Grant. –E D Townsend, A A G

FRI JUL 31, 1868
A young man named Gott accidentally fell against a circular saw in his mill, near Lebanon, Boone Co, Indiana, on Thursday, & died in a few minutes.

Promotions & appointments made in the ofc of the 6th Auditor of the Treasury for the Post Ofc Dept, since Jul 1: promoted from 2nd to 3rd class-Chas B R Colledge, W C Lipscomb, E G Blaine, Z Ellis, Chas Hendley, Henry Richter, John L Lake, E W Foster, W J Ketchum, John E O'Brien, J A Carpenter, C G McLeran, E C Tallmadge, Thos Gales Forster, Frank M Lalor, & Jas Balloch. From 1st to 2nd Class-D W Lathrop, John G Adams, Watkins Addison, Geo W Bridgeman, C W Banes, T L Lamb, J L Roosa, Wm Small, L O Sullivan, G L Starkey, L L Wynne, N B Milliken, Benj E McGrew, J S Woods, O T Thompson, & J H Wood. S B Morse, a 3rd class clerk on the rolls of the 2nd Auditor, is permanently transferred to this ofc.

Board of Police meeting yesterday. Additonal Pvt Edmond Young, guilty of conduct unbecoming an ofcr, was dismissed. Application of Geo Parkhurst, of Gtwn, for license to retail liquors was rejected, as was also the application of John W Kelly & Robt Aslow, of Gtwn. The official bonds of Justices Arthur Shepherd, Chas Walter & John C Cox were approved. John J Hill was reappointed an additional private for 6 months. Thos L Salkeld was appointed an additional private for 6 months. Private Timothy Brosnan, charged with conduct unbecoming an ofcr, was ordered to be admonished to be more careful in the future. In the case of complaint against Pvt Alfred Borden, charged with violating the rules & regulations, & disobedience of orders & conduct unbecoming an ofcr; sentence, that he be dismissed the force.

Died: on Jul 28, at Woodstock, Va, Milton M Welsh, late of New Market, Fred'k Co, Md, aged 62 years. [Balt Sun please copy.]

Died: on Jul 16, in Richmond Co, Va, Wm Bernard Berryman, native of Port Royal, Caroline Co, from early youth to near the close of 1858, a resident of Wash City, & for many years of the time a clerk in the Register's ofc of the Treasury Dept; emigrating to Kansas, after a residence of nearly 7 years, in that State he returned East, stopping in business in Balt, for a short time before going back to his native State to find a last resting place. He was in his 60th year.

New Orleans Crescent of Sunday. Duel yesterday between Paul Laresche, jr, & J S Bossier, below the city; weapons were double-barreled shot guns. Mr Laresche was shot through the abdomen, & died shortly afterwards. Mr Bossier was arrested & confined at the 2nd Dist Station-house. Mr Laresche's brother had been arrested before the duel, but he would not give any information & was put under bonds to keep the peace. The cause originated in a dispute relative to a lady. Mr Laresche was the challenging party. Bossier is a young man, about 25, & proved himself a gallant soldier on the losing side in the Confederate war; lost a leg at Fredericksburg; & was highly esteemed by his fellow soldiers & ofcrs. Laresche was also a brave soldier in the same army. His father & all the members of his family went out of the Federal lines to Richmond, when Banks sent out the registered enemies. No one laments the tragical result of the duel more than the survivor. He said all he had to live for is his aged mother.

Prince Napoleon employs 6 cooks, & spends $20,000 on his table.

Commencement at St John's College, Annapolis; address by Dr Welling the head of the institution; orator of the day, Hon Mr Howe, now a member of Congress.

In Canton, Ill, a few days ago, Mrs John Drummond was struck & instantly killed by lightning, while walking along the street. Her clothes were set on fire, & her body badly burned.

Public sale of valuable real estate; by decree of the Circuit Court for PG Co, Md, in Equity; sale at Beltsville, on Aug 5, **Chance & Chance Enlarged**-155¼ acres, & part of **Graney's Champion**-57 1/4th acres, adjoining each other, being the real estate of which Edw Marlow died seized & possessed, & upon which his wife, Tabitha Marlow, resided at the time of her death. The property has a small dwlg house, stable, meat-house, etc. -Danl Clarke, Geo Peter, trustees

Superior household & kitchen furniture at auction on Aug 1, the greater portion belonging to Mr Edw Thornton, the British Minister. Sale within our auction room. -Cooper & Latimer, aucts

Supreme Court of D C, Equity 1,048, Docket 8. Stoneman et al vs Hardesty et al. Ratify sale reported by G H Williams, trustee. –Geo P Fisher, Justice of Supreme Court, D C. -R J Meigs, clerk [No details given.]

Dept of the Interior, U S Patent Ofc, Wash, Jul 25, 1868. Ptn of Barnet L Solomon, of N Y, N Y, executor of the estate of Myer Phineas, dec'd, praying for the extension of a patent granted to said Myer Phineas, on Oct 24, 1854, for an improvement in Pen Holder, for seven years from the expiration of said patent, which takes place on Oct 24, 1868. -Elisha Foote, Com'r of Patents

SAT AUG 1, 1868

Adelina Patti, her marriage contract, disposal of her fortune. A Paris correspondent of the N Y Times writes: I have just heard the particulars of the marriage settlement between the Marquis de Caux & Adelina Patti, or rather enacted by Baron Jas Rothschild, as the friend & guardian of the latter. 500,000 francs, constituting the whole of the Diva's fortune, to be placed in trust for the benefit of herself & children. The principal is not to be touched under any circumstances whatever, Mlle Patti herself only enjoying the interest thereof. One-third of her future earnings to be set aside in the same manner, the remaining two thirds to be used as her husband & herself may decide. The father & mother of the bride are to each have a pension of 6,000 francs, which is to be allocated out of her income. This provision is honorable to Mlle Patti, whose sentiments of daughterly affection have always shown themselves superior to every other consideration. The Marquis de Caux asked to have the sum of 450,000 francs set aside for the payment of the mortgages on his estate, but on this point the Baron de Rothschild & Maurice Strakosch were inexorable; so that the property will have to be put up for sale, unless the creditors of the Marquis consent to wait for the chance of the repayment from Adelina' future earning, a contingency not very probable, from the known spend thrift habits of her future husband. It is calculated that at present Mlle Patti earns about 400,000 francs a year, which, with prudence, would soon enable the Marquis to pay off his debts. The marriage is to take place on Aug 1st.

Mr Jay Gould was on Thursday elected president of the Erie railroad, vice Mr S Eldridge, resigned.

The names of Dickens' children are Mary, Kate, Charles, Walter Laudor, Francis Jeffrey, Alfred Tennyson, Sydney Smith, Henry Fielding, & Edw Lytton Bulwer.

Calif papers of Jun 30. Harry Love, the Texas ranger, who obtained some notoriety a few years ago by claiming to be the slayer of Joaquin, the notorious robber, was living with his wife on a ranch owned by her, but they were not on friendly terms. Mrs Love employed a German, Eviersen, to work her place & Love became jealous. Evierson refused to leave the place & Love attempted to kill him. Shots were exchanged & Love's arm was shattered above the elbow, & Evierson beat him on the head with a pistol. Love's arm had to amputated, & he died from the operation & the wound on the head.

Thos Woodward, the coroner of this District, died at his residence in Gtwn yesterday, at age 76 years. He was a resident of this District for 58 years, & for 34 years past the coroner of the District. He was a deputy marshal under Marshal Tench Ringgold, who entered his duties in Jun, 1818. We believe he was a soldier in the war of 1812. He was one of the oldest members of the Methodist Church in the District.
+
Died: on Friday, in Gtwn, D C, Thos Woodward, aged 76 years; a resident of this District for over 58 years. His funeral at his residence this afternoon at 6 o'clock P M.

In the Circuit Court yesterday Judge Fisher had before him two women, Ella McCall & Clara Franklin, who were charged with abducting a little girl, Cora Aiken, from the custody of Mr F A Aiken, who had adopted her some 3 years since. Mrs McCall is the mother of the child, & it is claimed that while Cora, in company with Mr Aiken, was visiting her mother she was spirited away by Mrs McCall, who was aided by Clara Franklin. Judge Fisher issued an order requiring the woman McCall to be held to bail in the sum of 500, & that she be required to produce the child in court on Aug 14 next.

It is with regret we announce the death of Leonidas Coyle, who expired yesterday at his residence in Wash City. Mr Coyle was an old citizen of Wash, a gentleman of strict integrity, with a large circle of friends, who will mourn his loss.
+
Died: on Jul 31, Leonidas Coyle, in his 60th year. His funeral services will be Sunday next, at 4 P M, at his late residence, 419 E st.

Mr Wm Webster, a white man, & Wm Smith, colored, were severely injured on Thur by the explosion of a soda fountain in the cellar of the grocery store of Mr E G Stephens & Co, corner of 12th & H sts.

Criminal Court-Justice Wylie. 1-Lizzie Tilghman; larceny; guilty; a new trial granted, a *nolle pros* was entered. 2-Thos Hinton & Jas H Jones; assault & battery; guilty; sent to jail for 30 days. 3-Robt Gilmore; assault & battery; guilty; nominal sentence imposed. 4-Alice Garden; murder; plead not guilty; case continued. 5-Nathl T Ampey; keeping bawdy-house; acquitted. 5-Adolphus Bombay, H H Green, & Edw Talco; riot & affray; not guilty. 6-John Casey; assault & battery; *nolle pros*.

Died: on Jul 30, Dr Chas McCormick. His funeral will be from his late residence, 80 Gay st, Gtwn, on Sat, at 5 o'clock P M.

Memphis, Jul 31. Horse thieves hung by citizens. Last evening Christopher N Bender & Ben Whitfield, from Raleigh, were being taken to jail when 40 masked horsemen took the prisoners. This morning the men were found hanging from a tree.

Boston, Jul 31. Judge T D Bell, Chief Justice of the Supreme Judicial Court, died at his residence in this city today, aged 71 years.

Poughkeepsie Eagle: on Sat, in the little village of Carthage Landing, or Low Point, on the Hudson, two sisters drowned, Miss Christina-25 & Miss Josehine Rafael-17, residents of Cuba. They were accompanied by Mrs Bella Barquera & her husband, Carrie Somerndyke, & Kitty Bullis to the shore. Mrs Barquera is a sister of Christina & Josephine. Josephine was washed off a rock by the waves of a passing steamboat & was drowned. Saml Joyce, a young man, rescued Mrs Barquera who was trying to save Josephine. Mr Chas Joyce, brother of Saml, aided in the unsuccessful attempt. Christina Rafael, laboring under fear, suddenly sank. The Misses Rafael leave a father & mother in Cuba. The elder one was born in the U S, & the younger one in Mexico.

Frederick Female Seminary, Fred'k, Md, will commence its 26th scholastic year the first Monday in Sep. Board & Tuition per scholastic year, $250. For Catalogues address: Rev Thos M Carm, A M, President.

Victor Hugo's new book is to be called "The Exiles." He writes all his manuscripts in lead pencil.

MON AUG 3, 1868
Phil Enquirer, Jul 31. Many or our citizens have visited the Zoological Garden of Mr Chas E Becker, on 9th st, & this morning they will be surprised to hear of Mr Becker's death from a rattlesnake bite. He was about 40 years of age, & leaves a wife & family. The reptile, after inflicting the fatal wounds, was put to death.

Atlantic City, Aug 2. Henry Through, a Mr Van Kirk, & a son of Rev Hosea Ballew, all of Phil, were drowned here yesterday while bathing. Another case of drowning there yesterday, was Louis Morwitz, a nephew of Dr Morwitz, of the German Democrat, & an attache of that paper. He was a young unmarried man, much respected here. His immediate family are all in Germany.

Balt, Aug 1. Mrs ex-President Lincoln, who has been here since Thu, & had engaged passage on the same ship, under the escort of Mr Johnson, was taken suddenly ill last night. This morning she is better, & able to sit up, but too indisposed to undertake the voyage across the Atlantic at present.

Died: on Jul 19, after a short illness, at her residence in Montg Co, Md, Miss Julia Bradley, daughter of the late Abraham Bradley, of Wash City.

Died: on Aug 2, in Wash City, after a long illness, Malinda A, beloved wife of M E Bright, aged 43 years. Her funeral will take place on Aug 4 at 10 o'clock A M, from her late residence, 387 L st south, near 3rd st, & proceed to St Peter's Church, Capitol Hill.

Died: on Sunday, Susie May, aged 9 months, child of Marcus B & Susie Latimer. Her funeral will take place on Monday afternoon, from Mrs Lowe's, 297 Pa ave, between 9th & 10th sts.

Died: on Jul 21, Edward, infant son of Harvey John & Sarah Jane Hunt, aged 3 years & 6 months.

Leavenworth, Kansas, Aug 1. Gen Sheridan was arrested today, on complaint of Mr Dunn, for assault & battery. Dunn is postmaster at **Fort Leavenworth**, but was ordered off the reservation a few days ago, for alleged misconduct, & for refusing to obey the order was forcibly ejected; hence the action for assault.

At the funeral of M Viennet in Paris, the procession was one of the largest ever seen, &, what is very remarkable, many of the mourners were smoking.

Hon John A Kerr, of Lansing, one of the State printers of Mich, died on the Great Western railway train on Wed while on his way home from St Catherines, whither he had been for medical treatment.

The patent of A C Mellier, for making paper from wood & straw, has been extended for 7 years by the Com'r of Patents. This patent caused much litigation among various paper makers throughout the country.

M Aujac, the French tenor, while playing Bluebeard at Niblo's Garden, N Y, on Tue, was taken seriously ill. It was decided that he had been poisoned by the verdigris used to give lustre to Bluebead's beard.

Comrs' sale of valuable tract of land & fishery, known as ***Cockpit Point Fishery***, in Prince Wm Co, Va; by decree of the Circuit Court of Pr Wm Co, in the case of Wm Cleary against Wm Woodward & others; public auction on Aug 8, of ***Cockpit Point***, containing 525 acres. –Francis L Smith, Geo Wm Brent, Chas E Sinclair, Comrs of sale.

Public auction on Oct 5, by deed of trust executed to me on Jan 26, 1867, by John W Hoffocker & Rebecca his wife, of record in the Clerk's ofc of the County Court of Prince Wm Co, Va; sale of property known as ***God Ridge***, containing 600 acres of land; with a comfortable dwlg & outbldgs thereon. Mr Lebbens Ewell, who lives upon the property, will show it. For further information address Lebbins Ewell, or the trustee, Brentsville, Prince Wm Co, Va. –A Nicol, trustee

Orphans Court of Wash Co, D C. Letters of administration on the personal estate of Abraham F Kimmell, late of Wash City, D C, dec'd. –Mary A S L Kimmell, admx

Supreme Court of D C, Equity 1,244-docket 8. John W Wells et al vs Simeon Bronson et al. Ratify sales made & reported by the trustee, Wm Y Fendall. –Geo P Fisher, Justice Supreme Court, D C. –R J Meigs, clerk [No other information.]

TUE AUG 4, 1868
Thos Berry purchased a 3 story frame house & lot on Delaware ave, between B & C sts north, for $3,200.

Died: on Aug 2, John E Jackson, in his 27th year. His funeral will be from the residence of his mother, 354 E st, this afternoon, at 4 o'clock.

Died: on Aug 3, at ***Woodleigh***, at the residence of Hon R J Walker, his grand-daughter, Caroline Bayard Walker, infant child of Gen Duncan S Walker & Mary D Walker. The friends of the family are invited to attend the funeral which will move at 5 o'clock P M Tuesday, from ***Woodleigh*** to ***Oak Hill Cemetery***.

Supreme Court of D C, Equity 1,069-docket 8. Wm G Statter vs Catherine Bauman et al. Ratify sale made & reported by Wm F Mattingly & Fred'k Schmidt, trustees. [No other information.] -R J Meigs, clerk

The telegraph last night brought us the intelligence of the sudden death of Gen Chas G Halpine, editor of the N Y Citizen, & "Miles O'Reilly," of poetic fame. His death was the result of an overdose of choloroform, taken to alleviate neuralgic pains. [Aug 5th newspaper: Chas G Halpine was the son of a Protestant rector in the county of Waterford, Ireland, born in a delightful valley near the borders of the counties of Waterford & Cork, the very spot where Spencer wrote his "Fairy Queen." When about 18 he emigrated to this country; his first connection being with the Boston Post. He leaves a wife & 6 children to mourn his loss. N Y Express] [Aug 7th newspaper: The funeral of Gen Halpine will take place on Sat: the following will act as pall-bearers: Hon John T Hoffman, Maj Gen David Hunter, Jas T Brady, Hon Horace Greeley, Jas G Bennett, jr, Robt B Roosevelt, Peter B Sweeney, Richd B Connolly, Nelson J Waterbury, Richd O'Gorman, & Wm C Barrett.] [Aug 10th newspaper: N Y Express of Sat: The funeral of Maj Gen Chas Graham Halpine took place this morning from his late residence, 58 West Forty-seventh st; the remains were placed in the final resting place, *Cypress Hills Cemetery*. The deceased was attired in the military costume of a major general; the coffin bore the inscription: Charles Graham Halpine, Died August 3, 1868, aged Thirty-eight years and ten months.]

Criminal Court-Judge Wylie. 1-Amos Pratt, convicted of keeping a disorderly house; fined $50. 2-Geo Bath, Richd Brown, & Wm Simaker, indicted for riot & affray, convicted, & sentenced to jail for 60 days. 3-Danl Jackson, charged with forgery, brought in on a bench warrant, was released on giving $1,000 bail.

The wife of Senator Trumbull has been very ill for several days in this city, with scarcely any hope of her recovery. [Aug 5th newspaper: Mrs Senator Trumbull was yesterday somewhat better, & hopes are entertained of her recovery.]
[Aug 17th newspaper: Mrs Trumbull died yesterday; her remains will be taken to Springfield, Ill, for interment. Brief religious exercises will take place at the residence, 394 First st east, this afternoon, at 5 o'clock, previous to removal to the depot.]
[Aug 18th newspaper: The funeral of Mrs Senator Trumbull took place yesterday; services conducted by Rev John Chester, of the Capitol Hill Presbyterian Church. Senator Trumbull & his 2 sons, Mrs Trumbull's mother, & Dr Hood, the family physician, accompanied the body to Springfield, Ill. Mrs Trumbull was but 43 years of age. One of the sons of the Senator is now absent in Montana, & has not received the news of his mother's death.]
[Aug 21st newspaper: Mrs Trumbull was the daughter of Dr Garsham Jayne, of Springfield, & sister of Dr Wm Jayne, of the same city, who filled the ofc of Govn'r of Dakota during Mr Lincoln's first Presidency. For several months Mrs Trumbull had suffered from the painful affliction, an ovarian tumor, which resulted in her death. Springfield, Ill, was her childhood home. To her husband & children, her loss is irreparable. —Chicago Tribune]

Tom Placide, the famous old comedian, was married to a lady residing near New Orleans, a few days since.

Phil, Aug 3. Chas Buckwalter, a promising young lawyer, & Democratic politician of this city, died this morning of typhoid fever.

Boston, Aug 3. Catharine Glannon, a domestic discharged from the family of E W Burnstead, of Highland District, is in jail charged with trying to burn the Burnstead dwlg house.

Concord, N H, Aug 3. Wm H H Willey, aged 19, & Chas H Main, aged 9, were drowned while bathing in the Cochego river at Rochester yesterday.

WED AUG 5, 1868
Squa ga na ba, an old chief of the Ottawa Indians, died recently, & a medal was found hanging on his neck, which he had worn for 54 years, & which was presented to him in 1814 by the British Gov't, for the part which he took in killing & scalping American whites at the river Raisin massacre.

Orphans Court-Judge Purcell, Aug 4, 1868. 1-Clarence B Baker gave bond in the sum of $2,000 as collector of the goods, chattels, etc, of Owen Munson. John T Clark, & W L Bramhall, sureties. 2-The will of John Amrein was filed for probate. The testator bequeaths all his property to his wife, & names Geo Willner, exc. 3-The will of Judson Dover was filed for probate. The testator bequeaths all his property to his daughters, Mary Jane Grey & Sarah Dover, & appoints Wm Queen, exc. 4-The will of Margaret Golden was filed & partially proven. She names her sons Matthew & Michl excs. 5-Geo W Slidham gave bond in the sum of $300 as adm of Alex'r Berryhill, of the Creek Nation. R A Crawford & J B Luce, sureties. 6-Geo W Willner gave bond in the sum of $2,000 as exc of John Amrein. Jerome Browne, jr, & Chas Walter, sureties.

Died: on Aug 3, Jas F Dominic, the only son of Franciss D & Margaret A M Armstrong, aged 11 months & 3 days. His funeral will be from his late residence, 4½ & F sts, South Washington, this afternoon at 4 o'clock.

Died: on Aug 1, at St Paul, Minn, John B Hutchinson, aged 30 years, late of Wash, D C. His remains will be taken to Pepperell, Mass, for interment.

Executor's sale of real estate; by power contained in the last will & testament of Eliz Herbert, dec'd, on record in the ofc of the Register of Wills of Wash City, D C, & also on record in the ofcr of the Register of Wills of PG Co, Md: public sale on Aug 25 next, all that tract or parcel of land in PG Co, which said Eliz Herbert died seized & possessed, containing 167 acres, 2 roods & 3 perches; 2½ miles from the residence of Dr John H Bayne, & there is a good road, commonly called <u>New Cut Road</u>, leading from Wash, D C, to the premises; with a small dwlg house & outbldgs. –Asbury Lloyd, J Wesley Boteler, excs of Eliz Herbert, dec'd. [Marlboro Gaz copy & send bill to executors.]

Orphans Court of Wash Co, D C. Letters testamentary on the personal estate of John Amrein, late of Wash City, dec'd. —Geo Willner, exc

THU AUG 6, 1868
The President has appointed Hon Benj F James, of Ill, heretofore one of the principal examiners in the Patent Ofc, to be Examiner in Chief, in place of Hon Elisha Foote, appointed Com'r of Patents.

Hymenial. Married in Wash City, on Aug 4, by Rev Dr Sunderland, Mr Wolcott Lay, of N J, & Mrs Martha E Page.

Mr Henry S Barnes, a well known citizen & butcher of Wash City, died suddenly yesterday. Mr Barnes was a young man, energetic & courteous, beloved by a very large circle of friends.
+
Died: on Aug 5, after a brief illness, H S Barnes, aged 30 years. His funeral will take place today, Thursday, at 3 o'clock P M, from his late residence, 576 M st, from thence to *Oak Hill Cemetery*.

Association of the Oldest Inhabitants regular meeting was held yesterday; president, Dr J G Blake, in the chair; J Carroll Brent, sec. Mr Andrew Rothwell, from the cmte appointed to nominate ofcrs, reported the following, who were unanimously elected: Cor sec, Mountjoy Hanson; vice presidents, Richd Pettit, Jenkin Thomas, Peter G Washington, Edw Simms, Wm Gunton, John F Callan, Jas Adams, Erasmus J Middleton, John Purdy, Chauncey Bester, Wm Lord, Thos Havenner, & Francis Hanna. Mr S Masi was re-elected marshal of the assoc; Nicholas Callan renominated for the ofc of treasurer, but declined. Elected members of the association: Abel G Davis, Wm H Campbell, Lambert Tree, Wm H Parker, G W Harkness. Mr W W Cox presented the association with a fac simile lithograph copy of the Post Ofc Ledger Dept, by Dr Benj Franklin as Postmaster Gen, in 1776, 77, & 78, under the colonies; showing also the first Postmaster Gen appointed by Washington. This book was rescued from the burning of the Post Ofc Dept on Dec 15, 1836, by Mr Cox, as an employe of that ofc. Mr Jenkin Thomas, on behalf of Francis Dodge, of Gtwn, presented a copy of the constitution & by laws of the Columbia Fire Co, of Gtwn. Of the orginal signers, 95 in number, but one is now alive, Mr Chas Vincent. Mr Thomas also presented a copy of the Wash Directory for 1831. John Underwood, of Ill, was elected an honorary member several months since. Mr Wm Day was elected messenger of the association.

Mrd: on Aug 4, by Rev Byron Sunderland, Wolcott Lay, of Newark, N J, to Martha E Page, of Wash City.

Mrd: on Aug 1, by Rev Fr McNally, Mr A Otis Houghton, of Gtwn, D C, to Mrs Jennie T Tardy, of St Augustine, Fla. [N Y Herald Tribune & World please copy.]

Criminal Court-Justice Wylie. Edw Snowden & Alice Snowden, indicted for the grand larceny of clothing from Rebecca Hyatt, were tried, & the first was convicted, & the latter found not guilty.

Worcester, Mass, Aug 5. Washington Clapp, editor of the Natick Times, while walking from his dwlg to his ofc, in Natick, this morning, was seized with an apoplectic fit, & died in the street.

Hiram Callahan, of McHenry township, in this county, was bitten by a rattlesnake; while mowing in a field, a snake came in contact with the scythe & was cut in two. Later Hiram took hold of the piece to which the head was attached, to throw it away, & was quickly bitten. Reports said that he was dead, but we believe he is still alive.
–Jersey Shore Videtta

Phil Ledger. Sat last, at Atlantic City, four people well known citizens of Phil drowned, while bathing. Jos T Vankirk, aged 53 years; Mr G M Ballou, son of Rev Mr Ballou, pastor of the Second Universalist Church, in 8th st; Mr Henry C Trough, & Louis Morwitz, reporter on the German Democrat. Mr Vankirk & his youngest daughter, & young Mr Ballou & his mother, went to Atlantic City on Thu last, intending to remain a week or two, at the Mansion House. Mr Vankirk was at the head of the firm of Vankirk & Co, manufacturers of gas fixtures, at 912 Arch st. He resided at 444 Main st, Frankford, where he leave a wife & 6 children. G M Ballou, in his 22nd year, was the only son & living child of Rev Mr Ballou. He studied medicine & graduated with honors last spring, at the Univ of Pa. He was to have been married in a few months to the youngest daughter of Mr Vankirk, the one that accompanied her father to the sea-shore. Mr Henry R Trough's son was in the act of registering his name at the hotel, when news of the drowning of his father reached him. Mr Trough was of the firm of Trough & Lemmens, dealers in tinware, 523 South Second st. He leaves a wife & several children. He was about 50 years of age. Mr Morwitz was a German, about 26 years of age, unmarried; he was the brother of Dr Morwitz, the proprietor of the journal with which the dec'd was connected. Mr Morwitz was seen in the water endeavoring to save two men, one of whom he rescued, but the second, Mr Trough, was beyond his reach, & in his efforts, lost his own life.

Thos Fitzpatrick, aged 7 years, residing with his parents in Willoughby ave, near Skillman st, died of hydrophobia yesterday, from a dog bite he received in May last.
-N Y Com Advertiser.

FRI AUG 7, 1868
Thos Dowling, auct, sold the western 32 feet front of lot 16, in Holmead's addition to Gtwn, having a depth of 120 feet, improved with a comfortable brick dwlg, on Bridge st, near the bridge, to Mrs A McKeldry, for $1,900.

Portion of the late Saml DeVaughan estate sold yesterday, to John N Oliver, trustee, by Cooper & Latimer, aucts. Two houses on 9th st to Douglass Moore, for $10,850; house & lot on 9th st, to Alex'r R Shepherd, for $3,025.

Meeting of the Wash Schuetzen Verein on Wed: the vote for Pres stood: B Henze, 126; F Stosch, 105; Henze elected. Elected: Vice Pres, P Dill; Prot Sec, H Kendler, Financial Sec, R Springsguth; others elected to various offices: John Angermann, Aug Koch, V Helimuth, Chas Ebel, F Staley, F Huegle, C Kneessi, W Redgrave, A Cluss, John Kossell, John Kaiser, Lem Towers, Henry Govermann, Louis Beyer.

Died: on Aug 6, after a short illness, James Martin, infant son of Jos T & Margaret Ann Mitchell, aged 6 months & 13 days. His funeral is this Friday at 4 o'clock P M, from the residence of its parents, 6th & D sts.

Very Rev Dr Benedict J Spalding, brother of Archbishop Spalding, & administrator of the Diocese of Louisville, died on Tuesday at the Episcopal residence in that city, from the effects of injuries received by the accidental burning of a mosquito net on his bed. Dr Spalding was advanced in years. He was a most zealous laborer in the diocese, formerly presided over by the Most Rev Arshbishop. [Aug 10th newspaper: Fr Spalding was born in Marion Co, Ky, in 1810, & was the descendant of a noble race of Marylanders, who first established religious freedom in that colony. They belonged to the heroic age, & with Chas Carroll, of Carrollton, & the Howards, & others of the patriot order, gave tone to the liberal institutions of that State. In the Md Line the Spaldings were prominent soldiers of the War for Independence. Emigrating to Ky, they became conspiciuous leaders of society, politics, & religion. The founder of the family was Richd Spalding; his children partook of his features in a very remarkable degree. Dr Spalding was educated at St Mary's; went to the Theological Seminary, & graduated at the College of the Propaganda in Rome; in 1844 he was appointed Vicar General of Ky. His brother, Rt Rev Martin John Spalding, Archbishop of Balt, is the highest ecclesiastical functionary in America. A sister was for many years the chief of a religious society in the State, & the memory of her life is yet cherished. Another brother, Richd M Spalding, is a member of the Ky Legislatur. Ignatius A Spalding is the Senator from Union, & an elector for the State on the Democratic ticket. The most brilliant member of this remarkable family is Rev J Lancaster Spalding, who was utterly prostrated by the death of his uncle.] [Aug 11th newspaper: The funeral obsequies of the late Fr Spalding, on Friday, were most imposing. The Archbishop, expected from Balt, did not reach the city in time. The remains were taken to the new burial place, *St Louis Cemetery*, some 2 miles south of the city.]

Orphans Court of Wash Co, D C, Aug 4, 1868. In the case of Arsenius J Harvey, exc of Jas S Harvey, dec'd, the executor & Court have appointed Aug 25th next, for the final settlement of the personal estate of the said dec'd, of the assets in hand.
-Jas R O'Beirne, Reg/o wills

Phil, Aug 6. Geo Zimmerman, a cigar dealer of this city, committed suicide today by blowing out his brains.

SAT AUG 8, 1868

Gen Ellis Spear has been promoted to be a principal examiner in the Patent Ofc, vice Judge B F James, appointed examiner-in chief. Random Cook, first assistant to principal examiner, vice J M Blanchard, resigned.

Explosion of coal gas occurred in the basement of the Capitol bldg, in what is known as the Washington crypt. The funeral paraphernalia of the late Abraham Lincoln was placed for safe deposit in the crypt, & was ignited by the flames & partially destroyed. Diligent inquiry revealed nothing worse than the damages above mentioned.

Died: yesterday, Mrs Emily Brown, wife of Baley Brown, in her 50th year. Her funeral will take place from her late residence, on Md ave, between 12th & 13th sts, near the Bladensburg toll gate, on Sunday, Aug 9.

Albert Dick, 17, apprentice to Simms & Greer, carpenters, fell from the roof of the back bldg of Mr Jacob D Hutton, 7th st, below F, to the ground, 20 feet, & was injured seriously, if not fatally. He was removed to his father's residence, on N Y ave, between 4th & 5th sts. His skull is fractured, & it is feared he is injured internally.

Cincinnati, Aug 7. Thos B Page, President of the Third Nat'l Bank, & a prominent citizen, died today.

Trustee's sale of valuable real estate; by deed of trust from Edmund J Plowden, of St Mary's Co, Md, to Robt C Combs & Jas S Downs, trustees, for the benefit of all the creditors of said Edmund J Plowden, according to their original liens or priorities; public sale at the Court-house door, in Leonardtown, on Sep 1 next of *Brushwood Lodge*, containing 800 acres, more or less; *St Clement's Manor*, the *Glebe*, & the *Grubs*, containing 215 acres, more or less; & the wharf & bldgs, all these lands are location in the 4th Electon District of St Mary's Co. Property is located on the Potomac river, & has one of the finest dwlg houses in Southern Md upon it. It adjoins the fine estates of the late Wm H Garner, the late Wm H Thomas, & Wm Blair. –Robt C Combs, Jas S Downs, trustees

MON AUG 10, 1868

Despatch from Worcester, Mass: Michl Newman, aged 40 years, while attempting to get on a freight train at Websters, on Friday, fell on the track, & the wheels passed over him, crushing one of his legs, which was amputated. He died during the night.

Messrs Claggett & Sweeny, real estate brokers, sold part of lot 2 in square 408, & premises, being Nos 16 & 18 Market Space, for the sum of $36,000 to Thos L Hume, one of our most industrious & enterprising merchants. This property belonged to John F Clark, of Wash City.

Died: on Aug 9, after a long & painful illness, John Smith, one of the oldest residents of the eastern section of Wash City, in his 68th year. His funeral will take place from his late residence, 11th & M sts, on Tuesday, at 4 o'clock. He leaves a large family & numerous circle of friends to mourn their irreparable loss.

Died: on Aug 9, Isaac H Hopkins, in his 46th year. His funeral will take place on Aug 10, at 4:30 o'clock P M, from the residence of his uncle, G W Hopkins, on Conn ave, between Q & R sts.

Died: on Aug 9, John W Hodgson, in his 53rd year. His funeral will take place from his late residence, 6th & E sts, on Tuesday at 5 o'clock.

Died: on Aug 7, at Phil, Mary Grafton, wife of Henry J Thomas, & daughter of the late Thos G Addison, of Md.

Rev Chas Eagan, a Catholic priest in Augusta, Maine, has been indicted by the grand jury for libel.

Dr Herman Beslan, residing at 15 Amity st, N Y, committed suicide on Friday, by taking an overdose of morphine. Pecuniary difficulty prompted him to the act.

Robt Dunlap, late of Auburn, Me, died & left behind him $1,600 U S bonds. He willed $400 to his wife, one-half of the remainder to the Baptist Church in Buckfield, Me, & the balance to the Baptist Missionary Society. His wife waived the provisions of the will & asked an allowance. The Judge, after hearing the case, gave her the whole of $1,600.

Judge Chandler G Potter, of Hillsboro, N H, who died at Flint, Mich, on Monday, was a native of Concord, & graduated at Dartmouth in 1831.

Edwin A Stevens, the great millionaire of Hoboken, died in Paris on Friday. He had been afflicted with rheumatism for 2 years. When the news reached Hoboken on Sat the flags at the ferry, & all through the city, were displayed at half-mast.

Orphans Court-Judge Purcell, Aug 8, 1868. 1-Michl & Matthew Crane gave bond in the sum of $13,000, as excs of Margaret Golden. Jas White & Patrick White, sureties. 2-Wm R Woodward gave bond in the sum of $25,000, as adm of Thos Woodward. Amon Green & E J Middleton, sureties. 3-The will of John Morgan was filed for probate. He appoints Jas Morgan & Margaret Menney sureties. 4-Theodore Samuels gave bond in the sum of $300 as adm of Jos Barnes, alias Bowers. V R Freeman & Adam Miller, sureties. 5-The will of Jos Bowers was filed & fully proven. He names N H Miller exc. 6-The will of Leonidas Coyle was filed for probate. The testator bequeaths all his property to his wife, Harriet L Coyle, in fee simple, & names her executrix.

Orphans Court of Wash Co, D C. Letters testamentary on the personal estate of Margaret Golden, late of Wash City, D C, dec'd. –Michl Crane, Matthew Crane, excs

TUE AUG 11, 1868
Mike McCoole, the celebrated pugilist, has married a daughter of Danl Norton, a wealthy contractor of St Louis.

The body of a woman found in the lake at Chicago on Friday, & supposd to be that of one of the victims of the steamer **Sea Bird**, has been identified as that of the wife of Mr Martin Woodruff, who resides at Aurora, Ill. The lady committed suicide by drowning herself on the night of last Christmas, after being a week married. The day after her marriage she attempted to destroy herself by taking laudanum. She was insane at the time, & her husband had taken her to Chicago, intending to place her in an insane asylum.

Death of well known citizens. Mr John W Hodgson & Mr John Smith, both residents of the eastern portion of Wash City. Mr Hodgson, tinner, leaves an amiable wife & a family of children; Jos F Hodgson, late Intendant of the Wash Asylum, was his brother. Mr Smith, up to a few years ago, was employed in the Wash navy yard as master ship-carpenter, & engaged as a ship-builder for 45 years. The frig **Minnesota** was built under his supervision.

Died: on Aug 10, Anna Virginia, child of Jacob V & Virginia Vonderlehr, aged 1 year, 3 months & 10 days. Her funeral will be on Aug 11 at 3 o'clock P M, from the residence of her parents, 373 11th st, between K & L sts.

N Y, Aug 10. Fire broke out today at Hunter's Point, Long Island, destroying the varnish factory of Hobbs, Bligh, & Hubbard. Danl A Johnson, superintendent of the factory, was burned to death.

Cleveland, Aug 10. Mr Townsend, a bookkeeper of this city, & Mr Kennedy, a druggist, were blown off shore Sat, while in a small sailboat, & are supposed lost. Mr Townsend was the son of an old citizen of this place, & was celebrating his 21st birthday.

Valuable real estate at public auction; trustees in the case of Wm S Jones, in bankruptcy, will sell, on Aug 18, on the new or upper road from Gtwn to the Little Falls, 2 acres of land, improved by a new frame dwlg of 8 rooms, & numerous out bldgs. Also, one undivided half of lots 61 & 62, & part of lot 60, in Beatty & Hawkins' addition to Gtwn, fronting 150 feet on the south side of 3rd st, & 155 feet on the west side of Fred'k st. -Wm D Cassin, Wm R Woodward, trustees -Thos Dowling, auct

Louis Napoleon gets $14,240 a day; Queen Victoria, $6,027; Francis Joseph, $10,60; & the King of Prussia, $8,210.

Richmond, Aug 10. Intelligence has been received here of the accidental death, at Matoon, Ill, of Col T C Johnson, late president of the Randolph Macon College, Va.

Mrs Hole-in-the-day inherits one-half of her husband's property, estimated at about $2,000,000.

Jas Gordon Bennett, jr, manages the N Y Herald on board his yacht. Hence the politics of the paper are all at sea. -Ex

WED AUG 12, 1868
Orphans Court-Judge Purcell, Aug 11, 1868. 1-Henry Weaver gave bond in the sum of $4,000 as administrator of H S Barnes. Thos Weaver & Theodore Barnes, sureties. 2-Maria A Munson gave bond in the sum of $5,000 as admx of Owen Munson. Chas H Townsend & Thos M Shepherd, sureties. 3-The will of Jas Chapman was fully proven & admitted to probate. 4-The will of Ann Crown was fully proven & admitted to probate. 5-The will of Lewis Beard was fully proven & admitted to probate. 6-The will of Saml Brown was filed & partially proven. He appoints his wife sole excx. 7-Lena Brown gave bond in the sum of $5,000 as excx of Saml Brown. John Anderson & J C Clay, sureties. 8-Laura Pickens gave bond in the sum of $400 as guardian to the orphans of Lafayette & Laura Cameron. Saml Pickens, C H Osborne, & E McKenney, sureties. 9-The will of John Morgan was fully proven & admitted to probate. 10-Louis F Clements gave bond in the sum of $5,000 as adm d b n of Abner Brush. J T Clements & W R Baune, sureties.

Died: on Aug 11, Annie M, only daughter of Irwin S & Sarah E Barker, aged 10 months & 1 day. Her funeral will take place from the residence of Jas W Barker, 425 H st, this afternoon, at 4 o'clock.

Hon Stevens, whose illness has been reported for several days, died at midnight last night at his residence on Capitol Hill, in Wash City. His nephews, Simon Stevens & Thaddeus Stevens, jr; his housekeeper, Mrs Smith; Mr J Scott Patterson, of the Interior Dept; Sisters Loretta & Genevieve, of Providence Hospital; & the servants of his household, were at his bedside during his last moments. He passed away calmly as if asleep. He was born in Caledonia Co, Vt, Apr 4, 1793 & was almost 75 years of age; graduated at Dartmouth College in 1814, & immediately removed to Pa, where he studied law while teaching school; admitted to the bar 1816 in Adams Co, Pa; removed to Lancaster, Pa, in 1842; in 1842 & 1848 he was elected to Congress. [Aug 14th newspaper: The remains of Thaddeus Stevens will be taken to Lancaster. The funeral services will be held in the Rotunda at 8 A M & be conducted by Rev Dr Gray, of the E st Baptist Church, Chaplain of the Senate; Dr Boynton, Chaplain of the House, being out of the city.] [Aug 15th newspaper: funeral services were held on Aug 14 from the Capitol; conducted by Rev Drs Emery, Gray, & Hamilton, sermon by Dr Gray. Procession: the Butler Zouaves, [colored,] with arms reversed; & headed by King's colored band; & the Metropolian Police, under the command of Lt Noonan. The funeral ceremonies were under the direction of Lemuel Williams, undertaker. Burial will be in ***Shreiner's Graveyard***, Lancaster. His nephew Thaddeus Stevens, jr, was present at the funeral.]

Died: on Aug 8, at Warrenton, Fauquier Co, Va, Maggie Love, only daughter of Capt Jos S & Maggie L Sherrett, aged 10 months.

Orphans Court of Wash Co, D C. Letters of administration on the personal estate of Abner Brush, late of Wash City, D C, dec'd. –Louis F Clements, d b n & c t a

Orphans Court of Wash Co, D C. Letters of administration on the personal estate of Henry S Barnes, late of Wash Co, D C, dec'd. –Henry Weaver, adm

Orphans Court of Wash Co, D C. Letters of administration on the personal estate of Wm Northeridge, late of Wash City, D C, dec'd. –Jane Northeridge, admx

Orphans Court of Wash Co, D C. Letters testamentary on the personal estate of Saml Brown, late of Wash Co, dec'd. –Lenna Brown, excx

N Y, Aug 11. The body found last Sat in the East river proves to be that of Chas Ellet, formerly a judge in Calif, & for 9 years a member of the firm of Binninger & Co, in this city. Wounds were found on his person, & $4,000 in money & his watch were gone. He was undoubtedly robbed, murdered, & thrown into the river.

Letter dated London, Jul 29. The marriage of Adelina Patti, so often announced & so often denied, took place this morning at a Roman Catholic Church on the Clapham Park road. The bride was escorted by her father, Signor Patti. The Marquis de Caux was the happy bridegroom, & the Duke of Manchester & Mr ___, gave away the bride, who looked more beautiful than ever. Miss Maria Harris, Mlle Rita di Candia, daughter of Mario, Mlle Leuw, & Mlle Zanzy were the bridesmaids. The marriage ceremony of the Roman Catholic Church is a very short one, not occupying more than from 5 to 10 minutes. The party will leave at once for the Continent.

THU AUG 13, 1868
Nat'l Theatre: Stuart Robson' Burlesque Company are increasing nightly in popularity, & deservedly so; his personation of Wm Jones, in the farce of Jones' Baby is one of those laughable trifles that are always acceptable when given by an artist like Robson.

Mrd: on Aug 12, in Wash City, at the residence of Maj Perry Fuller, 365 K st, by Rev A W Pitzer, Mr Robt L Ream, jr, to Miss Anna A Guy.

Died: on Aug 12, Mary, youngest child of Alfred & Eugenie Gallagher, aged 2 years. Her funeral will take place from the residence of her grandfather, 314 4th st, between G & H sts, this afternoon, at 4 o'clock.
+
[Aug 15th newspaper:] Died: on Aug 14, Thomas, only son of Albert & Eugenie Gallagher, aged 4 years & 4 months. His funeral will take place from the residence of his grandfather, 314 4th st, on Saturday afternoon, at 3 o'clock.

Sale of Sir Walter Scott's Autograph Manuscripts, by auction, in London, recently by order of the trustees of the late Mr Robt Cadell, of Edinburgh.

1-"Quentin Durwood," L142. [Mr Toovey, of Piccadilly.]
2-"The Abbot," L50. [Mr J Murray, Albemarle st.]
3-"Woodstock," L120. [Thorpe.]
4-"The Betrothed," L77. [Lauder.]
5-"The Talisman," L70. [Lauder.]
6-"St Ronan's Well," L119. [Lauder.]
7-"Chronicles of the Cannongate," First & second series, L51. [Melville.]
8-"The Vision of Don Roderick," & other pieces; stanzas 19 to 54 in "Don Roderick," L57. A W [Elrick]
9-"Life of Napoleon Bonaparte," 9 vols 8vo-the proof sheets, with MS notes by Sir Walter Scott's friend & printer, Mr Jas Ballantyne, the margins covered with corrections & additions in the autograph of the author, L60. [Mr Bret.]
10-"Woodstock," 3 vols, in 2, 8 vo; the proof sheets of the first edition, with numerous MS notes by Mr John Ballantyne, & very extensive corrections & additions in the autograph of the author, L59. [Boone.]
11-"Tales of the Crusaders," "The Betrothed," & "The Talisman," 4 vols in 2, 8vo; the proof sheets of the first edition, with MS notes by Jas Ballantyne, & numerous corrections & additions in the autograph of the author, L40. [Mr Bret]
12-"Fortunes of Nigal," & "Quentin Durward," 6 vols in 3 8vo, the proof sheets of the first edition, with MS notes by Mr Jas Ballantyne, & numerous corrections & additions in the autograph of the author, L45. [Mr Toovey.]
13-"Paveril of the Peak," 4 vol in 2, 8vo, the proof sheets of the first edition, with MS notes by Mr Jas Ballantyne, & numerous corrections & additions in the autograph of the author, L26. [H Stevens.]
14-"The Pirate," 4 vols in 2, 8vo, the proof sheets of the first edition, with MS notes by Mr Jas Ballantyne, & numerous corrections & additions in the autograph of the author, L27. [Boone.]
15-" Ivanhoe," "Bride of Lammermoor," "Legend of Montrose," 8 vo. Fragments of the proof sheets, with MS notes by Mr Jas Ballantyne, & numerous corrections & additions in the autograph of the author, L21. [Mr Toovey.]
16-"Tales of a Grandfather," being stories from the history of Scotland, 6 vols, 12 mo, interleaved, with numerous corrections & additions by the author. Edinburgh, 1828. L100, to Mr Bret, of Bond st.

Emma Ames, daughter of Mrs Sarah F Ames, the well-known sculptor, will make her debut soon, under the name of Amy Girdlestone, at John Brougham's Theatre, N Y.

Mrs Cmdor Vanderbilt has been stricken with paralysis.

Indianapolis, Aug 12. Edw Reynolds, the father of Maj J J Reynolds, commanding the Dept of Texas, & of W F Reynolds, the former president of the Lafayette & Indianapolis Railroad Co, died this morning at Lafayette, Ind, aged 92 years.

U S Patent Ofc, Wash, , Aug 5, 1868. Ptn of Geo Miller, of Providence, R I, praying for the extension of a patent granted to him Nov 7, 1854, for an improvement in Manufacturing Leather Banding for Machinery. -Elisha Foote, Com'r of Patents

Supreme Court of D C, in Equity 1,355. Augusta McBlair et al vs Augusta Ten Eyck, Julia Ten Eyck, Jane Ten Eyck, Mary Ten Eyck, & others. Ordered that the above named dfndnts appear on the first rule day, 40 days after this day; otherwise the cause will be proceeded with as in case of default. –Geo P Fisher, Justice Supreme Court, D C -R J Meigs, clerk

Orphans Court of Wash Co, D C. Letters of administration on the personal estate of Thos Woodward, late of Wash City, D C, dec'd. –Wm R Woodward, adm

St Louis Republican. Married, on Sunday, Aug 9, at the Church of St Lawrence O'Toole, by Rev Fr Arthur Mulholland, Michl Alex'r McCoole to Miss Mollie Naughton, all of St Louis, Mo. The bride is a very pleasing looking girl, about 20 years of age. Long before the hour selected for the ceremony had arrived a vast crowd surrounded the church & the parsonage attached to see the great champion of America, McCoole, the pugilist.

FRI AUG 14, 1868
Board of Metropolitan Police. Chas Walter was appointed a police magistrate; Joshua B Stoops, lately appointed a private on trial, was dropped from the rolls. The following ofcrs were dismissed the force for the reasons specified: Pvt Augustus Westerfield, for inefficiency; Thos C Kelly, for violating rules & regulations; Benj C Berry, for gross neglect of duty; Wm Ryan & Wm Loring, for gross neglect of duty; Benj Leach, violating rules, intoxication & fighting; & J O Wallingsford, for gross neglect of duty. S S Lester, for inefficiency & conduct unbecoming an ofcr, was reprimanded, as was also Pvt J W Edmonson. New appointments made: Chas L Patton, Geo D Kenner, J H Yeager, H K Redway, Patrick O'Hare, & Jas Webb.

Alexandria, Aug 13. Mrs Richards, suffering from neuralgia, last night took an overdose of chloroform, from which she died. She was dead several hours before it was known.

Adah Isaacs Menkin falls over life's footlights into the grave. Her maiden name was Isaacs, & she was born in New Orleans, about 36 years ago; her first husband was Mr Menkin; in 1860 Mrs Menken was introduced to the N Y public by Mr Jas Nixon, then proprietor of the circus in 16th st. Previous to this her liason with John C Heenan in Calif, to whom she claimed to have married after her divorce from Menken, made her far from a stranger to the quidnunes of Gotham. Heenan's subsequent disavowal of the marriage will still be fresh in the public mind. About 1861 she became the better half of Mr R H Newell; this aliance lasted but a brief time. Paris, more than any other city, suited the peculiar genius of Adah. She must have felt at home among its scandals & eccentricities. -N Y Commercial Advertiser [No death date given-current item.]

A negro, Humphrey Mills, was arrested yesterday by Ofcr Huysman, of the 2nd Precinct, on the charge of trespassing on the grounds of Hon Amos Kendall, of **Kendall Green**; breaking down the fences, & carrying off the same for firewood. Mills was fined $10.

Mrd: on Aug 11, at the Foundry parsonage, by Rev Peyton Brown, Thornton F Hickey, of Wash, D C, to Miss Callista Conley, of Phil, Pa.

Died: on Aug 11, at the residence of his grandfather, Saml Cock, Harry Williams, aged 10 months & 14 days, only child of Silas H & Annie B Moore.

SAT AUG 15, 1868
Died: on Aug 12, at Richmond, Va, Miss Eliz Gwynn, sister of Gen Walter Gwynn, aged 75 years, 8 months & 19 days, a lady well known to many citizens of Wash & Gtwn, as well as Richmond & other parts of Va, her native State. For several years she had been declining in health.

Died: on Aug 14, Nellie, youngest daughter of Anthony N & Harriet A Trunnell, in her 4th year. Her funeral will be from the residence of her parents, 571 L st, between 6th & 7th sts, on Sunday afternoon at 4 o'clock. [Star & Express.]

Gen Imboden lately sold the Taylor land, 4,500 acres, adjoining West Point, Va, to a colonization company, for $60,000 cash, on delivery of the deed.

Maj Gen Canby yesterday assumed command of the Dept of Wash. Gen Orders, No 49. Headquarters Dept of Wash, Wash, D C, Aug 14, 1868. 2nd Lt Louis V Caziarc, 11th infty, & 2nd Lt Harry R Anderson, 6th infty, are announced as aides de camp. Brvt Lt Col M H Stacy, captain 12th infty, will report in person for special duty.
–Edwin Candy, Brvt Maj Gen U S Army

St Louis, Aug 14. A special to the Democrat, from Solomon City, Kansas, says Capt Moody reports that on Wed bands of Sioux, Cheyennes, & Arapahoes attacked a settlement on Solomon river, killing David Beaugardes & B B Bell. The Indians ravished 2 women on Plumb Creek, & carried off 2 little girls belonging to A A Bell, living on Mulberry Creek.

Albany, Aug 14. John Rathbone Schofield, the eldest son of Gen J M Schofield, Sec of War, died at West Point this morning. He was in the 11th year of his age.

I offer for sale the Bloomsgrove Brown-stone quarries, & 500 acres of land in Prince Wm Co, Va. –Francis L Smith, Post Ofc Box, 139.

Mrs Lincoln arrived at Bedford Springs, Pa, on Tuesday night.

Patrick H Jones, late Clerk of the Court of Appeals, has been appointed Register of N Y C, vice Gen Hapline, with the understanding that the fees, until Jan 1, are to be passed over to Mrs Halpine.

Tunnel City, Wisc, Jul 6. The death of the "Indian princess" & daughter of the head Winnebago Chief, Dandy, whose foot & leg were so badly injured by the cars at La Crosse, occurred at Tunnel City on Tuesday. Knowing she was dying, she shook hands with all, then kissed her children & her nurse. Whites & Indians alike assisted in dressing her for burial. Silver bobs were put in her ears, around her neck hung heavily with new beads; scarlet leggings, moccasins, blue petticoat, red calico skirt, & blanket, all new & decorated, completed her, & gave her a fitting dress for her appearance in the Spirit Land. As she lay in state a little sack of rice & tobacco was placed by her head side. She was put in a full length plain box & carried under a tree. The Indians gathered in a circle with their backs to the coffin & sang in a low chant. After the corpse was lowered into a grave that had been dug a few feet away, Dandy William, brother of the woman, stepped across the grave, dropping a handful of tobacco upon the coffin. He was followed by other Indians present. Chief Dandy arrived on the evening train; he had not heard a word of his daughter's death. When told he was filled with emotions & made his way to the grave. She left 2 orphan children. Old Dandy is 78 years old, & in failing health.

MON AUG 17, 1868.

On Sat Mr J Q Brigham, late deputy collector of the port of Richmond, Va, made a desperate attempt to commit suicide. He had lately been dismissed from the customs dept, owing to a reduction being made in the working force. He stopped at the Owen House, on Pa ave, & was in his own room, & stabbed himself, no less than 11 times. The chambermaid heard him fall to the floor & gave the alarm. Mr Brigham is about 45, unmarried, born in Mass; during the war served in various civil capacities with the army, was employed at Norfolk, whence he went to Richmond, where in 1865 he became deputy collector of the port. At a late hour last evening he was very low, & not expected to live through the night. [Aug 19th newspaper: Mr J Q Brigham died yesterday in his room in the Owen House. According to a despatch, his father-in-law is having the remains prepared for transportation to Boston, whither they will be taken charge of by E W Brigham, a brother of the deceased, who arrived here last evening.]

On Sat Justice Walter rendered a decision in the case of Maj Wm J McDonald, chief clerk of the Senate, charged with shooting a little girl, Mafilda Toner, who was treapassing upon his property with other children. He had loaded a shot-gun, intending to fire at them, solely to frighten them off the property. On Sat Maj McDonald was fined $15 for assault & battery on the girl, & $2 as the costs of the case.

Chas Morningstar, a laborer on the Wash branch of the Balt & Ohio railroad, was run over & instantly killed on Friday night, near *Jessup's Cut*. He was formerly a resident of Wash City, & a stone-cutter by trade. His body was brought to Wash City for interment.

Orphans Court-Judge Purcell, Aug 15, 1868. 1-Henry Wilson gave bonds in the sum of $500 as guardian of Lucy Pollard, orphan of John alias Jarrett Pollard; Andrew Lewis & Angeline Boswell, sureties. 2-The third account of Lucinda Ford, guardian to Annie Dorsey, infant of Hanson Dorsey, was filed & proved. 3-Chas Walker gave bonds in the sum of $2,000 as guardian to the orphans of Anthony Manyett; Geo Willner & John Van Riswick, sureties. 4-The will of John Smith was filed, in which he bequeaths all his estate, real & personal, to his wife, Margaret Smith, during her single life or widow hood, & thereafter to his children, Eliz Bentley, Cornelius Smith, Mary E Emrick, John T Smith, Margaret Watson, Adelaide Griffin, & Arabella Smith. He further appoints his wife, Margaret Smith, sole executrix. 5-Inventories of the personal property of Walter Harper & Henry S Barnes, dec'd, were presented by the respective appraisers. 6-The ptn of Ellen McCail was received, praying that Rev Jacob Walter may be appointed guardian to her child, Cora Anna Gerrish, said child having been committed by the Equity Court to the custody of said Walter, without prejudice to the jurisdiction of the Orphans Court. The ptn sets forth that Wm Gerrish, the father of the child in question, is deceased, & that she [petitioner,] has reason to believe that said child [Cora Anna Gerrish] is or may be entitled to personal property within the jurisdiction of the court. The hearing of the petition was set for 3 weeks from date. 6-Sarah E Crown gave bonds in the sum of $1,000 as excx of Ann Crown, dec'd; Jerome Brown & John J Johnson, sureties. 7-The will of Edmund Buckley was filed & partially proven, in which he bequeaths his estate to his wife & son, & appoints Thos Holden & Hugh McCaffery excs. 8-Jas Biggins gave bond in the sum of $500 as guardian to Patrick Hallaran, orphan of Thos & Mary Hallaran, dec'd; Patrick Muldoon & Michl Greeney, sureties.

Died: on Aug 16, Mary R, wife of Alfred B Talcott. Her remains will be taken to Connecticut for interment.

Died: on Aug 16, in Gtwn, D C, Mrs Ann E Booth, widow of the late Saml Booth, formerly of Pawtucket, R I, aged 46 years, 1 month & 29 days.

Rev Dr P D Gurley, pastor of the N Y Ave Presbyterian Church, is now lying very ill at Clifton Springs, N Y, whither he had gone in quest of relief. He arrived in Wash City nearly 15 years ago, & is universally beloved by vast numbers of our citizens.

John Putnam extinguished a gas-light in Portland, Maine, with his breath, instead of the stop cock, & died from its inhalation, the other day. He was a peddler, & belonged in Newcastle.

On Monday several pieces of rock broke loose from the side of Lookout Mountain, near Peep's Springs, Walker Co, Ga, & struck the dwlg of Mr Geo Acrofts, instantly killing Mrs Acrofts & an infant child. Three other children were injured, but not fatally.

N Y, Aug 15. 1-Dr Rice, Paymaster's Clerk Hendee, & 4 sailors died recently on the U S steamer **Ossipee**, on the coast of central America. 2-A Chinaman murdered Mr Lee & 3 children at the Iron Fork diggings.

Balt, Aug 15. The consecration of Rev Thos A Becker, as bishop of the new See of Wilmington, & Rev Jas Gibbons, as vicar apostolic, of N C, took place at the Cathedral today. The <u>See of Wilmington</u> embraces the State of Delaware, the Eastern Shore of Md, & the counties of Northampton & Accomac, Va.

Indian Superintendent Thos E Murphy, Atchison, Kansas, Aug 6, enclosed letters from John E Tappan, who was a member of the late Peace Commission, Jul 13 & 26, 1868, stating that the Kiowes had delivered up to him, as proof of their friendship for the whites, a boy about 4 years old, & a girl about 13, & he had handed them over to Gen Alfred Sully, commanding the Dist of the Upper Kansas. The children were seen by Murphy at **Fort Harker**. The girl said their name was Cordell, & her grandfather's name is Allwright; but she cannot tell what State or country they reside in.

TUE AUG 18, 1868

Died at Westminster, Md, on Jul 30, of paralysis, Lewis Beard, in his 67th year. He was born & raised in Leesburg, Loudoun Co, Va, & represented that county in the Legislature 11 years. He was a clerk in the Treasury Dept, under Mr Tyler's administration, where he remained, with the exception of the 4 years of Mr Polk's administration, until Jun, 1861, when he resigned.

Died: yesterday, Mrs H A Read, daughter of the late Capt Barclay Fanning, of the British army, in her 82nd year. Her funeral will take place this afternoon at 4:30 P M, from her late residence, at the Washington House, corner of 3rd st & Pa ave.

Died: on Aug 17, in Gtwn, Miss Harriet B Wilson, eldest daughter of the late Jas C Wilson. Her funeral will be from her mother's residence, 80 Gay st, on Tuesday, at 5 o'clock.

<u>List of ofcrs to which nominations were made & not confirmed during the second session of the 40th Congress, closed by a recess on Jul 27, 1868, to Sep 21, 1868.</u> Postmasters:

Allen, Thos C, Indianola, Texas
Bennett, Nathan B, Cambridge City, Ind.
Colt, Henry V, Geneseo, N Y
Champlin, Chas W, Waterloo, Iowa
Davis, Jas, Memphis, Tenn
Heffner, Wm, Shreveport, La
Hunt, Henry C, Delavan, Wisc
Little, Henry, Auburn, Maine

Johnson, David H, Griffin, Ga
Summers, Geo W, Augusta, Ga
Shea, Jas C, Milledgeville, Ga
Turner, A P, Idaho City, Idaho
Warfield, Beale A, Fredericksburg, Va
Whelan, John, Canton, Miss
Webster, Isaac W, Kenosha, Wisc

<u>Assessor of Internal Revenue:</u>
Abell, David H, 25th Dist, N Y
Chamberlain, Jos H, 5th Dist, Maine
Coulter, Jas E, 9th Dist, N Y
Smith, Lyndon A, 7th Dist, Ind

Simons, Lorenzo D, 1st Dist, N Y
Stevens, W T, Idaho
Treanor, John L, 5th Dist, Ky
Waddell, Lloyd D, 1st Dist, Ga

Collectors of Internal Revenue:
Burns, J, Irving, Idaho
Fithian, Wm, 7th Dist, Ill
Lacey, Alfred, 1st Dist, La
Spear, Percy B, 7th Dist, Pa
Smith, Robt M, 3rd Dist, Md

Justices of the Peace-Wash, D C.
Barnaclo, John W
Callan, Michl P
Callan, Nicholas
Cull, Jas
Douglass, Saml E
Lyles, Henry
Ryther, E A

Collectors of Customs:
Aiken, Wm, Charleston, S C
Smith, Jos E, Wiscassett, Maine
Hopkins, John D, Frenchman's Bay, Maine
Wisner, Wm H, New Orleans, La
Bradbury, Bion, Portland & Falmouth, Maine

Territories:
Gibbs, Isaac L, Govn'r, Idaho
Parker, W H, Sec, Idaho
Stafford, Wm M, Assoc Justice Supreme Court, Montana
Williston, Lorenzo, P, Assoc Justice Supreme Court, Montana
Pidgeon, Wm F, Sec, Idaho
Paddock, A S, Govn'r, Wyoming

Public Lands:
Chadwick, Stephen F, Receiver, Oregon
Caldwell, Jacob W, Register, Wyoming
Latham, Hiram, Surveyor General, Wyoming
Miller, Thos P, Receiver, Ind
Piatt, Robt F, Register, Arizona
Hawley, Geo A, Receiver, Wyoming

U S Marshals: Boone, J Rowan, Ky, Ky; Brown, H L, Western Pa; Rowland, Jos S C, Western Ark
U S Attys: Millson, John S, Va, Va; O'Neil, John P, Eastern, Pa; Smith, Benj H, West Va, West Va
Ministers Resident: Parker, Geo H, Ecuador; Stillwell, Thos N, Venezuela
Ministers Plenipotentiary: Rosecrans, Wm S, Spain
U S Consuls: Bradford, Oliver B, Brunai, Borneo; Smith, J, Albert, Mexico; & Webb, Francis R, Zanzibar
Indian Affairs: Collen, Wm J, Superintendent, Idaho & Montana
Manlove, Saml A, Agent, Osage & other Indians, Kansas
Surveyors of the Customs: Bowen, Wm, Hannibal, Mo; Rankin, Jas, Saybrook, Conn
Naval Ofcr: Fouke, Philip B, New Orleans, La
Com'r of Internal Revenue: Cummings, Alex'r S
2nd Auditor of the Treasury: Wilson, Luther D
Pension Agent: Gale, Geo S, N Y C, N Y
Com'r to examine into expenses incurred by the State of Indiana in enrolling & equipping troops to aid the Govn't in suppressing the rebellion: McConnell, Jos.
Military, Naval, & Revenue Cutter Service:
Sherman, Wm T, Lt Gen, Gen by brvt
Thomas, Geo H, Maj Gen, Lt Gen by brvt
Hawkins, Isaac R, late Lt Col, Col & Brig Gen by brvt

Fry, Jas B, brvt Brig Gen, Maj Gen by brvt.
Wallace, Geo W, brvt Col, Brig Gen by brvt
Wallace, Geo W, Lt Col, Col by brvt
Follet, Fred'k, late Capt 4th srtl, reinstatement
Stockton, Robt F, late 1st Lt 5th cavalry, reinstatement
Clifford, Jas A, 2nd Lt 3rd cavalry, 1st Lt
Garrett, Albert J, 2nd Lt 27th infty, transfer 1st regular cavalry
Rousseau, Richd H, 2nd Lt 17th infty
Armstrong, Jas F, Capt retired list, Capt active list
Clark, Robt M, 3rd Lt revenue cutter service
Owen, John, 3rd Lt revenue cutter service

Public sale: by decree of the Circuit Court for PG Co, Md, passed in a cause between Amelia H Chew & Richd B B Chew, adms c t a of L B Chew & others, cmplnts, & Thos F Bowie & others, dfndnts; public sale on Sep 9 next, in the town of Upper Marlboro, the dwlg house & lot of the said Thos F Bowie, in said village, called **Kinsale**, containing 340 acres, more or less. On Sep 10, public sale at the *Stone House* of John W Coff__e, at Croom, the real estate of the late Thos F Bowie, called **Brookefield**, containing 387 acres, more or less, & **Cheltenham**, contaning 752 acres, more or less. The dwlg house in Upper Marlboro is a commodious & elegant residence. **Kinsale** is 2½ miles from *Mount Calvert*; improvements are a dwlg house, meat house, corn house, stables, & quarters for servaants, & 3 large barns. **Brookefield** is 2½ miles from Nottingham. The bldgs are a tenant house, in good order; large corn house & stable, quarters for servants, & 2 large barns. **Cheltenham** is 7 miles from Nottingham; improvements are an excellent dwlg house, comparatively new, tenants' quarters, corn houses, stable, & 3 barns. -C C Magruder, Upper Marlboro -Peter W Crain, Balt City, trustees

WED AUG 19, 1868
Yesterday it was noticed that the restaurant & saloon of Henry Oentrich, at 11th & Pa ave, was not open for business as usual. Mr Julius Emmner & others forced their way into the house & found Oentrich dead on his bed, covered in blood. His right hand held a Colt's revolver; both hands were blackened with powder. The dec'd was 37 years of age, a native of Germany, & came to this country about 18 years ago. He leaves about $700 in the bank, besides other property, all of which he bequeathes, after payment of his debts, to his sister in Germany.

Orphans Court-Judge Purcell, Aug 18, 1868. 1-W E Mastin gave bond in the sum of $1,000 as guardian to orphans of Wm Mastin; John O'Neill & S H Sherwood, sureties. 2-Henry Vonder Heide gave bond in the sum of $2,000 as administrator of Anne Vonder Heide; Andress Spross & Louis Bayer, sureties. 3-The will of Charlotte Doubleday was filed & partially proven. The testatrix bequeathes her property to her daughter, Ann G McKinstry, & names her executrix. 4-The first & final account of Walter St Croix Redman, adm of J W Baker, was filed & passed.

Dr J S C Roland was yesterday appointed, by the President, U S Marshal for the Western District of Arkansas, vice Luther C White, suspended.

Lincoln Park, located just south of Lincoln Depot, is now being graded & beautified under the direction of Gen Michler, Superintendent of Public Bldgs & Grounds.

Mrs Cmdor Vanderbilt died of paralysis, on Monday, at the residence of her son-in-law, Hon Horace F Clark, 10 East 22nd st, N Y. She came down from Lebanon Springs on Aug 6, after her first attack, & for a day or two there was a fair promise of recovery. On Monday morning her complaint took a turn for the worse, & the result was announced.

Mrd: on Aug 16, in Wash City, at the residence of Col Henry R Clum, by Rev W W Dean, Mr ChasA Bates to Miss Alice A Lohness.

Died: on Aug 18, Kenneth Binoe, son of Dr J M & Helen H McCalla, aged 20 days. His funeral will take place from 404 C st, this morning at 10 o'clock.

Orphans Court of Wash Co, D C, Aug 18, 1868. In the case of Mary Essex & John T W Essex, admistrators c t a of Jas F Essex, sr, dec'd, the administrators c t a, & Court, have appointed Sept 15 next, for the final settlement of the personal estate of the said dec'd, of the assets in hand. -Jas R O'Beirne, Reg/o wills

THU AUG 20, 1868
Part of the will of the late Hon Thaddeus Stevens: admitted to probate on Tuesday; in his own handwriting. I bequeath to the trustees of title-holders of the graveyard in which my mother & brother, Alanson, are buried, in Peacham, Vt, $500 to keep their graves in order, & to plant roses & other cheerful flowers. I direct $100 to be paid to Thaddeus Stevens Brown, son of John E Brown, of Phil, at age. I give $2,000 to my nephew, Dr Thaddeus M Stevens, of Indianapolis. I give to his sister, Mrs Kauffman, $1,000. I give to Geo F Stevens, son of Simon Stevens, $1,000, to be put at interest, & paid to him by his father when he arrives at age. I give to Mrs Lydia Smith, my housekeeper, $500 a year during her natural life, to be paid semi annually; or, at her option, she may receive $5,000. I give to my nephew, Capt Thaddeus Stevens, now at Caledonia, my gold watch; also $800 a year to be paid half yearly. Mrs Smith may occupy the house the first year, & if Thaddeus, son of Morrill, prefers to keep house to boarding, he may keep house there with her, or with anyone else, during 3 years or part thereof. Executors & trustees, Anthony E Roberts, O J Dickey, & Edw McPherson, Jul 13, 1867. Witnessed in the presence of Edw Riley & Christopher Dice. Codicil: If my nephew, Maj Thaddeus Stevens, should get married before my decease, he will be at liberty to take possession of, & in fee, the house in which I now dwell, with the furniture thereof. –Thaddeus Stevens

Thos Dowling, auct, sold the property known as Jones' Soap Factory, on the upper road, above Gtwn, to Lewis Kengla, for $8,100. Also, the undivided 150 feet on the corner of Fred'k & 3rd sts, to Henry Whelan, for $19.25 per front foot.

The unexecuted portion of the sentences in each of the cases of Wm J Tolar, Thos Powers, & David Watkins, as mitigated on Nov 6, 1867, by Brvt Maj Gen E R S Canby, while commanding the 2nd Military Dist, is hereby remitted, & the Sec of War will issue the necessary orders for their release from military imprisonment. -Andrew Johnson [These prisoners were arrested & tried cojointly with Duncan G McRae & Saml Phillips, as to whom a nolle prosequi was entered, Phillips turning States evidence, & it being decided by the military commission that there was no evidence implicating McRae. The facts of the case: on Sunday, Feb 10, 1867, a respectable white girl, Miss Massey, returning from church to her home, in the vicinity of Fayetteville, N C, was met in the suburbs of the town, assaulted, dragged from the public highway, & brutally outraged; that on the same day, one Archie Beebe, a colored man, was arrested & charged with the crime; Beebe fully identified by the oath of the young lady; the prisoner, brought out a few minutes after the trial, was killed by a pistol shot, fired from the crowd. The dfndnts, Tolar, Powers, & Watkins were arrested by order of Gen Sickles. It does not appear that they had anything to do with the shooting; but it does appear that Phillips, who was acquitted, probably fired the pistol.]

Thos Dowling, auct, sold the property known as Jones' Soap Factory, on the upper road, above Gtwn, to Lewis Kengla, for $8,100. Also, the undivided 150 feet on the corner of Fred'k & 3rd sts, to Henry Whelan, for $19.25 per front foot.

Mrd: on Aug 18, at Rock Creek Church, by Rev Jas Bush, Dallas Johnson, M D, of Wash, D C, to Miss Lettie H Latimer, of Chas Co, Md.

Died: on Aug 19, of typhoid fever, Geo B Whiting, in his 24th year. His funeral will be from the residence of his father-in-law, Mr Evan Lyons, on Aug 21, at 10 o'clock A M.

Died: on Aug 16, Albert Edward, youngest son of Wm G & Catharine H Gallant, aged 11 months & 12 days.

FRI AUG 21, 1868
Titusville [Pa] Herald, Aug 17. Terrible collision on Sat, on the Oil Creek & Alleghany River railroad, at Rouseville. G E Marshall, of Corry, was killed outright. Jas Hare died on Sat night; Michl Perley died yesterday; Patrick Garvey died on Sunday; from their injuries. Michl Elliott was alive yesterday, but his recovery was pronounced impossible. He has a wife & several children. Dennis Sullivan; Jas Hollerin; Saml Poore, son of Conductor Poore; Patrick Lynch; John Murphy, Austin Carroll; Morris St Clair; & Mike Portland, were wounded.

Buffalo, Aug 19. Alleged fraud on the Gov't of a quarter of a million dollars, by a leading publishing house of this city. Messrs Calvin F S Thomas & Jas M Johnson, of the firm of Thomas, Howard, & Johnson, & A F Lee have been arrested, & held to bail in the sum of $10,000 each. Lee, late chief clerk of the Post Ofce, obtained receipts for a quarter of a million goods never furnished. The firm had a contract with the Post Ofc.

Augustin Iturbide, brother of the Prince Iturbide whom Maxilmilian adopted as his heir, now keeps a beer shop in the suburbs of Paris.

Boston, Aug 20. The examination of Dr Chas P Powers, on the charge of causing the death of Mrs Mary Abbie Bowen, by malpractice, resulted in his being committed for trial in default of bail.

Phil, Aug 20. Chas Cabot, president of the Allentown Rolling Mills, has absconded, leaving an indebtedness of from five hundred thousand to a million dollars. His partner in this city, L J Ettings, is believed to have been entirely ignorant of his indebtedness.

N Y, Aug 20. Wm P Holden, arrested on Aug 9 on a fictitious charge of stealing a carpet-bag from a train on the Erie road, is the robber of the American Express Ofc at Cedar Springs, Mich, on Mar 23, of a gold watch & $1,500. Deputy U S Marshal Cady, of Mich, is here awaiting a requisition to take Holden back.

Trenton, N J, Aug 20. Ralph A Shreve, Clerk of the U S Dist Court, died suddenly this afternoon. At one time he was a prominent Whig politician.

The following have been appointed store-keepers under the new internal revenue law: R H Cochrane, 6th Dist of Ky; Benj N Brooks, 1st Dist of Calif; Frank A Bayard, 1st Dist of Ill; John W Gregory, 12th Dist of Pa; C C Burr, 2nd Dist of Va; Uziah Stewart, 22nd Dist of Pa; & J J Tarman, 25th Dist of Pa.

SAT AUG 22, 1868
Died: on Aug 21, in Wash City, Annie T, only daughter of D M & Mollie Sylvester, aged 13 months & 2 days. Her funeral will take place from the residence of her parents, 155 5th st, between N & O sts, this afternoon, at 4 o'clock.

Hiram Ketchum, jr, of N Y, has been appointed Collector of Alaska.

Mrs Senator Sprague & Miss Chase were at Hudson, Wisc, a few days ago.

Lucerne, Aug 21. It became known to the Swiss authorities that an attempt was intended to have been made upon the life of the Queen of England during her recent sojourn in this place, & a strict search was made by the police for the parties concerned. Today a man, name not given, leaves no doubt that it was his deliberate design to assassinate Queen Victoria. He has been committed to prison to await a requisition from the British authorities.

Worcester, Aug 21. Two women & a boy were thrown from a carriage yesterday, while driving from Fayville to Ashland. The accident was caused by a harness breaking. Katy Dyer, 19 years of age, was instantly killed, & the other woman was seriously injured.

Catharine Chambers, deceased. Puruant to a decree of the High Court of Chancery of England, made, in a cause of "Eagles against Le Breton" the persons claiming to be the next of kin in America of Catharine Chambers, late of the town & county of Bedford, widow, dec'd, [who died in or about March, 1857,] or the present heir-at-law of the Catharine Chambers, are by their solicitors, on or before Dec 4, 1868, to come in & prove their claims at the chambers of the Master of the Rolls, in the Rolls Yard, Chancery La, Middlesex, England; or, in default thereof, they will be peremptorily excluded from the benefit of the said decree. Dec 18, 1868 is appointed for hearing & adjudicating upon the claims. –R B Church, Chief Clerk -Tamplin & Tayler, 159 Fenchurch st, Plaintiff's Solicitors

Supreme Court of D C, Equity 1,069. Wm Statter vs Catharine Baumann et al. Notice given to the parties in this cause, to the trustees appointed by the decree, to Chas Walter, guardian ad litem to the dfndnt Caroline Walter, & to such of the creditors of the late Paul Baumann, or of the said Catharine Baumann, devisee & excx of said Paul, as claim to have a lien upon the fund in the hands of said trustee, that on Aug 26 next, I shall proceed to state the account of said trustees, & the distribution of said fund. –W S Cox, auditor

N Y, Aug 21. Mr Elliott, the portrait painter, is reported to be at the point of death, at Albany.

The Sun says: Somewhere about 60 years ago Cornelius Vanderbilt commenced life by running a 'periauger' between Staten Island & N Y. During the day he plied his vocation & whenever his duties permitted visited his cousin, Miss Sophie Johnson, then a young & comely girl of 16, who also lived on the island. Perhaps it was the outburst of his first love that made the young sailor so ambitious, & inspired him with the energy & enterprise he has always exhibited. Certain it is, however, that the cousins married, & the old folks who knew them then speake with delight of the handsome pair, for they were admitted to be the comeliest couple Staten Island has ever produced. Cmdor Vanderbilt was once a ferryman until he was promoted, or more properly promoted himself to the position of captain of a steamboat, which he plied between this port & New Brunswick, N J. At the latter place he was proprietor of a hotel. His wife superintended the hotel while he was engaged in his active aquatic vocation. One evening at supper he told his wife he wished he had $5,000 to buy shares in the steamboat line. She consulted Mr Gibbons, & he advised the investment. The next evening at supper she gave him $5,000 to buy the shares. She had saved the money unbeknown to him, & it was probably this same money that floated the Cmdor into fame & fortune.

Col Jas N Caldwell has been detailed as Professor of Military Science at the Ky Univ, Lexington, Ky.

At Harmony Station, near Terra Haute, Ind, on Monday, Danl Diets, a butcher, cut his wife's throat with a butcher knife. The murdered woman was found soon afterwards by her husband's brother, & he gave the alarm, when a large crowd gathered & went in pursuit of the butcher. At last accounts he had not been caught.

John Kennedy was executed at Canton, N Y, on Thursday, for the murder of Thos Hand, in Feb, 1867.

MON AUG 24, 1868
Morweth Thame, a member of the Marine Corps, attempted to commit suicide on Sat, by taking a quantity of laudanum. He was found by Ofcr Stinchcomb in Jackson Square, &, but for prompt medical relief, would have died from the effects of the dose taken.

Mrd: on Aug 18, in Wash City, by Rev Mr Smith, Jos A Blain, of Richmond, Va, to Miss Emma C, youngest daughter of Dr John Stone, of Gtwn, D C. No cards. [Richmond, Petersburg, Phil, & St Louis [Mo] papers please copy.]

Died: on Aug 23, of consumption, Albert Fowler, in his 23rd year. His funeral will be from the residence of his father, Fred'k & 7th sts, Gtwn, on Aug 25 at 4 o'clock P M.

Died: on Aug 23, of brain fever, Rudolph, infant child of Rudolph & Annie Eichorn, aged 9 months & 24 days. His funeral will be from the residence of his parents, 3rd & F sts, this afternoon at 4:30 o'clock P M.

Reuben Sykes, of Bennington, Vt, in a recent fit of delirium tremens, chopped off the hands & feet of his infant child.

On Friday, Miss Isabella Smith, aged 17 years, daughter of Gen Kilby Smith, U S Consul at Panama, was accidentally drowned at Torresdale, on the Delaware river. Her body has not yet been recovered.

Chas B Lewis, local editor of a Michigan paper, who was crippled for life & greatly disfigured by the ship **Magnolia** disaster last spring, has brought suit against the owner of the boat for $30,000 damages.

TUE AUG 25, 1868
Died: on Aug 17, Jas De Shields, infant son of J Thomas & Mattie A Petty. [Va papers please copy.]

Died: on Aug 24, after a long & painful illness, Mrs Sarah Pickering, in her 79th year. Her funeral will be from the residence of her son-in-law, Wm Chambers, on 10th st, between O & P sts, this afternoon at 5 o'clock. [Alexandria Gaz copy.]

N Y, Aug 24. Prof Geo J Adler, a well-known author of several German scholastic works, died today.

Benj Bridley, 65, was shot in the head, severely injured, & robbed of $200 by Cornelius McQuirk, near the water works at Natick, Mass, on Sat. McQuirk is still at large.

The Treasury robbery-arrest of the wife of the accused thief, J H A Schureman, a colored messenger in the ofc of the Comptroller of the Currency, who was arrested some months since, charged with the abstracion of notes of various national banks from that bureau amounting to $12,000; & was held by the court to bail in the sum of $10,000, the case never being disposed of, the proof not being sufficient to convict, but the court refusing to discharge him. One day last week Mrs Georgia Schureman, his wife, called at the store of Mr Furst, on 9th st, & after making purchases, tendered a $50 note in payment. Mr Furst informed her that he didn't like the appearance of the note, & she said she received it in the market, & she would return & see the man there who gave it to her. Mr Furst sent word to the Treasury Dept, & it was identified as one of the missing notes. She was held in the sum of $1,000 for a further hearing. [Aug 29, 1868 newspaper: Examination resumed yesterday; Witnesses called-Jos Burroughs, Horatio Nater, J F Bates, [employed in the ofc of Comptroller;] John M Duncanson, teller in the Nat'l Bank of the Republic; Frank Newton; employed at Mr Brett's, 9th & F sts; Edw Myer, David Lewis, J W Griffin, J W Peck, A Magruder, Henry Kelly, & L M Price.] [Aug 31st newspaper: Miss Kate Vance was sworn; resides with Mrs A K Stuntz, on N Y ave, near 10th st; keeps a fancy store; Mary Witteraner, another young lady, was in the store at the time; Mary Witteraner, sworn; Mrs A E Stuntz, sworn; Mr Hurlburl recalled; Jos G Summers sworn-resides in Balt.] [Sep 1st newspaper: Sarah Boudine, colored, lives in Gtwn; was acquainted with Mrs Schureman; Miss Catharine Smith testified she lived with Mrs Schureman; was a dressmaker; Jos S Weems testified; Robt H Robertson & W S Dupuy testified.]

WED AUG 26, 1868
Perry Fuller to be Collector of Customs at New Orleans, vice Kellogg.

The Sec of the Treasury yesterday appointed John E Smith, Collector of Customs at Wiscasset, Maine; also, Henry J Goss Collector of Customs at St Augustine, Fla, vice E K Foster, resigned.

Lt McGee, 20th U S infty, "the drummer boy of Murfreesboro," is reported to have killed Dr Braman, surgeon of the post, at Baton Rouge, La, in a recent personal difficulty.

A telegram from Pittsfield, Mass: Jerry Murray, of Lowell, attempted to kill his wife in a train on the Pittsfield & North Adams railroad, by shooting her through the head. The wound is not fatal. In default of $10,000 bail, Murray was sent to jail to await trial.

Orphans Court-Judge Purcell, Aug 25, 1868. 1-The will of John Smith was admitted to probate & letters issued. 2-The will of Edw W Farley was fully proven, admitted to probate, & letters issued. 3-Edw Droop gave bond in the sum of $3,000, as administrator of Henry Oentrick. W B Todd, jr, & C M Baker, sureties. 4-Laura Farley gave bond in the sum of $20,000, as excx of Edw W Farley. Henry Turner & M A Turner, sureties.

Died: on Jul 29 last, in Upperville, Fauquier Co, Va, Mrs Frances S, beloved wife of Wm G Yerby, in her 69th year of age.

Died: on Aug 25, Maude Eliza, youngest daughter of Dr J Ford & Marion V Thompson, aged 13 months. Her funeral will from the residence of her grandmother, Mrs S A Greeves, 357 9th st, Mass ave, this afternoon at 3 o'clock.

Boston, Aug 25. Cmdor Jas Armstrong died in Charlestown today.

Miss J O Abbott will resume the duties of her School on Sep 7.

West St Academy, Gtwn, D C, Julius Soper, A M, Principal; will resume on Sep 1st. For particulars apply to the Principal, 59 First st, Gtwn, D C.

Prof Esputa's Musical Academy, will open on Aug 31, 1868. Call at his house, 513 8th st east, or at the Academy.

Prof Montgomery Johns, PH D, Boarding & Day School for Boys. Woodside School, near Hyattsville, PG Co, Md; fall session will open Sep 9.

Alnwick Seminary for Young Ladies, by M A Tyson & Sisters; Institution will be resumed on Sep 7. For circulars apply at Dr Tyson's drug store, 9th & L sts; or address Laurel P O, PG Co, Md.

Wesleyan Female College, Wilmington, Delaware; next session will begin Sep 10, 1868. -John Wilson, Pres

Orphans Court of Wash Co, D C. Letters testamentary on the personal estate of Edw W Farley, late of Wash Co, dec'd. –Laura Amney Farley, excx

Orphans Court of Wash Co, D C. Letters testamentary on the personal estate of John Smith, late of Wash Co, dec'd. –Margaret Smith, excx

Young Ladies Boarding & Day Seminary, Mrs General Wheeler, Principal, No 13 Third st, Gtwn, D C. The Seminary will be resumed Sep 7th.

The West End, Classical Mathematical & English Academy, will be opened in the Friends' Meeting House, I st, between 18th & 19th sts, on Sep 1. Apply to Rev C H Nourse, 349 N Y ave.

Frederick Female Seminary, Frederick, Md; will commence its 26th scholastic year the first Monday in Sept. Address Rev Thos M Cann, A M, Pres

Information wanted of Michl Glancy, aged 23; height 5 feet 8½ inches; hair, black; eyes grey; nose rather large; build, stout, forehead, average; became insane at Newport, Ky, while a soldier & escaped from guard while being transported to Gov't Insane Asylum at Wash. Any information will be thankfully received by his brother, John Glancy, 126 Cass st, Chicago, Ill.

Buel Hall, 322 I st; Mrs Rufus F Buel's Boarding & Day School for Young Ladies & Misses will reopen on Sep 22. Address Mrs Buel, by letter, as above.

St John's Hall, a Seminary for Young Ladies, 196 I st, between 20th & 21st sts, will be resumed on Sep 7. –Rev A J Faust, M A, Principal

Consolidated Business College, Wash, D C, will commence on Sep 1. Address at the College ofc, 7th & D sts, or address Henry C Spencer, Sec.

St Clement's Hall, Ellicott's Mills, Md, near Balt, Rev J Avery Shepherd, D D, Head Master. The third annual session will open on Sep 7.

Cumberland Valley Institute, for Young Gentlemen, Mechanicsburg, Pa, will commence Sep 7. -Rev O Ege & Son. Irving Female College, Rev T P Ege, A M, President.

THU AUG 27, 1868
Capt H B Nones, U S revenue cutter service, died at his residence in Wilmington, Del, on Tuesday, in his 65th year.

Chas Loring Elliott, one of the most distinguished of American portrait painters, died at his residence in Albany on Tuesday. He was born in Scipio, N Y, in 1812, but the greater part of his childhood was passed at Syracuse, where his father placed him at first in a store, &, when the boy's distaste for mercantile pursuits became too strong to be resisted, attempted to educate him in his own calling as an architect. The lad was quite averse to this profession & came to N Y & became a pupil of Trumbull & Quidor. He pursued his occupation in the western part of the State for about 10 years; making a reputation as a portrait painter. Among his last protraits was one of Erastus Corning; he was engaged upon one of Lt Govn'r Woodford, when seized with his final sickness, having suffered for some time from a tumor on the brain. [Aug 28th newspaper: He has left his wife & son well provided for, in independent circumstances. Of his family present during his illness was his wife & only son, his sister, Mrs Fitch, of Syracuse, & his sister-in-law. He will be buried in **Greenwood Cemetery**, which was his expressed wish.] [Aug 29th newspaper: Mr Elliott, it is said, left his family a property worth $80,000.] [Aug 31st newspaper: The funeral of Mr Elliott took place at the Academy of Design in N Y, on Sat; at his head was hung the palette, brushes, & mahlstick which he had formerly used; at the opposite end of the room was suspended an admirable portrait of the deceased, by Geo A Baker. The pall-bearers were the artists Gray, Hicks, Johnson, Palmer, Lang, Jas Hart, & Thayer. The remains were conveyed to **Greenwood Cemetery**.]

St Louis, Aug 25. Gen Sherman's daughter, Minnie, was thrown from a horse on Monday & badly bruised. The accident will detain Gen Sherman at **Fort Sanders** a few days.

New Orleans, Aug 26. Jos Mann, the only Democratic Representative in Congress from Louisiana, died this morning of congestion of the brain; age about 55 years.

Special Indian Agent W J Cullen writes to the Indian Bureau from *Fort Benton*, Montana, under date of Jul 27, enclosing letters which were found on the bodies of 7 men murdered by Indians at a place called Sanbiers' Woodyard, on the Missouri river, about 80 miles below *Fort Hawley*. They were buried by Capt Hovey, of the steamer **Levi Leoti**, on Jul 13. The names of 6 of them were: Henry Laubie, of Pittsburg, Pa; Wm Whittaker, of Phil; L Koysen, of St Louis; Frank L Burton, Lagrange, Tenn; Dowdell, St Louis; & Jones, home unknown.

Manayunk, Aug 26. Albert Tuckens, proprietor of the Fountain Hotel, was run over by the passenger cars last night & killed.

Phil, Aug 26. Dr L Q C Wishoot, manufacturer of tar cordial, died suddenly this afternoon in a drug store near his residence.

St Peter's Academy, in charge of the Sisters of the Holy Cross, will open on Sep 7, at 12 Duddington Pl, corner of First st east & C st south, Capitol Hill.

Boston, Aug 26. A young man, Geo Lackrider, a clerk in the employ of Lackrider & King, commission merchants, forged checks to the amount from $160,000 to $180,000, which were paid by the Market Bank, & then absconded. His whereabouts are unknown.

It is stated that Sec McCulloch accepted the resignation of Mr S M Clarke, Superintendent of the Printing Bureau, & appointed Mr Geo McCartee in his place.

Col Geo Hancock, of Jefferson Co, Ky, is said to have an original letter of Gen Washington, dated Mar, 1787.

Michl Doyle, residing near Towsontown, in Balt Co, was shot & killed on Aug 22 by John Carroll, a neighbor. A pig belonging to Carroll got into Doyle's cornfield. An action was brought against Carroll for damages, & a trial was had on Sat, after which the parties, as they were returning home, got into a quarrel, resulting in the killing of Doyle. Carroll was arrested, & is now in the Towsontown jail.

The *Herbart estate*, in PG Co, Md, 167 acres of farming land, was sold to Thos E Lloyd, for $21 per acre, $3,507.

FRI AUG 28, 1868
Michl Leonard & John Burns, of St Louis, got into an altercation on Wed in relation to some domestic matter. Leonard stabbed Burns with a bowie-knife, inflicting a wound from which he died. Burns' wife was also stabbed & killed.

Raleigh, N C, Aug 27. Hon David L Swain, LL D, late president of our university, died today, at his residence, at Chapel Hill. Some weeks ago he, with Prof Felton, were thrown from a wagon, & Mr Swain was seriously injured.

The Most Rev Archbishop Spalding made the following pastoral changes & appointments, to take effect immediately. Rev Desiderius De Wulf, now assistant pastor at St Matthew's, Wash, to be resident pastor of Westernport, attending the neighboring missions of Barton & Oakland, with its dependencies. Rev Laurence Malloy, now pastor of St Thos Aquinas, Hampden Village, to be pastor of St Joseph's, Texas, with the annexed missionary district. Rev Dwight E Lyman, to take charge as pastor of St Thos Aquinas, & the new chapel at Mount Washington, & the dependent missions, with Rev Francis P Duggan as assistant. Rev Edw Brennan, of St Patrick's, Cumberland, to be pastor of the neighboring churches of St Michael, Frostburg, & St Patrick's, Mount Savage, with Rev Jas P Carey & Rev Valentine F Schmidt, as assistants, besides Rev Jeremiah Hendricks, already associated with him. The new church at Lonaconing is also attached for the present to this mission. Rev L A Morgan, now pastor of St Michael's, Frostburg, is transferred to the Church of St Vincent de Paul, in Balt, having been appointed assistant to Rev Henry Myers. Rev Thos Lee, now assistant at St Vincent de Paul's Church, in Balt, is named secretary of the Most Rev Archbishop, & is transferred to the Metropolitan Church. Rev Jas F Mackin is appointed assistant to Rev Dr White, in the Church of St Matthew, Wash City. Rev Jeremiah O'Sullivan is named assistant to Rev Dr Chappelle, in the missions of Montgomery Co.

Board of Metropolitan Police: Pvt Robt French was fined $5 for violating the rules of the force. The following were appointed privates on the force: Lewis P Seibold, John R Allen, Robt W Dunn, & John Dailey. The following additional privates were appointed: John W Kitchen, for 6 months, to do duty on Water st, Gtwn; Henry E Norris, for 6 months, to do duty on Pa ave, between 12th & 13th sts; Hamlet Dixon, for 12 months, to do duty at Wisewell Barracks.

Mrs McClaning, an actress attached to the Boston Museum company, died on Wednesday, after a brief illness.

Maj Perry Fuller yesterday entered his bond, $100,000 as Collector of Customs for the port of New Orleans. He received his commission, & will leave for New Orleans today.

It is said the Oliver Dalrymple, who is the largest farmer in the State of Minnesota, having 1,700 acres devoted to wheat, will have cleared $100,000 from the last 2 harvests, which includes the one now being secured.

SAT AUG 29, 1868
Mrd: on Aug 23, at the residence of his father, Augustus P Webb, of Balt, Louis S Webb to Julia Van Ness Capron, of Wash, D C, daughter of the late Capt E A Capron, U S army.
+
Died: on Aug 25, in Balt, at the residence of his father, after a painful illness, Louis S Webb, eldest son of Augustus P Webb.

Mrd: on Aug 22, at Wash, by Rev C C Meador, R A Coates, of Fredericksburg, to Frances A Baldason, eldest daughter of Wm O Baldason, of Spottsylvania Co, Va. [Fredericksburg papers please copy.]

Wash, D C, Aug 24, 1868. In consequence of my failing health, necessitating my retiring from business, the copartnership existing between Geo Parker, Geo T Parker, & Saml G Parker, is this day dissolved by mutual consent. Geo Parker, sr, will pay all the indebtedness of said firm. –Geo Parker, Geo Thos Parker, Saml G Parker

The paving of 7th st to Boundary st is being rapidly pushed forward by the contractor, Mr J R Deeter, & will be completed this fall.

The School of the Good Shepherd, for Boarding & Day Scholars, Balt, is under the direction of the Sisterhood of the Good Shepherd; facing the s w corner of Franklin Square; religious teaching is in the hands of Rev C W Rankin, Rector of St Luke's Church. Application to be made to the Sister Superior, 594 West Fayette st, Balt, Md.

New Orleans, Aug 28. Wm O King, principal editor & proprietor of the New Orleans Times, died yesterday, after a lingering illness.

Louisville, Aug 27. Jos Rabbetti, aged about 68, for many years employed by the Western Union Telegraph Co, committed suicide this afternoon by shooting himself through the heart. Domestic troubles are said to have prompted the deed.

Harrison Young, a colored man, convicted 2 years since of murdering Mr Wooten, of Warwick Co, Va, was hung at Warwick Court-house on Tuesday.

Real estate. Perry W Lowe purchased a 2 story dwlg house, 39 south side First st, between Market & Potomac, Gtwn, for $5,200. E Kaufman purchased a 2 story brick dwlg, 291 Prospect st, between High & Potomac, for $4,325. The **Bell Farm**, near Falls Church, Fairfax Co, Va, containing 300 acres of land, improved by a dwlg, etc, was sold to Maj B C Whiting, of Mass, for $12,000.

MON AUG 31, 1868
Biographies of Grant: The soldiers will never fail to denounce Grant for having refused to make the exchanges of prisoners, which would have saved thousands from the sufferings that subsequently entailed disease & death. When gaunt disease was upon them, & death stared then in the face, & the grave yawned for its victims, the rebel Gov't, shown by Mr Ould & Gen Butler, besought our Gov't to send surgeons, food, medicine, & clothing to them, Gen Grant, to whom the matter was referred by our Gov't at Washington, refused to do so. He also refused to let the Confederate Gov't, upon their request for the purpose, have medicines, food, & clothing for the Union prisoners. For four long mortal months Grant refused to send steamships to take away the sufferers at Andersonville, whereby he became in effect the murderer of such as would have survived had transportation been previously sent, & of many of these who subsequently died.

Announcement yesterday in the Catholic churches of the District of the death of Mrs Fanny Keane, wife of Hugh Keane, of Balt, & mother of Rev J J Keane, assist pastor of St Patrick's Church, of Wash City.

Friends of the Marine Bank will be pained to learn that Prof M Perrez, who has for so many years played the octave flute in this band, is now confined in the Marine Hospital from a severe attack of paralysis, & but little hope is entertained of his recovery.

Orphans Court-Judge Purcell, Aug 29, 1868. 1-Jas Lackey relinquished his right to qualify as testamentary guardian to the orphans of Timothy Corcoran, [appointed under the will,] & letters testamentary were issued to Margaret Corcoran; bond $500. 2-Mrs R M McCulloch & her daughters renounced the right to administer on the estate of Jas Page McCulloch, in favor of M Ashford, who qualified by giving bond in $3,000. 3-The will of Patrick Corcoran, bequeathing his estate to his family, was filed & fully proven. 4-The will of the late Lewis Beard was fully proven. He bequeaths his estate to his family, & nominates Eliz R Beard & Jas Y Davis, excs, to whom letters testamentary were issued; bond $40,000. 5-The first & final account of C B Baker, collector of the personal estate of Owen Munson; of Jacob L Darwart, adm of Cornelia Martin; & of John Frizzell, adm c t a of John C Frizzell, were approved & passed. 6-The will of Laura Bell was filed & partially proven.

Last night Mr Williams, an elderly gentleman, employed as clerk for Gen Michler, Superintendent of Public Bldgs, died very suddenly. He was with his wife looking out the window, when blood suddenly issued from his mouth, & he fell upon the bed lifeless. Dr Toner pronounced the cause of his death hemorrhage of the lungs. Mr Williams leaves a wife & children, & a large circle of friends to mourn his loss.

Accidents: 1-On Sat Maj John T Clawson, of Va, stepping into a carriage, his foot slipped, & he fell with great force to the curbstone, between the wheels of the vehicle, injuring himself severely about the face & body. He was taken to the room of his brother-in-law, near by, & properly cared for. 2-Sat, as Mr R Wheatley was driving in a buggy on 7th st, the vehicle came into collision with a wagon, & was upset throwing Mr Wheatley out. He was slightly bruised. 3-A daughter of Mr McLinden was run over on Saturday & severely injured.

Mrd: on Aug 26, at Warrenton, Fauquier Co, Va, by Rev Mr Hubert, John W Wallace, of Christian Co, Ky, to Emma S Downman, daughter of the late John B Downman, of Fauquier Co. [Fredericksburg papers copy.]

Died: on Aug 30, in Wash City, after a long & painful illness, Frank T Sands, aged 34 years. He leaves a wife & 6 children. His funeral will take place at his late residence, 521 E st, between 8th & 9th sts, Navy Yard, at 11 o'clock, Monday, Aug 31, 1868.

Mme Amelie Strakosch, [sister of Adelina & Carlotta Patti,] is to make her debut as a contralto at the Italian Opera House in Paris.

Chicago, Aug 29. 1-Gen Grant was serenaded this evening at the residence of his brother by the tanners' organization of this city. He will return to Galena on Monday, & remain there a month or so longer. 2-Larkin G Meade, the Vt sculptor, has arrived here from Florence, with a design for the Lincoln monument at Springfield. 3-Adj Gen L Thomas arrived in this city this morning, on his tour of inspection of national cemeteries.

El Paso, Texas, Aug 12. The train of Mr Thos Everett, engaged in freighting flour to *Fort Cummings*, was attacked by Indians on his return trip 30 miles from the fort. After a desperate fight the train was taken by the Indians, with all the mules, & Mr Everett & 4 of his men were wounded, one mortally.

Detroit, Aug 30. Tragedy at Bell river, a small station on Great river, Canada. The saw & grist mill of E Van Orden was burned, & Van Orden, his wife, & nephew were burned. It is supposed they were robbed & murdered before the mills were fired.

Wm H C King, the principal editor & proprietor of the New Orleans Times, died on Thursday, after a lingering illness.

Wm H Ganley, 18 years old, son of Dominick Ganley, well-known citizen of Troy, N Y, was killed on Fri while attempting to jump on a passing train. Six cars passed over him.

Liverpool, Aug 29. Mr R A Curd, a prominent merchant of this city, died Aug 27th; the house of Curd & Co, is largely engaged in the cotton trade.

N Y, Aug 29. 1-Thos Collum, a letter carrier, was held to trial today for stealing letters. 2-Jas McMahon was found dead in West 20th st today, & his wife had been arrested for his murder. 3-Jas Colgan, the diver who was rescued from the diving bell at the navy yard, has remained partially unconscious until this morning, when he expired. 4-Patrick Morrissey, who stabbed his mother in court a few day ago, was sentenced to 6 months in the penitentiary. 5-Emil Ormsby, after endeavoring to kill his uncle, because the latter refused to allow him to address his daughter, cut his own throat. Both were found alive, the uncle with his head broken by a hammer, & it is thought that both will survive. Young Ormsby has been committed to jail to stand trial at the court in Chappagua, Westchester Co, where the attempted murder & suicide took place. 6-At the inquest at the lying-in hospital, in Amity st, over the body of a young girl, Susannah Latten, evidence was given showing that all the infants born were given away to unknown parties. It is a private concern, carried on by Dr Grindel & his wife, who are said to be now in Wisconsin. The place was patronized mostly by married ladies. The evidence relative to the girl Latten was the usual unfortunate history of seduction.

Orphans Court of Wash Co, D C. Letters of administration on the personal estate of Jas P McCulloch, late of Wash, D C, dec'd. –M Ashford, adm

Orphans Court of Wash Co, D C, Aug 29, 1868. In the case of Wm Albert King, adm of Thos Halloran, dec'd, the administrator & Court have appointed Sep 26 next, for the final settlement of the personal estate of the said dec'd, of the assets in hand.
-Jas R O'Beirne, Reg/o wills

Orphans Court of Wash Co, D C. Letters testamentary on the personal estate of Lewis Beard, late of Wash, D C, dec'd. –Jas Y Davis, Eliza R Beard, excs

TUE SEP 1, 1868
Louisville Courier, Aug 28. Dr Saml E McKinley, son of Judge McKinley, formerly Judge of the Supreme Court of the U S, & U S Judge of this circuit, was residing & practicing his profession at New Orleans when the city was captured by the Federal army; he was retained as surgeon for the Confederate sick, & afterward retained in the U S service. The doctor married a very wealthy heiress, Miss Morrison, of La, by whom he had 2 children, James, now with him in St Louis, & a daughter, E J Lyon McKinley, age 12 years. His wife dying during the infancy of the girl, the Dr, in 1864, moved to New Albany, Ind, taking with him his 2 children. About a year ago last winter, he moved to this city, where he remained till some time in 1867, & becoming desirous of going back to New Orleans to look after his property, left his little daughter at the Ursuline Academy, a Catholic female school in this city, for education, sending her from time to time money to pay her expenses. The Dr, having established himself in St Louis, requested Judge Taylor to send by Adams Express his little daughter to him, the Company agreeing to undertake the care & custody of the child. When Judge Taylor applied for the child, the Superior of the Academy objected to letting her go till her tuition should be fully paid. The Dr declared he had sent by mail the full amount, & then came for her himself. His counsel advising him that the Academy could not retain a lien on the child for their money, he sued out a writ of habeas corpus before his Honor Judge Bruce, & this case is the first broughr before Judge Bruce since qualifying as our Circuit Judge. The Superiors of the Academy, answering the writ, stated that the girl was named Lizzie Brown; that she was not the Dr's daughter; that she was 15 years of age, & that the Dr was drunken & unfit to control the child. It seems that the Superior applied to the county court to become her guardian, & exhibited, it is claimed, a printed envelope with the name of E J Lyon McKinley, in which her father had enclosed money to his daughter, this being the true name. It is also alleged he has letters from the Superior calling her, his daughter, Lyon. It is further said that she has become a Catholic, contrary to her father's wishes, who is an Episcopalian, & that she will, at her grandfather's death, become the heiress of more than a million. The Court ruled the answer of the respondent insufficient, & required her to be more explicit. This trial will develop some of the strangest points of law & fact known to jurisprudence. [Jan 18, 1869 newspaper: The "heiress case" in the Louisville courts has been decided against Dr S E McKinley, who petitioned for the custody of his daughter, aged 12, now held by the Mother Superior of the Ursuline Academy in that city. The Court held that the father was not a fit person to be entrusted with his daughter. She is a child by his third wife, who died in 1858, leaving a large fortune to her infant. The Doctor has been married five times in all, & is on the eve of a sixth matrimonial venture.]

A Rothschild has bought the whole vineyard of the Chateau Lafitte.

Robt Allen & Mathew Riley, while tearing down a portion of Coat-st Terrace, in Cincinnati, yesterday, were instantly killed by a falling bldg.

Mrs Gen Sherman arrived at Omaha on Friday, from Lancaster, Ohio, en route to *Fort Sanford*, where her daughter still remains very ill.

J Vincent Brown, collector for the 5th Mass district, died at Salem on Saturday.

Administrator's sale of handsome household & kitchen furniture at auction on Sep 3, at the late residence of Henry S Barnes, dec'd, on M st, between 7th & 8th sts.
–Henry Weaver, adm -Green & Williams, aucts

Boston, Aug 31. A train from Lawrence to Lowell yesterday ran into a crowd of boys gathering on the railroad bridge at Gorham Station, instantly killing Geo Lee, age 10 years, & Robt T Donly, age 7 years.

The cable announces the death of the wife of Victor Hugo. She had been the companion of Hugo from his earliest boyhood, being brought up in Paris in the former convent of the Feullantines. A mutual attachment sprang up between the playmates, which lasted through life. As he was poor, permission to marry the friend of his youth was for some time withheld, but the glory which was acquired ty the publication of the Odes et Ballades overcame all obstacles. The married life of Victor Hugo was one of great happiness, his wife being, in all the many vicissitudes which awaited the poet, his most devoted friend. While living with him in exile, she wrote, in 1863, a life of her husband, under the title, Victor Hugo raconte par un temoin de sa vie, 2 vols.

Internal Revenue appointments of gaugers & storekeepers:
Gaugers:
Timithy J Murray, Maine
John Hodgson, N H
Jas B Straw, N Y
Lucius H Goff, Vt
Geo B Isham, Vt
John O Pierce, Mass
Jas L Burbank, Mass
Henry M Phillips, Mass
Edw G Farmer, R I
Fred'k A King, Conn
David B Hale, Conn
John H Simmons, Conn
Wyatt C Martin, Conn
Wm H Doty, N Y
Jas Woods, N Y
Michl Mallon, N Y
Geo P Stewart, N Y
Robt M Myers, N Y
Chas Young, N Y
Stephen W Vandevanter, N Y
Elizur Wager, N Y
John Donahue, Dela
Thos H Walton, Pa
Chas P Durham, Pa
John H Sell, Pa
Chas A Lichtenhaler, Pa
Abraham H Seem, Pa
Am L Ritter, Pa
T Throp, Pa
R Graggin, Pa

Nathl B Reese, Va
Harvy Risk, Va
Louis H Porter, Va
Peter A Frercks, N C
Gerard Baucker, S C
Thos P Slider, S C
Edw T Pillsbury, Ga
Cornelius Van Arsdale, Ga
Edw Barinds, Miss
Everett W Foster, Ark
Henry C Hayman, Ark
John E Williamson, Ky
Nimrod B Allen, Ky
Jos V Hobson, Ky
Jas W Young, Ky
N A Rapier, Ky
Jas C Gill, Ky
Johnson Mason, Ky
Edw Martz, Ky
J B McClintock, Ky
B H Niemeyer, Ky
John W Wheeler, Ky
A H Sympson, Ky
Thos Kelly, Ky
Jas M Givens, Ky
Thos C Reed, Ky
Sidney K Turner, Ky
D M Lackey/Luckey, Ky
Thompson B Oldham, Ky
John E Browning, Ky
Jos D Wyatt, Ky
Robt Market, Mo
A J Sampson, Mo
Jas S Norton, Ill
A V Richards, Ill
Jas Scott, Ill
John H Holton, Ill
Jas C Starr, Ill
Otto Funky, Ill
Jas R Ashley, Ill
Wm J Florrer, Ill
Danl McKenzie, Ill
Jas L Briggs, Ill
David Armstrong, Ill
Robt E Haggard, Ill

Benedict Walter, Ill
August Fritz, Ill
Alfred Comings, Ill
Lucius S French, Ind
Jas M Riley, Ind
John G Sering, Ind
David B Wilson, Ind
R C Archibald, Ind
J W Eldridge, Ind
Sidney McGuire, Ind
Wm W Waddell, Ohio
Wm Rowe, Ohio
A D Brayden, Ohio
E H Osborn, Ohio
Alonzo Rogers, Ohio
David Hull, Ohio
Andrew Ingles, Ohio
J L Kessinger, Ohio
J H Officer, Ohio
Oliver C Carter, Ohio
Oliver Bourke, Ohio
Chas Bell, Ohio
Wm Page, Ohio
Edw Leavenworth, Ohio
Edw Welchman, Iowa
Edw Fay, Iowa
H C Darrah, Iowa
R B Stevenson, Iowa
A Newton, Iowa
Chas E Heath, Iowa
W T Palmer, Wisc
Wm L Norris, Wisc
Danl Brisbois, Wisc
F L Higbee, Wisc
Jas B Hunt, Wisc
W W Webb, Wisc
Alonzo Fulla, Kan
A J Edgertown, Minn
J V Daniels, Minn
B R McIntire, Dak
Geo E Crater, Colo
Benj Lowenstein, New Mexico,
Hugh Fulton, Neb
B S Prickett, Idaho

Storekeepers:
A D Johnson, Ky
H H Wayman, Ky
G M Thrasher, Ky
Jas H Bishop, Ky
E E Bowers, Ky
John B Hannah, Ind
Leander J Shepard, Ind
Wm T Suliwell/Sullwell, Ind

Abraham Kago, Ohio
Jas Segar, jr, Va
W W Bassett, Md
Albert Trego, Md
C G Fry, Va
Sanford E Chaffee, Va
John R Warneck

Died: on Aug 30, Thos J Williams, in his 60th year. His funeral will take place on Sep 3 at 2:30 P M, from the residence of Mrs C W Heydon, Pa ave, between 6th & 7th sts. [Sep 2nd newspaper: Masonic notice of the funeral of Past Deputy Grand Master, Brother T J Williams. –Noble D Larner, Grand Sec. Knights Templar: the Sir Knights of the Columbia Commandery, notice of the funeral of Frater, Sir T J Williams. –A T Longley, Recorder.]

Obit-drowned on Aug 21, Arabella Theresa, 2nd daughter of Gen Thos Kilby Smith, aged 16 years. Ask the "Sisters" under whose careful guidance she was placed, training both for earth & Heaven; ask her parents, to whom her presence was a light & joy; ask her brothers & her sister, & they will say she was as lovely in disposition & character as she was in that outward beauty of form & countenence, which could not fail to strike even the chance acquaintance & stranger. Yesterday she was carried to her quiet resting place, where, the full rites of the Church were pronounced.

Cold-blooded murder on Friday in Queen Anne's Co, Md: a man Reamy Gilmore, industrious, honest, & inoffensive farmer, aged about 40 years, residing on a farm belonging to the heirs of the Late Judge Chambers, on the road from Church Hill to Chestertown, was found dead & his wife lying in an insensible condition, but still alive, by a negro man & woman who had been engaged by Mr Gilmore to "save fodder" for him. They gave the alarm to Mr Gilmore's neighbors, who made the murder known to the ofcrs of the law; Justice Tarbutton, of Cumpton, summoned a jury of inquest, & among the witness was a negro woman, Martha Berwick, Mr Gilmore's cook, who finally confessed that a certain negro man in the neighborhood, who was in the habit of visiting her, named Michl Bell, & herself, had formed a plot to murder & rob Mr Gilmore. Bell attacked Mr & Mrs Gilmore with an axe in their bedrooms, killing Mr Gilmore instantly. Bell then searched for booty & left the premises. The woman was committed to jail. Michl Bell has not yet been caught. The murdered man was childless.

WED SEP 2, 1868
Albany, N Y, Sep 1. This afternoon a portion of a wall on the north side of Columbia st, west of Broadway, in progress of demolition, fell, burying people in the ruins. Robt Fitzgerald, a boy, was rescued with injury; the body of Miss Hogan, age 65 years, was found; & the body of Mrs McIntyre was brought from the ruins.

On Aug 18 nine negroes broke into Mrs Marks' house, near **Swain's Mill**, N C, violated her & her little daughter, & as the latter screamed, they tore her tongue from her mouth, & beat out her brains against the jamb of the fire-place. They then killed Mrs Marks' little boy, & set fire to the house. A servant, who had escaped from the house, gave the alarm to the neighbors, who extinguished the flames & released Mrs Marks, who was found insensible & tied by her hands & feet to the bed. The bodies of the girl & boy were buried, & measures were taken to arrest the negroes, who were supposed to be secreted in the woods.

Orphans Court-Judge Purcell, Sep 1, 1868. 1-The will of the late Jos Bradley, bequeathing his estate to his wife, was filed. 2-Mary A Ballinger was appointed guardian to the orphans of Geo W Ballinger; bond, $500.

Died: on Aug 31, after a lingering illness, Eliz L, wife of Saml W Pearson, of Wash City, in her 56th year. Her funeral is today at 2 o'clock P M, from her late residence, 326 G st, between 12th & 13th sts.

Died: on Sep 1, Peter W Miller, in his 23rd year, at his late residence, 12th & Boundary sts. His funeral will take place on Thursday morning at 9 o'clock.

Died: Sep 1, in her 33rd year, Georgie, wife of A Jackson Beall, & eldest daughter of Geo Hill, jr. Her funeral will take place Thursday morning, at 10 o'clock. The services will be held at **Oak Hill Chapel**. Friends of the family are invited without further notice.

Died: on Aug 31, in Gtwn, D C, Mary Ellen, infant daughter of Edw J & Indiana M Shoemaker, aged 1 year, 5 months & 27 days.

Died: on Sep 1, Helen J Mickle, youngest child of John & Jane Mickle, aged 10 months & 12 days. Her funeral will take place from the residence of her parents, 563 10th st, Island, on Sep 2 at 4 o'clock P M.

Hon Francis Granger died in Canandaigua on Friday, at the age of 81 years. He was a son of Hon Gideon Granger, who was Postmaster Gen under Jefferson. His father removed early in this century to Canandaigua from Conn. Mr Francis Granger was a member of Assembly in this State for 5 years from 1826; in 1830 & 1832, he was a candidate for Govn'r; was elected to Congress in 1835 & 1839; resigned to take the ofc of Postmaster Gen in the Cabinet of Mr Harrison; since 1841 he has lived retired from public life generally. His only daughter is the wife of Hon Robt C Winthrop, & is now in Europe. His only son, Gideon Granger, is a lawyer in Canandaigua. -N Y Commercial advertiser
+
Rochester, N Y, Aug 31. Gideon Granger, [the son of Hon Francis Granger,] who died at Canandaigua on Aug 28,] died this morning at the same place.

St Louis, Sep 1. More Indian outrages. A Denver despatch says that a family named Neff, numbering 9 persons, & residing at Kiowa, were found murdered on Saturday.

Ex-Govn'r Thos H Seymour, of Conn, is quite ill. His disease, at first taking the shape of a nervous fever, has now assumed a typhoid character.

Phil, Sep 1. Wm Horner, a gasfitter, injured by the explosion at the Mint, died last night.

Orphans Court of Wash Co, D C. Letters of administration on the personal estate of Mary Toumey, late of Wash, D C, dec'd. –John H Semmes, adm

Orphans Court of Wash Co, D C. Letters of administration on the personal estate of Wm J Smith, late of Wash, D C, dec'd. –Anna M Smith, admx

THU SEP 3, 1868
Real Estate: J B Wheeler & Co, aucts, sold a 3 story frame house & lot on 11th st, near Pa ave, to E S McClary, for $1,245.

Internal Revenue appointments: Storekeepers:

Garrett M Losse, N Y	A M Burdick, Wisc	Michl Kerwin, Pa
Bradford Knapp, N Y	Peyton Middleton, N Y	

Gaugers:

H R O Hertzog, N Y	John M D Ross, Ala
John W O'Brien, N Y	Wm Merrifield, N Y

Maj C G Megrem was yesterday appointed Assessor of Internal Revenue, vice Gaddes, resigned; & R J Feragenay, Assessor of Internal Revenue for Pa.

Christopher Coleman, colored, was killed on Tuesday by the falling of a bank on N Y ave, near 23rd st. The remains were taken in charge & buried by the Corp authorities.

Gonzaga College, F st, between 9th & 10th, will resume on Sep 7. For particulars apply to Rev B F Wiget, S J, President.

Orphans Court of Wash Co, D C. Letters of administration on the personal estate of Jas Chapman, late of Wash Co, D C, dec'd. –John Chapman, adm

FRI SEP 4, 1868
Mrd: on Sep 3, by Rev Mr Perinchield, C R Roelker, U S N, to Miss Parthenia M T, daughter of Dr L I Porter, of Gtwn, D C.

Mrd: on Aug 27, by Rev W A Smith, D D, Mr J T Berkley to Mrs Esther Moffett, all of Wash, D C. [Evening Star please copy.]

Died: on Sep 2, Chas G Weiss, in his 37th year. His funeral will be from his late residence, 19 & 21 K st, on Friday afternoon, at 3 o'clock.

Died: on Sep 3, Albert Henry, only & beloved son of M G & Mary Jane Copeland, aged 1 year, 9 months & 19 days. His funeral will be from the residence of his grandfather, 463 2nd st, between B & C sts, this afternoon at 4 o'clock.

Meeting on Wed of the Oldest Inhabitants' Association; president, Dr John B Blake, in the chair. Wm L Newton, Patrick O'Donohue, Chas P Sengstack, Isaac Birch, M V Buckey, & S Jerome Diggs were nominated & elected members. A paper was presented to them by Robt White, being the last letter written by Thos Jefferson, 10 days before his death. The letter was written to R C Weightman, Mayor of Wash, in answer to an invitation to participate in the celebration of the 4th of July; it was dated Monticello. Lewis Clephane, through the president, presented to the association an internal revenue receipt of May 28, 1816, signed by Jas H Blake, Collector of Internal Revenue for D C, from which it appeared that a 4 wheeled vehicle, termed a coachee, was taxed $16 per annum. Thanks were tender to Hon Hugh McCulloch for his kindness in allowing the association the use of this hall.

A young man's body washed ashore at Blackistone Island, which had been in the water but a few days. No marks of violence were found upon the body. The pockets contained letters dated in 1862, addressed to Miss Haynes, Annapolis, signed John D Hogan, in which the writer mentions being employed in the Treasury Dept. The body is supposed to have fallen from some steamer. The remains have been preserved on the island, & await requisition. Address Dr McWilliams, Post Ofc, St Mary's Co, for further information.

Hartford, Conn, Sep 3. Geo Hall, formerly of Savannah, Ga, but a native of this city, died at Norwich yesterday, aged 80. In his will he left $30,000 for charitable purposes in this city, & a like sum for the same object in Savannah.

<u>Internal Revenue appointments made yesterday of storekeepers & gaugers:</u>

Storekeepers

J W Lewellen, Richmond, Va	Jas S Mallory, Broklyn, N Y
David L Lee, Ohio	Wm H Martin, Ohio
Peter S Dowling, St Louis, Mo	Chester F Shelly, Lockport, N Y
J L P Defrees, St Mary's, Ohio	John W Redmon, Ill
Harvey Crampton, Ohio	C E Paddock, Louisville, Ky
Jesse Byrkett, Urbana, Ohio	Wm W Peterson, Ohio
Jules Mantanguier, Cincinnati, Ohio	Jesse F Madden, Brooklyn, N Y

Edw Mann, Otto Schadt, A E Harker, John W Connett, & F A Towner, Chicago, Ill

Gaugers:

John Barker, Ohio	Chas O'Hara, Ohio
Frank Koehl, Ohio	Jas Hunter, Calif
T O Ebaugh, N Y	

Bayard Taylor & family on Wed arrived in N Y from Europe.

In New Egypt, N J, during a thunder-storm on Monday, 2 daughters of Hon Thos B Jones, Associate Judge of Ocean Co, were instantly killed by a stroke of lightning. They were standing on the front of the piazza of their residence during the storm. They were aged 17 & 12 years old, & were standing with their arms entwined about each other's necks.

Trustee's sale; by decree of the Circuit Court for PG Co, in Equity, wherein Andrew Jamieson, trustee of Bryan Adams & Co & others are cmplnts, & Edgar W Wood, adm of W Tasker Wier, dec'd, & others are dfndnts: public sale on Sep 24, of that tract of land in Spalding's Election District, in said county, containing about 75 acres, of which the late W Tasker Weir died seized & possessed. Improvements consist of a dwlg house & kitchen, & some outbldgs. –Fendall Marbury, trustee

SAT SEP 5, 1868
N Y Herald. Information was received in this city late last night that Ex-Govn'r Thos H Seymour, of Conn, departed this life, after a painful illness, from typhoid fever, in his native city. He was born in 1808 in the city of Hartford, Conn, & was in his 61st year; he pursued his studies at the Military Academy at Middleton; commenced the practice of law; was quite successful, & realized a handsome income; he attached himself to one of the leading papers of his state, & in a short time filled the editorial chair; about the same time he filled the position of Judge of Probate; in Mar, 1846, the year after which his Congressional career was brought to a close, we find him in the Mexican campaign as a major of the 9th infty; the following year he was promoted to lt colonelcy of the 12th infty; on the death of Col Ransom he was promoted to the command of the regt; at the battle of Chepultepec, on Sep 13, 1847, he hightly distinguished himself, & was promoted. He was also with Gen Scott at the City of Mexico. The following year he returned home & was mustered out. He was a prominent member of the Masonic fraternity at the time of his death. [Sep 8th newspaper: Hartford: Thos H Seymour died Sep 3, 1868, aged 60 years. His remains were interred at *Cedar Hill Cemetery* Sep 7th.]

Chicago Journal, Cheyenne, Aug 26. Gens Sherman & Augur passed up on Sunday evening to **Fort Saunders**, on a trip to Idaho Springs, Colo. Gen Sherman brought with him 2 of his children, a young girl of 14 or 15 years, & a son. On Monday the girl took a horseback ride, escorted by Lt Male, of 20th infty. Not long after both horses came into the fort riderless. The Gen, with Gens Gibbons & Potter, being out hunting in an ambulance, were apprised of the circumstances & started in pursuit of the riders. The girl was found lying insensible, her head supported by Lt Male. The horse had run away, & the girl had jumped off, striking on her head & hands. The last report was that she was still insensible.

Brvt Brig Gen Geo W Balloch, commissary of subsistence, & Brvt Lt Col Edgar C Beman, commissary of subsistence, have been mustered out & honorably discharged on account of their services being no longer needed. Gen Balloch for some time past has been on duty in the Freedmen's Bureau, 19th & I sts.

Oak Hill Cemetery. At a meeting of the Board of Directors of this cemetery on Thursday evening, to consider the bids made some weeks since for the construction of a wall along Rock creek in front of the cemetery, no definite action was taken, & the bids were all referred to Capt Sanger, one of the members of the board. It is not likely that any action will be taken at present in the matter, and it is probable that the work, when commenced, will be done under the supervision of Mr Blundon, superintendent of the cemetery.

Col B A M Froiseth, who has been suffering from a severs illness for several weeks past, is convalescent, & his many friends will be glad to learn this.

Mrd: on Sep 3, at the Church of Epiphany, by Rev Dr C H Hall, S P Wrisley to Fannie, eldest daughter of the late Valentine Blanchard, all of Wash City. No cards.

Died: on Sep 2, at her home in Asbury, Wake Co, N C, Mrs Rosina Dowel, daughter of the late Geo Duffy, of Alexandria, Va, & wife of Albert H Dowell, late of that city, in her 40th year. She was a true Christian, an affectionate mother, & a loving wife. She leaves 9 children, an affectionate husband, & many friends in this city to mourn her loss.

T S Booth is to return to the stage, after 20 years retirement.

In Champaign Co, Ill, there is a farm 7 miles by 6 in size, & containing 23,000 acres; a stock farm, & most of it has been reclaimed from prairie grass, & sown in timothy & blue grass. The present owner is Mr John Alexander. The late owner was Mr Sullivant, who has sold out & taken a farm of 40,000 acres in Ford Co.

The Sec of the Treasury yesterday appointed the following:

Storekeepers:
Jas Shannon, N Y C
Washington Stark, Aurora, Ind
Jas Skelton, Lawrenceburg, Ind
Jos G O Harrington, Dover, Dela
John Holmes, Fayette Co, Pa
D D Brodhead, Phil, Pa
Cornelius Homan, texas

Gaugers:
Danl C Gibbony, Pa
H Meclay, Pa
C L Sayne, Ala
David Lostulter, Ind
Robt P Robinson, Pa
Jas S Gillam, Pa
Geo O Tiffany, Calif
Robt D Brown, Ind
John W Crump. N Y
Clesh Wilson, Pa

U S Patent Ofc, Wash, Sep 1, 1868. Ptn of Cyrenus Wheeler, jr, of Auburn, N Y, praying for the extension of a patent granted to him Dec 5, 1854, reissued Jan 3,1 1860, & in May 14, 1867, for improvement in Grain & Grass Harvesters, for seven years from the expiration of said patent, which takes place on. -Elisha Foote, Com'r of Patents

MON SEP 7, 1868
Gen McClellan, the distinguished soldier & patriot, expects to return to N Y in the ship **Cuba**, which is to sail from Liverpool on the 19th inst. N Y Tribune

Green & Williams, aucts, sold lot 6 in square 551, fronting on Q st north, between 2nd & 3rd sts west, improved by a 2 story frame house, to Robt F Muir, for $2,350.

Deserved promotion. We are pleased to note that Mr Louis P Seibold, who was recently appointed on the Metropolitan Police force, has been detained by Maj Richards as an assistant to Mr Hully, Superintendent of the Police Telegraph.

Denver [Col] News Aug 29. On the 27th a party of settlers, with Mr Bailey as leader, statrted in pursuit of the Indians, coming up with them at sunrise of the 28th, within 10 miles of Latham. Fighting commenced. Five Indians were killed, 15 wounded. The funeral of Wm Brush & the 2 men killed with him took place on the 26th, the settlers all over that section of the country being in attendance, & vowing vengeance.

Gen Gage, a member of the N J House of Asembly, from Morris Co, died on Saturday of typhoid fever.

Wm Crabtree, a brother of Miss Lotta, the actress, was run over by a train of cars at Tremont, on the Harlem road, on Saturday, & had a leg cut off.

The funeral of ex-Govn'r Seymour, of Conn, will take place today at 11 o'clock, at New Haven, Conn. Hon Horatio Seymour, cousin of the deceased, is expected to be present.

Hon Wm W Hooper, delegate to Congress from Utah, tripped & fell down the stairs in Salt Lake City, on Aug 19, while descending with his child in his arms, & in saving the child from being hurt, had a rib broken.

Wm M Stockton, a pilot, committed suicide in N Y on Saturday, the cause being grief at the death of his wife.

Died: on Sep 6, Mary Louisa Virginia, infant daughter of Isaac G & Mary Jaquette, aged 9 months & 10 days. Her funeral will take place on Sep 7 at 3 o'clock P M, from the residence of her grandmother, Mrs J L Anderson, 378 13th st, between N Y ave & I st. [Balt Sun & Phil Ledger please copy.]

Louisville, Sep 5. A German named Willeck, & his wife & 2 children, residing at Randolph, 10 miles below this city, on the Louisville & Nashville railroad, were found dead in their dwlg last Thursday morning. The murder is supposed to have been committed by negroes for the sake of $100, which Willeck is known to have possessed.

$10 reward for lost or stolen Newfoundland Dog, about 7 months old.
–Jas M Carlisle, 478 D st.

TUE SEP 8, 1868
Sec McCulloch yesterday made the following appointments: Storekeepers: Wm McConkey, N Y C; Rugus Motor, Lancaster, Ohio; Saml Johnson, Hamilton, Ohio. Gaugers: David Funk, Pa; Chas J Davis, Tenn; N W Thatcher, Ohio; E R McKean, Tenn; A J Chrisman, Pa; & H W Bunker, Tenn.

Phil, Sep 7. Alfred Alexander, under sentence of death & recently respited by the Govn'r, has been again indefinitely respited.

Died: on Sep 7, Robert Alexander, infant son of R S & Martha A Jordan. His funeral is this morning at 10 o'clock, from 326 9th st, between L & M sts.

One of the oldest citizens of the District, Wm Remington, died yesterday morning, at the residence of his son-in-law, Mr Z M Offutt, 64 Second st, Gtwn. Mr Remington was 105 years old; born in Montgomery Co, Md, but came when quite a young man to Gtwn, where he has lived ever since. His eyesight was unimpaired, & he never wore spectacles. During the war of 1812 he was for awhile in the ranks until relieved by his brother-in-law, Stephen Artes, who became his substitute. His funeral will take place from Trinity Church tomorrow, Wednesday morning, at 9 o'clock.

WED SEP 9, 1868
Sec McCulloch yesterday appointed the following, under the new internal revenue law:
Storekeepers:
Frank Wilson, Alexandria, Va
S F Cuyler, Phil, Pa
Bingham Eckert, Hamilton, Ohio
Wm Goodwin, Mass
Gaugers:
Jas Carson, Ohio
John Martz, Ky
Wm M Sleep, Pa

Wm Machier, Ohio
Thos M Johns, Dayton, Ohio
Enoch E Thomas, Mount Vernon, Ind

Madison Dye, Ohio
P Chesley, Mass
Wm Hergenrether, Ohio

Green & Williams, aucts, sold at private sale at 3 story brick house on 4th st west, between M & N sts south, to Thos Johnson, for $5,000.

Spelling awards: Best average spelling, Female Grammar School, Mollie M Bowen. Intermediate: Effie McFarlane. Grammar School contestants: Ellie Dunn; Mary McGill; Laura Bowen. Male School contestants: Wm A Dutton; Wm M Lyles; & Chas P G Scott.

Equity Court-Judge Fisher. 1-*In re.* Wm Redes, a lunatic; commission of lunacy. 2-Jouvenal vs Walter; order appointing Chas Walter guardian *ad litem.* 3-Drewry vs Drewry et al; order appointing commission to take answer of infant.

Columbia, Pa, Sep 8. Buckstable, owned by W G Case, of this borough, was burned today. A citizen, Isaac Dack was killed, & 2 firemen, named Clepper, were injured.

Orphans Court-Judge Purcell, Sep 8, 1868. 1-Second account of Benj F Bittenger, guardian to Chas T Bittenger. 2-Third individual account of Emma Gibbs, guardian to Chas T Gibbs. Fourth individual account of Emma Gibbs, guardian to Isabel B Gibbs. Fourth individual account of Emma Gibbs, guardian to Wm H Gibbs-all orphans of John H Gibbs, dec'd. 3-The will of Gustav C Weiss was admitted to probate & record as to personality. The testator names Gustav Hartig & Fred'k Schmidt as his execs, & bequeaths all the property he may inherit from his relations to his sister in Germany; & all his property in the U S, together with his life insurance of $5,000 to his wife. 4-The will of Jos Bradley, in which he bequeaths his estate to his wife, was partially proven. 5-Cornelius Stribling qualified in the sum of $1,300 as guardian to the minor heirs of Emma J Stribling, dec'd. Sureties, C K Stribling & Benj Darby. 6-The Court delivered an able opinion in the contested will of Eleanor Miller, dec'd, which has been before it for some time past, & has recently been elaborately argued by counsel. The Judge held that the testimony clearly established the testamentary capacity of the testatrix; that the will was executed according to the requirements of the statute, & that there was no undue influence exercised over her. He therefore decided it to be a valid will, & admitted it to probate. He said the case had been argued with great learning & ablility, in support of his positions he cited the case of Calvert vs Davis, 5 Gill & Johnson; 3 Washington's Circuit Court Reports; Swinburn on Wills; 1st Redfield on Wills, & numerous other authorities. At the conclusion of the decision, the counsel for the caveators took an appeal to the Supreme Court of the District. Robert Leach, for the will; M Thompson, for the caveators. On motion of Mr Leech, Chas Miller, the exec named in the will, was appointed collector of the personal estate of the testatrix, & gave bond in the sum of $20,000.

Concord, N H. Ex-President Pierce lies dangerously ill in this city. He was taken sick on Friday morning, but was comfortable all day Sunday & Monday morning. Yesterday afternoon & last night he was much worse.

Today we announce the demise of another old resident of Gtwn, who has gone down to the grave full of years, Elias Hutchins, a well known citizen of Gtwn, died unexpectedly at his residence on Washington st, Monday evening. He had been unwell only a few days, & friends who had visited him early in the evening were surprised at a later hour to hear of his death. He was born & raised in Gtwn, & was a member of Covenant Lodge of Odd Fellows, Hermion Lodge, Knights of Pythias, & the order of Red Men. His funeral is this afternoon at 3 o'clock.

Yesterday, on the grounds of the Executive Mansion, a number of boys were playing & by some means a pistol was discharged. Oliver Lydin, aged about 12 years, was seriously wounded & is now in critical condition. The pistol was either being handled by Oliver or one of his companions, in a careless manner.

On Sunday last, Dr Boynton, pastor of the First Congregational Church, resigned his position as such, to take effect May 6th next, when his term as Chaplain of the House will expire.

Balt, Sep 8. Yesterday 2 small boys, Alonzo Tichner & Chas Swab, aged 8 & 10, were engaged in a fight, when the latter struck the former with a stone weighing about 2 pounds & broke his neck. Swab has been committed for the action of the grand jury.

Mrd: Capt Geo R G Jones, late of Confederate army, to Miss Addie Eliza, daughter of Capt Wm J Ross, all of Mempis, Tenn. [No marriage date given.]

Died: on Sep 8, in his 24th year, of consumption, Edw Wm, son of Wm F & Mary L Hall. His funeral is tomorrow at 11 A M, from the Church of the Incarnation, 12th & N sts.

Died: on Aug 31, at Fremont, Neb, in his 17th year, Colville Dade, son of Eliz C & late Hunter Terrett, of Fairfax Co, Va. [Alexandria papers please copy.]

From Geo Washington's will we copy the following item: to each of my nephews Wm Augustine Washington, Geo Lewis, Geo Steptoe Washington, Bushrod Washington, & Saml Washington, I give one of the swords or cutteaux of which I may die possessed, & they are to choose in order they are named. These swords are accompanied with an injunction not to unsheath them for the purpose of shedding blood except it be for self defence, or in defence of their Country and it's rights, and in the latter case to keep them unsheathed, and prefer falling with them in their hands to the relinquishment thereof.

Jarvis Raymond, father of Henry J Raymond, of the N Y Times, died in Detroit on Sep 3.

Mr Dickens is said by English papers to have cleared $260,000 by his visit to this country. For his next [and last] reading in England he is to get L8,000.

The undersigned, residing within 4 miles of Warrenton, wishes to receive into his family about Oct, 4 or 5 boys, between ages of 14 & 16. He proposes to prepare them for the first year's course at the Va Military Institure, or at College. Address J C Pemberton, Warrenton, Fauquier Co, Va.

Phil, Pa, Sep 8. Last Sunday Mary *Moran, aged 6 years, residing with her parents, in the city, while sitting in front of the house, was accosted by a stranger, who asked the direction of a certain st. The mother sent the child to show him, as it was only a few steps distance, & the child was not afterwards heard of until today, when she was found in a brick pond, outraged, & dead. [Sep 10th newspaper: A little girl, Mary *Marman, whose mother, a widow resides at 2046 Orkney st, disappeared on Sunday last, & there was not trace of her until yesterday. Her body was found in a pond above Susquehannah ave, not far from her mother's residence, no doubt she had been outraged, murdered, & thrown into the pond. It appears that a man came along & asked directions to Dauphin st, & she walked with him to show him the way. The murderer has not yet been found. -Phil Ledger, Sep 9.] [Sep 10th newspaper: No arrests yet in the murder of Mary *Mohelman.] *Note: Mary Moran/Marman/Mohelman. Phil child murder case.

Partnership. Today I have associated with myself N H Huiton & John Murdoch, of Balt, Md, for the purpose of conducting within D C, the business of Architects & Civil Engineers. The firm will be Randolph Coyle & Co. –Randolph Coyle

Orphans Court of Wash Co, D C. Letters testamentary on personal estate of Edw Lacy, late of Wash Co, D C, dec'd. –Matthew Wait, Thos H Havenner, Chas H Lane, excs

THU SEP 10, 1868
Revenue appointments: Storekeepers: Frank Y Batchelder, Ohio; John Dougalss, Tenn. Tobacco Inspector: Thos Reed, Ky, vice G M Clark. Gauger: J Cruishank, Ohio.

Brvt Brig Gen Jos R Smith, U S A, retired, died at his residence, Monroe, Mich, Sep 3, 1868. He graduated from West Point in 1823; served gallantly through the Florida war; was breveted as major & lt colonel for gallant & meritorious conduct in the battles of Cerro Gordo, Contreras, & Churnbusco, in the latter of which battles he was twice severely wounded. He was breveted as colonel & brig gen for long & faithful service.

The rector of Christ Church, Rev Mr Olds, has for some time past been deeply afflicted with a malignant cancer, & the disease has assumed its worst form. There is but little hope of his recovery.

Mrd: on Sep 8, by Rev Chas J White, D D, Mr John A Milburn to Miss Emma F Chapman, all of Wash City.

Mrd: on Sep 8, at the residence of the bride's father, by Rev Mr Tudor, Chas Faris to Miss Emma Ashford, both of Va, now of Wash City.

Died: Katie Connelly, infant daughter of B F & Belinda Pumphrey, aged 5 months & 8 days. [No death date given-current item.]

Montgomery, Ala, Sep 9. Accident on the Montg & Mobile railroad this morning. Mr J F Warner, the express messenger, was instantly killed.

St Louis, Sep 9. Despatch from *Fort Wallace*, Kansas, says a few Indians attacked a hay train near Sheridan, & killed a man, Gardner E Carson.

Boston, Sep 9. Enoch Train, a well-known ship-owner, died yesterday of apoplexy, aged 67 years.

Musical. M Hassan Murray will resume tuition Sep 16. Vocalization taught in the Italian style, after the method of Perrell. Preparatory classes will be formed for Piano & Singing. Class terms moderate. Apply to 495 9th st, between D & E sts.

FRI SEP 11, 1868
Green & Williams, aucts, sold part of lot 10 in square 438, on G st, between 7th & 8th sts, 30 feet front, by 86 feet 4 inches deep, improved by a good frame dwlg, to Chas Jarvis, for $2,000.

Chas Christmas, for many years the managing partner in the house of A Belmont & Co, died in N Y a few days since, aged 77 years.

Sec McCulloch yesterday appointed the following:
Storekeepers:
Wm B Thompson, Columbus
David B Tiffany, Pa
David T Morseley, N Y
Wdwin T Williams, Ill
John Cahenover, Ill
J Koehler, Iowa
D A McKenzie, Iowa
Gaugers:
Martin Crane, N C
Valentine Walter, Ill

David Lowden, Ind
John F Kuhn, Pa
Robt Clements, Ohio
Saml N Adams, Oho
Wm Patton, Ohio
Myyron Bacon, Ohio
Wm F McIntire, Ill

Chas W Simpson, jr, Va

Board of Metropolitan Police: Pvt John W Hanes was fined $20 for conduct unbecoming an ofcr. Pvt Edw Blenet, for gross neglect of duty, was dismissed the force. Henry C Jones was reappointed an additional patrolman for 6 months, to do duty at Metropolitan Hall. F Le Payne was appointed additional patrolman for 6 months, to do duty on Pa ave, between 10th & 11th sts. Wm H Duffy was appointed a pvt on the force, vice Jas Webb, ineligible. The applications of the following for liquor licenses were rejected: Antoine C Miller, Michl Conner, Michl Hurley, Michl Murdoch, & D J O'Connell.

Concord, N H, Sep 8. Ex-Pres Pierce lies seriously ill at the house of Willard Williams, of this city, where he has boarded for several years. He returned from his cottage at Little Boar's Head, Hampton Beach, recently, & went on an excursion to Lake Winnipiseogee. He was taken down with an attack of cholera morbus on Sep 6. Dr Alpheus Morrill is in constant attendance on him. Sep 9: His condition is critical. His brother, Henry Pierce, of Hillsborough, arrived tonight. [Sep 14th newspaper: The only kindred now with the General are 2 of his nephews, John McNiel, of Hillsboro, & John F Aiken, of Andover, Mass. Hon Tappan Wentworth, of Lowell, & Thos W Pierce, of Boston, were with him yesterday. The sufferer converses a little from time to time with his attendants & relatives. His pastoral visitor is Rev Dr Eames, of St Pauls' Episcopal Church, of which Mr Pierce is a communicant.]

Montreal, Sep 10. Bishop Talford, of the Angelican Church, is dead.

Michl Harman, an Irishman, living on the Alexander farm in Woodford Co, Ky, was gored to death on Sat, by a vicious bull, which he was leading to water.

SAT SEP 12, 1868
Yesterday Mr John D Barclay, of the ofc of Com'r of Customs, celebrated the 64th anniversary of his entrance as a clerk in the Treasury Dept. He was appointed as a clerk on Sep 11, 1804; is yet hale & hearty, & discharges his official duty with clerical ability. As a relic of by-gone days, Mr Barclay still preserves on his desk a portion of the desk furniture given him upon his entering upon his duties as a clerk.

Hon Jonas D Sleeper, of Concord, N H, who died on Wed; was a prominent Democrat of his State; served 2 years in the State Senate, & at the time of his death was clerk of the Supreme Court.

Capt Jos Richd Wheatly, son of Mr Wheatly, of this place, formerly of Harrodsburg, Ky, has been appointed a lt in the Chirassiers of the Imperiale Gurade of the French army. The commission came from the Emperor himself. Capt Wheatly is the 3rd American who has received a commision from the present Emperor: the first being young Bonaparte, of N J, & the 2nd the son of Senator Mason, of Va. An ofcr in the Imperiale Guarde is a post of honor, as the individual becomes a member of the Emperor's household.
–Kansas [West Va] Republcan

Mrd: on Sep 8, at the Western Presbyterian Church, by Rev J M Coombs, pastor, Jas B Lambie, of Pittsburg, Pa, to Miss Mary M, eldest daughter of John B Turton, of Wash City. [Pittsburg papers please copy.]

Mrd: on Sep 10, by Rev E J Drinkhouse, Wm W Tucker to Mrs Celinda A Peddicord; all of Wash City.

Died: on Sep 11, Foster Thomas, son of Chas D & Anna E Pennabacker, in his 7th year. [Sunday Herald please copy.]

Cincinnati, Sep 11. Difficulty this afternoon at the Rail Mills between John Thompson & John Kember, when Thompson snatched a red hot iron rod, 6 feet long, & ran it through the body of Kember, killing him instantly. Thompson has been arrested. [Sep 22nd newspaper: Thomas, the man who killed Kimberley at the Cincinnati rolling mill, by thrusting a red hot iron through his body, had been acquitted on the ground of justifiable homicide.]

On Shippen st, Andrew O Kane keeps a pawnbroking establishement. He is a rich widower, about 60 years old; his family consists of 4 sons, two of them grown; his wife died over a year ago. About 5 months afterward, Mrs Anna M Smith, a widow, was engaged by him as a seamstress, or rather to repair & alter clothing which had been pawned & not been redeemed. O'Kane became much attached to her, & at length declared his intention to marry her. The sons resolved that he should not marry her & demanded that she go to her home. She had not stepped more than 2 feet when she was shot & fell to the sidewalk. Andrew O'Kane, jr, aged 17, is said to have fired the shot.
-Bulletin, Sep 5

MON SEP 14, 1868

Real estate. On Sep 9 P W Crain & C C Magruder, trustees for the sale of the estate of Gen Thos F Bowie, offered for sale the dwlg house situated in Marlboro. It was knocked down to Gen Bowie, at $3,501; *Kinsale* a tract of land near the village, containing 340 acres was offcered; it was purchased by Enoch Pratt, of Balt, for $25 per acre. On Sep 10 th residue of the real estate was offered at Croom, consisting of a tract called *Brookfield*, containing 387 acres. This tract was purchased by Enoch Pratt, at $29 per acre. The remaining tract, *Cheltenham*, containing 752 acres, was purchased by the same gentleman at $13.50 per acre. –Prince Georgian

Orphans Court-Judge Purcell, Sep 12, 1868. 1-Gustav Hartig, F Schmidt, & Maria Ann Weiss gave bail in the sum of $3,000 as adms of Gustav C Weiss. 2-The following accounts were filed & passed: First individual account of Augustus M Sprague, guardian to Marcella Spalding. Third general account of A M Sprague, guardian of John M, Jas F, & Marcella Spalding. First & final account of same, as administrator w a of Marcella Riley, [formerly Spalding.] 3-The will of Eliz Contee was filed & fully proven & admitted to probate & record. She appoints Ally Jackson administratrix.

Accidents. 1-Yesterday a little boy, son of John Connors, age about 2 years, was attacked by a vicious cow, & gored in a fearful manner. He was conveyed to his father's residence on North Capitol st, where his wounds were dressed by Dr Bond. His life is despaired of by his physician. 2-On Sat two colored men, Thos Richardson & N Somerville, in the employ of Mr Milburn, druggist on 15th st, were burned by the breaking of a carboy of vitriol which they were moving.

Mrd: on Sep 7, in Christ Church, by Rev Jno Pleasanton Du Hawel, Delaware City, Henry Clay Johannes, of the Treasury Dept, Wash, D C, to Adrianna Von Culin, of Delaware City, Dela.

Died: on Aug 25, at the residence of Z Tippett, in this county, John T Neale, of Wash City, in his 55th year.

Died: on Sep 12, Jane Adelaide, aged 20 years, 3 months & 9 days. Only daughter of Jas & Eliza Nokes, of Wash City. Her funeral will take place on Sep 15 at 4:30 P M, from the residence of her parents, 586 7th st, between G & I sts south.

Mrs Wishard, wife of the superintendent of the Soldiers' Home at Knightstown, Ind, died last Monday night, from the effects of morphine, taken to relieve neuralgic pains.

A child of Mr Dygan, of Springfield, Ohio, aged 3 years, was attacked with cerebro-spinal meningitis, or spotted fever, Thursday, & died in less than 5 minutes.

Orphans Court of Wash Co, D C. Letters testamentary on the personal estate of Gustav C Weiss, late of Wash Co, D C, dec'd. –Gustav Hartig, Fr Schmidt, Meria Ann Weiss, excs

Orphans Court of Wash Co, D C, Sep 12, 1868. In the case of Jilson Brown, exc of John Reed, dec'd, the executor & Court have appointed Oct 13th next, for the final settlement of the personal estate of the said dec'd, of the assets in hand. –Jas R O'Beirne, Reg/o wills

Trustees' sale of ***Norwood Beale***, valuable land near Annapolis; by decree of the Circuit Court for Anne Arundel Co, passed Jul 21st last, in the cause of the Farmers' Nat'l Bank of Annapolis vs Pinkney & others, the trustees will offer the land for sale at the Courthouse door, on Sep 30 next, the valuable real estate of which Jonathan Pinkney died seized, containing about 237 acres. ***Norwood Beale*** lies on the south side of Severn River, at ***Horse Shoe Point*** adjoining on the east the land recently purchased for the U S Naval Academy; the improvements consist of a small dwlg house, 2 barns, servants' quarters, corn house, & all necessary bldgs. Mr Phelps, the tenant, will give information to all desiring to examine the place. –Alex Randall, Alex B Hagner, trustees

TUE SEP 15, 1868
For sale: ***Richland***, a valuable West River plantation; by decree passed on Jul 20th last, by the Circuit Court of Anne Arundel Co, in the cause of the Farmers' Nat'l Bank of Annapolis, against Eliz Hamilton & others, the subscribers, as trustees, will offer at public sale, on Oct 1st next, ***Richland***, of which the late Saml H Hamilton died seized, consisting of 334¾ acres; lies at the intersection of the public road from Annapolis to Friendship with that from Owensville to Queen Anne, adjoining the farms of Edw Marriott, Jas Iglehart, jr, A C Gibbs, Geo B Stewart, & Danl Murray. The dwlg is large & commodious; with numerous out-bldgs. –A Randall, A B Hagner, trustees

Bridgeport, Conn, Sep 14. Rev H D Noble, rector of the Episcopal Church at Bridgewater, committed suicide this morning by cutting his throat with a razor, in the school basement. He kept a large boarding school in Brookfield, & was highly respected. He was 45 years of age & leaves a wife & 5 children. The cause was temporary insanity.

Cleveland, Ohio, Sep 14. Jos Skinner, of Independence, near this city, has been shot dead in his own house by burglars, who made their escape without committing robbery. Hatch Butler Field, a notorious character of this city; Robt McKearney, a painter, & N W Davis, a blacksmith, have been arrested for the murder of Skinner. The proof against two of them is positive.

Boston, Sep 14. Augustin Heard, an old china merchant, is dead.

N Y, Sep 14. D A Finney, member of Congress from the 20th [Pa] District, died at Brussels Aug 29.

Montreal, Sep 14. The funeral of the late Bishop Fulford took place yesterday.

By direction of the Sec of War, Brvt Maj Gen J Hooker, Brig Gen, will repair to N Y C & report for examination to Brvt Maj Gen Cooke, president of the Retiring Board, convened by Special Orders No 449, Sep 21, 1867.

Mrs Jacob Homan, of St Cloud, Minn, insane at the drowning of her two little girls in May last, poisoned herself & her only remaining child with strychnine last week.

Gen John A Logan is ill with fever at Joliet, Ill.

Gen Jas Shields, the veteran Irish soldier, is the Democratic candidate for Congress in the Independence [Mo] District, & is stumping it.

Public sale of *Enfield Chase*, residence of N H Shipley, PG Co, Md; on Oct 7 next, at Collington Post ofc, the estate of N H Shipley, containing 6_0 acres; improved by a good dwlg, several tenement houses, & outbldgs. –John Glenn & Co, 20 St Paul st.

Dissolution of copartnership between S A H Marks & Fred'k Stromberger, of Wash City; dissolved by mutual consent. The business will be continued by said S A H Marks, sr, at the old stand. –S A H Marks, F Stromberger

U S Marshal's sale on Oct 5, all Chauncey H Snow's right, title, claim, & interest in square known as square west of square 471, being an undivided 5th part of said square, with improvements thereon, in Wash City. Will be sold to satisfy execution 3,693, in favor of the Ocean Nat'l Bank of N Y C against Cornelius Wendell, Chauncey H Snow, & John F Coyle. –David S Gooding, U S, Marshal D C

WED SEP 16, 1868

The Sec of the Treasury yesterday made the following appointments: Mr John M Tobin, storekeeper, Mass; Mr W H McSpaden, gauger, Alabama.

A valuable piece of property on the s e corner of Gay & Green sts, Gtwn, has been sold by Judge Dunlop to A B Mullett, supervising architect of the Treasury Dept, for $12,000.

Chicago Tribune: We announce the death of Edw W Hall, & most highly esteemed member of the press of this city. He died on Tuesday, at the house of his parents in Washington, whither he had gone but a few weeks ago, as all who knew him were convinced, -to die. He was in his 24th year; when but 18 he entered the Ordnance Bureau at Washington as a clerk; in the winter of 1866 Mr Hall came to Chicago, & a little less than a year ago accepted a position on the Tribune.

Henry Wells, a citizen of Ramapo, Rockland Co, N Y, was taken sick of fever at his home on Monday. On Friday, while his attendant was dozing at his bedside, he disappeared, & there is no clue to his whereabouts.

Whalen, who is on trial for the murder of D'Arcy McGee, has been ironed in his cell, it is said, on account of proposed attempts to liberate him by bribing the sentry. Wade, one of the principal witnesses against him, has disappeared.

Comte de Corday d'Orbigny, first cousin of Charlotte Corday, died recently at his chateau, in Normandy, which he was never known to quit, except to attend the marriage or funeral of a relative in Paris. The aged Count was a French country gentleman.

Orphans Court-Judge Purcell, Sep 15, 1868. 1-The following accounts were filed & passed: First & final account of Eleanor Goodfellow, admx of Robt C Brent. Distribution account of the personal estate of Jas F Essex by Mary Essex, admx c t a. First & final account of Mary Essex, admx c t a of Jas F Essex. 2-Harvey P Lucas gave bond in the sum of $1,200 as exc of John Tappan; T R Rutherford & Delos Carpenter, sureties. 3-Robt J Powell gave bond in the sum of $1,200 as exc of Ann M Powell.

Mrd:on Sep 15, at St Matthew's Church, by Rev Fr White, John F Green to Celena A Appel, both of Wash City.

Mrd: on Sep 8, at the Western Presbyterian Church, by Rev J N Coombs, pastor, Thos J Barclay to Sophie D Jackson, daughter of the late I M Jackson, all of PG Co, Md.

Chas F Choteau, one of the wealthiest citizens of St Louis, has been refused registration. W H Lockland & R S McDonald, prominent lawyers, were also rejected, all on account of past alleged sympathy with "rebels."

St Jos, Mich, Sep 11, 1868. Loss of the propeller **Hippocampus**; the tug **W B Urmton** arrived at Sangatuck, bringing with her survivors from the wreck. Passengers saved: H Bailey, of St Jos; E N Hatch, St Jos; J Trumble, Pipestone; G A Fuller, Benton Harbor; J Riford, Benton Harbor; J Cooley, Chicago. Crew: Capt H M Brown; J P Bloom, clerk; Chas Morrison, wheelsman; C Ritterhouse, St Jos; Chas Russell, Benton Harbor; A Howard, Brainbridge; E N Cooper, Pipestone; Thos Johnson, Chicago; M Robinson, Chicago. Both of the latter were colored. Missing: A Burridge, Benton Harbor; W S Waterouse, do; A G Palmer, do; W Baugh, do; J A Marple, do; M Higbee, do; J K Burridge, Brainbridge; John Schrim, Chicago; A P Whitney, do; R M Burke, of Pipestone; ___ Richardson, St Jos; R Eustace, 1st engineer, Chicago; Wm Brown, 2nd engineer, do; B M Moore, do; ___ Cook, do; W B Brant, Brainbridge; Arthur Wooden, do; E Vanethroy, do; Murray Spirk, do; D James, do; F Mathews, Pipestone; ___ David, colored, Chicago; H Manuel, colored, Chicago; Jos Wright, Chicago. All but one, [Richardson,] from St Joseph were saved, while only one, [J Riford,] from Benton Harbor was rescued. Statement of Capt Brown: on the night of Sep 7, having been engaged by Capt Morrison, the regular master, to take charge of her on that trip, we left Benton Harbor at 10 P M, having on board 7,000 packages of peaches; heavy winds; the boat began rolling badly; water came through the engine room into the hold; within 5 minutes she had gone on her side & was totally submerged.

Explosion of a locomotive in Rochester, N Y, on Monday: killed-John Jones, engineer; Peter Armburst, brakesman; Ella Glasgow, 15; & Lizzie Sonne, aged 15. Mary Haney, aged 11 years, was killed by the falling down of the wall of her parents' house, which was thrown down by the explosion. Margaret Haney, another child, was badly injured.

U S Patent Ofc, Wash, Sep 11, 1868. Ptn of Geo W Hubbard & Wm E Conant, of N Y, N Y, praying for the extension of a patent granted to them Jan 9, 1855, & reissued Sep 18, 1866, for an improvement in Operating Slice Valves in Direct Action Engines. -Elisha Foote, Com'r of Patents

TUE SEP 17, 1868
Com'r Foote yesterday appointed J S Grinnell chief clerk of the Patent Ofc, vice A M Stout, resigned. Mr Grinnell was formerly chief clerk of the Dept of Agriculture.

Mr Jas Alston, in attempting to jump from a horse car while in motion, in Chicago, on Sat, slipped & fell under the car. Two wheels passed over his neck & breast, killing him instantly. Mr Alston was the son of John Alston, of the firm of Alston, Devoe & Co.

The death is announced of Mrs Eliz Emery, of Andover, Mass, at the advanced age of 91 years & 3 months. For 20 years she & her husband had charge of the Theological Institute, & she was universally known as "Mother Emery." She was the mother of Rev Joshua Emery, of North Weymouth, Mass, & of Rev S Hopkins Emery, of Ill.

Utica, Sep 16. Rear Admiral Wm Mervine died in this city last night, aged 78. He entered the navy when a lad; was engaged during the first year of the rebellion fighting for the Union, but his advanced age compelled an early retirement. His funeral is tomorrow.

U S Marshal's sale: Oct 7 next, of part of lot 1 in square 380, being the house & lot on Pa ave, between 9th & 10th sts, now occupied by J R ___, with improvements, in Wash City, seized & levied upon as the property of Walter Lenox, & will be sold to satisfy execution 268, in favor of Penniman, Stover, & Knight. –Ward H Lavon, late U S Marshal, D C

Trustee's sale of valuable property in Wash City; by deed of trust from Thos Edw Clark. Sale on Oct 17 next, the property known as the wharf & water privileges of lots 3 & 4 in square 826, with the warehouse, improvements rights, privileges, & appurtances. -Hugh Caperton, trustee -W L Wall & Co, aucts

FRI SEP 18, 1868
The funeral of Mr Edwin A Stevens took place at Hoboken on Wed, & was largely attended.

Green & Williams, aucts, sold the farm of Mr Wm P Hall, near Beltsville, Md, containing 138 acres, to Wm P Hall, for $1,200. They also sold lot 4 in subdivision of square 5, known as *Widow's Mite*, in the rear of the farm of Mr John Little, containing 43-10 acres, to Jos J Coombs, for $500 per acre.

The notorious negro thief, Tom Bowie, was arrested yesterday on a charge of assault & battery, with intent to kill, committed on a woman named Maria Shey. He is out on bail for a hearing.

Sec McCulloch yesterday made the following appointments:

Gaugers:
- Simeon Miller, Ind
- S M Weaver, Ind
- R C Peters, Ohio
- Wm R Martin, N H
- Alex J Todd, Ind
- C R Dimond, N Y
- John R Williams, N J
- Jas McKee, Ill
- Howard Shaw, N Y
- B F Mullen, Ind

Storekeepers:
- R D Pelsor, Ind
- J A Emrie, Ind
- C Merrill, Va
- M L Keith, Ill
- D Runnion, Ill
- Harry Pease, Ill
- Geo Hartrauft, Pa
- E C Dodds, Ohio

St Louis Republican: on Sat, in the vicinity of the Pond Store, south of Manchester road, owned by a respectable German, named Hildebrand, his residence was just across the street. One of the rooms was the scene of a shocking murder on Friday. Miss Caroline Drienhofer, a step daughter of Mr Hildebrand, a pretty young girl of 21 years, was murdered by a negro named Jordan Tyler. [Caroline's brother, Chas Drienhofer also lived there.] Tyler's weapon of destruction was a rifle. He was employed there as a general worker for the several months past; age about 35 and had a violent temper. Caroline had a great fear of him & told her step father that he ought to discharge Tyler. As Caroline was in the front room ironing some clothes, Tyler shot her. She died in 3 hours. Tyler was arrested; later a crowd collected & took him. Sunday morning his body was found partially burned, with a rope around the neck.

Public auction on Oct 10, at Milestown, St Mary's Co, Md, all the interest, right, & title which Robt M Shanks has in & to: *Little Hackley*, containing about 200 acres; *Church Swamp*, containing about 102 acres; *Battery Woods*, about 27 acres, more or less. *Little Hackley* farm is adjacent to the lands of Col Richd H Miles & Miss Mollie Shanks. Improvements are a new 2 story dwlg, with necessary outbldgs. –Jos H Key, Assignee of R M Shanks, Bankrupt

Boston, Sep 7. Lt Col R W Kenyon, a resident of Troy, N Y, died here last night at the Boston House, from the effects of laudanum. After taking the poison he informed the landlord what he had done, & said to him: "Do all you can to save me." A physician was called, who administered all the known remedies, without avail.

Col H M Beckley committed suicide last night at the Maltby House. He is a resident of Fincastle, Botetourt Co, Va, & arrived in this city about 2 weeks ago, & since then has been employed as a salesman in the dry goods house of Lanier & Co, West Balt st. A letter to his wife was found unopened in his room. Another letter said he had lost all his money gambling at the faro table, & could not survive the shame. During the war Beckley was colonel of a Va regt in the Confederate army. He leaves a wife & 2 children at Fincastle. His remains were taken thence by this morning's train.
–Balt American, 17th

N Y, Sep 17. Fire broke out this morning at the residence of Jas Gordon Bennett, on Washington Heights, caused by a defective flue. Damage about $20,000, which is fully covered by insurance.

Savannah, Ga, Sep 17. John E Hayes, editor of the Republican of this city, died yesterday.

SAT SEP 19, 1868
Rev M S Olds, D D, rector of Christ Church, Navy Yard, died yesterday; some 6 months ago a cancer appeared on his right cheek, which developed itself quickly. For 12 days prior to his death he has been unable to take nourishment of any kind, on account of a cancer which appeared on his tongue 2 months since. Dr Olds was 40 years of age, & was a son of Judge Olds, of Ohio. Early in life he moved from Ohio to Wisconsin, where he studied & practiced law. He served gallantly as a lt during the Mexican war, & at its close returned to Wisc. In 1855 he was ordained by Bishop Whipple. He leaves a wife, who is a daughter of Nathan Sargent, of this city, & 5 children. The funeral services will take place today, at 12 M, at Christ Church.
+
Died: on Sep 18, Rev Mark L Olds, rector of Christ Church, Wash Parish, aged 40 years, 8 months & 18 days. His funeral will be on Sep 19 at Christ Church at 12 M. [Sep 21st newspaper: The funeral process moved from the rectory to the street thence to the church yard into the church, up the right aisle, & the dead priest was duly placed with his head to the altar. The process then reformed & proceeded to the ***Congressional Cemetery***, where the final commital was said by by Mr Lewis, & the prayer by Mr Stearns.]

Clarence Fendall, of Wash City, died at Norfolk yesterday. He was the second son of the late Phillip R Fendall, of this city. For about 15 years past he has been attached to the U S Coast Survey, & was at the time of his death an assistant in command of the surveying schnr **Hassler**. During the war he was detailed for service under Gen Grant & Admiral Porter for duty as an engineer on the ship **Mississippi**, in the neighborhood of Vicksburg, & was officially recognized by Admiral Porter on more than one occasion. It was when on this duty he contracted the disease, chronic diarrhoea, of which he died. Mr Fendall was a graduate of Gtwn College; he was 33 years of age. His remains will arrive here this morning & will be taken to the family residence.

Died: on Sep 18, at ***Thorpland***, PG Co, the residence of the dec'd, Chas Hill, in his 82nd year. His funeral will take place on Sep 19 at 2:30 P M. [Balt Gaz & Sun please copy.]

Died: on Sep 18, Annie, daughter of J W & Annie Harrison, in her 5th year. Her funeral will be Sunday afternoon at 2 o'clock.

Died: on Sep 17, at his residence, Falls Church, Va, Mr T M De Cover, clerk A G O, in his 29th year. His funeral will take place from the residence of Mr Robt Cohen, 431 6th st, between F & G sts, on Sep 19, at 2:30 P M.

Died: on Sep 18, Wm Owner, aged 75 years. His funeral will take place from the residence of his sister, Mrs F F Cook, 520 Va ave, near 4th st, on Sep 20 at 3 o'clock P M.

Revenue appointments made yesterday:
Storekeepers:
Edw J Morgan, Ala
Henry Carpenter, Wisc
Edw Beebe, N Y
John L Morrison, West Va
John H Jessup, Va
John J Kelly, Pa
Danl Urich, Iowa

Inspector of Tobacco, Snuff, & Cigars: Gavin H Wood, Pa.

Gaugers:
John H Houseman, Calif
Timothy D Morris, Wisc
Darwin E Martin, Pa
Jas W Worden, West Va
Oliver M Clemens, West Va
Saml M McGough, Pa
Chas T Rock, Ill
Rufus W Dibble, Ill
O C Bosbyshell, Pa
Jas Gibson, Ala
John Keohler, Iowa
Chas J Bradley, Ill
Chas C Cummings, Ill
John D Keedy, Ill
Edw M Johnson, Ky

Ottawa, Sep 17. Patrick Blackley, one of the accomplices in the McGee murder, is said to be insane.

Miss Nellie Wade, to whom Mr Colfax is said to be engaged, is about 30 years of age.

Wm Abrams, of Indianapolis, Ind, has been arrested for the murder of Mr & Mrs Young, whose bodies were found, that of the woman horribly burned, in the woods last Sunday. Abrams is a street broker, said to be worth from $20,000 to $30,000. He had been an intimate friend of Young, & connected with him in business.

Mrs Stout, wife of the proprietor of the City Hotel of Des Moines, was burned so badly a few days ago at Indianola, that she died. She was mixing some medicine for a sick child, over the stove, when the oils exploded. She was immediately enveloped in flames.

MON SEP 21, 1868
Mr John Rainbow died on Friday, at the Brooklyn Navy Yard, where he has for some time been stationed as chief carpenter. The dec'd was a resident of this city, where his sister now resides. He had a host of friends here. It was he who constructed the full rigged ship **Constitution** that appeared in procession on the day of the inauguration of Pres Buchanan. His remains have been brought to Wash City & will be interred today.
+
Died: on Sep 18, at the Brooklyn Navy Yard, N Y, John Rainbow, U S N, in his 57th year. His funeral will take place in Wash City, from the residence of his nephew, Henry J Bright, 8th st east, near Pa ave, today, Sep 21, at 4:30 P M.

Chief Justice Chase arrived at Concord, N H, on Thu, on a visit to some of his relatives.

Col L B Grigsby has been appointed deputy collector of the port of N Y. Col Grigsby will have special charge of the transit of all merchandise, in the coastwise trade between the Atlantic & Pacific coasts.

Mrd: on Sep 15, at St Peter's Church, Phil, by Rev N P Tillinghast, Horace Hare, M D, of Phil, to Emily Power, daughter of Truxtun D Beale, of Wash City.

Died: on Sep 19, at his residence, at Fairfax Court House, Va, Dr Fred'k Baker, in his 59th year.

Died: on Sep 16, Claude Alexander, aged 13 months & 14 days, child of Danl B & Carrie V Little

Died: on Sep 19, in Balt, Henry Clay Tuttle, in his 24th year, son of the late Wm N Tuttle.

Died: on Sep 19, of consumption, Mrs Eliz Guerin, the beloved wife of Michl Guerin, aged 42 years. Her funeral will take place on Monday at 3:30 P M, from her late residence, on N st north, between 4th & 5th sts.

Died: on Sep 18, <u>Biddie</u> C, only daughter of Wm T & L Kelley, aged 9 months & 8 days. Her funeral will be today at 4 o'clock, from the residence of her parents, 1st st, between H & I. [Sep 22nd newspaper: Died: on Sep 18, <u>Bittie</u> E, only daughter of Wm T & L Kelley, aged 9 months & 8 days.]

Died: on Sep 20, John P, only son of John & Ann Pepper, aged 11 months & 2 days. His funeral will take place from the residence of his parents, 229 4½ st, between G & H sts, Island, this afternoon, Sep 21, at 4 o'clock P M.

Died: on Sep 19, John Vaughan, jr, youngest son of Amelia Goodrich & Rev John Vaughan Lewis, aged 1 year & 3 months. His funeral is on Tuesday at 10:30 A M, at St John's Church, 16th & H sts. [Sep 22nd newspaper: His funeral is on Tuesday at 3 o'clock P M.]

Interesting case. A H & Eliza T Morehead have, by their counsel, A G Riddle, entered a suit in the Circuit Court of D C, against Cornelius Boyle, formerly of Wash City, afterward of the Confederate army, the present owner of White Sulphur Springs, Va, for $35,000 damages. The plntfs allege that the dfndnt arrested Mrs Morehead & imprisoned her for the space of 3 years, from Jun, 1861, & prevented her from returning to the care & society of her husband & children. Dr Boyle was a provost marshal in the Confederate service, & alleges that under the orders of Gen Beauregard he prevented the plntf from crossing & recrossing the lines. Dr Boyle has retained Messrs R P Merrick & J F Ennis as his counsel.

Orphans Court-Judge Purcell, Sep 19, 1868. 1-Letters of administration on the personal estate of Jas E Triay, dec'd, were granted to Asbury Lloyd; bond, $3,000; Henry Lichau & Wm P Lassell, sureties. 2-First & final distribution accounts of A J Harvey, exc of Jas S Harvey, dec'd, were approved & passed. 3-Inventory of personal estate of G C Weiss, dec'd, returned by executor.

Yokohama, Aug 29. L H Grinnell, late acting lt in the U S navy, has been appointed overseer of the Japanese navy, under the Southern Gov't.

St Louis, Mo, Sep 19. An Omaha despatch says a party of Gov't surveyors were surprised by Indians at Republican river, south of *Fort Kearney*, on Wed, & Edw Malone, a flagman, was killed; the remainder escaped. They lost their instruments, supplies, & one team.

N Y, Sep 20. John Sefton, the well known comedian, died suddenly yesterday at his residence in this city.

Com'rs sale of that magnificent estate on Jas River, 35 miles above Richmond, called *Bolling Hall*, containing 1,561 acres; by decree of the Circuit Court of Goochland, pronounced Sep 8, 1868, in the case of Skipwith against Skipwith's execs; public auction, on the premises, on Oct 22 of *Bolling Hall*. The bldgs on the estate are numerous & mostly in good condition; the dwlg house is large & in excellent order. Messrs Woolfold & John P Dickinson, will show the place. –Jno H Guy, com'r

Public sale of valuable real estate; by decree of the Circuit Court for PG Co, in Equity, passed in a cause wherein Thos S Duckett & wife & others are cmplnts, & Danl Clarke, adm of Richd Duckett, & others are dfndnts. Sale on Sep 23, at the late residence of Richd Duckett, dec'd, in Queen Anne district, PG Co, Md, all the real estate of which Richad Duckett died seized & possessed, containing 600 acres of land, more or less. This farm is known as *Millford*, & adjoins the lands of the late Grafton, Tyler, R B Mullikin, & others. Improvements consist of a large & commodious brick dwlg house, comparatively new, with Garden, Meat-house, dairy, corn-house, stables, overseer's house, quarters for servants, & 3 large barns. –Danl Clarke, trustee

TUE SEP 22, 1868
The special term of the Criminal Court convened for the purpose of trying John H Surratt, either for murder or conspiracy, yesterday. The interest in the prosecution of Surratt has abated. The murder indictment was abandoned.

On Sunday, Wm Butler, residing on Md ave, between 8th & 9th sts, committed suicide by taking laudanum & strychnine.

Shepherd A Mount, the well-known artist, died at his residence, at Smithtown, Long Island, recently.

The following changes of clerks were made in the Patent Ofc last week: Saml J Frazier, chief messenger, dismissed; J J Ferrill, clerk, dismissed; Geo W Barter, clerk, resigned, to take effect in Oct; W S Parkhurst, appointed a clerk, after undergoing a creditable examination before the board of examiners.

Gen McClellan, with his wife & 2 children, sailed from Liverpool Sat, in the Cunard steamer **Cuba**, for N Y.

During an exciting race at an agricultural fair at Evansville, Ind, Dr Robt King, of Vincennes, getting upon the track, was struck by one of the horses & fatally injured.

Charges have been preferred against Mr J E Rice, the American Consul at Aspinwall, that he charges $2 for examining a passport, & $2,50 for signing a manifest.

Dr L A Biancini, an Italian homoeopathic physician of New Orleans, 65 years old, committed suicide a few days ago, at the grave of his wife, who died recently. Sorrow over her death was the cause of his action.

Geo Hickman was accidentally shot by a friend, Chas Rodgers, in Chatanooga, Tenn, on Sep 2. The two were practicing with revolvers on the river bank at the time. Hickman is not expected to recover from his wounds.

Improvements in Gtwn. We will not forbear to speak of the very elegant residences of Judge Peck & son, on the Senator Bright lot, though Judge Peck purchased & fitted up those handsome & delightful houses last year. They are an ornament to this elegant section of the city. Rev J E Nourse, chaplain of the navy, is bldg a handsome house at Stoddard & Green sts; & Stephen Brown, of the firm of Mayfield & Brown, is building another of like character on Washington st, between Congress & Gay. Mr Fowler, of ice fame, is bldg a very handsome house on the corner of Bell & Congress sts. Miss Readen is bldg a fine house on Gay st. Mr Jas Yates is bldg 2 on the same st, & Mr Richd Cruit is bldg still 2 more on that st. The most of these houses are of wood, but all all good bldgs, & some of them very elegant.

Indianapolis, Sep 21. John Haggerty shot & fatally wounded Murdy Conley while at work today, because Conley refused to drink beer with him.

Died: on Sep 20, Caroline De Rinzie, only child of Celestine & Rev A J Faust. Her funeral service will on Tues, Sep 22, at 3 P M, at St John's Church, 16th & H sts

Supreme Court of D C, Equity 1,316. John E Kendall vs John Gaynor et al. This cause is referred to me to state & settle the amount of indebtedness between the cmplnt & dfndnt John Gaynor, & to state the costs & expenses of this suit, & of the sale mentioned in the proceedings. Meeting on Sep 28 at 10 A M. –Walter S Cox, auditor

Orphans Court of Wash Co, D C, Sep 19, 1868. In the case of Thos Hutchingson, exc of Patrick Reynolds, dec'd, the executor & Court have appointed Oct 20th next, for the final settlement of the personal estate of the said dec'd, of the assets in hand.
-Jas R O'Beirne, Reg/o wills

WED SEP 23, 1868
Julia E Harshell, a Connecticut lady, lately received $150 damages & costs from the Shore Line railroad, for careless handling & smashing her trunk.

Providence Hospital & the Sisters of Charity. The Sisters ventured in 1863 to lay the foundations of an asylum on Capitol Hill; they purchased of Gerrit Smith, for $7,500, the old original residence of Danl Carroll, near the mansion which he subsequently built, & which is now known as the ***Carroll Mansion***. Gerrit Smith resided in this house while he was a member of Congress, &, we think Judge Cranch at one time resided there, & in this house Mrs Carroll died. In 1864 Congress gave them a liberal charter, & in 1866, an appropriation of $30,000 to aid in erecting a new & larger bldg. Hon Thaddeus Stevens & Senator John P Hale brought their humane enterprise to the attention of Congress. They have now torn away the old ***Carroll House***, & are putting in the foundations of a western wing; when this completed the structure will be some 180 feet long, with a wing at each & some 90 feet deep. Their original purchase of the ***Carroll House***, in 1833, by order of the Sisterhood, was occupied by them a while, & by them was surrendered, the field of their labors not then seeming to be fully prepared. This purchase was made under the guidance of Fr Peter Schriner, then pastor of St Peter's Church, on Capitol Hill, & subsequently pastor of St Vincent's Church, of Balt, where he died. The ***Providence Hospital*** is now under the supervision of Sr Loretto, superior, whose untiring, self denying energies & tender devotion to her work is known to all who familiarize themselves with the great enterprises of Christian benevolence in this District. Sr Mary Carroll is now at the Mother House in Emmitsbury. The bldg, with this new wing, will cost about $100,000.

Orphans Court-Judge Purcell. 1-The will of Florence Poe was filed, fully proven, & admitted to probate & record, & letters of administration c t a, were granted to Toulmin A Poe; bond, $20,000. 2-The first & final account of Jas Fulton, adm of Thos Chessaur, dec'd, was approved & passed.

San Bernardino [Calif] Guardian, Aug 24. Simon Bemis was killed by a grizzly bear on Friday week, in the mountains in the vicinity of Dunlap's ranch, within a couple of miles of the place where 2 brothers of the deceased, Parish & Whitesides, were murdered by the Indians in the spring of 1866. It appears that the deceased, in company with two of his brothers, went on the mountains after a load of posts, & while there he concluded to hunt, promising to return to camp in a shortime. He did not return home & his brothers became alarmed. His body was found on Sat, in a deep ravine, his skull in a shocking manner, & badly bitten & torn about the face & neck. His gun was nearby. On Monday his remains were conveyed to town, & born to their last resting place.

Sec McCulloch yesterday made the following appointments:
Storekeepers:
Wm L Ross, Ky   Frank T Reynolds, Ky   W S Nock, Ky
Edw P Calvert, Ky   Isaac Rosenburgh, NY C
L Varenzell Ky   Wm H R-dgeis, Va
Gauger: John K Lloyd, Ky
Tobacco Inspector: Wright Smith, Ky, vice G Youtsey, appointed assistant assessor.

Gen Clayton, of Ark, a few days since, while quail hunting, accidentally shot himself in the left hand, rendering amputation necessary.

John Boher, age 80, has been sentenced at Quincy, Ill, to 14 years in the State penitentiary for the murder of his son. His sister, 70 years old, will be tried next month for complicity in the offence.

Elmira, N Y, Sep 22. As the funeral procession of Mrs Carr was crossing the Erie railway a mile west of the painted post, the Rochester express came along & frightened the horse of a carriage in which was Mrs Drake, a sister of the deceased. She was thrown on the track, & had both feet cut off by the passing train. A child of the deceased was also run over, & literally cut to pieces.

Orphans Court of Wash Co, D C. Letters of administration on the personal estate of Florence Poe, late of Wash Co, D C, dec'd. –Toulmin A Poe, adm c t a

THU SEP 24, 1868
Dr Francis S Spring, of Boston, died last Saturday. He was 6 feet 5 inches in height, & weighed about 550 pounds. He possessed great skill in the treatment of cutaneous diseases.

Orphans Court-Judge Purcell, Sep 23, 1868. 1-The will of the late Florence Poe, bequeathing her personal property, jewelry, etc, to her family, was filed, fully proven & admitted to probate, & letters of administration c t a were issued to Toliman A Poe; bond, $20,000. 2-The will of the late Wm Remington, of Gtwn, was filed. He bequeathes his estate to his wife, during her life, & at her death to Jane Roberto Trunnell, Eliza Jane Offutt, Eliz L Rockaway, Ruth Ellen Chism, & others.

N Y Express: About the middle of August, Mary O'Connor, 5½ years old, Jas O'Connor, 3½ years old, children of Mr Jas O'Connor, residing in Walcott st, were bitten by a rabid dog, owned by Mrs Serlock. Mrs Serlock saw the dog bite the children, & made an attempt to rescue them, when the dog bit her. The little girl died on Sep 9, & the little boy died on Sep 19. Mrs Serlock is not considered in a dangerous condition.

Wilmington [N C] Journal. On Friday, in Fayetteville, a shooting took place at the Fayetteville Hotel between Mr R W Steadman & Dr W H Morrow, which resulted in the death of both parties. Politics was the mainspring of this action.

Fort Wallace, Kansas, Sep 23. Two scouts from Col Forsyth's command arrived here last night. They report that on Sep 17 the Indians tried to run off a portion of their stock, & half an hour later three or four hundred appeared on the bluffs, & made a dash for the camp. Col Forsyth had only 50 men; the Indians commenced firing on them, & kept it up fast & steadily. Col Forsyth had his left leg broken by a ball, & was also shot through the right thigh. Lt Beecher was shot in several places, & is supposed to be dying, as his back was broken. He begged his men to kill him. Dr Moore was shot in the head while dressing Col Forsyth's wounds. Two men were killed & 20 wounded. All the stock of the command was killed, & the men were living on horse flesh. Col Bankhead, commanding this post, sent out 100 men to his relief; scouts Col Carpenter, with his company, were to proceed to Col Forsyth's assistance. ***Fort Wallace***, Sep 23: 8 P M. Gen Nicols has just arrived from ***Fort Reynolds***. He reports Lt Beecher dead; Col Forsyth was nearly dying.

Lots in ***Peirce Place***, in square 206, opposite the State Dept, for sale. Price 28 cents per foot; one fourth cash; balance in 1, 2, 3, & 4 years. –Fitch & Fox, Real Estate Brokers & Aucts, 470 7th st.

FRI SEP 25, 1868
At 8 o'clock last evening Robt T Lincoln, eldest son of the late Pres Lincoln, was united in marriage with Miss Mary Harlan, only daughter of Senator Harlan, of Iowa. The marriage took place at the residence of the bride's father, in Wash City, Bishop Simpson, of the Methodist Episcopal Church, officiating. The ceremony was performed by Bishop Simpson in a very solemn & impressive manner. The bride was tastefully & handsomely dressed in rich white silk, trimmed with white satin & blond, with pearl ornaments. Among the distingushed persons present were Sec McCulloch, Sec Welles, Senator Ramsay of Minn, Rep Loughridge of Iowa, with their ladies; Mrs Abraham Lincoln, Senator Harlan, & Mrs Harlan. No cards of invitation were issued, & the party consisted of a few intimate personal friends of the two families. Mr & Mrs Lincoln leave today for the North, on their wedding tour.

Benj Teachout, age 60 years old, has been sentenced to be hung on Nov 13th by the Wyoming Co [N Y] court, for the murder of his wife. He is a well to do farmer & a member of the Baptist Church, but his wife being a confirmed invalid, he considered her a burden, & made away with her by a course of gradual poisoning.

Walnut Grove, Crooked Creek, Carroll Co, Ark, Sep 8. Five men shot down while in church on Sabbath last. No charges could be justly preferred, save only that they were Conservatives or Democrats. A Mr Ferrand, a young ex-Federal soldier, died instantly. Mr Thomas died the next day; Chas Lamb is not expected to live; while Wamic & Robt Lamb, are thought will recover. The assassins escaped.

The Pres has directed that the unexecuted portion of the sentence of the military commission in the cases of Wm J Tolar, Thos Powers, & David Watkins, citizens of S C, be remitted, & the prisoners be released from confinement.

Col Danl S Goodloe was on Wed appointed supervisor for the Dist of Ky.

It is said that ex- Govn'r Orr, of S C, has determined to take up his residence in St Jos, Mo, & to resume the practice of law.

Trial of John H Surratt, Sep 24, 1868. Discharge of prisoner. Judge Wylie: The only offence of which I am cognizant was committed over 2 years before the indictment was filed. I know nothing of his having fled from justice, the man may have been in the city all the time. I have decided the matter, & will listen to nothing further. The Court was adjourned. Surratt left the court room at the conclusion of the colloquy, receiving the congratulations of his friends.

Oak Hill Cemetery; The monument of Gen Reno stands upon the beautiful circle which crowns the heights of the new grounds, commanding a grand view of the Capitol in the distance. A mound at the foot of the monument shows the grave of the noble & lamented soldier, & near him the remains of his 3 young children-Alex'r, aged 15 months; Marion, aged 6 months, on one side; & Lewis aged 8 years, on the other. The inscription: "Major General Jesse Lee Reno, U S A. Born June 25, 1823. Killed at the battle of South Mountain, Sep 14,1863." Near the Reno memorial is the Hall monument column, with this inscription: "Edward Hall. Died September 25, 1866. Aged 54 years." One of the prettiest things in the new part of this cemetery is the little column upon the scroll resting upon the broken shaft, on which is inscribed, "Jennie, daughter of Octavius and Mary E Knight. Born April 11, 1863. Died Apr 24, 1867." There is much rivalry, we believe, between the lot-holders of the old & the new sections of the cemetery. The Libbey monument, on the declivity near the Chapel, is the finest memorial which has been recently raised in the older part of the cemetery, & is from the marble works of Maples, Phil. It is inscribed: "To the memory of Joseph Libbey, born in Dover, New Hampshire, February 3, 1793; died in Georgetown, D. C., August 24, 1866." The lots in the new addition are selling at about the rate of a thousand dollars' worth a month at the present time. The prices range from $1 to $1.60 per square foot; the & sizes of the lots range from 150 to 800 square feet each. A bank wall, 540 feet long & 6 feet high, on Mill st, has been constructed during this season, & they have now commenced a bank wall along Rock creek, which is to be 840 feet long & 15 feet high, at a cost of $15,000. A brick stable has been erected on the premises for the horses used upon the grounds. We believe there have been none but white marble monuments or memorials erected in the cemetery within the last year. An occasional monument of some other stone & color would break the wearisome monotony.

The body recently found on the shore of Lake Michigan has been fully identified as that of Miss Patchen, of Buffalo, one of the passengers on the steamer **Sea Bird**, lost in the lake in June last.

A despatch from St Louis states that Gen Hancock still remains at **Longwood**, at the residence of his mother-in-law, near Carondelet. He is suffering from the reopening of the wound he received at Gettysburg.

Rev J P Roles, who was deposed from the pastorate of the Church of the Holy Name, in Chicago, has been reinstated in his ecclesiastical functions, though he will be obliged to leave the diocese.

Toronto, Sep 24. A writ of habeas corpus was granted for Frank Reno & Chas Anderson, committed under the extradition law for shooting at Americus Wheldon with intent to kill, at Mansfield, Ind. The discharge was sought on the ground that shooting with intent to kill does not come under the Ashburton treaty.

Richmond, Sep 24. Capt Schultz, ex-capt of the Federal army, blew his brains out this morning in the garden of a citizen, from whose employment he had been discharged. He leaves a family in N Y.

Trustee's sale of real estate; by deed of trust executed to me by John Murphy & Mary his wife, dated Apr 21, 1866, recorded in Liber R M H No 15, folio 251; public sale, on Oct 6 next, at the premises, lot 12, in square 62_, with the improvements.
-John E Norris, trustee -Green & Williams, aucts

SAT SEP 26, 1868
Memphis Appeal, Sep 7. Mr T A Alexander, a peaceful gentleman, who lived on the Hernando road, was attacked & shot by 4 negroes who burst into his house. Mrs Alexander ran out the back door when she heard the shots. They plundered the house, set the house on fire, & made their departure, leaving Mr Alexander senseless & helpless at the mercy of the flames. Owing to the dampness of the inflammable material used, the fire had not made much headway. Neighbors arrived & attended to Mr Alexander. Mr W J Saint, the neighbor who assisted Mr Alexander, along with others, from the description given by Mrs Alexander, arrested Moses Crockett, & deposited him in the Station-house. On Monday night, one of the murderers, Henry Groves, was shot dead as he tried to run & escape. Another outrage: from the Memphis Appeal, Sep 7. On Sat 4 negroes went to the house of Mrs Viney Jones, on President's Island, plundered her house; attempted to quiet her screams, but she had armed herself with a knife & drove into the groin of one of them, penetrating the kidneys, & making a terrible wound. The whole party was captured: Edwin Hall, Feter Ford, Thos Boone, Caesar Stinson, the latter being the wounded man. Outraged: Schenectady Star, Sep 14. This morning an outrage was perpetrated upon an aged German woman, named Louckes, in Van Zandt's woods, on the Albany turnpike, by a brute of negro, who overtook the woman in the woods, knocked her down, ravishing her person several times & then fled. She was found by a neighbor who notified her husband. Mrs Louckes lies in a very precarious condition, & it is thought her injuries will result fatally. A warrant has been issued for the negro. Little Rock, [Ark] Gaz. Aug 2. On Friday last a negro, Jas Warner went to the residence of O Strange, & told Mrs Strange that her husband was ill, & desired her to come to him. Mr Strange often stayed at his brick kiln, at Fourche bridge. Mrs Strange left with the negro, her "blue box" with about $150, with her. On Sat morning she was found dead. Warner had been in her husband's employ & had been discharged. Mrs Strange's 9 year old little girl was present when they started. Maj Strange was an ofcr in the U S service; he was

educated in Coblentz, on the Rhine, & is an engineer of merit. His late wife was a lady of culture. Chattanooga [Tenn] Union, Sep 19. On Sat last, a family named Gardner, from North Alabama, arrived at the Camp Ground, as the village is known, intending to make a permanent settlement. The family consisted of Hiram Gardner, age about 60, & 3 daughters, all who had attained womanhood. They slept in the wagon that night; they were awakened by loud noises, & found a number of negroes around the wagon. They seized Mr Gardner & the youngest daughter, aged about 25; the other two women were bound to trees & their screams went unanswered. At daylight a farmer went to the assistance of the helpless couple. They searched for the father & daughter, & came upon them lying on the ground covered with blood. They appeared to be dead, but when whiskey was applied, in a short time, they were able to be moved. It is doubtful his daughter, who had been ravished by the 5 negroes, will recover. One of the negroes has been arrested & is in jail in Harrison. Georgia Clarion: Outrages & double murder near Swain's Mill, N C, on Tues last. Mrs Marks, a young & beautiful widow lady, about 30 years of age, a hired woman, Mrs Grally, & 2 children, a little boy of 5 & a little girl of 8, living with her. On Sep 21st, at 9 P M, a negro knocked on the door & said he had a letter for Mrs Marks; as the door was opened, 9 negroes made a rush into the house. Mrs Marks was tied to the bed & violated in turn by all 9 of the negroes. The screams of the little girl were fearful; they beat her brains out. The little boy with tied with cords, & proceeded to commit a nameless outrage upon his body. The hired woman had escaped & fled toward Stover Station. She lost her way & in the morning arrived at Mr Appleby's, the nearest neighbor. He called up his men & when they arrived at Mrs Mark's, they found the house on fire. Mrs Marks was insensible; Geo, the little boy, was found on the floor; the dead body of Annie, the little girl, was found in the yard. The negro who pretended to have the letter was recognized by Mrs Grally, as Bill Batson. Batson's wife said he was going to Milberry to a negro meeting. Life & property are at the mercy of the blacks in nearly the whole South. No one has been arrested as yet.

Revenue appointments were made yesterday by Sec McCulloch: Gaugers: J W Manley, N Y; J W Stevens, N Y; Jacob Boon, Pa. Storekeepers: W H Hilleary, Fred'k, Md; Jas Corning, Richd Romons, & John Ruedi, St Louis; Geo H Walker, Milwaukie; T C Kendall & W D Hibburd, Chicago; J D Leland, N Y; J H Kyle, Columbus, Ohio.

Died: on Sep 23, in Harrisburg, Pa, Kate, wife of Col O A Mack, U S A, & daughter of Gen Justin Di__ick, U S A, aged 30 years.

London, Sep 25. Rev Henry Hart Milmau, deacon of St Paul's Church, is dead.

Delaware Water Gap, Pa, Sep 25. The Brainard House was robbed this morning, & Thos Broadhead, the proprietor, with his brother, started in pursuit of the robbers. Thos Broadhead took hold of one of them, when the other drew a revolver & shot Thos, wounding him; Theodore Broadhead was shot & killed. The murderers are supposed to be Irish; they were captured & lodged in Strandsburg jail. Thos Broadhead will probably recover.

Orlando Sheldon, of Somers, Conn, was found nearly insensible in his room at Massasoit House, Springfield, Mass, on Wed morning, from inhaling gas which had escaped during the night. He had probably failed to turn off the gas on retiring. He is not expected to recover.

MON SEP 28, 1868

Wheeling, West Va, Sep 27. A disastrous fire occurred this morning in Culbertson's Star Foundry. Chief of Police Shanley had both thighs broken; Policeman Bradley was instantly killed while endeavoring to enter a window.

At a fireman's celebration at St Anthony, Minn, a small cannon prematurely discharged, horribly mangling two gunners, Wm Palmer & Vorman Ross. They are still alive.

Worcester, Mass, Sep 26. Silas & Chas T James, who murdered Jos G Clark, in this city, on Feb 28 last, were executed on Friday. The scaffold used was the same upon which Prof Webster, Green, & other murderers were executed. The bodies were delivered to their relatives.

Died: on Sep 26, in Balt, Mrs Ann R Poole, aged 58 years.

Died: on Sep 26, Maggie Johnson, beloved wife of Albert Johnson, & daughter of M B Clark, after a short but painful illness. Her funeral will be from her late residence, 274 7th st, between L & M sts, on Sep 28 at 2 o'clock P M.

Died: on Sep 27, at the residence of her son, Jane E Brewer, widow of the late Wm Brewer, of Fairfax Co, Va, in her 64th year. Her funeral will be from the residence of C J Brewer, 567 12th st, between B & C sts, at 3 o'clock P M.

Died: on Sep 27, John Bennett, son of Thos & Sarah A Dennis, aged 7 years, 1 month & 28 days. His funeral will be this afternoon, at 3 o'clock, from the residence of his parents, 386 G st south, between 6th & 7th sts east.

Died: on Sep 26, John M, infant son of J M & Susan Stake; aged 8 months & 3 days. His funeral will take place from his parents' residence, 117 Prospect st, Gtwn, D C, this evening, at 4 o'clock.

Orphans Court-Judge Purcell, Sep 26, 1868. 1-Jos J Waters gave bond in the sum of $300 as administrator d b n of Paul Hess. R N Jackson & H E Waters, sureties. 2-The following accounts were filed & passed: Distribution account of the personal estate of Thos Halloran, by W A King, adm. Second individual account of J L Hawkins, guardian to Russel Brown & F L Brown. Second individual account of M J Braxton, guardian to I J Braxton & Sarah A Braxton. Second general account of M J Braxton, guardian to R F, L C, & S A Braxton. First account of Wm Chambers, guardian to Capston K & Henry McDonald. 3-Thos Cowling gave bond in the sum of $1,000 as administrator of Ed Cowling, jr. Atwell Cowling & G H Turton, sureties.

TUE SEP 29, 1868

Portsmouth, N H, Sep 28. Among the deaths of men connected with the press, we notice that of Abner Greenleaf, of Portsmouth, N H, father of Albert Greenleaf, late of Wash City. The former had reached the advanced age of 84 years, & preserved his faculties in a most remarkable manner down to a late date. He was long connected with the old N H Gazette, which is, or was, one of the very oldest papers of the country.

Richmond, Sep 28. On Sat, in New Kent Co, Mrs Stewart, a widow, was murdered, & the corpse burnt with the dwlg. John Baker, her farm manager, was also murdered & robbed of $500 in gold.

Memphis, Sep 28. Avalanche's Helena [Ark] letter, dated yesterday: Deputy Sheriff J W Maley, with a posse, surrounded the cabin of a notorious negro, Lee Morrison, who had killed several persons last winter; shot & maimed for life Sheriff Bart Taylor, while attempting to arrest him; recently knocked the jailor on the head, & escaped to the hills. No sooner had they knocked on the door yesterday than Morrison fired, instantly killing Sheriff Maley. He severely wounded Perry Neagle & Andy Barnes, colored. He escaped & was later found when 100 men scoured the woods for him. A vote was taken, & he was hung on the spot.

Died: on Sep 28, at the residence of John E Norris, in Wash City, Mrs Annie R Norris, beloved wife of Jas L Norris, of Fred'k City, Md. [Fred'k, Md, & Cleveland, Ohio, papers please copy.]

Died: last evening, Mrs Harriet C Risley, wife of Hon H A Risley, Assist Solicitor of the Treasury; after a painful illness of more than 3 weeks, of typhoid fever, at their residence, 90 Pa ave, Wash City. The funeral will be announced hereafter. [Sep 30th newspaper: The funeral of Mrs Harriet C Risley will take place this afternoon at 2 o'clock, from the residence of her husband, Mr H A Risley, 90 Pa ave.]

Memphis, Sep 28. Gen T C Hindman, late C S A, was assassinated at his residence in Helena last night. A man named Robbins, from Springfield, Mo, who served under Hindman, was arrested. He stoutly denies being the murderer. [Sep 30th newspaper: Gen Thos C Hindman was assassinated on Sunday, at his residence in Helena, Ark, while sitting in the midst of his family, smoking. His left hand, which held the pipe, was carried away by the the charge of buckshot, two of which entered his neck, inflicting a wound from which he died 8 hours later. It is believed he was assassinated by a political enemy.] [Oct 14th newspaper: After he was shot, Mr Hindman survived about 8 hours, during which time he conversed calmly in relation to business matters; & spoke with touching beauty & affection to his wife & 4 little children, who have been so inhumanly bereaved.]

Phil, Sep 28. Chas H Graffen, of the Sunday Mercury, & Robt P King, of the firm of King & Baird, died here yesterday.

Paris, Sep 28. Count Walewski, formerly Pres of the Corps Legislatif, & lately a member of the Privy Council, died yesterday, aged 58. [Sep 30th newspaper: His mother, the Countess Walewski, a Polish lady of great beauty, attracted the special attention of Napoleon I at a fete at Warsaw in 1800. Napoleon won her affections, & on May 4, 1810, she gave birth to the Count. He was educated in Geneva, & returned to Poland in 1824. In Dec, 1831, he married a daughter of the sixth Earl of Sandwich, & after her death married a decendant of the last King of Poland.]

Bethlehem, Pa, Sep 28. A North Pa train ran over a cow yesterday & a passenger car was upset. Henry Dotts, the brakesman, was killed; Chas Keechline, of Bethlehem, & Jos Shawdt, of Phil, were badly hurt. Chas Bowman & D G Maglathory were severely injured.

Lewiston, Me, Sep 28. T A D Fessenden, formerly a member of Congress, died this morning, after a brief illness. Among the members of the family present during his last moments was his brother, Senator Fessenden.

Balt, Sep 28. Capt Fred'k M Brand died suddenly in this city this morning, of paralysis. He had just returned from Europe, where he went for the benefit of his health. He was captain of the First German Guards, organized in this city in 1837. His body was taken charge of by the Masons. He was 70 years of age.

Newark, N J, Sep 28. Four miners, Wm Moore & Richd Sampson, from Bristol, England, & Jas Richards & Jas Thomas, from Cornwall, England, were instantly crushed to death on Thursday by falling into the shaft of an iron mine at Mount Hope, Morris Co, near Jersey City. They were buried on Sunday. The bodies were buried in one grave.

WED SEP 30, 1868
Detachment of U S Troops, Day Fork of the North Fork of the Republican River, Sep 26, 1868. Col Forsythe sends his love. He is badly wounded, but will be able to travel tomorrow. Lt Beecher, 3rd infty, & Dr Moore died of their wounds, & are buried. Lt Col Carpenter arrived here yesterday. Forsythe's men fought desperately. I cannot remove the dead, but the doctors say I can remove the wounded tomorrow to **Fort Wallace**. Col Forsythe estimates the number of Indians at 600. They were Cheyennes, Arapahoes, & Sioux. Killed: Lt F H Beecher, Acting Surgeon Moore, T W Culver, Wm Wilson, & Louis Farley. Wounded: Col G A Forsythe, [twice,] Wm Armstrong, G B Clarke, Barney Day, H Farley, Richd Gant, John Haley, Frank Harrington, W H H McCall, Howard Martin, Thos O'Donnel, H H Tucker, Louis McLaughlin, Harry Davenport, & S R Davis. -Henry C Bankhead, Brvt Col Commanding

Madison, Wisc, Sep 29. Mrs Anne Wallace, of Richland Co, was murdered yesterday by a young man named Neville. Neville was caught & lynched by the citizens. The object of the murder was money.

Orphans Court-Judge Purcell, Sep 29, 1868. 1-Letters of adm were granted to Chas S Wallach on the estate of Wm Owner, dec'd; bond $3,000. 2-Letters of adm were granted to Nathl Pitts, jr, upon the estate of Nathl Pitts, sr, dec'd, late of the U S navy; bond $1,200. 3-Letters of adm were granted to Helen E Morgan on the personal estate of T C Morgan; bond $3,000. 4-Michl Talty was appointed guardian to the orphans of John Talty dec'd; bond $1,000. 5-First account of Wm Emmert, guardian to Lewis H Emmert, orphan of Henry & Louisa Emmert, dec'd, was approved & passed. 6-First & final account of Wm Edelin, exc of Henry Carrack, dec'd, was approved & passed.

Fatal railroad accident: the train from this city containing the 29th infty, en route for Memphis, Tenn, ran off the track on Monday, near Keswich, Va, owing to one of the switch bars breaking. The following privates were killed: Geo Hewitt, co C; & Leopold Marcus, co I. Wounded: Privates Jos Myer, Ira U Blan, Jas Cosgrove, & Lewis Beaufela, co B; John Baker, Henry Schlerker, J Holden, Edwin Snow, & T Kelley, co C; Wm Ramsay, John Farlayer, Thos Kelly, T Anderson, D Rat-ay, & A Francis, co A; Jas Martin, co I; Cpl Peter Troy, co G; one brakeman. The wounded men were placed on a train & conveyed to Lynchburg.

Mrd: on Sep 29, at the Church of the Epiphany, by Rev C H Hall, D D, & Rev Reeve Hobbie, Chas F Rockwell, U S A, to Ellen G, daughter of the late Hon S R Hobbie.

Died: on Sep 23, in Front Royal, Va, of pulmonary consumption, Miss Mattie C Reynolds. [Va, Md, & Pa papers please copy.]

Died: Sep 29, Jas H Wheeler, in his 49th year, formerly of Balt, Md. His funeral will be from the residence of his son-in-law, W T Johnson, 464 3rd st, betwee Pa ave & East Capitol st, on Sep 30 at 3:30 P M.

Died: on Sep 29, in Gtwn, D C, Miss Mary Ann Beall. Her funeral will take place from the residence of her brother, Wm D Beall, 118 West st, this afternoon, at 4:30 P M.

Died: on Sep 27, in Cumberland, Md, at the residence of Gen Thruston, Mrs Sidney A Bradley, relict of the late Wm A Bradley, & eldest daughter of Hon Buckner Thruston, dec'd. Her funeral will be on Oct 1, 2 P M, at the family residence, 336 N Y ave.

Died: on Sep 26, Thos Robbins, in his 74th year. His funeral will be from his late residence, corner of 12th & Mass ave, on Sep 30 at 2 o'clock P M, to proceed to **Holyrood Cemetery**, Gtwn. "Dearest father, thou hast left us, We thy loss most deeply feel; Tis the Lord that hath bereft us, He can all our sorrows heal."

Obit-died: on Sep 28, in Phil, Richd W Pearson, formerly of Wash, in his 28th year. Mr Pearson came to Wash in 1862, & up to the beginning of the present year was connected with the banking house of Jay Cooke & Co, as teller of that institution. He was overtaken by the disease which but a few hours ago terminated his life; he was compelled to abandon his business, & left us for the quiet & comfort of his home.

Richmond Whig, Sep 28. From Constable Robt S Taylor, of New Kent Co: on Sat last John Baker, a colored man, after coming from the woods where he had been cutting poles, stopped at his hog pen, on the land of Mrs Julia Stewart, a white widow woman, in New Kent Co; while resting on his axe, he was shot from behind; he was then dragged to Mrs Stewart's landing 400 yards distant, stripped of his clothes, to see if he had money; he was then tied & thrown into the river. His body was discovered Sunday. John D Christian, coroner of the county, summoned a jury, as directed by law. The following jury was procured: John D Odell, foreman, Robt Wright, Jas Chandler, Richd L Gilliam, Eppa Gilliam, Wm T Call, Richd Boswell, Jas A Austin, Thos W Austin, & Wm A Burnett; veridict–death by gun-shot wound, inflicted by person unknown. The deceased was a mixture of negro & Indian blood, prompt & reliable. He owned a farm, but rented & worked a part of the land of Mrs Stewart, on which he resided & on which he was killed. The same evening, Mrs Stewart, referred to above, was murdered, robbed, & then burned up in her house. There are parties strongly suspected, but no arrests have been made. Mrs Stewart had lived alone for some time, except for Baker, hence the murderers were able to accomplish their hellish purpose without any danger of discovery.

Hon Geo W Summers died at his residence, near this place, on Sep 19. He had been in declining health for some time. –Kannawha Republican

Executor's sale of the estate of Wm Gaul, dec'd, on Oct 22, on the premises, n e corner of New Market & Callowhill sts, Phil; mules, wagons, casks, tools, a lease & the goodwill of one of the largest breweries in the U S; together with the malt house. –Sarah Gaul, Simon Delbert, Geo H Osertuffer, Peter L Snyder, excs -M Thomas & Sons, aucts, 139 & 141 South 4th st.

THU OCT 1, 1868
Gen Frank P Blair spent yesterday at *Silver Spring*, on a visit to his parents, & passed through this city last evening on his way to Bedford, Pa, where he speaks today. He is fresh from the canvass in Ohio, Indiana, & Pa, of which he gives most gratifying accounts.

Rev Dr Phineas D Gurley the beloved pastor of the N Y Ave Presbyterian Church, died at the residence of Judge Casey, on C st, between 4½ & 6th sts, yesterday. He was in the 52nd year of his age. He had been in bad health for a year past, from a derangement of the stomach. Drs C H Nichols, Edwards, [of the army,] & A Y P Garnett attended him. Dr Gurley was born at Hamilton, Madison Co, N Y, Nov 12, 1816, & graduated at Union College in 1837. His funeral will not take place until Saturday, it being the dying wish of Dr Gurley that sufficient time should be allowed for the arrival of relatives. [Oct 3rd newspaper: Funeral of Dr Gurley. At the conclusion the cortege proceeded to *Glenwood*, where the remains were interred.]

Boston, Sep 30. By the falling of the wall of the skating rink last night, Geo Gookin, of Chelsea, was killed, & Madison Putnam & Elisha Saville were injured, but not seriously.

Richmond, Sep 30. Jas K Caskie, a prominent tobacco merchant, died today.

Mrd: on Sep 7, in Rowe, Mass, Dr Julian W Dean, of Wash, D C, to Kate Wells, daughter of the late Horace Browning, of R. No cards.

Died: on Sep 30, Isabella Souter, a native of Scotland. Her funeral is this evening at 3 o'clock, from the residence of Jos Shillington, 510 G st.

Died: on Sep 30, in Phil, Wm B Malcolm, for many years a resident of this city.

FRI OCT 2, 1868
Cooper & Latimer, aucts, sold west half of lot 8 in square 815, improved by a 2 story frame house, to Mr J H Meed, for $610.

Robt Brown, an old resident of the Fifth Ward, of Wash City, died on Oct 1, at the advanced age of 84 years. He was the superintendent of construction of the Capitol bldg until the present new wings were added; he was also superintendent of the erection of the Pres' House, the dry dock at the Gosport Navy Yard, & one of the contractors for the completion of the Gen Post Ofc bldg.
+
Died: on Oct 1, Robt Brown, aged 84. His funeral will take place from his late residence, 25 south A st, Capitol Hill, this evening, Friday, at 3 o'clock.

Mrd: on Sep 30, at the Church of the Ascension, by Rev Dr Pinckney, Geo A Wadsworth, of Allin, Ill, to Mary Bell, daughter of the late Capt T S Everett, of Md.

Died: on Sep 13, near Bastrop, Texas, Roscoe T Wilson, late of Norfolk, Va. [Norfolk papers please copy.

Trustee's sale of personal property; by deed of trust executed to me by P B Brown, dated Jun 12, 1868, recorded in Liber 6 of Chattel Records; public sale on Oct 16 next, at 261 F st, household & kitchen furniture. –R Ross Perry, trustee -Green & Williams, aucts

U S Patent Ofc, Wash, Sep 21, 1868. Ptn of Hannah M Brown, of Woonscoket, R I, admx of the estate of John E Brown, dec'd, & Wm E Barrett, of Providence, R I, exc of the estate of Stephen S Bartlett, praying for the extension of a patent granted to them Jan 2, 1855, in three divisions, for an improvement in Grain & Grain Harvesters.
–S D Hodges, Acting Com'r of Patents

Headquarters of the Potomac, Warrenton, Nov 10, 1862. It was nearly midnight on Friday, the 7th instant, when Gen Buckingham handed the order of the President to Gen McClellan, relieving him from command of the Army of the Potomac, & directing him to report at Trenton, N J. It was entirely unexpected by everyone here.

SAT OCT 3, 1868
Capt Albert G Ryan was today appointed Collector of Internal Revenue for the First District of Arkansas.

Geo D Prentice has retired from the Louisville Journal.

M F Maury has undertaken a physical survey of the State of Va, under appointment of the Va Military Institute.

By deed of trust executed to me on Jan 26, 1867, by John W Boffocker & Rebecca his wife, of record in the Clerk's ofc of the County Court of Prince Wm Co, Va, I shall sell, before the door of the Court-house, on Oct 5, 1868, the property known as *Gold Ridge*, containing 650 acres of land. Improvements include a comfortable dwlg & the usual outbldgs. Mr Lebbens Ewell, who lives upon the property, will show it.
-A Nicol, trustee, Brentsville, Prince Wm Co, Va.

Sec McCulloch yesterday appointed the following internal revenue ofcrs:
Storekeepers:
Horatio C McCorkhill, Ky
Thos W Pritchett, Ky
Herman Blodgett, N Y
Bernard Biglin, N Y
York A Woodward, La
Gaugers:
Lucian J Wright, Calif
Wm Jennings, Calif
Byron P Cordwell, Oregon
Owen B Gilson, Oregon
Simon Goodrich, Ill
C M Patterson, Calif
S B Davenport, Calif
S F Childs, Calif
Jas J Felter, Calif
Saml Rorer, Ky
Geo W Jolly, Ky
Saml A Pearce, R I
C A Woodrich, Md
John Shisaler, Pa
Oscar T Linsey, Ohio
Jas A Dall, Md
French McDowell, Pa
D B Ainger, Ohio
R C Algee, Tenn
C O Wilbur, Tenn
R L Tomlin, Mo
F H Vanderburgh, Mich
John M Hauck, Md
Wm S Hilleary, Md
P B Hunt, Ky
E E Wells, Ky
G M Barth, Ky

Saml Babcock was appointed Collector of Internal Revenue for Conn, vice John Woodruff, dec'd.

Norfolk, Oct 1. The two men, John Perkins, white, & Benj Jefferson, colored, sentenced to be hanged tomorrow for the outrage on Miss Sarah Eliz Ford, at her home, in Norfolk Co, on Jun 9 last, have just been respited by telegraph by Govn'r Wells to Oct 9. Perkins was formerly a Federal soldier, & was well known as the leader of a gang of predatory negro thieves in N C, his accomplice being one of the band. The characters of both are extremely bad.

Topeka, Kan, Oct 1. The Adj Gen received information that a party of from 25 to 40 Indians, supposed to be Pawnees, had carried off Mr & Mrs Bossett from their home, 25 miles from Salina. Mrs Bossett had her baby with her, 2 weeks old, & was not able to travel. She was left on the prairie with her child, entirely stripped of her clothing.

MON OCT 5, 1868

The funeral of Rev Phineas D Gurley, D D, pastor of the N Y ave Presbyterian Church took place on Sat. The remains were kept on ice until Sat when they were encased in a handsome coffin of fine walnut, the silver plate inscribed: "Rev Phineas D Gurley, D D, born November 12, 1816, died September 30, 1868. The corpse was attired in a suit of black. The following gentlemen acted as pallbearers: P M Vearns, Prof Henry E D Gilman, A R Shepherd, Gen Vincent, Geo Lowry, Mr Willard, Mr Blagden, T C Theaker, Mr Ballantyne, Mr F_nt, Paymaster Jackson. Reserve: D McClellan, B F Winslow, Mr Ogden, Mr Barr, Mr Kelly, & Judge Lawrence.

Green & Williams, aucts, sold part of lot 5 in square 771, improved by a 2 story brick dwlg to Mrs Ann Bean, for $1,000. Cooper & Latimer, aucts, sold the south part of lot 10 in square 100, on 21st st, between L & M sts, improved by a 2 story frame dwlg, to H Clay Stewart, for $700.

Dr J A Chamberain, formerly a clerk in the Post Ofc Dept, in Wash City, died at Manchester, N H, Sep 27, in his 36th year, after an illness of nearly 2 years, confined to his room for 17 months. He formerly practiced dentistry in Wash City; afterwards graduated at the Medical College, Gtwn, D C. Autopsy revealed the cause of death was cancer of the right lung. He leaves a wife & child. The funeral will take place Wed, at 1½ o'clock, from the residence of Franklin Tenney, on Myrtle st, & will probably be conducted by the Masons, of which order deceased was a brother.

Orphans Court-Judge Purcell, Oct 3, 1868. 1-J V Coburn gave bond in the sum of $1,500 as administrator of John Coburn; O W Marsh & W Rutherford, sureties. 2-Annie E Raybold gave bond in the sum of $500 as administratrix c t a, of H S Raybold; J B Patterson & G P Fisher, sureties. 3-The first & first general & final accounts of Catharine Barrett, guardian to the orphans of T J Barrett, dec'd, were filed & passed.

Died: on Oct 3, at the residence of his brother-in-law, Dr R K Stone, in Wash City, Geo Harrison Ritchie, youngest son of the late Thos Ritchie, of Richmond, Va.

Died: on Oct 2nd, at Poughkeepsie, N Y, Mrs Dr Taylor, aged 86 years, a native of Lancashire, England, mother of Franck, Henry, & Hudson Taylor, of Wash City.

Ex parte Saml A Mudd, Saml Arnold, & Edw Spangler. Judge Boynton: This is an application for a writ of habeas corpus to release from imprisonment Saml A Mudd, Saml Arnold, & Edw Spangler, who were sentenced by a military commission sitting in the city of Washington, in the spring of 1865, to military confinement at ***Fort Jefferson***, within this judicial district.

Geo W Janieson, a well known actor, was run over & instantly killed at Yonkers this evening by the express train on the Hudson river road.

Edw Ware, general ticket agent of New Orleans, Jackson, & Great Northern railroad, attempted to commit suicide in New Orleans on Sat by shooting himself in the head.

Orphans Court of Wash Co, D C. Letters of administration on the personal estate of John Coburn, late of Wash Co, D C, dec'd. –J V Coburn, adm

Orphans Court of Wash Co, D C, Oct 3, 1868. In the case of Jas W White, administrator of Wm J Toomy, late of Wash, D C, dec'd, the administrator & Court have appointed Oct 27 next, for the final settlement of the personal estate of the said dec'd, of the assets in hand. -Jas R O'Beirne, Reg/o wills

Com'rs sale of valuable real estate; by decree of the Circuit Court of Montg Co, in Equity, wherein Wm S Offutt & Sara J Offutt his wife, are cmplnts, & Luther M Offutt & others are dfndnts, the subscriber will offer at public sale, on Oct 28, 1868, on the premises, all the real estate of which Wm H Offutt, late of said county, deceased, died seized & possessed. Lot No 1 contains 178½ ares, more or less. Lot 2 contains 119 acres, more or less. The property is located on the main road leading from Wash City to Seneca Mills, commonly called the <u>River road</u>. Lot No 1 is improved by a comfortable frame dwlg house, & all necessary out-bldgs. Lot No 2 has no bldgs on it. –Hazel B C Shell, John L DuFief, Elbert Perry, Com'rs. N B: Mr H C Fawcett, residing thereon, or Mr N D Offutt, in the town of Rockville, will show the land.

Valuable real estate at public vendue; by power & authority vested by the heirs of Elijah Thompson, late of Montg Co, deceased, the undersigned, as com'rs to divide & sell the real estate will offer the real estate, on the premises, on Oct 31; all the real estate of which said Thompson died seized & possessed, lying in said county. Lot 1 contains 184¼ acres, more or less, improved by a large & commodious 2 story rough cast brick mansion, containing 8 rooms. Lot 2 contains 126½ acres, more or less, lies on the n e side of Fred'k road; has a small log house thereon. Lot 3 adjoining lot 2, contains 181 acres, more or less with large tobacco house thereon. Lot 4, adjoins lot 3, contains _52 acres, more or less. Lot 5 adjoins the village of Gaithersburg, & contains 3½ acres, more or less, with a good frame bldg thereon, suitable for dwlg & store. Lot 6 consists of a house & lot in the village of Gaithersburg, & contains 1½ acres, more or less; improved by a 2 story frame house with back bldg, & is occupied at present as a store. Lot 7 adjoins the land of Hazel B Cashell, Edwin M Muncaster & others, & contains 201¼ acres of land, more or less; with a good frame house, tobacco house, & other bldgs. Lot 8 contains 30 1/8 acres, more or less; is near the village of Unity; with 2 dwlg houses & necessary out houses. –Hazel B Cashell, N C Dr Kerson, Wm Musser, Com'rs

TUE OCT 6, 1868
Mrd: on Oct 1, at St Paul's English Lutheran Church, by Rev Dr Finckel, John W Nairn to Fanny, eldest daughter of the late Coleby Young, all of Wash City.

Albany Argus, Sep 16. Outrages have been perpetrated by the suddenly liberated blacks all over the Southern States, robberies, murders, rapes of the white wives & daughters, have become common occurrence. The women are subjected to indignities worse then death. Monday last, an aged & repectable German woman, while in the country between Albany & Schnectady, engaged picking berries was outraged by a negro from Florida, John Williams. Thinking her dead, he fled through the town of Niakayuna, where he committed another crime. He was found yesterday & doubtless will spend the balance of his miserable life in State prison.

Nashville, Jul 13. A young man named Fredand was murdered by 3 negroes on Sat night, who entered his room & cut his throat & hacked him to pieces. One of the negroes was arrested, taken to Columbia, seized by a party of white men, & supposed killed.

Washington, Jul 21. Early today Capt J C Queen was discovered with his throat cut, in a lot east of the Executive Mansion. He had since been restored to consciousness, & relates that he was attacked by 1 white man & 2 colored men. One colored man held him, while the other with a razor, & the white man with a knife, disabled him, gashing his throat. They robbed him of $200, & a gold watch.

The beautiful little girl, age about 9 years, daughter of Mr Wm Lieth, living on Fairhaven's turnpike, 3 miles from here, was sent last Sat to a neighbor's, about a half a mile distant, on an errand Her mother became alarmed when she did not return & went in search of her. She was found near a clump of bushes, moaning, terribly mutilated, in a dying condition. She said a large negro dragged her into the bushes & committed a most horrid outrage upon her person. He then cut off one of her arms, broke one of her legs, & then terribly mutilated her face. She lived but a few minutes after her mother found her. -Dallas [Ala] Herald

Fort Monroe, Sep 17. Yesterday, a young girl residing about 4 miles from Hampton, on the Yorktown, was outraged by two negroes, Henry Harrison & Wm Jones. The perpetrators were arrested, & are now held in military prison, awaiting their trial by the civil authorities.

Thos Johnson, 24, residing at 27 Laurence st, went into the house 43 Laurence st, N Y, where a large number of colored families reside, & beat Mrs Ellen May, age 39, an invalid. She died soon after supposedly of hemorrhage of the lungs. Mrs May was a widow, an inoffensive & quiet woman. Johnson was locked up at the Police Station.

Evansville Courier, Sep 13. Yesterday a party of negroes employed as deck hands on the steamer **Linton**, threw an Irishman named Carney overboard. His only offence was his nationality. All of the negroes concerned in the murder have been arrested.

Hon Julius Bing, formerly U S consular representative at Smyrna, Asia Minor, has just been appointed diplomatic agent of the Provisional Cretan Gov't in this country.

N Y, Oct 5. The coroner's jury in the case of Jas Hamilton, supposed to have been poisoned by a mistake of a druggist, have rendered a verdict exonerating the latter from blame.

Thomson, Ga, Sep 9, 1868. Bloody tragedy yesterday near this place. Negro Sam Wilson, a stock cutter for the mill of Stoval & Wilson, with an axe, killed Mr Faulkner, formerly of S C. He then struck Mr Lowe with the axe-he lived but 3 hours. He then proceeded in the direction of Mr Thomson, with axe in hand, pursued by negroes. The negroes caught him & hung him. Mr Lowe was from Missouri & will be buried with Masonic Honors this day at 11 o'clock. –John M Curtis

Orange Springs, Fla, Jul 22. Adolphus, a negro, 18, formerly a slave of Gen W Owens, of Marion Co, Fla, visciously murdered Mrs Nancy Dupree, wife of Erastus D Dupree, formerly Miss Colson, born in Twiggs Co, Ga, Oct 22, 1845. Knowing Mr Dupree was away, Adolphus came to Mrs Dupree demanding 75 cents owed him for some work. Mrs Dupree said she there was not money in the house to pay him with, & ordered him off. He then shot her with a musket, taking off the top of her head, & kicked & beat her until she was in a dying condition. A few days more & she would have been a mother for the first time. Adolphus was taken the next day. The sheriff demanded the prisoner, but Mr Dupree's brother & friends refused to give him up; he was dealt with by lynch law. Many of the negroes wanted to burn him alive. Mrs Dupree was a member of the Union Baptist Church; a good wife, a spotless Christian. –D L Branning

Nashville, Jul 20. Jeremiah Ezell, [white man] was shot Sat near Franklin, Tenn. Ezell & others patrolled the streets on horseback, & rode out from town; they were fired on by 18 negroes in ambush. Ezell died from his wound Sunday.

Revenue appointments made yesterday by Sec McCulloch:
Storekeepers: A A Terrell, Ill; O B Stone, Ohio; Robt Terrell, Va
Gaugers: Chas E Dimmitt, Ohio; H H Brown, Mich
Tobacco Inspectors: Allen O Binckley, Mo; Saml Reynolds, N Y; Dennis Hogan, N Y; H J McMahon, N Y; John F Coulter, N Y.

The Balt Sun of yesterday says: Mrs Lincoln, widow of the late Pres, with her youngest son, after the marriage of Capt Robt Lincoln, her eldest son, at Wash, on Sep 24, returned to this city on the 26th, & took rooms at Barnum's City Hotel, where she remained in comparative retirement, being visited only by a few personal friends, until Thu last, when she left with her son, & was driven directly to **Locust Point**. Veiled & unknown to the crowd, the widow & son of the late President went on board the steamship **Baltimore**, bound to Bremen. She at once went to the her state room; her name did not appear on the passenger list. Those intimately acquainted with Mrs Lincoln aver that her visit to Europe at this time is for the purpose of placing her youngest son at school in Germany, after which she will probably spend the winter in the south of France.

Died: on Oct 4, Augustus Stuart, youngest son of Augustus E & Aietta Le Merle, aged 2 months & 15 days. His funeral is this evening at 1 o'clock, from 238 6th st.

Died: on Sep 9, at Salt Springs, Greenwood Co, Kansas, Geo McLeran, aged 66 years.

Died: on Oct 2, at Bristol, R I, Fannie C Campbell, daughter of Albert H & Mary P Campbell, & granddaughter of Judge Mason Campbell of the Treasury Dept, aged 8 years & 3 months.

Trustee's sale of valuable improved real estate on 7th st road, in Wash Co, D C; by deed of trust from Nicholas Lochboehler & his wife Caroline Lochboehler, to the subscriber, dated Sep 19, 1868, recorded among the land records of Wash Co, D C, in Liber R M H, No 14, folios 191 thru 193. Public auction on Nov 4, part of a piece of ground known as *Mount Pleasant*, [lot 39;] with bldgs thereon. –John Killian, trustee
-Green & Williams, aucts

Orphans Court of Wash Co, D C, Oct 3, 1868. In the case of Sarah Green, admx c t a of Edwin Green, dec'd, the administratrix c t a & Court have appointed Oct 27 next, for the final settlement of the personal estate of the said dec'd, of the assets in hand.
-Jas R O'Beirne, Reg/o wills

Orphans Court of Wash Co, D C, Oct 3, 1868. In the case of John A Ruff, exc of Andrew Small, dec'd, the executor & Court have appointed Nov 21 next, for the final settlement of the personal estate of the said dec'd, of the assets in hand.
-Jas R O'Beirne, Reg/o wills

WED OCT 7, 1868

The fine residence of Mr Penlezey, on Congress st, Gtwn, has been sold at private sale for $7,500.

Equity Court-Judge Wylie. 1-Finch et al vs May et al. Appointing R T Morsell trustee to sell. 2-Hines vs Hines et al. Appointing a commission to appoint a guardian ad litem. 3-Mulligan et al vs Mulligan et al; pro confesso vs Sarah Mulligan, & reference to auditor.

Orphans Court-Judge Purcell, Oct 6, 1868. 1-Michl Talty gave bond in the sum of $1,000 as administrator of John Talty; Martin Connolly & John Riley, sureties.
2-The first & final account of the executor of Jas Fullalove, & distributions of the estate were approved & passed. 3-Rev Jacob A Walter was appointed guardian to the infant Ela McCall, baptized Cora Anna Garrish. Bond, $300.

Mrd: on Oct 6, at the M st Methodist Church, by Rev Mr Tudor, Mr A M Hughes, jr, of Columbia, Tenn, to Miss Lillie T Smoot, of Wash, D C.

Died: on Aug 15, at Oaxsca, Mexico, Jas Dempsey Hutton, a native of Wash, D C.

N Y, Oct 6. Wm Barker, superintendent of the Panama railroad, was assassinated by J L Baldwin, a civil engineer in the employ of the company. Baldwin was suffering from mania potu & subsequently shot himself, & will probably die.

Savannah, Ga, Oct 6. The Savannah Republican was sold by the administrator today, & goes into the hands of Col J R Sneed, the former editor & proprietor, who takes possession immediately.

Horses for sale: J B Olcott & Son, Livery & Sale Stables, 469, 471, & 473, 8th st, between D & E sts.

U S Patent Ofc, Wash, Oct 2, 1868. Ptn of Ambrose Foster, of Lauraville, Md, for himself & the reps of J A Messenger, dec'd, praying for the extension of a patent granted to said Ambrose Foster, on Jan 16, 1855, for an improved Building Block.
-S H Hodges, Acting Com'r of Patents

Supreme Court of D C, Oct 6, 1868; in Equity No 1,409. Geo M Weston & Bethshebe his wife, plnts, vs Albert Moore, Lt Col Edw Williston & Helen Beatrice his wife; John Washburn & Robt C Washburn, minors under the age of 21 years, children of Alge___ Washburn & Ann Sarah Washburn his wife, but now deceased, Frank Moore, Cyrus Moore & Albert P Moore, minors, under 21 years of age, & children of Orrin Moore, now dec'd, & his wife, Frank F Moore, dfndnts. Dfndnts to appear on or before the first rule day occurring 40 days after this day, which will be the first Tuesday of Dec, 1868, otherwise the cause will be proceeded with as in case of default.

THU OCT 8, 1868
At the corner of Third & E st, Wm B Todd is erecting 2 neat residences, designed to be occupied by his two sons, Dr Seth Todd & Wm B Todd, jr. The bldgs are being built in the best possible manner.

Ex-Govn'r L W Bartley, of Ohio, lately purchased from Messrs Sykes, Chadwick & Co, the valuable property opposite the Treasury Dept, fronting on Pa ave & Lafayette Square, long occupied as the headquarters of the Dept of Wash. The price paid was, we understand $75,000. Judge Bartley intends to improve the property, with a view to making it his residence in the future.

Hymenial. John T Given, a gentleman highly esteemed & respected in this community, was on Tuesday evening united in marriage to Miss Amanda C Walters. The ceremony was performed by Rev Geo W Samson, assisted by Rev Dr Ames, at the residence of Mrs Ross, corner of 9th & I sts. The happy couple left in the 8:30 P M train, enroute for a honeymoon trip to the North.

Prof Edw Foreman, formerly of the Wash Univ, Md, & now professor in the Smithsonian Institute, has also been appointed Professor of Chemistry in the Medical Dept of Gtwn College, of Wash City.

The following appointments & promotions have just been made in the Post Ofc: Theodore L Holbrook, appointed temporary clerk in money order ofc-salary $1,200 per annum; Alex'r Somerville, promoted from regular laborer to temporary clerk same of-salary $900 per annum; J P Chestnut, appointed regular labor.

Yesterday decrees of divorce were issued in the Circuit Court divorcing Lucy Reese from the bonds of matrimony with John P Reese. Also, divorce granted to Chas P Wannell, jr, from Letitia Wannell.

N Y, Oct 7. Brig Gen Wm Gater, U S A, died in this city this afternoon, after a short illness, aged 80 years. [Oct 12th newspaper. N Y, Oct 11. The funeral of Brvt Brig Gen Gates, U S army was largely attended this afternoon. All the U S troops from Govnr's Island acted as an escort, & the body was taken to Govn'r Island for interment.] Note: Gater/Gates: copied as written.

Died: on Oct 7, Mrs Matilda Coyle, relic of the late Francis Coyle, aged 79 years. Her funeral will take place on Friday, from the residence of Mr B Bayliss, 257 I st, between 17th & 18th sts, at 10 o'clock, requiem mass will be celebrated at St Aloysius Church at 11 o'clock.

Died: on Sep 29, in Macon, Miss, of congestive fever, Mrs Sarah Townsend Ferris, formerly of Wash, D C.

Dissolution of partnership, by mutual consent, of Moses T Parker & Chas MacNichol, Wash, D C, Oct 1, 1868. –M T Parker, C MacNichol

Supreme Court of D C, Equity 1,235. Francis Wheatley vs Eliza M Clampitt et al. Statement of the account of sales & distribution among the heirs of Wm H Clampitt; meeting on Oct 12, at 10 o'clock. –Walter S Cox, auditor

Supreme Court of D C, Equity 341, docket 7. Matilda Grammer vs Todd & Prebasco. Ratify sales made by the trustee, to Jas P Kelleher, of the north half of lot 12 in square 377, in Wash City, for $530.45; & to Jona _ Collins, the south half of lot 12, in square 377, for $530.45. –R J Meigs, clerk

FRI OCT 9, 1868
Association of the Oldest Inhabitants, Wed; Dr John B Blake, pres, in the chair; Rev Randolph Gurley was elected a member of the association, & the following nominated for membership: Mr Middleton nominated Edgar Patterson, of Wash Co; Mr Simms nominated Wm H Upperman; Mr Brent nominated Dr Chas E W Davis; Dr BlakeCmdor Levin Powell, U S N; all of which were laid over for one month, under rule. On motion by Mr Jenken Thomas, Judge Jas Dunlop, of Gtwn, was elected an honorary member. Dr Tustin moved that a cmte of two, be appointed by the chair to procure a suitable room for the meeting; Messrs J Carroll Brent & John F Callan were appointed. Dr Gunton moved that the meetings be held at 4 o'clock instead of 5 o'clock; which was adopted.

Messrs J B Wheeler & Co, aucts, sold at private sale a 3 story brick house & lot on Bridge st near Green st, Gtwn, to Jas Goddard, for $1,625. Also, a vacant lot on Green st, near Bridge, to Wm H Godey, for $16.50 per front foot.

Regular session of the Board of Police, yesterday. Pvt Silas H Sherwood, charged with gross violation of the rules, was admonished to be more careful for the future. The annual reports of T A Lazenly, sec of the Board; of Geo R Herrick, property clerk; & C Noonan, lt in charge of the sanitary company, were approved. Adolph Kreas, Michl McSweeny, & Patrick Fitzgerald were appointed privates on the force. Francis Quinn was appointed an additional private for 6 months, to do duty at the Ebbitt House. The official bond of Pvt Detective Geo F Gibbons was received & approved. Applications for liquor licenses disapproved: John Mooney, Edw McCormick, Jas O Reinzel, L P Keach, Mrs D Lang, C H Reinzel, [of Gtwn] & Geo Mueller, Henry Koch, Michl Connor, John Loeliger, & J Joseph, of Wash.

Mrd: on Oct 8, at the residence of the bride's brother by Rev Fr Boyle, E P McManus, of Balt, Md, to Mary A, only daughter of the late Martin King, of Wash, D C. No cards. [Balt, Phil, & N Y papers please copy.]

Mrd: on Oct 8, at Wesley Chapel, David A Burr, of Wash City, to Miss *Juda M Mothershead, of Indianoplis, Ind. [Star copy.] [*Possibly Juda. Difficult to read.]

Died: on Oct 5, at his late residence, **Belle Haven**, Richmond Co, Va, Mr Robt K Nevitt, formerly of Wash, D C.

Died: on Sep 30, in Macon, Miss, of congestive fever, Mary Ann, eldest daughter of Henry C & the late Mary Ferris, formerly of Wash City.

Died: on Oct 8, Anne, the eldest daughter of Bernard & Sarah V Bryan, aged 6 years, 2 months & 9 days. Her funeral will take place this afternoon, at 4:30 P M, from her parents; residence, 8th & L sts, No 457, Navy Yard.

Trustee's sale of valuable brewery with all the fixtures & machinery; by certain deeds of trust to the undersigned, among the records of the Dist of Columbia; formerly known as the Metropolitan Brewery, & now occupied by Louis Beyer, embracing lots 18 thru 21, & part of lot 22, in square 535, in Wash City. –Fred W Jones, Whitman C Bestor, John Boyd, jr, Fred W Jones, Chas Klomann, F Schmidt, trustees. -Green & Williams, aucts

SAT OCT 10, 1868
John J Bogue, real estate agent, Gtwn, sold to Messrs Dungan & Quigley, of the Alexandria Canal & Aqueduct Co, that valuable property on **Arlington Heights** formerly known as **Hoover's farm**, upon which **Fort Corcoran** is located. The estate contains 141 acres, which, with the improvements, was sold for $16,000 cash, in gold.

Died: on Oct 9, in Wash City, Philip Seebold, in his 30th year. His funeral will take place from his late residence, 263 N Y ave, between 6th & 7th sts, on Sunday at 3 o'clock P M.

Richmond, Oct 9. John Perkins was executed in the jail yard at Portsmouth, Va, today, for violating Sarah J Ford. He addressed the crowd, saying he expected to be before God in a few minutes, & declared that he was innocent, & did not know whether Sarah Ford was a man or a woman. Perkins was from Wakefield, N H.

Boston Post, Sep 17. The supposed perpetrator of the brutual rape upon Mrs Wildman, in Brookfield, Conn, has ben arrested in New Haven & will be taken to Dansbury for trial. He is a young strongly built negro about 25, represent himself as a former slave in Va.

Memphis, Jul 22. 1-On Monday night Saml McSwain, living near Granada, Miss, was shot & mortally wounded by a negro, Sam McLean, who was pursued by the citizens & a party of soldiers. He was captured & brought back to Grenada. 2-Gus Benton, a well known confectioner, was severely stabbed this morning by Chas Gustman.

Fortress Monroe, Va, Aug 26. Yesterday Harrison Young, a colored man, was hanged for the murder of Mr Wooten, of Warwick Co, 2 years ago. [Oct 24th newspaper: **Fortress Monroe**, Oct 23. Two negroes, Abel Williams & Henry Young, sentenced to death for the murder of Mr Wooten, 2 years ago, in Warwick Co, who were to have been hung today, have been respited by the Govn'r until Nov 27.]

We scarcely heard of the arrival of Hon Howell Cobb at N Y when came the stunning news of his sudden death on Oct 9th. He dropped dead in the corridor of the Fifth Avenue Hotel. Mr Cobb was in the pride of life, full of physical health & mental force. Howell Cobb was born at Cherry Hill, Jefferson Co, Ga, Sep 7, 1815; when a child, his father removed to Athens, Ga, where he has since resided. He graduated at Franklin College in 1834; admitted to the bar in 1836; in 1837 was appointed Solicitor Gen of the Western Circuit, which he held 4 years; was elected a Rep in Congress in 1842, re-elected in 1844, 1846, & 1848; was chosen Govn'r of Ga; in 1855 was elected to Congress, & on the accession of Mr Buchanan to the Presidency, Govn'r Cobb went into his Cabinet as Sec of the Treasury. He took a prominent part in the rebellion of 1861, & was a member of the so-called Confederate Congress, & brigadier general. [Oct 12th newspaper: Mr Cobb had been stopping at the Fifth Avenue Hotel for the past 4 weeks together with his wife, Mrs Mary A Cobb & his eldest daughter, Mary Ann, 19 years old. They met Col J J William, of Fla, who was formerly an ofcr on Gen Cobb's staff, & Bishop Beckwith, of Ga, on their return to their room from breakfast. Mr Cobb stopped to introduce Mr Beckwith to his wife. They conversed but a short time, when Mr Cobb turned to address his wife, but, without uttering anything, put his hand to his head, swooned, & sat down upon the step. Mrs Cobb knowing of her husbands' vertigo, expected he would revive. Col Williams saw instantly that he was seriously ill, & hastened to get a physician. Mr Cobb expired in 20 minutes. –N Y World, Saturday]

Memphis, Oct 9. 1-Geo W Stockton, bookkeeper of Gibbon & Bro, was found drowned in Wolf river. Supposed suicide. 2-Mollie Everett, a negro woman, died this afternoon from the effect of a beating administered by her husband with a boot-jack.

The case of Eliz C Chessman vs Bertram Leins, action for breach of promise, was finished yesterday, the jury returning a verdict for the plntf of $2,000 damages, with costs. Exceptions were filed, & the case will go the the Court of General Term.

Mr T A Tolson, who was severely injured about 2 months since in being thrown from his buggy, is confined to his bed with an attack of billious intermittent fever, & is very low.

Phil, Oct 9. Rev Thos H Stockton, for several terms Chaplain of the House of Reps, & well known as a minister of the Methodist Episcopal Church, died this evening, in this city, aged 60 years.

Yazoo [Miss] Banner, Sep 25. On Sep 18, near Yazoo City, Mrs Fannie Richardson, age 68, infirmed, was outraged and badly beaten by a negro man, John Nance, as she walked to her home, with the aid of a cane. Her son, Mr Jas Richardson went in pursuit of him. When found, Esquire Ratcliffe took charge of him & sent him to Yazoo City, to be lodged in jail. From his statements, he was guilty.

Boston, Oct 9. Geo L Richardson, of the firm of Richardson & Co, of this city, residing at Longwood, arose from his bed this morning, while laboring under a temporary fit of insanity, deliberately cut the throats of two of his children. The oldest, a boy of 13 years, is dead, but the other may recover. Richardson fled from the house & was found in his barn, & sent to the insane asylum. Last summer Richardson was sun-struck, & has had trouble with his head ever since He had been absent from business for more than a week. [Oct 13th newspaper: Mr Richardson has a wife & 4 children; the lad who is dead was 14 years of age; beloved by all.]

Arthur D Witzleben, having disposed of his entire stock in trade, Wines, Liquors, etc, the business will continue under the firm of A De Witzleben & Co. -Alfred De Witzleben, Chas F Myers.

MON OCT 12, 1868
Davenport Gaz, of Monday. Last Sat the splendid team of P L Mitchell, of Rock Island, was being driven down the street with a carriage, in which were seated Mrs P L Mitchell & her 3 daughters, Miss Laura, Mrs H T Wadsworth, & Mrs W C Wadsworth, [the two last of this city] & Mrs W Grenell, of Rock Island. The driver halted for the approaching train, & the animals gave a sudden plunge to the left & went on a mad run; the carriage was thrown at least 6 feet in the air. Mrs Mitchell expired on Sunday. Mrs Grenell was taken to her home with a bad wound at the back of the head. The other ladies received cuts & bruises. Mrs Mitchell has lived for more than 10 years in Rock Island; she was the mother of Mrs H T & Mrs W C Wadsworth, & had extensive acquaintance in Davenport also. Her age was 55 years. Mrs Grenell is still in a stupid state.

Orphans Court-Judge Purcell, Oct 10, 1868. 1-The will of the late August Dorges, of company F, 44th U S infty, was filed for probate. 2-Gotlieb Weiner was appointed administrator of the estate of Clarence Fendall, late of the U S coast survey. Bond was entered into by W Y Fendall in the sum of $1,800. 3-Letters of administration were granted to Chas Graham on the personal estate of Hannibal Graham; bond, $800. 4-Hiram Berner was appointed guardian to Maria Jane Felson & Henry Felson, orphans of Henry & Eliz Felson, late of this city; bond $1,500. 5-Chas Augustus Hooe aged 17 years, was bound as an apprentice to Leonard C Bailey till his 21st year.

Died: on Oct 10, Mrs Eliz Wright, wife of Chas J Wright, aged 45 years & 5 months. Her funeral will take place from her late residence, on 6th st, between I & K sts, this evening, at 3 o'clock.

Henry W Grinnell, a son of Henry Grinnell, of N Y, late a lt in the American navy, has been constituted Inspector Genr'l of the Japanese navy; salary $15,000 per annum.

Wm H Horton, Sub Assist Com'r Bureau of Refugees, Freedmen & Abandoned Lands, in Texas, has been dishonorably discharged the service of the bureau by command of Brvt Maj Gen Reynolds. It is charged that in the summer of 1867 he received a bribe.

Ex-President Pierce is now able to ride out.

N Y, Oct 11. The funeral of Brvt Brig Gen Gates, U S army was largely attended this afternoon. All the U S troops from Govnr's Island acted as an escort, & the body was taken to Govn'r Island for interment.

N Y, Oct 11. Walter B Griffin, a passenger by the steamer **Guiding Star**, was arrested at midnight on a charge of embezzling money from the North American Ins Co of Calif.

Orphans Court of Wash Co, D C. Letters of administration on the personal estate of Clarence Fendall, late of U S Coast Survey, dec'd. —W Y Fendall, adm

Orphans Court of Wash Co, D C, Oct 10, 1868. In the case of Christina V N Callan, excx of Teresa Hill, of Wash City, D C, the executrix & Court have appointed Oct 21 next, for the final settlement of the personal estate of the said dec'd, of the assets in hand. -Jas R O'Beirne, Reg/o wills

Orphans Court of Wash Co, D C, Oct 10, 1868. In the case of A Thos Bradley & Wm A Bradley, jr, excs of Wm A Bradley, sr, dec'd, the executors & Court have appointed Oct 31st next, for the final settlement of the personal estate of the said dec'd, of the assets in hand. -Jas R O'Beirne, Reg/o wills

TUE OCT 13, 1868
Boston, Oct 12. Jos Warren Revere, a well known merchant of this city, died at Canton, Mass, aged 91. He was a son of Paul Revere, of the Revolutionary War.

La Crosse Democrat: on Friday a band of 5 robbers went to the house of an old man named Klum, a German, who resides on the old Scott farm, in Vernon Co, tied the old man & his wife to a bed, robbed them, then set the bed & house on fire. They were rescued by the neighbors, but the house was burned. The robbers took $1,700 & 22 gold watches, which Klum brought from Germany; jumping into a wagon, made their escape.

Mr Thos Stanley, an old & highly respected citizen of Wash, was quite serverely injured yesterday by falling from the steps of his residence, seriously fracturing one of his limbs.

Mrd: on Oct 8, at Phil, by Rev D A Cunningham, Geo D Patton, jr, of Wash, to Louisa/Louise, daughter of Henry R Ayres, of Phil. No cards.

Died: at his residence, on 9th st, Wm Souness, native of Haddington, Scotland. His funeral will take place this Tuesday evening, at 2 o'clock. [No death date given.]

Died: on Oct 12, Bertha Mead, the youngest daughter of Jas H & Julia Mead, aged 19 months. Her funeral will be today at 3 o'clock, from the residence of her parents, 6th & B st.

U Augustus Burgdorf, 453 Pa ave, furnishing Undertaking in all its branches promptly attended to.

Trustee's sale of valuable bldg lot in south Wash, at auction; by decree of the Supreme Court of D C, wherein Geo W Howard & others are cmplnts, & Wm J Howard & others dfndnts; public auction on Oct 29, of lot 6 in square 265, in Wash City; lot fronts 50 feet on 14th st, between C & D sts. –M H Stevens, trustee -Green & Williams, aucts

Trustee's sale of valuable lease-hold; by deed of trust dated Apr 2, 1868, recorded in Liber E C E, No 2, folios 442 etc, of the Chattel records of Wash Co, D C; public auction on Oct 19, all the unexpired term of Adolph Miller in a certain lease from John Moore to the said Miller of part of lot 515 fronting on N Y ave, beginning at the n w corner of Margaret Mullanys' lot; improved by a small frame house. –John D Ellis, trustee -Green & Williams, aucts

WED OCT 14, 1868
St Louis Republican: inquest on Sat on Bertha Gebhart, age 14 years. She was a "sewing girl," & resided with her parents at 2626 Carondelet ave. She slept in the same room with her grandmother, & accidentally overturned a small night lamp, the floor & oil catching fire. Her father Henry Gebhart ran to her help. She died on Saturday.

Rock Island [Ill] Union, Oct 7. On Monday last, in Mercer Co, Martha Martindale, 18, was living with her step-father, Chas Williams, a farmer. John G Allsworth, a German, aged 22, about 2 years on this country, was working for another farmer of the vicinity, named Ketzel. John was smitten with Martha, & he stated that she had promised him her hand in marriage, & rented a farm in Iowa, to which he proposed to move when their nuptials were consumated. However, the course of love did not run smooth, & John blamed Martha of fickleness. Some two weeks ago they had an altercation, in which he struck her in the face. John was arrested, tried, & fined $20 for the assault. On Sat last, John went to Andalusia, bought a Colt's revolver of Mr Jones, on which he paid $9, & pawned 2 rings for the balance. Sunday he went to her house; her bedroom on the first floor, he pushed back the curtain & fired at her as she lay in bed. Allsworth then shot himself in the head with fatal effect. He was buried the same day, on a piece of unknown prairie east of Benj Dunn's. Martha's wound is not dangerous, & she will recover.

Mr John J Bogue, of Gtwn, sold the fine brick dwlg with the spacious grounds attached, on the northeast corner of Third & Fayette sts, to E B Barrett, for $20,000.

Orphans Court-Judge Purcell, Oct 13, 1868. 1-The following were filed & passed: First & final account of Henry C Brown, adm of Jonathan Nichols; First account of Augustus Brown, guardian of Victoria Brown; second account of Emma Ten Broeck, admx of Saml C Smoot; second individual account of Emma Ten Broeck, guardian to Kenneth R & Matilda Smoot. 2-S W Pearson gave bond in the sum of $2,000 as adm of Eliz A Cross, H O Wood, W B Entwisle, sureties. 3-The argument of the case of Crown vs Crown, which is an application for the removal of a guardian on the ground that he was appointed during the lifetime of the minor, & without his consent, was commenced. Judge Leach & Mr J E Williams for petitioner; & Lloyd & Lascelle for respondent.

Mrd: on Oct 12, at the Church of the Ascension, by Rev Dr Addison, Adelbert Gordon, of Wash City, to Miss Bessie Laws, formerly of Hampton, Va. [Norfolk papers please copy.]

Died: on Oct 13, in PG Co, Md, at the residence of his grandfather, R W Bates, Robert Francis, only child of Frank A & Virginia B Springer, aged 1 year, 3 months & 2 days. His remains will be at **Congressional Cemetery** for interment at 3 o'clock this evening, Wednesday, Oct 15.

Plumbing, Gas, & Steam Fitting, by A R Shepherd & Bros, Dealers in Metals & Mscl Hardware, 269 Pa ave, near 11th st. [Ad]

Dr Simeon Smith, at the time of his death, 60 years ago, bequeathed $1,000 to the town of West Haven, Vt, to be kept at compound interest till this time, when it should be expended in establishing a grammar school in the town. By poor investment $100 of the principal was lost, some years ago, & it has not always been possible to invest the interest promptly, so that not the full value has been secured, but, as it is, the fund amounts to nearly $23,000.

For Stoves & Tinware go to H I Gregory, dealer in Stoves, Tinware, & Housekeeping Goods, 321 Pa ave, near 7th st. [Ad]

THU OCT 15, 1868
Govn'r Clayton, of Ark, accidentally shot himself in the wrist the other day. The hand has been amputated.

Equity Court-Judge Fisher. 1-Murray et al vs Murray et al; appointing J B Donnaly trustee, instead of J N Fearson, dec'd. 2-Brady vs Brady; order that the parties live apart; the eldest child to defendant; alimony, $30 per month. 3-Leynard vs Leonard; order appointing W B Drayton to take testimony.

Attention is called to the advertisement of the extensive & complete dying & scouring establishment of Mr A Fisher, whose ofc is at 448 7th st, opposite the Patent Ofc.

On Monday afternoon a litte daughter of Sgt Robt Johnson, of the 7th Precinct Police, was run over by a street car on the 7th st line, & her left foot was badly crushed.

Mrs Mary L Hutchinson, the mother of the Hutchinson family singers, died recently of paralysis at Milford, N H, aged 83. She was the mother of 16 children, to whom the musical powers with which she was naturally gifted were generously transmitted.

Mrd: on Oct 14, at the Ninth st Presbyterian Church, Wash City, by Rev Dr J C Smith, Saml Francis Rynex, of Wash City, to Adela F Reddick, 3rd daughter of Mr David Reddick, of Ill. No cards.

Died: on Oct 12, at Phil, Wm R Edes, of Gtwn, D C. His funeral will take place from the residence of his brother, David Edes, Washington st, near West, Gtwn, on Thursday, Oct 15, at 1:30 o'clock P M.

Macon [Ga] Journal of Sat: Triple execution on Sat of Amos Gorman, Levi Jenkins, & Robt Whitus, convicted of the murder of Jonathan Sheffield, on Aug 25 last, near that city. The execution took place on Oct 9, at the city jail. Three ropes hung from rings attached to the cross beam; the whole was veiled with a curtain. Three plain pine coffins were passed in. The prisoners came out all dressed in a white shroud; their faces plainly showed the trace of tears. Fr Collana, of the Catholic Church, offered to baptize them in that faith, to which Whitus said: "Well, if it will do any good." It was done; they all knelt & repeated a prayer after him.

Phil, Oct 14. Two brothers, Christian & Edw Byrnes, were shot dead, & Chas Specht & J Toland were wounded, last night in the 4th Ward, in a political row, the origin of & actors in which are unknown. Policeman John Young, who was wounded in a row in the 7th Ward last night, died this morning. Saml Holt & Chas Powell have been arrested, charged with murdering the brothers Byrnes. Holt was a sheriff's deputy.

Phil, Oct 14. The lad Perkins, who was shot yesterday by Deputy Sheriff Flanagan, died today at the hospital.

Savannah, Ga, Oct 14. The steamer **San Salvador** arrived this morning with the remains of Hon Howell Cobb. Flags in the city are displayed at half mast. Augusta, Ga, Oct 14. The remains of Gen Cobb arrived here this morning, escorted by cmtes from Savannah & Macon.

FRI OCT 16, 1868
Yesterday John Philp, a young Englishman, committed suicide, at his boarding house, [kept by Mrs Cudlipp,] on Pa ave, between 3rd & 4½ sts. He had been residing there about 18 months; employed for some months past in one of the ofcs of the Freedmen's Bureau, but was discharged on Oct 3 on account of excessive use of intoxicating liquors. Mr Chas Cudlipp handed him a letter from England & he went to his room. He was found with his throat cut, just before he breathed his last.

Mrd: on Oct 14, by Rev John Conron, pastor of New Brighton Church, Staten Island, N Y, Chas K Landis of Vineland, N J, to Clara F Meade, daughter of Capt R W Meade, U S N.

Mrd: on Oct 14, at the parsonage, by Rev P B Brown, Lloyd P Locke to Miss Teany E Dice.

Mrd: on Oct 15, at the Church of the Ascension, by Rev Dr Pinckney, Leonard O Bowie to Miss Willie B Drew, both of Wash City. No cards.

Mrs Geo Francis Train has purchased 2 acres on the Bellevue beach at Newport for $15,000.

Some 2 weeks ago Mr A Von Zarboni, who occupied the position of stage manager at the Apollo Garden Theatre, died. His wife, Rosina Von Zarboni, so distressed at the death of her husband, committed suicide from the effects of prussic acid, on Sunday. On Friday she had ordered two tombstones to be placed over the graves of herself & husband. -St Louis Republican

SAT OCT 17, 1868
Thos R Laird was on Thursday appointed Supervisor of Internal Revenue for the district of Va & West Va.

The funeral of Mr Wm T French, a well know citizen of Wash, took place yesterday from his late residence, & was attended by large delegations of Odd Fellows & members of the Grand Encampment of the Dist, in which organization he held the position of Grand Marshal. The remains were deposited in **Glenwood Cemetery**.

The death of Count Waleski, the son of Napoleon I, by a Polish lady, already recorded, was very sudden. He arrived at Strasburg with his wife, who was quite ill. He entered the apartment to inquire after her health, & passed into an adjoining room, where he exclaimed, "A glass of water-quick-a doctor," & expired. [Oct 20th newspaper: Count Waleski died a poor man, & the expense of his funeral had to be defrayed out of the civil list.]

Died: on Oct 15, in Richmond, J C Douglas, aged 29 years, the eldest son of the late Wm & S E Douglas. His funeral will take place on Sunday, at 2:30 P M, from the residence of his mother, 591 H st north.

The family of the late Nathaniel Hawthorne are about to sail for Germany to reside.

Supreme Court of D C, Equity No 500. John A Middleton et al vs Eliza T Berry et al. Statement of the account of the trustees with the trust fund, & the balance for distribution; parties interested are to appear on Oct 22, at 1 o'clock. –Walter S Cox, auditor

MON OCT 19, 1868
Revenue appointments: Storekeepers:

J P Johnson, Ohio	John W Fisher, Ill
Henry A Homen, Mass	Jos W Thompson, N Y
John B Evans, Ky	W P Miller, Kan
John C Burton, Ind	

Gaugers:

Walker J Budington, N Y	W P Floyd, Pa
Robt B Lamon, Ill	Wm Wilson, Ohio
F B McElroy, Mo	

D H Ketchum has been appointed inspector of tobacco & cigars for the 6th Dist of Wisc.

Gen Hooker has been placed on the retired list, with full rank of Major General.

Orphans Court-Judge Purcell, Oct 17, 1868. 1-Gotlieb Wiener was appointed executor of the estate of August Dorges, dec'd; bond $500. 2-Susan Allison was appointed guardian to W Allison, orphan of John W Allison, late of Fairfax Co, Va; bond $2,500. 3-The will of Mary Frank was filed & fully proven. She bequeaths to her daughter, Ann Eliz Nolan, & her heirs & assigns, all her property of every description. Also, the claim which is pending in the Supreme Court of D C against Wm F Gardner, as well as all property & estate which may be awarded her by or under said cause. 4-A petition for the sale of the real estate of the orphans of Caleb Delaney, & order was granted to Ann Delaney.

Mrd: on Oct 15, by Rev E L Wells, of Pittsfield, Silas Wright Gillet to Abbie P Wood, daughter of Henry R Wood, all of New Lebanon, N Y. No cards.

Mrd: on Oct 15, at the residence of the bride's mother, by Rev Mr Duncan, David S Holland, of Wash, D C, to Mary E Hutton, of Montg Co, Md.

Mrd: on Oct 15, at the First Presbyterian Church, by Rev Dr Sunderland, John A Marchand, of Greensburg, Pa, to Mary E, only daughter of the late David S Todd, of Greensburg, Pa.

Mrd: on Oct 14, by Rev Chas H Nourse, at his residence, Maj John B Stanard, of Culpeper Court House, Va, to Miss Bettie K Peter, 4th daughter of the late John P C Peter, of Md.

Died: on Oct 18, in Gtwn, in his 83rd year, Geo Hill, sr, a native of Portsmouth, England, but for the last 50 years a citizen of Alexandria & Wash, D C. His funeral will take place on Oct 20 at 10:30 A M, from the residence of his son, Geo Hill, jr, 160 Bridge st, Gtwn. [Oct 21st newspaper: the funeral of the late Geo Hill, sr, took place yesterday, from the residence of his son, Geo Hill, jr; Rev Dr Perinchief, rector of St John's Church, [Episcopal,] preached the funeral sermon; after which the cortage moved to ***Oak Hill Cemetery***, where the remains were interred in the family burying ground. Mr Hill was a highly esteemed citizen of Gtwn, & for many years had been known in that community as a gentleman of honor & intelligence.]

N Y, Oct 18. At an altercation last night, in a liquor store, John McAdam was shot & fatally wounded by Michl Mulligan.

Memphis, Oct 18. A notorious character, Bill Porter, was shot & killed by a man named Carline last night, near the old Fair Grounds. An old feud existed between them. Carline was arrested & committed.

St Louis, Oct 18. Gen E B Brown, U S pension agent here, was required to plead yesterday to an indictment against him for conspiracy to defraud the Gov't, in connection with distilled spirits. The General's brother, Dr Brown, was also arrested for complicity in tobacco frauds.

TUE OCT 20, 1868
PG Co, Md: in the Circuit Court-State vs Wm Aken & John McNally, of Wash, D C. Presented & indicted for assault with intent to kill J W Burch, of this county. Tried by jury. Guilty of assault & battery. Fined $30 each, & costs.

Victor Hugo has been profoundly melancholy since his wfe's death. He talks only of his own probable decease, & his inability to work. The publication of his new novel, "1793," has been postponed.

New Orleans, Oct 19. The body of Sheriff Pope, of St Mary's parish, killed Sat night, arrived here this evening under charge of his wife, en route for Para, Ill, his home. Mr Pope was formerly colonel of the 29th Ill regt. No clue to his assassins has been obtained.

Lynchburg Republican, 18th. The engine **Washington**, attached to one of the special trains which left here yesterday, conveying the delegates from the Norfolk convention to their homes, exploded near Elk Creek Bridge, on the Tenn road, instantly killing Jerome Stout, the engineer, & Wm Beckham, the fireman. Mr Stout was unmarried. Mr Beckham leaves a wife & 2 children, who reside in this city.

Worcester, Mass, Oct 19. Fr O'Keefe, a Catholic priest at Clinton, Mass, died suddenly this morning.

Supreme Court of D C, Oct 19, 1868, Equity 1,402, Docket 9. John Deinhardt vs Louise Deinhardt. On motion of cmplnt by Mr Schmidt, his solicitor, it is ordered that the dfndnt cause her appearance to be entered herein on or before the first rule day occurring 40 days after this day; otherwise the case will be proceeded with as in case of default.
-R J Meigs, clerk

Peremptory sale of a valuable tract of land in PG Co, Md, at auction, on Oct 28, on the premises, that valuable tract of land known as *Conjurors Defeated*, containing 100 acres of land, adjoins the lands of Thos Jenkins & others, on the road leading to Good Hope. By order of the heirs, W L Wall & Co, aucts

WED OCT 21, 1868
Watson Freeman, for many years U S Marshal for the Dist of Mass, died on Oct 19 at this farm, in Sandwich, Mass; he was a native of Boston, & resided there most of his life. He was a worthy representative of a distinguished colonial ancestry. Of late years, he has passed the winter with his daughter & son-in-law, Mr Edw Clark, at their hospitable mansion in Washington.

Green & Williams, aucts, sold a 2 story frame house, with lot fronting on Q st north, between 1st & 2nd sts west, to John Dries, for $2,000; also part of lot 5 in square 771, improved by a brick house, to Mrs Ann Bean, for $1,000; & south part of same lot to Jas Fullalove, for $525; also lot adjoining the above, improved by a frame house, to Jas Myers, for $235. By same aucts, a 10 years' leasehold of Adolph Miller in part of lot 6, in square 515, fronting on N Y ave, was sold to G W Uttermehle, for $450. Fitch & Fox, real estate brokers & aucts, as agent for Mr Joshua Peirce, sold square 193 for $42,000. [This ground is in the northwest part of the city, having a frontage of 450 feet on 16th st, & will, when subdivided, furnish handsome sites for residences.]

Leonie Leblanc, a Parisian actress, recently lost 300,000 francs at roulette, in Baden-Baden; & Prince George won 160,000 francs at the same place.

Orphans Court-Judge Purcell, Oct 20, 1868. 1-Jas H Luxen gave bond in the sum of $2,000 as guardian to the orphans of Jas Beckert. 2-First & final account of Thos Hutchinson, exc of P Reynolds, filed & passed. 3-Fourth account of same as guardian to orphans of John Robinson, filed & passed. 4-Ann E Noland gave bond in the sum of $1,000 as admx c t a of Mary Frank.

Promotions made in the Treasury Dept from Oct 1 to Oct 15:
Second Auditor's ofc: H L Shepherd, 1st to 2nd class, vice J H Claflin, resigned.
Ofc Comptroller of Currency: J W Griffin, to 4th class; Edw Denig, to 3rd class; Wm Cruikshank, to 2nd class; J S Langworth, to 2nd class. Third Auditor's Ofc: J C Fay, to 2nd class.
Internal Revenue Bureau: Saml Wilcox, appointed head of division, to take effect from Jul 1, 1868.
Register's Ofc: Frank P Norton, to 3rd class.
Resignations:
Second Auditor's Ofc: J H Claflin, S Smolinski, J Irving Burns, J A Beck, L M Van Gorden, Geo T Colwell, & E B Williams.
Register's Ofc: Mrs M P Ratcliffe, R McAllister, & Geo R Ball.
Ofc Comptroller of the Currency: A A Miller, E A McKay, Geo Sage, & Mrs Mary G Mahon.
Internal Revenue Bureau: Miss M Kimball & Miss N A Hanna.
Treasurer's Ofc: M J O'Shaughnessy.
Third Auditor's Ofc: Chas H Beach & C T Wyman.
Second Comptroller's Ofc: W D Morris.
Sec's Ofc: W S Hineline & Mrs M W Smart.
Assist Supervising Architect's Ofc: B Oertley.
Wm C Burnell, of Oregon, a clerk in the Pension Bureau, has been transferred to a clerkship in the Third Auditor's Ofc of the Treasury Dept.
Com'r Cox, of the Pension Ofc, has appointed Mr W L Hinds, of N Y, a clerk in the Pension Ofc, vice Burnell, transferred.

Mrd: on Oct 20, at Wash, D C, at the residence of the bride's father, by Rev S D Finckle, D D, Frank H Finkel, of Wash City, to Miss Lottie Brady, daughter of Hon Jasper E Brady, formerly of Pittsburg, Pa. No cards. [Pittsburg & Harrisburg papers please copy.]

Dayton, Ohio, Oct 20. A woman named Warriman murdered her husband near this city this morning. She first shot him with a revolver, & then struck him several times on the head with an axe. Cause, domestic troubles.

St Louis, Oct 20. Ben Cutler, the Surveyor General of New Mexico, & formerly Adj Gen of Calif, died on Sunday last at Santa Fe.

Boston, Mass, Oct 20. Alfred Green, negro, was sentenced to 4 months in the House of Correction for throwing stones at a Democratic procession last night.

From the Pacific. San Francisco, Oct 20. 1-Rev Lorrin Andrews died on Sep 29. The dec'd was a native of Connecticut, but a resident of the islands since 1828. 2-The flag of the North German Confederation was raised over the residence of Theo C Henck, recently appointed consul of that power.

Springfield, Mass, Oct 20. Jas Dyer was arrested at Holyoke today for the rape & murder of Catharine McCabe, whose dead body was taken from the canal last night. The parties were seen together on Friday night. Dyer has a wife & 6 children.

THU OCT 22, 1868
Where has C Baum removed his Hoop-skirt & Corset Manufactory? To 513 7th st, Intelligencer Bldg, where he always keeps the best goods at the lowest prices. [Ad]

China, Glass, & Housefurnishing Goods: Thos Pursell & Son's, 351 Pa ave, opposte Metropolitan Hotel. Stoneware at factory prices.

Best French & American Confectionary; refreshment of all kinds; oysters & game. Wedding & reception parties furnished by J H Shaffield, 246 Pa ave, near 12th st.

Public sale of 40 acres of land near Contee's Station; on Nov 4, at Beltsville, the farm of the late Thos H Worthington, directly on the railroad between Muirkirk & Contee's Stations. –John Glenn & Co, 68 Fayette st, Balt.

In addition to their other duties, the detectives of the Metropolitan Police have now to take their turn in standing guard over the prisoner E B Olmsted, the alleged defaulting postal disbursement clerk who is still confined at Gov't expense at the hotel of Mr Bunker, 6th & Pa ave. Mr Olmstead is having quite a pleasant time as the guest of the Treasury Dept, which department has engaged Maj Richards to act as host. That gentleman, by proxy, sees that everything necessary for the comfort of his guest is provided, & that every attention is paid the prisoner. We understand that yesterday Mr Burr, of the Treasury Dept, [who seems to be judge, jury, & manager in this case] fixed the amount of bail necessary to be entered by Olmsted at $20,000. If, as was reported by the Post Ofc Dept, the defalcation was but $9,000. Why this enormous bail! Is the prisoner a criminal, or not? And why is he not treated as other criminals are? Or is the whole procedure a farce?

FRI OCT 23, 1868
Cmdor C H Poor, U S navy, promoted to the position of rear admiral, vice Read Admiral H K Hoff, who has been placed on the retired list.

John Williams appointed Collector of Internal Revenue for the Second Dist of Tenn, vice Abernethy, resigned.

Despatch from Boston: 6 men fishing in dories were drowned & a 7th knocked over board by the main boom: Jas Burke, Jas Driscoll, Jas Hobert, John Lyden, Patrick Hinds, Flaterty, & Logan. They were all residents of or near Boston, & most had families.

Mr Geo W Childs has given the Philadelphia Typographical Society a lot of ground in **Woodlands Cemetery**, for which he paid $8,000.

Yesterday Chas Ellis, a colored man, was brought before Justice Clark, on the charge of assault on Mr Thos Young, a private watchman at Centre Market. Ellis cut Young severely with a bowie knife in several places.

The President has pardoned Maj Gen Wm Preston, of Ky, formerly of the Confederate army. The pardon is granted under the third exception of Pres Lincoln's amnesty proclamation, excepting all above the rank of colonel, & was recommended by ex-Atty Gen Speed, Hon Montgomery Blair, & others.

Mrd: on Oct 16, in Balt, by Rev Dr Bullock, Geo C Henning, of Wash, D C, to Mrs Sue A Parker, of Accomac C H, Va.

M H Stevens & Co offer their entire stock, fixtures, & good will for sale. The declining health of Mr Stevens is the reason for selling. The business has been conducted by Mr Stevens for over 25 years. 360 Pa ave, Metropolitan Hotel.

The monument to the memory of the late Maj Gen John Sedwick, U S Volunteers, was unveiled & solemnly inaugurated Oct 21st at the U S Military Academy at West Point. Inscription on the pediment: [Metal plate inserted in the south panel.]

     Major General
     JOHN SEDGWICK
    United States Volunteers,
     Born Sept 13, 1813
   Killed in battle at Spotsylvania, Va,
     May 9, 1864,
  While in command of the Sixth Corps,
    Army of the Potomac.
    The Sixth Army Corps,
  In loving admiration of its Commander,
    Dedicates this Statue
     to his
     Memory

Mr Geo W Childs, proprietor of the Phil Ledger, sailed for Europe on Wednesday.

Fashionable ladies in Paris wear small gilt champagne bottles for earrings.

San Francisco, Oct 21. Capt Mitchell, cmder of the U S steamer **Saginaw**, was murdered tonight at Sutler & Stockton sts, in the centre of this city. His body was robbed. Nov 12th newspaper Lt Cmder Mitchell, who was murdered on Oct 21 in San Francisco, was considered the finest mathematician in the navy. He fell in with a pair of villains, with whom he stood treat, & subsequently quarrelled. No marks of violence could be found on the body of the victim, though he died a few moments after the assault. Deceased stood first on the list of lt cmders. He graduated in 1854.]

For sale: the stock, fixtures, & good will of a Grocery Store. Apply to W H Clagett, at Clagett & Sweeney's, No 4 Market Space.

$100 reward for estrayed Roan Mare & one Grey Mare. Apply at my place, 12th & K sts, Navy Yard. –M H Homiller

Guardians sale of a fine bldg lot in the neighborhood of St Aloysisus Church; by decree of the Orphans Court of D C., dated Aug 29, 1868; public sale on Oct 10 next, all the right, title, interest & estate of Ida J & Ella Louise Mills, minor children of John & Mary Mills, of, in, & to the south part of lot 34 in square 557, on First st west, just above L st north, with a depth of 105 feet. –Saml C Mills, guardian

U S Patent Ofc, Wash, Oct 21, 1868. Ptn of Geo A Brown, of Middletown, R I, praying for the extension of a patent granted to him Jan 23, 1855, for an improvement in Hay Making Machine. –Elisha Foote, Com'r of Patents

For sale: valuable farm in PG Co, Md, on the road leading from **Riggs' Mill** to Colesville, containing about 279 acres, more or less. Public auction on Nov 4 next, the farm of Jas Owens, adjoining the farms of Wm Sibley & Wm Rapley, known as the homestead of the late Col Jackson, dec'd. Improved by a dwlg house, barn, & stable, in good repair. -Green & Williams, aucts

Extensive sale of hardware & agricultural implements on Nov 5, at the warehouses & store of J P Batholow, opposite the Centre Market, on 7th st, between Pa ave & the canal, commencing at 10 A M, & continuing from day to day. -Green & Williams, aucts

SAT OCT 24, 1868
Tomorrow afternoon the corner-stone of St Joseph's German Catholic Church will be laid with imposing ceremonies by Bishop Gibbons, of N C. The Church is located at the corner of Second st east & C st north. The work was started by Rev B F Wiget, president of Gonzaga College, & the bldg enterprise was entrusted to St Joseph's Society of Wash City, of which Mr Michl Stegmaier is president, & architect of the church.

Yesterday the jurors for the Circuit Court, [Nov] were drawn at the Clerk's ofc, by the Register, Mr Boswell; the Clerk of Gtwn, Mr Laird; & the Clerk of the Levy Court, Mr Callan, as follows:

Geo H Hamilton	C W Dawes	Fielder Magruder
H N Wadsworth	Geo W Emmerson	Wm Barnaclo, sr
Andrew Rothwell	Jonathan Kirkwood	Danl J Serrin
Z M Offut	G K Dater	Wm Hess
E A Rosenthal	Jacob F King	Hilleary Smith
Wm Warder	W H Robbins	Owen Lovengood
David L Shoemaker	A H Pickrell	J S McKenny
Jas Carroll	Judson E Brown	John R Zimmerman
Isaiah E Brissey	Thos B Creighton	

Board of Police Com'rs meeting: Pvt D G Noble, for neglect of duty, was dismissed. The resignation of Pvt Geo L Arnold was received & accepted. Christopher Fitzpatrick, J H Myers, & John McDonald were appointed privates on the police force. Thos Young was appointed an additional private for duty in the Centre Market for 3 months. C W O'Key was reappointed an additional private for 12 months' duty in the Navy Yard. The applications of Geo W Theeker, Geo Kraft, John T Scrivener, & S P Keach, residents of Gtwn, for liquor licenses, were disapproved. The applications of Jos Freundt & J J Heck, of Wash, for licenses, were disapproved, & the partition of Henry Koch & John Loeliger, for a reconsideration of their applications for licenses, rejected at a previous meeting, were laid on the table.

Yesterday E B Olmsted was released on bail, & his is now at his home with his family. The following became his surety in the sum of $10,000, $2,000 each: R M Hall, Hellett Kilbourne, Geo Chorpenning, Jas M Latta, & Adele Salger. Olmsted was charged with feloniously embezzling & converting to his own use the sum of $44,646 of the Govn't funds.

Sunday last Mrs Martha F Mason, an elderly widow lady, residing on the Potomac, near **Budd's Ferry**, Chas Co, Md, was brutally treated by a negro man, who afterwards robbed her. He stole $25 from her trunk; & a gold watch & gun belonging to her son. She was alone at the time & is recovering from the blow on her head & the choking. –Balt Gaz

Died: on Oct 22, Charles Edwin, son of C E & S M Rittenhouse, in his 14th year. His funeral will take place from the residence of his parents, Stoddart & Montgomery sts, Gtwn, this afternoon, at 4 o'clock.

Died: on Oct 23, Jonathan Brewer, aged 29 years, formerly of Fairfax Co, Va. His funeral is on Sunday at 2 o'clock, from the residence of his brother, C J Brewer, 567 12th st, between B & C, Island.

Our esteemed fellow citizen, Jas M Carlisle, has returned from his European trip, & the complete restoration of his health, which had been impaired by his professional labors.

Cincinnati, Oct 23. Hon Geo H Pendleton has been confined to his bed since Tuesday last by inflamation of the lungs, & has been compelled to give up his appointments to speak in Missouri, Michigan, & N Y.

Mr Nevile Bullitt, an old citizen of Louisville, has died there of a tight boot, which produced mortification.

Country residence for sale; the large Family Mansion now occupied by Hon Amos Kendall, at **Kendall Green**, about 2 miles from Wash City Post Ofc; the house & back bldg contain 13 rooms with gas, bathroom, etc, A bowling alley, & if desired, a horse & cow will be rented with the premises. –Wm Stickney, Wash City

Gen Prim is one of the richest men in Spain. He owns 10 houses in Madrid. Gonzales Bravo did not dare confiscate them, Prim having written to him that if he in any way molested his wife or laid hands on his property, his life would be taken. Prim's threats were always carried out to the letter. His famous menace addressed to Queen Isabella 2 years ago, "Change you system now, madame, or I swear that you shall all flee from Spain," terrified the Queen at that time so much that O'Donnell was scarcely able to dissuade her from acceding to Prim's request.

N Y, Sep 28, 1868. Letter to Hon Wm M Evarts, from brethren of the N Y bar, inviting him to a complimentary dinner on his accession to the ofcr of Atty General of the U S.

B F Cutting	E G Benedict	G N Titus
J W Gerard	Chas Donohue	Joshua M Van Cott
Ch O'Conor	S P Nash	Clarkson N Potter
Edwards Pierrepont	John E Develin	I T Williams
Wm Mitchell	B W Griswold	John Jay
Henry E Davies	Henry Nicoll	John N Whiting
Wm Fullerton	C Van Santvoord	Richd H Bowne
Chas A Peabody	A P Man	Isac P Martin
John K Porter	G M Spier	C A Seward
Hooper C Van Vorst	Edgar S Van Winkle	John Ef Ward
Wm H Leonard	Wm Betts	J P Girard Foster
Jas T Brady	Wm M Prichard	S Cambreleng
John H Anthon	John Slesson	F F Marbury
Danl D Lord	Henry Hilton	W F Allen
Chas P Kirkland	Jas C Carter	Saml L M Barlow
S J Tilden	Jas Thomson	E L Fancher
Richd O'Gorman	E W Stoughton	Jas Emott
Aaron J Vanderpool	Chas E Sanford	Freeman J Fithian
Saml G Courtney	E Delafield Smith	J W Edmonds
E H Owen	Augustus F Smith	

Reply: Wash, Oct 17, 1868. I am quite sure that I may, without misgiving, accept this genial invitation as heartily as it has been offered, etc. –Wm M Evants

Horatio Browning & Alpheus Middleton have leased the store, 343 Pa ave, lately occupied by Geo & Thos Parker & Co, & have formed a copartnership conducting a wholesale & retail Grocery Business. [Alpheus Middleton, is late of Montg Co, Md.]

MON OCT 26, 1868
Gen Cassius Fairchild, U S Marshal, died at Milwaukie, on Sat, from a wound received in the battle of Shiloh.

Dr S A H McKim, of the eastern section of Wash City, has been appointed by Mr Bowen as physician to the Wash Asylum, vice Dr S S Bond, who was ordered to vacate a few days ago, on account of his participation in the recent disclosures before the investigation cmte appointed by the joint convention of the City Councils.

Pres Buchanan's farm sold for $133 an acre.

Died: on Sunday, the *28th instant, Susan Ellen, infant child of J Ledyard & Susan S Hodge, aged 23 months. Her funeral will take place from her parents' residence, 401 N Y ave, on Oct 27, at 12 o'clock. [*Sunday was Oct 25th. Copied as written.]

Died: on Oct 23, Jas B Munro, aged 37 years. His funeral will take place from his late residence, 322 Mass ave, on Monday at 11 o'clock.

N Y, Oct 25. Robt G Gamble & Mrs Hujup, charged with poisoning Gamble's wife, have been acquitted & honorably discharged.

Sale of fast horses on Oct 28, in front of the stables of John C Howard, on G st, between 6th & 7th sts. These horses are the property of Col C M Alexander, City Postmaster, & are sold to reduce his stock. -Green & Williams, aucts

Albany, Oct 24. Terrible accident last night about 12 o'clock, to the express train from N Y, on the Hudson River railroad, 3 miles below Greenbush, caused by a broken rail. Mrs M C Tyler, of Northeastern Pa, who was making purchases in N Y, was killed outright. John Davidson, railroad conductor, of Lyons, Wayne Co, was fatally injured and died this morning. Injured: Mrs John Davidson, of Lyons Wayne Co; Pliney T Sexton, of Palmyra, N Y; E M Bailey, of Rochester, N Y; John Hermeston, wife, & 3 children, of Phil, Pa, Mr H severely burned & bruised, Mrs H slightly injured, the children are unhurt; J Adolphus, of Auburn, N Y, badly injured; his wife, slightly; Jerome W Rogers, of Rochester, N Y, dangerously injured; Julius Riamann & Otto Riamann, father & son, of N Y C, father internally injured, the son not seriously. The engineer Wm H Reese escaped injury.

Sale of improved real estate on 7th st west, Wash City; by 3 deeds of trust to me, recorded in the land records of Wash Co, D C; public auction of lots 14 & 15 in square 471, at L st & an alley, between 6th & 7th sts; with a frame bldg that is used as a dwlg & restaurant. –W Y Fendall, trustee -J T Coldwell & Co, aucts

Orphans Court of Wash Co, D C. Letters of administration on the personal estate of Isabella Suter, late of Wash Co, D C, dec'd. –Jos W Nairn, adm

Orphans Court of Wash Co, D C. Letters of administration d b n on the personal estate of Walter S Chandler, late of Gtwn, D C, dec'd. –Wm Chandler, adm d b n

Orphans Court of Wash Co, D C, Oct 24, 1868. In the case of Jabez P Colby, exc of Stoddard B Colby, dec'd, the executor & Court have appointed Nov 24 next, for the final settlement of the personal estate of the said dec'd, of the assets in hand.
-Jas R O'Beirne, Reg/o wills

St Louis, Oct 24. 1-The Democrat's special Little Rock despatch says Hon Jas Hinds, member of Congress from the 2nd Dist, was assassinated today while traveling through Monroe. Hon Jos R Brooks, who was travelling with Mr Hinds, was wounded, but it is supposed not fatally. 2-Jas Coolsey, an outspoken Republican, was murdered in the same county, near Clarendon, a few days since. 3-The Republican has a special from Little Rock, Ark, which says the report of the assassination of Hinds & the wounding of Brooks, is distrusted. [Oct 29th newspaper: The body of Hon J Hinds arrived at Little Rock, Ark, Oct 27, & lay in state for several hours in the State House.]

Trustees' sale of valuable real estate; by decree of the Circuit Court for PG Co, in Equity, wherein Dennis B Lyles & others are cmplnts, & Fendall Marbury, adm of Wm Lyles, Caroline Lyles, & others, are dfndnts; public sale, on Nov 17, of that celebrated Shad & Herring Fishery, known as the **Tent Landing**, with 30 acres, & necessary outhouses attached thereto. This Fishery is on the Md shore, 4 miles below Alexandria, Va. -Fendall Marbury, Saml B Hance, trustees

Trustees' sale of valuable real estate; by decree of the Circuit Court for PG Co, in Equity, wherein Dennis B Lyles & others are cmplnts, & Fendall Marbury, adm of Wm Lyles, Caroline Lyles, & others, are dfndnts; public sale, on the premises, on Nov 26, of **Auburn**, containing about 1,000 acres, of which the late W Lyles died seized & possessed. This land has been greatly improved by the fact that it was occupied by the Govn't during the war & large herds of cattle were fed on it. The improvements consist of a comfortable cottage, brick stable & carriage house, corn-house, tenant-house, tobacco barns & other outbldgs. The elegant Mansion was burnt during the war. -Fendall Marbury, Saml B Hance, trustees. [Creditors of Wm Lyles, dec'd, to file their claims in the ofc of the Clerk, with the vouchers thereof, within 3 months from the dale of sale.]

TUE OCT 27, 1868
Rochester, Oct 26. 1-The arch of a blast furnace at Charlette fell today killing a man named Meacham, & injuring 2 others. 2-A man, John Watts, who had his arm crushed while coupling a train of cars last Sat on the Central railroad, in this city, died today.

Concord, N H, Oct 26. Deacon Alvale Kimball, a prominent citizen of Nassau, died in a prayer meeting last night, at the age of 64 years.

Revenue appointments made yesterday: Storekeepers: Jos L McNeil, Pa; Geo Starrett, Pa; Jas L Bradbury, Ill; Henry Y Graham, Ohio. Gaugers: J Henry Miller, Pa; J F Chenoweth, Ill; John Reily, Md; Carlos P Merwin, Conn; David M Rue, N Y; Thos Churchill, Ill; Robt Wallace, Md; Wm B Lyons, Md. Tobacco Inspector: Timothy W Kelly, N Y.

Household & kitchen furniture, Rosewood case piano, at auction, at the late residence of Col D F Hamlink, being house 227 on Bridge st, between Fred'k & Fayette sts; sale on Oct 30th. -Thos Dowling, auct

We regret to announce the death of Mr John T Garner, an old & much respected citizen of the Third Ward, which occurred yesterday. Mr Garner was originally a native of PG Co, Md, but has for many years past resided in Wash City, where he has engaged in contracting for paving & grading the streets & alleys. For years he was Com'r of the Third Ward, & performed the duties of that ofc with strict fidelity & intelligence, making for himself hosts of friends in every station of life.

+

Died: on Oct 26, John T Garner, in his 58th year, a native of PG Co, Md, but for the last 18 years a resident of Wash. His funeral will take place from his late residence, 276 8th st, between M & N sts, on Oct 27, at 2 o'clock P M; the funeral services to take place at McKendree Chapel, Mass ave, between 9th & 10th sts.

N Y, Oct 26. 1-Hiram C Corwin, an ex-Alderman of N Y C, committed suicide this morning by cutting his throat. 2-Danl Burke has been arrested for shooting private watchman Kane during the progress of a fire. Kane died shorly afterwards. 3-At noon today a boy, John Condon was shot at Pier 52, East River, by a young woman, the wife of a canal boat capt. The dec'd with other boys, made an attack on the canal boat, where the woman was alone & unprotected, & that he was shot by her in self defence. The woman was arrested & held to await the coroner's investigation.

At a stated convocation of **Mount Vernon R A Chapter**, held on Oct 26, the following were elected & installed for the ensuing Masonic year: Dolson B Searle, Most Excellent High Priest; Jos Daniels, Excellent King; John W Griffin, Excellent Scribe; Nathan B Clarke, Treasurer; Wm H Fry, Sec; Saml Baxter, Capt of the Host; Wm J Hay, Principal Sojourner; Wm A Farlee, Royal Arch Capt; Chas L Patten Grand Master of the First Veil; John H Pickell, Grand Master of the Second Veil; Norris Thorn, Grand Master of the Third Veil; Leonard Stoddard, jr, Janitor.

F M Clark, for a long time past clerk in the ofc of the Sec of the Interior, has been placed in charge of the "slave trade division" of the Interior Dept.

Mrd: on Oct 22, at St Aloysius Church, by Rev Fr Stonestreet, Thos E McGraw to Miss Ella Richardson, both of Wash City.

Mrd: on Oct 22, at St Aloysius Church, by Rev Fr Stonestreet, Jas McGraw, jr, to Miss Emma Ragan, both of Wash City.

Died: on Oct 23, of paralysis, Mrs Sydney Edelin, consort of Edw H Edelin, in her 68th year. She was formerly of PG Co, Md.

Died: on Oct 28, Susan Ellen, infant child of J Ledyard & Susan S Hodge, aged 23 months. Her funeral will take place from her parents' residence, 401 N Y ave, on Oct 27th, at 12 o'clock.

Elmira, Oct 26. Chas Huston, 70 years of age, was run over by the cars on the Erie railroad, near the city, & killed today.

Hartford, Oct 26. Chas Gilbert, sentenced 3 years ago to the State Prison for life for murder, escaped from the prison in Wethersfield today.

WED OCT 28, 1868
Sec McCulloch yesterday made the following appointments of Internal Revenue ofcrs: Storekeepers: W C Johnson, Calif; Thos Eagan, N Y; John W Leggett, N Y; Robt Turniss, N Y; John Simpson, Pa; Thos Crosby, Conn; Asa M Van Sickles, Ohio; L S Coleman, Ky; Wm P Dougherty, Pa. Gaugers: Thos Colton, N Y; Saml Dremman, Calif; Adam H Sowers, Ohio; Wm H Wyant, Ohio; Wm C Rhodes, N Y; A L Bergfeld, Mo; Jos Shultz, Ill; Jas H Hendricks; Ind; John Watts, Ind; Jas A Crafton, N C; B A Beardsley, N Y, R H Sturgess, Ill; Jas Mitchell, Ill; T T Holcomb, Conn. Tobacco Inspectors: Saml M Hoff, Iowa; T W Scott, Ind.

The Board of Guardians of the Public Schools of Gtwn awarded the contract for bldg a new school house, to Messrs Wm J Dyer & Son; contract given is a trifle about $9,000.

Andrew Rowland, a farmer, residing 4 miles from Hagerstown, Md, was mysteriously murdered on Sunday night week. Mrs Rowland said her husband had been with Lewis Snyder Sunday in Boonsboro; he returned home, they had supper, & all retired. She was awakened by the groan of her husband, tried to awaken him, & he didn't respond. She then aroused her father, Mr Chas F Gelwicks, who saw that Mr Rowland had been brutally murdered. No clues could be found in the testimony of Mrs Rowland, Mr Gelwicks, a son & daughter of Mr Rowland, or Mr Louis Snyder. Mr Rowland has life insurance in the sum of $5,000; one half for the benefit of his wife, & the remainder for the benefit of his children by his former wife. At his death, his wife would be entitled to a $100 from the treasury of the Odd Fellows, besides the $2,500 insurance, which will doubtless be paid her, if her innocence is established.

Orphans Court-Judge Purcell, Oct 27, 1868. 1-The will of the late Jonathan Brewer, bequeathing his estate to his brother, sister, & nephew, was filed & proven, & letters testamentary were issued to Chas I Brewer; bond $8,000. 2-The will of the late Wm Remington was fully proven & admitted to probate. 3-The first & final account of the admx of Woodford Stone, & second account of the admx of Edw Hall, were approved & passed.

Mrd: on Oct 27, at the residence of Wm R Woodward, Wash, D C, by Rev O Perrinchief, Geo Waters, of Gtwn, D C, to Catherine F, daughter of the late Wm Redin, of the same place.

Died: on Oct 26, at her residence, in Fairfax Co, Va, Mrs Lucy Henry Cutts, widow of the late Hon Chas Cutts, formerly U S Senator from N H.

Buffalo, Oct 27. A German, Louis Metzger, set fire to his dwlg this morning, & then shot himself, fatally.

Diabolical murder. Montgomery Mail, Oct 21. Macon Co, in the neighborhood of Salem Church, about 5 miles from the village of Notasulga. Last year a young couple, Wm Duke, 18, & Miss Low, 16 wanted to marry, but her family objected. They eloped. After the honeymoon they resided with his family; the husband & his family treated the young bride with harsh treatment. The young couple went to housekeeping & invited the preacher to dinner the next Sat night. When the preacher arrived he found the young wife suspended by the neck with a cord from one of the joists of the house, her body cold & stiff. Their sleeping baby was the only sound of breathing in the house. The father of the husband was seen leaving the house before that day. The husband had been absent for 2 days, but returned on Sat night. The matter is being investigated.

Dr John Burr Hereford, of Woodyard, PG Co, Md, fell suddenly dead while talking to Mr Long, at Cameron & Wash sts, about 5 o'clock yesterday afternoon. Dr Burr had just inquired of a gentleman the route to the residence of W D Corse, & was soon borne thither a corpse. His remains are now at the residence of Mr Corse; they will be conveyed to his Md home for repulture. -Alexandria Advertiser, 27th

Art Gallery, 394 Pa ave, between 9th & 10th sts, Wash, D C. Paintings, French, German, & American Chromos, Engravings, Photographs, Stereoscopes, Stereoscopic Views, Parlor Brackets, & a full assortment of best quality Black Walnut & Gilt oval & square picture frames, constantly on hand. –A V S Smith, proprietor

THU OCT 29, 1868

Yesterday Patrick Fitzgerald, watchman at the canal docks of the Cumberland Coal & Iron Co, in Gtwn, was found in an insensible condition on the dock, by an employe, Edw Patterson, & taken to a room near by, where he died in less than an hour. Thursday night a fight occurred between a colored boatman & a young man, Jake Trimble, also employed on a boat. Fitzgerald had interfered to quiet the parties, who left at a late hour. Trimble was held for a hearing on the charge of disorderly conduct.

The Com'r of Patents, Hon Elisha Foote, appointed Henry H Bates a Second Assist Examiner of Patents, he having past a satisfactory examination for that position.

Late Tuesday a huckster, Gila Tucker, attempted to commit suicide by swallowing a dose of laudanum. A physician administered an antidote, & the attempt was frustrated. Cause, domestic troubles.

Sec McCulloch yesterday appointed the following internal revenue ofcrs:
Storekeepers: H W Purdy, Ky; H S Mansur, Ohio; Wm Cock, Wash Territory; Jos F Pusey, Va; Jos H Means, R I; Frank Zerbe, Pa.
Gaugers: J H Murray, Ky; C W Short, Ohio; Chas P Moyer, Pa; Nathan K Lytle, Ohio; Robt T Campbell, Wash Territory; Chas G G Merrill, Conn; John W Corley, Ky.

John G Green, of Buffalo, had the reputation of being the best diver on the lakes; a few days since he committed suicide. Early in life he became deeply attached to a young lady in Chelsea, Mass, the beautiful daughter of a wealthy citizen; the attachment was reciprocated; Green pledged never to claim the hand of his affianced until he had accumulated sufficient to enable him to retire from a vocation so full of peril in nature. When he undertook to rescue the treasure from the sunken steamer **Atlantic** he meant that it should be his last job of diving. He imprudently insisted on descending while warm; he was seized with paralysis, & was dragged to the surface more dead than alive. From that attack he never recovered. Moody & disconsolate, he sought in the intoxication glass temporary relief from the sorrow which oppressed him. At length he has rashly ended his misery & his life, & found in the suicide's grave the peace he vainly sought elsewhere.

Died: on Oct 28, after a long & painful illness, Catharine A Harbin, in her 38th year. Her funeral will take place from her late residence on 8th st, on Friday, at 9:30 o'clock, & proceed to St Peter's Church.

Died: on Oct 28, Percival Winfield, son of Geo R & Maria A Hall, aged 7 years & 5 months. His funeral will be tomorrow at 3 o'clock P M, from the residence of his parents, 11th & Mass ave.

Died: on Oct 26, near Groveton, Prince Wm Co, Va, Sallie F Bronaugh, 3rd daughter of John O Bronaugh, of Va. "Blessed are the pure in heart, for they shall see God."

<u>Sec McCulloch yesterday appointed the following internal revenue ofcrs:</u>
Storekeepers: H W Purdy, Ky; H S Mansur, Ohio; Wm Cock, Wash Territory; Jos F Pusey, Va; Jos H Means, R I; Frank Zerbe, Pa.
Gaugers: J H Murray, Ky; C W Short, Ohio; Chas P Moyer, Pa; Nathan K Lytle, Ohio; Robt T Campbell, Wash Territory; Chas G G Merrill, Conn; John W Corley, Ky.

Boston, Oct 28. At the annual meet of the board of overseers of Harvard College, Hon John H Clifford, was re-elected president of the board, & Dr N B Shutrliff sec. The election for president was deferred for the present.

Marlboro Gaz: The little boy, Thos Knode, who fell from the balustrade at the Md Agricultural College, about 40 feet, reported dead, is still living, & hopes are entertained for his recovery. Dr King removed from the skull a large piece of bone.

Extensive sale of country sites & market gardens, between Uniontown & Benning's Bridge, at auction, on Nov 9; the tract belonging to Capt Krouse, subdivided into lots 2 thru 9 front on River road & are for the most part 40 feet front by 200 feet deep. Lots 10 thru 22 are between the 2 roads, & contain 1 acre each; except lots 17 & 18 are fractional parts of an acre. -Cooper & Latimer, aucts

Trustees' sale of real estate; by decree of the Circuit Court for PG Co, Md, in Equity, wherein Jas H Burch & others are cmplnts, & Arthur P West & others are dfndnts; public sale on Nov 24, of land known as ***Westwood***, now in the possession of Nathl Soper, containing 210 acres of land, more or less & being a portion of the same real estate which was purchased by the said Nathl Soper of the undersigned, trustees, in 1859. This property is in Nottingham district, near T B & Brandywind, & adjoins the lands of Mrs Araminta Brooke, John Tayman, & ***Cheltenham***, recently purchased by Enoch Pratt, of Balt City. There is a small dwlg-house, with out-bldgs, attached, on the premises. -Wm D Bowie, Thos H Clagett, trustees

FRI OCT 30, 1868
Sec McCulloch on Tuesday made the following appointments of internal revenue ofcrs: Storekeepers: David Roath, Pa; Chas A Van Horn, Mo; Robt Davidson, Ohio; Thos Harper, Ohio; Benj H Hair, Ohio; David Gordon, Ohio; Wm Yorke Atlee, La; Jas Ells, N Y; J R Baker, Ohio; V B Carey, Ohio; Jas Maguire, Va. Gaugers: Jos B Lathrop, N Y; Asa W Cash, N Y; Jas A Garland, Conn; L T Campbell, Conn; Geo P Leonard, Ohio; Walter A Edwards, N Y. Tobacco Inspector: David Pulman, Va.

Promotions in the navy just made by the Sec of the Navy. Lt Cmder Jos P Fyffe, to be cmder from Dec 2, 1867; Passed Assist Surgeon Thos C Walton, to be surgeon from Oct 22, 1868; Passed Assist Paymasters D B Batione/Ratione & W F A Torbert, to be paymasters from Aug 26 & Sep 16, 1868; Assist Paymasters Henry Gerrard & John F Tarbell, to be passed assist paymasters.

C Goodwin Clark, principal of the Lincoln Grammar School at Boston, has been sued for $2,000 damages for whipping a pupil, as is claimed, excessively. The case is on trial.

Michl Lynch purchased part of lot 213, fronting 16 feet on Fred'k st, with a depth of 96 feet, improved by a 3 story frame house, for $1,185. Part of lot 215, fronting 14 feet on Fred'k st, with a depth of 96 feet, improved by a small frame house, was purchased by Jas Calhoun, for $800.

Equity Court-Judge Olin, Oct 29, 1868. 1-Larkin against Laughlin; decree appointing Jos Gawler trustee. 2-*In re* estate of Corbet Dulaney; decree ratifying proceedings of Orphans Court. 3-Estate of Saml De Vaughn; decree ratifying trustee's report *nisi*.

Mrd: on Oct 28, at ***Bellevue***, Gtwn Heights, the residence of the bride's father, by Rev Pelham Williams, of Boston, Leonard C Gunnell to Mary, daughter of C E Rittenhouse. No cards.

Mrd: on Oct 29, in Wash, D C, by Rev A H Ames, Wm H Arrington to Sarah H Pulling, both of Prince Wm Co, Va.

The executors of Edwin A Stevens estate have employed Gen McClellan, at an annual salary of $10,000, to superintend the completion of the famous Stevens battery at Hoboken, & which, when afloat, is to be tendered as a free gift to the State of N J.

Balt, Oct 29. 1-The distillery of Schilling & Williar was burned this afternoon; loss, $10,000. 2-Mathias Rochester, a member of Hook & Ladder company No 1, was thrown from the truck & killed this morning.

SAT OCT 31, 1868
Died: on Oct 29, at Carmelite Convent, Balt, Md, Helen Mary Riordan, in religion Sister Baptiste, eldest child of the late Jas Riordan, of Wash City.

Died: on Sep 30, 1868, at Guadalajara, Mexico, Maria, wife of Robt G Loweree, & eldest daughter of John Major, lately a resident of Gtwn, D C.

Sec McCulloch yesterday made the following appointments of Internal Revenue: Gaugers: Henry C De Ahra, N Y; Braxton Baker, Ind; Ezra M Beardsley, Ill. Storekeepers: Saml Radesky, N Y; Jas N Mills, Va; Geo Slothower, Md; Rudolph Blumenburg, Md; Jas A Bloomer, Pa; W S Crosby, Pa; Dwight Graves, Mass; Chas Carples, Ill.

Mademoisele Christine Nilsson has received an offer in England of $20,000 in gold, per month, for a series of 4 months.

Geo C Henning's one-price clothing store is at 511 7th st.

Supreme Court of D C, Oct 29, 1868; in Equity 1,401; Docket 9. Timothy McCarthy vs Patrick McCarthy & Julia McCarthy, his wife, & Wm Graham. On motion of the cmplnt by W F Mattingly, his solicitor, it is ordered that the dfndnts appear on or before the first rule day occurring 40 days after this day; otherwise the cause will be proceeded with as in case of default. –A B Olin, justice -R J Meigs. clerk

Two valuable farms, stock, crop growing, farm implements, wagons, carts, household & kitchen furniture, on Nov 18; public auction of the tracts of land adjoining the farms of W A Batchelor, Thos W Riley, & Mr Clark, one containing 74 acres & improvements; another adjoining, containing 58 acres. –W L Wall & Co, aucts

MON NOV 2, 1868
Last night Detectives Coomes & Miller were passing along C st, when they found a man besmeared with blood & mud, suffering very much. He was Andrew A Barnaclo, who resides on 4½ st, between H & I sts, who had been attacked & knocked out of the buggy he hired from a livery stable in Jackson Hall alley. Barnaclo is said to be a quiet, inoffensive young man, a clerk in the shoe store of Mr Geo B Wilson, under Odd Fellows' Hall. He does not know who attacked him.

Treasury Dept: The following resignations have been received & accepted within the past few days. Second Auditor's Ofc: W G Tack, S W Ward, W P Tisdell, Byron Sykes, C E Prentice, John E Crooks, R E H Wing, Jas M Cushing, Thos L Wilson, Joel G Floyd, G C Whitehall, Geo W Starr, H E Hoffman, B C Bristol, W W Hobbs, G R Richmond, Chas Sprawl, John C Gallagher, Geo H Henderson, W F Lee, L C Hootce, J N Sparks, John A Mullen, John T McDowell, T S Boston, & Isaac Nesmith.
Register's Ofc: Miss Mary E Delaney, Mrs L J Bush.
Third Auditor's Ofc: Benj E Smith.
Bureau of Statistics: H H Bates.
Treasurer's Ofc: Miss F M Bailey.
[Another reduction will be made on Dec 1st, when about 200 males & female clerks will be dismissed from the Second Auditor's, Sixth Auditor's, & Register's ofc.]

Orphans Court-Judge Purcell, Oct 31, 1868. 1-S Kerr gave bond in the sum of $5,000 as guardian of the orphans of G A Munro. Same party gave bond in the sum of $1,000 as adm of B Munro. 2-Valentine Hornbush gave bond in the sum of $1,000 as executor of Geo Deufel. The will of Geo Deufel was filed, fully proven, & admitted to probate & record.
3-The following accounts were filed & passed: First & final account of O W White, adm of W J Toonery. First & final account of C H Cragin, exc of S T McKenny.

Mrd: on Oct 29, by Rev Mr Wiley, at the residence of the bride's father, Dr W H Taylor, of Chapel Hill, Montg Co, Md, to Eliz Blackston Riley, daughter of Thos W Riley, of Wash City, D C. No cards. [Brooklyn papers please copy.]

Died: on Oct 22, in New Orleans, of congestion, Miss Millie E Carter, of Woodstock [paper folded], Wash Co, Miss. [Warrenton, Va, papers please copy.]

Orphans Court of Wash Co, D C. Letters testamentary on the personal estate of Geo Deufel, late of Wash City, D C. –Valentine Hornbush, exc

Trustee's sale of valuable improved real estate on Pa ave; by deed of trust recorded in Liber R M H No 25, folio 442, of the land records of the Dist of Columbia; public auction on Nov 10, of part of lot 5 in square 118; being the same property that was conveyed by Saml Davidson to Saml Duvall by deed dated Apr 4, 1844, & recorded in Liber W B No 111, folio 239, of said land records. Also, parts of lots 6 & 8 in said square; being the same property that was conveyed by Margaretta Mechlin to the said Saml Duval, by deed dated May 21, 1850, recorded among said land records in Liber J A S No 15, folio 183, except so much of said lot No 6 as was subsequently conveyed by the said Duvall & wife to one David Hines, by deed dated Feb 21, 1859, & recorded in Liber J A S, No 170, folio 109, of said land records. The amount due under the deed of trust is $7,997.86 with interest from Jul 30, 1867. –E Carusi, trustee -Cooper & Latimer, aucts

TUE NOV 3, 1868
Meeting of the Industrial Home School, at the Home, in Army Square, the vice president, A M Gangwer, in the chair, annual report presented. The following ofcrs were elected for the ensuing year: Pres, Henry D Cooke; Vice-Presidents, A M Gangewer, D M Kelsey, H H Tilley; treasurer & solicitor, pro tem, John Hitz; sec, W L Waller. Trustees for 3 years: Z Richards, F H Smith, Judson S Brown, & John Hills, to fill the vacancy occasioned by the removal from the District of J H Deitrich. Executive Cmte:

Mrs Z Richards	Mrs John Hitz	Miss Sally Magruder
Mrs C L Cartter	Mrs R B Clark	Miss J Nourse
Mrs M A Blackford	Mrs G A Hall	Mrs H Randsley
Mrs M C Hart	Mrs Wm L Waller	Mrs L Richards
Mrs A M Gangewer	Mrs John R Elvans	Mrs R Doolittle
Mrs D W Bliss	Mrs J A Howes	
Mrs H Creecy	Miss Kate Denham	

Advisory Cmte:

Mrs H D Cooke	Miss Mary Thompson	Mrs E. D. E. N.
Mrs C B Boynton	Mrs C Robbins	Southworth
Mrs H A Brewster	Mrs Byron Sunderland	
Mrs J C Smith	Mrs Kidwell	
Mrs W W Webb	Mrs C S Cox	

Gtwn turnpike directors meeting held at Falls Church, on Sat, the following ofcrs elected for the ensuing term: Pres, Wm D Shepherd; Directors: W W Dungan, John M McCormick, W H Jolan, Isaac Crossman, David Edes, Allen Pierce, Geo B Whiting, & H Febre.

Catholic Churches in Wash:
St Patrick's, corner of 10th & F sts; Rev Jacob A Walter, pastor; Rev John J Keare, assist.
St Peter's, Capitol Hill; Rev F X Boyle, pastor; Rev Jeremiah Henricks, assist.
St Matthew's, 15th & H sts; Rev Chas T White, D D, pastor; Rev Desire C De Wulf, assist.
Church of the Immaculate Conception, 8th & N sts; Rev P F McCarthy, pastor.
St Stephen's, 21st & Pa ave; Rev John T McNally, pastor.
St Dominick's, on 6th st, Island; Rev T A Bokel, O S D, pastor; Rev N D Young, O S D; Rev J Cary, O S D; Rev J Rooney, O S D; Rev P O Call, O S D, assists.
St Aloysius, on North Capitol st, corner of I; Rev Bernardinus Wiget, S J, pastor; Rev O H Stonestreet, Rev Aloysius Roccofort, Rev D Lynch, assists.
St Mary's, [German] on 5th st, near H; Rev Mathias Alig, pastor.
Methodist Episcopal:
Mission Chapel of the Wash Convocation, Capitol Hill; services at 7:30 P M.
East Wash, 4th st, between G & S C ave; Rev Wm Holliday, pastor.
Foundry Meeting House, G & 14th sts; Rev B P Brown, pastor; N Brown, assist.
Wesley Chapel, 5th & F sts; Rev A H Ames, pastor.
Mckendree Chapel, on Mass ave, 9th st; Rev Wm Krebs, pastor.
Fletcher Chapel, N Y ave & 4th st; Rev Job Lambeth, pastor.

Union Chapel, 20th st, Pa ave; Rev Chas A Ried, pastor.
Ryland Chapel, 10 st, Island, corner of L; Rev Wm Hamilton, D D, pastor.
Gorsuch Chapel, 4½ st, between Canal & Arsenal; Rev J N Davis, pastor.
Waugh Chapel, Captiol Hill, east of Old Capitol; Rev Geo G Markham, paster.
Providence Chapel, on the hill just at the point where the cars from Balt turn to come into the city; Rev John Lighter, pastor.
First Congregational Methodist Chapel, M st, near 9th; Rev W V Tudor, pastor.
Hamline Church, 9th & P sts; Rev J W Hoover, pastor.
Wesley Chapel Mission, 9th & S sts; Rev Jas G Hening, pastor.

Episcopal:
St Paul's Church, 23rd st between I st & Pa ave; Rev Augustus Jackson, rector; seats free.
Church of the Incarnation, 12th & N sts; Rev R W Lowrie, rector.
Christ Church, G st, between 6th & 7th sts; Rev M L Olds, rector.
St John's, opposite the Pres' Mansion: Rev J V Lewis, rector.
Trinity, 3rd & C sts; Rev Mr Addison, rector.
Church of Epiphany, G st, between 13th & 14th sts; Rev Dr Hall, rector.
Church of the Ascension, H st, between 9th & 10th sts; Rev Dr Pinkney, rector.
Grace Church, Island; Rev A Holmead, rector.
Rock Creek Church, near Soldiers' Home.

Baptist:
First Baptist, 13th between G & H; Rev A D Gillette, D D, pastor.
Second Baptist, 4th st Va ave, near the Navy Yard; Rev P Warren, pastor.
E st Church, near the Gen Post Ofc; Rev E H Gray, D D, pastor.
Fifth Baptist, D st, near 4½, Island; Rev C C Meador, pastor.

Presbyterian:
North Presbyterian, N st, between 9th & 10th; Rev Mr Fox, pastor.
Western Presbyterian, H st, between 19th & 20th sts; Rev J M Coombs, pastor.
First Presbyterian, 4½ st, near City Hall; Rev Dr Sunderland, pastor.
N Y Ave Church, between 13th & 14th sts.
Fourth Presbyterian, 9th st, north of the Patent Ofc; Rev John C Smith, D D, pastor.
Assembly Church, 5th & I sts; Rev Wm Hart, pastor.
Sixth Presbyterian, 6th st, near Md ave; Rev Geo H Smyth, pastor.
Capitol Hill Presbyterian, 4th st, between B & Pa ave; Rev John Chester, pastor.
Presbyterian Church, 7th st, Island, between D & E sts.

Lutheran:
German Evangelical Congregation of Trinity, Unaltered Augsburg Confession 4th st west, corner of M; Rev E M Buerger, pastor.
German Evangelical, G st, corner of 20th; Rev Saml Finckel, pastor.
St Paul's 11th & H sts; Rev J G Butler, pastor.
Evangelical Lutheran, [German,] St John's Church, 4½ st, Island; Rev W Frey, pastor.

Central Presbyterian Church:
Columbia Law College, 5th st, between D & E; Rev A W Pitzer, pastor. Seats free.

Methodist Protestant:
Methodist Protestant, 9th st, between E & F; Rev S J Drinkhouse, pastor.
Methodist Protestant, near the Navy Yard, Va ave; Rev Jas Thompson, pastor.

Potomac, of North Washington, near *Holmead's old burial ground*; Rev S A Hoblitzell & Rev O Cox.
Friends Meeting House:
Orthodox, 9th st, near F.
Meeting House, on I st, between 18th & 19th sts.
Unitarian:
Unitarian Congregational Church, D & 6th sts; service every Sunday.
New Jerusalem:
Church on North Capitol st, between B & C sts. Seats free.
Christian Church:
The Christian Church meets in the Supreme Court, City Hall, on every Lord's Day, at 11 o'clock; Rev Henry T Anderson, pastor.
First Reformed Church:
Corner of 6th & N sts; Rev J W Ebbinghouse, pastor.
Congregational Church:
First Congregational: services at Hall of Reps; evening services at Columbia Law Bldg. Services at the Capitol-Preaching in the Hall of Reps; Rev C B Boynton, D D, chaplain.
Hebrew Synagugue:
Washington Hebrew Congregation, 8th st, second square north of the Patent Ofc.
Churches in Gtwn:
Trinity, Roman Catholic, near the College.
St John's [Protestant Episcopal] Rev Mr Tillinghurst, pastor.
First Baptist Church, Market st, near 4th; Rev Jas Nelson, pastor.
Presbyterian, Rev Mr Taylor, pastor.
Christ Church, P E, Rev Walter Williams, pastor.
St Alban's; Rev Mr Chew, rector.
Methodist Episcopal, Dunbarton st; Rev E B Edwards, D D, pastor.
Methodist Protestant, Congress st; Rev D A Sherman, pastor.
West Gtwn, M E; Rev G M Berry, pastor.
Episcopal Mission, South High st; Rev Mr Brown, pastor.
Churches in Alexandria:
First Presbyterian; Rev C C McCampbell, pastor.
Second Presbyterian; Rev J T Leftwich, pastor.
Methodist Episcopal: Rev Jas R Walker, pastor.
Methodist Episcopal South; Rev Mr Muney, pastor.
Methodist Protestant; Rev Mr Jones, pastor.
Christ Church-Episcopal; Rev Mr McKim, pastor.
St Paul's Church-Episcopal; Rev S W Norton, pastor.
Grace Church-Episcopal, Rev D T Sprigg, pastor.
Baptist Church; Rev Mr Williss, pastor.
Catholic Church; Rev Fr Kroes, pastor.

Worcester, Mass, Nov 2. Bridget Murray was killed last Sat while in a cabbage field, by the owner, Batholomew O'Donnel, who shot her with a pistol. She was celebrating Hallow Eve, & with some other girls went to the field to get cabbage.

Sec McCullock yesterday made the following appointments of internal revenue ofcrs: Storekeepers: John Markell, Pa; Geo D Phelps, Ill; John Kinney, Pa; Louis Dorman, Mo; Geo E Parshall, Pa; Harrison Hippell, Pa.
Gaugers: Joshua Webster, Miss; Wm Clotworthy, Tenn; Geo Ryan, Mo; Richd K Baird, Miss.

Young Catholics' Friends Society, of Gtwn: following ofcrs were elected for the ensuing year: Pres, W A King; Vice-Pres, J D McGill; Corr Sec, J J Kane; Rec Sec, John Sis; Bookkeeper, John Walsh; Treasurer, M O Donoghue; Steward, J J Reily; Trustees, Saml Hein, J A Reily, Dennis Horrigan, M F Moran, Perry W Lowe, & M McNally. The society numbers 135 members. They have under their charge a large & flourishing school of children. Many of these children are clothed from the treasury of the society.

A few days ago we announced the death of a bright & beautiful boy, a son of Col C D Pennebaker. Today we are called upon to chronicle the death of his last born. The bereaved father & mother have the sincerest sympathy of all their friends who knew their pets-Foster & Freddy- & they have, also, the consolation that these little loved ones have escaped the ills of life, &, like the violets of the early spring, have rendered their sweetness for a while to those who cherished & loved them, but have gone to join the angel choir to which are admitted only the innocent & good.

Died: on Nov 2, Saml F Savage, aged 32 years, late of the U S navy. [Nov 4 newspaper: Died: on Nov 2, Saml F Savage, U S Navy, aged 32 years, youngest son of Geo Savage. His funeral will take place on Thursday, Nov 5, at 10 o'clock, at St Aloysius Church.]

Died: on Nov 2, Fred'k James, youngest son of Col C D & Anna E Pennebaker, aged 20 months & 7 days. His funeral will be performed at the residence of Col Pennebaker, Mass ave & 10th sts, at 2 o'clock, today, after which the remains will be conveyed immiediately to **Cave Hill Cemetery**, Louisville, Ky, for interment.

Cincinnati Commercial: on Thursday, as a special freight train lay on the side track at Gravel Pit, a station on the Ohio & Miss railroad, 18 miles west of this city, when the engine exploded her hot boiler; The conductor, Mr Mills Howe, the fireman, John Mulane, & 3 little boys who were standing nearby, were hurled into the air & killed. Jos Gardner, engineer, & Henry Howe, brakesman, brother of the conductor, were severely injured. One of the boys was John Smith, age 12; his brother also died; Thos Murphy, age 15, was the other boy killed; his little brother, age 6 years, was slightly injured. Mr Murphy, father of the boys, resides at North Bend, about 5 miles from the disaster. Mullane was a single man; his mother lives at Mattoon, Ill.

WED NOV 4, 1868
Balt, Nov 3. Jas H Stevens was run over & killed yesterday by a locomotive at the depot of the Northern Central railroad, in this city. He was one of the oldest engineers on the road, but was lately acting as a watchman.

Sec McCulloch yesterday made the following appointments of internal revenue ofcrs: Storekeepers: Timothy M Corley, Mass; Robt Hastings, N Y; M J Counts, Ohio; Clifton Morton, Ala; John Fitzgerald, Pa; Henry Martin, Pa; David Young, Pa; John Baker, Pa; John F King, Ill; John B Moulton, Ill; Jas A McGreen, Ill; Wm Glenzer, Ill; Andrew C Smith, Ill. Gaugers: Henry Maranville, Ohio; B F Halls, Ga; Robt S Anthony, Va; Alfred K Nichols, Va; Thos Dornan, Pa; Peter Shiner, Pa; F W Grinnell, Pa; Geo Fehr, Pa.

Balt American, Nov 3. This morning Lloyd G Ridgely, a boarder at the Susquehanna Hotel, leaped from the rear roof of the hotel, on Davis st, elevated 45 to 50 feet above the ground, to cause almost instant death. The deceased was about 45 years of age & unmarried. He has a mother & other relatives residing in thie city. He was a member of the firm of Ridgely & Co, merchant tailors.

Wash City Post Ofc-Quarterly Bulletin-Oct 1, 1868.
C M Alexander, Postmaster
Lambert Tree, Chief Clerk
Nathan H Barrett, Assist Chief Clerk
T D Dow, Cashier
Jas A Kennedy, Superintendent Post Ofc
Geo H Plant, jr, Chief Assorting Clerk for City Delivery
Simeon H Merrill, Superintendent Money Order Dept
S R Kilby, Clerk of Registry Dept
Jas E Bell, Superintendent of Letter Carriers
Richd Lay, Chief of Mailing Dept
Fred Depro, Special Agent

Louisville Courier, Oct 30. Yesterday the locomotive & 3 cars were blown to fragments on the Louisville & Nashville railroad, a mile south of Memphis Junction. Killed: Engineer J Dezeotell; Jerry Huggins, fireman; John Brown, brakeman; wood passer, J Carroll. John Welsh, brakeman, died later from his injuries. Conductor Dearman & a brakeman, the only remaining men on the train, were in no way injured, having been in the caboose at the rear of the train when the explosion took place.

Green & Williams, aucts, sold lot 11 in square 38, being 23½ feet front by 79 feet deep, on 24th st west, between Pa ave & L st north, improved by a 2 story brick dwlg, to Patrick Murray, for $3,425. They also sold half of lot 10 in square 100, on 21st st west, between L & M sts north, improved by a 2 story frame dwlg, to G W Steward, for $800.

Orphans Court-Judge Purcell, Nov 3, 1868. 1-The will of David Fitzgerald, dec'd, was filed, fully proven, & admitted to probate & record. 2-Dorethea Ripetti was appointed guardian to Rita Triay; bond $3,000. 3-The second account of Cassandra O Buck, guardian to Margaret Buck, was approved & passed.

N Y, Nov 3. Hon Saml R Betts, for more than 40 years Judge of the U S Dist Court of this district, died last night, at New Haven, Conn, from an attack of apoplexy.

Wm B Astor, the richest man in America; his life is little, but his property is great. His chief distinction is that he is John Jacob Astor's son. Wm B has been preserved by his temperament from all extravagances & excesses; he has the cool head & calm blood of his German ancestors, to whom irregularity was unknown, & temptation impossible. He has been associated in business with his father from his early years, he learned his habits, & followed his example. In his 76th year, he takes more note of a trifling expenditure than a clerk whose annual salary is not much beyond his hourly income. John Jacob Astor, at age 20, left his village home in Baden, so poor that he walked to the nearest seaport, with a small bundle, containing his wordly goods, spent his last penny for a passage in the steerage, sailed for N Y, & would have arrived here with nothing but youth & health, had he not sold on the voyage half-dozen flutes given him by his brother in London. For the flutes he received $12, & having made the acquaintance of a furrier on board the ship, & talked with him about the trade, he invested his small capital, on debarking, in furs. From the small beginning he steadily & rapidly rose, until he founded the American Fur Co, sent his ships to every sea, & died worth $50,000,000. Wm, the son, has spent the 20 years since the death of his father, devoted constantly to swell the fortune. Astor was born in a small brick house, built by his father, & occupied as a fur store, but long since torn down, at Broadway & Vesey, the site of the present Astor House. Astor's ofc is in Prince st, Broadway, a one story brick, with heavy shutters, that remind you of a village bank. Astor lives in Lafayette Place, in a handsome, though somewhat old fashioned brick house, adjoining the Astor Library. His residence was built for & given to him by his father. He is very fond of walking; a tallman, fully 6 feet, of heavy frame, large & rather course features; small eyes, cold & sluggish looking, much more German than American. He has 2 sons, John Jacob & Wm B Astor, jr, both of whom are as close applicants to business as their father; & several daughters, all married to wealthy gentlemen. Mrs Astor is the daughter of Gen Armstrong, Jas Madison's Secretary, a woman of culture & accomplishement. It is said he is very anxious to live, to see how many of his investments will turn out; but, at 76, that rare pleasure cannot be forever enjoyed. Sentence him to idleness tomorrow, & before the Christmas chimes were rung from Trinity, the family lot in **Greenwood** would have another occupant.

Supreme Court of D C; Equity 1,418-docket 9. Ellen M Cotter vs Margaret Fitzgerald et al. The object of this suit is to have a partition or sale of lot 16 in square 562, in Wash City, whereof Richd Cotter, the father of the cmplnt, died seized, & it appearing to the court that a subpoena has been duly issued & returned by the Marshal of D C, "not to be found." It is ordered that the dfndnt, Richd Brosnan, cause his appearance to be entered herein on or before the first rule day occurring 40 days after this day; otherwise the case will be proceeded with as in case of default. -A B Olin, Justice -R J Meigs, clerk

Died: on Nov 3, Gertrude T Clements, aged 4 years & 9 months, the youngest child of Ignatius & Jane Clements. Her funeral will be Nov 5, at 3 o'clock, from her late residence on H st, between 18th & 19th sts.

THU NOV 5, 1868
The President today directed the assignment of Brvt Maj Gen Edw R S Canby to the Military District & Dept of Texas, with instructions to relieve Gen Reynolds of the command as soon as practicable. This is a severe & merited rebuke to Gen Reynolds, who, in his proper sphere the colonel of a regt of 800 men, when assigned to the post of commander of a district embracing a State, assumes the power of an autocrat, stalks into civil courts, & peremptorily orders the continuances of cases; &, in defiance of the Federal Constitution, which requires that "each State shall appoint a number of electors equal to the whole number of Senators & Representatives to which the State may be entitled in Congress," issues his proclamation absolutely prohibiting any assemblages, proceedings, or acts in Texas having in view the election of electors of a Chief Magistrate for the naiton. This "proud man," dressed in a little brief authority, has at length had his "fantastic tricks" brought to an inglorious termination; & it is hoped he may never again have an opportunity of playing the part of a petty despot. The people of the Dist of Columbia regret to part with such an accomplished officer & affiable gentleman as Gen Canby. Brvt Brig Gen Wallace, by seniority of rank, succeeds to the command of the Dept of Washington.

Sec McCulloch yesterday made the following appointments of internal revenue ofcrs: Storekeepers: J F McKenna, Va; C N Discoll, Calif; Thos Murray, Iowa. Gaugers: Addison Martin, Calif; Wm H Alden, Iowa. Tobacco Inspector, H F Wilkins, Va.

The funeral of Mrs Harriet Murphy, wife of Francis J Murphy, who died yesterday, will take place from St Patrick's Church tomorrow morning at 9 o'clock. Mrs Murphy had been an invalid for over 20 years, during which time she was constantly under medical treatment, & her long, lingering illness is perhaps one of the most remarkable known to the physicians of the District. +Died: on Nov 4, after a long & painful illness, Harriet, beloved wife of Francis J Murphy, in her 64th year.

Yesterday Coroner W W Potter held an inquest on the body of Absolem Conrad, who died at the station-house, in Gtwn, from the effects of injuries received in a brutal attack made by Geo W Clementson. The deceased had on his person discharges from the army of the following dates: Jun 3, 1863; Jul 24, 1865; Nov 3, 1867; Oct 9, 1868; about $50 in money, besides a pocket knife & a note to Eliza Conrad, Christline, Ohio. He was apparently a man of about 45 years of age. Clementson is held for examination.

Madison, Wisc, Journal. On June 1, 1868, in Grant Co, Miss Catharine Jordan was killed by her lover, Wm E Kidd, in Glen Haven; large rewards for offered for the arrest of the murderer. Mr Delaware, a resident of the town where the murder was committed, learned of the presence of a man answering his description in Gtwn, Colo. Mr Delaware, with the assistance of Frank Winship, of Sioux City, Iowa, arrested him in Noble Co, Minn, on Oct 8. He was taken to the cars, & on Oct 14, near Jefferson, Green Co, Iowa, committed suicide by taking strychnine. He had confessed that he cut Miss Jordan's throat; "killed her for love." His last words: "Tell mother that I killed her for love."

Rev Henry H Millman died recently; his loss was not only to the pulpit, but to poetry & drama. [Death date not given-current item.]

Presidential Election. N Y Herald, Nov 4. The battle is over & the victory won. Grant & Colfax have been chosen by the people of the U S our next President & Vice President.

Among the passengers who sailed on Sat last, in the steamer **Berlin**, from Balt, was the Countess de Pourtales & family, for some time past residents of Wash. The family expects to remain in Europe about one year.

Memphis, Nov 4. In a difficulty on Main st last night, Dan Earle shot a German, Geo Rendihuber, inflicting a fatal wound. Earle was arrested & lodged in jail.

Lucy Stone & Mrs Blackwell, her mother-in-law, offered their votes in the 11th Ward of Newark, N J, on Tuesday, but the judges refused to receive them.

Mrs Mary Sharkey was accidentally killed in Augusta, Ga, last Wed. A negro was in her store making some purchases, & was negotiating for a pistol with the daughter of the deceased, a girl about 13 years of age, & while she was exhibiting the pistol it was discharged, the contents passing through Mrs Sharkey's heart.

Excellent piano & household & kitchen furniture at auction-Nov 12, at the residence of the late Wm A Bradley, 336 N Y ave, between 9th & 10th sts. One inlaid table purchased at the sale of Sir Henry Bulwer. -Cooper & Latimer, aucts

Mrd: on Oct 7, by Rev R H McKim, Capt H A F Worth, formerly of the 6th U S infty, to Mary E, daughter of John B Peyton, of Wash, D C.

Mrd: on Nov 3, by Rev J J Keane, Edw R Loxbury, of Wash City, to Mrs Martha W Smart, of Leesburg, Va.

FRI NOV 6, 1868
Regular meeting of the Oldest Inhabitants' Association, the Pres, Dr John B Blake, in the chair; Mr J F Callan reported that it was inexpedient to change the place of meeting. Messrs Wm Nourse, Gen Wm H French, Levi Davis, Thos R Brightwell, & Patrick Sweeney were nominated.

Yesterday Policeman Owens accidently shot himself theough the hand with his pistol at the station-house. The wound was painful, but not dangerous. Dr R C Crogon dressed his wound.

Alex Williamson, employed in the Kissington Rolling Mill, Pittsburgh, was instantly killed Monday by being caught in some of the machinery. He was 45 years old, & leaves behind him a wife & 3 children.

Sec McCulloch yesterday made the following appointments of internal revenue ofcrs:
Storekeepers: Thos Fair, Pa; Howard Allen, Pa; Joshua S Fletcher, Pa; Jos R Matthews, Pa; Clay H Deckert, Ohio; W H Schaffer, Ohio; John E Keider, Ohio; Clifton Lowe, Ohio; F W Ames, La; Patrick Dunles, Ill; John Tiermeyrs, Mo; J H Hogan, Mo; C A Corbet, Mo; Hugh Watson, Mo; Thos Wilkinson, Mo; John S Matthews, Mo; John W Young, Mo; Dennis Holland, Pa; J P Ward, La; Harvey George, Mo; Walter Capehart, Va; Jesse S Mapes, N Y; Wm H Kniffen, N Y.
Gaugers: Gideon Cornell, Ariz; F R Strange, Maine; Geo Gold, New Mexico; Pelig Fiske, Md; Jas Steele, Ohio.
Tobacco Inspector: F R Miller, Pa

Board of Police meeting yesterday. Pvts John Zirwes & C C Langley, charged with neglect of duty, were sentenced to be admonished. Pvt Jas B O'Brien, charged with violation of orders & neglect of duty, was dismissed the force. Pvt Wm H Lusby, charged with violation of the rules & regulations, neglect of duty, & conduct unbecoming an ofcr; to be dismissed the force. The following were appointed privates on the force: Chas W O'Neil & Chas Brandengeyer. The following additional privates were appointed, on condition that they pass the required examination: J T Gatewood, for duty at H D Cooke's residence in Gtwn, for 6 months; Thos Colter, for duty at Wisewell Barracks, for 6 months. Pvt L S Pond, having served the probationary term satisfactorily, was ordered to be commissioned. The resignation of Pvt Richd A Frere was received & accepted, to take effect at once. The following applications for liquor licenses were disapproved: Wm McGuire, Burns Connelly, Ernest Wangeman, Patrick Conway, John Noonan, Robt Billow, Jos Freundt, Bernard Bryan, E Kottmann, John Schotterbeck, Chas Schuster, John Lolliger, Romanus Rudhardt, & Francis Ochsenreiter, of Wash; & Z Williams & R F Martin, of Wash Co.

Mrd: on Oct 22, at St Mary's Church, Alexandria, Va, by Rev Fr Kroes, John S Greene to Mary T Roach, daughter of the late Jas Roach, all of Alexandria. [Balt papers please copy.]

Died: on Nov 5, Mrs Mary Eliz King, widow of the late Wm W King, in the 74th year of her age. Due notice of the funeral will be given hereafter. [Nov 7th newspaper: Mrs M E King's funeral will take place at 10 o'clock on Nov 7, from St Matthew's Church, corner of H & 15th sts.]

Died: on Nov 2, at Brooklyn, N Y, Frances Annie Fisher, aged 2 years, 8 months & 23 days, only daughter of Louis H & Katie L Fisher. [Nov 7th newspaper: Died: on Nov 2, at Brooklyn, N Y, Frances Amili Fisher, aged 2 years, 8 months & 23 days, only daughter of Louis H & Katie L Fisher.]

Equity Court-Judge Olin. 1-Mackenbur vs Carpenter et al. Order appointing B C Lovejoy guardian *ad litem*. [Mackenbur/Mackenburg: space enough for a "g."]

Chancery sale, on G st, between 12th & 13th sts; by decree of the Supreme Court of D C; wherein Robt B Clokey is cmplnt & Wm N Clokey et al are dfndnts; Equity No 1,328; public auction, on Nov 18, of part of lot 6 in square 288, in Wash City, with improvements. Also, all the right, title, interest, & estate of Jane W Wakefield, dec'd, as "reversionary lessor," of, in, & to the west half of lot 7 in square 288.
–A Thos Bradley, trustee -Cooper & Latimer, aucts

Gen Van Wyck has been defeated for Congress in the 11th Dist of N Y.

Mrs Lincoln arrived in Paris on Wed, & took private apartments in the Champe Elysees.

On Monday engine 502, attached to a freight train on the Central Ohio division of the Balt & Ohio railroad, exploded near Claypoel station, 12 miles east of Zanesville. The fireman, John Harley, was thrown & severely bruised. The engineer, Robt Brown, of Zanesville, & the brakeman, Wilson Gardner, of Patasksia, were instantly killed.

SAT NOV 7, 1868
Ex-Pres Pierce was well enough to ride to the polls in Concord, N H, on Tuesday, & vote for Seymour & Blair.

Gen Grant & family are expected to arrive in Chicago yesterday, en route for Washington. The General has declined any public reception here on his return.

Col Drake, who sunk the first oil well on Oil Creek, & gave the world the benefit of his discovery, is at Titusville, living in extreme destitution.

Sec McCulloch yesterday appointed the following internal revenue ofcrs:
Storekeepers: Robt O Dennett, N H; Frederick Fuller, N C; Andrew M Smith, Miss; Wm R Bear, Ill; Nathan Briggs, N Y; John C Le Ferre, Wisc.
Gaugers: Jerry Weakley, Ind; Geo K Crutchfield, Va; Theophilus Pratt, N Y; John Hilliard, Pa; Jas F Caulk, Md.

Since the overthrow of the Bourbon monarchy in Spain, five hundred Jesuits have fled across the frontier to Portugal.

Mrs Jas Rice, of Newark, N J, was probably fatally burned by a kerosene accident on Wednesday night. She had filled her lamp & she overturned it on the mantel. Two of her children, who were with her, were slightly injured.

Died: on Nov 5, John Francis McNerhany, aged 22 years & 11 months, eldest son of John & Rachel McNerhany. His funeral is this morning, at 9 o'clock, from the residence of his parents, 134 5th st west, between O & P sts north.

Died: on Nov 5, Maude Eliza, infant daughter of Dr J Ford & Marion V Thompson, aged 1 month. Her funeral will be from the residence of her grandmother, 357 9th st, on Nov 7, at 11 o'clock.

Boston, Nov 6. At West Townsend, today, the train on the Peterboro & Shirley road ran over & killed John Hyde, road repairer in the employ of the Fitchburg railroad.

On Wednesday, Mrs Sophia Hecht, wife of Mr L Hecht, a merchant of this city, residing at 459 North 6th st, came to her death in a most distressing manner. Mrs Hecht was suffering from a nervous disorder; her doctor gave her a prescription; she took it to the drug store of Mr H A Bower; he was absent from the city, & his son, Mr Jos A Bower, a young man, made the fatal mistake of reading the abbreviation of assafoeida for atrophia, a narcotic poison, & this he put in the pills in the quantity prescribed for assafoeida. Mrs Hecht died after severe suffering. –Phil Ledger, Nov 6.

On Friday, Oct 2, a son of Mr Ickes, of Fremont, Ohio, aged 9 years, was taken sick with diptheria, & on Sunday died. His sister, aged 7 years, was taken sick on Sat & died on Monday. They were both buried in one grave. On Oct 12 Mr Ickes himself died of the same disease, after an illness of 48 hours. On Sat, Oct 31, an infant of 1 year, the last one of the family, was deposited in the tomb beside the father, sister, & brother. Mrs Ickes is in poor health. She is an entire stranger in Fremont, having come from Pa with her husband in the spring.

MON NOV 9, 1868
Real estate. 1-Cooper & Latimer, aucts, sold part of lot 5 in Reservation B, fronting 24½ feet on Missouri ave, between 4½ & 6th sts west, running back 127 feet 5 inches to a 30 foot alley, improved by a 3 story brick dwlg, to Geo W Cochran, for $9,200. 2-Green & Williams, aucts, sold the western part of lot 3 in square 198, on I st, between 15th & 16th sts, improved by a 2 story brick house, to Jas Wormley, for $3,200.

Gen U S Grant, President elect, accompanied by his wife & son, Gens Smith, Comstock, & Badeau, of his staff, & J Russell Jones, of Chicago, arrived in Washington Sat, from Galena, Ill. The party drove to Gen Grant's residence, on I st.

On Saturday Mrs Mary White, wife of Henry A White, residing at 153 K st, between 19th & 20th sts, committed suicide. Mr White was a clerk under Gen Miller, in the Quartermaster's Dept. She cut her jugular vein. Mrs Mary White was between 45 & 50 years of age. Ever since she buried her child in 1850 she has been mentally depressed. In Texas, when she lost her child, she, every moonlight night, would go to the graveyard, one & a half miles from the encampment, & sit on the grave until he took her away. He was then in the 2nd dragoons. She drank sometimes.

Died: on Nov 7, of typhoid fever, Ellen, beloved wife of John Hogan, in her 54th year. Her funeral will be at St Peter's Church, Capitol Hill, this evening at 2 o'clock P M.

Died: on Nov 8, at his residence, in Wash City, in his 52nd year, John T Bradley, of Pa, late clerk in the U S Patent Ofc. His funeral will take place at 3 o'clock P M, today. [Phil & Lancaster, Pa, papers please copy.]

Died: on Nov 7, Agnes May, only child of Franklin & Julia A Barrett, aged 2 years, 1 month & 13 days. Her funeral will take place from the residence, 504 12th st, Monday, at 3 o'clock P M.

The murderess Kate Johnston was on Saturday sentenced to be hung at Buffalo, N Y, on Dec 18th.

Orphans Court-Judge Purcell, Nov 7, 1868. 1-Jas M Miflin qualified as guardian of Alice M, orphan of Wm N Odell; bond $500; sureties, Anson Gale & Sylvester T F Sterick. 2-Dorothea Repetti qualified as guardian of Reta Triay, orphan of Raphael T & Reta Triay; bond $3,000; sureties, Jas Repetti, John Levezzie, & Wm P Lasselle. 3-The renunciation of Rachel Miller as guardian to Alice M, orphan of Wm N Odell, was filed. 4-Petition of Isabella K Thompson, widow of Wm Thompson, for authority to sell certain real estate, was filed & decree of sale awarded.

A young lady, Miss Lulie Daniel, daughter of Maj Wm Daniel, of Edgefield District, S C, was burned to death last Sunday. Her garments caught fire from the kitchen fire.

Augustus Kutzbock, a well known citizen & architect of Madison, Wisc, drowned himself last Saturday, on account of business reverses. The water where he threw himself in was but two or three feet deep.

Buffalo, N Y, Nov 8. S V Ryan, the new Bishop of Buffalo, was consecrated today with splendid & imposing ceremonies at St Joseph's Cathedral; 7,000 were present. The sermon was preached by Rev Wm Ryan, of St Louis. The ceremonies were 5 hours.

Supreme Court of D C. Michl Gore vs Susana J Snyder & others. Creditors of John H Snyder, dec'd, & others interested, are to appear before me on Nov 12, on the premises, to ascertain the value of the land & improvements mentioned in the bill, & the liens on the same, stating their priorities. –Walter S Cox, auditor

Orphans Court of Wash Co, D C, Nov 7, 1868. In the case of Wm H Dougal, exc of Philip Harry, dec'd; the executor & Court have appointed Dec 1 next, for the final settlement of the personal estate of the said dec'd, of the assets in hand.
-Jas R O'Beirne, Reg/o wills

Orphans Court of Wash Co, D C, Nov 7, 1868. In the case of Jos Redfern & Wm Wilson, adms of Saml Redfern, dec'd; the administrators & Court have appointed Dec 1 next, for the final settlement of the personal estate of the said dec'd, of the assets in hand.
-Jas R O'Beirne, Reg/o wills

Wanted, a private Tutor, to teach 2 boys the usual branches of a liberal education. For particulars apply to W P Brooke, at John A Bakers Agricultural Store, Wash.

TUE NOV 10, 1868
Sec McCulloch yesterday made the following appointments of internal revenue:
Gaugers: David B Risley, Mo; Julius Strouge, Mo; J F Hoyt, Ill; AB Smith, Ill; L A Mixer, Ill; Geo Eicher, Pa; John H Roberts, Pa; Wm M Russell, Ohio.
Storekeepers: St Clair Sutherland; Ill; Humphrey Best, Ky; John Quinn, Pa; Wm Bucks, Pa; Bert Grant, Pa.

Frank Walker, of Adams, Mass, was shockingly burned, at the west shaft of the Hoosac Tunnel, recently, by explosion of benzine, which he used kindling a fire under a boiler.

Died: on Nov 9, Emily Beale, second daughter of John H & Gertrude P Houston. Notice of the time of the funeral will appear in tomorrow's papers. [Nov 11th newspaper: Her funeral will be from the residence of her father, 177 G st, on Nov 12, at 2 o'clock P M.]

Died: on Nov 7, suddenly, Mary White, of Wash City, aged 50 years.

Atlanta, Ga, Nov 9. Govn'r Bullock has offered a reward of $5,000 for the arrest & conviction of the person or persons who caused the death of Albert G Ruffin, sheriff of Richmond Co, who was killed in the election riot at Augusta.

Greenleaf's Point, in the southernmost extremity of Wash City, at the junction of the Potomac & Anacostia rivers, was selected as the site for an arsenal intended for the manufacture & depository of military stores, as early as 1804, & was used exclusively for that purpose till 1812, when, immediately on the declaration of war with England, the Gov't proceeded to erect, on the side approachable by water, strong batteries to protect the arsenal, & also to guard the river channels leading to the Navy Yard, & other sections of the city & District. Notice of Jul 19, 1815: It is proposed to construct at **Greenleaf's Point** some temporary works for the further defence of the city; the patriotic citizens turned out in large numbers with their implements, & did good service; it was then known as **Fort Washington**; it had not the slightest preparation for defence on the land side. When the British troops repulsed out forces at Bladensburg, Aug 24, 1814, & were moving upon the city, the authorities had nothing better to do than to prepare to evacuate the premises. That night the American troops, under command of Col Bomford, removed what property they could, burnt the workshops, & on Aug 25 a detachment of 200 British troops marched to the fort & commenced the destruction of what had been left; they found some 18 pounder guns, they attempted to destroy them by discharging one against the trunnion of the other; before evacuating a large amount of powder was concealed in a dry well; the wadding from the first gun fired in attempting to destroy these 18 pounders fell into this well, producing a tremendous explosion. Half of the men were killed; among them was Capt Frazer, Acting Adj Gen of the British forces. The British had 12 killed & 30 wounded. The fort below Alexandria now **Fort Washington**, was in 1814 a mere water battery of a dozen or fifteen guns, was called **Fort Warburton** in 1814, &, we think, its name was not changed till the fort was rebuilt, in 1818. In 1823-24 the garrison was withdrawn. About this time ***Greenleaf's Point*** became the seat of the penitentiary of the District, located on the northern border of the Arsenal grounds. Chas Ralfinch was the architect of the Penitentiary; he consulted with Elam Lynds, the father of the Auburn system, & adopted that plan. Jas Greenleaf, as head of a large business firm, came here soon after the place was permanently fixed as a capital. The company, Morris, Nicholson & Co, consisted of Robt Morris, the great Phil financier, illustrious in the days of the Revolution for both his personal devotion to the cause & the offering of his great wealth to the same cause, but who, in a shipwreck of his fortune in his last days, closed his life in prison for debt in Phil. John Nickolson & Jas Greenleaf purchased lots here on an immense scale. Oliver Walcott, Sec of the Treasury, on Jul 4, 1800, wrote a long letter to his wife in Conn, describing thie famous place, the permanent seat of the American Gov't. Greenleaf's enterprise broke down. The funds were exhausted when one row of his fine houses had been completed, & these are still standing at the entrance to the Arsenal grounds. Gen Wm Henry Terrett, of Fairfax, Va, came over here with hundred or two of the surplus servants from his plantations, & had a brick yard on a scale of great magnitude. He was of one of the old Va families, & owned an estate of great value. Among the leading spirits of the city were also Dr Henry Huntt, Abraham Young, Wm Deakins, Lynch & Sands, & Wm Duncanson, the guardian of Marcia Burns, & manager of her vast estate after the death of her father, till she was married to Van Ness; & last, not least, Thos Law & Danl Carroll, of Duddington. Greenleaf was bred to the bar; the son of Wm Greenleaf, who was at one period sheriff of Suffolk Co, Mass, & born in Boston in 1765. He was Consul in Holland before coming here; married in that country, lost his wife, & left his only child, a son, there, who never came to America. Wm Cranch, Chief Justice of this Dist for half a century, who came here in 1794, was much employed by Greenleaf in the first years of his residence in the Dist. He was a native of Mass, a son of Harvard; his wife, Nancy Cranch, the sister of Greenleaf, died Sep 16, 1843, at the age of 71 years, leaving in this community a name hallowed with whatever most dignifies & adorns a Christian woman, & on the next day, Sep 17, her brother, Jas Greenleaf, died here at the late of 78 years, after a long life of turmoil. Cmdor Rogers resided some years in the house at the west end of a row of brick residences close to the present entrance to the Arsenal permises. Indian Camping Ground: was a well known fishing ground & hunting ground occupied by the Indians prior to the advent of the Europeans. Cmdor John Rodgers was the senior ofcr of the navy, & when he died in 1838, was not on duty, having in 1837 resigned his navy commision on account of failing health. He did good service in the war of 1812. Cmder Rodgers died in Phil, & his remains were brought to his home at ***Greenleaf's Point***, & buried at the ***Congressional Burying Ground***. He was a native of Md, born in 1771, & 67 at the time of his death.

Tallahassee, Fla, Nov 6. A German, Nicholas Simon, living in the country west of this city, was found dead in the road yesterday, with his skull broken; his pockets rifled.

Herr Werder, of Nuremberg, has invented an improvement on the Prussian needle-gun. It weighs only 8½ pounds, & requires a smaller charge, & has been fired 20 times in a minute, without attaining the maximum of speed.

Victor Hugo, for his new work, "Par ordre du Roi," just finished, receives from his publisher, M Lacroix, the sum of 300,000 francs.

Extensive sale of boots & shoes, store fixtures, safe, & stove, at auction, of Nov 17, at the store of H Burns & Co, 408 Pa ave, between 4½ & 6th sts. -Cooper & Latimer, aucts

WED NOV 11, 1868
N Y Times, Nov 10. The screw frigate **Franklin**, flagship of the European squadron, passed Sandy Hook late yesterday, in-bound, having on board the first of American seamen, Admiral David G Farragut, & the members of his family. The **Franklin** is first rate, carrying 39 guns & about 800 men. Annexed is a partial list of her ofcrs: Cmdor Alex'r M Pennock; Cmder Jas W Shirk; Lt Cmders Edw E Potter, J Crittenden Watson, Fred'k Pearson, Ira Harris, jr, & Wm Bainbridge Hoff; Lt Jacob M Little; Ensigns Saml N Kane, Hugh W McKee, & Gifford D Gill; Assist Surgeon Fred'k W Winderlich; Paymaster, Capt John A Bradford; Engineers, Lt Geo P Hunt, Master Geo W Slivers, Wm A Windsor, & Henry L Slosson; Chaplain. Lt Cmder John P Wallace; Marine Corps, Lt Col Chas Heywood & Manuel C Goodrell.

Wm Preston Hilliard died in Columbus, Ga, in Nov, after a brief illness. He was a man of genius & high culture, having been for some time at school in Gtwn, D C, a student at Princeton, N J, where he graduated with distinction. He served with great gallantry in the Confederate army; was present at the defence of *Fort Sumter*; was with Early in the valley of Va, & with Lee in the final struggle at Petersburg.

On Oct 23, Frederic Wm Dickens, latest surviving brother of Mr Chas Dickens, who has residing in Darlington during the last 12 months, & had for 3 weeks before his death suffered from an abscess in the lung. -Darlington [England] Times

Henry Polkinhorn has purchased the Sunday Herald & Intelligencer job printing ofc. -Evening Star There is not a word of truth in the above statement.

Died: on Nov 10, of consumption, in his 27th year, George W, eldest son of George B Smith, of Wash City. His funeral will be from the residence of his father, 3rd & N st, this evening, Nov 11, at 2 o'clock.

Died: on Nov 10, of hemorrhage, Miss Caroline Nalley, daughter of the late Aaron & Eliz Nalley. Her funeral will take place on Nov 12 at 2 o'clock P M, from 494 12th st.

Orphans Court-Judge Purcell, Nov 10, 1868. 1-The will of the late Eliz Mary King was filed & partially proven. She bequeathes the largest part of her estate to her daughter, Mrs Rutherford, & Miss Redgate. 2-Dorothea Repetti was appointed guardian to Rita Triay, orphan of Raphael R Triay; bond $3,000. 3-The first & final accounts of executor of Basil Fletcher, & excx of Teresa Hill, were approved & passed.

Mr Thos Cooke, a famous mechanician, died a fortnight since, at York, England, in the 63rd year of his age; was the most celebrated manufacurer of astronomical instruments in Great Britain, & was, besides, a man of large scientific attainments.

Two weeks ago Mr Edwin Forrest paid, through Jay Cooke, at Phil, $65,000, the amount in full of the accumulated alimony due to his late wife under the decision in the divorce decree, which has at last been made final. Mr Forrest has expended, it is estimated, upwards of $300,000 in this painful divorce suit.

Executor's sale of leather sewing machines, leather & tools, on Nov 13, on account of the executor of Geo Deufel, dec'd, at the store at 9th & D sts. –John B Wheeler& Co, aucts

Chancery sale of valuable property on H st, between 15th & 16th st; by decree of the Supreme Court of D C, passed Oct 29, 1868; wherein Mary V Larkin is cmplnt, & Jos F Loughron & others are dfndnts, Equity 1,321; sale Nov 25 next, the west 22 feet 6 inches on M st, part of lot 21 in square 161. –Jos Gawler, trustee -J B Wheeler & Co, aucts

Trustee's sale of valuable real estate in Chas Co, Md; by decree of the Circuit Court for Chas Co, in Equity; public sale on Nov 27, lot 44, & part of tract of land called **Mount Pleasant**, containing about 600 acres, more or less. This land adjoins the land of John D Bowling, T Elzan Gardiner, & others, & was formerly owned by Dr John H Robertson & wife. Improvements include a fine dwlg house. –F Stone, trustee

THU NOV 12, 1868
Sec McCulloch has confirmed the appointments of John G Noah, to be Supervisor of Internal Revenue for the State of Tenn; Judge Saffold to be Supervisor for the States of Ala, Ga, & Fla; & Jas R Bayley, for Oregon, Wash, Idaho, & Montana.

Sec McCulloch yesterday made the following appointments of internal revenue ofcrs:
Storekeepers: Geo H Barnes, Ky; G C West, Ky; E S Mansfield, Montana Territory; Jas A Mann, Mo; States Barton, N Y; Jos C Carr, Ill; Edw Keyser, Pa.
Gaugers: Jos Kelly, Ohio; John J McLean, Ill; Geo E Slothower, Md; Leonard Martin, Mo; Geo W Haws, Dakota; Jasper H Altemus, Pa; Thos Leddy, Fla.

The two story & basement brick house, 36 Fayette st, Gtwn, was disposed of at private sale for $4,000. [Name of purchaser not given.]

Yesterday Mr Nicholas B Ray, a member of the Metropolitan Police force, died at his late residence on L st, between 4th & 5th sts, after an illness of several months, in his 35th year. He was a native of Balt, & had been a resident here over 15 years; appointed an ofcr of the force Dec 14, 1865; & was a good & faithful ofcr. He leaves an affectionate wife & 3 small children to mourn his loss. His funeral will take place from his late residence tomorrow, at 3 o'clock P M.

John Quincy Adams, the Democratic candidate for Governor in Mass, ran 10,000 ahead of his ticket at the recent election.

A jury recently rendered a verdict against the town of Walpole, N H, in favor of Miss Ella A Gates for $5,168, to compensate her for injuries sustained in consequence of driving against a post which the authorities had permitted to remain in the road.

Gen Kilpatrick has been granted 3 months' leave of absence from the Chilian mission, & has returned to N J.

Our cable despatches this morning contain the brief announcement of the death in London yesterday of the Marquis of Hastings, but 26 years of age. He inherited at an early age a large fortune; consisting principally of landed estates. He married Lady Flora Paget, who was at the time engaged to another gentleman, but who preferred to walk from a milliner's shop into the arms of her more youthful lover. There was some scandal attached to this marriage, which his subsequent failure served to aggravate. –N Y Times

Died: on Nov 11, after a long & painful illness, Mrs Mary E Parker, aged 57 years. Her funeral will be from her son's [John C Parker's] residence, 205 5th st, between M & N sts, this evening at 3 o'clock P M.

Troy, N Y, Nov 11. Mary E Magee, daughter of Capt Magee, of this city, committed suicide this morning by shooting herself through the heart with her father's revolver. The act was caused by temporary insanity. Miss Magee was 20 years of age. [Nov 17th newspaper: Mary Eliza Magee committed suicide in the family at 195 8th st, opposite Anthony place, on Nov 11. No cause can be assigned for the act, unless it may be temporary insanity. Her mother heard the report of the revolver & found her daughter in the agonies of dissolution. Capt Magee is at present residing in Chicago, & has been summoned by telegraph to return to his terribly bereaved family. –Troy Times, Nov 11]

Orphans Court of Wash Co, D C. In the matter of the petition of Saml C Mills, guardian. Said guardian reported he sold part of lot 34 in square 557 to Wm P Lasselle, as trustee for Mary A Mills; & the terms have been complied with. –Wm F Purcell, Judge of Orphans Court -Jas R O'Beirne, Reg/o wills

FRI NOV 13, 1868
The Sec of the Treasury yesterday made the following appointments of internal revenue ofcrs:
Storekeepers: W E Dubant, Va; F L Sarmiento, Va; Thos S Duvall, Ky; Wm R Letcher, Ky; E S Metzger, Pa; E D Reynolds, Pa; Chas N Aykroyd, Pa; John Barker, Ohio; John Shaw, Md; Jas S Wright, Ala.
Gaugers: Robt Nelson, Pa; Oliver C Lock, Ill; Jas E Rathburn, Ill; A C Parks, Ind; Draper A Dewees, Ohio; Delaware Milton, Ohio; Lineback E S Butler, Ohio; Geo L Mitchell, Ga; L C Cherry, 2nd Ala. Tobacco Inspector: Danl Urich, Iowa.

Fred Boehmler, postmaster at Cedar Falls, Iowa, has been arrested for robbing the mails passing through his hands. Several plundered letters were found on his person, one of them containing $500. The extent of his robberies has not yet been ascertained.

In the case of ex-Judge Sidney A Hubbell, of New Mexico, against the Western Union Railroad Co, to recover for personal injuries received by an explosion & burning of the steamboat **Lansing** on the Mississippi river, the jury awarded $12,000 to the plntf for damages a few days since at Chicago.

The first instance of a Chicago pulpit being occupied by a <u>female preacher</u> occurred on Sunday last in the Church of the Redeemer, [Universalist,] where Rev Mrs Chapin, of **Mount Pleasant**, Iowa, addressed very large audiences in the morning & evening, with considerable effect.

John M Kills, who, with his accomplices, forged nearly $70,000 in Gov't vouchers during the war, was brought up for trial at Nashville last week. He pleaded guilty, & was recommitted to jail to await sentence. At the time the forgeries were committed, Kills was a quartermaster in the army.

Mrd: on Nov 10, at **Avalon**, near Wash, the residence of the bride's mother, by Rev Wm Hodges, Phil C Riley, of Wash, to Virginia Covington, second daughter of the late Benj P Smith, of the former place. [Balt papers please copy.]

Mrd: on Nov 6, by Rev J A Jefferson, at Washington st M E Church, Mr Chas E Luckett, of Wash, D C, to Miss Sarah F Whitlock, of Petersburg.

Mrd: on Nov 11, by Rev Vaughn Lewis, of St John's Church, John B Patterson to Mrs Annie E Raybold, both of Wash City. No cards.

Rambles among the Schools. Female Grammar School of the 4th District: Mrs M A Amidon first entered the schools of this district in 1849 as Miss Margaret A Milburn, principal of Primary School No 3, holding this place till she was promoted to her present position in 1854. In that year a second story was added to the grammer school. The Female Grammar School of the First District: Miss Annie E Evans, who entered the public schools of Wash City as a teacher of secondary school in 1802, was promoted to her present place in the course of that year, & is doing superior work. Secondary School No 5, Girls' School of the 1st District, occupies a frame bldg, formerly a small church, halfway between Pa ave & the canal; teacher is Mrs M E Rodier who has been in the public schools since 1849. Primary Colored School is in charge of Miss Rebecca H Elwell, which is further on the same st. The Stevens' School House is on 22nd st, near K, adjoins the lot occupied by the feed store & house of Mr Alfred Jones. Mr Jones assented that the house should have been set at least 5 feet higher, with a cellar under it. The Board of Trustees last year consisted of Sayles J Bowen, Alfred Jones, & A G Hall, & they were the trustees when this location was selected.

Died: on Nov 11, Thos Bartlett, in his 64th year. His funeral will be from his late residence, 12th & Mass ave, this evening, Nov 13, at 2 o'clock.

Balt, Nov 12. 1-Josiah Gordon, a well known character of this city, was shot & killed last night by Michl Keho, proprietor of a drinking saloon. Keho was committed for the action of the grand jury. 2-This morning the body of Jas Glenn, the engineer of the Holliday st distillery, was found in the machinery, crushed to a shapeless man. It is supposed that he was caught accidentally by the crank.

Albany, Nov 12. The second trial of Geo W Cole for the murder of L Hiscock commenced this morning, Judge Hogebook presiding. No jurors have as yet been sworn.

SAT NOV 14, 1868
Sec McCulloch yesterday made the following appointments of internal revenue ofcrs:
Storekeepers: W N Berkley, La; John R Winder, Utah Territory.
Gaugers: W F Districht, Pa; W A Sands, Pa; John A Baiteman, Pa; Jacob Reif, Ind; John F Brand, Ohio; Robt Campbell, Utah Territory; B B Bitner, Utah Territory; J C Barber, Ill; J A Zabel, Ill; Wm M Brown, Ill, G W Hotaling, Ill.

Messrs Jones & Richardson, aucts, at Marlboro, Md, sold the farm belonging to James Naylor, of James, known as the ***Milltown farm***, on the Patuxent river, containing about 350 acres, to Mr Geo R Herrick, of Wash City, for $4,100 cash.

The divorce suit which has been pending for some time between Maria M Waldron & Hamyden Waldron, terminated by a decision in favor of the petitioner, & a divorce was granted *a vinculo*. It was ordered that her maiden name of Maria Madeleine Sedogard be restored to her.

Gen McClellan is about to take up his residence permanently at Hoboken.

Thurlow Weed & his daughter returned from Europe on Wednesday. The health of Mr Weed is somewhat improved.

Mrs Harriet Hewlett, of Merrick, Long Island, on Friday of last week, saturated her clothing with kerosene, & then set fire to them. She was burned to death. She was about 30 years of age.

Mrd: on Nov 12, at St Peter's Church, Capitol Hill, by Rev Fr Boyle, Dr F S Walsh, jr, of Wash, D C, to Miss Mary E Talburtt, of Wash Co.

Mrd: on Nov 12, in Balt, at the residence of the bride's sister, by Rev Dr Roberts, R W Carter, of Wash, to Susan G Carter, of Balt. No cards. [Balt papers copy.]

Died: on Nov 13, David, infant child of Francis & Annie E Lamb, aged 20 months.

Salvator Taglioni just died at Naples, aged 78 years. He composed more than 200 ballets. During the disorders in Italy, in 1848, Taglioni, who was a great friend of the King, was taken by the insurgents & shot. He, however, survived, in spite of 14 wounds which he received.

Columbus [Ga] Sun & Times, Nov 7. Mr Owen Thomas died several weeks ago; only one will has been found, it was made in 1852; he desired that about 25 of his negroes be carried by his executor, after his death to Liberia, as they might elect, & there set free, they & their posterity forever. He then desired the residue of his property, including some 60 other negroes, who also were his slaves, to be reduced to money. He required that his debts, which are small, his executors & the expenses of transportation of the negroes to be free, be first paid, & then the remainder of the funds to be divided among the negroes thus set free, & divided in specified proportions, on their arrival at their new homes. There now remain 19 negroes who claim the property of deceased under his will, which his relations are endeavoring to break. The estate is worth at least $50,000, & may exceed this sum by many thousands. Mr Jas K Redd, who is the only surviving executor of the will, has presented it for probate. Gen H L Benning & Jas M Russell, counsel for caveators, proposed to introduce him to prove that Owen Thomas had often said that he no longer considered the document his will; that he had made another will. Williams & Thornton & Ramsey & Ramsey represent the negroes; Ingram & Crawford, the executor; Jas M Russell, Mrs Hargroves, [the only surviving sister of Owen Thomas] & Gen H L Benning & Peabody & Bannon, the heirs of Mrs M W Tweat, dec'd, another sister. The array of counsel is imposing.

Trustees' sale of valuable hotel & real estate; by decree of the Circuit Court for PG Co, Md, in Equity, wherein Geo H Calvert, exc of Chas B Calvert & others are cmplnts, & John H Surratt, Isaac Surratt, & others are dfndnts, the subscribers, as trustees, will offer at public sale, on the premises, on Dec 9, 1868, a tract of land in PG Co known as part of **His Lordship's Kindness**, containing 200 acres, more or less, of which the late John H Surratt died seized & possessed. This property is more commonly known as **Surrattsville** & is on the stage road from Wash City to **Fort Tobacco** & Leonardtown, 10 miles from Wash City. The property is improved by a commodious Hotel, well kept, yields a handsome profit to any enterprising man, with outbldgs attached & a Blacksmith's Shop. -C C Magruder, Danl Clarke, trustees

Youngstown, Ohio, Nov 13. Ex-Govn'r David Tod, of Brier Hill, died very suddenly this morning, while preparing to take the train for Cleveland. The disease is yet unknown.

Boston, Nov 13. Phineas Slowe, pastor of the Baptist Bethel for seamen, died today, aged 56.

Cleveland, Ohio, Nov 13. The sentence of Mrs Victor, to be hanged on Nov 20 for the murder of her brother, Wm Pacquet, was commuted yesterday by Govn'r Hays to imprisonment for life.

MON NOV 16, 1868

Cooper & Latimer, aucts, sold lot 3 in square 530, on 4th st west, between F & G sts north, improved by a 2 story frame dwlg, to Jeremiah D Long, for $3,125.

On Wednesday difficulty occurred at the grocery store of Wm Shaugnesy on Dela ave, near I st, between the proprietor & a man named Michl Nash. It appears that Nash had been drinking, & while in the store used insulting language, which caused *Shaugnesy to put him out. Nash returned & hurled a brick at Shaugnesy, which hit him over the eye, fracturing his skull, from the effects of which he died yesterday. Nash was committed to jail to await the result of the inquest. Shaugnesy leaves a wife & 2 children. [Nov 19th newspaper: Coroner Potter yesterday held an inquest over the body of Mrs Bridget *Shaunnessy, whose death on Tuesday morning led to the belief she died from injuries received. A verdict was returned that she came to her death from disease of the heart & lungs, in conjunction with the excitement caused by the affray in which her husband was killed.] [Nov 25th newspaper: Michl Nash, charged with the murder of Wm Shaunnessey, has been committed to jail.] *Two spellings of: Shaugnesy/Shaunnessy.

On Sat a boy, Jerry Sullivan, aged 11 years, while with Frank Cassady, was painfully wounded in the right foot by the accidental discharge of a shot gun in the hands of Cassady. The boys were hunting just outside the city limits, when the accident occurred.

Sec McCulloch on Sat made the following appointments of internal revenue ofcrs: Storekeepers: John E Murray, Ky; S E Underhill, Ill; Benj Fouke, Md; H J Fach, Mo; A W Holeman, Ky; Benj Wallace, Pa; Wm Williams, Iowa; Jos Campbell, Pa; Jas Good, Ky; Simon Jones, La; D L McFarland, La; H W Purdy, Ky. Gaugers: John Ivers, Mo; Henry Harger, Iowa; A H Delano, Mass; C F Levy, S C.

On Nov 6 Chas & Amelia Medford, of Wash City, lost an interesting child, their daughter, Mary Theodosia, 10 years old-by diptheria. On Nov 11, two more of their children, Chas Franklin & Jas Frederick, ages 7 & 2 years respectively, died of the same terrible disease; & on Sat the afflicted parents mourned the loss of yet another child, Grant Medford, aged 5 years, who was stricken down by this dreadful scourge-making 4 deaths in one family in little more than a week. The physician who attended this family is now very ill with the same complaint. He was taken shortly after the death of the first child, & learning of the fate of the other, he requested that the bodies should be promptly removed from the house without the delay of funeral services. Yesterday the sorrowful duty of interring 3 children was performed at **_Glenwood Cemetery_**, the services being conducted by Rev J W Hoover, the pastor of Hamlin Church.

Orphans Court-Judge Purcell, Nov 14, 1868. 1-Rosa McKenna was appointed guardian of the orphan of Wm Moore; bond $500. 2-Letters of administration on the estate of Julia Prout; bond $5,000. 3-Annie M Rimans, on estate of J A Bemas; bond $500. 4-Hermoine C Fleet was appointed guardian to the orphans of M B Street; bond $3,000.

N Y Post of Sat evening; this morning at Fulton Ferry, on the N Y side, the ferry boat **Hamilton** left her slip on the Brooklyn side with a great number of passengers, & as she neared the N Y side encountered the flood tide. She was then headed down stream; at this time, it is alleged, a Southern propeller, endeavoring to enter a neighboring slip, let go her stern line & swung around, thus blocking up the entrance to the Fulton Ferry slip. There was not sufficient room, & disaster was unavoidable; the ferry boat **Hamilton** crashed against the ferry boat **Union**, which lay chained in a slip adjoining her own. The forward deck of the **Hamilton** sunk several inches below the guards of the Union, which latter vessel had a light load on board. The ladies' cabin of the **Hamilton** was crushed in; terrified women & children screamed. Geo Brewer, a printer boy, who stood on the forward part of the boat with his dinner pail in hand, ready to spring ashore, was caught between the boats, & literally crushed to death. Geo Devoe, a working man, was crushed & mortally wounded; resided at 346 Tillary st, Brooklyn. Mrs Hart, 127 Plymouth st, Brooklyn, had one of her feet cut off; she has since died. John Thompson, janitor of the Sun Bldg, living at 157 Navy st, Brooklyn, is fearfuly injured. Also killed: Carlos Kraus, 257 Atlantic st, Brooklyn, mortally wounded. Margaret Mullie, East N Y, mortally wounded. Also wounded: Julia Darbey, a young girl, fatally; taken to her home, Franklin & Flatbush aves, Brooklyn. Alfred Hart, son of Mrs Hart, reported dead; his feet & legs were badly crushed; residence Thompkins ave & Hickory st, Brooklyn. Eliza Campion, seriously; home-10 Lawrence st, Brooklyn. Chas Gross, a German, taken to the Long Island College Hospital; badly injured as to be unable to give his residence. Francis N Skerritt, Kent ave, Bookyln; seriously. Catherine Farrell, 112 Navy st, Brooklyn, badly injured. Wm Cunningham, 146 Portland ave; taken home. Mrs Corrigan, 119 Bridge st, Brooklyn. Wm Brock, printer boy, in company with boy Brewer, badly injured, taken to the hospital. Nature of injuries & residence not given: Mrs Asburgh. Francis M Scammel, Brooklyn; Sarah Clark & Lizzie Clark, girls, Pearl st, Brooklyn; & Catherine McNeely, 228 Front st, Brooklyn, injured. Julia Mahan, 232 Hudson ave, slightly injured; Mrs Quimby, 82 Cranberry st, Brooklyn; Mr Monell, 257 Atlantic st, Brooklyn, foot crushed; Miss Bond, Smith st, Brooklyn, slightly; Chas Gencloth, Sumter st, Brooklyn, seriously injured

Boston, Nov 14. Judge Clifford, U S Circuit Court, this morning delivered his opinion in the great Howland will case, in which Betty Robinson, now Mrs Edw H Green, was the cmplnt, against Thos Mandell & others, excs under the last will of Silvia Ann Howland, to have the will set aside. The whole case rested on the admission of the deposition of Mrs Green, & this the Court decided inadmissable so far as related to a contract between her & Miss Howland, & the bill of cmplnt was dismissed, with costs. An appeal to the Supreme Court was taken for the complnt. [Nov 17th newspaper: Plntf, Mrs Green, nee Hetty H Robinson, is in her own right the richest woman in America; on Jul 2, 1865, Sylvia Ann Howland, of New Bedford, a somewhat eccentric maiden lady, died in that city, & left a property of over $2,000,000, to be distributed according to the provision of her will, to her niece, Mrs Green, & several friends, servants, & public objects. In Sep, 1860, Mrs Green was possessed in her own right of a large amount of property derived from her mother, the sister of Miss Howland & at that time her aunt was at variance with her father, & the two ladies adopted the plan of making mutual wills, in order to effectually prevent the inheritance by that gentleman of any part of the estate of Miss Howland having promised that if Mrs Green would comply with that request she would make a will bequeathing her all she possessed. Mrs Green that day made a will in favor of Miss Holland, excluding her father from all benefit from the will; Miss Howland, at the same time, caused a draft of her own will, not then completed, to be executed. Howland seemed to have ignored this will, for on Sep 1, 1863, made another will, appointing Thos Mandell et al execs of this will, & in Nov, 1864, she added a codicil, devising a large part of her property to several persons & corporations, to the exclusion of her niece. The Court's opinion is that the evidence is not sufficient to prove the alleged contract, & does not indicate any contract that would be recognized in law. The bill of complnt was dismissed with costs. An appeal was claimed by the cmplnt to the U S Supreme Court, & allowed.]

Valuable country residence at public auction; Nov 30th, the beautiful Farm owned by T L Hume, near Bladensburg, Md, containing about 35 acres, more or less; improved by a large dwlg house-11 rooms; manager's house-4 rooms; servants house-2 rooms; brick smoke house; ice-house; & other outbldgs. Also, will be sold 3 first rate mules, 3 wagons, 1 cart, agricultural & garden implements; poultry & hogs. Apply to Thos L Hume, on La ave, or the gentleman living on the premises. -Green & Williams, aucts

TUE NOV 17, 1868

Speaker Colfax will be married to Miss Wade at Andover, Ohio, tomorrow.

Boston, Nov 16. 1-Impressive funeral services were held today in the Bethel Church over the remains of Rev Phineas Stowe. Several hundred people more than the church could hold filled the streets in the neighborhood. 2-John Crane, of Cambridge, was today sentenced to two years' hard labor for criminally omitting certain property from his bankruptcy schedule.

Bethlehem, Pa. Nov 16. Bishop Stevens fell on the sidewalk in South Bethlehem last Sat night, & broke his arm & leg. He is at the residence of Prof Coffee, his brother-in-law, receiving surgical aid.

Public sale of 50 acres of land, within 3 miles of Wash, on Nov 26, on the premises, known as *Cedar Hill*; adjoins the farms of Messrs Allen Dodge & Clarke Mills-the railroad passing through it divides it in two nearly equal sites. Improvements consist of a small dwlg house upon each division. –Geo H Calvert, jr, agent for Geo H Calvert, exc -Green & Williams, aucts

Mr Jas Burrow, of Troy, N Y, aged 25 years, was killed on Sunday, while about to land on the N Y side from one of the Barclay st ferry-boats. As the boat was about to land, he fell or was pushed off the boat, & was crushed to death between the boat & the wharf.

The funeral of ex-Govn'r Tod took place at Youngtown, Ohio, on Sunday; no less that 15,000 persons were present. The funeral services were held in the Govnr's cottage at **Brier Hill**. Rev Saml Maxwell, of St John's Church, Youngstown, officiated.

Trustee's sale of property on 4½ st; by decree passed by the Supreme Court of D C, in Chancery No 192, wherein Richd H Clark et al are cmplnts, & Rice W Payne et al are dfndnts; public sale on Dec 8, of part of lot 12, square A, in Wash City; improved with a 2 story brick house. –Wm F Mattingly, trustee -Cooper & Latimer, aucts

Three story new brick dwlg on U st, between 13th & 14th sts, at auction, on Nov 27 next; we shall sell lots 24 thru 27 in Chas J White's subdivision of square 235; house has gas & water-pipes. Also, vacant lot adjoining on the west side, near 14th st, fronting 20 x 145 feet. -Cooper & Latimer, aucts

WED NOV 18, 1868
Obit-died: Gioacchino Rossini, the greatest composer for the Italian stage since Mozart, died in Paris on Saturday, at the age of nearly 77. Rossini was born in Pesaro, near Bologna, Feb 29, 1792; his mother was a singer, his father a player on the horn. Rossini married Signora Colbran, a well known prima donna, who had taken leading parts in a great number of his operas, & in 1824 they went to London under an engagement, he to compose an opera & she to sing The promised opera was not written; the prima donna, who certainly was not in the heyday of her charms, did not please, & the lessees of the King's Theatre were ruined by their costly importation. In 1845, Signora Colbran being dead, Rossini married Madame *Oympo Pellisier, & passed his time in Paris. The catalogue of Rossini's works comprises 38 operas, & a great variety of miscellaneous music. [*This could possibly be Oympo or Olympo.] [Dec 12th newspaper: Mr Rossini's last 2 days were a slow agony, & he suffered actual martyrdom. His body was literally on fire, so greatly did the inflammation consume him, that from time to time he moaned out, "I burn; ice, ice!" This was readily given him. He sometimes took the hand of his wife, who never left his bedside, & covered it with kisses. On Friday the Cure of Passy administered extreme unction, & half an hour later the patient lost consciousness. At ten at night he uttered his wife's name, & that was the last word that passed his lips.]

Orphans Court of Wash Co, D C. Letters testamentary on the personal estate of Eleanor Miller, late of Wash City, D C, dec'd. –Chas Miller, exc

Orphans Court of Wash Co, D C. Letters of administration on the personal estate of Wm R Edes, late of Gtwn, D C, dec'd. –David Edes, A Hyde, adms

THU NOV 19, 1868
Coroner Potter yesterday held an inquest over the body of Mrs Bridget Shaunnessy, whose death on Tuesday morning led to the belief she died from injruies received. A verdict was returned that she came to her death from disease of the heart & lungs, in conjunction with the excitement caused by the affray in which her husband was killed.

Mrd: on Nov 17, in Wash, by Rev T R Howlett, Jas E Leggard to Cornelia A Triplett, both of Va.

I forewarn all persons from trusting my wife, Mary Ann Orme, on my account, as I will pay no bills of her contraction after this date-Nov 18, 1868. –Thos P Orme

August Harper, a young German of Chicago, while out hunting Sunday, near Ainsworth, accidentally shot himself dead.

Mary McElrey & her sister, two domestice servants in Lee, Mass, have just received intelligence that a wealthy old relative has died & left them $70,000 each.

The Cathedral in Balt was crowded yesterday by a gay & animated throng, to witness the marriage of John T M Orendorff to Miss Maria Bohrer.

Geo P Sanglon, cashier of the Commercial Bank of St John, N B, has absconded, leaving defalcations to the amount of $90,000.

The President has appointed Wm H Russell to be Collector of the 2nd Dist of Conn, vice Woodruff, dec'd. Mr Babcock, recently appointed, declines.

Gen Grant breakfasted on Tuesday at Delmonico's with Gen Badeau & Horace Greeley. It is said this was the first time that Gen Grant & Mr Greeley had met each other.

A mass meeting of foreign born citizens was held in Richmond on Monday to raise funds to purchase a homestead for Gen H A Wise, for his services in the campaign of 1855 against the Know Nothings. A cmte of Irish, Germans, & Israelites was appointed to collect funds in that city.

Mrs J J Audubon, the widow of the naturalist, for whom an appeal was gotten up in Savannah, writes to the editor of a paper in that city that she knows nothing of the signer of the appeal, & is in no need of assistance, as she is boarding comfortably in N Y C, & her 13 grandchildren are independent of her.

Valuable improved property for sale at auction at H & 21st st; by decree of the Supreme Court of D C, in Equity, Jarboe & Junius J Boyle; public auction on Dec 21, all the right, title, & interest of Junius J Boyle in lots 19 & 20 in square 79 in Wash City, with improvements, or so much thereof as may be necessary, to pay a debt of $2,500.
-Saml L Phillips, trustee -W L Wall & Co, aucts

Valuable improved property at N Y & 10th sts at auction; by decree of the Supreme Court of D C, in Equity No 1,050, Yates & Selby cmplnts, against Geo Seitz et al; public auction on Dec 10, all the right, title, & interest of Geo Seitz in part of lot 1 in square 343. -Saml L Phillips, trustee -W L Wall & Co, aucts

Jas Molan, Dealer in Wines, Liquors, & Cigars: 372 Pa ave, adjoining the Metropolitan Hotel. Store & Sample room superintended by Wm H Conroy.

Orphans Court of Wash Co, D C, Nov 17, 1868. In the case of Jos F Kelley, adm of Hannah Fraser, dec'd, the administrator & Court have appointed Dec 15 next, for the final settlement of the personal estate of the said dec'd, of the assets in hand. -Jas R O'Beirne, Reg/o wills

FRI NOV 20, 1868
The dead body of Miss Esther Kendall, a lady about 60 years of age, who lived alone in Sterling, Mass, was found on the floor of her sleeping room on Tuesday, where it had probably lain several days. The cause of her death is unknown.

London, Nov 17. Messrs Baring Brothers, bankers, drew one million pounds sterling from the Bank of England yesterday for the Russian Gov't. It is said that this was on an American account, the money being in part payment for the Territory of Alaska. There must surely be some error about this. It is known that the Russian Govn't is drawing in gold as rapidly as possible.

Cooper & Latimer, aucts, sold part of lot 6 in square 288, on G st, near 13th st west, with improvements, to Robt B Clokey for $2,525.

Died: on Nov 19, W Ashton Fitzgerald, aged 59 years, of typhoid fever, at his residence, 353 F st. Mr Fitzgerald was a native of Boston, but for the last 30 years has been a resident of Wash City. [Boston papers please copy.]

Died: on Nov 19, at Key West, Fla, in his 56th year, Capt Benj More Dove, U S N, a native & resident of Wash City. [Nov 23rd newspaper: Benj More Dove: his naval record extended from 1826, commencing with his first duty as a midshipman, then to the higher grades of lt cmder, & capt. He was an affectionate son, kind & gentle as a husband, & a devoted brother. –X]

Havana, Nov 19. The steamer **Star** of the Union was lost on Friday; she lies where she struck on Morrill's Reef. A boat which was put out was capsized by the surf, while attempting to land, & 2 passengers, Geo Johnson, of Phil, & ___ Clark, of San Francisco, were drowned. Their bodies have not yet been recovered.

Board of Police meeting yesterday: applications for approval of their applications for liquor licenses were rejected: Lucy Reese, Elbert Keip, Jas Larin, Thos McCann, Bernard Henze, Bligh & McConnell, Sykes. Chadwick & Co; John Roonly, Michl Conner, Jas Flannagan, Peter Kilmahan, Jas White, Patrick Murphy, Peter Carlin, John B Burk, Wm Kennedy, Jas McGuire, S W Owen, Chris Mades, Margaret Burns, Matthew Byrnes, Ferd Butler, Richd D Lacy, J J Heck, Mark Lorenzie, Thos Green, N Zange, Henry Kochs, & Casper Herbert.

Cleveland, Nov 19. The Central Ohio Lunatic Asylum, at Columbus, was totally destroyed by fire last night. Mary Bropley, Mrs Bridget Bropley, of Columbua; Clara Bradford, Lizzie *Harrold, Caroline Conner, & Susan Parker were smothered to death. The inmates were removed to other public institutions. There were 350 patients confined there. [Nov 21st newspaper: Also suffocated-Lizzie *Herald, of Athens; Mrs Ansel, Mrs Parker, an old woman known as Mother Murray. Mrs Bain was seriously injured.] [*Two spellings: Harrold/Herald.

SAT NOV 21, 1868

Henry Sommers, late capt 2nd U S infty, was this morning arraigned before Justice David R Smith, on the charge of having forged the name of Thos Swords, Assist Quartermaster General, U S army to two drafts on the U S Depository at Louisville, Ky. The accused is a German by birth, & was appointed from the army as 2nd lt on Feb 19, 1863, & 1st lt Feb, 1865, having been brevet captain May 12, 1861.

Com'r Rollins yesterday sent to the Sec of the Treasury the nomination of Jas Belger, of Md, as supervisor for the Texas district.

W H Rozar, a law student at Griffin, Ga, fell off the Atlanta train last Sunday, at the first Chickamauga bridge, & was instantly killed.

Rev Mr Hall, of Guilford, Conn, was dismissed from his society recently, for hanging out a political banner on election day.

Sec McCulloch has appointed Wm H Lambert, John A Graham, Reuben Thorp, Jas Tilghman, L A C Gerry, J T B McMasters, & Robt J Waller, gaugers in the First Md Dist.

Household & kitchen furniture at auction on Nov 24, at 432 1st st east, between Pa ave & East Capitol st, known as **Carroll Place**. -Cooper & Latimer, aucts

Trustee's sale of valuable tract of land on old Bladensburg road, 3 miles from the Centre Market, public auction, on the premises, on Nov 20, recorded in Liber N C T 37, folio 166, in Wash Co, adjoining the land of Henry Queen & McCeney, containing 18 acres, more or less, with a 2 story dwlg house, corn-house & stable. It is known as the country residence of the late Mitchell H Miller, dec'd. –Wm Newman, trustee
-Green & Williams, aucts

MON NOV 23, 1868

Mr John S Pendleton died at Redwood, near Culpeper Court-house, on Thursday last. He had been in failing health for some time & his decease was not unexpected. He was generally known in Washington previous to the war; an intimate friend of Mr Snowden; served for several sessions in the Legislature of Va; for several terms as a Representative in Congress; also Minister to one of th South American Governments.

The funeral of the late Wm A Fitzgerald, formerly of Boston, Mass, but for the past 30 years a citizen of Washington, took place yesterday from his late residence, 353 F st, between 9th & 10th sts. For 20 years he was employed in the Nat'l Intelligencer ofc.

Mrd: on Nov 19, at the residence of the bride's father, by Rev J N Coombs, Mr H F Ellis, of Balt, to Sarah, eldest daughter of Jos E Rawlings.

Mrd: on Nov 18, at St Peter's Church, by Rev Fr Boyle, Jos H Hilton, of Wash City, D C, to Miss Alice Jane Mardes, daughter of the late Capt Wm Mardes, of Richmond, Va. [Fredericksburg & Richmond papers please copy.]

Died: on Nov 21, Mrs F Buxenstein, late from Balt, aged 65 years. She will be buried from the residence of Wm Emmert, near **Glenwood Cemetery**, on Nov 23 at 3 o'clock. [Balt Sun please copy.]

Obit-died: on Oct 6, 1868, in Richmond Co, Va, in his 54 year, Robt K Nevitt. He was born in PG Co, Md, & removed with his father to Fairfax Co, Va, in 1826; here he resided until 1838, when he removed to Wash Co, D C; in 1836 he married Miss L C Moore, who died in 1864; in 1866 he married Miss Mary E Ramsey, both of Wash, D C. In 1865 he purchased & moved to **Naylor's Hold**, in Richmond Co, Va. His last illness was of 2 weeks' duration; his wife & daughter were unavoidably absent. For 30 years he was an active & consistant member of the Methodist Episcopal Church.

Orphans Court-Judge Purcell, Nov 21, 1868. 1-Annie M Remas gave bond in the sum of $800 as admx of Isaac A Remas, dec'd. 2-Geo Thomas gave bond in the sum of $500 as guardian to the heir-at-law of Margaret A Thomas. 3-The following accounts were filed & passed: first account of Esther Humbert, excx of Wm Humbert; second general account of Sarah L Parkhurst, guardian to orphan of W G Parkhurst; second account of John A Ruff, exc of Andrew Small.

In accordance with the resolution of the Councils, Mayor Bowen has offered a reward of $500 for the apprehension & conviction of the murderer of John H Faulkner, who was killed on Jun 21 last.

Col J Whitehead Bryson, late of the 88th N Y volunteers, & now a prominent member of the Fenian Brotherhood, has been appointed brig genr'l in the U S army by the President. [Nov 24th newspaper: The announcement by telegram from Buffalo, that Col J Whitehead Bryson has been appointed brig genr'l, is without any foundation.]

U S Patent Ofc, Wash, Nov 19, 1868. Ptn of Thos C Ball, of Bellow's Falls, Vt, praying for the extension of a patent granted to him on Feb 27, 1855, for an improvement in Screw Jacks. –Elisha Foote, Com'r of Patents

Peremptory sale of the entire stock of prime family groceries, liquors, fixtures, horses, wagons, & harness, on Nov 27, the entire stock of Messrs Sioussa & Ennis, 320 Pa ave, between 6th & 7th sts. —W L Wall & Co, aucts

TUE NOV 24, 1868
Michl Shearer, who resides near Gtwn, was seriously wounded on Sunday by the accidental discharge of a pocket pistol. The ball lodged in his head; the wound may prove fatal.

Dr John Mayo, a brother of ex-Mayor Mayo, of Richmond, died in that city on Sat.

Mrs Pattie B Johnson, the widow of Thos C Johnson, has commenced suit against the Indianapolis & St Louis Railroad Co for $25,000 damages, on the ground that her husband was killed through the criminal negligence of the employes of that road. He was in a sleeping-car, which was to be left off at Matoon. While he was passing from that to another car the cars were suddenly uncoupled, throwing him upon the track, where he was run over & killed.

Died: on Nov 23, at the residence of her aunt, Mrs Kinsley, Mary, daughter of the late Wm & Mary T Bush, in her 17th year. Her funeral will take place from 531 L st, between 8th & 9th sts, at 2 o'clock on Nov 25.

Trustee's sale of valuable real estate; by decree of the Circuit Court for PG Co, Md, in Equity, wherein Eleanor L Lee & W Seaton Belt, adms of Benj Lee, & others are cmplnts, & Mary L Contee & Danl Clarke, adms d b n, of John Contee, & others are dfndnts; public sale on Nov 30th next of: all that tract of land called & known as *Arthur's Sealed Enlarged*, or *Webbs*, containing 238 acres, more or less. Also, all that tract of land called *Woodland*, adjoining the above, containing 294 acres, more or less.
–Richd B B Chew, Danl Clarke, trustees.

Phil Inquirer of Monday. Last night at 10th & Pine sts, an elderly lady, Mrs Mary E Hill, was killed & her body thrown out of a second story window. Geo S Twitchell, a son-in-law of the murdered woman, with his wife, Mrs Hill's daughter, resided with the deceased, the 3 being the only occupants of the large & very handomely furnished house. Mr Twitchell [about 32] was taken to the 8th Ward Station house. Mrs Twitchell seemed more concerned about her husband than her murdered mother.
+
Phil, Nov 23. Mrs Twitchell is in custody on suspicion of participating in the murder. The dec'd was very wealthy, which was inherited from her last husband. Mrs Twitchel was a daughter of the deceased by her former husband. [Nov 25th newspaper: Phil, Nov 24. The coroner rendered a verdict that Mrs Hill came to her death at the hands of Geo Twitchell & his wife Camilla. Both of them were committed for trial. The evidence given today completely destroys the theory of robbery & murder by outsiders.]

Orphans Court of Wash Co, D C. Letters of administration on the personal estate of Wm B Malcom, late of Wash Co, D C, dec'd. –Wm A Austin, adm

Tallahassee, Fla, Nov 23. Gen Waddy Thompson, who in Calhoun's time was Congressman from S C, & afterwards Minister to Mexico, died here this afternoon, aged about 70 years.

WED NOV 25, 1868
Sec McCulloch yesterday appointed C E Creecy, Supervisor of Internal Revenue for the District of Lousiiana & Arkansas. Mr Creecy has been for several years at the head of the Appointment Bureau of the Treasury Dept.

Green & Williams, aucts, sold the south half of lot 32 in square 107, with improvements fronting on 19 st west, between K & L sts, to Dr C Miller, for $1,200.

Philip Hanson, colored, found dead on Sat last, near Lincoln Barracks, died from drunkeness & exposure.

Jas Gore, proprietor of a retail cigar establishment on 6th st, Louisville, committed suicide on Thursday by shooting himself with a pistol.

A few friends of Miss Alice Carey have shown their appreciation of her works & worth by presenting her with $1,000. The gift was made through Mr Greeley, in a very delicate & pleasant manner.

Henry E Hill, a well known druggist in Detroit, committed suicide last Thursday by blowing out his brains with a pistol. He had failed in business the previous day. He leaves a wife, to whom he was married only a year ago.

Orphans Court-Judge Purcell, Nov 24, 1868. 1-The will of the late Patrick Moroney was fully proven. 2-Mrs Kate Savage, widow of the late Saml F Savage, renounced her right to administer on the estate of her husband in favor of Jos L Savage & Wm B Reaney, to whom letters were issued; bond $20,000. 3-Mrs Mary Eliz Wilson renounced her right to qualify as admx d b n & c t a on the estate of her deceased husband, in favor of John Wilson, father of deceased, to whom letters were issued; bond $2,000. 4-The first & final accounts of the executor of S B Colby & fourth account of guardian to the infants of Saml Crown, & legal heirs of G W Crown, were approved & passed. 5-The will of the late John Howes was filed. He bequeathes his household furniture & personal property to his wife, as also his real estate during her natural life, & at her death to go to his nieces, daughters of John L Gilbert, of Wash Co, Md. He nominates his wife as executrix.

Mrd: on Nov 24, at the residence of the bride's mother, by Rev E P Phelps, Mr John P D Phelps to Miss Kate S, 3rd daughter of the late Wm H Bayne, of Fayetteville, N C. No cards.

Died: on Nov 15, at her residence, Mantua, Northumberland Co, Va, Mrs Nannie Ogle Smith, wife of Dr Jas Smith, & daughter of H G S Key, Leonardtown, Md. [Balt papers please copy.]

Died: on Nov 23, in Fairfax Co, Va, Mrs Amelia T Young, in her 68th year.

Died: on Nov 23, Olive Morton Hall, aged 2 years, youngest daughter of Mr & Mrs R M Hall. Her funeral will be at the residence of Mr Cushing, 358 C st, between 4½ & 6th sts, on Nov 26, at 2 o'clock.

Orphans Court of Wash Co, D C. Letters of administration on the personal estate of Saml F Savage, late of Wash Co, D C, dec'd. –Jos L Savage, W B Reaney, adms

Supreme Court of D C; in Equity 1,442-docket 9. Wm M Galt & Co, cmplnts, vs Henry W Thies et al, dfndnts. On motion of cmplnt by Fendall & Fendall, his atty, it is ordered that the dfndnt, Henry W Thies, cause his appearance to be entered herein on or before the first rule day occurring 40 days after this day; otherwise the case will be proceeded with as in case of default. –A B Olin -R J Meigs, clerk

Richmond, Nov 21. H Rives Pollard, editor of the Southern Opinion, was shot & killed this morning by Jas Grant. The cause of the shooting was the publication of an article in the Opinion of Sat last, relative to the elopement of the daughter of Wm H Grant, a wealthy tobacconist of this city. "An elopement, so called, on Clay st-an upper ten famly concerned-dreadful denouement." Jas Grant, a brother of the lady, Miss Mary Grant, was taken to the station house.

Albany, Nov 21. The residence of Elisha Fiero, at West Davenport, Delaware Co, was the scene of a most brutal murder last night. Fiero & his wife had retired, & during the night the burglars entered their sleeping apartment, one of whom put his hand under their pillow, causing them to awake, & when Mr Fiero raised his arm, the burglar discharged a pistol. The ball passed between his fingers & entered the head of Mrs Fiero, killing her almost instantly. The burglars then fled & escaped.

THU NOV 26, 1868
Mr John T Berret has purchased, at private sale, the residence of Maj Chas S Jones, on H st, near 10th, for the sum of $10,000 cash. This is considered very cheap for property in that desirable locality.

Mrd: on Nov 24, at St Peter's Church, by Rev Fr Boyle, Mr Theodore F King, of Atchison, Kansas, to Miss M Isadore Serra, of Wash, D C, niece of Thos McDonnell, of the U S Coast Survey. No cards.

Died: on Nov 25, Mary Lacy, in her 20th year. Her funeral will take place at 3 o'clock P M today, from St Peter's Church.

Died: on Nov 18, at Houghton, Mich, Hon Clarence E Eddie, aged 34 years. His funeral will take place on Nov 27 at 2 o'clock, from the residence of Mrs Edw C Eddie, 596 M st, between 6th & 7th sts.

Sec McCulloch has assigned H C Niles to duty as chief of the Appointment Bureau at the Treasury Dept, vice C E Creecy, appointed supervisor. Mr Niles for some time past has been chief clerk of the bureau.

The body of a murdered man, Wm E Burton, was found on Friday, on the side of a road near Gordonsville, Va, not far from the depot of the Chesapeake & Ohio railroad. It was ascertained that he lived near Milboro, Va, & had been a brakeman on one of the freight trains. He had a family in Milboro. Why the murder was committed is not known yet.

N Y, Nov 25. Felix Larkin, O'Baldwin's backer, went into Campbell's oyster saloon, Hudson & Canal st, this morning, & got into an altercation with the proprietor, who stabbed him repeatedly, & clubbed him, fracturing his skull. Larkin died almost instantly. Campbell was arrested, but states that he acted in self defence. David C O'Day & John Burns, of this city, & John McClown, of Phil, were injured in the melee. [Nov 30th newspaper: N Y, Nov 28. O'Baldwin, the Irish giant, was arrested today in consequence of the death of his bail bondsman, Felix Larkin, & being unable to procure other bail in $1,000 to keep the peace, was committed to the Tombs. The inquest in the case of Larkin was commenced today.] [Dec 1st newspaper: N Y, Nov 30. The coroner's inquest in the case of the Larkin homicide resulted in a verdict that the deceased came to his death by stabs at the hands of Robt Campbell, John Berrigan, & Ann Hines, & they were committed to await the action of the grand jury.]

Milwaukee, Nov 25. J M Lyon, proprietor of the Daily News, was found dead last night at the foot of his stairs. It is supposed that he died from a fit of apoplexy.

Phil, Nov 25. A boy named Copley, aged 12 years, employed in a drug store, committed suicide last night by swallowing some drugs, supposed to be strychnine. [Nov 30 newspaper: Phil Ledger, Nov 28: A boy named Robt Crossly, aged 14, who died from poison on Wed last, was employed by Mr Lungren. He was often beaten by his father & his mother had beaten him with a whip or cowhide. Death was caused by taking strychnine.]

Rockland, Me, Nov 25. Deputy Marshal Weeks today arrested Ezra Turner, of Isle au Haut, on the charge of smuggling.

Trustee's sale of house & lot in square 107, L & 19th sts; by deed of trust from John Cunningham, dated Oct 22, 1862, & recorded in Liber N C T No 7, folio 240; auction on Dec 30 next, of lot 34, with a frame house & brewery thereon, to be sold for the payment of 2 notes, of $400 each, with the unpaid interest thereon. –A Hyde, trustee
-Cooper & Latimer, aucts

Trustee's sale; by decree of the Circuit Court for PG Co, in Equity, public sale at the late residence of John Higgins, dec'd, on Dec 17 next, of a part of the estate consisting of about 400 acres, located adjacent to *Scagg's Station*; a first-class farm, improved by a comfortable frame dwlg & all necessary out-bldgs. The residue of said real estate contains about 200 acres, 3 miles from the village of Laurel.
–N C Stephen, Henry L Carlton, trustees

SAT NOV 28, 1868
The family of Mr Kreslusky, living on K st, between 4th & 5th sts, have been the victims of poisoned flour, & have been suffering from the effects of using the article, in which was found a large quantity of arsenic.

On Thu, Geo Repetti, about 19, residing near the Navy Yard, was severely injured in the left eye. He was out gunning near the Insane Asylum with a companion, who was in the act of discharging his gun, when the nipple blew out, striking Repetti in the eye.

Robt Diggs, about 19, was attacked on Thu, while going to his home in the First Ward, & stabbed in several places. He is not expected to recover. Assaulting party is unknown.

Yesterday the slaughter-house belonging to Mr Homing, & occupied by Chas Able, on *Buzzard's Point*, was totally destroyed by fire, caused by the careless use of matches.

Maj John H Downing, a well known politician of Schuylkill Co, Pa, died on Thursday at Pottsville.

Wm Price, an old citizen, a member of the bar, & U S Dist Atty during Pres Lincoln's administration, died in Balt on Thursday.

Intelligence of the murder of Capt Edw W Thompson, Acting Dist Atty in Arkansas, is received from Portland, Me. It is stated that he was killed by persons who took offence at his voting for Gen Grant in the recent elections.

Board of Police-meeting yesterday. Pvts appointed on the force: H L Chubbeck, John Liscombe, & Michl Towers. Robt Brown was appointed an additional private for 6 months, for duty between Vt ave & 10th st, & P & Q sts. Application for liquor licenses were disapproved as follows:

John Neenan	Rudolph Bleifus	Jas Green
Hugh Murray	Mark O'Hollaran	Wm J Watts
Michl McKim	Tim McCormick	John Southey
John Pella	Geo Schnell	Jas Barrett
Wm H Simpson	Wm Sweeny	Peter Dirning
Thos Morrow	J J Flanigan	Martin Cady
Henry Sievers	Dennis Dunn	J H Middleton
Michl Hallihan	Wm Haggerty	Fred Stinzing
John Holyschuh	Michl McCartney	Peter H Reeves

Fred Moehlich	Geo Wallacher	Jas McCarty
Casper Ruppert	John Imrie	Anna McArdle
John Flanigan	Chas H Parker	Maj John Watt
P Huhn	Martin Raynor	Danl O'Leary
Michl Donahue	Wm Henry	Jas Kane
Jas Biggins	Tom Flynn	Wm H Jackson
Michl Flynn	Wm Ryan	Patrick McHugh
Thos Biggins	Patrick Corcran	John Fegan
R J Borden	Jas Cole	Francis Armstrong
Barney Hart	Barth Shea	Barbery Wail
Owen McQuade	Antony Miller	Chas Hartmann
David McCarty	Hugh McCaffrey	Darby Cohen
Bernard Fitzpatrick	Felix Martin	Michl Leahey
Geo N Herrells	Bartley Knox	L Martin
Mary McQuillan	Patrick Collins	Matthew Pepper
John F Murray	Francis Keough	John Corigan
Jas McLaughlin	John McCarthy	Jas McCarthy
Frank Gallaher	Anna Doyle	R A Golden & Bro
John Hartnett	Geo A Shekell	Wm Washington
John Thomas	Taylor & Dye	David Welsh
N N H Maack	Geo Weld	Chas Eisenhute

Mrd: on Nov 26, at the Church of the Incarnation, by Rev A L Lowry, Brvt Maj Evan Thomas, U S A, to Josephine D C Foster.

Died: on Nov 6, at Vancouver, Rhoda, the wife of Jos Fletcher, Register of the Land Ofc, Wash Territory, & daughter of Jos Fawcett Cameronia, Montg Co, Md.

Died: on Nov 22, at Coalsmouth, Kanawha Co, West Va, Agnes, daughter of Robt MacLeod, & grand-daughter of the late John MacLeod, of Wash City.

N Y, Nov 27. Geo B Harlson, many years president of the Atlantic Mail Co, died today.

Oakwood, the late residence of Hon John Scott, dec'd, in Fauquier Co, Va, for sale; consists of 700 acres of land; a commodious Mansion house of stone, stuccoed, & all necessary out bldgs, & is well fenced. Apply to John A Spilman, or Brooke & Scott, Warrenton, Va.

Superior assortment of household & kitchen furniture at auction on Dec 10, at the residence of Mrs M Bevan, 307 Pa ave, between 9th & 10th sts. -Cooper & Latimer, aucts

Norwood School, Nelson Co, Va; Preparatory to the Univ of Va; six accomplished Instructors. Students received at any time. –Wm D Cabell, Principal, Norwood, Va

Slate Roofing, Mr John J Harvey, having charge of my Slating in Wash City, will attend to orders left at his residence, 404 6th st. Repairing promptly attended to.
-Matthew Gault

MON NOV 30, 1868
E L Huffman, one of the most prominent merchants & pork packers of Louisville, died on Friday.

Mr John T Clark has sold his homestead, with 40 acres of land, situated near St Lawrence's Chapel, about one mile from Jessup's Cut, Anne Arundel Co, to Mr Blacklock, of Balt, for $8,000. Mr Blacklock intends to erect a fine residence on the place, & make it a most attractive seat.

Board of Police meeting on Sat last. Applications for licenses disapproved, as follows:

Dennis Connell	P O'Connor	Fred Stosch
Lewis Nowrath	John Rochford	John C Howard
Groton Schutz	Coris Boyle	John T Martin
Morris Roach	Michl McCormick	John Shanahan
Peter Conlan	Peter Schafer	Mathias Papst
H H Byer	Lena Heidinger	Cornelius Sullivan
Patrick E Welch	Jesse Williams	Geo Forth
John H Hill	John McGran	Catharine Maroney
Henry Lichan	Michl Dailey	Geo A Haske
Jos Platz	John Moore	Henry Briggerman
Gotleib Welner	Cornelius Shea	Peter Fox
Wm Langdon	H Keiser	Bertram Leins
Henry Newkirk	Geo Juenemann	Fielder Magruder

Promotions in the Treasury Dept made since Nov 15. Third Auditor's Ofc-Wm B Shaw, from 1st to 2nd class; Calvin C Wilson, from 3rd to 4th class. Fourth Auditor's Ofc-John Cook, from 1st to 2nd class. Sec's Ofc: W H Cook, from 2nd to 3rd class.

Equity Court-Judge Olin. 1-Falconer vs Utermehle et al: order appointing W Y Fendall guardian *ad litem*. 2-Holiday et al vs Holiday et al: order reinstating Chas S Wallach as trustee for resale. 3-Hess vs Hess: decree appointing R P Jackson trustee to sell. 4-Adams vs Adams: order discharging M A Donaldson for contempt.

Orphans Court-Judge Purcell, Nov 28, 1868. 1-The last will & testament of Margaret C Grimes was filed, fully proven, & admitted to probate & record. 2-The will of Wm A Fitzgerald, who bequeathes his estate, real & personal, to his wife, Mary W Fitzgerald, was filed & fully proven. 3-Thos Moreland qualified as guardian to Annie Moreland; bond $600. 4-Jeanette Reid qualified as guardian to Eliz Reid, monor child of Wm Reid, dec'd; bond $1,000. 5-The eighth account of Jemima Ball, [late Brown,] guardian to Reuben M Brown, orphan of Reuben Brown, dec'd, was filed & approved by the court.

Died: on Nov 2, at her residence, near Kabietown, Jefferson Co, West Va, Mrs Mary Osburn, in her 69th year.

Died: on Sunday, Mrs Julia Ann Ingman, aged 66 years. Her funeral will take place from the residence of her brother, I F Mudd, 134 D st, between 9th & 10th sts, at 3 o'clock P M.

Richmond, Va, Nov 28. Dr Arthur E Peticolas, superintendent of the Eastern Lunatic Asylum, at Willaimsburg, committed suicide there this morning by leaping from a window of the asylum, & dashing his brains out on the bricks below. The deceased was a distinguished physician, & a former professor in the medical college here. His mind has been unsettled for some time past. [Dec 2nd newspaper: Dr Peticolas leaves a wife & one child, a daughter, nearly grown.]

Jas Palmer, of the firm of Palmer & Phillips, Pittsburg auctioneers, committed suicide on Thursday, by swallowing a quantity of laudanum.

Hon W M Butts, a member of the Ga House of Reps, from Marion Co, died suddenly of apoplexy, while out hunting last week.

Mrs Thos Williams, the wife of a St Louis huckster, gave birth to 4 living children last Tuesday, 3 girls & 1 boy. Two of the children have died.

TUE DEC 1, 1868
Green & Williams, aucts, sold 18 acres of land, with improvements, on the old Bladensburg road, Wash Co, known as the residence of the late Mitchell H Miller, to John Lord, for $5,000.

Bishop H C Lay, lately elected bishop of the newly constituted Diocese of the Eastern Shore, is a native of Powhatan Co, Va, & 9 years ago was elected missionary bishop of Arkansas by the Episcopal General Convention, then sitting in Richmond. Dr Lay had been previously rector of the Episcopal Church in Huntsville, Ala.

The following persons have been appointed justices of the peace for the Dist of Columbia: Saml C Mills, J W Barnaclo, & Richd B Nixon.

Wash Ads:
1-I must have a suit of clothes, but where will I find a fashionable tailor whose charges are reasonable? Why, don't you know? Of N Thorson, Merchant Tailor, 286 Pa ave.
2-Where can I find the largest assortment of hard & soft Lumber, on the most reasonable terms? At C B Church & Co, 11th st & Md ave.
3-Where can I purchase a Looking-Glass? Of Francis Lamb, dealer in Looking-glasses, Portrait & Picture Frames, 237 Pa ave, near 13th st.
4-The Place to get First-Class Carriages of all styles; also, Horses & Buggies, & Saddle Horses for ladies & gentlemen, & to by a good Horse, is at J B Olcott & Son's, 469 8th st, between D & E.

5-Where is the best place to see the largest assorted stock of Leather & Shoe Findings? At Thos G Ford's, 430 7th st, between G & H sts.

6-Where is an Iron-Founder, Machinist, Engineer, Boiler-maker to be found? At Gray & Noyes, corner Maine ave & 3rd st.

7-Where do you get your Horse Shod; Mine is lame & can't travel. Go to John F Doran, D st, between 13½ & 14th sts. He will obviate all difficulties.

8-Gentleman: Where may I obtain the latest style Hat? Lady: Go to Stinemetz, Hatter & Furrier, 234 Pa ave, where I intend to purchase a handsome set of Mink Furs.

9-Who sells the best & cheapest Harness in the city? Why, Jas S Topham & Co, manufacturers of all kinds of goods in their line, & sell at manufactory prices.

10-Where is the best place to get Guns & Sporting Material? At Peabody's, 414 D st, between 6th & 7th sts.

11-Where has Lockwood, Hufy, & Taylor, removed their Ladies & Gentlemen's Furnishing Store: To 354 Pa ave, adjoining the Metropolitan Hotel.

12-Where can I find the Largest & Cheapest assortment of Zephyr Worsted? At M Silver's, 413 7th st, between G & H; & 30 Market Space, 7th & 8th.

13-Where is the best place to buy Fancy & Millinery Goods, Laces, & Trimmings, & the best & most reliable Sewing Machines? At Davis & Gaither's, 20 Market Space.

14-Where will I find a Reliable Electrotyper & Stereoptyper? Why, C W Murray, 273 Pa ave, between 10th & 11th sts.

15-Perry & Bro, Extensive Dealers in Dry Goods of the best class for general family consumption; Dress Goods, Rich Shawls, Cloaks, & Embroideries. Perry Bldg, Pa ave & 9th st.

16-Who keeps the largest stock of Patent Medicine, Perfumery, & Fancy Articles? S Calvert Ford, Chemist & Druggist, 286 Pa ave

17-Where can you have your Teeth extracted without pain or injury, & all kinds of Dental work performed in the best manner? At the Howland Dental Association, 27 4½ st.

18-Where has Moxley removed his costume Manufactory to? Why to 445 10th st, between F & G sts.

19-The best French & American Confectionary, Fruits, Refreshments of all kinds. Oysters & Game. Wedding & reception parties furnished by J H Shaffield, 246 Pa ave, between 12th & 13th sts.

20-Where shall I buy my China, Class, & Housefurnishing Goods? At Thos Pursell & Son's, 351 Pa ave, opposite Metropolitan Hotel. Stone ware at factory prices.

21-Buy your Wood & Coal of G L Sheriff, 437 Pa ave, between 3rd & 4½ sts. Kindling & Stove Wood prepared in the best manner, cheap for cash.

22-Why can Geo W Cochran & Co, 276 Pa ave, furnish "Cigar Tobacco" & other articles pertaining to their business at less rates than others? Because their stock is larger, & bought for cash.

23-Carriages. Carriages. Carriages. We are now offering at our extensive salesroom, 477 & 479 14th st, the largest & most complete selection of Carriages ever offered in this District.

24-Where shall I buy my Carpets, Curtains, etc? At W S Mitchell & Co, Perry Bldg, Pa ave & 9th st. They have a beautiful & extensive assortment at the lowest prices.

25-Who Will Build Me a House Right cheap? Why, Jas G Naylor, Carpenter & Builder & General Contractor, 18 Louisiana ave, & opposite 5th st.
26-C Schnieder, Practical Bell Hanger, 271 Pa ave. Bells hung in the most approved style, with or without tubing. Lightning Rods, with Platina Points, put up in the best manner.
27-Where can we find the best assortment of Builders', Blacksmiths', & Wheelwright's Hardware? At L C Campbell's, 351 Pa ave, fourth door from 6th st. Sign of the Golden Anvil.
28-Go to Housekeeping! Why, Where can I get my Kitchen Utensils, Wooden & Willow Ware? Why, at Finckle's New Store, 316 F st, between 10th & 11th sts.
29-Where is the finest N Y Butter to be had? At the Northern Produce Co, Pa ave, between 10th & 11th sts, wholesale dealers in Produce Provisions, Foreign & Domestic Fruits.
30-Who keeps the Best Beef, Mutton, Veal & Lamb? Hoffman & Hunt, stalls Nos 59 & 61, Centre Market, & No 60 Northern Market.
31-C F Cummins, 347 7th st, two doors south of Northern Market, an extensive & reliable Boot & Shoe House, receiving daily the latest styles & most celebrated makes.
32-Who makes the best fitting Boots & Shoes? Wm Young, E st, between 8th & 9th sts, who warrants entire satisfaction upon the easiest terms.
33-Where is the largest assortment of Builders' Material to be found; Sash, Doors, Blinds, Slate, Mantles, & Hardware? At Builders' Depot, 562 7th st, opposite Centre Market. W W Hamilton & Co.
34-Where can I purchase a corn-sheller? At John A Baker's, La ave, near 9th, dealer in Agricultural Implements, Seeds, & Grain, Hay-cutters, & Hay-presses.
35-You can have Fresco, Decorative, & every description of Ornamental Painting executed in the best style by Shutter & Bakeman, Artists, 425 9th st, between G & H sts.
36-At Philp & Solomons' Metropolitan Bookstore, 332 Pa ave, cane be found new & standard Books, a large assortment of fashionable & staple Stationery, Engraving, Lighographing, Printing, & Binding in every style.
37-H R Searle, Architect, 421 E st, between 7th & 8th sts.
38-The Equitable Life Assurance Society. Cash assets $8,000.000; Annual Income $5,000,000. Is the best company in which to insure. Don't let another day pass. F Heyer, Agent, 476 7th st.
39-Who are the proper persons to secure Letters Patent of the U S or Europe? Alexander & Mason, Attys, 469 7th st.
40-Augustus Burgdorf, 453 Pa ave. Furnishing Undertaking in all its branches promptly attended to.
41-Messrs M W Galt & Bro, 280 Pa ave, are the agent of the American Watch Co, Waltham; Patek, Philippe & Co, celebrated watchmakers, Geneva; & for the Gorham Manufacturing Co, Providence, R I.
42-Where can you get all kinds of Mill Word done; also, Brackets, Newels, Ballusters, & Moulding? At Danl Smith's, Phoenix Planing Mills, corner 12th st & Canal.
43-T M Harvey's Iron-clad, 267, corner of Pa ave & 11th st, Ladies' & Gentlemen's Oyster Saloon. All delicacies of the season from Northern & Southern markets served in first-class style.

44-Franklin & Co, Opticians, 244 Pa ave, are manufacturing the Brazilian Pebble Spectacles & Eye-glasses, in gold, silver, steel, vulcanized rubber, or shell frames, & suit them properly & scientifically to every eyesight.
45-Plumbing, Gas, & Steam Fitting, Brackets, Slate Mantels, Mscl Stores. Alex R Shepherd & Bros, 269 Pa ave.
46-Where can I get a Good Photograph? At the old established Gallery of Brady & Co, 352 Pa ave, between 6th & 7th sts.
47-Where shall I go to find the largest assortment of Picture Frames? At Markriter's. Who can paper my rooms & halls neat & cheap: Why, Markriter, 486 7th st.
48-For Stoves & Tinware go to H L Gregory, dealer in Stoves, Tinware, & Housekeeping Goods, 321 Pa ave, near 7th st.
49-Connecticut & Mayfield Brown, Stone, Seneca Stone, Granite, & Marble Flagging, Curbing, Marble Tiling, etc, furnished prepared for all purposes by M G Emery & Bro, 172 2nd st, between B & C sts.
50-The American Tea Co, 213 & 215 Pa ave, opposite Willard's Hotel.
51-Where can I get the best Trunk in Wash? At Jas S Topham & Co, 500 7th st. They use McMurray's Patent Stay in all their Trunks, & no extra charge.

China & Glass. We ask buyers of China, Glass, Plated Wares, & House-Furnishing Goods, to examine our stock & prices. Cortlan & Co, Importers, 216 & 218 Balt st, Balt, Md.

Gen Sheridan, with his staff & 2 battalions of cavalry, have arrived at **Camp Supply**, Indian Territory. Gen Custer was to start immediately on a chase after the Indians, which would probably last all winter. Snow was falling.

Double murder at Prestonburg, Ky, a few days since. A constable, John Moore, while striving to collect a debt from Wm Huff, had a quarrel with him. Moore then armed himself, & meeting Huff, shot him dead in the street. Moore was arrested, but a son of Huff, fearing the murderer of his father would escape, went to the jail, & calling Moore to the window of his cell, shot him in the head, inflicting a fatal wound. Public opinion there was very strong against Moore, & justifies his murderer.

A nurse girl, age 18 years, left in charge of 3 children of the McCulloch family, near Corning, N Y, last Wed, in a fit of rage at the youngest child for being fretful, threw it upon the floor, stamped upon it until is was lifeless. When its mother returned home at night it was dead. The girl was arrested.

Ofcrs elected at the meeting of the St Andrew's Society on Friday last: Wm R Smith, president; Fred B McGuire, Gen Geo W Balloch, vice presidents; Alex'r Gardner, treasurer; David Knox, recording sec; Wm Small, corr sec; Fred D Stuart, John Cameron, John H Barry, Jas Cummings, John Small & Alex'r Williamson, managers.

Equity Court-Judge Olin. In re, bankruptcy of C P & W H Banres; order of reference to auditor.

Police orders: yesterday Maj Richards directed Lt M A Austin to assume command of the 8th Precinct. In the order relieving Lt Harbin, of that precinct, the Major assures him that his course while in command is heartily approved. Sgt C T Crump, promoted last week from the ranks, is assigned to duty in the First Precinct, & Sgt M B Gorman is assigned to the 6th Precinct, relieving Sgt A A Greer, who is transferred to the 5th Precinct.

Mrd: on Nov 30, in Wash City, by Rev A H Ames, Thos Hanson, of N Y, to Miss Kate B, 3rd daughter of Abner Stephenson, of Fairfax Court House, Va.

Died: on Nov 29, M R Roche, in his 41st year. His funeral will be from his late residence on 8th st, between M & N sts, at 2½ o'clock P M, today, Dec 1.

Died: Monday, at her residence, on 14th st, Rosa, wife of Lewis Shotts, late of Montg Co, Md. Her funeral will take place tomorrow, Wed, at 10 o'clock, from the Church of the Immaculate Conception, where a requiem mass will be sung for the repose of her soul.

Died: on Nov 30, George W, eldest son of George M & Frances D Arth, in his 4th year. His funeral will take place from the residence of his father, 9th st, tomorrow at 10½ A M.

Died: on Nov 15, at *Queensboro*, the residence of his brother-in-law, R H Burr, Wm H Fenwick, in his 30th year.

N Y, Nov 30. Geo W McLean, of Wash, corresponding clerk of the U S secret service dept, was today committed to jail by U S Com'r Jackson, of Jersey City, on the charge of passing a counterfeit $10 nat'l bank bill at a drinking saloon yesterday. The accused said he was intoxicated at the time, & had no knowledge of the act.

Milwaukie Sentinel, Nov 23. The body of J M Lyon, senior editor of the Milwaukie News, & a prominent & highly respected citizen, was found at the foot of a pair of staris leading into a bldg on Maine st, now occupied by Elisha Starr, but generally known as the Louis House. There are other circumstances connected with the affair of which it is not proper to speak at this time. Mr Lyon was last seen alive at 11:30 o'clock. He leaves 2 daughters, aged about 6 years & 14 years. He came to this city from the State of N Y, about 6 years since.

Jacob Barker, of New Orleans, now in his 86th year, on Thursday received his final discharge in bankruptcy from all his liabiities, which, according to his amended schedule, exceeded in amount a half million of dollars.

Notice. The connection of F A McGee with the agency of the N Y Life Ins Co is this day terminated. The business of the Company in this District will hereafter be conducted by the undersigned. –J M Grasser, Genr'l Agent

Supreme Court of D C; Equity 1,050. Yates & Selby vs Geo Seitz et al. Parties to this cause, & the creditors of Geo Seitz, to meet on Dec 7 at my ofc, 8 Columbian Law Bldg, to ascertain the amount of the debts due by the said Geo Seitz. –C Ingle, special auditor

Adms sale of nearly new household & kitchen furniture at auction on Dec 4, at the residence of the late S F Savage, 501 K st, between 4th & 5th sts. –J Savage, adm -Cooper & Latimer, aucts

WED DEC 2, 1868
Thos Dowling, auct, Gtwn, sold lot 18, in Beall's addition to Gtwn, fronting 20 feet on Wash St, & 39 feet deep, with improvements, together with the interest therein of the orphan children of Jas H Fleet, to Mr Chas Peters, for $1,800. Messrs Kilbourn & Latta, real estate brokers, have sold to Mayor S J Bowen, the residence of Gen Grant, on I st, for $40,000. This fine house is one of the 3 known as the ***Douglas Row***, one of the other 2 being occupied by ex-Mayor Wallach, & the other as the Protestant Orphan Asylum. They were originally built by Senators Douglas, Rice, & Breckinridge, 10 years ago.

Liquor licenses granted by the Police Com'rs to the following parties to sell liquor:

John Reamy	Caspar Keller	Mrs Augusta Kroeger
John Cumiskey	Wm Shoomaker	Rudolph E Peterson
Louis Betz	Rosa A Eisenbeis	Edw Gaetz
Thos McCormick	Herbert Harris	E Cullinan
Geo W Bauers	John Schwartz	John P Hamlin & Bro
Godden & Norris	Conrad Yost	Anthony Bragazzi
Victor Roux	John J Centner	Theodore Johansan
Patrick Brennan	Peter F Genty	Scott & Broughton
Wm Greason	C C Willard-hotel	W W Laskey
John G Killians	John Hancock	Jas Molan
Wm Scherger	Sebastian Aman	Chas Mades
Adam Reinhart	Ed Kolb	Matthew Ruppert
Fred'k Ruple	Fred G Rohr	John Sherr
John A Gray	Saml G Langley	John O'Leary
M M Force	Fred'k Kohler	Jas A Crane
Peter Vernum	John Buchler	Jos Joseph
Geo Dill	Cenard Berins	Thos Kelly

Henry Sommers arrested about 2 weeks since on the charge of having forged the name of Assist Quartermaster Gen Swords to 2 drafts on the U S depository at Louisville, was committed to jail in default of bail-$1,000 being required in one case & $500 in the other.

We call attention to the sale by Cooper & Latimer, aucts, this morning at 307 Pa ave, between 9th & 10th sts, the residence of Mrs M Bevan.

Equity Court-Judge Olin, Dec 1, 1868. 1-Hines vs Hines; decree appointing R T Morsell trustee to sell. 2-Gocklin agt Widmayer; order appointing E Carusi guardian *ad litem* to C H Utermehle, jr.

Orphans Court-Judge Purcell, Dec 1, 1868. 1-The will of John Hames was fully proven & admitted to probate & record.

By the death of Antoine Pierre Berryer, which occurred in Paris on Sat, France had lost one of its most celebrated lawyers & politicians. The dec'd was born in Paris on Jan 4, 1790, & received his education at a Jesuit college. Berryer wanted to devote himself to the service of the Church, but his father, himself an eminent lawyer, prevailed upon him to adopt the legal profession.

N Y, Dec 1. In the U S Dist Court today the jury returned a verdict of guilty against Garner C Baker, late teller of the Tradesman's Bank, indicted for embezzling.

Phil, Dec 1. On Fri last a man named Engleman, living at Carlinville, Ill, cut the throat of his divorced wife, nearly severing the head from the body. Engleman was arrested & lodged in jail. Yesterday a mob of country people took him from jail & hung him.

Mr Alden Goldsmith, of N Y, sold his celebrated trotting mare, Goldsmith Maid, for $20,000.

Supreme Court of D C, Equity 1,459, docket 9. Mary E Owner vs Jas Owner et al. It is ordered that the dfndnt, Jas Owner, cause his appearance to be entered herein on or before the first rule day occurring 40 days after this day; otherwise the case will be proceeded with as in case of default. –A B Olin, Justice -R J Meigs, clerk

Mr Elisha Riggs, of this city, has obtained a judgment of $70,000 against the city of Dubuque, Iowa.

Capt Allen B Snow, a veteran sea captain, died in Boston on Saturday. He had long been engaged in trade with Cuba, & had made 131 voyages in succession.

Mr Edw A Pollard & J Marshall Hanna, left Richmond last Saturday by the Chesapeake & Ohio railroad, with the remains of the late H Rives Pollard. The interment was made on Sunday, in the family burying ground at Alta Vista, Nelson Co.

THU DEC 3, 1868
Mr Wm Arnold has purchased the country seat, about a mile west of Alexandria, known as **Maple Grove**, from Maj Jas Gleason, of the firm of Gleason & Glenn, of Wash City, for $10,000. There are 22 acres of land in the tract, & a handsome dwlg, with all necessary outbldgs. Messrs Green & Wise, real estate agents, in Alexandria, sold on Nov 30th, 88 acres of land in Loudoun Co, at the Guilford depot, to Mr Denmead, for $2,500.

Green & Williams, aucts, sold the 22 acres of the farm known as ***Cedar Hill farm,*** lying between Wash & Balt railroad & the turnpike adjoining the farms of Messrs Allen & Dodge & Clark Mills, to Col Wright Rives, for $200 per acre-$4,400.

List of approvals of liquor licenses by the Metropolitan Police Board:

Geo H Smart	Geo W Harvey & Co	Geo H Whitney
Anton Roths	Jacob Horner	H Clay Simpson
Richd Robbs	Wm Helmes	Jackson Cole
Thos McKeever	Jas W Gibson	Wm G Yost
Matthew McDonnough	Geo F Bincher	August Seebros
Chas Klotz	John D Beckley	John Mager
Wm Fagan	Wm Burchard	Albert Leubner
Wm Cary	Francis Brandner	John Freeman
F Beckart	R E Peterson	Mrs M Ruthford
J A Gray	Edw Goetz	Wm Sanderson
Chas H Saur	Jos Garhardt	Jas A Branson
John Tearny	Wm McGuire	Jas Casparis
John Cummisky	J Snow	Wm E Schoonsborn
Louis Betz	J C Gaekler	W C Christman
J J Flannigan	Patrick Ragan	H C Young
J J Heck	John Schultz	Jas Steel
Oliver Donn	Wm Schwing	Catharine Boarman
F Rappie	Julius Esenbeiss	Henry Briggerman
Wm Shoemaker	M B Bean	John Wunderitch
Casper Keller	W G Hurley	Theo Lewis
Geo Dell	Henry Buscher	Fred'k Myer
M M Force	Adolph Kraeutler	Robt Bello
John W Usher	John Beck	John Wail
Herman Schmidt	Peter Boyle	Geo A Shekell
Jas A Powers	Ernest Wangiman	J W Ridgely
Chas Essing	Edw Foreham	T B Pumphrey
Bernard Henzl	Leopold Kolipinki	McCullum & Brady
Harris & Wambold	Chas Berg	Jas H Lewis
Edw McCarthy	Henry Vonderhide	A Herforth
F Herman	John Lynn	Wm Herforth
Jas T Radd & Son	Henry F Schoubern	H A Hudson
Rudolph Richards	A B Copps	Jos Englehart
Julius Rivier	H S Benson	Henry Groverman
Dennis O'Neal	Mrs A F Beveridge	Chris Dickson
Andrew Nepath	C G Lederer	Thos Coleman
A D Hilton & A Moore	August Backus	M DeAtley
Louis C Kranch	Fred Martin	

Wm Dickson & J W C Colgan; Wm H Garbuit & Jas T McGowan; Shelly & Potts-Metropolitan Hotel

Oldest Inhabitants Association meeting yesterday: Pres Dr John B Blake, in the chair; J Carroll Brent, sec. Nathan Magruder & Wm Orme were nominated for membership. The death of Capt Benj T Dove was announced. A letter from John Underwood was read, giving reminisences of the early history of Washington. Nicholas F Callan read a paper on the life & services of Gen John P Van Ness, who died in this city in 1846; which was warmly applauded.

Died: on Dec 2, after a protracted illness, Josephine Eliz, the wife of R R Warner, in her 31st year. Her funeral will be tomorrow at 11 A M, from Columbia Hospital, 14th st. [Star & Express copy.]

Died: on Dec 2, Mrs Rachel Grove Lindemood, aged 57 years. Her funeral will be from the residence of her sister, Mrs Lambright, 387 9th st, near I, Dec 4 at 11 o'clock.

Patents to Washingtonians: 1-Julius Edwards Dutch, for preserving meats; P J Turney, machine for sawing marble; D E Somes, construction of rubber & other elastic springs.

Mr Edw A Pollard announces the Southern Opinion will be issued on Saturday next, as a mark of respect to the memory of his brother, & that its publication will be discontinued.

Fendall Marbury & Saml B Hanes, as trustees, sold, on Nov 26, the real estate of Wm Lyles, dec'd, as follows: lot 1, 217 acres, to John H Underwood, $17.50 per acre; Lot 2, 256 acres, to Dennis B Lyles, of Wash, D C, $31 per acre; lot 3, 305 acres, to Dennis B Lyles, $18 per acre. The same trustee, on Nov 30th, sold to Thos Seabrook, the real estate of the late John Contee, called **Webb's**, containing 238 acres, at $15 per acre. Mr Seabrook is the principal contractor of the Balt & Potomac railroad.

Mrs Leslie & her 2 children were burned to death at Sing Sing, N Y, on Sat, in consequence of the upsetting of a kerosene lamp.

Mobile, Dec 2. Augusta J Evans, the well known authoress, was married last night to L M Wilson, president of the Mobile & Montgomery railroad.

Wilmington, Del, Dec 2. A special despatch to the Commercial, from Princess Anne, Md, states that a warrant has been received for the execution of Wm Welles, Wm Wilsen, & Geo Pounds, for the murder of the captain & mate of the schnr **Brave**, in Chesapeake bay, on Mar 31st last. The warrant fixes Jan 8 as the day of execution.

N Y World. Suicide yesterday at the boarding house of Mrs Letitia Morris, 41 South Wash Square. Mrs Mary A Gatewood, a boarder, cut her throat with a razor while under arrest for larceny. She was a niece of ex-Senator Guthrie, of Ky; a widow, about 38 years of age; when married she resided in Louisville, Ky; after the death of her husband, some years ago, she came to N Y. The dec'd was a victim of kleptomania, with an invincible desire to steal.

A little daughter of Mr John W Brown, of Vincentown, N J, was attacked by a game cock recently, & picked so severely that lockjaw set in & resulted in her death.

Rothschild's disease was inflammation of the liver.

Supreme Court of D C; Poulus Thyson, plntf, vs John Lincoln, dfndnt. No 5,271-at law. On motion by Mr Wm F Mattingly, his atty, it is ordered that the dfndnt cause his appearance to be entered herein on or before the first rule day occurring 40 days after this day; otherwise the case will be proceeded with as in case of default.
-D K Cartter, Chief Justice -R J Meigs, clerk

Supreme Court of D C; Edw Mulligan, plntf, vs Denis Byrne, dfndnt. No 5,241-at law. On motion by Mr Wm F Mattingly, his atty, it is ordered that the dfndnt cause his appearance to be entered herein on or before the first rule day occurring 40 days after this day; otherwise the case will be proceeded with as in case of default.
-D K Cartter, Chief Justice -R J Meigs, clerk

FRI DEC 4, 1868
Gen Sheridan has forwarded a report of the fight which Custer's command of cavalry had with Indians on the Washita river on Nov 27. Black Kettle & 102 warriors were killed, & 53 women, many children, horses, robes, arms, & lodges captured. Maj Elliott, Capt Hamilton, & 19 enlisted men were killed, & 3 ofcrs & 11 men wounded.

Jas Maize McCrae, a veteran newspaper contributor, & for many years a respected resident of this city, died yesterday. He was born in Fairfax Co, Va, Nov 22, 1801, & was in his 68th year at the time of his death. His father was the first postmaster at Alexandria, Va, appointed by Gen Washington, & he was the nephew of the celebrated Col McCrae who fought with such distinguished gallantry under Gen Jackson at the battle of New Orleans. His brother, Wm Allison McCrae, when a cadet at West Point, was expelled for refusing to testify against a classmate, as was the whole of the class for following his example. He was afterwards appointed U S Dist Atty for Florida, & was killed by Col Hawkins, with whom he fought 5 separate duels. [Dec 5th newspaper: The funeral of Maj McCrae will take place this morning at 11 o'clock, at his house, opposite the Franck Taylor Bookstore, Pa ave.]

Nothing remains of *Fort Lafayette* but a ruined mass of brick & mortar. The loss, from the fire, to the Gov't, will be about $250,000.

Ten years ago a man named Jaques Constadt murdered, from jealousy, a young & beautiful Italian girl in New Orleans. He was convicted of the crime, but escaped punishment by some legal quibble, only to become insane. He died last week.

Mrd: on Dec 2, by Rev Mr Lewis, Byron Seuff, of Chillicothe, Ohio, to Estelle Louisa Fleury, of Wash City.

Board of Police: 1-Pvt Thos M Williams, charged with violating the rules & regulations, was sentenced to be admonished by the Major. 2-Pvt Jas W Atwell, charged with intoxication, was dismissed the force. 3-The name of Pvt Wm H Duffy was dropped from the rolls of the force.

Died: on Dec 2, Benj S Bayly, in his 68th year. His funeral is this afternoon at 2 o'clock, from his late residence, 5th st, between H & I sts. [Dec 5th newspaper: The funeral of the late Benj S Bayly took place yesterday, largely attended. Columbian Encampment & Columbia Lodge of Odd Fellows, headed by Heald's Band, were present. The services at the house were conducted by Rev W Mead Addison, of Trinity Church. The remains were interred at *Congressional Cemetery*.]

John S Elliott died at his residence, Dixon's tavern, Queen Anne's Co, on Sunday last, of pneumonia, aged 59 years. He was the largest man ever raised in Md, & perhaps in the U S. A few years ago he weighed nearly 500 pounds; of late he had fallen off, & his weight was reduced to less than 400 pounds. In height he was 5 feet 10 inches. He was a native of this county. –The Crumptonion

SAT DEC 5, 1868

W L Wall & Co, auctioneers, have sold at auction part of lot 10 in square 77, fronting 25 feet on 22nd st west, by a depth of 52 feet, improved by a 3 story brick dwlg house, to Jas Morgan, for $5,550. Also, part of same lot, fronting 25 feet on 22nd st, by a depth of 52 feet on H st north, for 52 cents per foot, to Jas Biggins. Also, 25 feet adjoining same, to Jas Biggins, for 28 cents per square foot.

Mrd: on Dec 3, at Trinity Church, Upper Marlboro, by Rev H J Kershaw, T Somerville Dorsett to Miss Bede McGregor, all of PG Co, Md. No cards.
+
Mrd: on Dec 3, at Trinity Church, Upper Marlboro, by Rev H J Kershaw, T F S Bowie to Miss Aggie W McGregor, all of PG Co, Md. No cards.

Mrd: on Dec 3, by Rev B N Brown, Mr Wm Burnell, of N Y, to Miss Julia A Little, daughter of the late Saml J & Margaret D Little, of Wash.

Mrd: on Dec 2, at the residence of the bride, by Rev Mr Lewis, Byron Seneff, of Chillicothe, Ohio, to Estelle Louise Fleury, of Wash City.

Died: on Dec 4, Wm Benj Jackson, in his 88th year. His funeral will take place from his late residence, 333 Pa ave, tomorrow, Sunday, at 2 o'clock P M.

J Marshall, a bookkeeper of the U S Treasury Dept in New Orleans has been held for trial for abstracting gold coin & replacing it with silver, in order to secure for himself the difference in premium. The amount so manipulated is said to be $30,000.

Wanted, a room, with board, in a private family near 14th & N Y ave. Address Geo G Gaither, Dept of Stae, stating kind of room & terms.

Information received at the Brooklyn Police Headquarters yesterday: a paymaster's clerk absconded from the navy-yard with $12,000, of which he was the custodian. The defaulter was R D Bogert, stationed on the U S receiving ship **Vermont**. He abstracted the amount from the safe on Tuesday A year past he had been in the habit of visiting gambling houses & his losses largely exceeded his gains. He is short in stature, slim figure, sandy hair, light complexion, & wears spectacles; his is age 26 & is married. During the war Bogert was paymaster on the vessel **Cmdor Barney** & other vessels attached to the Potomac Flotilla. -N Y Tribune, Dec 4

Boston, Dec 4. It is Dennis Reeme, & not Keene, who is suspected of the murder of Dennis Gronau, in Charlestown. He voluntarily surrendered himself, & denies the crime. He is held for examination. The murder took place in Furbisher's sausage & lard factory, & the position of Gronau's body indicated that he was stooping over the chopping block at work, when a blow was given him from behind, severing his head from his body. The murder causes great excitement in Charlestown.

Harrisburg, Pa, Dec 4. A cmte of ladies from N Y called upon the Governor this morning to urge the pardon of Hester Vaughn. They were courteously informed that their action had long since been quietly anticipated by thousands of humane & philanthropic citizens, mostly ladies of Pa, & any further agitation of the subject was unnecessary, as the case was throughly understood, & his acton determined on. [Dec 11th newspaper: Govn'r Geary assured his visitors that he would never sign Hester Vaughan's death warrant.]

1835 was the inauguration of the Florida, or Seminole war. Gen Thompson was killed by the outraged Oceola. On Aug 11, 1835, Pvt Dalton was killed, & the Florida war began, & extended through a period of 7 years. The great Sioux war of 1852 had its immediate origin in a trivial incident. An Indian, impelled by the fierce gnawings of hunger, killed a cow belonging to a Mormon emigrant near **Fort Laramie**. The Indians offered remuneration for the cow; this was rejected. A lt, with 20 men pursued the Indians, & demanded the surrender of the offender; the tribe refused, & the ofcr ordered his men to "fire." In less time than it requires to write the sad story the entire party were killed. Thus began the Sioux war, which lasted 4 years. The war was finally terminated at the battle of "Ash Hollow," by that old veteran, Gen Harney. This little brush of 4 years with the Sioux cost the Treasury $40,000,000. The Navojoe war was began by a trivial incident. A negro boy offered some indignity to an Indian, who let fly an arrow with fatal effect. The murderer fled to his tribe. An ofcr demanded the surrender of the culprit. The demand was refused, & as usual rashness precipitated a conflict. This war cost $30,000,000. The Arapahoe & Cheyenne war was commenced in 1864, & desolated the Plains for 2 years, originated when: some stock, [we believe an old "hoss",] was supposed to have by stolen by the noble red men. An ofcr demanded not the surrender of the animal, but the disarming of the Indians. A fight ensued, of course. There was a cold blooded massacre of old men, squaws, & pappoosas at Sand Creek, in Colorado

Territory. The Indians exasperated by this unprovoked murder by Col Chivington & his troops, sought & obtained the aid & protection of the Camanches & Kiowas. This led to the confederation of nearly all the tribes & bands from the Red River of the North to the Red River of the South, & to the terrible Indian war of 1865. The war taxed the U S Treasury from forty to fifty million dollars. This disaster was closed by the treaty concluded in Oct, 1865, at the mouth of the Little Arkansas. A second war with the southern Cheyennes & Arapahoes was inaugurated in 1867. In Apr, 1867, a military command, without any known cause, attacked & burned their village of 300 lodges, including about 100 lodges of friendly Sioux, consuming every vestige of provisions, clothing, & implements of every description, thus forcing them to resume the war path or starve. The war raged for 7 months. This war was terminated by the treaty of Oct, 1867, at Medicine Lodge creek. The present war, with the Cheyennes, Apaches, Arapahoes, Kiowas, & Comanches, has been in progress for several months. Entire settlements have been depopulated, & scores of U S troops killed at a single dash; vast trains of horses, mules, oven, & wagon loads of merchandise captured; locomotives & trains of cars thrown from the track, & pasengers massacred. This conflict has cost the U S from $1,500,000 to $2,000,000 per week. The savages are in better fighting trim, finer morale, & better supplied with the bone & sinew of war than ever. Several heavy detachments of troops, under the noble little Phil Sheridan & the veteran Sulley, & others, are scouring the Plains in search of the wily foe. There are about 350,000 Indians in the U S, [leaving out those recently bought from the Czar of Russia, who didn't get $7,200,000 for Alaska,] to feed & clothe as wards of the nation; cost about $30,00,000 per annum. From long observation on the frontier we know the Indian never goes on the war path if left alone, when his maw is well filled & his limbs well clad.

Memphis Appeal, Nov 20. The absurd proclamation of martial law by the so called Governor of Arkansas could hardly have other results than bloodshed. On Nov 10 a band of two to three hundred men entered the little town of Centre Point, Sevier Co, & took possession of the place. The citizens were marshalled en masse in an open field while the town was ransacked & plundered. They called themselves the Clayton militia. Finally one Capt Reeves addressed the captive citizens telling them that Gov Clayton had declared martial law in Sevier Co, & they were there to enforce the proclamation. Next day hordes of thieves & assassins entered the town. They commenced an indiscriminate onslaught, shooting those who could not escape. They selected 3 citizens, Hester, Anderson, & Gilbert, & shot them down like dogs. The militia are still in possession of Centre Point.

MON DEC 7, 1868
Died: on Dec 5, Harriet Helena Paulina, daughter of Julia & Hon Jos S Wilson, Com'r Gen Land Ofc, aged 4 years & 11 months. Her funeral is today, Dec 7, at 1 o'clock.

Died: on Dec 5, of consumption, Rosa E Lowrie. Her burial services will be at the Church of the Incarnation, today, the 7th, at 11 A M.

Journeymen Bookbinders' Society elected the following for the ensuing year: Pres, Archibald Hullett; Vice Pres, Wm Bullock; Rec Sec, John Perkins; Financial Sec, Thos Stewart; Treasurer, Dr McFarland.

Orphans Court-Judge Purcell, Dec 5, 1868. 1-The will of Mrs Rachel Grove Lindamond, bequeathing her property to Mrs Emily S Shepherd, her niece, was filed & partially proven. The testatrix names Arthur Shepherd & Silas Marchant excs. 2-The will of the late Sophia Taylor, bequeathing a house & lot in Williamsport, Md, to her daughter; a life estate in a half lot to her son, then to revert to her grand-daughter, to whom he also leaves half a lot, was filed & fully proven. 3-The first & final account of W H Dougal, exc of Philip Harry, dec'd; first of Jos Redfern & Wm Wilson, adms of S Redfern, dec'd; third account of Eliza McDuell, excx of John McDuell; & second account of Arlemesia Bean, guardian to orphans of Benj Bean, were approved & passed.
4-Letters testamentary were issued to Mary W Fitzgerald on the estate of Wm A Fitzgerald; bond $3,000. 5-Letters testamentary were issued to Dickerson Naylor on the estate of Margaret C Grimes; bond $15,000.

Madison, Ind, Dec 5. Collision of steamers on the Ohio River last night. The steamer **United States** & the steamer **America** collided near Rael's Landing, about 2 miles above Warsaw, on the Indiana side. It is said that some mistake was made in the signals. It is supposed that 75 or 80 persons are lost. Mr & Mrs Inskens jumped from the **United States** to the deck of the **America**, 15 feet, & were saved. Also known to have been saved on the **United States**: Jas Sickles & wife, Fremont, Ohio; Jas Price & brother, Louisville; Lee Kahn & Dr Leslie, Cincinnati; B Nelson, Allegheny City; Master Pearce saved, but mother & brother lost; Capt Robert, McCamont, Cincinnati, burned about the neck; Robt Nelson, Newport, Ky, slightly injured; G W Green & lady, Col Harris, Louisville; Geo H Middleton, Cincinnati; Wm Chamberlin, Cincinnati; Mr McFarrall & wife, Nashville; Mr Hoy, Louisville; J B Fisher, N Y; S H Clark, Memphis. The following are missing but supposed to be safe: M Crawford & lady, Mr Ragge & wife, Mr Huddle, wife & daughter, B F Morris, B Sleshmyer, Mr Otter, J Maddox, & P Hartman. Those lost on the **United States** were Mrs R H Jones & daughter, Eva, of Waynesville, Ohio; Elijah Fort, colored. The rest of the **United States**' passengers cannot be correctly given, owing to the loss of the clerk's books. Rev Mr Parrin & Rev Mr Risley, of N Y, are missing; also, Mrs Harriet Warring & white servant, of New Albany; *Mr Bigley, John L Burns, John M Lowdower, M J Look, Mr Garvin, Mr Johnson, Mrs G W Griffin, O Heidelberg, Miss Mary L Johnson, Steele Bright, O B Sappington, L H Vance, Mr Hammers, Wm Briggs, Chas Runk, Mr Pope, & Mr Hegan are supposed to be saved. The ofcrs lost are John Fennell, steward; Richd Marshall, 2nd do; Jas Johns, 3rd clerk; Jas Fennell, barkeeper; & Dan, colored barber. Mr Hayes, of Nashville, was severely bruised. Ola Bull was among the passengers saved. The wife of Cmdor Thompson, & a lady travelling with her were lost. Mrs Hayes, Nashville, missing; John Moore, Owingsville, Ohio, lost; Harris, of Brunswick's billard manufactory of this city, missing. There were 96 passengers on the **America**, only one of whom is known to be lost. The **United States** lies in 8 feet of water. [Dec 8th newspaper: N Y, Dec 7: John H Weber, of the firm of Oliver, Carpenter & Co, of N Y C, who was on board the steamer **America**, arrived here safe. Phil, Dec 7: Geo W Fahnestock, lost on the steamboat **United States**, with his daughter, was a well known druggist of Phil. The two ladies put on board at Cincinnati by Mr Wheeling were Mrs Thomson, wife of Cmdor Edw R Thomson, of the U S navy, & Mrs Griffin, niece of W R Lesse. They were reported to be on their way to join Cmdor Thomson, who is on duty at New Orleans. Madison, Ind, Dec 7: A body, supposed to be that of Mrs Pearce, of Louisville, has been recovered. Seven other recovered bodies cannot be recognized. Mr Fisher, of Pa, a passenger on board the **United States**, was badly burned about the face & hands. Mr Cunningham, of Alleghany City, Pa, is in the hospital, badly burned. *Mr Bigley, of Pittsburg, mentioned as having been lost, is safe.] [Dec 11th newspaper: Cincinnati, Dec 10. The body of Mrs Peace, of Louisville, found in good condition. John Malgengroft, of Louisville, who was supposed to have been lost, turned up all right. Mrs Eliza House & son, of Birmingham, Pa, are among the lost. The body of the late Mr Fahenstock, of Phil, & also an Italian named Domines, were among the bodies recovered. Domines had a large amount of gold upon his person. Fears were entertained that Jacob S Golladay, member of Congress from Ky, was lost; letters have been received from him stating he was on the steamboat **America** at the time of the collision & escaped injury, suffered nothing worse than the loss of his baggage.] [Dec 13th newspaper: Mr & Mrs Hutchins, of Concord, N H, were passengers in the mail steamer **United States**; the steamer had a large quantity of coal oil on her deck, which was ignited, & in less than 30 seconds after sunk. Mr Hutchins was born in Concord, Oct 21, 1797, where he has since resided; he married Miss Sarah Tucker, of Boston, in 1820, by whom he had 11 children, of whom the following are still living: Mr Abel Hutchins & Col Geo H Hutchines, of this city; Maj Ben T Hutchins, of New Orleans; Rev Chas L Hutchins, of Lowell, & Dr Edw R Hutchins, of Phil. Mr Hutchins was the oldest merchant of our city until 2 years ago, when he relinquished his business to two of his sons. For some years he has suffered from severe rheumatism, & was on his way to New Orleans, where he was intending to spend the winter.] [Dec 12th newspaper: Louisville Journal of Wed: Capt R H Woodfolk, who was a passenger on the steamer **United States**, arrived home yesterday. He saw Mr Geo Northrup, railroad agent, & Mr Inskip, of Madison, jump from the hurricane deck to the lower deck of the **America**, neither were badly hurt. Mr Green & bride, of Madison, procured life preservers, but did not know how to fasten them. He found some bits of rope with which he fastened the life preservers around himself & wife, & then tying their arms together, leaped into the water & reached the shore in safety. Ole Bull swam ashore with all his clothing on & his diamond studded fiddle in his hand. A little son Mr Jack Pearce, only 11 years old, jumped from the hurricane roof & swam ashore. His mother & younger brother perished. Capt Pearce, Wm Taylor, clerk, & other ofcrs of the American got ashore from the stern of that boat. He saw a yawl containing 10 or 12 ladies drawn under the suction of the moving wheel by the **America**, & crushed. He has not seen his room-mate Mr Hart, & supposed that he is among the lost. He has a brother here awaiting some tidings of the ill fated one.] [Dec 17th newspaper: Among the passengers in the steamer **United States**, was a young clog-dancer, Billy Barker, well known in negro minstrelsy.]

N Y, Dec 6. Under the final decision of the Court of Appeals, Mrs Sinclair recently obtained from her former husband, Edwin Forrest, $85,000, costs, & hitherto unpaid alimony.

Jas Fisk, one of the Erie directors, has commenced an action for damages $100,000, against the N Y Tribune, for publishing a statement to the effect that he had run off with $8,000,000 belonging to the fund of the company.

Mrs Clark Whittier, wife of the well-known specialty physician, obtained a divorce in St Louis on Friday, with alimony of $12,000 per annum for 4 years, $15,000 at the end of that time, & permission to resume her maiden name of Camilia Wall.

Mayor L Stanton, of Cleveland, together with his wife & 2 children, were badly poisoned last Sunday by partaking of a stew in which a diseased chicken was served up. The family were very ill for 48 hours, but all are now convalescent. Many chickens around Cleveland are dying of diptheria.

J G W Mauk, who commanded a colored regt at the close of the rebellion, was made brig general by brevet, & afterwards appointed registry clerk in the New Orleans post ofc, has been arrested by Messrs Hobbs & Shallcross, special agents of the Post Ofc Dept, & indicted for purloining money orders to the amount of $5,515. The ex-brigadier has given bail in the sum of $10,000, & his trial is set down for Dec 14.

Public sale of the valuable real estate of the late Zachariah B Beall, containing 1,005 acres of land about 2 miles from Forestville, in PG Co,Md, on Dec 29 next.
–C C Magruder, trustee

U S Marshal's sale of steam tug **Katy Wise**; by order from the Clerk's ofcr of the Supreme Court of D C; public sale, for cash, at J S Davidson's wharf, in Gtwn, D C, on Dec 11, of the **KatyWise**, her tack & apparel; No 202 Admiralty, in favor of Henry J Devinney. –David S Gooding, U S Marshal, D C

Orphans Court of Wash Co, D C. Letters testamentary on the personal estate of Wm A Fitzgerald, late of Wash Co, D C, dec'd. –M W Fitzgerald, excx

U S Marshal's sale of all of square 7_8, with improvements thereon, in Wash City, seized & levied upon as the property of the Balt & Ohio Railroad Co, & will be sold to satisfy execution No 1,741, Supreme Court, in favor of Ellen T Harris, admx of John O Harris, against said railroad. –David S Gooding, U S Marshal, D C

TUE DEC 8, 1868
The President received the resignation of Gen J B Steadman, Collector of Internal Revenue for First Dist of Louisiana, & it has been accepted; to take effect Dec 31st.

N Y, Dec 7. In the case of Cmdor Meade, who is alleged to be illegally restrained on the pretended ground of insanity, affidavits were filed by B F Bache & Mrs Cmdor Meade, declaring that it is their belief that the Cmdor is insane. Affidavits were also filed to the effect that he presents no appearance of insanity. The case has been postponed for one week.

Mr J E Van Steenburgh, for 18 years cashier of the bank at Fishkill, N Y, met with a fatal accident on Thursday last; he left N Y on the Poughkeepsie special train Thur, & before reaching there he fell asleep, not being aroused till after the train had left the station. He got the idea to get off the train, but it was going faster than he expected, & was thrown under the wheels, both legs were crushed, & he died on Friday morning.

Died: on Dec 5, Mrs Mary Bender, wife of the late Maj Geo Bender, in her 60th year. [Dec 11th newspaper: The relatives & friends of the late Mrs Mary Bender are invited to attend her funeral on Sat, Dec 12, at 1 o'clock, from her late residence, 198 I st, between 20th & 21st st.]

Died: on Dec 7, Timothy J Lane, aged 54 years. His funeral will be from his late residence, 21st st, between E & F sts, on Dec 8, at 1:30 P M.

Died: on Dec 1, at **Woodley**, D C, Henry White, aged 8 years.

U S Patent Ofc, Wash, D C, Dec 5, 1868. Ptn of J J Anderson, of Rochester, Beaver Co, Pa, praying for the extension of a patent granted to him on Mar 6, 1855, for an improvement in Cook Stoves. -Elisha Foote, Com'r of Patents

WED DEC 9, 1868
The Board of Police at the last meeting approved the following liquor licenses:

A Woodley	Ernest Lofileir	John H Semmes
Geo Schnell	Edw Engels	J L Miller
Henry Miller	Mary Weiss	Andrew Sprohs
John Fredericks	Mathias Pfeffer	Henry Wills
Francis Buehler	John Schlotterbeck	Wm Rullman
John Paxton	Burns Connely	Wm Carey
John Welcker	John Shea	Geo W Bunker & Co
Peter Jouvenal	John Ready	Henry B__zeholz
Wm Finley	Geo G Dubant	Wm H Edelin
John Baiel	John E Behrend	Thos Stackpole
Jas Flannigan	Michl Hiel	Chas Eisenhut
Christoper Mades	Jas W Taylor	

Annual meeting of the Wash Dental Association, held Monday; ofcrs elected: Pres, Dr R F Hunt; Vice Pres, Dr T O Hills; Sec, Dr J C Smith; Treasurer, Saml Lewis; Librarian, Dr H N Wadsworth; Exec Cmte: Drs Noble, Hills, & Dawes. The annual address was delivered by Dr H N Wadsworth.

Mrd: on Dec 2nd, at St Charles' Church, Cornwallis' Neck, Chas Co, Md, by Rev Fr Vetermele, John Francis Hickey, of Wash, to Nannie C Jenkins, of Chas Co, Md. [Balt papers please copy.]

Died: on Dec 8, Robt Israel, in his 44th year. His funeral will take place from the M st Methodist Church, between 9th & 10th sts, on Dec 10 at 2 o'clock.
+
Mr Israel was for more than 16 years an attache of this ofc, & by his fidelity & integrity gained the esteem of all connected with it. Relinquishing his connection with this ofc to engage in mercantile pursuits, he soon ranked among our most active & enterprising merchants. He was a devoted husband & father.

Meeting of the ofcrs of the 12th infty, held at **Lincoln Barracks**, Wash, D C, upon the occasion of the death of Brvt Lt Col Henry E Maynadier, major of the regt, which sad event took place at Savannah, Ga, Dec 3, 1868. Resolved, that we tender our hearfelt sympathy to the family of the deceased in this their bereavement. –Geo W Wallace, Lt Col 12th infty, Commanding Regt, Chairman [Dec 11th newspaper: The funeral of Brvt Lt Col Henry E Maynadier, Major 12th infty, will take place at the Church of the Epiphany this morning, at 10 o'clock.]

Criminal Court-Judge Fisher. 1-Thos Bowie, indicted for an asault with intent to kill Bernard West with a razor on Jul 4th last, was found guilty of assault & battery; fined $1. 2-John Shoter & Lewis Medley; grand larceny; guilty; sentenced to the penitentiary for 1 year. 3-W H Winfield; grand larceny; plead guilty. 4-Harris Carroll; larceny; *nolle pros*. 5-Robt Richardson; larceny; *nolle pros*.

Orphans Court-Judge Purcell, Dec 8, 1868. 1-Mary E Grimes gave bond in the sum of $2,500, as guardian to the orphans of A T Grimes. 2-The will of Benj S Bayley was filed & fully proven. The testator names his wife as excx & bequeaths her all his property, with the exception of $1,000 to Jane Eaton. 3-The following accounts were filed & passed: First & final account of Sarah Ellen Herbert, excx of S M Herbert. Third account of D W McFarlan, guardian to Ida M Baldwin. Silas Merchant gave bond in the sum of $300 as exc of R G Lindermood. Theodora Dausch gave bond in the sum of $800 as admx of Nicholas Dausch.

Orphans Court of Wash Co, D C, Dec 8, 1868. In the case of Susan Brayfield, admx c t a of Saml De Vaughan, the administratrix c t a & Court have appointed Jan 2nd next, for the final settlement of the personal estate of the said dec'd, of the assets in hand.
-Jas R O'Beirne, Reg/o wills

Orphans Court of Wash Co, D C, Dec 8, 1868. In the case of Lewis A Edwards & John L Edwards, adms of Jas L Edwards, dec'd, the administrators & Court have appointed Jan 2nd next, for the final settlement of the personal estate of the said dec'd, of the assets in hand. -Jas R O'Beirne, Reg/o wills

Phil, Dec 8. A wood train on the Cleveland & Toledo railroad was thrown from the track yesterday. John Niland & Michl Costello were killed; John Maloney seriously wounded.

Trustee's sale of valuable bldg lot near the War Dept; by decree of the Supreme Court of D C, wherein Terence Drury is cmplnt, & Mary M Drury et al are dfndnts; Equity No 1,351; sale on Dec 21, of lot 6 in square 168, fronting on north G st, between 17th & 18th sts. –Saml T Drury, trustee -Green & Williams, aucts

THU DEC 10, 1868

Pres Johnson, accompanied by his grandchildren, attended the Nat'l Theatre last night.

Sec McCullock yesterday appointed Ira M Harrison supervisor of N J.

The ship **John Duncan**, from St John's, N B, for Liverpool, capsized in the Atlantic & was lost. The captain, his wife, & a crew of 9 were lost.

Liverpool, Dec 9. The following persons on board the ill fated steamer **Hibernia**, were saved in the captain's & boatswain's boats: A Mason, Miss Rogerson, Catharine Boyle, Geo C Forbes, Mrs E Morrell, Ann Webb, John A Bethel, Mrs Bethel, Patrick Brewster, Mrs D N Nulvin, John Robinson, Bernard McFeely, Rev M O Connor, Josiah Cooks & wife, all cabin passengers; Campbell, Direny, Rogers, Dickett, Dohn, Mosier, Austin, McGown, wife & child & infant, McIntosh, & Irvine, all steerage passengers.

Plymouth, Dec 9. The jury in the case of Deacon Andrews returned a verdict of guilty of manslaughter, & the prisoner was sentenced to 20 years imprisonment.

Mrd: on Dec 1, by Rev Dr Burgett, at the residence of the bride's mother, in Mobile Co, Mr L M Wilson to Miss Augusta J Evans.

Died: on Dec 8, Robt Israel, aged 44 years. His funeral will take place from the M st Methodist Church, between 9th & 10th sts, today, at 2 o'clock P M.

Orphans Court of Wash Co, D C. Letters of administration on the personal estate of Nicholas Dausch, late of Wash Co, D C, dec'd. –Theodora Dausch, admx

FRI DEC 11, 1868

Louisville Courier Journal. A little over a week ago,in Fentress Co, Tenn, near the Ky line, lived an old lady, some 80 years of age, & her 3 grandchidren, a young lady, a boy of 12, & the third a small girl. In the neighborhood was a man named Logsdon, who murdered the grandmother & grand-daughter, & left the boy for dead; all the money he found was $75. The grandmother was thought to have the back pay of her dead son, who had been a soldier. The boy survived & told the sheriff of Fentress Co the whole bloody story. Logsdon was arrested & will doubtless be made to suffer the extreme penalty of the law.

Sale of a large & desirable double dwlg house & vacant lots, near the War Dept, by decree of the Supreme Court of D C, in Chancery, No 495; public auction of brick dwlg house with back bldg, possession promised on or before Jan 1, 1869, belonging to the estate of the late Gen Lawson, known as the *Wirt House*; lot fronts 93 feet on north G st, & runs back 113 feet 9 inches. Also, lots 26 & 28 of part of same square, fronting 30 feet & 56 feet 11 inches on said G st, running back about 113 feet 9 inches, adjoining the first mentioned. This property is in the same square as *Winder's Bldg*. —W Y Fendall, trustee -J T Coldwell & Co, aucts

Cleveland, Ohio, Dec 6. Last night the elegant residence of L M Hubby, on Euclid st, was entirely destroyed by fire, & Mr Hubby was so seriously injured, that recovery is considered doubtful. The house being outside the city limits of the city, is not supplied with gas from the gas-works, & Mr Hubby had introduced into it Pierce's patent gasoline; the instrument was outside the house, & the main pipe in the basement The gas being out of order, Mr Hubby went into the basement with a candle, to see if he could discover the leak, & immediately the explosion followed. Mrs Hubby was uninjured; Mr Hubby's son & son's wife, & Miss Ella Hubby, a beautiful & accomplished girl of 20, were thrown to the ceiling by the explosion, falling back into the basement. Miss Ella was terribly burned & will probably not live. Mr Hubby & wife escaped with slight injuries. The house, valued at $50,000, was a total loss.

SAT DEC 12, 1868
Miss Helen Western, a well known star actress, died yesterday at the Kirkwood House, in this city. She was taken sick in Pittsburg, about 5 weeks since, & came here to fulfill an engagement at Wall's Opera House, during which time her illness developed itself into conjestion of the bowels, causing her death. She was about 23 years old, sister of Lucille Western, daughter of Mrs English, of Boston, by a former husband. She was born in N Y. Her only relatives now living are her mother, Mrs English, in Boston, & her sister Lucille, now at San Francisco. Her remains were taken to Boston yesterday by Mr Chas F Wing, who had acted as Miss Western's agent for several years past, & will be interred in *Mount Aubutn Cemetery*, near Boston.

The funeral of Brvt Maj Gen Henry E Maynadier, 12th infty, who died in Charleston, S C, on Dec 3, took place yesterday from the Church of the Epiphany, on G st. The following gentlemen acted as pall bearers: Col Mason, Maj Graham, Capt Fillebrown, Maj Eddy, Mr Edwards, & Mr W D Davidge; services conducted by Rev C H Hall, assisted by Rev Mr Jackson & Rev Mr Holly. The deceased was about 38 years of age, & leaves a widow & 5 children to mourn his loss. The body was interred at *Kalorama*.

When Pres Johnson leaves the *White House* it will be with clean hands, & we trust a pure heart. The ladies of his household have the credit in Washington of discharging the duties of their position with a degree of order, elegance, & grace never exceeded in the White House. Much as the President has been persectued politically, no taint of corruption, or meanness, or selfishness clings to him.

Mr Gaylord Clarke, for many years conductor of the old Knickbocker, was so severely injured in his fall down stairs, some 30 feet, at his home at Piermont on Wednesday, that a fatal result is apprehended.

Mr Douglas Love, foreman of the Detmold coal mine, on George's Creek, about 8 miles from Frostburg, Md, was murdered at his house on Sunday. He was called to the door by 2 strangers, & as soon as he appeared was fired at from pistols in the hands of each, killing him almost instantly. No clue to the murderers, but it is thought they were men who had recently been discharged from work by Mr Love.

Montgomery, Ala, Dec 11. Hon W B Fannin, for many years a prominent member of the Ga Legislature, was buried in this city today. He died suddenly, of apoplexy. [Death date not given.]

Died: on Dec 11, Henry A Weedon, aged 58 years. His funeral will be Sunday at 2 P M.

MON DEC 14, 1868

Louisville, Dec 13. Capt Edwin Torrill, who led the raiding party against Shelbyville about 2 years ago, died of his wounds today.

Phil, Dec 13. Henry M Flint, whose letters over the signature of Durid, during the war, attracted much attention, died yesterday at Camden, N J.

Orphans Court-Judge Purcell, Dec 12, 1868. 1-Jas Nokes gave bond in the sum of $400 as guardian to the orphans of John Karr. 2-Richd H Burr gave bond in the sum of $6,000 as administrator of W H Fenwick.

Equity Court-Judge Olin, Dec 12, 1868. 1-Hilton against Hilton; order allowing $100 per month to complainant. 2-Smith against Smith; order appointing John C Wilson guardian *ad litem* to infants.

Mrd: on Nov 12, at the bride's residence, 247 west 21st st, N Y C, by Rev Dr Burchard & Rev Franklin Rising, the Rev Jas A Little to Miss Sarah J Cooper, all of N Y.

Louisville, Dec 12. Tragedy at New Albany today; Luther Whitten, outside guard of the jail, was met at the entrance by a party of men, who presented pistols at him, demanding silence or death. He shouted & was seized & knocked down. Sheriff Fullalove came down from his sleeping apartment & when he refused to give them the keys, he was shot in the right arm, inflicting a painful wound. His wife who was in bed, refused to tell them where the keys were; they searched & found them in a drawer. Thos Matthews, inside guard, was compelled to open the cells. Frank & Wm Reno were dragged out & hung. Simon Reno was then suspended between the ceiling & the floor. Chas Anderson was hung at the corner of the jail. They intended to hang a man named Clark, the murderer of Gen Tilli, but feared they had remained too long.

Norfolk, Dec 13. A man named Jaques, from N Y, & Thos Moore, from Balt, were drowned in the harbor today by the overturning of a yawl boat in the gale.

Richmond, Dec 12. Geo W Cook was today sentenced by the U S Dist Court to 10 years imprisonment in the Albany penitentiary for robbing the mail.

Phil, Dec 12. The jury in the case of Jos Hart, for the murder of Wm McKieve, returned a verdict of manslaughter, with a recommendation for mercy. Hart is 18. Seven other boys are to be tried for participation in the fight which resulted in the death of McKieve.

TUE DEC 15, 1868
Mrd: on Dec 11, at the Trinity parsonage, by Rev Mr Addison, Wm H Moore to Miss Alice Burch, both of Bryantown, Chas Co, Md.

The President yesterday sent to the Senate the following nominations: Alex'r Cummings, of Pa, to be Com'r of Internal Revenue; Henry A Smythe, now Collector of N Y, to be Minister to Russia, vice Mr Clay; Wm J Cullen, to be Superintendent of Indian Affairs for Montana & Idaho; Benj F James, to be Chief Examiner of the Patent Ofc.

Cornelius Wendell, one of the com'rs of the Union Pacific railroad, & F J Brooks, of Wash, returned to the city yesterday from a trip over that road. Mr Wendell states that the road is built in a first-class manner.

Washington City. 1-Gen Frank P Blair arrived in the city yesterday.
2-Cyrus W Field is in the city, the guest of his brother, Judge Field.

In regard to the alleged insanity of Cmdor Meade, his son-in-law, Mr Chas K Landis, says that his confinement was made by his son, Lt Cmder Meade, & approved by his brother, Gen Meade, & Sec Welles, of the navy, on the grounds of humanity. Mr Landis knew nothing of the confinement until the day of his marriage, when he was informed of it by Lt Cmder Meade, & urged to delay the marriage.

Trustee's sale of property on 10th st west; by deed of trust from Thos Chase & wife, dated Apr 15, 1868, recorded in Liber E C E No 31, folios 486 etc, of the land records of Wash Co, D C, & by order of the *cesturi qui* trust; sale on Dec 22 next, of lot 27 in square 340, in Wash City. –Wm D Cassin, Wm A Gordon, trustees -W L Wall & Co, aucts

Trustee's sale of private residence on E st north between 6th & 7th sts; by deed of trust from Alex'r McD Davis & wife, dated Jun 5, 1857, recorded in Liber J A S No 197, folio 54; public auction on Dec 28, next, of part of lot 17 in square 467; the house is 443 E st north, 4 stories high; will be sold to pay an indebtedness of $1,000 with interest from Jun 5, 1858. –Thos J Fisher, trustee -Cooper & Latimer, aucts

WED DEC 16, 1868

A Buffalo detective who has been in pursuit of a thief who robbed Mr Wm Fargo of $200,000 in bonds, in Jan last, returned & reports that he found his man, H V Clinton, at Aspinwall, & left him locked up in jail. The detective also saw the stolen bonds.

Mrd: on Dec 10, at the Fourth Presbyterian Church, by Rev John C Smith, D D, John L Caldwell to Miss Hattie E Williamson, daughter of John B Williamson. No cards.

Mrd: on Dec 14, at the residence of the bride's brother, by Rev Dr Tudor, Mr Jas M Sinclair to Miss Loula Latimer, both of Va.

Died: on Dec 15, Dr Geo L Pancoast. His funeral will be on Thursday, at 1:30 P M, from the residence of his mother, on 14th st, between R & S sts. [Phil papers please copy.]

Died: on Dec 15, Mary Virginia Ball, the beloved wife of Chas G Ball. Her funeral will be from St Patrick's Church, on Dec 17 at 10 o'clock.

M Berryer, the greatest ornament of the Paris law courts, died on Sunday, at his chateau of Augerville, in his 79th year.

Chancery sale of valuable real property, by decree of the Orphans Court of D C., passed Dec 12, 1868, & of the Supreme Court of D C, dated Dec 15, 1868, Equity No 1,481, I will as guardian sell at public auction, on the premises, Dec 31, 1868, the real property on 22nd st, between I & Pa ave: part of lot 13 in square 54; improved by a substantial frame house. –M Thompson, guardian -John B Wheeler, aucts

THU DEC 17, 1868

The only daughter of Hon John D Defrees was married last evening, at the residence of the bride's father. Hon Hugh McCulloch & wife, Speaking Colifax & wife, & Postmaster General Randall, Senator Sherman & wife, Senator Anthony, & a large number of other distinguished persons were present.

A portion of the **Granby tract**, adjoining **Fort Saratoga**, north of this city, containing about 40 acres, was sold by John Patch, real estate agent, to Maurice Pechin, for $6,000.

Mrd: on Dec 15, by Rev Geo H Ray, of Va, assisted by Rev Mr Tudor, pastor of M st Methodist Church, Mr Jas E Ray to Miss Gurtie E Shreve, all of Wash, D C.

Dr Pancoast, late of the U S army, died on Tues, at his residence on 14th st, near R st; he was a nephew of the celebrated surgeon of that name in Phil, & although only 23 years of age, had attained such a reputation that he was made medical director of the cavalry command of the U S army during the late rebellion, since the termination of which he has been engaged with Dr Johnson, in Wash City, in the practice of medicine & surgery. He was 30 years of age & unmarried, at the time of his death. His funeral will take place this afternoon at 2 o'clock, when the interment will take place in **Glenwood Cemetery**.

Trustee's sale of valuable farm known as *Joseph's Park*, in Montg Co, Md, on the Rockville road, about 7 miles from Gtwn, D C; on Dec 30, on the premises, by deed of trust dated May 12, 1859, recorded in Liber J G M, No 7, folios 465 thru 467, of the land records of the Circuit Court of Montg Co, Md, all that part & parcel of land known as *Joseph's Park*, adjoining Saml Perry's. The above farm contains 112 acres, more or less, improved by a comfortable dwlg, barn, & stable. –B Milburn, surviving trustee
-Cooper & Latimer, aucts

Kansas City [Missouri] Times gives an account of a horrible affair which recently occurred in Jasper Co, Mo: Mr Turner, of Clay Co, Mo, purchased a lot of cattle some months ago of Col J C McCoy & others, at Dallas, Texas, the cattle to be paid for at a pointed called Dexter Springs. Col McCoy sent his nephew, quite a young man, with the cattle, to receive his portion of the money, about $1,500 & the others also sent agents. After receiving pay for the cattle, young McCoy, ___ Jones, & 3 others started back to Texas, & while encamped at Buckhar's Prairie, Jasper Co, were fired upon by 5 men, & two of the party killed & one mortally wounded. McCoy & one other man escaped & went to a farm house near by. The men followed & demanded McCoy's money, which was given up, & then placed him & his comrade in a school-house, & kept guard. They shot McCoy & left him for dead; he was not killed & found the next morning in the house of a settler, but there is little hope of his recovery. The other man, Jones, escaped.

Legacy duty on estate of the late Baron Rothschild is upwards of twenty million francs.

The funeral of Helen Western took place at the Unitarian Chapel, in Pitts st, Boston, Tuesday, Rev S H Winkley officiated. The remains were deposited at *Mount Auburn*.

FRI DEC 18, 1868
Board of Police meeting yesterday: Applications from the following persons for liquor licenses were rejected: Chas McHugh, Jas Donnelly, Michl Breen, Jas Cantwell, John Davison, Geo A Haske, & Jas Kane.

Yesterday Mr F G McNamara, a clerk in the 2nd Auditor's ofc, was found dead in his bed at his room, 456 10th st, adjoining *Ford's Theatre* bldg, & the corner. Dr W W Potter was called on to hold an inquest. Verdict: death was caused by apoplexy. The deceased was about 32 years of age, & a native of Charleston, S C.

John Loeliger, proprietor of Lutz' Hotel, C & 10th sts, was arrested on Tuesday for selling liquor without a license. Loeliger was fined $20 & costs.

Hon Fernando Wood purchased from S P Brown, the corner house in the new & elegant block just completed at the corner of I & 15th sts, immediately opposite Senator Morgan's, for $40,000. Mr Wood will furnish the house immediately in the very best manner, & will occupy it as a private residence.

The President sent to the Senate on Wed the following nominations: Thos C Call, to be Collector of Internal Revenue for the 6th Dist of Iowa; Jas N Marks, Collector of Customs at Phil, in place of Cake, to be removed; Archibald M Green, Collector of Internal Revenue for 24th Dist of N Y; Saml T Maddox, Assessor of Internal Revenue for 3rd Dist of N Y, vice Wattmore, suspended; Jose Manuel Gallegos, Superintendent of Indian Affairs, New Mexico; Isaac Newton, Warden of the Jail for the Dist of Columbia; Saml T Hooper, Marshal for Wisc; Fred'k N Dockery, Marshal for the Southern Dist of Fla; G Gordon Adams, atty for the Southern Dist of Miss; John P O'Neill, Atty for the Southern Dist of Pa; Walter M Smallwood, Postmaster at New Orleans, vice Taliaferro.

Mrs Abraham Lincoln, while recently making some purchases in a fancy good store at Frankfort-on-the-Main, suddenly fainted away. She was removed to her hotel, where, at last accounts, she was lying in a condition which gave rise to great apprehension.

The Portsmouth Chronicle says ex-Pres Pierce was much overcome by the death of Mr & Mrs Hutchins, [in the Ohio river disaster,] & he is prostrated by sickness. Mr Hutchins had kindly invited him to accompany himself & wife to New Orleans, & for several weeks Mr Pierce thought of accepting the invitation.

One of the most accomplished stars of the Australian theatrical world, Mme St Denis, has committed suicide. She took poison, & states in a letter she left, that the motive was an unrequited passion for a gentleman, whose name has not been made public. She was born at Malines, in Belgian, her father being a surgeon in the French army, & her mother an English woman.

Mrd: on Dec 16, at the Fourth Presbyterian Church, by Rev John C Smith, D D, Wm A Meloy to Emmie N Stewart, both of Wash City. No cards.

N Y Tribune says Mrs Lewis Jennings, [Miss Henriques,] intends to return to the stage.

To the editors of the Evening Post: The recent outrage perpetrated upon me, which has had such full exposure, & awakened so widely the public indignation, will be reconciled to my mind if it tend to prevent similar conspiracies. As the pieces of silver given to Judas displayed the motives for the betrayal of the Saviour of mankind, so did the marriage of my daughter the morning after my entrapment shed all the light needed upon that atrocity. I may find reason for speaking more at large upon this subject hereafter. My immediate purpose in this card is to tender my thanks to my true & warm personal friends, to the public press, & to an independent judiciary, as vindicated through a warm-hearted, honest, bold, & clear-sighted judge. As it is not always the good fortune of victims to be rescued, as I have been, by humane & voluntary hands, from a living tomb, it will be some consolation if my case shall be among the last of its kind in Christendom. In order that it may have this blessed result, I may be required, in a further communication, to allude to the circumstances which prove it to be a transaction of unmitigated cruelty, & without a shadow of legal or reasonable excuse. Yours truly, R W Meade, Dec 14, 1868.

N Y, Dec 17. Pres Johnson has pardoned John Osbrey, who was recently fined $1,000 for presenting fraudulent whiskey bonds.

SAT DEC 19, 1868
The Senate yesterday confirmed the nomination of John W Rowland to be a member of the Levy Court for the District of Columbia.

Mr Wm McMahon, a poor lithographic printer in Louisville, recently, by the decease of a relative in Manchester, England, fallen heir to 8,000 pounds sterling or $40,000 in gold.

Mrd: on Dec 17, in Balt, Md, at the Church of the Ascension, by Rev Dr Custis, Miss Anna M, daughter of Gen A K Smith, to Thos O Taylor, of Va. The happy couple left Balt in the 11 o'clock A M train for their home in the sunny south. [Alexandria & Leesburg, Va, papers please copy.]

Died: Dec 18, after a long & painful illness, Mrs Mary Ann Scrivener, aged 53 years. Her funeral is today from her late residence, 591 M st, between 6th & 7th sts, at 2:30 P M.

Richmond, Va, Dec 18. The farm of ex-Govn'r Wise, in Princess Anne Co, which was so long held by the Gov't, was yesterday surrendered to the owner by order of U S authorities.

Supreme Court of D C, in Equity No 263. Grove et al vs S S Parker et al. Wm F Mattingly, trustee, sold lot 15 in square 79, in Wash City, to Edw C Carrington, for $4,570. –A B Olin, Justice -R J Meigs, clerk

Supreme Court of D C, in Equity No 1,115. David L Morrison, cmplnt, vs Wm Harris et al, dfndnts. It is ordered that the sale made by Michael Thompson, trustee, of the real estate of Thompson Javins, dec'd, be ratified & confirmed. –A B Olin, Justice -R J Meigs, clerk

MON DEC 21, 1868
Judge Anthony L Robertson, a distinguished lawyer of N Y, died on Friday.

Cooper & Latimer, aucts, sold lot 22 in square 412, on 8th st, between E & F sts, South Washington, containing 2,159 square feet, to Wm Kettler, for $1,075.

Sat a man named Chas E King went into the grocery store of Roach & Co, in Pa ave, & after taking a drink of liquor, sat down, & immediately expired. He was removed to his late residence, 511 17th st, between Pa ave & H st. He died from heart disease.

The new organ for Trinity Church, Gtwn, ordered more than a year ago, has at length been completed, & reached its destination on Wed last. It is from the manufactory of Henry Erben, of N Y, & contains 34 stops. The organ will be ready for Christmas Day.

On Sat afternoon Edw E Trimble, the fireman of Union Engine Co, attempted to commit suicide by taking laudanum. Drs Draper & Hagner attended him, & by prompt medical assistance saved his life.

Mr Sidney I Wales, late receiver & inspector of stores at the Navy Yard, resigned that position on Dec 15, to accept a position as special mail agent of the Post Ofc Dept.

The wife of Rev F Rominies, of the Dutch Reformed Church, committed suicide in Columbus, on Thursday, by hanging herself to some hooks in the wall. She had recently buried a child, & of late had shown symptoms of derangement. Mr Rominies & 3 children remaining are down with scarlet fever.

The President on Sat sent to the Senate the following nominations: Thos N Stilwill, for Minister Resident in Venezuela; Jas Davis, for postmaster at Memphis, Tenn; Robt D Andrews, for coiner in the U S Mint at Denver, Colo; & the following collectors of Internal Revenue: P B Spear, Pa; Chas C Dane, Mass; G W Colby, Ala; Arthur D Markly, Pa; O H Russell, Conn; Robt K Byrd, Tenn; & the following assessors: W C Tulley, Pa; C C Megrue, Ohio; Thos A Burdett, Miss; Lloyd D Waddell, Ga.

Orphans Court-Judge Purcell, Dec 19, 1868. 1-A renunciation of the heirs of W H Fenwick in favor of Richd H Burr was received, & letters of administration were issued to him; bond $5,000. 2-*In re*. Ptn of Spalding & Rapley et al, for citation on Mrs Joliffe, widow of John Joliffe, to show cause why she should not take letters on the estate, was taken up & argued by Messrs Morsell & Miller for petitioner, & Messrs Leach & Beard for respondent.

Mrd: on Dec 17, at the residence of Dr Boyle, in Aldie, Loudoun Co, Va, by Rev Jos S Brown, Patrick H Conway of Stafford Co, Va, to Millie M, daughter of the late Thos S Hall.

Died: on Dec 19, Chas Kirby King, the eldest son of the late C K King, of Norfolk, Va, aged 28 years. His funeral will take place from the residence of his mother, 511 17th st, Tuesday, at 12 o'clock M. [Dec 22nd newspaper: Mr Chas K King, whilst visiting his brother at his ofc, of the house of Messrs Roach & Co, on Dec 19, was taken suddenly ill & expired in a short time. He graduated at the U S Naval Academy, & resigned a few years since, & has since been connected with the mercantile service. He was a gentleman of unusually good health & temperate habits.]

Richmond, Dec 20. E H Gill, superintendent of the Richmond & Petersburg railroad, died this morning.

Providence, R I, Dec 19. Dr A Parsons, an eminent & venerable physician of this city, died today, aged 88 years. He was surgeon on the flagship **Lawrence** in the battle of Lake Erie, & was the last surviving ofcr of Perry's fleet.

On Saturday as Mr Geo Brady was returning from Wash City with his team, in some way or other he fell from his seat, & his feet entangled in or bout the bounds of the wagon; the horses became frightened & dashed off at full speed. When his body was found he was most horribly mangled. He was a tenant of Mr Robt Clagett, & a most excellent citizen. He leaves a widow & 4 or 5 children. –Marlboro Gaz

TUE DEC 22, 1868
Yesterday as laborers were bldg the hospital & medical dept attached to Howard University, on the grounds near the Park Hotel, the side walls fell, precipitating 10 workmen to the ground, nearly 40 feet. Benj Wheatley, a colored laborer, had one leg broken; Jos Wimsatt, bricklayer, residing in Gtwn, was seriously injured; Albert H Hilliary, Andrew Ferguson, J C Donohoe, Robt J Armsted, Robt Torogmorton, John Reed, Wm Mahoney & Israel Baker, a colored man, were injured & bruised. The cause of the accident is attributed to the effects of the frost on the brick of which the bldg was constructed, known as the patent brick, composed of water, lime, & sand. The material has been considered by many as unfit for bldg purposes, & the fall of the walls was predicted by a number of persons some time since. The building was being erected under the direction of Gen Howard. Police will investigate other bldgs in Wash City erected of the same material.

Police Matters. 1-Henry McPherson, of Gtwn, was arrested for assault & intent to kill Isaac Corry, & held in $500 bail to appear at court for trial. 2-Yeterday the case of A Holsten, charged with selling liquor without license was resumed; case was dismissed.

The New Orleans Bee states that Gen Rousseau has purchased the magnificent ***Belle Isle*** plantation, near Brashear City, Berwick's Bay, in Louisiana, & has made arrangements to cultivate sugar-cane next season.

Mrd: on Dec 21, at the residence of the bride's father, by Rev Mr Jackson, Jos M Wright, of Balt, Md, to Miss Lottie, daughter of Rear Admiral Chas H Poor, U S N. [Balt & Phil papers please copy.]

Died: after a short illness, Emma, daughter of Isaac & Johanna Hill. Her funeral will take place from the residence of her parents, $9t^h$ st, near N Y ave, on Dec 23, at 2 P M. [Death date not given.] [Dec 23rd newspaper: Her funeral will take place from St Patrick's Church, 10th & F sts, on Dec 23 at 2 P M.]

Chicago, Dec 21. Chas H Wagual/Wigual, for the past 11 years Commercial of the Chicago Journal, died of consumption yesterday, aged 30.

Providence, R I, Dec 21. Rev Wm O'Leary, pastor of St Mary's Catholic Church, in Newport, & Vicar General of the diocese of Hartford, died suddenly Sunday morning.

Rothschild left 2,500 francs annuity to every clerk who had been 10 years in his service.

WED DEC 23, 1868
Assist Surgeon Wm V Marmion has been detached from the receiving ship Ohio, & ordered to the Naval Hospital, Wash, D C.

Orphans Court-Judge Purcell, Dec 11, 1868. 1-Mary R Phillips gave bond in the sum of $500 as administratrix of Sarah Gates. 2-Emeline Richie gave bond in the sum of $400 as guardian to G W Hall. 3-Jas B_iggins gave bond in the sum of $1,500 as guardian to the orphans of Thos Holloran. 4-Eliz L Oates gave bond in the sum of $800 as admx of Thos Oates. 4-Nathl Kelley gave bond in the sum of $500 as adm of W McKelley.

The beautiful church, at the corner of 25th & Pa ave, St Stephen's Church, which was commenced in 1865, is sufficiently near completion to be dedicated on Sunday next, St Stephen's day, at 10 o'clock. When completed this edifice will cost about $20,000, very nearly all of which has been paid up; & a very handsome residence for the pastor has been erected by the congregation of St Stephen's. [Dec 28th newspaper: Dedication of St Stephen's Church on Dec 27th; Rev Thos Foley, D D, Vicar Gen of this diocese, dedicated the church; the pastor of St Matthew's Church, Rev Dr C J White, celebrated the solemn high mass; the orchestra was under the direcion of Prof Thos N Caulfield. The church is 53 feet wide on Pa ave, with a projection 19 feet wide by 9 feet deep in centre of front, which forms part of the ground work of the tower. The depth of the bldg on 25th st is 115 feet. The bldg is heated by hot-air furnaces.]

Criminal Court-Judge Fisher, Dec 22, 1868. 1-Christopher Bohlayer, indicted for an assault & battery with intent to kill: not guilty. 2-Isaac Landis was convicted of larceny, as also Jas Sanders, John Johnson, Chas Hagan, Maria Bailey, & Geo Warner. Chas Harris was found not guilty on a charge of pettit larceny.

Edw E Trimble, foreman of No 1 Engine Co, took laudanum on Sat last, died from the effects of the poison, at his residence on K, between 19th & 20th sts, Monday. His funeral will take place this morning, & will be attended by members of the Fire Dept.

Maj Gen O O Howard has requested the following gentlemen to serve on a board for the investigation of the accident to the hospital bldg in process of erection near Campbell Hospital & Howard Univ; Gen Nathan Michler; Edw Clark, architect of the Capitol extension; J W Rumsey & Francis Wivel, builders; Chas Webster, mason.

Sec McCulloch yesterday confirmed the nomination of Julius C Burroughs to be Supervisor of Internal Revenue for the States of Mich & Wisc. C E Creecy, Supervisor of Internal Revenue for the State of Louisiana, has suspended E M Boulguy, Collector of the 2nd Dist of that State, on the charge of malfeasance in ofc.

Died: on Tuesday, Briscoe S Mitchell, son of Rev Geo W & Cornelia D Mitchell, aged 18 years. His funeral will take place from the residence of his father, on K st, between 11th & 12th sts, this evening at 2 o'clock P M.

Died: Dec 20, at the residence of A B Fuller, 140 Clinton Pl, N Y, John Osgood, late a clerk of the Interior Dept.

Yesterday Mr Geo W Adams, for many years the Washington correspondent of the N Y World, & now owner of the Evening Star, was married to Miss Jennie Barclay, at the residence of the bride's father, John M Barclay, journal clerk of the House of Reps. Owing to a recent domestic affliction, the wedding was attended by only the immediate friends & relatives of the groom & bride, who, after receiving congratulations from those present, left last evening for the North on a wedding tour.

The Senate Cmte on Naval Affairs held a meeting Wed & agreed to report the following names for promotion in the naval service: [the rear admiral & cmder lines were too light to read;] to be lt cmders, Edw Hooker, Alonzo Muldeans, Chas O'Neill, N Mayo Dier, F M Green, & H H Gorrigan; to be captains, Rich & T Ronshaw; Johnson B Creighton; to be lts, Edw S Keyser, Deewitt C Kell, Geo A Durand, Jas G Green, Thos M Gardner, Chas M Anchory, Feliz McCurley, John McGowen, Richd H Miller, Thos Wilson, H G Neill, Chas H Rockwell, Gerhardt C Schulze, C A Salizky, Thos F Wade, John K Wynn, Geo F Wilkins, Geo E Wingate; to be 1st lts in the marine corps: Jas M T Young & A S Taylor.

Mr Brooks Bennett, of Shrewsbury, Vt, while trading at a store in Rutland on Thu, was taken with an epileptic fit, & fell heavily on his face, apparently dead. Medical aid was summoned, & he was revived. His first words were, "What did you say that was a yard?"

Public sale of valuable lot & improvements on Gay st, in Gtwn, D C, on Dec 29. The subscriber, as atty for the owner, Hezekiah Miller, will offer that lot being part of Beall's addition to Gtwn, 87 Gay st, fronting 42 feet & 2¾ inches on Gay st, running back 120 feet; improved by a good two story frame dwlg house, with back bldg of brick, in good order, now occupied by H C Weste_belt. –M Bannon, 32 St Paul's st, Balt, Md. -Thos Dowling, auct

THU DEC 24, 1868
Yesterday Mr Edw Preston, who had for the past 4 years resided with his brother, Wainwright Preston, on 1st st, between O & P sts, commited suicide by shooting himslef over the right ear with a single-barrelled pistol, causing instant death. He was about 58 years of age, a carpenter by trade, & has wife in Balt, where he resided until about 4 years ago. The cause of this distressing affair was attributed to spinal disease.

Trustee's sale of very valuable improved property on F st north, between 11th & 12th sts; by deed of trust from John S Tyson, Fannie A Ellicott, & others, dated Nov 29, 1857, recorded in Liber E C E No 22 folio 152: sale on Jan 6, 1869, of part of lot 1 in square 320, together with the appurtenances, to pay an indebtedness of $8,388.19, with interest from Dec 8, 1868. –H Wm Ellicott, trustee -W L Wall & Co, aucts

FRI DEC 25, 1868

Chicago Journal of Tuesday; a hurricane visited this city on Sat & last night, it's fury scarcely abating a minute until 4 o'clock this morning. One tremendous bldg fell & buried several surrounding structures, in one of which were a number of human beings. A one story house, comprising Nos 71 & 73 Adams st, used as a tenement house, was buried. It was occupied by Mrs Rouche, an aged widow; Mr S Heath & his wife, Mrs Tillotson, Jacob Waters, his wife, & 2 children, one of them a baby, & his sister, Mrs Dingman. These persons were in the house at the time of the crash. The searchers were rewarded by the discovery of the suffers, still alive. The little girl had numerous flesh wounds; Mrs Waters is in critical condition, & it is feared she will die.

Mr A P Gould, of Nashua, N H, recently died, leaving a will depriving his daughter of all interest in a policy of insurance on his life, which he had attained for the benefit of his wife & children. His executor collected the insurance, amounting to $1,400, & refused to pay the daughter any portion of that sum. Thereupon she sued him, & the court has given a decision in her favor, holding that an insurance policy cannot be changed by a will.

Mrs Matilda Heron is to withdraw from the stage & lecture on her experiences thereupon.

Mortgage sale of valuable property in Bladensburg, at auction, on Jan 14, 1869; part of lot 4; part of lot 5; the improvement, a large frame house containing 22 rooms, stable, & other outbldgs. –Emeline T Howell -Green & Williams, aucts

MON DEC 28, 1868

Phil, Dec 27. Wm Curtis, R W Grand Sec of the Grand Lodge of Pa, & Grand Scribe of the Grand Encampment I O O F, died suddenly this morning at his home in this city. He has been an active & prominent member of the Order for over 35 years.

Orphans Court-Judge Purcell, Dec 26, 1868. 1-Eliz Oates gave bond in the sum of $1,500 as guardian to the orphans of Thos Oates. 2-The will of Mary A Scrivener was fully proven. 3-The following accounts were filed & passed: 1st account of John R Adams, guardian to the orphans of John Wells. Second account of Wm Keenan, guardian to Margaret Byrne. First account of same, as administrator of P W Byrne.

Mrd: on Dec 22, in St Paul's Church, Royalton, Vt, by Rev Thos Gallaudet, D D, rector of St Ann's Church, N Y, assisted by Rev Jas Batchelder, rector, Edw M Gallaudet, president of the Nat'l Deaf Mute College, Wash, D C, to Susy, daughter of the late Dr Jos A Denison, jr, of Royalton.

Died: on Dec 27, Geo C B Mitchell, son of Rev Geo W & Cornelia D Mitchell, aged 34 years, 4 months & 16 days. Her funeral will take place from the residence of her father, 364 K st, between 11th & 12th sts, this day at 2 o'clock.

Died: on Dec 24, at Drainesville, Fairfax Co, Va, Jos Henry Wheat, formerly of Wash City. His funeral will be at Trinity Church, 3rd & C sts this day, at 2 o'clock P M.

Chicago, Dec 26. Mrs Augustus N Dickens, widow of Augustus Dickens, the brother of Chas Dickens, the celebrated novelist, committed suicide yesterday at 568 north Clark st, by taking an overdose of morphine. She sent her children to the home of her brother-in-law, Mr Lawrence, on Christmas evening, to take part in getting up a Christmas. They remained there over night, & on returning home next morning discovered their mother on the floor dead. Mrs Dickens was 35 years of age. She leaves 3 children. She has suffered much lately from poverty, being dependent at most entirely upon friends for the necessaries of life. The acrimonious controversy growing out of the conduct of her distinguished brother-in-law, Chas Dickens, towards Mrs Dickens on the occasion of his late visit to this country, will be remembered by all.

John Taylor, of Parkersburg, Va, while cleaning his gun, accidentally shot dead his little step-daughter, aged 7 years.

Rev Dr Dunne, of Chicago, who was at the head of the controversy with Bishop Duggan, died on Wednesday, in his 45th year.

Gabriel Martin, & 2 maiden sisters, residing in Columbia Co, Ga, were robbed & murdered last Thursday night. Their house was set on fire & their bodies consumed.

The family of John McDonald, of Phil were suffocated on Thursday night by the gas from a coal stove, which was burning all night in their bedroom. One daughter is dead, & another is not expected to recover.

Public sale of highly improved land in Fairfax Co, Va; by decree of the Circuit Court of Fairfax Co, rendered at its June term, 1868, in the cause of R M Mott, use of N Demeritt vs Anna Sackett; sale on Jan 18 next, of the tract of land in said county, on which Mrs Gen Sackett resides, containing 210 acres, situated at Spring Vale, on the Gtwn & Leesburg Turnpike, formerly owned by John F Webb; highy improved by an excellent dwlg, outhouses & barn. Also, the tract of 948 acres on the opposite side of the turnpike, with a small house. –M Dulany Ball, Com'r, Fairfax Co, Va.

TUE DEC 29, 1868
The Cincinnati papers of last Saturday announce the death, at Greenville, Miss, of Chas S Moorehead, ex-Govn'r of Ky. He was born in Nelson Co, Ky, in 1802, & was admitted a member of the legal profession; after he engaged in politics. He was one of the most eloquent speakers that have made Ky famous for splendid oratory.

Complications connected with the ***St Thomas*** purchase are attracting much attention. It was Mr Seward who first applied to the Danish Gov't to sell the island. Denmark refused, not seeming anxious to part with the property. After Russia had agreed to sell Alaska, this opinion changed. –Wash Cor N Y Tribune

Criminal Court-Judge Fisher. 1-Eliz Cavanaugh; larceny; not guilty, on account of a faulty indictment. 2-Annie Hamilton; assault & battery; guilty.

Children's Party at the Executive Mansion. The children of the President's family have issued cards of invitation to young misses & masters of an age corresponding with their own, to a dancing party on Tuesday evening next, at 6 o'clock. Invitations have gone out to about 350 children, embracing families in official position & in private life, from Gen Grant's children to those of the humblest parentage. –Wash Despatch to Balt Sun

London, Dec 28. Sir Richd Mayne, who made himself notorious not long since in breaking up Sunday night meetings in *Hyde Park*, died yesterday. [Dec 31st newspaper: Sir Richd Mayne, the Chief Com'r of the Metropolitan Police of London, whose death, on Dec 27th, is announced by the Atlantic cable, was born in Ireland, in 1796. He was the 4th son of Mr Justice Mayne, one of the judges in the Court of King's Bench, Ireland, & graduated at Trinity College, Dublin. Just before his death he was made baronet by Mr Diarseli.]

Died: on Dec 28, in Gtwn, D C, at the residence of her son, Geo Hill, in her 83rd year, Ann Warne, wife of the late Geo Hill, sr, a native of Portsmouth, England, but for the last 50 years a resident of Alexandria, Va, & Wash D C. Her funeral will take place on Dec 30, at 3 o'clock P M, from the residence of her son, Geo Hill, jr, 160 Bridge st, Gtwn.

Died: on Dec 28, Henry King, in his 56th year. His funeral will take place from the residence of his son-in-law, Stoddard st, Gtwn, on Dec 30 at 11 o'clock A M.

Shocking accident at Miller farm, on Oil creek, on Sat last; a benzine tank exploded killing Geo Knowlton & injuring Geo Bartlett. Loss, $$,4,000.

Vanderbilt is said to have made between $5,000,000 & $6,000,000 by his last stroke in N Y Central.

The benefactions of Mr Geo Peabody amount to about $7,735,000 in gold.

Mr Henry R Reynolds, one of the most successful builders in Balt, died quite suddenly yesterday morning.

WED DEC 30, 1868

Police Matters. 1-Levi Smith, arrested on the charge of setting fire to the carpenter's shop on Sat last, was committed to jail for court. 2-Yesterday L M Crist was arrested, on charge of forging a check purporting to be signed by J H Squier, who pronounced it was a forgery. Crist is held for a further hearing.

Mr Geo F Hammond, an Inspector of the Treasury Dept, who was recently murdered near Brownsville, Texas, was formerly a resident of Wash City, & married here. He was well known in this city, & left here last spring for duty in Texas.

London, Ontario, Dec 29. Mr Jones, the murderer of his niece, was executed this morning. Many thousands of people collected about the scaffold. He denied his guilt to the last.

Orphans Court-Judge Purcell, Dec 29, 1868. 1-*Julia Flanahan gave bond in the sum of $1,000 as admx of John Flanahan. 2-Robt Johnson gave bond in the sum of $20,000 as exc of Mary Ann Scrivener. 3-Helen B Nilliston filed a renunciation of right of administration on the estate of Cyrus Moore in favor of Henry S Davis. 4-The will of Jos M Downing was filed for probate. The testator bequeathes all his property to his wife, & named her executrix. 5-First individual account of Geo L Sheriff, guardian to John S & Doll E Killmon, orphans of John T Killmon, was filed & passed. 6-Robt Johnson gave bond in the sum of $10,000 as guardian to Ella R Scrivener, orphan of Mary Ann & Chas Scrivener. [*Looks like it is Julia-letter was missing.]

There seems to be some doubt whether the death of Mrs Augustus Dickens, the sister-in-law of Chas Dickens, resulted from premeditated self destruction, or from the indiscreet use of morphine. She had been in the habit of using the drug for some time past for neuralgic pains, & a few days before her death she had borrowed a book of a neighbor which treated of poisons, & had read it carefully, so that she must have been pretty well informed upon the character of the poison she was using. Still, there was no seeming reason for committing the deed. Although poor, she was beyond the reach of want, & had only the day before received a remittance of a certificate of deposit for $100 from some friendly source. The verdict of the coroner's jury: the decease came to her death by an overdose of morphine, administered by herself while in a state of mental aberration. This means the belief of the jury to be that Mrs Dickens committed suicide. Mrs Dickens was buried on Sunday. Her children will be carefully provided for.

Chicago, Dec 29. A fire broke out this morning in Franklin st, which orginated by the careless use of kerosene. Three men & a woman jumped from a 4th story window upon the roof of a 2 story bldg, & escaped with slight injuries. Wallace & Lewis Cane, brothers, joined hands & leaped headlong into the street, one being instantly killed, & the other dying in about 15 minutes after.

N Y, Dec 29. 1-Thos Eagan was arrested last night in Jersey City for stabbing Patrick H Feary. Eagan claimed that he was assaulted by Feary with a knife. 2-A German sailor, John Sebatsol, was killed early this morning at a dance house on Grand st, in Hoboken. Several arrests have been made.

Orphans Court of Wash Co, D C. Letters of administration on the personal estate of Jos H Wheat, late of Fairfax Co, Va, dec'd. –Albert J Wheat, adm

Orphans Court of Wash Co, D C. Letters of administration on the personal estate of Cyrus Moore, late of Wash Co, D C, dec'd. –H S Davis, adm

Roanoke Valley Land Agency, I have established at Boydton, Mecklenburg Co, Va, an agency to be devoted exclusively to the purchase of real estate in the counties of Mecklenburg, Halifax, Charlotte, Lunenburg, & Brunswick. –Thos F Goode

THU DEC 31, 1868

Sudden deaths. 1-The cause of the sudden death of Mrs Martin, on Sunday last, & who was buried on Tuesday at **Glenwood Cemetery**, is to be investigated by Dr Potter, the coroner, at the request of Maj Richards. 2-Dr Potter held an inquest on the body of the colored man, Moses Turner, who died on Sunday night, & after a post mortem examination, a verdict of death by rupture of a blood vessel to the brain was rendered.

Criminal Court-Judge Fisher. In the case of Danl Jackson, on trial for the past 2 days for forgery, the jury returned a sealed verdict of not guilty.

Cincinnati, Ohio, Dec 30. This morning, in this city, Wm Ashback killed his wife, Josephine, by blows on the head with a hatchet, & stabbing her once in the left side with a butcher knife. He then shot himself with a rifle, scattering his brains all over the room.

Chicago, Dec 30. It has been proved in court that the late Mrs Dickens left property worth $3,800. An acquaintance of Chas Dickens, in this city, says that Mr Dickens' brother fled from England with the deceased lady, deserting his wife, whom the novelist supported comfortably.
+
Chicago Tribune, Dec 30. Mrs Dickens lived at 568 North Clark st, in this city. She & her children were invited to a party given on Christmas eve by Mrs Lawrence, cousin to her husband, who lives on the West Side. Mrs Dickens did not go herself, but sent her children, & a note: Dear Emily, Somebody relieved me of my purse & its contents. The affair has worried me so that I have concluded not to accept your invitation for myself, but to let the children come. Please see them safely to the cars, or if too late after your festivities, keep them all night; but be sure & send them home early in the morning, as we are anticipating a merry little dinner tomorrow. –Bertha [By the side of the bed were found 2 bottles, one of them nearly full of morphine, & the other empty. An empty wine glass, in which traces of morpine were descernible, stood near the bottles. Mrs Dickens has been taking morphine for about 8 months to allay pain of severe attacks of neuralgia, to which she was a victim. It would seem she took too much of the narcotic by mistake. The turkey was ready for roasting, the children's candy, & the raisins for plum pudding were in the house.]

Worcester, Mass, Dec 30. Ichabod Washburn, originator & head of the extensive wireworks of Washburn & Moen Manufacturing Co, of this city, died at his residence this morning, after a protracted illness.

Cleveland, Ohio, Dec 30. Lewis Davis, for the murder of D R Skinner, of Independence, this fall, was today sentenced to be hanged on Feb 4.

An old man, Michl Soden, living in New Albany, Ind, died from hemorhage last week, resulting from a piece of meat which lodged in his windpipe 2 weeks before, producing partial strangulation, & rendering him unable to take other than liquid nourishment.

U S Patent Ofc, Wash, D C, Dec 26, 1868. Ptn of Thos Crossley, of Bridgeport, Conn, praying for the extension of a patent granted to him Jun 20th, 1854, & ante-dated Apr 5, 1854, for an improvement in Machines for Printing Woollen & other Goods.
-Elisha Foote, Com'r of Patents

Emil Deschamps has become blind.

The oldest man in Minnesota, Louis La Bonte, aged 104 years, died at the residence of his son-in-law, at Fairmount, last week. His wife, still living, is 99 years of age. Eight years ago Mr La Bonte began to grow childish, though he still possessed intelligence. Three years ago he lost his power of speech, & with it apparently his reason. On the Saturday before he died he went out of doors barefooted. He was a Frenchman & a Catholic, & was in the British service in the war of 1812.

Homicide in Missouri. St Joseph Herald, Dec 24. Last evening there was a fatal encounter between two lawyers of the St Joseph bar, Messrs A T Green & Jos L Earley. Early struck Green; Early, with a heavy cane, struck Green's arm, & his head; Green fired at Earley, from a small Smith & Wesson revolver, the ball striking him in the left breast; Mr Earley breathed his last. The body of the dec'd was taken to his residence on 5th st. Mr Green delivered himself to the custody of the sheriff & is now in the county jail. Mr Earley was 28 years of age, born in Ireland, & came to this country about 10 years ago. Soon after he arrived he married a lady in Balt, who survives him. Mr Early came to this city from Nebraska about 2 years ago; he was a cousin of P H Earley, Councilman from the 5th Ward. Mr Green is a lawyer, & came to St Joseph from Galena, Ill, about 18 months ago. Soon after his arrival he formed a partnership with Mr Early, the deceased.

Mrd: on Dec 29, at the residence of the bride's father, by Rev Dr McCauley, Wm H Shryock, of Balt, to Miss Marah Thorn, daughter of Henry Thorn, of Wash City.

Richmond, Va, Dec 30. 1-Sally Anderson, who was released from the execution of the death sentence by Judge Underwood, & afterwards rearrested by the Major, was today finally set free. 2-Wm Greanor, one of the oldest tobacco manufacturers in this city, died today. 3-Mosly Clark, born Jun, 1747, died yesterday, aged 121 years & 6 months. He was a wagon driver during the Revolutionary war.

Fifteen years ago a young & brilliant pianist, Mlle Herseilie Rony disappeared from Paris; no trace of her could be obtained. She has just made her appearance again, after 14 years incarceration in a hospital for the insane, where she was detained under a different name. This case is to be brought before the criminal courts.

Thos Dowling, auct, has sold the 2 story frame house of Hezekiah Miller, on Gay st, with lot, 42 feet front & 120 feet deep, to Wm King, for $4,400.

The funeral of Mrs Ann Warne Hill took place yesterday afternoon from the residence of her son, Maj Geo Hill, 160 Bridge st. The remains were incased in a walnut coffin covered with black cloth, on the lid of which was a silver plate inscribed with the name & age of the dec'd. After the services were performed at the house, the interment took place at *Oak Hill Cemetery*.

A

Abbot, 117
Abbott, 69, 81, 117, 201, 280
Abell, 26, 210, 271
Abernethy, 346
Abert, 74
Able, 392
Abner, 18
Abrams, 310
Academy of the Visitation, 134, 212
Acker, 64, 142, 199
Acrofts, 270
Action, 232
Adams, 17, 34, 35, 39, 51, 63, 80, 89, 92, 121, 132, 139, 141, 142, 186, 212, 224, 234, 240, 250, 258, 294, 301, 376, 394, 419, 424, 425
Adamson, 212, 248
Addis, 193
Addison, 9, 24, 25, 98, 134, 250, 262, 339, 361, 405, 416
Adler, 189, 278
Adoe, 99
Adolphus, 330, 351
Agassiz, 3
Agg Farm, 151
Ahera, 155
Ahern, 154
Aigler, 136
Aiken, 162, 196, 253, 272, 301
Ainger, 326
Aken, 343
Akins, 175
Alaska, 90, 97, 276, 385, 407, 426
Albrighton, 31
Albro, 162
Alden, 366
Aldridge, 3
Aldrige, 121
Alexander, 33, 59, 64, 141, 142, 194, 198, 201, 210, 240, 242, 243, 295, 297, 318, 351, 364, 397
Alexandria Cemetery, 203
Algee, 326
Alig, 360
Allabach, 199
Alleg, 15
Allen, 32, 40, 52, 80, 91, 100, 170, 174, 196, 197, 199, 201, 211, 231, 237, 239, 240, 271, 283, 288, 289, 350, 368, 402
Allender, 85
Allison, 342
Allsworth, 339
Allwright, 271
Alman, 91
Alnwick Seminary, 280
Alsier, 121
Alson, 50
Alston, 307
Altemus, 375
Alvord, 118, 168
Alymer, 78
Aman, 400
Ames, 30, 71, 142, 183, 188, 266, 332, 357, 360, 368, 399
Amidon, 377
Amos, 202
Ampey, 253
Amrein, 257, 258
Anchory, 424
Anderson, 20, 79, 89, 136, 192, 224, 230, 237, 264, 268, 296, 318, 323, 362, 407, 411, 415, 430
Andrew, 3, 142
Andrews, 15, 21, 79, 82, 83, 147, 156, 164, 184, 230, 345, 413, 421
Andrus, 25
Angerman, 142
Angermann, 260
Angus, 33, 64
Ansel, 386
Anthon, 350
Anthony, 122, 180, 364, 417
Antisell, 137, 153
Antonette, 133
Appel, 195, 306

Appleby, 17, 44, 80, 90, 319
Appletons, 104
Arapahoe & Cheyenne war, 406
Archibald, 289
Arlington Heights, 334
Armadie, 137
Armburst, 306
Armsted, 422
Armstrong, 93, 139, 226, 228, 257, 273, 280, 289, 322, 365, 393
Arne, 43
Arnold, 32, 96, 122, 147, 164, 198, 327, 349, 401
Arrington, 357
Arrison, 63, 109
Art Gallery, 355
Artes, 297
Arth, 399
Arthur, 109, 228, 249
Arthur's Sealed Enlarged, 388
Asboth, 170
Asburgh, 381
Ashback, 429
Ashburn, 115, 201
Ashby, 6, 222
Ashford, 64, 285, 286, 300
Ashley, 239, 289
Ashton, 160, 241
Aslow, 250
Asten, 15, 170
Astor, 22, 38, 64, 365
Astor House, 54
Atchinson, 108
Atkins, 110, 197
Atkinson, 137, 173
Atlee, 137, 357
Attley, 210
Atwater, 233, 238
Atwell, 405
Auburn, 352
Audubon, 384
Augur, 294
Aujac, 255
Auld, 247
Aulick, 141, 174, 176, 192

Austin, 2, 153, 324, 389, 399, 413
Avallon, 18
Avalon, 377
Avers, 238
Avireth, 211
Axtell, 223, 240
Aykroyd, 376
Aylmer, 103, 210
Ayres, 213, 338
Azadia/Axadia, 23

B

B__zeholz, 411
B_iggins, 423
Babcock, 230, 326, 384
Bache, 3, 61, 411
Backus, 402
Bacon, 136, 142, 171, 172, 301
Badeau, 370, 384
Baden, 65
Baiel, 411
Bailey, 44, 77, 117, 121, 142, 146, 153, 171, 238, 296, 306, 337, 351, 359, 423
Bain, 386
Bainbridge, 112
Baine, 56
Baird, 321, 363
Baiteman, 378
Bake, 236
Bakeman, 397
Baker, 43, 49, 56, 94, 99, 118, 121, 124, 137, 140, 142, 200, 211, 245, 257, 273, 279, 281, 311, 321, 323, 324, 357, 358, 364, 397, 401, 422
Bakers, 372
Baldason, 284
Baldwin, 23, 71, 83, 84, 118, 142, 199, 215, 332, 391, 412
Ball, 5, 82, 91, 113, 115, 133, 141, 166, 210, 218, 345, 387, 394, 417, 426
Ballantine, 193
Ballantyne, 112, 206, 247, 266, 327
Ballard, 130
Ballenger, 41, 203
Ballentyne, 193

Ballew, 254
Ballinger, 291
Balloch, 250, 294, 398
Ballou, 259
Balmain, 221, 224
Balt flood, 242, 245
Bamberger, 222
Banes, 250
Bang, 192
Bangs, 72
Bankhead, 316, 322
Banks, 198, 251
Bannister, 26
Bannon, 13, 20, 42, 176, 379, 424
Banres, 398
Barbee, 186
Barber, 147, 378
Barbour, 8, 87, 117, 141, 166, 178, 189, 241
Barcalow, 238
Barclay, 10, 11, 135, 224, 302, 306, 424
Barinds, 289
Baring, 385
Bark, 33
bark **Cortland**, 192
bark **Gangenolf**, 63
bark **Rover**, 4
Barker, 58, 101, 114, 121, 135, 143, 164, 219, 264, 293, 332, 376, 399, 409
Barlow, 350
Barmore, 191
Barnabe, 55
Barnaclo, 73, 150, 272, 348, 358, 395
Barnard, 44
Barnes, 142, 200, 258, 262, 264, 265, 270, 288, 321, 375
Barnett, 187
Barney, 73, 79
Barnum, 72, 160, 178, 330
Baron, 184
Barquera, 253
Barr, 92, 164, 327
Barrand, 66
Barrell, 233
Barret, 120, 162, 249

Barrett, 24, 59, 75, 77, 192, 256, 325, 327, 339, 364, 371, 392
Barron, 30
Barry, 142, 171, 398
Barth, 326
Bartholomew, 86
Bartholow, 212
Bartlett, 2, 80, 122, 214, 237, 325, 378, 427
Bartley, 332
Barton, 30, 173, 178, 375
Bascom, 143, 147
Bass, 249
Bassett, 290
Bastianelli, 212
Batchelder, 249, 300, 425
Batchelor, 358
Bateman, 2
Bates, 33, 90, 132, 142, 187, 274, 279, 339, 355, 359
Bath, 256
Batham, 182
Batholow, 348
Batione, 357
Batson, 319
Battery Woods, 308
Baucker, 289
Bauers, 400
Baugh, 306
Baugher, 119
Baukhages, 183
Baum, 18, 346
Bauman, 21, 214, 223, 256
Baumann, 163, 277
Baune, 264
Baxter, 72, 353
Bayard, 255, 276
Bayer, 273
Bayley, 83, 152, 249, 375, 412
Bayliss, 141, 201, 333
Bayly, 150, 223, 405
Bayne, 257, 389
Bazin, 16
Beach, 92, 122, 198, 235, 345
Beale, 81, 311, 372

Beall, 8, 73, 111, 136, 142, 243, 291, 323, 410
Beall's Manor, 73
Bean, 231, 327, 344, 402, 408
Bear, 369
Beard, 142, 264, 271, 285, 287, 421
Beardsley, 121, 122, 354, 358
Beare, 126
Beasley, 111
Beatty, 87, 94
Beaufela, 323
Beaugardes, 268
Beaumont, 216
Beauregard, 311
Beavans, 143
Beaver Dam, 13
Bebb, 45
Beck, 226, 345, 402
Beckar, 208
Beckart, 402
Beckenbaugh, 194
Becker, 254, 271
Beckert, 344
Becket, 60
Beckham, 344
Beckley, 197, 308, 402
Beckwith, 127, 191, 335
Beebe, 275, 310
Beech, 35
Beecher, 43, 316, 322
Behrend, 411
Behrins, 202, 229
Belger, 133, 386
Belie, 199
Bell, 57, 81, 97, 108, 111, 114, 122, 152, 197, 202, 210, 224, 232, 253, 268, 285, 289, 290, 325, 364
Bell Farm, 284
Belle, 199
Belle Haven, 334
Belle Isle plantation, 422
Bellevue, 357
Bellinger, 214
Bellis, 137
Bello, 402

Belmont, 147, 301
Belt, 108, 153, 164, 209, 213, 388
Beman, 294
Bemas, 380
Bemis, 314
Bencock, 238
Bender, 253, 411
Benedict, 24, 350
Bennett, 91, 113, 127, 147, 179, 256, 264, 271, 309, 424
Benning, 59, 356, 379
Benson, 126, 142, 198, 402
Bent's Fort, 165
Bentley, 167, 270
Benton, 103, 335
Berg, 191, 402
Bergfeld, 354
Berins, 400
Berkeley, 118, 122
Berkley, 292, 378
Berner, 337
Berret, 56, 390
Berrigan, 391
Berry, 13, 37, 130, 131, 142, 156, 189, 204, 219, 255, 267, 342, 362
Berryer, 59, 401, 417
Berryhill, 257
Berryman, 28, 250
Berwick, 290
Beslan, 262
Best, 372
Bester, 258
Bestor, 140, 143, 334
Bethel, 413
Betts, 83, 350, 364
Betz, 400, 402
Bevan, 393, 400
Beveridge, 33, 142, 402
Bey, 129
Beyer, 260, 334
Biancini, 313
Biddie, 103
Biddle, 87
Biden, 245
Bidwell, 15, 219

Bielby, 118
Big Spring Mill, 61
Bigby, 15
Bigelow, 7, 66, 121
Bigger, 41
Biggins, 270, 393, 405
Bigler, 235
Bigley, 408, 409
Biglin, 326
Billings, 30, 105
Billow, 368
Bincher, 402
Binckley, 17, 220, 330
Bing, 329
Binning, 58
Binninger, 265
Binoe, 274
Birch, 53, 293
Bird, 46, 189
Birge, 135
Bishop, 32, 49, 143, 290
Bishop of Buffalo, 371
Bissell, 79
Bissett, 194
Bitner, 378
Bittenger, 298
Bittinger, 159
Black, 119, 220
black bass, 228
Blackburn, 91, 138
Blackford, 360
Blackley, 310
Blacklock, 394
Blackman, 137
Blackwell, 367
Bladen, 96
Blagden, 25, 30, 33, 54, 140, 141, 327
Blain, 278
Blaine, 250
Blair, 14, 141, 173, 198, 202, 223, 233, 235, 241, 261, 324, 347, 369, 416
Blake, 29, 30, 54, 56, 82, 88, 97, 142, 213, 241, 258, 293, 333, 367, 403
Blakely, 177
Blan, 323

Blanchard, 93, 141, 192, 261, 295
Blaney, 109
Bleecker, 15, 170, 216
Bleifus, 392
Blenet, 301
Bletz, 123
Bligh, 263, 385
Bliss, 51, 117, 360
Bloch, 247
Block, 104
Blodgett, 8, 220, 326
Blondon, 142
Bloom, 41, 306
Bloomer, 358
Bloomgart, 130
Blossom, 121
Blount, 40
Blout, 60
Blumenburg, 358
Blundon, 295
Bly, 96
Boag, 221
Board of Police, 4, 18, 52, 81, 186, 210, 250, 334, 349, 368, 385, 392, 394, 405, 411, 418
Boardman, 140
Boarman, 57, 83, 138, 402
boat **Hamilton**, 381
boat **Little Western**, 197
boat **Union**, 381
Bock, 115
Bodfish, 249
Boehmler, 377
Boffocker, 326
Bogan, 32, 113, 142
Bogert, 406
Boggs, 142
Bogue, 19, 43, 82, 125, 181, 220, 334, 339
Bogy, 1
Boher, 315
Bohlayer, 210, 423
Bohrer, 21, 79, 109, 162, 172, 384
Boisseau, 172
Bokel, 360

Bolling Hall, 312
Bolton, 43
Bombay, 253
Bomford, 372
Bonaparte, 48, 113, 134, 175, 302
Bond, 20, 99, 142, 156, 172, 303, 381
Bonnell, 180
Bonner, 147
Boon, 319
Boone, 131, 199, 238, 266, 272, 318
Booth, 42, 71, 88, 248, 270, 295
Boothby, 43
Bopp, 172
Borden, 18, 52, 236, 246, 250, 393
Borland, 16, 24, 181
Borrows, 142
Bosbyshell, 310
Boss, 181
Bossett, 327
Bossier, 251
Boston, 197, 359
Bosts, 64
Boswell, 136, 270, 324, 348
Boteler, 141, 257
Boudine, 279
Bouie, 197
Bouldin, 106
Boulguy, 423
Bourke, 289
Bowen, 123, 154, 156, 186, 189, 197, 199, 242, 272, 276, 297, 350, 377, 387, 400
Bower, 370
Bowers, 229, 262, 290
Bowie, 5, 64, 236, 273, 303, 307, 341, 357, 405, 412
Bowie's Purchase, 175
Bowling, 375
Bowman, 96, 322
Bowne, 350
Boyce, 64
Boyd, 7, 36, 86, 110, 205, 334
Boyden, 132, 211
Boyer, 236
Boyle, 18, 20, 37, 52, 54, 64, 102, 142, 159, 173, 208, 223, 236, 311, 334, 360, 378, 384, 387, 390, 394, 402, 413, 421
Boynton, 122, 147, 264, 298, 327, 360, 362
Brackenridge, 162
Bracker, 95
Bradbury, 15, 272, 352
Bradford, 83, 87, 94, 188, 272, 374, 386
Bradley, 3, 16, 24, 33, 67, 71, 92, 122, 130, 136, 142, 151, 196, 200, 254, 291, 298, 310, 320, 323, 337, 367, 371
Brady, 192, 200, 227, 256, 340, 350, 398, 402, 422
Bragazzi, 400
Bragg, 249
Braine, 12, 152
Braman, 279
Bramhall, 257
Branaugh, 65
Brand, 322, 378
Brandengeyer, 368
Brandner, 402
Brandon, 44
Branning, 330
Branson, 184, 402
Brant, 306
Brashahan, 136
Bravo, 350
Brawner, 62
Braxton, 122, 320
Bray, 136
Brayden, 289
Brayfield, 412
Brayley, 101
Brecker, 55
Breckinridge, 400
Breen, 418
Brennan, 115, 283, 400
Brenner, 155
Brent, 16, 29, 30, 54, 63, 100, 140, 210, 212, 213, 220, 255, 258, 306, 333, 403
Brentwood, 170
Bret, 266

Brett, 142, 247, 279
Brewer, 63, 320, 349, 354, 381
Brewster, 52, 360, 413
Brice, 62, 82
Brick House Farm, 182
Bridgeman, 250
Bridget, 142
Bridley, 278
Brielmayer, 178
Brien, 219
Brier Hill, 383
brig **Amherst**, 101
brig **Washington**, 192
Briggeman, 21
Briggerman, 394, 402
Briggs, 289, 369, 408
Brigham, 269
Brigham Young, 114
Bright, 215, 254, 310, 408
Brightwell, 367
Brightwood, 202
Brisbois, 289
Briscoe, 119, 225
Brissey, 348
Bristol, 359
Britt, 23
Britton, 11, 142
Broadhead, 69, 319
Brock, 73, 381
Brockman, 45
Broderick, 187, 200, 250
Brodhead, 174, 295
Brokenborough, 13
Bronaugh, 42, 356
Bronson, 255
Bronte, 183
Brooke, 98, 124, 357, 372, 393
Brookefield, 273
Brookeville Academy, 232
Brookfield, 303
Brooks, 49, 88, 100, 108, 173, 198, 276, 352, 416
Bropley, 386
Brosnan, 250, 365
Bross, 5

Brothers of the Christian Schools, 208
Brough, 3, 192
Brougham, 148, 266
Broughan, 81
Broughton, 400
Brours, 180
Brown, 1, 8, 13, 19, 24, 32, 33, 53, 54, 55, 72, 75, 80, 85, 88, 99, 103, 105, 109, 111, 117, 128, 132, 136, 141, 142, 143, 147, 149, 151, 154, 156, 159, 179, 182, 195, 196, 197, 199, 203, 204, 213, 214, 219, 233, 236, 240, 256, 261, 264, 265, 268, 270, 272, 274, 287, 288, 295, 304, 306, 313, 320, 325, 330, 339, 341, 343, 348, 360, 362, 364, 369, 378, 392, 394, 398, 404, 405, 418, 421
Browne, 3, 4, 24, 32, 78, 179, 257
Browner, 184
Browning, 79, 105, 142, 161, 183, 198, 209, 224, 289, 325, 350
Brownlow, 109
Bruce, 36, 68, 287
Bruckheimer, 72
Brunai, 272
Brundage, 223
Brunet, 177
Brunto, 43
Brush, 39, 264, 296
Brushwood Lodge, 261
Bryan, 103, 131, 141, 334, 368
Bryson, 387
Buchanan, 157, 166, 167, 169, 181, 310, 351
Bucher, 213
Buchler, 400
Buchnan, 181
Buck, 74, 364
Buckalew, 243
Buckey, 45, 129, 184, 185, 233, 293
Buckingham, 180, 325
Buckley, 104, 109, 196, 270
Buckner, 74, 137
Bucks, 372
Buckwalter, 257

Budd's Ferry, 349
Buehler, 411
Buel, 32, 128, 281
<u>Buel Hall</u>, 281
Buell, 8, 17, 108
Buerger, 361
Buffington, 243
Buhler, 104
Bulfinch, 3
Bulger, 111
Bulkley, 142
Bull, 44, 104
Bullett, 170
Bullis, 253
Bullitt, 349
Bullock, 216, 347, 372, 408
Bulwer, 252, 367
Bundy, 4, 142
Bunker, 297, 346, 411
Burbank, 288
Burch, 21, 343, 357, 416
Burchard, 402
Burche, 142
Burchell, 114, 118, 142
Burdett, 219, 421
Burdette, 143
Burdick, 292
Burgdorf, 338, 397
Burgee, 156
Burgett, 413
Burk, 385
Burke, 127, 191, 192, 218, 306, 346, 353
Burkhardt, 3
Burlingame, 166
Burnell, 345, 405
Burnett, 219, 324
Burnham, 240
Burnman, 10
Burns, 27, 70, 115, 153, 192, 237, 272, 282, 345, 373, 374, 385, 391, 408
Burnside, 93, 218, 221
Burnstead, 257
Burr, 63, 203, 213, 276, 334, 346, 399, 415, 421
Burrass, 119

Burrell, 18, 241
Burrett, 173
Burridge, 306
Burrington, 121
Burritt, 175
Burroughs, 46, 279, 423
Burrow, 382
Burrows, 238
Burt, 56, 80, 142
Burton, 92, 94, 282, 342, 391
Buscher, 402
Bush, 275, 359, 388
Busher, 183
Bushnell, 208
Busk, 11
Buss, 95
Busteed, 3, 5, 47
Butler, 11, 32, 83, 104, 105, 111, 113, 132, 191, 284, 312, 361, 376, 385
Butt, 75, 233
Butts, 395
Buzzard's Point, 392
Buzzer, 39
Byer, 394
Byrd, 421
Byrkett, 293
Byrne, 81, 135, 163, 172, 199, 404, 425
Byrnes, 110, 340, 385
Byron, 102, 176

C

Cabell, 393
Cabot, 276
Cadell, 266
Cady, 392
Cagger, 214, 220
Cahenover, 301
Cahoon, 137
Cake, 419
Caldwell, 12, 20, 35, 93, 136, 272, 277, 417
Calhoun, 389
Call, 324, 360, 419
Callaghan, 107, 128
Callahan, 143, 177, 205, 225, 259

Callan, 10, 12, 15, 29, 63, 80, 93, 114, 126, 140, 158, 212, 258, 272, 333, 337, 348, 367, 403
Callen, 33
Calvert, 18, 38, 155, 206, 298, 315, 379, 382
Cambreleng, 350
Camels, 46
Cameron, 8, 90, 132, 219, 264, 398
Cameronia, 393
Cammack, 17, 143, 181
Camp, 222
Camp Cook, 159
Camp Supply, 398
Camp Vere, 46
Campbell, 22, 26, 91, 116, 122, 143, 200, 230, 258, 331, 355, 356, 357, 378, 380, 391, 397, 413
Campion, 381
Canby, 134, 268, 275, 366
Candia, 265
Candy, 268
Cane, 428
Cann, 280
Cannon, 72
Cantwell, 418
Capehart, 368
Caperton, 208, 307
Capin, 92
Cappenger, 24
Capron, 83, 283
Captiol Hill, 125
Carbery, 29
cardinals, 105
Carey, 58, 283, 357, 389, 411
Carlin, 93, 174, 385
Carline, 343
Carlisle, 54, 56, 141, 296, 349
Carlton, 174, 392
Carm, 254
Carmelite Convent, 358
Carmony, 26
Carne, 210
Carney, 134, 329
Carothers, 80

Carpenter, 15, 31, 115, 133, 250, 306, 310, 316, 322, 368, 408
Carples, 358
Carr, 87, 108, 109, 190, 245, 315, 375
Carrack, 323
Carrico, 59, 75
Carrigan, 52
Carrington, 25, 100, 119, 141, 154, 184, 420
Carroll, 4, 15, 17, 107, 116, 126, 158, 173, 186, 196, 199, 212, 242, 260, 275, 282, 314, 348, 364, 373, 412
Carroll Mansion, 314
Carroll Place, 386
Carson, 165, 297, 300
Carswell, 139
Carter, 14, 16, 17, 45, 58, 64, 65, 86, 91, 96, 143, 289, 350, 359, 378
Cartter, 25, 33, 54, 63, 71, 75, 86, 89, 95, 99, 100, 128, 152, 171, 360, 404
Cartwright, 10
Caruis, 100
Carusi, 17, 25, 67, 83, 143, 152, 211, 359, 401
Carver, 218
Cary, 176, 177, 360, 402
Case, 93, 297
Casey, 239, 253, 324
Cash, 118, 357
Cashell, 328
Caskie, 325
Casparis, 76, 402
Cass, 34
Cassady, 380
Cassel, 135
Cassell, 181, 224
Casserly, 210
Cassidy, 173
Cassin, 111, 172, 224, 263, 416
Castel, 214
Castello, 17
Castle, 126
Castle Hill, 132
Castleman, 143, 199
Cathcart, 15, 135, 225

Catholic Cemetery, 231
Caton, 150, 171, 239
Caulfield, 423
Caulk, 369
Cavanaugh, 426
Cave Hill Cemetery, 130, 363
Caziarc, 268
Cedar Grove, 42
Cedar Hill, 294, 382
Cedar Hill Cemetery, 294
Cedar Hill farm, 402
Centner, 400
Centre Market House, 201
Chace, 80
Chadwick, 33, 141, 272, 332, 385
Chaffee, 9, 290
Chamberain, 327
Chamberlain, 115, 271
Chamberlin, 408
Chambers, 89, 150, 174, 277, 278, 290, 320
Champlin, 189, 271
Chance, 41, 159
Chance & Chance Enlarged, 251
Chancy, 10, 17
Chandler, 11, 17, 155, 324, 351
Chapin, 78, 377
Chapman, 42, 123, 212, 221, 264, 292, 300
Chappelle, 283
Charleton, 143
Chase, 39, 146, 198, 276, 311, 416
Cheesman, 243
Cheever, 126
Cheltenham, 273, 303, 357
Cheney, 80, 210
Chenoweth, 352
Cherry, 376
Cheseline, 172
Chesley, 297
Chesley property, 124, 128
Chessaur, 314
Chessem, 43
Chessman, 336
Chester, 91, 122, 197, 256, 361

Chestnut, 81, 333
Chevalier, 88
Chevallie, 96
Chew, 51, 107, 273, 362, 388
Cheyenne Indians, 58
Children's Party, 427
Childs, 6, 81, 326, 346, 347
Chilson, 180
Chilton, 212
Chinn, 104
Chipman, 119, 148
Chippewa Chief, 207
Chisein, 181
Chisholm, 197
Chism, 315
Chittenden, 192
Chivington, 407
Chorpenning, 349
Choteau, 306
Chrisman, 87, 297
Christ Church, 189
Christian, 324
Christman, 402
Christmas, 301
Chubbeck, 392
Church, 143, 277, 395
Church Swamp, 308
Churchill, 352
Ciaflin, 130
Cissel, 97
Cissell, 63
Clabaugh, 208
Claflin, 345
Clagett, 140, 233, 348, 357, 422
Claggett, 33, 261
Clampit, 206
Clampitt, 333
Clapp, 259
Clark, 10, 15, 24, 31, 51, 91, 92, 94, 109, 116, 122, 137, 143, 181, 184, 194, 237, 241, 243, 249, 257, 261, 273, 274, 300, 307, 320, 344, 347, 353, 357, 358, 360, 381, 383, 385, 394, 408, 415, 423, 430
Clark Mills, 204

Clarke, 14, 33, 64, 87, 135, 136, 163, 187, 190, 191, 194, 197, 212, 251, 282, 312, 322, 353, 379, 388, 415
Clarkson, 81
Clarrisson, 187
Clarvoe, 23
Clary, 139, 194
Clawson, 64, 87, 285
Clay, 44, 49, 97, 133, 264, 416
Clayton, 111, 143, 315, 340, 407
Cleary, 19, 159, 199, 208, 255
Cleaver, 121
Clemens, 310
Clement, 161
Clements, 65, 128, 137, 264, 265, 301, 365
Clementson, 366
Clemm, 39
Clendenin, 113
Clendening, 95
Clephane, 29, 32, 61, 293
Clepper, 297
clerk, 313
Cleveland, 213
Clifford, 273, 356, 381
Clifton, 234
Clinkett, 237
Clinton, 417
Clokey, 169, 369, 385
Close, 13, 135, 151
Closs, 135
Clotworthy, 363
Cluberla, 26
Clum, 274
Cluss, 143, 260
Clymer, 143
Coates, 284
Coats, 60
Cobb, 3, 121, 335, 341
Cobleigh, 124
Coburn, 240, 327, 328
Cochran, 121, 141, 245, 370, 396
Cochrane, 230, 276
Cock, 268, 355, 356
Cockpit Point, 255

Cockpit Point Fishery, 255
Coff__e, 273
Coffee, 125, 382
Coffin, 197
Cogan, 21
Coghan, 224
Cohen, 80, 309, 393
Coit, 4
Colbran, 383
Colburn, 18
Colby, 5, 8, 351, 389, 421
Coldwell, 116, 123, 351, 414
Cole, 4, 39, 52, 378, 393, 402
Coleman, 133, 210, 292, 354, 402
Colemen, 97
Coles, 211
Colett, 226
Colfax, 137, 310, 367, 382
Colgan, 286, 402
Colifax, 417
Coliwell, 196
Collana, 340
Colledge, 250
Collen, 272
Collier, 210
Collington, 135
Collingwood, 193
Collins, 4, 23, 25, 59, 61, 65, 178, 199, 208, 210, 219, 333, 393
Collison, 136
Collum, 286
Colson, 330
Colt, 271, 273, 339
Colter, 368
Coltman, 141, 146
Colton, 354
Columbia Hospital, 64
Columbian College, 111, 176, 197, 200
Colwell, 200, 345
Combe, 102
Combs, 26, 28, 49, 194, 261
Comfort, 41
Comings, 289
Commager, 153
Comstock, 115, 370

Conant, 192, 307
Condie, 137
Condon, 353
Congressional Burying Ground, 116, 226, 373
Congressional Cemetery, 39, 71, 83, 91, 120, 185, 231, 236, 309, 339, 405
Conjurors Defeated, 344
Conklin, 193
Conkling, 216
Conlan, 116, 394
Conley, 101, 268, 313
Conn, 28
Connell, 394
Connelly, 5, 300, 368
Connely, 411
Conner, 129, 153, 223, 301, 385
Connett, 293
Connick, 51
Connolly, 133, 178, 256, 331
Connor, 93, 214, 315, 334, 394, 413
Connors, 303
Conrad, 137, 366
Conron, 341
Conroy, 148, 197, 385
Constadt, 404
Contee, 51, 303, 346, 388, 403
Conway, 187, 368, 421
Cook, 19, 34, 63, 100, 178, 212, 218, 220, 261, 306, 310, 394, 416
Cooke, 32, 46, 48, 199, 214, 304, 323, 360, 368, 375
Cookey, 134
Cookley, 241
Cooks, 141, 413
Cool, 207, 214
Cooley, 1, 306
Coolsey, 352
Coombs, 33, 68, 71, 121, 202, 249, 302, 306, 307, 361, 387
Coomes, 358
Cooney, 139
Cooper, 10, 40, 41, 77, 148, 214, 232, 306
Copeland, 132, 293
Copley, 391
Copp, 143
Coppinger, 78
Copps, 402
Corbet, 357, 368
Corbin, 73, 186
Corcoran, 18, 53, 54, 56, 70, 82, 117, 141, 143, 154, 155, 179, 195, 205, 285
Corcran, 393
Corday, 306
Cordell, 271
Cordwell, 326
Corigan, 393
Corley, 355, 356, 364
Cornell, 368
Cornesser, 173
Corning, 121, 281, 319
Cornley, 41
Corrigan, 381
Corry, 422
Corse, 84, 355
Corss, 84
Cortlan, 236, 244, 398
Corwin, 121, 353
Corydon, 17
Cosgrove, 323
Coskery, 208
Costello, 413
Cottage Grove, 197
Cotter, 365
Cotton, 219
Cottrell, 153
Coulter, 271, 330
Counts, 364
Courtney, 350
Couse, 122
Cover, 173
Covington, 377
Cowes, 179
Cowling, 6, 37, 320
Cox, 2, 14, 18, 28, 63, 93, 117, 121, 126, 129, 137, 143, 179, 204, 207, 212, 221, 232, 235, 236, 240, 250, 258, 345, 360, 362

Coyle, 33, 125, 204, 253, 262, 300, 305, 333
Crabtree, 118, 159, 167, 296
Crafton, 354
Cragen, 65
Cragin, 91, 172, 359
Craig, 63
Crain, 207, 273, 303
Crampton, 293
Cranch, 8, 314, 373
Crane, 262, 301, 382, 400
Crater, 289
Craton, 63
Crauford, 177
Craufurd, 91
Craven, 43, 77
Crawford, 1, 25, 138, 143, 201, 240, 257, 379, 408
Crawshay, 47
Creecy, 360, 389, 391, 423
Creighton, 348, 424
<u>Cremona violins</u>, 209
Crendiropulo, 197
Criminal Court-Judge Olin, 2, 4, 7, 8, 9, 13, 14, 17, 97
Crindall, 192
Cripps, 143
Crismond, 95
Crist, 427
Crockett, 318
Crockston, 151
Crogan, 170
Croghan, 81, 176, 206
Crogon, 367
Crolly, 199
Cromwell, 183, 212
Cronice, 13
Cronin, 16, 18, 187
Crook, 5
Crooks, 359
Cropley, 1, 27, 213, 228
Crosby, 62, 213, 247, 354, 358
Cross, 21, 23, 37, 46, 47, 59, 70, 172, 181, 205, 339
Crossley, 430

Crossly, 391
Crossman, 360
Crossty, 194
Crouse, 39, 129
Crowley, 46, 133, 157
Crown, 52, 73, 223, 243, 245, 264, 270, 339, 389
Cruikshank, 345
Cruishank, 300
Cruit, 143, 313
Crumnut, 73
Crump, 295, 399
Cruse, 88
Crutchett, 148, 155
Crutchett Cottage, 148
Crutchfield, 369
Cruttenden, 139
Cruzat, 60
Cudlipp, 341
Cuittenden, 154
Culbertson, 320
Culinan, 147
Cull, 73, 80, 96, 101, 272
Cullen, 282, 416
Cullinan, 64, 400
Cullinane, 120
Cullom, 118
Culver, 12, 59, 80, 83, 322
<u>Cumberland Valley Institute</u>, 281
Cumiskey, 400
Cummings, 20, 240, 249, 272, 310, 398, 416
Cummins, 397
Cummisky, 402
Cunningam, 143
Cunningham, 65, 66, 171, 214, 338, 381, 391, 409
Cuppy, 240, 243
Curd, 286
Curran, 94
Curry, 179, 192
Curtis, 55, 113, 114, 156, 214, 330, 425
Cushing, 215, 359, 390
Cushman, 48, 167
Custar, 34

Custer, 19, 398, 404
Custis, 8, 18, 197, 244, 420
Cutler, 153, 345
cutter **Lawrence**, 235
cutter **Noesha**, 50
cutter **Northerner**, 51
Cutting, 9, 18, 59, 350
Cutts, 56, 354
Cuyler, 297
Cypress Hills Cemetery, 256

D

d'Orbigny, 306
D'Ourches, 90
Dack, 297
Daggett, 115
Dahlgren, 163, 249
Daiger, 208
Dailey, 283, 394
Daily, 34, 52, 93, 95, 210
Dakin, 63
Dale, 235
Dall, 326
Dallenger, 171
Dalrymple, 283
Dalton, 136, 406
Daly, 134
Dana, 34, 80, 95
Dandy, 269
Dane, 11, 421
Danenhower, 143
Daniel, 371
Daniels, 17, 289, 353
Dansch, 171
Darbey, 381
Darby, 65, 79, 143, 298, 393
Darity, 4
Darlington, 23, 178
Darnall, 114
Darrah, 289
Darrow, 109
Darwart, 285
Dater, 348
Daughton, 65
Dausch, 412, 413

Davenport, 12, 93, 135, 322, 326
David, 306
Davidge, 28, 100, 141, 156, 414
Davidson, 83, 115, 143, 351, 357, 359, 410
Davies, 152, 350
Davis, 10, 11, 14, 21, 24, 29, 32, 61, 65, 80, 86, 90, 95, 97, 103, 118, 120, 135, 137, 143, 156, 162, 169, 170, 172, 173, 178, 182, 187, 188, 194, 196, 198, 204, 221, 224, 232, 233, 238, 245, 258, 271, 285, 287, 297, 298, 304, 322, 333, 361, 367, 396, 416, 421, 428, 429
Davison, 13, 194, 418
Dawes, 348, 411
Dawson, 91, 198, 232
Day, 3, 24, 229, 258, 322
De Ahra, 358
de Berg, 95
De Camp, 226
De Cover, 309
De Frees, 212
De Hass, 140
de Irisor_i, 178
De Leon, 46
de Morny, 48
de Pourtales, 367
De Puebla, 210
De Rinzie, 313
de Seato, 48
De Selding, 25
De Vaughan, 412
De Vaughn, 357
De Waldeck, 112
De Wolf, 187, 194
De Wolff, 1
De Wulf, 283, 360
Deacon, 157
Deakins, 373
Dean, 77, 80, 92, 274, 325
Dearman, 364
DeAtley, 402
Debant, 143
Debauvais, 216

Decamp, 183
Decker, 121
Deckert, 159, 368
decorating the graves, 130
Dederick, 74
Deeble, 122, 162
Deely, 60, 135
Deering, 246
Deeter, 284
Deford, 245
Defrees, 293, 417
Degges, 180
DeHaas, 105
Deinhardt, 344
Deitrich, 360
Deitz, 58
Delacroix, 224
Delafield, 141
Delaney, 249, 342, 359
Delano, 380
Delaware, 366
Delbert, 324
Dell, 402
Delwig, 77
Dement, 63, 95, 172
Demeritt, 80, 426
Demick, 143
Demonet, 123, 131
Demonett, 126
Dempsey, 15, 143, 192
Denham, 37, 360
Denhane, 88
Denig, 345
Denin, 173
Denison, 425
Denman, 190
Denmead, 401
Dennett, 369
Dennis, 320
Dennison, 179, 249
Dent, 39, 133, 229
Denver, 1, 141
Denville, 171
Depeyster, 160
Depro, 172, 364

Depue, 181
Dernelman, 60
Derrick, 87
Deschamps, 430
Desher, 249
Detmold, 415
Deuer, 170
Deufel, 359, 375
DeVaughan, 246, 260
Devaughn, 186
Develin, 42, 214, 350
Devine, 241
Devinney, 410
Devlin, 214
Devoe, 307, 381
Dewdney, 160
Dewees, 221, 376
Dewey, 3
DeWolf, 198
DeWolff, 143
Dexer, 148
Dezeotell, 364
Di__ick, 319
Diarseli, 427
Dias, 97
Dibble, 310
Dice, 274, 341
Dick, 10, 261
Dickens, 1, 34, 35, 39, 44, 48, 52, 59,
   71, 95, 104, 109, 114, 118, 127, 163,
   252, 299, 374, 426, 428, 429
Dickerson, 55
Dickett, 413
Dickey, 239, 243, 274
Dickins, 37
Dickinson, 96, 250, 312
Dicks, 8
Dickson, 143, 402
Dier, 424
Dietrich, 136
Dietrick, 172
Diets, 277
Digg, 17
Diggs, 81, 293, 392
Dikeman, 141

446

Dill, 260, 400
Dillon, 127, 244
Dimmitt, 330
Dimond, 308
Dingman, 425
Dinin, 49
Direny, 413
Dirning, 392
Discoll, 366
Dissosway, 221
Distin, 192
Districht, 378
Ditch, 249
Dix, 50, 124
Dixon, 53, 80, 95, 99, 140, 146, 181, 283
Dixon's tavern, 405
Dobbins, 40
Dobler, 66
Dockery, 419
Dodd, 4, 179
Dodds, 308
Dodge, 49, 122, 235, 258, 382, 402
Dodson, 100, 118, 143, 196
Doherty, 212
Dole, 1, 123, 139, 143
Dolen, 30
Domines, 409
Donahue, 121, 288, 393
Donald's Grove, 175
Donaldson, 64, 67, 143, 394
Donegan, 16
Donly, 288
Donn, 21, 34, 73, 78, 172, 402
Donnaly, 340
Donnelly, 213, 218, 228, 418
Donoghue, 363
Donohoe, 422
Donohue, 350
Donovan, 91, 192
Doolittle, 167, 360
Doran, 190, 396
Dorges, 337, 342
Dorman, 1, 363
Dorn, 186
Dornan, 364

Dorrs, 147
Dorsett, 140, 405
Dorsey, 7, 13, 18, 103, 148, 196, 270
Dotts, 322
Doty, 179, 288
Doubleday, 273
Dougal, 143, 371, 408
Dougall, 44, 143
Dougalss, 300
Dougans, 241
Dougherty, 95, 201, 354
Douglas, 71, 73, 342, 400
Douglas Row, 400
Douglass, 5, 88, 100, 121, 160, 199, 272
Dove, 59, 62, 385, 403
Dover, 257
Dow, 364
Dowdell, 282
Dowel, 295
Dowling, 16, 21, 27, 36, 91, 124, 128,
    135, 158, 160, 176, 185, 200, 207,
    220, 236, 259, 263, 274, 275, 293,
    352, 400, 424, 431
Downey, 155, 191, 192, 221
Downing, 105, 199, 213, 392, 428
Downman, 108, 285
Downs, 261
Doyle, 52, 66, 112, 220, 282, 393
Drabell, 93
Draine, 180
Drake, 77, 161, 315, 369
Draper, 137, 421
Drayton, 59, 340
Dremman, 354
Drenham, 180
dressing her for burial, 269
Drew, 212, 244, 341
Drewry, 297
Drienhofer, 308
Dries, 344
Drinkhouse, 105, 302, 361
Driscoll, 346
Driver, 232
Droop, 143, 279
Drummond, 251

Drury, 15, 43, 160, 196, 200, 413
Dryer, 219
Du Hawel, 303
Dubant, 168, 206, 224, 376, 411
Dubois, 121, 224
Duckett, 312
Dudley, 104
Duff, 48
Duffield, 202
Duffin, 60
Duffy, 295, 301, 405
DuFief, 328
Duggan, 283, 426
Duggen, 39
Duhamel, 3, 103
Duhigg, 173
Duke, 355
Dulaney, 357
Dulany, 221
Duley, 155
Dull, 63
Dumas, 17, 42, 161
Dumpter, 115
Duncan, 11, 13, 24, 80, 81, 343
Duncanson, 118, 171, 279, 373
Dundas, 225
Dungan, 334, 360
Dunham, 121
Dunlap, 141, 143, 262, 314
Dunles, 368
Dunlop, 54, 110, 150, 151, 305, 333
Dunn, 18, 143, 152, 177, 254, 283, 297, 339, 392
Dunne, 426
Dunning, 2
Dupree, 330
Dupuy, 279
Durand, 87, 424
Durant, 141
Durham, 174, 181, 288
Durid, 415
Dutch, 403
Dutton, 68, 194, 297
Duval, 6, 49, 110, 111, 359

Duvall, 6, 14, 30, 40, 135, 175, 242, 245, 359, 376
Dwinelle, 200
Dworak, 136
Dwyer, 244
Dye, 297
Dyer, 57, 62, 64, 68, 83, 96, 130, 138, 200, 208, 210, 276, 346, 354
Dygan, 303
Dyson, 122

E

Eagan, 262, 354, 428
Eagles, 277
Eames, 301
Eardley, 32
Earl of Sandwich, 322
Earle, 367
Earley, 430
Early, 83, 374
earrings, 347
Easby, 172, 212, 221, 236
East Capitol barracks, 84
Eastman, 215
Eaton, 32, 59, 62, 146, 147, 153, 183, 412
Ebaugh, 118, 293
Ebbinghouse, 362
Ebel, 260
Eber, 230
Eberly, 143
Ebert, 136
Echols, 16, 17, 24, 45, 215
Eckelman, 93
Eckels, 120, 162, 187
Eckert, 297
Eckhard, 219
Eckloff, 68, 121, 207, 208, 210, 236
Eckly, 71
Eddie, 65, 86, 88, 103, 391
Eddins, 5
Eddy, 243, 414
Edelen, 184
Edelin, 119, 154, 214, 323, 353, 411
Edes, 202, 340, 360, 383

Edgely, 212
Edgertown, 289
Edmonds, 350
Edmonson, 9, 267
Edmonston, 17, 28, 30, 42, 65, 107, 143, 154
Edwards, 9, 26, 80, 108, 178, 193, 218, 324, 357, 362, 412, 414
Egan, 143
Egbert, 12
Ege, 281
Eicher, 372
Eichern, 143
Eicholds, 218
Eichorn, 278
Eisenbeis, 400
Eisenhut, 411
Eisenhute, 393
Eisnagle, 79
Ekin, 10, 11
Eldridge, 17, 80, 89, 252, 289
Eliot, 64, 80, 82, 83, 143, 208, 241
Ellet, 265
Ellets, 234
Ellicott, 424
Ellicott's Mills, 239
Elliot, 212
Elliott, 93, 135, 168, 212, 234, 275, 277, 281, 404, 405
Ellis, 2, 85, 90, 91, 100, 122, 143, 166, 250, 338, 347, 387
Ells, 357
Ellsworth, 41
Elmwood Home School, 203
Elrick, 266
Elrod, 10
Elvan, 202
Elvans, 141, 360
Elverson, 6
Elwell, 377
Elwood, 212
Elzey, 20
Emerson, 161, 214
Emery, 115, 141, 143, 264, 307, 398
Emmerson, 348

Emmert, 129, 323, 387
Emmner, 273
Emmons, 63
Emory, 105, 108, 109, 189
Emott, 350
Emrich, 75, 129
Emrick, 270
Emrie, 308
Enfield Chase, 305
Engelman, 137
Engels, 411
engine **Washington**, 344
Engle, 51, 124
Englehart, 402
Engleman, 401
English, 53, 65, 75, 414
Engly, 110
Ennis, 102, 241, 311, 388
Eno, 147
Enos, 26, 121, 208
Entwisle, 88, 339
Epler, 194
Erben, 213, 420
Ernst, 232
Esenbeiss, 402
Espey, 184
Esputa, 280
Essex, 6, 91, 274, 306
Essing, 402
Estelle, 98
Estill, 44
Etheridge, 169
Ettings, 276
Eunson, 34
Eustace, 306
Eustis, 53, 56
Evans, 3, 10, 32, 92, 93, 106, 126, 141, 143, 189, 194, 206, 244, 342, 377, 403, 413
Evants, 350
Evarts, 195, 350
Eve, 122
Evening Star, 424
Everett, 286, 325, 336
Evers, 187

Eversfield, 153
Eviersen, 252
Ewell, 255, 326
Ewing, 39, 143, 171
Executive Mansion, 44, 427
Ezell, 330

F

F_nt, 327
Fach, 380
Fagan, 402
Fahenstock, 409
Fahnestock, 409
Faily, 125
Fair, 368
Fairchild, 350
Falconer, 97, 98, 126, 394
Fallon, 192
Fancher, 350
Fannin, 415
Fanning, 271
Fant, 236, 241
Faraday, 3, 61, 119
Fargo, 417
Faris, 300
Fariswe, 45
Farlayer, 323
Farlee, 353
Farley, 31, 68, 128, 135, 242, 279, 280, 322
Farmer, 288
Farrae, 212
Farragut, 250, 374
Farran, 53
Farrar, 35
Farrell, 136, 154, 381
Farren, 43, 245
Farrer, 242
Farwell, 84
Fast, 201
Faulkner, 168, 169, 330, 387
Fauntz, 106
Faust, 281, 313
Fauth, 101
Fawcett, 328, 393

Fay, 129, 289, 345
Fearce, 14
Fearson, 59, 75, 77, 340
Feary, 428
Febiger, 194, 213
Febre, 360
Febrey, 119
Fechet, 249
Fegan, 208, 393
Fehr, 364
Feinour, 171
Felardo, 173
Felson, 337
Felter, 326
Felton, 176, 243, 282
Female Grammar School, 206
female preacher, 377
Fendall, 17, 54, 66, 70, 123, 186, 225, 255, 309, 337, 351, 390, 394, 414
Fenianism, 112
Fenn, 146
Fennell, 408
Fenton, 43
Fenwick, 19, 72, 73, 83, 143, 159, 186, 213, 237, 399, 415, 421
Feragenay, 292
Ferguson, 73, 173, 237, 243, 422
Fernley, 237
Ferrand, 316
Ferrill, 313
Ferris, 237, 333, 334
Fessenden, 146, 152, 209, 322
Fetty, 218
Ficklen, 183
Ficklin, 122
Field, 3, 37, 60, 80, 134, 137, 230, 304, 416
Fiero, 390
Fillebrown, 414
Fillson, 178
Finch, 49, 184, 238, 331
Finckel, 328, 361
Finckle, 345, 397
Fine, 109
Fink, 50, 64, 81, 89

Finkel, 345
Finley, 411
Finney, 88, 304
Finnicum, 60
Finnigan, 98
Fish, 87
Fisher, 44, 54, 57, 63, 83, 93, 99, 100, 102, 119, 148, 232, 233, 251, 253, 255, 267, 327, 340, 342, 368, 408, 409, 416
Fisk, 41, 179, 410
Fiske, 368
Fitch, 40, 80, 87, 119, 124, 133, 136, 143, 218, 246, 281, 316, 344
Fithian, 272, 350
Fits, 94
Fitzgerald, 121, 194, 290, 334, 355, 364, 365, 385, 387, 394, 408, 410
Fitzhugh, 2, 74, 111, 143
Fitzpatrick, 97, 250, 259, 349, 393
Flagg, 29
flagship **Hartford**, 57
flagship **Lawrence**, 421
Flammers, 159
Flanagan, 341
Flanahan, 428
Flanders, 158
Flanigan, 392, 393
Flannagan, 192, 238, 385
Flannery, 120
Flannigan, 233, 402, 411
Flashman, 247
Flaterty, 346
Fleet, 380, 400
Fletcher, 140, 164, 201, 212, 249, 368, 374, 393
Fleury, 404, 405
Flint, 212, 415
Flores, 113
Florid, 121
Florrer, 289
Floyd, 342, 359
Flynn, 40, 393
Foley, 5, 187, 208, 423
Follet, 273

Foot, 52, 83
Foote, 43, 84, 198, 232, 240, 248, 251, 258, 267, 295, 307, 348, 355, 387, 411
Forbes, 122, 413
Forbush, 249
Force, 26, 29, 32, 34, 143, 181, 196, 215, 400, 402
Ford, 59, 61, 64, 70, 71, 119, 122, 124, 143, 210, 237, 247, 270, 280, 318, 326, 335, 370, 396
Ford's Theatre, 61, 418
Fordyce, 107
Foreham, 402
Foreman, 10, 13, 121, 237, 332
Forest, 86
Forge, 138
Forman, 210
Formes, 104
Forney, 57
Forrest, 21, 47, 49, 89, 143, 221, 224, 375, 410
Forster, 250
Forsyth, 178, 316
Forsythe, 322
Fort, 408
Fort Benton, 159, 282
Fort Cobb, 3
Fort Corcoran, 334
Fort Cummings, 286
Fort Dodge, 46
Fort Ellis, 159
Fort Foot, 94
Fort Foote, 108, 130
Fort Harker, 271
Fort Hawley, 282
Fort Jackson, 57
Fort Jefferson, 327
Fort Kearney, 312
Fort Lafayette, 404
Fort Laramie, 406
Fort Leavenworth, 254
Fort Lyon, 165
Fort McHenry, 108
Fort McPherson, 128
Fort Monroe, 329

Fort Pulaski, 22
Fort Reynolds, 316
Fort Ripley, 198
Fort Sanders, 281
Fort Sanford, 288
Fort Saratoga, 417
Fort Saunders, 294
Fort St Philip, 57
Fort Sumter, 374
Fort Tobacco, 379
Fort Wallace, 19, 34, 300, 316, 322
Fort Washington, 83, 94, 108, 130, 372
Fort Wayne, 26
Forth, 394
Fortress Monroe, 50, 55, 335
Fosdick, 77
Fossett, 122
Foster, 4, 14, 80, 250, 279, 289, 332, 350, 393
Foster's Neck, 229
Fouke, 272, 380
Fountain, 245
Foutz, 10
Fowler, 143, 184, 185, 198, 227, 233, 241, 249, 278, 313
Fox, 13, 22, 40, 66, 81, 87, 95, 119, 124, 133, 136, 140, 210, 246, 316, 344, 361, 394
Foxall, 63
France, 197, 206
Francis, 143, 323
Franey, 136
Frank, 57, 153, 242, 342
Franklin, 21, 110, 118, 253, 258, 398
Franseker, 198
Fraser, 235, 237, 385
Fraunces, 176
Frazer, 372
Frazier, 109, 176, 313
Fredand, 329
Frederick, 192
<u>Frederick Female Seminary</u>, 280
<u>Frederick Female Seninary</u>, 254
Fredericks, 411
Fredrich, 37

Freeman, 5, 141, 262, 344, 402
Freer, 179
Fremont, 140, 155, 165
French, 80, 92, 93, 94, 189, 221, 240, 283, 289, 341, 367
Frercks, 289
Frere, 210, 368
Freundt, 4, 349, 368
Frey, 41, 247, 361
Frick, 210
Fridley, 196, 211
Friess, 6, 12
frig **Minnesota**, 263
frigate **Franklin**, 374
Frisbie, 10
Fristoe, 197
Fritz, 289
Frizele, 246
Frizzell, 168, 285
Froiseth, 102, 295
Fromming, 136
Frost, 122, 242
Fry, 171, 219, 273, 290, 353
Fugitt, 50, 143
Fulford, 304
Fulla, 289
Fullalove, 176, 331, 344, 415
Fuller, 43, 201, 265, 279, 283, 306, 369, 424
Fullerton, 184, 350
Fulton, 93, 225, 289, 314
Fultz, 215
Funk, 297
Funky, 289
Furbisher, 406
Furgerson, 45
Furnace, 121
Furness, 3
Furst, 279
Fust, 217
Fusting, 208
Fyffe, 357

G

Gabbrel, 245

Gabriel, 245
Gaddis, 143
Gaekler, 402
Gaetz, 400
Gage, 296
Gail, 41
Gailor, 13
Gaines, 184
Gaiser, 202
Gaither, 396, 406
Gale, 272, 371
Gales, 129
Galfardi, 112
Gallagher, 115, 265, 359
Gallaher, 111
Gallaher, 393
Gallant, 275
Gallaudet, 425
Gallegos, 419
Galligan, 171, 205
Galsey, 121
Galt, 23, 33, 124, 140, 141, 143, 180, 199, 245, 390, 397
Gamble, 351
Gambrell, 156
Gambrill, 20, 245
Gambrills' gate, 20
Gangwer, 360
Ganin, 244
Ganley, 286
Gans, 220
Gant, 322
Gantt, 44
Ganzevoort, 228
Garachanin, 217
Garagnon, 50
Garbuit, 402
Garden, 140, 253
Gardiner, 375
Gardner, 91, 92, 108, 132, 153, 176, 319, 342, 363, 369, 398, 424
Garhardt, 402
Garland, 357
Garner, 167, 261, 353
Garnett, 324
Garowski, 160
Garrard, 201
Garratt, 137
Garret, 197
Garretson, 241
Garrett, 17, 147, 193, 273
Garretty, 250
Garrigues, 123
Garrish, 331
Garrison, 56, 241
Garrity, 58
Garvey, 275
Garvin, 408
Gaston, 198
Gater, 333
Gates, 333, 337, 376, 423
Gatewood, 368, 403
Gauginagel, 233
Gaul, 324
Gault, 22, 394
Gavit, 18
Gawler, 357, 375
Gaylord, 115
Gaynor, 313
Gayson, 192
Geary, 51, 58, 406
Gebhart, 338
Geer, 30
Geier, 15, 16, 22, 37, 39
Gelwicks, 354
Gencloth, 381
Gensler, 219
Genty, 400
George, 368
Gerard, 350
Gerhardt, 101, 172
<u>German Methodist Church</u>, 160
Gerrard, 15, 357
Gerrish, 270
Gerry, 386
Gerther, 219
Gest, 44
Getchell, 11
Gheen, 241
Gibbings, 55, 111

Gibbon, 336
Gibbons, 82, 271, 277, 294, 334, 348
Gibbony, 295
Gibbs, 25, 154, 235, 241, 272, 298, 304
Giberson, 73, 179
Gibson, 64, 93, 106, 107, 150, 166, 227, 310, 402
Gideon, 41, 46, 161
Gier, 32
Giesboro, 73, 98, 237
Gilbert, 102, 121, 136, 354, 389, 407
Gill, 31, 46, 114, 289, 298, 374, 421
Gillam, 295
Gillard, 237
Gillem, 52
Gillespie, 7
Gillet, 342
Gillett, 120
Gillette, 105, 197, 361
Gilliam, 324
Gilliams, 48
Gilliman, 94
Gillis, 94
Gillroy, 101
Gilman, 33, 155, 158, 173, 327
Gilmore, 3, 188, 253, 290
Gilson, 326
Ginnsler, 178
Girdlestone, 266
Gittings, 70, 179, 205
Given, 191, 208, 332
Givens, 289
Gladmon, 213, 228
Glancy, 280
Glannon, 257
Glasco, 181
Glascoe, 213
Glasgow, 132, 306
Gleason, 9, 176, 401
Glebe, 261
Glenn, 10, 305, 346, 378, 401
Glennon, 115
Glenubuth, 115
Glenwood, 88, 324

Glenwood Cemetery, 23, 28, 30, 54, 78, 105, 112, 113, 156, 234, 341, 380, 387, 417, 429
Glenzer, 364
Gobright, 144, 162, 196
Gockeler, 223
Gocklin, 401
Goddard, 154, 172, 224, 334
Godden, 400
Godey, 143, 210, 334
Godhelp, 247
Goelet, 147
Goetz, 402
Goff, 174, 288
Goggin, 80
Gold, 200, 368
Gold Ridge, 326
Golden, 18, 106, 246, 257, 262, 393
Goldsborough, 57
Goldschmidt, 88, 111
Goldsmith, 401
Golladay, 409
Gonigle, 248
Gonzaga College, 292
Good, 380
Good Hope Tavern, 200
Good Luck, 13
Goodall, 8, 136, 143
Goode, 429
Gooden, 82
Goodfellow, 306
Gooding, 6, 77, 86, 113, 123, 202, 305
Goodloe, 317
Goodman, 121
Goodrell, 374
Goodrich, 115, 224, 311, 326
Goodrick, 55
Goodwin, 36, 297
Gookin, 324
Goolinski, 212
Gorbutt, 224
Gordan, 89
Gordon, 56, 68, 134, 339, 357, 378, 416
Gore, 77, 232, 371, 389
Gorman, 16, 214, 256, 340, 350, 399

Gormon, 21
Gorrigan, 424
Gosler, 181
Goss, 115, 179, 279
Gott, 250
Gould, 243, 252, 425
Gouverneur, 124
Gove, 206
Gover, 168
Govermann, 260
Gowing, 188
Graffen, 321
Grafton, 137, 262, 312
Graggin, 288
Graham, 15, 30, 35, 46, 125, 187, 208, 337, 352, 358, 386, 414
Grally, 319
Grammer, 63, 194, 333
Granby tract, 417
Graney's Champion, 251
Granger, 291
Grant, 1, 7, 24, 37, 39, 49, 56, 74, 84, 95, 104, 133, 157, 170, 176, 198, 203, 205, 214, 228, 243, 247, 249, 250, 284, 286, 309, 367, 369, 370, 372, 384, 390, 392, 400
Grason, 182, 219
Grasser, 399
Grau, 196
Graves, 173, 358
Gray, 39, 48, 67, 129, 136, 143, 158, 189, 213, 228, 264, 281, 361, 396, 400, 402
Greanor, 430
Greary, 73
Greason, 194, 400
Greeley, 256, 384, 389
Green, 32, 33, 46, 52, 53, 58, 63, 69, 80, 87, 106, 126, 129, 141, 143, 152, 237, 238, 244, 253, 262, 306, 320, 331, 345, 356, 381, 385, 392, 408, 409, 419, 424, 430
Greene, 3, 11, 71, 368
Greeney, 270
Greenfield, 227

Greenleaf, 321, 373
Greenleaf's Point, 372
Greenough, 48
Greenwell, 68
Greenwood, 1, 188, 365
Greenwood Cemetery, 228, 281
Greer, 212, 261, 399
Greeves, 141, 280
Gregory, 276, 340, 398
Greir, 221
Grenell, 336
Grennel, 50
Grenup, 78, 112
Grey, 196, 204, 257
Gridley, 219
Grier, 249
Griffin, 3, 91, 179, 270, 271, 279, 337, 345, 353, 408, 409
Griffing, 208
Griffith, 79, 223
Grigsby, 311
Grimes, 394, 408, 412
Grindel, 286
Grinder, 143
Grinnell, 307, 312, 337, 364
Griswold, 95, 179, 350
Groding, 147
Groesbeck, 233
Gronau, 406
Gross, 111, 137, 381
Grosts, 48
Grove, 420
Grover, 99
Groverman, 402
Groves, 318
Grow, 248
Grubs, 261
Gtwn College, 80, 147, 209, 210, 237, 309, 332
Gudgin, 6, 37
Guerin, 311
Guest, 246
Guidicini, 12
Guild, 30
Guilford, 87

Guinand, 167
Guinard, 144
Guinity, 129
Guipe, 96
Gulick, 143
Gunn, 150
Gunnell, 64, 143, 357
Gunston Hall, 42
Gunther, 121
Gunton, 30, 32, 54, 141, 258, 333
Guoyle, 207, 214
Gurley, 3, 41, 87, 118, 192, 270, 324, 327, 333
Gurr, 110
Gustman, 232, 335
Guthrie, 42, 117, 123, 178, 185, 403
Guy, 265, 312
Gwynn, 268

H

Hable, 157
Hackenyas, 244
Hackett, 87, 192, 193
Hackman, 181
Hadaway, 134
Haden, 249
Hadley, 12, 37, 46, 47
Hadly, 3
Hagan, 423
Hagans, 152
Hagemann, 18
Haggard, 289
Haggerty, 313, 392
Hagner, 64, 144, 153, 169, 209, 304, 421
Hahyaktakee, 48
Hail, 214
Hair, 357
Haldredge, 178
Hale, 131, 288, 314
Hall, 4, 14, 15, 21, 33, 49, 56, 67, 103, 128, 144, 150, 169, 171, 172, 181, 204, 218, 224, 232, 249, 250, 293, 295, 299, 305, 307, 317, 318, 323, 349, 354, 356, 360, 361, 377, 386, 390, 414, 421, 423

Halladay, 161
Hallaran, 206, 270
Halleck, 3, 4, 38, 90
Halley, 171
Hallihan, 392
Halloran, 287, 320
Halls, 364
Halpine, 256, 269
Ham, 249
Hamel, 218
Hames, 401
Hamil, 137
Hamilton, 63, 85, 105, 144, 189, 218, 264, 304, 330, 348, 361, 397, 404, 426
Hamlin, 134, 150, 224, 400
Hamline, 131
Hamlink, 352
Hammack, 69, 126
Hammer, 137
Hammers, 408
Hammond, 25, 134, 210, 427
Hamstead, 179
Hance, 352
Hancock, 10, 29, 71, 87, 98, 107, 185, 187, 282, 317, 400
Hand, 187, 278
Handly, 170
Handy, 50, 133, 197, 212
Hanen, 87
Hanes, 301, 403
Haney, 91, 306
Hanks, 81
Hanlin, 121
Hanlon, 109
Hanna, 258, 345, 401
Hannah, 290
Hannan, 244
Hannebury, 115
Hanner, 64
Hannon, 236
Hansmann, 119
Hanson, 2, 144, 193, 213, 258, 389, 399
Hapgood, 177
Hapline, 269
Hapwood, 250

Harbaugh, 136
Harbin, 37, 46, 47, 356, 399
Harbottle, 192
Hard, 17
Hardesty, 118, 175, 188, 251
Harding, 245
Hare, 275, 311
Harger, 380
Hargroves, 379
Harker, 293
Harkness, 144, 212, 258
Harlan, 104, 316
Harley, 369
Harlowe, 45
Harlson, 393
Harman, 81, 122, 128, 301
Harmon, 235, 241
Harmonial Cemetery, 88, 190
Harney, 31, 406
Harper, 3, 164, 170, 199, 222, 223, 270, 357, 384
Harrington, 10, 34, 295, 322
Harris, 1, 13, 39, 97, 106, 115, 119, 121, 185, 219, 228, 236, 244, 245, 246, 250, 265, 374, 400, 402, 408, 410, 420, 423
Harrison, 56, 61, 76, 160, 174, 183, 309, 329, 413
Harriss, 137
Harrold, 386
Harrover, 144, 247
Harry, 371, 408
Harshell, 314
Hart, 5, 9, 26, 133, 199, 281, 319, 360, 361, 381, 393, 409, 416
Harte, 201
Hartig, 298, 303
Hartley, 4, 102, 141
Hartman, 67, 121, 408
Hartmann, 393
Hartnett, 208, 393
Hartrauft, 308
Hartshorn, 137, 248
Harvey, 1, 7, 30, 54, 62, 88, 147, 158, 191, 260, 312, 394, 397, 402

Haseltine, 5
Haske, 394, 418
Haslup, 166
Hastings, 43, 55, 364, 376
Hatch, 137, 306
Hatter, 155
Hauck, 326
Hauptman, 213
Haven, 164
Havenner, 258, 300
Haverstack, 174
Havlick, 192
Haw, 182
Hawes, 9, 94
Hawk, 245
Hawkins, 21, 30, 43, 235, 243, 272, 320, 404
Hawks, 127, 239
Hawley, 36, 272
Haws, 375
Hawthorne, 342
Hay, 137, 149, 240, 353
Hayes, 239, 309, 408
Hayman, 82, 289
Hayne, 74, 77
Haynes, 293
Hays, 86, 144, 229, 379
Hayward, 76
Hazard, 150, 158, 171, 194, 216
Hazel, 24, 67
Hazeltine, 212
Head, 223
Heald, 405
Heard, 137, 304
Heath, 249, 289, 425
Hecht, 370
Heck, 9, 349, 385, 402
Hed_epeth, 238
Hedrick, 210
Heenan, 121, 183, 267
Hefelfinger, 157
Heffner, 271
Hegan, 408
Heiberger, 144
Heide, 273

Heidelberg, 408
Heidinger, 394
Hein, 363
Heine, 144
Heinecke, 164
Heise, 162
Heiskell, 192
Heitmilier, 144
Helen, 241
Helimuth, 260
Hellen, 97
Heller, 177
Helmes, 402
Helmick, 141, 191
Henck, 345
Henderson, 121, 122, 198, 359
Hendley, 250
Hendren, 116
Hendricks, 198, 283, 354
Hendrickson, 128
Hening, 361
Hennage, 59
Hennessy, 178
Henning, 100, 144, 196, 347, 358
Henricks, 360
Henriques, 419
Henry, 24, 30, 53, 83, 100, 101, 112, 144, 181, 196, 221, 244, 393
Henson, 142, 192
Hention, 121
Henze, 171, 260, 385
Henzl, 402
Hepburn, 89, 129, 172, 248
Herald, 386
Herard, 73
Herbart estate, 282
Herbert, 52, 212, 257, 385, 412
Hereford, 355
Herforth, 402
Hergenrether, 297
Herman, 402
Hermeston, 351
Herndon, 243
Heron, 210, 425
Herr, 125, 141

Herran, 210
Herrell, 176
Herrells, 393
Herrick, 44, 334, 378
Herring, 1
Herron, 96
Hertzberg, 144
Hertzog, 292
Hess, 65, 88, 204, 320, 348, 394
Hessler, 95
Hester, 407
Heuisler, 208
Heustis, 3
Hewett, 186
Hewitt, 323
Hewlett, 378
Heydon, 290
Heyer, 397
Heywood, 243, 374
Hibben, 218
Hibberd, 137
Hibbs, 166
Hibburd, 319
Hickey, 268, 412
Hickman, 313
Hicks, 192, 281
Hiel, 411
Higbee, 289, 306
Higgenson, 57
Higgins, 56, 165, 178, 218, 392
Hilbush, 183
Hildebrand, 308
Hildreth, 137
Hill, 18, 24, 44, 60, 65, 128, 144, 162, 172, 237, 243, 244, 250, 291, 309, 337, 343, 374, 388, 389, 394, 422, 427, 431
Hilleary, 91, 319, 326
Hillgen, 44
Hillgren, 5
Hilliard, 201, 369, 374
Hilliary, 422
Hilliery, 181
Hills, 249, 360, 411

Hilton, 63, 78, 114, 186, 199, 350, 387, 402, 415
Hinckle, 59
Hindman, 127, 321
Hinds, 67, 345, 346, 352
Hineline, 345
Hines, 331, 359, 391, 401
Hinton, 201, 253
Hippell, 363
His Lordship's Kindness, 379
Hiscock, 39, 378
Hitchcock, 125, 179
Hitz, 83, 84, 144, 360
Hobbie, 323
Hobbs, 263, 359
Hobert, 346
Hoblitzell, 362
Hobson, 289
Hocker, 226
Hocklin, 115
Hodge, 26, 27, 28, 86, 121, 165, 243, 351, 353
Hodges, 115, 189, 248, 325, 332, 377
Hodgson, 91, 262, 263, 288
Hoff, 346, 354, 374
Hoffer, 212
Hoffman, 101, 128, 256, 359, 397
Hoffocker, 255
Hogan, 132, 184, 187, 195, 211, 290, 293, 330, 368, 370
Hoge, 26, 96
Hogebook, 378
Hohonan, 164
Holbrook, 333
Holcomb, 354
Holcombe, 219
Holden, 270, 276, 323
Hole-in-the-day, 264
Holeman, 380
Holiday, 394
Holland, 5, 343, 368
Hollerin, 275
Holliday, 360
Holliday's Choice, 175
Hollidge, 16

Hollingshead, 199
Hollister, 41
Hollon, 111
Holloran, 423
Holly, 414
Hollywood, 203
Holmead, 76, 111, 195, 201, 361
Holmead's old burial ground, 362
Holmes, 164, 184, 230, 238, 295
Hololan, 106
Holstein, 147, 181
Holsten, 422
Holt, 141, 340
Holton, 289
Holyrood Cemetery, 323
Holyschuh, 392
Homan, 295, 305
Homberger, 137
Home Farm, 182
Homen, 342
Homiller, 348
Homing, 392
Honchen, 115
Hood, 69, 80, 137, 171, 256
Hooda, 222
Hooden, 109
Hooe, 209, 337
Hoogs, 212
Hooker, 81, 167, 233, 304, 342, 424
Hoolehan, 26
Hooper, 115, 194, 196, 213, 296, 419
Hoop-skirt, 346
Hoop-skirts, 104
Hootce, 359
Hoover, 171, 183, 198, 225, 361, 380
Hoover's farm, 334
Hopkins, 11, 12, 15, 18, 68, 103, 166, 189, 224, 236, 262, 272
Hopper, 182
Horgesky, 192
Hornbush, 359
Horner, 292, 402
Horrigan, 363
Horsch, 101
Horse Shoe Point, 304

Horsford, 227
Horton, 121, 209, 337
Horwitz, 33
Hosch, 146
Hoskins, 249
Hosmer, 5, 59, 103, 199
Hotaling, 378
Hotchkiss, 224
Hough, 144
Houghton, 153, 258
Houk, 151
Houndschild, 64
House, 172, 193, 409
Houseman, 310
Houser, 10
Houston, 80, 372
Hovey, 282
Howard, 45, 47, 64, 103, 115, 122, 125, 136, 137, 141, 144, 147, 150, 166, 172, 174, 213, 218, 236, 249, 260, 275, 306, 338, 351, 394, 422, 423
Howard Univ, 423
Howard University, 422
Howe, 3, 86, 128, 251, 363
Howell, 95, 248, 425
Howes, 63, 360, 389
Howett, 113
Howland, 4, 218, 235, 381, 396
Howlett, 176, 224, 384
Hoxie, 249
Hoy, 408
Hoyt, 121, 372
Hubbard, 14, 102, 153, 189, 210, 263, 307
Hubbell, 377
Hubble, 88, 164
Hubby, 414
Hubert, 285
Huddle, 408
Hudson, 402
Huegle, 260
Huesties, 10
Huff, 398
Huffman, 394
Hufty, 33

Hufy, 396
Huggan, 164
Huggins, 364
Huggon, 88
Hughes, 31, 39, 44, 74, 77, 105, 122, 128, 203, 222, 331
Hugo, 35, 51, 254, 288, 343, 374
Huguenot, 186
Huhn, 393
Huiton, 300
Hujup, 351
Hull, 4, 94, 174, 289
Hullett, 408
Hully, 296
Humbert, 387
Hume, 18, 144, 233, 261, 382
Humphrey, 140, 144
Humphreys, 21
Humphries, 135, 183, 232
Hunneburg, 115
Hunt, 3, 4, 24, 28, 130, 137, 182, 216, 247, 254, 271, 289, 326, 374, 397, 411
Hunter, 80, 82, 98, 106, 122, 144, 210, 230, 256, 293
Hunter's Mill, 98
Huntington, 33, 153
Huntly, 91
Huntt, 373
Hunyday, 217
Hurdle, 63, 86, 122
Hurlburl, 279
Hurlburt, 134
Hurley, 66, 86, 301, 402
Hustin, 93
Huston, 354
Hutchings, 170
Hutchingson, 314
Hutchins, 298, 409, 419
Hutchinson, 37, 155, 193, 194, 237, 257, 340, 344
Hutton, 5, 35, 147, 189, 245, 261, 331, 343
Huyck, 129
Hyam, 140
Hyatt, 259

Hyde, 144, 201, 370, 383, 391
Hyde Park, 89, 427
Hydeley, 105
Hyland, 60

I

Iardella, 224, 228
Ickes, 370
Iddings, 193
Iddins, 100, 163
Iglehart, 304
Imboden, 268
Impeach, 49
impeachment, 65, 69, 74, 84, 97, 147, 155, 159
Impeachment, 152
Improvements in Gtwn, 313
Improvements in Washington, 199
Imrie, 393
Indian princess, 269
Ingersoll, 61, 179
Ingle, 32, 57, 91, 98, 144, 205, 224, 225, 227, 400
Ingles, 289
Ingman, 395
Ingraham, 57, 177
Ingram, 201, 379
Inskens, 408
Inskip, 409
Ireland, 144
Irvine, 413
Irving, 89, 230
Irving Female College, 281
Isaacs, 267
Isham, 288
Isherwood, 33
Israel, 412, 413
Iturbide, 276
Ivers, 380
Ives, 5, 175

J

Jackson, 1, 5, 9, 12, 16, 17, 44, 56, 86, 94, 95, 97, 128, 133, 135, 144, 172, 200, 255, 256, 303, 306, 320, 327, 348, 361, 393, 394, 399, 404, 405, 414, 422, 429
Jacob, 20
Jacobs, 20, 134, 171
Jagerisky, 37
James, 76, 98, 111, 140, 242, 258, 261, 306, 320, 416
Jamieson, 149, 294
Jamison, 219
Janes, 137
Janieson, 328
Janney, 61
Jaques, 416
Jaquette, 296
Jarboe, 81, 384
Jardin, 152
Jarret, 72, 120
Jarvis, 299, 301
Javins, 420
Jay, 225, 350
Jayne, 256
Jefferds, 154
Jefferies, 122, 241
Jefferson, 63, 88, 203, 291, 293, 326, 377
Jeffrey, 66, 148, 252
Jeffries, 50, 237
Jenkins, 115, 172, 200, 340, 344, 412
Jenks, 248
Jennings, 326, 419
Jerome, 127
Jerrell, 234
Jessup, 310
Jessup's Cut, 20, 269, 394
Jesuits, 369
Jewell, 47, 144, 189
Jewett, 10, 121
Jewish Democratic Club, 247
Joaquin, 252
Jocelyn, 44
Jocknick, 212
Johannes, 303
Johansan, 400
John W Vanhook's Hill, 66

Johns, 54, 131, 280, 297, 408
Johnses, 28
Johnson, 6, 9, 12, 16, 17, 19, 26, 29, 32, 34, 44, 45, 46, 53, 56, 63, 64, 81, 82, 83, 85, 88, 91, 94, 97, 106, 108, 117, 133, 141, 144, 146, 147, 152, 154, 155, 169, 171, 172, 175, 176, 179, 181, 184, 193, 194, 196, 197, 198, 204, 207, 214, 219, 220, 223, 236, 237, 240, 241, 242, 243, 245, 249, 254, 263, 270, 271, 275, 277, 281, 290, 297, 298, 306, 310, 320, 323, 329, 340, 342, 354, 385, 388, 408, 413, 414, 417, 420, 423, 428
Johnson's Island, 231
Johnston, 11, 371
Jolan, 360
Joliffe, 421
Jolly, 326
Jones, 2, 3, 6, 7, 15, 21, 26, 28, 37, 44, 52, 54, 58, 81, 92, 93, 99, 118, 137, 154, 172, 205, 206, 210, 212, 220, 231, 232, 238, 244, 249, 253, 263, 265, 269, 274, 275, 282, 294, 299, 301, 306, 318, 329, 334, 339, 362, 370, 377, 378, 380, 390, 408, 418, 428
Jones' Loss/Less, 175
Jordan, 297, 366
Joseph, 263, 334, 400
Joseph Park, 202
Joseph's Park, 418
Joslin, 12
Jouvenal, 297, 411
Joy, 26
Joy's Bldg estate, 48
Joyce, 20, 82, 151, 153, 172, 253
Juarez, 50
Judd, 161
Juenemann, 394
Julian, 62, 135
Julien, 3
Just, 144

K

Kago, 290

Kahn, 408
Kaiser, 213, 260
Kalb, 229
Kalorama, 414
Kane, 5, 8, 10, 19, 249, 302, 353, 363, 374, 393, 418
Karr, 415
Kaufffman, 274
Kaufman, 284
Kavanaugh, 67, 245
Kay, 161
Kayne, 193
Keach, 334, 349
Kean, 31, 59
Keane, 126, 285, 367
Keare, 360
Kearney, 91
Keasbey, 81
Keathley, 242
Keating, 75, 91, 129, 160, 187, 205
Kechley, 225
Keech, 191
Keechline, 322
Keedy, 310
Keefe, 56, 64, 344
Keeler, 148, 210
Keeling, 237
Keen, 6
Keenan, 10, 134, 425
Keene, 406
Keese, 12, 23, 238
Kehl, 236
Keho, 378
Keickhoefer, 141
Keider, 368
Keip, 385
Keiser, 394
Keith, 308
Keleher, 155
Keliher, 149
Kell, 424
Kellaher, 168, 224
Kelleher, 168, 206, 333
Keller, 200, 400, 402

Kelley, 23, 29, 32, 35, 62, 109, 176, 192, 202, 218, 311, 323, 385, 423
Kellogg, 279
Kelly, 13, 20, 23, 32, 60, 62, 63, 65, 81, 132, 134, 141, 144, 149, 179, 214, 231, 236, 250, 267, 279, 289, 310, 323, 327, 352, 375, 400
Kelsey, 147, 360
Kember, 302
Kendall, 3, 95, 141, 197, 268, 313, 319, 349, 385
Kendall Green, 52, 125, 268, 349
Kendall Green Barracks, 125
Kendler, 260
Kengla, 86, 274, 275
Kennedy, 33, 105, 129, 136, 141, 263, 278, 364, 385
Kenner, 267
Kennon, 8
Kent, 10, 89, 90
Kenyon, 21, 134, 192, 308
Keohler, 310
Keough, 393
Kepner, 16
Kerr, 62, 93, 144, 230, 255, 359
Kersey, 184
Kershaw, 405
Kerson, 328
Kervand, 116, 119, 126, 131
Kerwin, 292
Kessinger, 289
Ketchum, 144, 250, 276, 342
Kettler, 95, 420
Ketzel, 339
Key, 308, 390
Keyser, 375, 424
Keyworth, 86, 140
Kibbey, 21, 33, 141
Kidd, 366
Kidwell, 33, 103, 134, 144, 146, 360
Kieckhoefer, 210
Kiekhoefer, 33
Kilbourn, 33, 111, 139, 400
Kilbourne, 349
Kilburn, 144

Kilby, 364
Kilgore, 15
Killian, 118, 221, 331
Killians, 400
Killmon, 428
Kills, 377
Kilmahan, 385
Kilpatrick, 376
Kimball, 124, 201, 208, 215, 345, 352
Kimberley, 302
Kimmell, 9, 204, 229, 230, 255
King, 3, 8, 25, 32, 51, 56, 82, 84, 100, 113, 119, 125, 141, 151, 157, 214, 215, 225, 227, 235, 246, 264, 282, 284, 286, 287, 288, 313, 320, 321, 334, 348, 356, 363, 364, 368, 374, 390, 420, 421, 427
King of Prussia, 263
Kingsbury, 81
Kingsley, 121
Kingwalt, 204
Kinney, 41, 247, 363
Kinsale, 273, 303
Kinsella, 11
Kinsley, 17, 110, 131, 388
Kintzing, 80
Kirby, 202
Kirk, 197
Kirkland, 350
Kirkpatrick, 59
Kirkwood, 124, 348
<u>Kissington Rolling Mill</u>, 367
Kit Carson, 165
Kitchen, 68, 283, 397
Klerlein, 224
Klief, 184
Kline, 128
Kloman, 205
Klomann, 334
Klopfer, 46, 73
Klotz, 402
Klum, 338
Knable, 22
Knap, 173
Knapp, 121, 174, 292

Kneessi, 260
Knickbocker, 415
Kniffen, 368
Knight, 144, 166, 202, 249, 307, 317
Knights, 3, 176
Knode, 356
Knowles, 229
Knowlton, 427
Knox, 122, 393, 398
Kobb, 113
Koch, 260, 334, 349
Kochs, 385
Koehl, 293
Koehler, 301
Koenig, 40
Kohler, 400
Kolb, 400
Kolipinki, 402
Konstantinovich, 217
Koontz, 68, 114
Koppel, 210
Korts, 24
Kortwright, 124
Kossell, 260
Kottmann, 368
Kotty, 218
Koysen, 282
Kraeutler, 402
Kraft, 349
Kranch, 402
Kraus, 381
Krause, 205
Kreas, 334
Krebs, 360
Kreslusky, 392
Kretchmar, 19
Kriel, 76
Kroeger, 400
Kroes, 362, 368
Krouse, 225, 356
Krumme, 72
Kuhn, 301
Kurtz, 121
Kutzbock, 371
Kyle, 319

L

L'Heritier, 163
La Bonte, 430
La Croix, 112
La Mothe, 12
Lacey, 272
Lackey, 285, 289
Lackrider, 282
Lacroix, 374
Lacy, 174, 247, 300, 385, 390
Laden, 187
Lafayette, 140
Lafayette Square, 205
Lafferty, 248
Lafitte, 187, 288
Lainhart, 109
Laird, 341, 348
Lake, 250
Lalor, 228, 250
Lamar, 219
Lamarsh, 218
Lamb, 250, 316, 378, 395
Lambell, 166, 191, 204
Lambert, 386
Lambeth, 360
Lambie, 302
Lambright, 129, 244, 403
Lamon, 202, 342
Lancaster, 15, 196, 237, 247
Lander, 154
Landis, 341, 416, 423
Landsford, 236
Lane, 105, 169, 181, 218, 233, 300, 411
Laney, 25
Lang, 281, 334
Langdon, 394
Lange, 24
Langley, 51, 88, 136, 147, 236, 246, 368, 400
Langly, 52
Langstaff, 132
Langtry, 44
Languish, 43
Langworth, 345

Langworthy, 153
Lanman, 99, 118
Lansdale, 152
Lansingbock, 237
Lapan, 94
Lapham, 121
Laresche, 251
Larin, 385
Larkin, 286, 357, 375, 391
Larman, 210
Larned, 20, 79
Larner, 24, 46, 171, 290
LaRoche, 207
Lascelle, 339
Lashhorn, 157
Laskey, 211, 229, 400
Lassell, 312
Lasselle, 196, 371, 376
Latham, 272
Lathrop, 32, 113, 114, 141, 156, 250, 357
Latimer, 254, 275, 417
Latrobe, 24
Latta, 33, 84, 111, 139, 144, 349, 400
Latten, 286
Lattimore, 144
Laubie, 282
Lauck, 212
Lauder, 266
Laughlin, 138, 357
Lavender, 12
Lavens, 238
Lavon, 307
Law, 64, 94, 135, 373
Lawler, 238
Lawless, 92
Lawlor, 184, 228
Lawrence, 135, 141, 144, 163, 191, 327, 426, 429
Laws, 18, 339
Lawson, 36, 414
Lawton, 192
Lay, 32, 153, 258, 364, 395
Lazenly, 334
Le Breton, 277
Le Ferre, 369
Le Grimes, 88
Lea, 1, 219
Leach, 46, 51, 113, 267, 298, 339, 421
Leahey, 393
Leary, 44, 393, 400
Leavan, 67
Leavenworth, 289
Leblanc, 344
Leckie, 235
LeCompte, 81, 212
Leddy, 375
Lederer, 65, 402
Lee, 10, 14, 56, 68, 96, 137, 144, 152, 178, 190, 204, 207, 236, 238, 270, 275, 283, 288, 293, 359, 374, 388
Leech, 6, 36, 144, 161, 190, 197, 225, 230, 245
Leffingwell, 42
Leftwich, 362
Legendre, 197
Leggard, 384
Leggett, 354
Leghton, 17
Leibrich, 43
Leich, 40
Leiffert, 204
Leighton, 114
Leins, 336, 394
Leisher, 245
Leizer, 147
Leland, 211, 319
Leman, 154, 155, 160
Lemmens, 259
Lenman, 141, 194
Lennox, 54
Lenox, 202, 307
Lenthall, 33
Leonard, 21, 115, 123, 231, 282, 340, 350, 357
Lerman, 247
Lesh, 194
Lesiardi, 117
Leslie, 144, 228, 403, 408
Lesse, 409

Lester, 115, 136, 267
Letcher, 173, 376
Leubner, 402
Leutze, 231
Leuw, 265
Leveridge, 15
Levers, 110
Levezzie, 371
Levi, 94
Levy, 247, 380
Lew, 83
Lewellen, 293
Lewis, 5, 42, 61, 87, 88, 136, 144, 176, 179, 180, 188, 199, 203, 222, 270, 278, 279, 299, 309, 311, 361, 377, 402, 404, 411
Leynard, 340
Libbey, 76, 111, 144, 194, 317
Libby, 111
Liberman, 64
Lichan, 394
Lichau, 67, 166, 312
Lichau House, 67, 87
Lichtenhaler, 288
Lichtenuhaler, 131
Lidball, 240
Lieberman, 144
Lieth, 329
Lightbody, 187
Lighter, 361
Lightner, 4
Lilly, 5, 65
Limaker, 233
Lincoln, 43, 64, 85, 90, 115, 120, 152, 157, 164, 188, 208, 254, 256, 261, 268, 286, 316, 330, 347, 369, 392, 404, 419
Lincoln Barracks, 108, 412
Lincoln Monument, 120
Lincoln Park, 274
Lind, 5, 44, 88
Lindamond, 408
Linde_kohl, 184
Lindemood, 403
Lindenkohle, 225

Lindermood, 412
Lindner, 107
Lindsay, 113, 169
Lindsey, 80
Lindsley, 73, 144, 171, 224
Linedick, 240
Linkins, 144, 172, 199
Linsey, 326
Linthicum, 28, 141
Linville, 104, 106
Lipman, 120
Lippincott, 188
Lipscomb, 105, 250
Liscomb, 238
Liscombe, 392
Liston, 193
Litchfield, 63, 181
Little, 103, 154, 271, 307, 311, 374, 405
Little Hackley, 308
Littlewood, 81
Livermore, 153, 166
Livingston, 59
Livingston Manor, 157
Livingstone, 206
Lloyd, 5, 24, 55, 67, 81, 89, 199, 200, 206, 257, 282, 312, 315, 339
Lobdell, 14
Lochboehler, 331
Lock, 376
Lockbeiller, 43
Locke, 341
Lockland, 82, 306
Lockwood, 33, 396
Locust Point, 330
Lodor, 108
Loeliger, 334, 349, 418
Lofileir, 411
Logan, 104, 151, 305, 346
Logsdon, 413
Lohness, 274
Lohse, 26
Lolliger, 368
Lone Mountain Cemetery, 200
Long, 75, 124, 179, 380
Longley, 290

Longwood, 317
Lontain, 193
Look, 408
Loomis, 41, 121
Lord, 73, 82, 171, 206, 258, 350, 395
Lorenzie, 385
Loring, 15, 58, 267, 281
Losse, 292
Lostulter, 295
Lott, 87, 140
Lottar, 37
Lotts, 118
Louckes, 318
Loughborough, 130, 155
Loughridge, 316
Loughron, 375
Louis, 115
Love, 252, 415
Lovejoy, 16, 122, 204, 368
Lovengood, 348
Lover, 224
Low, 355
Lowden, 301
Lowdower, 408
Lowe, 12, 254, 284, 330, 363, 368
Lowenthal, 37, 59, 75, 119, 155
Loweree, 358
Lowndes, 1
Lowndeses, 28
Lowrie, 118, 361, 407
Lowry, 10, 14, 47, 68, 141, 155, 159, 327, 393
Lowther, 5
Loxbury, 367
Lucas, 7, 60, 106, 306
Luce, 257
Luckett, 202, 377
Luddarth, 72
Ludwig, 98, 104, 213
Lumsden, 172, 184, 243
Lumsdon, 153
Lungren, 391
Lusby, 18, 174, 207, 214, 368
Luskey, 210
Lutz, 141, 418

Luxen, 344
Lyden, 346
Lydin, 298
Lyles, 73, 111, 210, 272, 297, 352, 403
Lyman, 134, 283
Lynch, 2, 4, 6, 8, 21, 32, 101, 192, 208, 210, 275, 357, 360, 373
Lynds, 373
Lynn, 402
Lyon, 160, 391, 399
Lyons, 121, 153, 352
Lytle, 355, 356
Lytton, 85, 252

M

Maack, 393
Mabie, 185
Macadams, 249
Macauley, 245
Macduff, 71
Machier, 297
Machievel, 177
Mack, 9, 319
Mackall, 144, 210, 249
Mackay, 95
Mackel, 96
Macken, 187
Mackenbur, 368
Mackenburg, 368
Mackenzie, 197
Mackin, 283
MacLeod, 393
MacNichol, 333
Macpherson, 52
Mactavish, 168
Macy, 109
Madden, 293
Maddox, 61, 408, 419
Maden, 190
Mades, 385, 400, 411
Madigan, 5
Madison, 132, 365
Magaw, 181
Magee, 32, 63, 97, 376
Mager, 402

Magins, 226
Maglathory, 322
Magruder, 9, 23, 37, 74, 106, 111, 124, 135, 144, 156, 209, 232, 273, 279, 303, 348, 360, 379, 394, 403, 410
Maguire, 41, 80, 83, 89, 106, 147, 184, 209, 357
Mahan, 381
Mahew, 179
Mahon, 137, 144, 345
Mahoney, 422
Main, 257
Major, 358
Malady, 175
Malcolm, 325
Malcom, 389
Male, 294
Maley, 321
Malgengroft, 409
Mallery, 249
Mallon, 288
Mallory, 115, 210, 293
Malloy, 283
Malone, 41, 105, 115, 132, 312
Maloney, 413
Man, 350
Manadier, 83
Mandell, 381
Mangan, 106
Mankin, 229
Manley, 319
Manlove, 272
Mann, 51, 281, 293, 375
Manney, 202
Manning, 3, 12, 37, 52
Mansfield, 52, 375
Mansur, 355, 356
Mantanguier, 293
Manuel, 306
Manyett, 270
Manypenny, 1
Mapes, 368
Maple Grove, 401
Maranville, 364
Marble, 81

Marbury, 51, 54, 64, 70, 86, 124, 142, 144, 195, 205, 294, 350, 352, 403
Marchand, 343
Marchant, 408
Marcher, 217
Marcott, 62
Marcus, 323
Marden, 158
Mardes, 387
Mare, 136
Marion, 166
Markell, 363
Market, 289
Markham, 361
Markly, 421
Markriter, 33, 142, 398
Marks, 100, 144, 291, 305, 319, 419
Markwalder, 83, 84
Marle, 199
Marll, 36
Marlow, 251
Marman, 299
Marmion, 118, 423
Maroney, 394
Marple, 306
Marquis de Caux, 252, 265
Marr, 235, 240
Marriott, 304
marrying a white woman, 35
Marsh, 65, 87, 249, 327
Marshall, 13, 55, 83, 93, 249, 275, 405, 408
Martin, 56, 80, 93, 105, 148, 172, 195, 197, 199, 210, 238, 249, 285, 288, 293, 308, 310, 322, 323, 350, 364, 366, 368, 375, 393, 394, 402, 426, 429
Martindale, 339
Martine, 78
Martz, 289, 297
Masi, 140, 258
Mason, 42, 47, 81, 111, 118, 144, 150, 169, 204, 241, 289, 302, 349, 397, 413, 414
Masonic Temple, 157
Massey, 122, 275

Mastin, 273
Mather, 186
Mathews, 306
Matlocks, 102
Matthews, 51, 58, 120, 121, 147, 154, 173, 241, 246, 368, 415
Mattingly, 17, 33, 40, 83, 113, 142, 144, 163, 167, 200, 227, 256, 358, 383, 404, 420
Mattoon, 147
Mattson, 9
Matur, 4
Maugle, 158
Mauk, 410
Maury, 144, 163, 166, 326
Mausen, 39
Maxilmilian, 276
Maxwell, 27, 215, 228, 245, 246, 383
May, 33, 43, 54, 82, 88, 134, 142, 186, 214, 229, 329, 331
Mayfield, 313
Mayhead, 221
Maynadier, 412, 414
Maynard, 96, 100, 102
Mayne, 427
Mayo, 137, 388
McAdam, 343
McAlister, 40, 136
McAllister, 345
McArdle, 393
McArena, 73
McAvoy, 239
McBlair, 267
McBrainey, 24
McBride, 173, 229
McCabe, 218, 346
McCaffery, 270
McCaffrey, 393
McCail, 270
McCall, 67, 150, 253, 322, 331
McCalla, 274
McCamant, 164
McCamont, 408
McCampbell, 362
McCandless, 236

McCann, 174, 385
McCarnant, 26
McCartee, 282
McCarthy, 78, 98, 186, 208, 236, 358, 360, 393, 402
McCartney, 392
McCarty, 14, 42, 140, 191, 393
McCathran, 159
McCatran, 181
McCauley, 7, 17, 80, 229, 245, 430
McCavrin, 75
McCawley, 118
McCeney, 25, 386
McClaning, 283
McClary, 292
McCleary, 86
McClellan, 8, 60, 101, 159, 174, 296, 313, 325, 327, 358, 378
McClelland, 17, 63, 89, 207
McClernand, 232, 241
McClery, 71, 100, 107, 127
McClintock, 289
McClish, 122
McClown, 391
McColgan, 208, 229
McConkey, 297
McConnell, 81, 179, 227, 272, 385
McCook, 223
McCoole, 263, 267
McCoole, the pugilist, 267
McCorkhill, 326
McCorkie, 200
McCormick, 43, 91, 188, 245, 253, 334, 360, 392, 394, 400
McCowan, 94
McCoy, 418
McCrae, 404
McCrea, 213, 230
McCulloch, 176, 282, 285, 286, 293, 297, 301, 308, 315, 316, 319, 326, 330, 354, 355, 356, 357, 358, 364, 366, 368, 369, 372, 375, 378, 380, 386, 389, 391, 398, 417, 423
McCullock, 413
McCullom, 144

McCullum, 402
McCurcy, 164
McCurdy, 26
McCurley, 424
McDaniel, 39, 144
McDaniels, 91
McDermail, 136
McDermot, 201
McDermott, 88, 172, 208, 213
McDevitt, 152, 206, 224, 226
McDonald, 38, 83, 193, 269, 306, 320, 349, 426
McDonnell, 390
McDonnough, 402
McDonough, 56
McDougall, 3, 200
McDowel, 133
McDowell, 144, 326, 359
McDuell, 2, 32, 184, 408
McElrey, 384
McElroy, 342
McEven, 118
McFadden, 184
McFarlan, 412
McFarland, 172, 380, 408
McFarlane, 194, 297
McFarrall, 408
McFeely, 413
McFerran, 60, 108
McGarvey, 99, 155
McGee, 112, 212, 279, 305, 310, 399
McGhee, 225
McGill, 33, 44, 144, 206, 222, 297, 363
McGilton, 109
McGlue, 5
McGolgan, 33
McGough, 310
McGowan, 153, 157, 402
McGowen, 424
McGown, 413
McGran, 394
McGrann, 8
McGrath, 56
McGraw, 353
McGreen, 364

McGregor, 8, 405
McGrew, 250
McGrorty, 173
McGuire, 30, 54, 92, 122, 141, 187, 289, 368, 385, 398, 402
McHugh, 393, 418
McIlhenney, 138
McIllhenny, 139
McIllheny, 144
McIlvaine, 51
McIntire, 289, 301
McIntosh, 64, 89, 201, 413
McIntyre, 8, 81, 193, 290
McKay, 345
McKean, 45, 53, 59, 61, 122, 185, 297
McKearney, 304
McKee, 308, 374
McKeean, 61
McKeever, 402
McKelden, 105, 142
McKeldon, 33
McKeldry, 259
McKelley, 423
McKenna, 366, 380
McKenney, 18, 63, 91, 264
McKenny, 348, 359
McKenzie, 4, 122, 289, 301
McKieve, 416
McKillip, 218
McKim, 46, 350, 362, 367, 392
McKinley, 287
McKinnon, 123
McKinstry, 200, 273
McKnew, 144
McKnight, 122, 153
McLaughlin, 6, 27, 58, 160, 192, 322, 393
McLaughly, 223
McLaurin, 123
McLean, 118, 144, 188, 189, 335, 375, 399
McLeod, 97, 121
McLeran, 250, 331
McLinden, 285
McMahon, 169, 203, 206, 286, 330, 420

McManus, 208, 334
McMasters, 386
McMcPherson, 73
McMeir, 209
McMovens, 5
McMurray, 174, 398
McNabb, 98
McNair, 109, 189
McNally, 258, 343, 360, 363
McNamara, 418
McNanny, 6
McNaughton, 218
McNeely, 381
McNeil, 352
McNeir, 178
McNerhany, 157, 369
McNett, 109
McNiel, 301
McNight, 122
McPherson, 6, 10, 11, 12, 17, 25, 30, 44, 75, 90, 92, 139, 142, 146, 274, 422
McPhersons, 147
McQuade, 393
McQuillan, 393
McQuirk, 278
McRae, 275
McSherry, 8, 29
McSpaden, 305
McSwain, 335
McSweeny, 334
McVey, 194
McWilliam, 8
McWilliams, 293
Meacham, 352
Mead, 5, 133, 136, 338
Meade, 8, 246, 286, 341, 411, 416, 419
Meador, 284, 361
Meagher, 3
Meakin, 175
Mealey, 210
Means, 355, 356
Mears, 100, 144
Mechlin, 359
Meclay, 295
Medary, 140

Medford, 380
Medill, 1
Medjid, 222
Medley, 412
Meech, 240
Meed, 325
Meeks, 233
Meem, 225
Meggins, 226
Megrem, 292
Megrue, 421
Meigs, 22, 123, 144, 235, 243
Melcher, 71
Mellen, 189
Mellier, 137, 149, 255
Mellon, 43
Meloy, 419
Melton, 90
Melville, 266
Melvin, 22
Menden, 186
Mendenhall, 108, 137
Menken, 59, 267
Menkin, 267
Menney, 262
Mercer, 12, 80, 184, 190, 195
Merchant, 173, 412
Meridian Hill, 14
Merle, 331
Merrell, 176
Merrick, 100, 142, 152, 208, 224, 311
Merrifield, 292
Merrill, 89, 90, 308, 355, 356, 364
Merriman, 142
Merriwether, 26
Mervine, 307
Merwin, 352
Messenger, 332
Metcalf, 150, 249
Metropolis View, 156, 171
Metzerott, 33, 83, 141, 150
Metzger, 355, 376
Mexwell, 140
Meyer, 14
Michie, 215

Michler, 274, 285, 423
Mickle, 291
Micks, 194
Middleton, 3, 114, 116, 118, 123, 125, 141, 156, 204, 258, 262, 292, 333, 342, 350, 392, 408
Miflin, 371
Milburn, 89, 144, 172, 209, 231, 300, 303, 377, 418
Miles, 308
Mille, 184
Miller, 16, 17, 22, 26, 40, 49, 56, 64, 67, 74, 75, 81, 83, 89, 92, 94, 126, 137, 144, 172, 180, 187, 188, 191, 213, 223, 224, 225, 236, 245, 262, 267, 272, 291, 298, 301, 308, 338, 342, 344, 345, 352, 358, 368, 370, 371, 383, 386, 389, 393, 395, 411, 421, 424, 427, 431
Millford, 312
Milligan, 240
Milliken, 50, 250
Millman, 367
Mills, 48, 62, 86, 101, 105, 140, 238, 268, 348, 358, 376, 382, 395, 402
Millson, 272
Milltown farm, 378
Millville Flour Mills, 86
Millward, 131
Milmau, 319
Milton, 376
Miner, 23, 32, 191, 196
Minor, 10, 79
Miramon, 42
Mitchell, 4, 7, 13, 33, 35, 53, 54, 107, 112, 114, 142, 186, 187, 189, 207, 222, 223, 228, 260, 336, 347, 350, 354, 376, 396, 423, 425
Mix, 1, 39, 100, 198
Mixer, 372
Moehlich, 393
Moen, 429
Moffett, 292
Mohelman, 299
Mohne, 210

Mohun, 2, 13, 18, 142, 148
Molan, 385, 400
Molen, 93
Moncrieff, 121
Monell, 381
Monroe, 191, 225
Montague, 80
Monteith, 129
Montgomery, 108, 189
Montose, 73
Montrose, 83, 266
Moody, 268
Mooney, 334
Moore, 9, 30, 33, 56, 84, 98, 103, 118, 126, 129, 144, 151, 166, 189, 220, 232, 234, 238, 260, 268, 306, 316, 322, 332, 338, 380, 387, 394, 398, 402, 408, 416, 428
Moorehead, 426
Moran, 99, 122, 144, 155, 217, 299, 363
Morand, 75, 103
Mordaunt, 43
Morehead, 311
Moreland, 394
Moreton, 193
Morgan, 109, 117, 241, 262, 264, 283, 310, 323, 405, 418
Morison, 184
Morley, 178
Mormons, 35, 201
Morningstar, 269
Moroney, 389
Morrell, 413
Morrice, 119
Morrill, 274, 301
Morris, 56, 67, 127, 175, 310, 345, 373, 403, 408
Morrisey, 115
Morrison, 27, 59, 113, 115, 118, 122, 144, 181, 225, 249, 287, 306, 310, 321, 420
Morrissey, 286
Morrow, 315, 392
Morse, 154, 188, 250
Morsel, 171

Morseley, 301
Morsell, 25, 33, 37, 54, 89, 111, 113, 117, 171, 243, 331, 401, 421
Morton, 38, 138, 192, 249, 364
Morwitz, 254, 259
Moscheles, 212
Mosely, 86
Moses, 201
Mosher, 91, 122, 144, 208
Mosier, 5, 413
Moss, 100
Mothershead, 334
Motor, 297
Mott, 159, 163, 426
Mould, 151
Moulder, 69, 189
Moulton, 202, 364
Mount, 312
Mount Air, 42
Mount Airy, 96
Mount Auburn, 418
Mount Aubutn Cemetery, 414
Mount Calvert, 273
Mount Olivet Cemetery, 19, 62, 65, 158
Mount Pleasant, 331, 375, 377
Mount Vernon, 22, 66, 94, 130
Mount Vernon Ladies' Association, 66
Mount Vernon R A Chapter, 353
Mountain View, 233
Mowry, 174
Moxley, 144, 396
Moyer, 355, 356
Moylan, 19
Mozart, 383
MrTudor, 169
Mudd, 327, 395
Mudge, 70
Mueller, 52, 334
Muir, 296
Mulane, 363
Muldeans, 424
Muldoon, 270
Muldrow, 23
Mulford, 203
Mulhany, 5

Mulharn, 30
Mulhern, 211
Mulholland, 267
Mullany, 152
Mullanys, 338
Mullen, 308, 359
Muller, 11, 157
Mullett, 305
Mullie, 381
Mulligan, 111, 196, 331, 343, 404
Mullikin, 312
Muncaster, 328
Munck, 71
Mundoe, 11
Muney, 362
Mungen, 174
Munro, 351, 359
Munsen, 184
Munson, 19, 159, 229, 237, 257, 264, 285
Munson Hill Farm, 19
Munson's Hill, 159
Murchison, 119
Murdoch, 189, 300, 301
Murdock, 144
Murphy, 42, 75, 87, 94, 113, 206, 209, 233, 245, 271, 275, 318, 363, 366, 385
Murray, 21, 53, 142, 148, 222, 226, 232, 266, 279, 288, 300, 304, 340, 355, 356, 362, 364, 366, 380, 392, 393, 396
Murrray, 386
Murtagh, 24, 227
Muse, 88
Muser, 51
Musgrave, 101
Musgrif, 4, 52
Mussard, 166
Musser, 328
Muth, 183
Myer, 279, 323, 402
Myers, 12, 16, 34, 36, 53, 77, 157, 183, 189, 283, 288, 336, 344, 349
Myerson, 119

N

Nachman, 52
Nagle, 71, 92, 118
Nairn, 223, 328, 351
Nalle, 209
Nalley, 81, 374
Nance, 336
Nantier-Didice, 3
Naphegyi, 138
Napoleon, 251, 263
Napoleon I, 322
Narvaez, 128
Nash, 18, 350, 380
Nater, 224, 279
Naughton, 267
Navojoe war, 406
Naylor, 3, 25, 55, 142, 178, 378, 397, 408
Naylor's Hold, 387
Neagle, 321
Neale, 134, 213, 303
Needwood, 124
Neenan, 392
Neff, 249, 292
Neighbor, 115
Neill, 424
Nelma, 149
Nelson, 75, 168, 173, 362, 376, 408
Nemegezele, 230
Nepath, 402
Neruda, 95
Nesmith, 359
Neville, 322
Nevitt, 334, 387
New Cut Road, 257
new organ, 420
Newberg, 87
Newburg, 174
Newell, 235, 238, 267
Newkirk, 394
Newman, 65, 144, 172, 192, 218, 261, 386
Newmeyer, 199
Newton, 81, 87, 95, 121, 199, 244, 279, 289, 293, 419
Niah, 380
Nibbing, 15
Niblo, 34, 120
Nichols, 117, 125, 136, 324, 339, 364
Nicholson, 10, 62, 109, 172, 173, 178, 373
Nickens, 86
Nickolson, 373
Nicodemus, 108
Nicol, 255, 326
Nicoll, 350
Nicols, 316
Nicolson, 10, 66, 239
Nieman, 115
Niemeyer, 289
Niland, 413
Niles, 53, 141, 391
Nilliston, 428
Nillson, 5
Nilsson, 106, 358
Nisbet, 32
Nisbett, 43
Nixon, 186, 267, 395
Noah, 375
Noble, 304, 349, 411
Nobles, 219
Nock, 315
Noerr, 172
Nokes, 68, 91, 303, 415
Nolan, 29, 75, 342
Noland, 344
Nones, 281
Noonan, 224, 264, 334, 368
Noonon, 196
Noonson, 39
Norment, 1, 64, 105, 141, 189, 225
Norris, 17, 18, 34, 73, 100, 125, 129, 135, 195, 283, 289, 318, 321, 400
North German Confederation, 345
Northeridge, 265
Northrup, 409
Norton, 23, 32, 51, 118, 216, 236, 244, 263, 289, 345, 362

Norwood Beale, 304
Norwood School, 393
Nosh, 247
Nourse, 138, 139, 280, 313, 343, 360, 367
Nowlan, 68
Nowrath, 394
Noyes, 10, 91, 144, 189, 241, 396
Nugent, 200, 219
Nulvin, 413
Nutting, 52

O

O'Brien, 115, 154, 169, 204, 250, 292, 368
O'Connell, 301
O'Conor, 350
O'Day, 391
O'Donnel, 322, 362
O'Donnell, 187, 350
O'Donohue, 293
O'Farrall, 15
O'Halloran, 154
O'Hara, 293
O'Hare, 100, 114, 222, 267
O'Harra, 55
O'Hollaran, 392
O'Key, 349
O'Leary, 422
O'Neal, 402
O'Neale, 187
O'Neil, 58, 272, 368
O'Neill, 43, 122, 208, 210, 273, 419, 424
O'Rourke, 25
O'Shaughnessy, 345
O'Toole, 15, 144, 267
Oak Hill Cemetery, 56, 72, 153, 162, 195, 255, 258, 295, 317, 343, 431
Oak Hill Chapel, 291
Oakwood, 393
Oates, 423, 425
O'Beirne, 2
O'Beirne, Reg/o wills, 6, 7, 8, 9, 13, 27, 31, 35, 43, 56, 57, 59, 71, 75, 76, 84, 97, 99, 113, 117, 120, 124, 126, 130, 138, 139, 150, 162, 174, 175, 184, 191, 215, 242, 260, 274, 287, 304, 314, 328, 331, 337, 351, 371, 376, 385, 412
Oceola, 406
Ocha, 94
Ochsenreiter, 368
Ockert, 89
Octagon, 96
Odell, 324, 371
Oentrich, 273
Oentrick, 279
Oertley, 345
Officer, 289
Offley, 168
Offut, 348
Offutt, 18, 52, 62, 224, 297, 315, 328
Ogden, 81, 327
Ogle, 96, 189, 390
Oilrich, 214
Okeson, 30
Okey, 128
Oland Farm, 109, 176
Olcott, 109, 209, 332, 395
old burying ground, 158
Old Parsonage Lot, 166
Oldest Inhabitants, 29, 63, 140, 213, 215, 258, 293, 333, 367, 403
oldest man, 430
Oldham, 289
Olds, 110, 300, 309, 361
Ole Bull, 409
Olin, 33, 54, 171
Oliphant, 206
Oliver, 45, 100, 121, 163, 246, 408
Olmstead, 4, 346
Olmsted, 346, 349
Onderdock, 92
Orendorff, 384
Orme, 40, 142, 194, 384, 403
Ormsby, 286
Orphans Court-Judge Purcell, 1, 6, 8, 12, 15, 21, 24, 30, 32, 37, 46, 51, 59, 65, 83, 96, 100, 103, 111, 119, 126, 135,

137, 148, 154, 155, 160, 165, 167,
172, 184, 191, 196, 204, 207, 214,
223, 225, 235, 245, 257, 262, 264,
270, 273, 279, 285, 291, 298, 303,
306, 312, 314, 315, 320, 323, 327,
331, 337, 339, 342, 344, 354, 359,
364, 371, 374, 380, 387, 389, 394,
401, 408, 412, 415, 421, 423, 425, 428
Orr, 317
Osborn, 289
Osborne, 91, 164, 264
Osbrey, 420
Osburn, 81, 395
Osertuffer, 324
Osgood, 424
Ossinger, 172
Ost, 221
Otis, 3
Ott, 89
Otter, 408
Otterback, 144
Ould, 284
Outcalt, 116
Overby, 182
Owen, 9, 33, 58, 59, 66, 144, 179, 194, 204, 273, 350, 385
Owens, 11, 25, 63, 144, 172, 239, 330, 348, 367
Owings, 242, 245
Owner, 310, 323, 401

P

P O Ws, 231
P_fferling, 125
Pacha, 222
Packard, 115, 127
Pacquet, 379
Padden, 199
Paddock, 240, 272, 293
Paganini, 95
Page, 126, 127, 137, 148, 150, 258, 261, 285, 289
Pagels, 7
Paget, 376

Palmer, 3, 34, 88, 92, 99, 119, 120, 121, 137, 177, 211, 281, 289, 306, 320, 395
Palmerston, 161
Pancoast, 417
Papst, 394
Paquet, 206
Parafine, 38
Parish, 102
Park, 56
Parke, 96
Parker, 4, 16, 30, 32, 33, 37, 39, 54, 63, 75, 83, 85, 99, 105, 109, 136, 153, 169, 181, 193, 243, 258, 272, 284, 333, 347, 350, 376, 386, 393, 420
Parkhurst, 250, 313, 387
Parkington, 11
Parks, 83, 376
Parrin, 408
Parshall, 363
Parson, 140
Parsons, 109, 137, 212, 421
Partridge, 242, 245
Parvin, 137
Passmore, 47
Patch, 189, 417
Patchen, 193, 317
Paterson, 225
Patsey, 220
Patten, 203, 353
Patterson, 64, 88, 124, 127, 145, 175, 181, 198, 201, 204, 207, 225, 235, 242, 245, 264, 326, 327, 333, 355, 377
Patti, 252, 265, 285
Patton, 267, 301, 338
Paul, 85
Paul Revere, 338
Paulding, 3, 51, 89
paving of 7th st, 284
Paxson, 52, 146
Paxton, 30, 159, 177, 411
Payne, 133, 146, 149, 196, 301, 383
Payson, 249
Peabody, 37, 82, 135, 149, 169, 224, 350, 379, 396, 427
Peach Lot, 13

Pearce, 326, 408, 409
Pearson, 144, 170, 198, 204, 207, 208, 291, 323, 339, 374
Pease, 308
Peaslee, 66, 173
Peaster, 18, 229
Pechin, 417
Peck, 26, 65, 141, 145, 215, 279, 313
Peddicord, 302
pedestrians, 149
Peifner, 206
Peirce, 344
Peirce Place, 316
Peirce's Mill, 23
Pella, 392
Pelletier, 89, 126
Pellisier, 383
Peloaza, 200
Pelsor, 308
Pemberton, 299
Pendleton, 23, 349, 386
Penlezey, 331
Penn, 12
Pennabacker, 302
Pennebaker, 363
Penniman, 202, 307
Pennington, 26
Pennock, 163, 174, 194, 374
Pepper, 10, 106, 192, 236, 311, 393
Perinchief, 38, 122, 343
Perinchield, 292
Perkins, 50, 68, 200, 326, 335, 341, 408
Perley, 275
Pernichief, 36
Perrell, 300
Perrez, 285
Perrin, 194, 241
Perrinchief, 153, 354
Perrington, 28
Perry, 11, 96, 115, 145, 211, 218, 245, 325, 328, 396, 418
Peter, 251, 343
Peterkin, 241
Peters, 15, 23, 235, 243, 308, 400
Peterson, 293, 400, 402

Peticolas, 395
Petipa, 61
Petitt, 222
Peto, 224
Pettit, 189, 201, 223, 258
Petty, 278
Peyton, 199, 367
Pfeffer, 411
Pfluger, 214
Pheffer, 189
Phelan, 212
Phelps, 154, 304, 363, 389
Philip, 33, 204, 207
Phillip, 225, 235
Phillips, 41, 83, 96, 144, 154, 203, 219, 244, 275, 288, 384, 395, 423
Philp, 33, 37, 142, 341, 397
Phineas, 251
Piatt, 272
Pickell, 353
Pickens, 264
Pickerell, 145
Pickering, 278
Pickrell, 142, 145, 189, 348
Pidgeon, 235, 272
Pierce, 63, 140, 146, 172, 188, 249, 288, 298, 301, 337, 360, 369, 414, 419
Pierrepoint, 25
Pierrepont, 350
Pierson, 81, 145
Pike, 47, 149, 249
Pilling, 145, 180
Pillow, 46
Pillsbury, 289
Pilson, 131
Pinckney, 54, 56, 62, 118, 137, 138, 139, 221, 325, 341
Piney Point, 228
Pinkerton, 82
Pinkney, 49, 304, 361
Pitcher, 140
Pitts, 101, 323
Pitzer, 265, 361
Placide, 257

Plant, 32, 64, 75, 97, 103, 114, 141, 223, 364
Plants, 93
Plantz, 164
Plater, 17
Platz, 27, 394
Pleasant Plain mill, 136
Pleasants, 138, 197
Plowden, 209, 229, 261
Plowman, 199
Plum, 218
Plummer, 187
Pochon, 210
Poe, 39, 233, 241, 314, 315
Pohlers, 184
Pohlmeyer, 140
Poland, 249
Polk, 185, 235, 271
Polkinhorn, 144, 374
Pollak, 144
Pollard, 33, 168, 197, 270, 390, 401, 403
Pollock, 248
Polzinhorn, 212
Pomeroy, 192
Pond, 21, 186, 219, 368
Pool, 32, 215
Poole, 30, 320
Poor, 346, 422
Poore, 275
Pope, 106, 112, 131, 249, 250, 343, 408
Porter, 62, 81, 213, 289, 292, 309, 343, 350
Portland, 275
Posey, 214, 219
Post, 11, 17, 137
Poston, 64
Potter, 62, 262, 294, 350, 366, 374, 380, 383, 418, 429
Potts, 136, 141, 402
Poulliet, 192
Pounds, 403
Powell, 39, 40, 59, 98, 138, 306, 333, 340
Power, 311

Powers, 5, 17, 133, 186, 226, 275, 276, 316, 402
Prandel, 44
Prather, 93, 94, 200, 204, 222
Prathers, 92
Pratt, 26, 178, 200, 214, 256, 303, 357, 369
Pratton, 83
Prebasco, 333
Preble, 246
Prentice, 130, 182, 326, 359
Prentiss, 81, 140
Prescott, 230
Preston, 220, 347, 424
Price, 3, 5, 32, 38, 68, 189, 230, 279, 392, 408
Prichard, 350
Prickett, 289
Priest, 161
Prim, 180, 350
Prince, 14, 204, 206, 244
Prince Michael, 217
Pringle, 16
Pritchett, 326
Probasco, 194
Procter, 93, 98
Proctor, 52, 58
Proomskall, 115
propeller **Governor Cushman**, 136
propeller **Hippocampus**, 306
propeller **Lynhaven**, 55
Prosise, 66
Prospect Hill, 175
Prout, 380
Provest, 141, 142
<u>Providence Hospital</u>, 264, 314
Pugh, 112, 175
Pulling, 357
Pulman, 357
Pumphrey, 300, 402
Purcell, 32, 55, 93
Purdy, 71, 142, 200, 258, 355, 356, 380
Purnell, 52
Pursell, 346, 396
Pusey, 355, 356

Pushee, 102
Putnam, 81, 270, 324
Pyewell, 135
Pyle, 249
Pyles, 6
Pywell, 6, 37, 155

Q

Qintinna, 243
Quayle, 207
Queen, 123, 172, 214, 241, 257, 329, 386
Queen Isabella, 180, 350
Queen of England, 276
Queen of Spain, 166
Queen Victoria, 77, 263
Queensboro, 399
Quicksall, 145
Quidor, 281
Quigley, 334
Quimby, 381
Quinlan, 13
Quinn, 210, 334, 372

R

Rabbetti, 284
Rabbit Island, 101
Rabbitt, 208
Rabelais, 177
Radcliffe, 36
Radd, 402
Radesky, 358
Radovanovich, 217
Rael's Landing, 408
Rafael, 253
Raffery, 218
Ragan, 111, 167, 184, 353, 402
Ragge, 408
Rainbow, 310
Raine, 92
Rainey, 158
Ralfinch, 373
ram **Arkansas**, 57
Ramsay, 74, 316, 323

Ramsburg, 65
Ramsey, 22, 121, 379, 387
Ramus, 223
Rand, 9
Randall, 102, 145, 169, 174, 176, 304, 417
Randolph, 35, 74, 149, 153, 165, 167
Randsley, 360
Ranelagh, 31
Rankin, 272, 284
Ransom, 294
Ransone, 66
Raphael, 195
Rapier, 289
Rapley, 348, 421
Rappie, 402
Rat-ay, 323
Ratcliffe, 336, 345
Rathbone, 187, 268
Rathburn, 376
Ratione, 357
Raub, 136
Rawlings, 26, 206, 387
Rawlins, 176
Ray, 28, 75, 129, 141, 172, 375, 417
Raybold, 119, 148, 327, 377
Raymond, 37, 248, 299
Raynor, 393
R-dgeis, 315
Read, 271
Reade, 60
Readen, 313
Ready, 80, 411
Reagan, 158
Real, 240
Ream, 265
Reamy, 400
Reaney, 389, 390
Reay, 121
Red Hill, 24
Red House, 183
Redd, 248, 379
Reddick, 340
Redes, 297
Redfern, 371, 408

Redgate, 374
Redgrave, 260
Redin, 158, 354
Reding, 190
Redman, 273
Redmon, 293
Redmond, 13
Redstrake, 82
Redway, 267
Redwood, 140
Reed, 12, 48, 57, 106, 118, 136, 145, 151, 169, 172, 181, 197, 233, 244, 289, 300, 304, 422
Reeme, 406
Reems, 219
Rees, 92
Reese, 142, 202, 230, 242, 245, 289, 333, 351, 385
Reeves, 115, 392, 407
Regney, 159
Reid, 49, 394
Reif, 378
Reilly, 218, 256
Reily, 210, 352, 363
Reims, 238
Reinhart, 400
Reinzel, 334
Reiss, 206
Remas, 387
Remington, 297, 315, 354
Rencher, 74
Rendihuber, 367
Reno, 234, 317, 318, 415
Repetti, 371, 374, 392
Resley, 142
Rets, 244
Revere, 338
Reynolds, 1, 11, 65, 100, 118, 121, 196, 214, 266, 314, 315, 323, 330, 337, 344, 366, 376, 427
Reynolds Barracks, 108
Rhea, 232
Rheinhard, 153
Rheinhart, 5
Rhodes, 215, 232, 354

Riamann, 351
Rice, 8, 9, 30, 270, 313, 369, 400
Richards, 1, 8, 23, 32, 63, 100, 145, 181, 209, 267, 289, 296, 322, 346, 360, 399, 402, 429
Richardson, 72, 136, 137, 145, 150, 179, 218, 241, 244, 303, 306, 336, 353, 378, 412
Richie, 423
Richings, 175
Richinson, 179
Richland, 304
Richmond, 359
Richter, 250
Riddall, 21
Riddel, 246
Ridder, 119
Riddle, 25, 33, 59, 189, 311
Ridenour, 93
Rider, 72
Ridgely, 47, 138, 224, 364, 402
Ridgeway, 214
Ridgway, 181
Ridner, 247
Ried, 361
Riford, 306
Riggs, 30, 32, 33, 56, 141, 190, 223, 401
Riggs' Mill, 348
Riley, 33, 36, 64, 79, 145, 176, 214, 250, 274, 288, 289, 303, 331, 358, 359, 377
Riley's Neglect, 175
Rimans, 380
Ringgold, 3, 252
Rinker, 61
Riordan, 242, 358
Ripetti, 364
Rise, 223
Risk, 289
Risley, 321, 372, 408
Risque, 210
Ritchie, 327
Rittenhouse, 209, 227, 349, 357
Ritter, 288
Ritterhouse, 306
<u>River road</u>, 328

Rives, 37, 130, 132, 145, 204, 390, 401, 402
Rivier, 402
Roach, 187, 368, 394, 420, 421
Roath, 357
Robbins, 10, 32, 145, 321, 323, 348, 360
Robbs, 402
Roberts, 1, 7, 9, 37, 51, 108, 140, 274, 372, 378
Robertson, 6, 12, 30, 35, 148, 279, 375, 420
Robinett, 250
Robinson, 8, 12, 15, 24, 43, 49, 62, 123, 129, 145, 151, 179, 221, 248, 295, 306, 344, 381, 413
Robinson Crusoe's island, 241
Robson, 265
Roccofort, 360
Roche, 65, 73, 399
Rochester, 358
Rochford, 394
Rock, 147, 310
Rock Creek Church Cemetery, 74, 82
Rock Creek College, 208
Rock Hall, 86
Rockaway, 315
Rockbridge Alum Springs, 215
Rockwell, 323, 424
Roden, 173
Rodgers, 313, 373
Rodier, 52, 157, 377
Rodman, 39, 250
Roe, 249
Roelker, 292
Roeper, 115
Rogers, 5, 48, 61, 109, 125, 170, 173, 178, 289, 351, 373, 413
Rogerson, 225, 413
Rohr, 400
Rohrer, 31, 194
Roland, 274
Roles, 318
Rollins, 36, 175, 386
Rolman, 93
Rominies, 421

Romons, 319
Ronshaw, 424
Rony, 430
Rook, 219
Rooney, 179, 222, 360
Roonly, 385
Roop, 30
Roosa, 250
Roosevelt, 147, 256
Rorer, 326
Roscol, 187
Roscrans, 240
Rose, 11, 38, 41, 94, 218
Rose Hill Estate, 47
Rosebery, 234
Rosecrans, 232, 243, 272
Rosenburgh, 315
Rosenheim, 247
Rosenthal, 348
Roseti, 183
RosettaWatkins, 17
Ross, 3, 32, 42, 68, 81, 93, 129, 148, 171, 189, 204, 231, 292, 299, 315, 320, 332
Rosseau, 112
Rossini, 383
Rossiter, 68, 101
Rothermel, 249
Roths, 402
Rothschild, 163, 252, 288, 404, 418, 422
Rothwell, 80, 258, 348
Rouche, 425
Rourke, 25, 115
Rouse, 104
Rousseau, 106, 236, 249, 273, 422
Roux, 133, 400
Rover, 208
Rowan, 272
Rowe, 289
Rowland, 69, 110, 167, 272, 354, 420
Rozar, 386
Rucker, 11
Rudd, 210
Rudhardt, 368
Rue, 352

Ruedi, 319
Ruff, 114, 126, 145, 155, 331, 387
Ruffin, 372
Rugby House, 114
Ruggles, 145
Rullman, 411
Rumsey, 147, 423
Runk, 408
Runnion, 308
Rupert, 203, 221
Ruple, 400
Rupley, 123
Ruppert, 10, 145, 393, 400
Rush, 96, 212
Russell, 137, 138, 139, 162, 192, 194, 198, 214, 236, 249, 306, 372, 379, 384, 421
Russell Barracks, 108
Ruth, 33
Rutherford, 17, 89, 197, 306, 327, 374
Ruthford, 402
Ryan, 39, 59, 211, 212, 267, 326, 363, 371, 393
Rynderson, 46, 112
Rynerson, 46
Rynex, 340
Ryon, 119, 149, 180, 214, 215
Ryther, 272

S

Sackett, 426
Sacred College, 105
Sacred Heart, 233
Saffold, 116, 375
Safford, 151
Sage, 345
Sager, 137
Saint, 318
Saint Puderitius, 113
Salger, 349
Salizky, 424
Salkeld, 146, 250
Sampson, 65, 289, 322
Samson, 54, 72, 197, 208, 332
Samuels, 262

Sanders, 139, 423
Sanderson, 402
Sands, 158, 210, 285, 373, 378
Sanford, 350
Sanger, 295
Sanglon, 384
Santa Anna, 138
Sappington, 408
Sargent, 309
Sarmiento, 376
Sarsfield, 126
Sauer, 95
Saul, 142, 167, 212
Saunders, 73, 126, 129, 157
Saur, 402
Savage, 33, 60, 126, 142, 249, 363, 389, 390, 400
Saville, 324
Savre, 137
Sawtelle, 81
Sawyer, 153, 200, 210
Saxton, 145, 192
Sayne, 295
Scagg's Station, 392
Scala, 236
Scammel, 381
Scanlon, 191
Schaaf, 22
Schadt, 293
Schaeffer, 72
Schafer, 33, 154, 203, 394
Schaffer, 135, 142, 203, 368
Schaum, 47
Schayer, 4
Schemborn, 106
Scherer, 223
Scherger, 400
Scheutzen Verein, 171
Schilling, 358
Schlerker, 323
Schlotterbeck, 411
Schmidt, 79, 163, 172, 191, 256, 283, 298, 303, 334, 344, 402
Schneider, 145
Schnell, 392, 411

Schnieder, 397
schnr **Ada Medora**, 193
schnr **Brave**, 403
schnr **Cordelia**, 115
schnr **Evening Star**, 175
schnr **Flounder**, 108
schnr **Growler**, 132
schnr **Hassler**, 309
schnr **Nautilus**, 192
schnr **Peter A Keyser**, 44
schnr **Walton**, 150
Schofield, 64, 99, 118, 122, 131, 133, 137, 149, 150, 176, 268
Scholer, 187
School of the Good Shepherd, 284
Schooley, 248
Schoonsborn, 402
Schott, 90, 100
Schotterbeck, 368
Schoubern, 402
Schrim, 306
Schriner, 314
Schrock, 22
Schrode, 206
Schroder, 51
Schroeder, 7, 102, 126, 171, 193
Schultz, 150, 318, 402
Schulze, 424
Schureman, 279
Schuster, 368
Schute, 197
Schutter, 145
Schutz, 394
Schwartz, 400
Schwing, 172, 402
Sclater, 45
Scott, 28, 41, 46, 80, 88, 91, 109, 115, 148, 152, 188, 212, 227, 229, 239, 266, 289, 294, 297, 338, 354, 393, 400
Scrivener, 40, 154, 349, 420, 425, 428
Scroggins, 65
Scull, 230
Seabrook, 403
Searle, 14, 64, 147, 193, 353, 397
Seaton, 10

Seavey, 135
Sebatsol, 428
Sedgwick, 3
Sedgwick Barracks, 108
Sedogard, 378
Sedwick, 347
See of Wilmington, 271
Seebold, 335
Seebros, 402
Seeley, 15, 187
Seem, 288
Sefton, 312
Segar, 290
Seibel, 199
Seibold, 283, 296
Seigert, 210
Seitz, 83, 154, 384, 400
Selby, 83, 384, 400
Selden, 91, 146, 235, 243
Sell, 288
Sellman, 224
Seminole war, 406
Semken, 33
Semmes, 33, 59, 68, 86, 118, 142, 210, 292, 411
Sempkin, 145
Seneff, 405
Sener, 122
Sengstack, 293
Senior, 219
Senneff, 76, 77, 151
Senseney, 70
Sensner, 109
Sering, 289
Serlock, 315
Serra, 390
Serrin, 348
Seuff, 404
Seufferle, 86, 145
Sewall, 103
Seward, 97, 193, 198, 350, 426
Sexton, 351
Seyfert, 210
Seymour, 2, 131, 136, 216, 292, 294, 296, 369

Shack, 152
Shackelford, 140
Shackleford, 222
Shacklin, 212
Shade, 39
Shafer, 212
Shaffield, 346, 396
Shallcross, 410
Shanahan, 55, 191, 222, 394
Shanklin, 3
Shanks, 308
Shanley, 320
Shannon, 295
Shares, 13
Sharkey, 367
Sharpe, 115
Sharpley, 134
Sharretts, 206
Shaugnesy, 380
Shaunnessy, 380, 383
Shaw, 45, 93, 106, 113, 178, 308, 376, 394
Shawdt, 322
Shea, 62, 233, 244, 271, 393, 394, 411
Shearer, 246, 388
Shears, 173, 249
Sheckells, 199
Shedd, 145
Sheets, 218
Sheffield, 340
Shekell, 393, 402
Shelan, 116
Sheldon, 320
Shell, 328
Shelley, 243
Shelly, 145, 293, 402
Shelton, 96
Shenig, 8
Shepard, 290
Shepardson, 30
Shepherd, 33, 65, 112, 127, 141, 145, 172, 217, 224, 226, 233, 250, 260, 264, 281, 327, 339, 345, 360, 398, 408
Shepherd place, 114
Sheppard, 22

Sherer, 223
Sheridan, 254, 398, 404
Sheriff, 91, 136, 396, 428
Sherman, 26, 52, 60, 71, 99, 111, 198, 272, 281, 288, 294, 362, 417
Sherr, 400
Sherrett, 265
Sherwood, 45, 273, 334
Shey, 307
Shibant, 249
Shields, 80, 162, 199, 226, 278, 305
Shier, 77
Shillington, 180, 325
Shiner, 13, 364
Shinkle, 93
Shinn, 142
ship **Ansel**, 148
ship **Constitution**, 310
ship **Costa Rica**, 4
ship **Cuba**, 296
ship **General Grant**, 101
ship **Hartford**, 4, 57
ship **Hermit**, 173
ship **John Duncan**, 413
ship **Magnolia**, 278
ship **Mississippi**, 309
ship **Ocean**, 57
ship **Princeton**, 51
ship **Saranac**, 192
ship **Sheboygan**, 115
ship **Vermont**, 406
ship **Washusett**, 61
ship **Wyoming**, 192
Shipley, 65, 305
Shippen, 75, 82
Shirk, 374
Shisaler, 326
Shoemaker, 23, 65, 172, 249, 291, 348, 402
Shonnard, 216
Shoomaker, 400
Short, 98, 355, 356
Shoter, 412
Shotts, 399
Showell, 41

Shreeve, 145
Shreiner's Graveyard, 264
Shreve, 238, 276, 417
Shriver, 145
Shrode, 196
Shryock, 430
Shugree, 194
Shultz, 354
Shuster, 33, 118, 145
Shutrliff, 356
Shutter, 397
Shuttleworth, 213
Sibley, 136, 145, 208, 348
Sickles, 42, 71, 275, 408
Siddons, 102
Sievers, 392
Sigler, 26
Silliman, 34, 180
Silver, 396
Silver Spring, 14, 324
Silvey, 219
Sim, 56, 164
Simaker, 256
Simmons, 199, 288
Simms, 8, 63, 65, 87, 128, 145, 194, 196, 210, 258, 261, 333
Simon, 373
Simons, 271
Simpson, 6, 7, 9, 60, 62, 65, 86, 115, 145, 301, 316, 354, 392, 402
Sinclair, 216, 255, 410, 417
Sioussa, 388
Sioux war, 406
Sipes, 225
Sis, 363
Sister Baptiste, 358
Sister Loretta O'Reilly, 64
Sisterhood of the Good Shepherd, 284
Sisters Loretta & Genevieve, 264
Sisters of Chariety, 64
Sisters of Charity, 314
Sisters of Mercy, 245
Sisters of the Holy Cross, 282
Sitgreaves, 209, 238
Skelton, 295

Skerritt, 381
Skinner, 81, 159, 218, 304, 429
Skippon, 23
Skipwith, 312
Slack, 125
Slade, 85, 88, 96, 99, 100, 205
Slater, 192
Sledge, 199
Sleep, 297
Sleeper, 302
Sleshmyer, 408
Slesson, 350
Slider, 289
Slidham, 257
Slivers, 374
Sloat, 3
sloop **Marion**, 192
Slosson, 374
Slothower, 358, 375
Slough, 46, 112
Slowe, 379
Small, 114, 126, 155, 250, 331, 387, 398
Smallwood, 132, 419
Smart, 44, 210, 345, 367, 402
Smith, 3, 7, 11, 15, 18, 20, 28, 31, 33, 38, 41, 42, 48, 54, 56, 58, 75, 82, 86, 88, 93, 95, 97, 100, 101, 103, 107, 111, 116, 121, 126, 127, 136, 138, 139, 142, 145, 150, 156, 167, 189, 190, 192, 201, 204, 207, 212, 216, 218, 220, 222, 233, 235, 236, 240, 241, 244, 249, 252, 253, 255, 262, 263, 264, 268, 270, 271, 272, 274, 278, 279, 280, 290, 292, 300, 302, 314, 315, 339, 340, 348, 350, 355, 359, 360, 361, 363, 364, 369, 370, 372, 374, 377, 386, 390, 397, 398, 411, 415, 417, 419, 420, 427, 430
Smithgall, 181
Smithson, 63
smoking, 31, 254
Smolinski, 345
Smoot, 17, 53, 113, 114, 122, 133, 145, 156, 208, 211, 331, 339
Smyth, 164, 361

Smythe, 416
Sneed, 332
Snow, 71, 121, 125, 305, 323, 401, 402
Snowden, 21, 58, 259, 386
Snyder, 31, 52, 127, 172, 206, 245, 324, 354, 371
Soden, 430
Sohier, 186
Sohn, 214
Soldiers' Home, 123
Solomon, 251
Solomons, 33, 37, 141, 397
Somerndyke, 253
Somers, 135
Somerville, 238, 303, 333, 405
Somes, 41, 140, 403
Sommers, 386, 400
Sonne, 306
Sonnenschmidt, 50, 172
Soper, 146, 280, 357
Sothoron, 206, 207
Soule, 24
Souness, 338
Souter, 325
South Danvers, 82, 149
Southall, 99, 176
Southey, 392
Southwick, 248
Southworth, 117, 360
Sowers, 197, 354
Spaids, 102
Spalding, 40, 125, 184, 231, 240, 243, 260, 283, 303, 421
Spangler, 327
Sparks, 234, 359
Spaulding, 118, 180
Spear, 261, 272, 421
Specht, 340
Speed, 347
Speke, 94
Spencer, 90, 121, 256, 281
Spier, 350
Spilman, 140, 393
Spindler, 111
Spirk, 306

Sprague, 64, 115, 276, 303
Sprawl, 359
Sprigani, 212
Sprigg, 362
Sprigman, 230
Spring, 315
Spring Mill, 61
Springer, 339
Springsguth, 260
Sprohs, 411
Spross, 273
Spurrier, 124
Squa ga na ba, 257
Squier, 427
Sr Loretto, 314
Sran, 96
St Aloysius parachial Schools, 208
St Ann's Church, 237
St Anna's Hall, 35
St Clair, 3, 275
St Clement's Manor, 261
St Denis, 419
St John, 44
St John's College, 251
St Joseph's German Catholic Church, 348
St Louis Cemetery, 260
St Marie, 213
St Mary's Retreat, 105
St Paul's Day, 27
St Peter's Academy, 282
St Stephen's Church, 423
St Thomas purchase, 426
St Vincent's Academy, 199
Stacey, 108
Stackpole, 94, 130, 411
Stacy, 268
Stadfeldt, 29
Staetter, 163
Stafford, 42, 109, 160, 176, 229, 272
Stake, 27, 320
Staley, 260
Stalley, 171
Stanard, 343
Stanbery, 79, 163

Stanford, 98
Stang, 22
Stanley, 338
Stansbury, 245
Stanton, 11, 49, 65, 69, 76, 93, 152, 157, 240, 249, 410
Stark, 295
Starkey, 250
Starks, 111
Starkweather, 199
Starnes, 104
Starr, 150, 289, 359, 399
Starrett, 352
Statter, 256, 277
Steadman, 68, 174, 315, 410
steamer **America**, 408
steamer **Ariel**, 192
steamer **Arrow**, 94, 130
steamer **Atlantic**, 356
steamer **Berlin**, 367
steamer **Chesapeake**, 12
steamer **City of Boston**, 212
steamer **Connecticut**, 190
steamer **Cuba**, 97, 313
steamer **Express**, 131
steamer **George Leary**, 44
steamer **Guiding Star**, 337
steamer **Hartford**, 51
steamer **Hibernia**, 413
steamer **Keyport**, 167
steamer **Knight**, 150
steamer **Levi Leoti**, 282
steamer **Linton**, 329
steamer **Magnolia**, 92, 93
steamer **Morning Star**, 192
steamer **Neusho**, 51
steamer **Ossipee**, 270
steamer **R N Rice**, 193
steamer **Raleigh**, 4
steamer **Russia**, 109, 127
steamer **Sacramento**, 61
steamer **Saginaw**, 347
steamer **San Salvador**, 341
steamer **Scotia**, 127
steamer **Sea Bird**, 115, 123, 263, 317

steamer **Star**, 385
steamer **State of N Y**, 212
steamer **Stephen Low**, 226
steamer **Vidette**, 218
steamship **Australian**, 248
steamship **Baltimore**, 330
Stearns, 81, 309
Stebbins, 5
Stedpole, 245
Steedman, 55
Steel, 97, 245, 249, 402
Steele, 210, 368
Steens, 121
Steepleton, 219
Steer, 145
Stegmaier, 348
Stein, 115
Steinmetz, 160, 234
Steinway, 150
Stephen, 37, 114, 146, 177, 392
Stephens, 43, 81, 83, 198, 201, 240, 253
Stephenson, 90, 145, 399
Steptoe, 299
Sterick, 371
Stern, 122
Sterrett, 186
Stetson, 47, 84, 214
Stettinius, 172
Stevens, 14, 18, 32, 52, 66, 92, 93, 94, 104, 124, 126, 145, 147, 192, 202, 262, 264, 266, 271, 274, 307, 314, 319, 338, 347, 358, 363, 382
Stevenson, 289
Steward, 364
Stewart, 49, 64, 91, 118, 121, 122, 136, 145, 171, 176, 183, 203, 208, 219, 276, 288, 304, 321, 324, 327, 408, 419
Stickney, 145, 349
Stieren, 162
Stillmore, 138
Stillwell, 272
Stilwill, 421
Stimpson, 18
Stinchcomb, 278
Stinemetz, 32, 126, 145, 214, 396

Stinson, 219, 318
Stinzing, 392
Stockpole, 137
Stockton, 4, 273, 296, 336
Stoddard, 82, 353
Stokely, 9
Stokes, 92, 131
Stone, 5, 81, 124, 145, 207, 278, 327, 330, 367, 375
Stone House, 273
Stoneman, 118, 175, 188, 225, 251
Stoner, 181
Stonestreet, 19, 99, 353, 360
Stoops, 128, 210, 212, 267
Storer, 137
storeship **Supply**, 197
Storm, 240, 243
Storms, 52, 187
Storrs, 114
Story, 4, 5, 71, 132
Stosch, 260, 394
Stotler, 79
Stott, 98, 145
Stoub, 91
Stoughton, 103, 137, 142, 350
Stout, 34, 218, 231, 307, 310, 344
Stout, Acting Com'r, 40, 41, 43, 45, 47, 49, 50, 53, 57, 59, 63, 66, 68, 72, 74, 76, 77, 78, 84, 85, 86, 101, 103, 107, 113, 114, 116, 117, 120, 122, 123, 126, 130, 131, 132, 136, 140, 146, 149, 151, 154, 156, 158, 159, 161, 162, 168, 175, 177, 180, 185, 193, 195, 196, 200, 209, 210, 215, 216, 217, 220, 225, 227, 229
Stoutenburgh, 122
Stoval, 330
Stove, 202
Stover, 88, 307, 319
Stowe, 382
Stoze, 17
Straitner, 10
Strakosch, 252, 285
Stramore Hall, 157
Strange, 318, 368

Strauss, 50
Straw, 288
Strawberry Hill, 113
Street, 380
street railroad, 103
Streeter, 238
Stribling, 157, 298
Strimel, 237
Stromberger, 305
Strong, 42, 99
Stroud, 50
Strouge, 372
Stuart, 331, 398
Stubblefield, 240
Stubbs, 223
Stucher, 135
Stuntz, 279
Sturgeon, 204
Sturgess, 354
Sturgis, 242
Sugs, 23
Suliwell, 290
Sulley, 407
Sullivan, 4, 78, 110, 111, 115, 124, 145, 148, 149, 154, 155, 187, 199, 212, 232, 234, 245, 246, 250, 275, 283, 380, 394
Sullivant, 295
Sullwell, 290
Sully, 271
Summerfield, 153
Summers, 8, 46, 245, 247, 271, 279, 324
Summit Point, 86
Sunderland, 54, 88, 91, 127, 164, 189, 197, 258, 343, 360, 361
Sunnis, 100
Surratt, 25, 152, 213, 312, 317, 379
Surrattsville, 379
Suter, 351
Sutgreaves, 145
Sutherland, 372
Suton, 111
Swab, 299
Swagert, 249

Swain, 51, 54, 58, 113, 117, 133, 145, 184, 282, 319
Swain's Mill, 291
Swallow, 206
Swan, 30, 76
Swarr, 181
Swartwort, 179
Sweeney, 33, 70, 256, 348, 367
Sweeny, 261, 392
Sweet, 121, 183, 220
Swinburn, 298
Swinton, 37
Switzer, 219
Swords, 386, 400
Sykes, 33, 94, 130, 278, 332, 359, 385
Sylvester, 276
Sympson, 289
Syphax, 106
Sypherd, 194

T

Tabler, 10, 155, 158
Tabor, 209
Tack, 359
Taggart, 107
Taglioni, 379
Talbert, 220
Talbot, 91
Talburt, 13
Talburtt, 378
Talco, 253
Talcott, 270
Talford, 301
Taliaferro, 419
Tallifero, 137
Tallmadge, 250
Talty, 145, 323, 331
Tamplin, 277
Tanney, 128
Tansell, 204
Tappan, 95, 271, 306
Tarbell, 357
Tarbutton, 290
Tardy, 258
Tarman, 276

Tasker, 67
Tayler, 277
Tayloe, 96, 141, 145, 222, 223
Taylor, 1, 5, 18, 27, 33, 39, 47, 58, 62, 72, 87, 93, 108, 109, 114, 118, 134, 138, 145, 147, 153, 154, 159, 205, 206, 210, 212, 222, 244, 249, 268, 287, 294, 321, 324, 327, 359, 362, 393, 396, 404, 408, 409, 411, 420, 424, 426
Tayman, 357
Teachout, 316
Tearny, 402
Teel, 137
Teice, 166
Tekner, 82
Templeman, 28, 232
Ten Broeck, 44, 339
Ten Eyck, 267
Tenbrook, 208
Tenneson, 203
Tennesson, 203
Tenney, 63, 74, 92, 327
Tennison, 203
Tent Landing, 352
Terrell, 330
Terrett, 232, 299, 373
terrier slut, 166
Terry, 8
Thacher, 6
Thame, 278
Thatcher, 81, 164, 297
Thayer, 281
The Cottage, 225
The Ridge, 200
Theaker, 58, 71, 327
Theaker, Com'r of Patents, 2, 7, 8, 9, 12, 13, 14, 15, 16, 18, 31
Thecker, 176
Theeker, 349
Thian, 210
Thies, 390
Thoma, 16, 22, 32, 37, 39
Thomas, 4, 8, 13, 14, 15, 29, 65, 67, 69, 97, 100, 105, 108, 111, 137, 140, 156,

160, 165, 179, 188, 194, 196, 199,
204, 211, 222, 240, 246, 258, 261,
262, 265, 272, 275, 278, 286, 297,
302, 316, 322, 324, 333, 379, 387, 393
Thompson, 9, 24, 47, 59, 64, 72, 78, 81,
111, 114, 120, 129, 136, 145, 152,
162, 166, 183, 187, 192, 194, 196,
200, 206, 224, 225, 245, 249, 250,
280, 298, 301, 302, 328, 342, 360,
361, 370, 371, 381, 389, 392, 406,
408, 417, 420
Thoms, 203
Thomson, 350, 409
Thorn, 33, 145, 178, 353, 430
Thornley, 193
Thornton, 44, 65, 209, 251, 379
Thorp, 192, 386
Thorpe, 207, 266
Thorpland, 309
Thorson, 395
Thrasher, 290
Throop, 117
Throp, 288
Through, 254
Thruston, 151, 323
Thurlow, 43
Thurston, 103, 111, 140
Thyson, 142, 404
Tibbetts, 213
Tiber Creek, 67, 198, 228
Tichner, 299
Ticknor, 7, 55, 104
Tidball, 151
Tiermeyrs, 368
Tietsort, 193
Tiffany, 121, 193, 295, 301
Tilden, 350
Tilghman, 182, 253, 386
Tilley, 145, 360
Tilli, 415
Tillinghast, 311
Tillinghurst, 362
Tillotson, 425
Tilston, 12
Tilton, 165

Tippett, 303
Tipton, 225
Tisdel, 196, 200
Tisdell, 121, 359
Titus, 26, 350
Toban, 196, 235
Tobin, 305
Tobriner, 145
Tod, 379, 383
Todd, 32, 118, 133, 142, 146, 186, 194,
279, 308, 332, 333, 343
Toland, 340
Tolar, 275, 316
Tolson, 336
Tomley, 245
Tomlin, 326
Tomlinson, 33
Tompkins, 75
Toner, 137, 150, 228, 269, 285
Toombs, 127, 246
Toomy, 328
Toonery, 359
Toovey, 266
Topham, 145, 174, 396, 398
Torbert, 357
Tormey, 5
Torney, 212
Torogmorton, 422
Torrens, 4
Torrey, 15, 230
Torrill, 415
Totten, 145, 187
Toumey, 292
Towers, 260, 392
Towles, 145, 237
Towner, 293
Townsend, 26, 52, 109, 125, 148, 159,
250, 263, 264, 333
Townshend, 171, 205
Tracey, 153
Tracy, 212
Train, 156, 300, 341
Travers, 179
Traverse, 145
Travis, 60, 88

Treanor, 189, 271
Tree, 31, 258, 364
Trego, 290
Triay, 7, 126, 312, 364, 371, 374
Trimble, 225, 355, 421, 423
Triplett, 203, 384
Tripp, 192
Tritt, 193
Trollope, 127
<u>Trotting Stallion</u>, 151
Trough, 259
Trout, 25
Troxel, 96
Troy, 323
Truax, 173
Trueman, 100, 163
Truesdale, 62
Truman, 8, 218
Trumble, 306
Trumbull, 206, 256, 281
Trunnel, 33
Trunnell, 210, 268, 315
Tuay, 51
Tuck, 159
Tuckens, 282
Tucker, 38, 58, 66, 75, 145, 204, 302, 322, 355, 409
Tuckerman, 48, 78
Tudor, 36, 59, 150, 300, 331, 361, 417
tug **Katy Wise**, 410
tug **W B Urmton**, 306
tug-boat **James A Wright**, 63
Tulley, 421
Tultavull, 89
Tuohy, 210
Turkey Thicket, 123
Turner, 9, 41, 122, 147, 154, 163, 170, 193, 214, 240, 271, 279, 289, 391, 418, 429
Turney, 403
Turniss, 354
Turpin, 119, 168, 206, 224
Turtle, 249
Turton, 14, 194, 206, 302, 320
Tustin, 11, **88**, 333

Tuttle, 52, 103, 311
Tuturville, 64
Twain, 61, 78
Tweat, 379
Twichell, 160
Twitchell, 388
Tyler, 8, 62, 64, 137, 159, 271, 308, 312, 351
Tyng, 70
Tyson, 280, 424

U

Ullman, 172
Underhill, 380
Underwood, 26, 69, 258, 403, 430
Uniontown, 66
United States, 408
Upham, 177
Upperman, 63, 83, 333
Upshur, 8, 10, 12, 110, 150
Upson, 229
Urich, 310, 376
<u>Ursuline Academy</u>, 287
Usher, 222, 402
Utermehle, 79, 141, 158, 394, 401
Uttermehle, 21, 100, 344

V

Valentine, 63
Valkmer, 249
Van Arsdale, 289
Van Buren, 190, 211
Van Cott, 350
Van Gorden, 345
Van Hook, 22
Van Horn, 63, 357
Van Kirk, 254
Van Master, 214
Van Ness, 373, 403
Van Nest, 170
Van Orden, 286
Van Riswick, 2, 105, 116, 145, 204, 270
Van Santvoord, 350
Van Sickles, 354

Van Steenburgh, 411
Van Syckle, 213
Van Vliet, 62
Van Vorst, 350
Van Winkle, 69, 80, 350
Van Wyck, 369
Van Zanwick, 182
Vance, 279, 408
Vanderbilt, 35, 64, 104, 125, 266, 274, 277, 427
Vanderburgh, 326
Vandergriff, 15
Vandergrift, 15
Vanderpool, 350
Vanderwerken, 172
Vandevanter, 288
Vanethroy, 306
VanGuilder, 218
Vanhook, 66
Vankirk, 259
Varenzell, 315
Varnell, 113, 158
Vaughan, 311
Vaughn, 189, 406
Vearns, 327
Veasey, 181
Veitch, 37, 135, 232
Venneren, 118
Verdi, 160
Vermeren, 188
Vernon, 172
Vernum, 400
Verschel, 91
Vert, 128
vessel **Cmdor Barney**, 406
Vetermele, 412
Vetter, 187
Victor, 206, 229, 379
Viennet, 254
Vierbuchen, 184
Viger, 192
Vincent, 122, 258, 327
Vineyard, 151
Viser, 213, 238
Voll, 31

Von Culin, 303
Von Essen, 8
Von Valkenburg, 4
Von Zarboni, 341
Vonder Heide, 273
Vonderhide, 402
Vonderlehr, 263
Voss, 146, 159
Voultair, 33
Vroman, 62

W

Wackeman, 239
Waddell, 201, 240, 271, 289, 421
Wade, 108, 133, 305, 310, 382, 424
Wadsworth, 145, 199, 325, 336, 348, 411
Wager, 288
Wagner, 62, 89, 91, 95
Wagoner, 170
Wagual, 422
Wail, 393, 402
Wair, 95
Wait, 300
Wakefield, 131, 369
Walbridge, 250
Walcott, 49, 62, 373
Walden, 153
Waldron, 378
Wales, 421
Waleski, 342
Walewski, 322
Walker, 13, 41, 51, 58, 86, 135, 156, 199, 212, 235, 249, 255, 270, 319, 342, 362, 372
Wall, 31, 33, 70, 81, 116, 142, 224, 344, 410
Wallace, 7, 31, 81, 108, 146, 178, 200, 224, 249, 273, 285, 322, 352, 366, 374, 380, 412
Wallach, 30, 88, 146, 154, 172, 191, 198, 214, 224, 244, 323, 394, 400
Wallacher, 393
Waller, 360, 386
Wallingsford, 267

Walls, 221
Walsh, 65, 111, 124, 155, 204, 212, 363, 378
Walt, 50
Walter, 15, 73, 81, 88, 106, 148, 250, 257, 267, 269, 270, 277, 289, 297, 301, 331, 360
Walters, 179, 332
Walton, 154, 288, 357
Walworth, 3
Wambold, 402
Wamelink, 193
Wamlet, 193
Wands, 219
Wangeman, 368
Wangiman, 402
Wangman, 223
Wannall, 52, 73
Wannell, 333
Ward, 3, 14, 15, 22, 32, 66, 81, 95, 105, 146, 164, 222, 230, 350, 359, 368
Warder, 348
Ware, 111, 328
Warfield, 20, 271
Waring, 248
Warn, 82
Warne, 427
Warneck, 290
Warner, 10, 65, 177, 223, 300, 318, 403, 423
Warren, 81, 96, 135, 222, 223, 361
Warriman, 345
Warring, 408
Warrington, 2
Washburn, 15, 332, 429
Washburne, 205
Washington, 21, 35, 46, 63, 87, 116, 132, 136, 196, 201, 233, 247, 258, 282, 299, 393, 403, 404
Washington crypt, 261
Waterbury, 256
Waterouse, 306
Waters, 2, 38, 63, 89, 146, 172, 212, 228, 320, 354, 425
Waterson, 145

Watkins, 4, 106, 115, 275, 316
Watson, 70, 71, 147, 192, 212, 270, 368, 374
Watt, 393
Wattmore, 419
Watts, 93, 111, 232, 240, 352, 354, 392
Waugh, 18
Waverley Seminary, 191
Way, 184, 217
Wayman, 290
Wayne, 3, 24
Weakley, 369
Weaver, 58, 146, 181, 264, 265, 288, 308
Webb, 32, 65, 145, 173, 229, 230, 267, 272, 283, 289, 301, 360, 403, 413, 426
Webbs, 388
Weber, 78, 137, 408
Webster, 73, 77, 86, 171, 179, 185, 189, 210, 229, 240, 253, 271, 320, 363, 423
Weed, 55, 219, 378
Weeden, 69
Weedon, 415
Weeks, 209, 238, 249, 391
Weems, 279
Weightman, 293
Weiles, 118
Weiner, 337
Weisel, 38
Weiss, 293, 298, 303, 312, 411
Weisse, 178
Welch, 5, 198, 394
Welchman, 289
Welcker, 34, 145, 411
Weld, 393
Weller, 65
Welles, 176, 316, 403, 416
Welling, 200, 251
Wellman, 81
Wells, 32, 81, 82, 115, 140, 219, 229, 232, 235, 238, 255, 305, 325, 326, 342, 425
Welner, 394
Welsh, 25, 142, 250, 364, 393
Wendell, 71, 75, 125, 305, 416

Wenderstraut, 154
Wentworth, 301
Werder, 373
Wesley, 9
Wesleyan Female College, 280
Wesson, 103, 430
West, 19, 30, 63, 145, 154, 172, 357, 375, 412
West Point, 227
West Point cadet, 230
Westcall, 225
Westerfield, 165, 166, 267
Western, 414, 418
Westmoreland, 148
Weston, 137, 149, 332
Westwood, 357
Wetherell, 172
Wetzell, 18
Whalen, 305
Whaley, 15, 118
Whann, 246
Wharten, 82
Wharton, 21, 75, 209, 222
Wheat, 233, 425, 428
Wheatland, 166, 169, 181
Wheatley, 36, 53, 120, 142, 146, 285, 333, 422
Wheatly, 302
Wheeler, 5, 22, 35, 43, 44, 60, 95, 108, 133, 136, 142, 154, 157, 190, 280, 289, 295, 323, 334, 375, 417
Wheeling, 409
Wheelock, 178
Whelan, 89, 112, 184, 185, 233, 271, 274, 275
Wheldon, 318
Whidney, 153
Whipple, 249, 309
White, 7, 23, 88, 104, 122, 146, 147, 194, 198, 203, 210, 243, 262, 274, 283, 293, 300, 306, 328, 359, 360, 370, 372, 383, 385, 411, 423
White House, 414
Whitehall, 359
Whiteley, 161
Whitely, 196
Whitfield, 253
Whiting, 17, 275, 284, 350, 360
Whitlock, 377
Whitnell, 49
Whitney, 5, 10, 242, 306, 402
Whittaker, 282
Whitten, 415
Whittier, 36, 410
Whittingham, 168
Whittington, 244
Whittle, 131
Whittlesey, 229
Whitus, 340
Whyte, 74, 223
Wickerson, 90
Widenayer, 12
Widmayer, 401
Widow's Mite, 195, 307
Wiekel, 39
Wiener, 342
Wier, 294
Wiget, 20, 41, 208, 211, 292, 348, 360
Wigfall, 174
Wight, 209
Wigual, 422
Wilber, 223, 238
Wilbur, 326
Wilcox, 240, 345
Wilder, 94
Wildman, 335
Wiles, 93
Wiley, 99, 182, 359
Wilker, 182, 185
Wilkins, 3, 366, 424
Wilkinson, 87, 174, 183, 368
Willard, 33, 41, 114, 141, 199, 249, 327, 400
Willeck, 296
Willeston, 173
Willett, 213, 221, 236
Willey, 137, 250, 257
William, 188, 269, 335
Williams, 8, 10, 12, 13, 17, 22, 29, 34, 36, 63, 64, 70, 89, 110, 118, 125, 130,

136, 145, 149, 150, 171, 172, 175,
180, 183, 194, 196, 200, 211, 212,
213, 218, 220, 241, 245, 246, 251,
264, 268, 285, 290, 301, 308, 329,
335, 339, 345, 346, 350, 357, 362,
368, 379, 380, 394, 395, 405
Williamson, 27, 28, 245, 289, 367, 398, 417
Williar, 358
Willis, 3, 19, 86, 87, 100, 196, 200
Williss, 362
Williston, 223, 229, 272, 332
Willner, 135, 257, 258, 270
Willow Grove, 98
Wills, 28, 411
Willson, 33
Wilmot, 90
Wilsen, 403
Wilson, 3, 4, 33, 51, 53, 87, 95, 127, 136, 137, 142, 146, 148, 154, 169, 180, 184, 187, 196, 197, 198, 199, 206, 212, 234, 236, 240, 243, 270, 271, 272, 280, 289, 295, 297, 322, 325, 330, 342, 358, 359, 371, 389, 394, 403, 407, 408, 413, 415, 424
Wiltberger, 63
Wiltburger, 202
Wilton, 199
Wimer, 240
Wimsatt, 422
Winchell, 134
Winder, 119, 378
Winder's Bldg, 414
Winderlich, 374
Windsor, 374
Winfield, 356, 412
Wing, 359, 414
Wingate, 424
Winkley, 418
Winn, 25
Winninger, 20
Winship, 366
Winslow, 3, 327
Winter, 81, 142, 215
Winthrop, 55, 85, 291

Wirt House, 414
Wise, 145, 163, 384, 420
Wisewell, 69
Wisewell Barracks, 125
Wishard, 303
Wishoot, 282
Wisner, 272
Witherow, 33, 146
Witteraner, 279
Witzleben, 336
Wivel, 423
Wolf, 218
Wolfe, 147
Wolfley, 80, 243
Wollard, 172
Wood, 15, 31, 50, 62, 177, 181, 182, 238, 250, 294, 339, 342, 418
Wooden, 306
Woodfolk, 409
Woodford, 281
Woodhull, 145
Woodland, 388
Woodland Cemetery, 54
Woodlands Cemetery, 346
Woodleigh, 255
Woodley, 156, 228, 411
Woodman, 130
Woodrich, 326
Woodruff, 121, 126, 223, 263, 326, 384
Woods, 119, 225, 250, 288
Woodward, 20, 90, 119, 137, 142, 190, 195, 225, 252, 255, 262, 263, 267, 326, 354
Woody, 246
Woolard, 212
Wooldridge, 187
Woolfold, 312
Wooten, 218, 284, 335
Worden, 163, 170, 194, 310
Wormely, 244
Wormer, 6
Wormley, 96, 244, 370
Worrell, 115
Worsch, 171
Worster, 73

Worth, 367
Worthington, 25, 89, 98, 135, 142, 163, 170, 198, 240, 346
Wright, 3, 13, 24, 62, 184, 230, 233, 306, 324, 326, 337, 342, 376, 422
Wrisley, 295
Wroe, 106
Wroten, 122
Wunderitch, 402
Wurdeman, 145
Wyant, 354
Wyants, 17
Wyatt, 289
Wyckoff, 12
Wyette, 159
Wylie, 31, 33, 54, 192, 317
Wyman, 345
Wyndham, 23
Wynn, 167, 424
Wynne, 66, 250

Y

Yale, 3, 200
Yates, 44, 46, 83, 115, 154, 181, 237, 313, 384, 400
Yeager, 267
Yearley, 168
Yeatman, 134, 214
Yerby, 279
Yorke, 357
Yost, 8, 400, 402
Young, 3, 35, 54, 55, 64, 73, 80, 83, 109, 114, 122, 131, 134, 138, 142, 146, 154, 161, 172, 176, 186, 188, 201, 208, 237, 250, 284, 288, 289, 310, 328, 335, 340, 347, 349, 360, 364, 368, 373, 390, 397, 402, 424
Young Catholics' Friends Society, 363
Youtsey, 315

Z

Zabel, 378
Zange, 385
Zanzy, 265
Zeouth, 135
Zerbe, 355, 356
Zimmer, 17, 42
Zimmerman, 109, 199, 261, 348
Zirwes, 18, 368
Zolinger, 202

Other Heritage Books by Joan M. Dixon:

National Intelligencer *Newspaper Abstracts Special Edition: The Civil War Years Volume 1: January 1, 1861–June 30, 1863*

National Intelligencer *Newspaper Abstracts Special Edition: The Civil War Years Volume 2: July 1, 1863–December 31, 1865*

National Intelligencer *Newspaper Abstracts Jan. 1, 1869–Jan. 8, 1870*

National Intelligencer *Newspaper Abstracts Volume 1866–Volume 1868*

National Intelligencer *Newspaper Abstracts Volume 1840–Volume 1860*

National Intelligencer *Newspaper Abstracts, 1838–1839*

National Intelligencer *Newspaper Abstracts, 1836–1837*

National Intelligencer *Newspaper Abstracts, 1834–1835*

National Intelligencer *Newspaper Abstracts, 1832–1833*

National Intelligencer *Newspaper Abstracts, 1830–1831*

National Intelligencer *Newspaper Abstracts, 1827–1829*

National Intelligencer *Newspaper Abstracts, 1824–1826*

National Intelligencer *Newspaper Abstracts, 1821–1823*

National Intelligencer *Newspaper Abstracts, 1818–1820*

National Intelligencer *Newspaper Abstracts, 1814–1817*

National Intelligencer *Newspaper Abstracts, 1811–1813*

National Intelligencer *Newspaper Abstracts, 1806–1810*

National Intelligencer *Newspaper Abstracts, 1800–1805*

www.ingramcontent.com/pod-product-compliance
Lightning Source LLC
Chambersburg PA
CBHW051333230426
43668CB00010B/1250